W9-ATT-138

LIFE

STORIES

LIFE

STORIES

PROFILES FROM *THE NEW YORKER*

EDITED BY

DAVID REMNICK

THE MODERN LIBRARY
NEW YORK

2001 Modern Library Paperback Edition

Copyright © 2000 by The New Yorker Magazine

All rights reserved under International and Pan-American Copyright Conventions.
Published in the United States by Random House, Inc., New York,
and simultaneously in Canada by Random House
of Canada Limited, Toronto.

MODERN LIBRARY and colophon are registered trademarks of Random House, Inc.

All of the pieces in this collection were originally published in *The New Yorker.*
The publication date of each piece is given at the end of the piece.

This work was published, in hardcover and in different form,
by Random House, Inc., in 2000.

Library of Congress Cataloging-in-Publication Data

Life stories : profiles from The New Yorker / edited by David Remnick.
p. cm.
ISBN 0-375-75751-1
1. Biography—20th century. 2. United States—Biography. I. Remnick, David.
CT220.L54   2000
920.073—dc21   99-053712

Modern Library website address: www.modernlibrary.com

Printed in the United States of America

68975

Book design by Jo Anne Metsch

To Eleanor Gould Packard,
guardian of the sentence

ACKNOWLEDGMENTS

Dozens of *New Yorker* staffers—editors, writers, assistants, fact checkers—gave me lists of their favorite Profiles. I am very grateful for the suggestions. Pamela Maffei McCarthy and Eric Rayman at *The New Yorker* made the happy arrangement with Daniel Menaker and Ann Godoff at Random House for this volume and for *Wonderful Town*, a companion collection of short fiction set in New York City. Susan Choi, Dorothy Wickenden, Henry Finder, and Roger Angell worked especially hard in sorting through these Profiles, and Brenda Phipps, Beth Johnson, Chris Shay, and the magazine's library staff were also of great help to me and to this project.

CONTENTS

INTRODUCTION

DAVID REMNICK

It used to be said around the *New Yorker* offices that our founding editor, Harold Ross, invented the Profile. But if a Profile is a biographical piece—a concise rendering of a life through anecdote, incident, interview, and description (or some ineffable combination thereof)—well, then, it's a little presumptuous to stick Ross at the front of the queue, ahead of Plutarch, Defoe, Aubrey, Strachey, or even *The Saturday Evening Post*. And yet in 1925, when Ross launched the magazine he liked to call his "comic weekly," he wanted something different—something sidelong and ironical, a form that prized intimacy and wit over biographical completeness or, God forbid, unabashed hero worship. Ross told his writers and editors that, above all, he wanted to get away from what he was reading in other magazines—all the "Horatio Alger" stuff.

James Kevin McGuinness, a staffer in the earliest days of the magazine, suggested the rubric "Profiles" to Ross. By the time the magazine got around to copyrighting the term, it had entered the language of American journalism. Most of the initial Profiles in the magazine were fairly cursory and bland (and not worth anthologizing). The first was a sketch of the Metropolitan Opera's impresario Giulio Gatti-Casazza; it ran just over one page and showed scant evidence of even the most rudimentary reporting. It wasn't terribly funny, either. By 1927, however, the reporting was getting stronger and the writing more irreverent. John K. Winkler's Profile of William Randolph Hearst, a five-part piece, was both uproarious and well researched, and Janet Flanner had begun perfecting a shorter form, with a Profile of Edith Wharton.

The most influential of the early Profiles was Alva Johnston's delightful dissection, in 1932, of a phony Russian prince named Michael Dmitry Obolensky

Romanoff. The prince's real name was Harry F. Gerguson, late of Illinois. (Like Joseph Mitchell's great subject, Joe Gould, Gerguson was an irresistible fake. He was so irresistible, in fact, that Ross eventually befriended him and sent him off to Los Angeles, where he could mooch off Dave Chasen, the restaurateur; eventually, Obolensky mooched off enough of Chasen's customers to open his own place.) While the mainstays of Ross's *New Yorker*, E. B. White and James Thurber, did the most to develop the magazine's urbane tone and sensibility, Johnston, who had won a Pulitzer Prize as a reporter at *The New York Times* in 1923 and later moved to the *Herald Tribune*, gave the Profile form real literary and journalistic weight. Johnston was the first to combine a natural wit and sense of storytelling with the legwork of a first-class newspaperman. His Profiles, especially those of Obolensky and the Florida architect Addison Mizner, influenced generations of *New Yorker* writers and Profile masters, from A. J. Liebling to John McPhee to Mark Singer. His obituary in the magazine read, in part, "When *The New Yorker* in its earliest days was trying to establish the Profile as a new journalistic form, it was Alva Johnston more than anyone else who set the pace, clarified the idea, and produced the pieces. He gathered and assembled facts in such a way as to give a fresh, candid, gay, and occasionally satirical picture of an individual."

Ross was a man of enormous social energy and mischief, and he was not reluctant to use pieces in *The New Yorker* as a means of settling feuds and even starting them. St. Clair McKelway's Profile of Walter Winchell enumerated hundreds of errors and bogus items in Winchell's gossip column; the piece was so thorough a trouncing that it provoked Winchell to report in the *Mirror* that Ross wore no underwear. Evidently, Winchell had erred again; Ross mailed him the very pair of undershorts he was wearing when he read the offending column. Winchell, for his part, demanded that the owner of the Stork Club ban Ross from his tables.

Wolcott Gibbs's skewering of Henry Luce in 1936 heightened the rivalry between *The New Yorker* and the Time-Life empire, a rivalry that had started with a long, nasty, and well-informed piece on Ross and *The New Yorker* in *Fortune* by one of Ross's earliest colleagues, Ralph Ingersoll. Gibbs's Profile, which enjoyed Luce's cooperation, made a buffoon of its subject and, even more effectively, undermined "Timespeak," the queerly stentorian, neologism-studded artificial language of his magazines. (In Gibbs's devastating summary, "Backward ran sentences until reeled the mind.") Leaning heavily on the reporting of his colleague John Bainbridge, Gibbs subjected Luce to a reportorial strip search, detailing his income, the décor of his colossal apartment, his odd habits in the office, his taste for pompous middlebrow journalism, and his megalomania. The Profile ended with a stunning flourish: "Certainly to be taken with seriousness is Luce at thirty-eight, his fellowman already informed up to his ears, his future plans impossible to contemplate. Where it all will end, knows God!"

When Luce was shown the galleys he was furious and demanded a meeting with Ross. "There's not a single kind word about me in the whole Profile," he complained at the late-night summit.

"That's what you get for being a baby tycoon," Ross replied, showing his command of Timespeak.

"Goddamit, Ross, this whole goddam piece is ma . . . ma . . . malicious, and you know it!"

Ross hesitated. Finally, he said, "You've put your finger on it, Luce. I believe in malice."

The *New Yorker* Profile has expanded in many ways since Ross's time. What had been conceived of as a form to describe Manhattan personalities now travels widely in the world and all along the emotional and occupational registers. There are Profiles of malice (Gibbs on Luce) and Profiles of praise (Joan Acocella on Mikhail Baryshnikov). There are Profiles about identity (Gates on Broyard) and Profiles about the strangeness of American fame (Tynan on Carson). One quality that runs through nearly all the best Profiles—the Profiles represented here and the many, many more for which there was, finally, no room this time—is a sense of obsession. So many of these pieces are about people who reveal an obsession with one corner of human experience or another. Richard Preston's Chudnovsky brothers are obsessed with the number pi and finding the pattern in randomness; Calvin Trillin's Edna Buchanan is an obsessive crime reporter in Miami who visits the scenes of disaster four, five times a day; Calvin Tomkins's Philippe Petit has walked from one World Trade Center tower to the other on a tightrope and now wants to walk across the Grand Canyon; Mark Singer's Ricky Jay is obsessed with magic and the history of magic. In every great Profile, too, the writer is equally obsessed. It's often the case that a writer will take months, even years, to get to know a subject and bring him or her to life in prose.

The Profile is ubiquitous in modern journalism. We are awash in pieces calling themselves profiles that are about the inner thoughts of some celebrity; more often than not they are based on half-hour interviews and the parameters set down by a vigilant publicist. *The New Yorker* has not been the only home for better work. But whether it's in *The New Yorker* or elsewhere, the Profile is a terribly hard form to get right. Susan Orlean manages it with a subject who can only bark; Nancy Franklin does it with a subject who has been dead for many years. Janet Malcolm, in her piece about the painter David Salle, says a great deal about the difficulty of settling on the right details, the right angle of vision in a Profile that consists, as she says, of "Forty-one False Starts."

In trying to assemble a collection of Profiles that would represent, to some degree, the form as it developed over the seventy-five-year history of the magazine, I needed at least a couple of guidelines to limit myself and the book. After gathering suggestions from colleagues on the staff of *The New Yorker* and from contributors around the country, I discovered that, with the help of our library,

I had amassed a box of photocopied Profiles larger than one's first refrigerator. Rule No. 1 was that no writer could appear more than once. Even more painful, I decided to publish pieces only in full. I wanted the reader to get the real thing—no excerpts, no snippets. As a result the reader will have to go elsewhere for a range of long or multipart Profiles: Dwight MacDonald on the Ford Foundation; John Betjeman's self-Profile in verse; George W. S. Trow on Ahmet Ertegun; Arlene Croce on Edward Villella; Rachel Carson on the sea; Marshall Frady on Jesse Jackson; Liebling on Earl Long; Susan Sheehan on Carmen Santana; William Whitworth on Roger Miller; Jane Kramer on Allen Ginsberg; Alec Wilkinson on a bounty hunter; Hannah Arendt on Bertolt Brecht; Jervis Anderson on Ralph Ellison; Janet Malcolm on the psychoanalyst "Aaron Green"; S. N. Behrman on Joseph Duveen; Lawrence Weschler on Robert Irwin; Brendan Gill on Tallulah Bankhead; John Bainbridge on Toots Shor; Connie Bruck on Hillary Clinton; St. Clair McKelway on Walter Winchell; Philip Hamburger on John P. Marquand; Richard Rovere on William F. Howe and Abraham H. Hummell; Pauline Kael on Cary Grant; and Joseph Mitchell on Joe Gould. As you can see, the history is rich. Some of these, like Malcolm's "Psychoanalysis" or McPhee's many Profiles, are in print and fairly easy to come by in bookstores; some, like Mitchell's Joe Gould, have recently emerged in new editions; finding many of the others will depend on the industry of the reader, the local library, the serendipity of used-book stores, and the increasing quality and range of the various on-line Web sites for used books.

Beyond giving pride of place to Joseph Mitchell's "Mr. Hunter's Grave" (because I love it so), I have arranged the pieces mainly to vary lengths and tone and, sometimes, to compare treatments of a similar theme, as with the two dance pieces and a few of the pieces about public success (Capote on Brando) and public failure (Angell on Blass). The truth is, however, that this is an anthology designed strictly for pleasure. There are no hidden lessons.

LIFE

STORIES

JOSEPH MITCHELL

MR. HUNTER'S GRAVE

WHEN things get too much for me, I put a wild-flower book and a couple of sandwiches in my pockets and go down to the South Shore of Staten Island and wander around awhile in one of the old cemeteries down there. I go to the cemetery of the Woodrow Methodist Church on Woodrow Road in the Woodrow community, or to the cemetery of St. Luke's Episcopal Church on the Arthur Kill Road in the Rossville community, or to one on the Arthur Kill Road on the outskirts of Rossville that isn't used any longer and is known as the old Rossville burying ground. The South Shore is the most rural part of the island, and all of these cemeteries are bordered on at least two sides by woods. Scrub trees grow on some of the graves, and weeds and wild flowers grow on many of them. Here and there, in order to see the design on a gravestone, it is necessary to pull aside a tangle of vines. The older gravestones are made of slate, brownstone, and marble, and the designs on them—death's-heads, angels, hourglasses, hands pointing upward, recumbent lambs, anchors, lilies, weeping willows, and roses on broken stems—are beautifully carved. The names on the gravestones are mainly Dutch, such as Winant, Housman, Woglom, Decker, and Van Name, or Huguenot, such as Dissosway, Seguine, De Hart, Manee, and Sharrott, or English, such as Ross, Drake, Bush, Cole, and Clay. All of the old South Shore farming and oyster-planting families are represented, and members of half a dozen generations of some families lie side by side. In St. Luke's cemetery there is a huge old apple tree that drops a sprinkling of small, wormy, lopsided apples on the graves beneath it every September, and in the Woodrow Methodist cemetery there is a patch of wild strawberries. Invariably, for some reason I don't know and don't

want to know, after I have spent an hour or so in one of these cemeteries, looking at gravestone designs and reading inscriptions and identifying wild flowers and scaring rabbits out of the weeds and reflecting on the end that awaits
me and awaits us all, my spirits lift, I become quite cheerful, and then I go for
a long walk. Sometimes I walk along the Arthur Kill, the tidal creek that separates Staten Island from New Jersey; to old-time Staten Islanders, this is "the
inside shore." Sometimes I go over on the ocean side, and walk along Raritan
Bay; this is "the outside shore." The interior of the South Shore is crisscrossed
with back roads, and sometimes I walk along one of them, leaving it now and
then to explore an old field or a swamp or a stretch of woods or a clay pit or an
abandoned farmhouse.

The back road that I know best is Bloomingdale Road. It is an old oyster-shell
road that has been thinly paved with asphalt; the asphalt is cracked and pocked
and rutted. It starts at the Arthur Kill, just below Rossville, runs inland for two
and a half miles, gently uphill most of the way, and ends at Amboy Road in the
Pleasant Plains community. In times past, it was lined with small farms that
grew vegetables, berries, and fruit for Washington Market. During the depression, some of the farmers got discouraged and quit. Then, during the war, acid
fumes from the stacks of smelting plants on the New Jersey side of the kill
began to drift across and ruin crops, and others got discouraged and quit. Only
three farms are left, and one of these is a goat farm. Many of the old fields have
been taken over by sassafras, gray birch, blackjack oak, sumac, and other
wasteland trees, and by reed grass, blue-bent grass, and poison ivy. In several
fields, in the midst of this growth, are old woodpecker-ringed apple and pear
trees, the remnants of orchards. I have great admiration for one of these trees,
a pear of some old-fashioned variety whose name none of the remaining farmers can remember, and every time I go up Bloomingdale Road I jump a ditch
and pick my way through a thicket of poison ivy and visit it. Its trunk is hollow
and its bark is matted with lichens and it has only three live limbs, but in favorable years it still brings forth a few pears.

In the space of less than a quarter of a mile, midway in its length,
Bloomingdale Road is joined at right angles by three other back roads—
Woodrow Road, Clay Pit Road, and Sharrott's Road. Around the junctions of
these roads, and on lanes leading off them, is a community that was something
of a mystery to me until quite recently. It is a Negro community, and it consists
of forty or fifty Southern-looking frame dwellings and a frame church. The
church is painted white, and it has purple, green, and amber windowpanes. A
sign over the door says,

"AFRICAN METHODIST EPISCOPAL ZION."

On one side of the church steps is a mock-orange bush, and on the other side is
a Southern dooryard plant called Spanish bayonet, a kind of yucca. Five cedar

trees grow in the churchyard. The majority of the dwellings appear to be between fifty and a hundred years old. Some are long and narrow, with a chimney
at each end and a low porch across the front, and some are big and rambling,
with wings and ells and lean-tos and front porches and side porches. Good pine
lumber and good plain carpentry went into them, and it is obvious that attempts
have been made to keep them up. Nevertheless, all but a few are beginning to
look dilapidated. Some of the roofs sag, and banisters are missing on some of the
porches, and a good many rotted-out clapboards have been replaced with new
boards that don't match, or with strips of tin. The odd thing about the community is it usually has an empty look, as if everybody had locked up and gone off
somewhere. In the summer, I have occasionally seen an old man or an old
woman sitting on a porch, and I have occasionally seen children playing in a
back yard, but I have seldom seen any young or middle-aged men or women
around, and I have often walked through the main part of the community, the
part that is on Bloomingdale Road, without seeing a single soul.

For years, I kept intending to find out something about this community, and
one afternoon several weeks ago, in St. Luke's cemetery in Rossville, an opportunity to do so presented itself.

I had been in the cemetery a couple of hours and was getting ready to leave
when a weed caught my eye. It was a stringy weed, about a foot high, and it had
small, lanceolate leaves and tiny white flowers and tiny seed pods, and it was
growing on the grave of Rachel Dissosway, who died on April 7, 1802, "in the
27th Yr of her Age." I consulted my wild-flower book, and came to the conclusion that it was peppergrass (*Lepidium virginicum*), and squatted down to take a
closer look at it. "One of the characteristics of peppergrass," the wild-flower
book said, "is that its seed pods are as hot as pepper when chewed." I deliber-
ated on this for a minute or two, and then curiosity got the better of me and I
stripped off some of the seed pods and started to put them in my mouth, and at
just that moment I heard footsteps on the cemetery path and looked up and
saw a man approaching, a middle-aged man in a black suit and a clerical collar. He came over to the grave and looked down at me.

"What in the world are you doing?" he asked.

I tossed the seed pods on the grave and got to my feet. "I'm studying wild
flowers, I guess you might call it," I said. I introduced myself, and we shook
hands, and he said that he was the rector of St. Luke's and that his name was
Raymond E. Brock.

"I was trying to decide if the weed on this grave is peppergrass," I said.

Mr. Brock glanced at the weed and nodded. "Peppergrass," he said. "A very
common weed in some parts of Staten Island."

"To tell you the truth," I said, "I like to look at wild flowers, and I've been
studying them off and on for years, but I don't know much about them. I'm
only just beginning to be able to identify them. It's mostly an excuse to get out
and wander around."

"I've seen you from a distance several times wandering around over here in the cemetery," Mr. Brock said.

"I hope you don't mind," I said. "In New York City, the best places to look for wild flowers are old cemeteries and old churchyards."

"Oh, yes," said Mr. Brock, "I'm aware of that. In fact, I'll give you a tip. Are you familiar with the Negro community over on Bloomingdale Road?"

I said that I had walked through it many times, and had often wondered about it.

"The name of it is Sandy Ground," said Mr. Brock, "and it's a relic of the old Staten Island oyster-planting business. It was founded back before the Civil War by some free Negroes who came up here from the Eastern Shore of Maryland to work on the Staten Island oyster beds, and it used to be a flourishing community, a garden spot. Most of the people who live there now are descendants of the original free-Negro families, and most of them are related to each other by blood or marriage. Quite a few live in houses that were built by their grandfathers or great-grandfathers. On the outskirts of Sandy Ground, there's a dirt lane running off Bloomingdale Road that's called Crabtree Avenue, and down near the end of this lane is an old cemetery. It covers an acre and a half, maybe two acres, and it's owned by the African Methodist church in Sandy Ground, and the Sandy Ground families have been burying in it for a hundred years. In recent generations, the Sandy Grounders have had a tendency to kind of let things slip, and one of the things they've let slip is the cemetery. They haven't cleaned it off for years and years, and it's choked with weeds and scrub. Most of the gravestones are hidden. It's surrounded by woods and old fields, and you can't always tell where the cemetery ends and the woods begin. Part of it is sandy and part of it is loamy, part of it is dry and part of it is damp, some of it is shady and some of it gets the sun all day, and I'm pretty sure you can find just about every wild flower that grows on the South Shore somewhere in it. Not to speak of shrubs and herbs and ferns and vines. If I were you, I'd take a look at it."

A man carrying a long-handled shovel in one hand and a short-handled shovel in the other came into the cemetery and started up the main path. Mr. Brock waved at him, and called out, "Here I am, Joe. Stay where you are. I'll be with you in a minute." The man dropped his shovels. "That's Mr. Damato, our gravedigger," said Mr. Brock. "We're having a burial in here tomorrow, and I came over to show him where to dig the grave. You'll have to excuse me now. If you do decide to visit the cemetery in Sandy Ground, you should ask for permission. They might not want strangers wandering around in it. The man to speak to is Mr. George H. Hunter. He's chairman of the board of trustees of the African Methodist church. I know Mr. Hunter. He's eighty-seven years old, and he's one of those strong, self-contained old men you don't see much any more. He was a hard worker, and he retired only a few years ago, and he's fairly well-to-do. He's a widower, and he lives by himself and does his own

cooking. He's got quite a reputation as a cook. His church used to put on clambakes to raise money, and they were such good clambakes they attracted people from all over this part of Staten Island, and he always had charge of them.
On some matters, such as drinking and smoking, he's very disapproving and
strict and stern, but he doesn't feel that way about eating; he approves of eating. He's a great Bible reader. He's read the Bible from cover to cover, time and
time again. His health is good, and his memory is unusually good. He remembers the golden age of the oyster business on the South Shore, and he remembers its decline and fall, and he can look at any old field or tumble-down house
between Rossville and Tottenville and tell you who owns it now and who
owned it fifty years ago, and he knows who the people were who are buried out
in the Sandy Ground cemetery—how they lived and how they died, how
much they left, and how their children turned out. Not that he'll necessarily
tell you what he knows, or even a small part of it. If you can get him to go to
the cemetery with you, ask him the local names of the weeds and wild flowers.
He can tell you. His house is on Bloomingdale Road, right across from the
church. It's the house with the lightning rods on it. Or you could call him on
the phone. He's in the book."

I thanked Mr. Brock, and went straightway to a filling station on the Arthur
Kill Road and telephoned Mr. Hunter. I told him I wanted to visit the Sandy
Ground cemetery and look for wild flowers in it. "Go right ahead," he said.
"Nobody'll stop you." I told him I also wanted to talk to him about Sandy
Ground. "I can't see you today," he said. "I'm just leaving the house. An old
lady I know is sick in bed, and I made her a lemon-meringue pie, and I'm going
over and take it to her. Sit with her awhile. See if I can't cheer her up. You'll
have to make it some other time, and you'd better make it soon. That cemetery
is a disgrace, but it isn't going to be that way much longer. The board of
trustees had a contractor look it over and make us a price how much he'd
charge to go in there with a bulldozer and tear all that mess out by the roots.
Clean it up good, and build us a road all the way through, with a turn-around
at the farther end. The way it is now, there's a road in there, but it's a narrow
little road and it only goes halfway in, and sometimes the pallbearers have to
carry the coffin quite a distance from the hearse to the grave. Also, it comes to
a dead end, and the hearse has to back out, and if the driver isn't careful he's liable to back into a gravestone, or run against the bushes and briars and scratch
up the paint on his hearse. As I said, a disgrace. The price the contractor made
us was pretty steep, but we put it up to the congregation, and if he's willing to
let us pay a reasonable amount down and the balance in installments, I think
we're going ahead with it. Are you busy this coming Saturday afternoon?" I
said that I didn't expect to be. "All right," he said, "I tell you what you do. If it's
a nice day, come on down, and I'll walk over to the cemetery with you. Come
around one o'clock. I've got some things to attend to Saturday morning, and I
ought to be through by then."

· · ·

SATURDAY turned out to be nice and sunny, and I went across on the ferry and took the Tottenville bus and got off in Rossville and walked up Bloomingdale Road to Sandy Ground. Remembering Mr. Brock's instructions, I looked for a house with lightning rods on it, and I had no trouble finding it. Mr. Hunter's house is fully equipped with lightning rods, the tips of which are ornamented with glass balls and metal arrows. It is a trim, square, shingle-sided, two-story-and-attic house. It has a front porch and a back porch, both screened. The front porch is shaded by a rambler rose growing on a trellis. I knocked on the frame of the screen door, and a bespectacled, elderly Negro man appeared in the hall. He had on a chef's apron, and his sleeves were rolled up. He was slightly below medium height, and lean and bald. Except for a wide, humorous mouth, his face was austere and a little forbidding, and his eyes were sad. I opened the door and asked, "Are you Mr. Hunter?" "Yes, yes, yes," he said. "Come on in, and close the door. Don't stand there and let the flies in. I hate flies. I despise them. I can't endure them." I followed him down the hall, past the parlor, past the dining room, and into the kitchen. There were three cake layers and a bowl of chocolate icing on the kitchen table.

"Sit down and make yourself at home," he said. "Let me put the icing on this cake, and then we'll walk over to the cemetery. Icing or frosting. I never knew which was right. I looked up icing in the dictionary one day, and it said 'Frosting for a cake.' So I looked up frosting, and it said 'Icing for a cake.' 'Ha!' I said. 'The dictionary man don't know, either.' The preacher at our church is a part-time preacher, and he doesn't live in Sandy Ground. He lives in Asbury Park, and runs a tailor shop during the week, and drives over here on Sundays. Reverend J. C. Ramsey, a Southern man, comes from Wadesboro, North Carolina. Most Sundays, he and his wife take Sunday dinner with me, and I always try to have something nice for them. After dinner, we sit around the table and drink Postum and discuss the Bible, and that's something I do enjoy. We discuss the prophecies in the Bible, and the warnings, and the promises—the promises of eternal life. And we discuss what I call the mysterious verses, the ones that if you could just understand them they might explain everything—why we're put here, why we're taken away—but they go down too deep; you study them over and over, and you go down as deep as you can, and you still don't touch bottom. 'Do you remember that verse in Revelation,' I say to Reverend Ramsey, 'where it says such and such?' And we discuss that awhile. And then he says to me, 'Do you remember that verse in Second Thessalonians, where it says so and so?' And we discuss that awhile. This Sunday, in addition to the preacher and his wife, I've got some other company coming. A gospel chorus from down South is going to sing at the church Sunday morning, a group of men and women from in and around Norfolk, Virginia, that call themselves the Union Gospel Chorus. They sing old hymns.

Reverend Ramsey heard about them, and got into some correspondence with them. There's seven of them, and they're coming up on the bus today, and they'll spend the night in Asbury Park, and tomorrow, after they sing, they're coming to my house for Sunday dinner. That'll be ten for dinner, including the preacher and his wife and me, and that's nothing. I have twenty to dinner sometimes, like at Thanksgiving, and do it all myself, and it doesn't bother me a bit. I'm going to give them chicken fricassee and dumplings for the main course. Soon as I finish this cake, I'll take you in the dining room and show you what else I'm going to give them. Did you have your lunch?"

"I had a sandwich and some coffee on the ferryboat coming over," I said.

"Now, you know, I like to do that," Mr. Hunter said. "I never go cross on the ferryboat without I step up to the lunch counter and buy a little something—a sandwich, or a piece of raisin cake. And then I sit by the window and eat it, and look at the tugboats go by, and the big boats, and the sea gulls, and the Statue of Liberty. Oh, my! It's such a pleasure to eat on a boat. Years and years ago, I was cook on a boat. When I was growing up in Sandy Ground, the mothers taught the boys to cook the same as the girls. The way they looked at it—you never know, it might come in handy. My mother was an unusually good cook, and she taught me the fundamentals, and I was just naturally good at it, and when I was seventeen or eighteen there was a fleet of fishing boats on Staten Island that went to Montauk and up around there and fished the codfish grounds, and I got a job cooking on one of them. It was a small boat, only five in the crew, and the galley was just big enough for two pots and a pan and a stirring spoon and me. I was clumsy at first. Reach for something with my right hand and knock something else over with my left elbow. After a while, though, I got so good the captain of the biggest boat in the fleet heard about my cooking and tried to hire me away, but the men on my boat said if I left they'd leave, and my captain had been good to me, so I stayed. I was a fishing-boat cook for a year and a half, and then I quit and took up a different line of work altogether. I'll be through with this cake in just a minute. I make my icing thicker than most people do, and I put more on. Frosting. Speaking of wild flowers, do you know pokeweed when you see it?"

"Yes," I said.

"Did you ever eat it?"

"No," I said. "Isn't it supposed to be poisonous?"

"It's the root that's poisonous, the root and the berries. In the spring, when it first comes up, the young shoots above the root are good to eat. They taste like asparagus. The old women in Sandy Ground used to believe in eating pokeweed shoots, the old Southern women. They said it renewed your blood. My mother believed it. Every spring, she used to send me out in the woods to pick pokeweed shoots. And I believe it. So every spring, if I think about it, I go pick some and cook them. It's not that I like them so much—in fact, they give me gas—but they remind me of the days gone by, they remind me of my mother. Now, away down here in the woods in this part of Staten Island, you might think you were fifteen miles on the other side of nowhere, but just a little ways up Arthur Kill Road, up near Arden Avenue, there's a bend in the road where you can sometimes see the tops of the skyscrapers in New York. Just the tallest skyscrapers, and just the tops of them. It has to be an extremely clear day. Even then, you might be able to see them one moment and the next moment they're gone. Right beside this bend in the road there's a little swamp, and the edge of this swamp is the best place I know to pick pokeweed. I went up there one morning this spring to pick some, but we had a late spring, if you remember, and the pokeweed hadn't come up. The fiddleheads were up, and golden club, and spring beauty, and skunk cabbage, and bluets, but no pokeweed. So I was looking here and looking there, and not noticing where I was stepping, and I made a misstep, and the next thing I knew I was up to my knees in mud. I floundered around in the mud a minute, getting my bearings, and then I happened to raise my head and look up, and suddenly I saw, away off in the distance, miles and miles away, the tops of the skyscrapers in New York shining in the morning sun. I wasn't expecting it, and it was amazing. It was like a vision in the Bible."

Mr. Hunter smoothed the icing on top of the cake with a table knife, and stepped back and looked at it. "Well," he said, "I guess that does it." He placed a cover on the cake, and took off his apron. "I better wash my hands," he said. "If you want to see something pretty, step in the dining room and look on the sideboard." There was a walnut sideboard in the dining room, and it had been polished until it glinted. On it were two lemon-meringue pies, two coconut-custard pies, a pound cake, a marble cake, and a devil's-food cake. "Four pies and four cakes, counting the one I just finished," Mr. Hunter called out. "I made them all this morning. I also got some corn muffins put away, to eat with the chicken fricassee. That ought to hold them." Above the dining-room table, hanging from the ceiling, was an old-fashioned lampshade. It was as big as a parasol, and made of pink silk, and fringed and tasselled. On one wall, in a row, were three religious placards. They were printed in ornamental type, and they had floral borders. The first said "JESUS NEVER FAILS." The second said "NOT MY WILL BUT THINE BE DONE." The third said "THE HOUR IS COMING IN WHICH ALL THAT ARE IN THE GRAVES SHALL HEAR HIS VOICE, AND SHALL COME FORTH; THEY THAT HAVE DONE GOOD, UNTO THE RESURRECTION OF LIFE AND THEY THAT HAVE DONE EVIL, UNTO THE RESURRECTION OF DAMNATION." On another wall was a framed certificate stating that George Henry Hunter was a life member of St. John's Lodge No. 29 of the Most Worshipful Prince Hall Grand Lodge of Free and Accepted Masons. While I was looking at this, Mr. Hunter came into the room. "I'm proud of that," he said. "There's several Negro Mason organizations, but Prince Hall is the biggest, and I've been a member since 1906. I joined the Masons the same year I built this house. Did you notice my floors?" I looked down. The floor boards were wide and made of some kind of honey-colored wood, and they were waxed and polished. "Virgin spruce," he said. "Six inches wide. Tongue and groove. Built to last. In my time, that was the idea, but in this day and time, that's not the idea. They've got more things nowadays—things, things, things; kitchen stoves you could put in the parlor just to look at, refrigerators so big they're all out of reason, cars that reach from here to Rossville—but they aren't built to last, they're built to wear out. And that's the way the people want it. It's immaterial to them how long a thing lasts. In fact, if it don't wear out quick enough, they beat it and bang it and kick it and jump up and down on it, so they can get a new one. Most of what you buy nowadays, the outside is everything, the inside don't matter. Like those tomatoes you buy at the store, and they look so nice and shiny and red, and half the time, when you get them home and slice them, all that's inside is mush, red mush. And the people are the same. You hardly ever see a son any more as good as his father. Oh, he might be taller and stronger and thicker in the shoulders, playing games at school and all, but he can't stand as much. If he tried to lift and pull the way the men of my generation used to lift and pull, he'd be ruptured by noon—they'd be making arrangements to operate. How'd I get started talking this way? I'm tired, that's why. I been on my feet all morning, and I better sit down a few minutes." He took a tablecloth from a drawer of the sideboard and shook it out and laid it gently over the cakes and pies. "Let's go on the back porch," he said.

THERE were two wicker rocking chairs on the back porch, and we sat down. Mr. Hunter yawned and closed his eyes and slowly lowered his chin to his chest. I looked at his back yard, in which there were several rows of sweet potatoes, a row of tomatoes, a weeping willow, and a feeding table for birds. Mr. Hunter dozed for about five minutes, and then some blue jays flew into the yard, shrieking, and they aroused him. Pressing his elbows against the chair, he sat up, and followed the jays with his eyes as they swooped and swirled about the yard. When they flew away, he laughed. "I enjoy birds," he said. "I enjoy their colors. I enjoy the noise they make, and the commotion. Even blue jays. Most mornings, I get up real early and go out in the yard and scatter bread crumbs and sunflower seeds on the feeding table, and then I sit up here on the porch and watch. Oh, it's nice out here in the early morning! Everything is so fresh. As my mother used to say, 'Every morning, the world anew.' Some mornings, I see a dozen different kinds of birds. There were redbirds all over the yard this morning, and a surprising number of brown thrashers and red-winged blackbirds. I see a good many I don't recognize; I do wish I knew their names. Every so often, a pair of pheasants land on the feeding table. Some of the old fields around here are full of them. I was picking some tomatoes the other day, and a pair of pheasants scuttled out from under the tomato bushes and flew up right in my face. Whoosh! Up goes the cock bird. A second later—whoosh! Up goes the hen bird. One of her wings brushed against me. I had my mind on something else, or I could've caught her. I better not get on the subject of birds, or I'll talk your ears off. You said on the phone you wanted to know something about Sandy Ground. What do you want to know? How it began?"

"Yes, sir," I said.

"Oysters!" said Mr. Hunter. "That's how it began." There was a fly swatter on the floor beside Mr. Hunter's chair, and a few feet in front of his chair was an old kitchen table with a chipped enamel top. He suddenly reached down and grabbed the swatter and stood up and took a step toward the table, on which a fly had lit. His shadow fell on the fly, and the fly flew away. Mr. Hunter stared wildly into space for several moments, looking for the fly and muttering angrily, and then he sat back down, still holding the swatter.

"It's hard to believe nowadays, the water's so dirty," he continued, "but up until about the year 1800 there were tremendous big beds of natural-growth oysters all around Staten Island—in the Lower Bay, in the Arthur Kill, in the Kill van Kull. Some of the richest beds of oysters in the entire country were out in the lower part of the Lower Bay, the part known as Raritan Bay. Most of them were on shoals, under ten to twenty feet of water. They were supposed to be public beds, open to anybody, but they were mainly worked by Staten Islanders, and the Staten Islanders considered they owned them. Between 1800 and 1820, all but the very deepest of these beds gradually petered out. They had been raked and scraped until they weren't worth working any more. But the Staten Islanders didn't give up. What they did, they began to bring immature oysters from other localities and put them on the best of the old beds and leave them there until they reached market size, which took from one to four years, all according to how mature the oysters were to begin with. Then they'd rake them up, or tong them up, and load them on boats, and send them up the bay to the wholesalers in New York. They took great pains with these oysters. They cleaned the empty shells and bottom trash off the beds that they put them on, and they spread them out as evenly as possible. Handled this way, oysters grew faster than they did all scrouged together on natural beds. Also, they grew more uniform in size and shape. Also, they had a better flavor. Also, they brought higher prices, premium prices. The center of the business was the little town of Prince's Bay, over on the outside shore.

"At first, the Staten Islanders used sloops and bought their seed stock close by, in bays in New Jersey and Long Island, but the business grew very fast, and in a few years a good many of them were using schooners that could hold five thousand bushels and were making regular trips to Maryland and Virginia. Some went into inlets along the ocean side of the Eastern Shore, and some went into Chesapeake Bay. They bought from local oystermen who worked natural beds in the public domain, and they usually had to visit a whole string of little ports and landings before they got a load. At that time, there were quite a few free Negroes among the oystermen on the Eastern Shore, especially in Worcester County,

Maryland, on the upper part of Chincoteague Bay, and the Staten Island captains occasionally hired gangs of them to make the trip North and help distribute the oysters on the beds. Now and then, a few would stay behind on Staten Island for a season or two and work on empty beds, cleaning them off and getting them ready for new seed stock. Late in the eighteen-thirties or early in the eighteen-forties, a number of these men left their homes in and around Snow Hill, Maryland, the county seat of Worcester County, and came up to Staten Island to live. They brought their families, and they settled over here in the Sandy Ground section. The land was cheap in Sandy Ground, and it was in easy walking distance of Prince's Bay, and a couple of Negro families were already living over here, a family named Jackson and a family named Henry. The records of our church go back to 1850, and they show the names of most of the original men from Snow Hill. Three of them were Purnells—Isaac Purnell, George Purnell, and Littleton Purnell. Two were Lambdens, spelled L-a-m-b-d-e-n, only their descendants changed the spelling to L-a-n-d-i-n—Landin. One was a Robbins, and one was a Bishop, and one was a Henman. The Robbins family died out or moved away many years ago, but Purnells, Landins, Bishops, and Henmans still live in Sandy Ground. They've always been the main Sandy Ground families. There's a man from Sandy Ground who works for a trucking concern in New York, drives trailer trucks, and he's driven through Maryland many times, and stopped in Snow Hill, and he says there's still people down there with these names, plenty of them, white and Negro. Especially Purnells and Bishops. Every second person you run into in Snow Hill, just about, he says, is either a Purnell or a Bishop, and there's one little crossroad town near Snow Hill that's named Bishop and another one that's named Bishopville. Through the years, other Negro families came to Sandy Ground and settled down and intermarried with the families from Snow Hill. Some came from the South, but the majority came from New York and New Jersey and other places in the North. Such as the Harris family, the Mangin family, the Fish family, the Williams family, the Finney family, and the Roach family."

All of a sudden, Mr. Hunter leaned forward in his chair as far as he could go and brought the fly swatter down on the table. This time, he killed the fly.

"I wasn't born in Sandy Ground myself," he continued. "I came here when I was a boy. My mother and my stepfather brought me here. Two or three of the original men from Snow Hill were still around then, and I knew them. They were old, old men. They were as old as I am now. And the widows of several others were still around. Two of those old widows lived near us, and they used to come to see my mother and sit by the kitchen range and talk and talk, and I used to like to listen to them. The main thing they talked about was the early days in Sandy Ground—how poor everybody had been, and how hard everybody had had to work, the men and the women. The men all worked by the day for the white oystermen in Prince's Bay. They went out in skiffs and anchored over the beds and stood up in the skiffs from sunup to sundown, raking oysters off the bottom with big old claw-toothed rakes that were made of iron and weighed fourteen pounds and had handles on them twenty-four feet long. The women all washed. They washed for white women in Prince's Bay and Rossville and Tottenville. And there wasn't a real house in the whole of Sandy Ground. Most of the families lived in one-room shacks with lean-tos for the children. In the summer, they ate what they grew in their gardens. In the winter, they ate oysters until they couldn't stand the sight of them.

"When I came here, early in the eighteen-eighties, that had all changed. By that time, Sandy Ground was really quite a prosperous little place. Most of the men were still breaking their backs raking oysters by the day, but several of them had saved their money and worked up to where they owned and operated pretty good-sized oyster sloops and didn't take orders from anybody. Old Mr. Dawson Landin was the first to own a sloop. He owned a forty-footer named the Pacific. He was the richest man in the settlement, and he took the lead in everything. Still and all, people liked him and looked up to him; most of us called him Uncle Daws. His brother, Robert Landin, owned a thirty-footer named the Independence, and Mr. Robert's son-in-law, Francis Henry, also owned a thirty-footer. His was named the Fannie Fern. And a few others owned sloops. There were still some places here and there in the Arthur Kill and the Kill van Kull where you could rake up natural-growth seed oysters if you spliced two rake handles together and went down deep enough, and that's what these men did. They sold the seed to the white oystermen, and they made out all right. In those days, the oyster business used oak baskets by the thousands, and some of the Sandy Ground men had got to be good basket-makers. They went into the woods around here and cut white-oak saplings and split them into strips and soaked the strips in water and wove them into bushel baskets that would last for years. Also, several of the men had become blacksmiths. They made oyster rakes and repaired them, and did all kinds of ironwork for the boats.

"The population of Sandy Ground was bigger then than it is now, and the houses were newer and nicer-looking. Every family owned the house they lived in, and a little bit of land. Not much—an acre and a half, two acres, three acres. I guess Uncle Daws had the most, and he only had three and three-quarter acres. But what they had, they made every inch of it count. They raised a few pigs and chickens, and kept a cow, and had some fruit trees and grapevines, and planted a garden. They planted a lot of Southern stuff, such as butter beans and okra and sweet potatoes and mustard greens and collards and Jerusalem artichokes. There were flowers in every yard, and rosebushes, and the old women exchanged seeds and bulbs and cuttings with each other. Back then, this was a big strawberry section. The soil in Sandy Ground is ideal for strawberries. All the white farmers along Bloomingdale Road grew them, and the people in Sandy Ground took it up; you can grow a lot of strawberries on an acre. In those days, a river steamer left New Brunswick, New Jersey, every

morning, and came down the Raritan River and entered the Arthur Kill and
made stops at Rossville and five or six other little towns on the kill, and then
went on up to the city and docked at the foot of Barclay Street, right across
from Washington Market. And early every morning during strawberry season
the people would box up their strawberries and take them down to Rossville
and put them on the steamer and send them off to market. They'd lay a couple
of grape leaves on top of each box, and that would bring out the beauty of the
berries, the green against the red. Staten Island strawberries had the reputation of being unusually good, the best on the market, and they brought fancy
prices. Most of them went to the big New York hotels. Some of the families in
Sandy Ground, strawberries were about as important to them as oysters. And
every family put up a lot of stuff, not only garden stuff, but wild stuff—wild-
grape jelly, and wild-plum jelly, and huckleberries. If it was a good huckleberry
year, they'd put up enough huckleberries to make deep-dish pies all winter.
And when they killed their hogs, they made link sausages and liver pudding
and lard. Some of the old women even made soap. People looked after things in
those days. They patched and mended and made do, and they kept their yards
clean, and they burned their trash. And they taught their children how to conduct themselves. And they held their heads up; they were as good as anybody,
and better than some. And they got along with each other; they knew each
other's peculiarities and took them into consideration. Of course, this was an
oyster town, and there was always an element that drank and carried on and
didn't have any more moderation than the cats up the alley, but the great majority were good Christians who walked in the way of the Lord, and loved Him,
and trusted Him, and kept His commandments. Everything in Sandy Ground
revolved around the church. Every summer, we put up a tent in the churchyard
and held a big camp meeting, a revival. We owned the tent. We could get three
or four hundred people under it, sitting on sawhorse benches. We'd have visiting preachers, famous old-time African Methodist preachers, and they'd
preach every night for a week. We'd invite the white oystermen to come and
bring their families, and a lot of them would. Everybody was welcome. And
once a year, to raise money for church upkeep, we'd put on an ox roast, what
they call a barbecue nowadays. A Southern man named Steve Davis would do
the roasting. There were tricks to it that only he knew. He'd dig a pit in the
churchyard, and then a little off to one side he'd burn a pile of hickory logs
until he had a big bed of red-hot coals, and then he'd fill the pit about half full
of coals, and then he'd set some iron rods across the pit, and then he'd lay a
couple of sides of beef on the rods and let them roast. Every now and then, he'd
shovel some more coals into the pit, and then he'd turn the sides of beef and
baste them with pepper sauce, or whatever it was he had in that bottle of his,
and the beef would drip and sputter and sizzle, and the smoke from the hickory
coals would flavor it to perfection. People all over the South Shore would set

aside that day and come to the African Methodist ox roast. All the big oyster captains in Prince's Bay would come. Captain Phil De Waters would come, and Captain Abraham Manee and Captain William Haughwout and Captain Peter Polworth and good old Captain George Newbury, and a dozen others. And we'd eat and laugh and joke with each other over who could hold the most.

"All through the eighties, and all through the nineties, and right on up to around 1910, that's the way it was in Sandy Ground. Then the water went bad. The oystermen had known for a long time that the water in the Lower Bay was getting dirty, and they used to talk about it, and worry about it, but they didn't have any idea how bad it was until around 1910, when reports began to circulate that cases of typhoid fever had been traced to the eating of Staten Island oysters. The oyster wholesalers in New York were the unseen powers in the Staten Island oyster business; they advanced the money to build boats and buy Southern seed stock. When the typhoid talk got started, most of them decided they didn't want to risk their money any more, and the business went into a decline, and then, in 1916, the Department of Health stepped in and condemned the beds, and that was that. The men in Sandy Ground had to scratch around and look for something else to do, and it wasn't easy. Mr. George Ed Henman got a job working on a garbage wagon for the city, and Mr. James McCoy became the janitor of a public school, and Mr. Jacob Finney went to work as a porter on Ellis Island, and one did this and one did that. A lot of the life went out of the settlement, and a kind of don't-care attitude set in. The church was especially hard hit. Many of the young men and women moved away, and several whole families, and the membership went down. The men who owned oyster sloops had been the main support of the church, and they began to give dimes where they used to give dollars. Steve Davis died, and it turned out nobody else knew how to roast an ox, so we had to give up the ox roasts. For some years, we put on clambakes instead, and then clams got too dear, and we had to give up the clambakes.

"The way it is now, Sandy Ground is just a ghost of its former self. There's a disproportionate number of old people. A good many of the big old rambling houses that used to be full of children, there's only old men and old women living in them now. And you hardly ever see them. People don't sit on their porches in Sandy Ground as much as they used to, even old people, and they don't do much visiting. They sit inside, and keep to themselves, and listen to the radio or look at television. Also, in most of the families in Sandy Ground where the husband and wife are young or middle-aged, both of them go off to work. If there's children, a grandmother or an old aunt or some other relative stays home and looks after them. And they have to travel good long distances to get to their work. The women mainly work in hospitals, such as Sea View, the big t.b. hospital way up in the middle of the island, and I hate to think of the time they put in riding those rattly old Staten Island buses and standing at bus stops in all kinds of weather. The men mainly work in construction, or in factories across the kill in New Jersey. You hear their cars starting up early in the morning, and you hear them coming in late at night. They make eighty, ninety, a hundred a week, and they take all the overtime work they can get; they have to, to pay for those big cars and refrigerators and television sets. Whenever something new comes out, if one family gets one, the others can't rest until they get one too. And the only thing they pay cash for is candy bars. For all I know, they even buy them on the installment plan. It'll all end in a mess one of these days. The church has gone way down. People say come Sunday they're just too tired to stir. Most of the time, only a handful of the old reliables show up for Sunday-morning services, and we've completely given up Sunday-evening services. Oh, sometimes a wedding or a funeral will draw a crowd. As far as gardens, nobody in Sandy Ground plants a garden any more beyond some old woman might set out a few tomato plants and half the time she forgets about them and lets them wilt. As far as wild stuff, there's plenty of huckleberries in the woods around here, high-bush and low-bush, and oceans of blackberries, and I even know where there's some beach plums, but do you think anybody bothers with them? Oh, no!"

MR. Hunter stood up. "I've rested long enough," he said. "Let's go on over to the cemetery." He went down the back steps, and I followed him. He looked under the porch and brought out a grub hoe and handed it to me. "We may need this," he said. "You take it, if you don't mind, and go on around to the front of the house. I'll go back inside and lock up, and I'll meet you out front in just a minute."

I went around to the front, and looked at the roses on the trellised bush beside the porch. They were lush pink roses. It was a hot afternoon, and when Mr. Hunter came out, I was surprised to see that he had put on a jacket, and a double-breasted jacket at that. He had also put on a black necktie and a black felt hat. They were undoubtedly his Sunday clothes, and he looked stiff and solemn in them.

"I was admiring your rosebush," I said.

"It does all right," said Mr. Hunter. "It's an old bush. When it was getting a start, I buried bones from the table around the roots of it, the way the old Southern women used to do. Bones are the best fertilizer in the world for rosebushes." He took the hoe and put it across his shoulder, and we started up Bloomingdale Road. We walked in the road; there are no sidewalks in Sandy Ground.

A little way up the road, we overtook an old man hobbling along on a cane. He and Mr. Hunter spoke to each other, and Mr. Hunter introduced him to me. "This is Mr. William E. Brown," Mr. Hunter said. "He's one of the old Sandy Ground oystermen. He's in his eighties, but he's younger than me. How are you, Mr. Brown?"

"I'm just hanging by a thread," said Mr. Brown.

"Is it as bad as that?" asked Mr. Hunter.

"Oh, I'm all right," said Mr. Brown, "only for this numbness in my legs, and I've got cataracts and can't half see, and I had a dentist make me a set of teeth and he says they fit, but they don't, they slip, and I had double pneumonia last winter and the doctor gave me some drugs that addled me. And I'm still addled."

"This is the first I've seen you in quite a while," said Mr. Hunter.

"I stay to myself," said Mr. Brown. "I was never one to go to people's houses. They talk and talk, and you listen, you bound to listen, and half of it ain't true, and the next time they tell it, they say you said it."

"Well, nice to see you, Mr. Brown," said Mr. Hunter.

"Nice to see you, Mr. Hunter," said Mr. Brown. "Where you going?"

"Just taking a walk over to the cemetery," said Mr. Hunter.

"Well, you won't get in any trouble over there," said Mr. Brown.

We resumed our walk.

"Mr. Brown came to Sandy Ground when he was a boy, the same as I did," Mr. Hunter said. "He was born in Brooklyn, but his people were from the South."

"Were you born in the South, Mr. Hunter?" I asked.

"No, I wasn't," he said.

His face became grave, and we walked past three or four houses before he said any more.

"I wasn't," he finally said. "My mother was. To tell you the truth, my mother was born in slavery. Her name was Martha, Martha Jennings, and she was born in 1849. Jennings was the name of the man who owned her. He was a big farmer in the Shenandoah Valley in Virginia. He also owned my mother's mother, but he sold her when my mother was five years old, and my mother never saw or heard of her again. Her name was Hettie. We couldn't ever get much out of my mother about slavery days. She didn't like to talk about it, and she didn't like for us to talk about it. 'Let the dead bury the dead,' she used to say. Just before the Civil War, when my mother was eleven or twelve, the wife of the man who owned her went to Alexandria, Virginia, to spend the summer, and she took my mother along to attend to her children. Somehow or other, my mother got in with some people in Alexandria who helped her run away. Some antislavery people. She never said so in so many words, but I guess they put her on the Underground Railroad. Anyway, she wound up in what's now Ossining, New York, only then it was called the village of Sing Sing, and by and by she married my father. His name was Henry Hunter, and he was a hired man on an apple farm just outside Sing Sing. She had fifteen children by him, but only three—me, my brother William, and a girl named Hettie—lived past the age of fourteen; most of them died when they were babies. My father died around 1879, 1880, somewhere in there. A few months after he died, a man named Ephraim Purnell rented a room in our house. Purnell was an oyster-man from Sandy Ground. He was a son of old man Littleton Purnell, one of the

original men from Snow Hill. He had got into some trouble in Prince's Bay connected with stealing, and had been sent to Sing Sing Prison. After he served
out his sentence, he decided he'd see if he could get a job in Sing Sing village
and live there. My mother tried to help him, and ended up marrying him. He
couldn't get a job up there, nobody would have him, so he brought my mother
and me and William and Hettie down here to Sandy Ground and he went back
to oystering."

We turned off Bloomingdale Road and entered Crabtree Avenue, which is a
narrow dirt road lined on one side with sassafras trees and on the other with a
straggly privet hedge.

"I didn't like my stepfather," Mr. Hunter continued. "I not only didn't like
him, I despised him. He was a drunkard, a sot, and he mistreated my mother.
From the time we landed in Sandy Ground, as small as I was, my main object in
life was to support myself. I didn't want him supporting me. And I didn't want
to go into the oyster business, because he was in it. I worked for a farmer down
the road a few years—one of the Sharrotts that Sharrott's Road is named for.
Then I cooked on a fishing boat. Then I became a hod carrier. Then something
got into me, and I began to drink. I turned into a sot myself. After I had been
drinking several years, I was standing in a grocery store in Rossville one day,
and I saw my mother walk past outside on the street. I just caught a glimpse of
her face through the store window as she walked past, and she didn't know
anybody was looking at her, and she had a horrible hopeless look on her face.
A week or so later, I knocked off work in the middle of the day and bought a
bottle of whiskey, the way I sometimes did, and I went out in the woods between Rossville and Sandy Ground and sat down on a rock, and I was about as
low in my mind as a man can be; I knew what whiskey was doing to me, and yet
I couldn't stop drinking it. I tore the stamp off the bottle and pulled out the
cork, and got ready to take a drink, and then I remembered the look on my
mother's face, and a peculiar thing happened. The best way I can explain it, my
gorge rose. I got mad at myself, and I got mad at the world. Instead of taking a
drink, I poured the whiskey on the ground and smashed the bottle on the rock,
and stood up and walked out of the woods. And I never drank another drop. I
wanted to many a time, many and many a time, but I tightened my jaw against
myself, and I stood it off. When I look back, I don't know how I did it, but I stood
it off, I stood it off."

We walked on in silence for a few minutes, and then Mr. Hunter said, "Ah,
well!"

"From being a hod carrier, I became a bricklayer," he continued, "but that
wasn't as good as it sounds; bricklayers didn't make much in those days. And
in 1896, when I was twenty-seven, I got married to my first wife. Her name was
Celia Ann Finney, and she was the daughter of Mr. Jacob Finney, one of the oystermen. She was considered the prettiest girl in Sandy Ground, and the situation I was in, she had turned down a well-to-do young oysterman to marry me,

a fellow with a sloop, and I knew everybody thought she had made a big mistake and would live to regret it, and I vowed and determined I was going to give her more than he could've given her. I was a good bricklayer, and I was especially good at arching and vaulting, and when a contractor or a boss mason had a cesspool to be built, he usually put me to work on it. We didn't have sewers down in this part of Staten Island, and still don't, and there were plenty of cesspools to be built. So, in 1899 I borrowed some money and went into business for myself, the business of building and cleaning cesspools. I made it my lifework. And I made good money, for around here. I built a good house for my wife, and I dressed her in the latest styles. I went up to New York once and bought her a dress for Easter that cost one hundred and six dollars; the six dollars was for alterations. And one Christmas I bought her a sealskin coat. And I bought pretty hats for her—velvet hats, straw hats, hats with feathers, hats with birds, hats with veils. And she appreciated everything I bought for her. 'Oh, George,' she'd say, 'you've gone too far this time. You've got to take it back.' 'Take it back, nothing!' I'd say. When Victrolas came out, I bought her the biggest one in the store. And I think I can safely say we set the best table in Sandy Ground. I lived in peace and harmony with her for thirty-two years, and they were the best years of my life. She died in 1928. Cancer. Two years later I married a widow named Mrs. Edith S. Cook. She died in 1938. They told me it was tumors, but it was cancer."

We came to a break in the privet hedge. Through the break I saw the white shapes of gravestones half-hidden in vines and scrub, and realized that we were at the entrance to the cemetery. "Here we are," said Mr. Hunter. He stopped, and leaned on the handle of the hoe, and continued to talk.

"I had one son by my first wife," he said. "We named him William Francis Hunter, and we called him Billy. When he grew up, Billy went into the business with me. I never urged him to, but he seemed to want to, it was his decision, and I remember how proud I was the first time I put it in the telephone book— George H. Hunter & Son. Billy did the best he could, I guess, but things never worked out right for him. He got married, but he lived apart from his wife, and he drank. When he first began to drink, I remembered my own troubles along that line, and I tried not to see it. I just looked the other way, and hoped and prayed he'd get hold of himself, but there came a time I couldn't look the other way any more. I asked him to stop, and I begged him to stop, and I did all I could, went to doctors for advice, tried this, tried that, but he wouldn't stop. It wasn't exactly he wouldn't stop, he couldn't stop. A few years ago, his stomach began to bother him. He thought he had an ulcer, and he started drinking more than ever—said whiskey dulled the pain. I finally got him to go to the hospital, and it wasn't any ulcer, it was cancer."

Mr. Hunter took a wallet from his hip pocket. It was a large, old-fashioned wallet, the kind that fastens with a strap slipped through a loop. He opened it and brought out a folded white silk ribbon.

"Billy died last summer," he continued. "After I had made the funeral arrangements, I went to the florist in Tottenville and ordered a floral wreath and picked out a nice wreath-ribbon to go on it. The florist knew me, and he knew Billy, and he made a very pretty wreath. The Sunday after Billy was buried, I walked over here to the cemetery to look at his grave, and the flowers on the wreath were all wilted and dead, but the ribbon was as pretty as ever, and I couldn't bear to let it lay out in the rain and rot, so I took it off and saved it." He unfolded the ribbon and held it up. Across it, in gold letters, were two words. "BELOVED SON," they said.

MR. Hunter refolded the ribbon and returned it to his wallet. Then he put the hoe back on his shoulder, and we entered the cemetery. A little road went halfway into the cemetery, and a number of paths branched off from it, and both the road and the paths were hip-deep in broom sedge. Here and there in the sedge were patches of Queen Anne's lace and a weed that I didn't recognize. I pointed it out to Mr. Hunter.

"What is that weed in among the broom sedge and the Queen Anne's lace?" I asked.

"We call it red root around here," he said, "and what you call broom sedge we call beard grass, and what you call Queen Anne's lace we call wild carrot."

We started up the road, but Mr. Hunter almost immediately turned in to one of the paths and stopped in front of a tall marble gravestone, around which several kinds of vines and climbing plants were intertwined. I counted them, and there were exactly ten kinds—cat brier, trumpet creeper, wild hop, blackberry, morning glory, climbing false buckwheat, partridgeberry, fox grape, poison ivy, and one that I couldn't identify, nor could Mr. Hunter. "This is Uncle Daws Landin's grave," Mr. Hunter said. "I'm going to chop down some of this mess, so we can read the dates on his stone." He lifted the hoe high in the air and brought it down with great vigor, and I got out of his way. I went back into the road, and looked around me. The older graves were covered with trees and shrubs. Sassafras and honey locust and wild black cherry were the tallest, and they were predominant, and beneath them were chokeberry, bayberry, sumac, Hercules' club, spice bush, sheep laurel, hawthorn, and witch hazel. A scattering of the newer graves were fairly clean, but most of them were thickly covered with weeds and wild flowers and ferns. There were easily scores of kinds. The majority were the common kinds that grow in waste places and in dumps and in vacant lots and in old fields and beside roads and ditches and railroad tracks, and I could recognize them at a glance. Among these were milkweed, knotweed, ragweed, Jimson weed, pavement weed, catchfly, Jerusalem oak, bedstraw, goldenrod, cocklebur, butter-and-eggs, dandelion, bouncing Bet, mullein, partridge pea, beggar's lice, sandspur, wild garlic, wild mustard, wild geranium, rabbit tobacco, old-field cinquefoil, bracken, New York fern, cinnamon fern and lady fern. A good many of the others were unfamiliar to me, and I broke off the heads and upper branches of a number of these and stowed them in the pockets of my jacket, to look at later under a magnifying glass. Some of the graves had rusty iron-pipe fences around them. Many were unmarked, but were outlined with sea shells or bricks or round stones painted white or flowerpots turned upside down. Several had fieldstones at the head and foot. Several had wooden stakes at the head and foot. Several had Spanish bayonets growing on them. The Spanish bayonets were in full bloom, and little flocks of white moths were fluttering around their white, waxy, fleshy, bell-shaped, pendulous blossoms.

"Hey, there!" Mr. Hunter called out. "I've got it so we can see to read it now." I went back up the path, and we stood among the wrecked vines and looked at the inscription on the stone. It read:

DAWSON LANDIN

DEC. 18, 1828

FEB. 21, 1899

ASLEEP IN JESUS

"I remember him well," said Mr. Hunter. "He was a smart old man and a good old man—big and stout, very religious, passed the plate in church, chewed tobacco, took the New York *Herald,* wore a captain's cap, wore suspenders *and* a belt, had a peach orchard. I even remember the kind of peach he had in his orchard. It was a freestone peach, a late bearer, and the name of it was Stump the World."

We walked a few steps up the path, and came to a smaller gravestone. The inscription on it read:

SUSAN A. WALKER

MAR. 10, 1855

MAR. 25, 1912

A FAITHFUL FRIEND

"Born in March, died in March," said Mr. Hunter. "Fifty-seven years and fifteen days, as well as I can figure it out in my head. That hardly seems the proper thing to pick out and mention on a gravestone. Susan Walker was one of Uncle Daws Landin's daughters, and she was a good Christian woman. She did more for the church than any other woman in the history of Sandy Ground. Now, that's strange. I don't remember a thing about Uncle Daws Landin's funeral, and he must've had a big one, but I remember Susan Walker's funeral very well. There used to be a white man named Charlie Bogardus who ran a store at the corner of Woodrow Road and Bloomingdale Road, a general store, and he also had an icehouse, and he was also an undertaker. He was the undertaker for

most of the country people around here, and he got some of the Rossville business and some of the Pleasant Plains business. He had a handsome old horse-
drawn hearse. It had windows on both sides, so you could see the coffin, and it
had silver fittings. Bogardus handled Susan Walker's funeral. I can still remember his two big black hearse-horses drawing the hearse up Bloomingdale Road,
stepping just as slow, the way they were trained to do, and turning in to
Crabtree Avenue, and proceeding on down to the cemetery. The horses had
black plumes on their harnesses. Funerals were much sadder when they had
horse-drawn hearses. Charlie Bogardus had a son named Charlie Junior, and
Charlie Junior had a son named Willie, and when automobile hearses started
coming in, Willie mounted the old hearse on an automobile chassis. It didn't
look fish, fowl, or fox, but the Bogarduses kept on using it until they finally gave
up the store and the icehouse and the undertaking business and moved away."

We left Susan Walker's grave and returned to the road and entered another
path and stopped before one of the newer graves. The inscription on its stone
read:

FREDERICK ROACH

1891–1955

REST IN PEACE

"Freddie Roach was a taxi-driver," Mr. Hunter said. "He drove a taxi in
Pleasant Plains for many years. He was Mrs. Addie Roach's son, and she made
her home with him. After he died, she moved in with one of her daughters.
Mrs. Addie Roach is the oldest woman in Sandy Ground. She's the widow of
Reverend Lewis Roach, who was an oysterman and a part-time preacher, and
she's ninety-two years old. When I first came to Sandy Ground, she was still in
her teens, and she was a nice, bright, pretty girl. I've known her all these years,
and I think the world of her. Every now and then, I make her a lemon-
meringue pie and take it to her, and sit with her awhile. There's a white man in
Prince's Bay who's a year or so older than Mrs. Roach. He's ninety-three, and
he'll soon be ninety-four. His name is Mr. George E. Sprague, and he comes
from a prominent old South Shore family, and I believe he's the last of the old
Prince's Bay oyster captains. I hadn't seen him for several years until just the
other day I was over in Prince's Bay, and I was going past his house on Amboy
Road, and I saw him sitting on the porch. I went up and spoke to him, and we
talked awhile, and when I was leaving he said, 'Is Mrs. Addie Roach still alive
over in Sandy Ground?' 'She is,' I said. 'That is,' I said, 'she's alive as you or I.'
'Well,' he said, 'Mrs. Roach and I go way back. When she was a young woman,
her mother used to wash for my mother, and she used to come along sometimes
and help, and she was such a cheerful, pretty person my mother always said it
made the day nicer when she came, and that was over seventy years ago.' 'That
wasn't her mother that washed for your mother and she came along to help,' I

said. 'That was her husband's mother. That was old Mrs. Matilda Roach.' 'Is that so?' said Mr. Sprague. 'I always thought it was her mother. Well,' he said, 'when you see her, tell her I asked for her.' "

We stepped back into the road, and walked slowly up it.

"Several men from Sandy Ground fought in the Civil War," Mr. Hunter said, "and one of them was Samuel Fish. That's his grave over there with the ant hill on it. He got a little pension. Down at the end of this row are some Bishop graves, Bishops and Mangins, and there's Purnells in the next row, and there's Henmans in those big plots over there. This is James McCoy's grave. He came from Norfolk, Virginia. He had six fingers on his right hand. Those graves over there all grown up in cockleburs are Jackson graves, Jacksons and Henrys and Landins. Most of the people lying in here were related to each other, some by blood, some by marriage, some close, some distant. If you started in at the gate and ran an imaginary line all the way through, showing who was related to who, the line would zigzag all over the cemetery. Do you see that row of big expensive stones standing up over there? They're all Cooleys. The Cooleys were free-Negro oystermen from Gloucester County, Virginia, and they came to Staten Island around the same time as the people from Snow Hill. They lived in Tottenville, but they belonged to the church in Sandy Ground. They were quite well-to-do. One of them, Joel Cooley, owned a forty-foot sloop. When the oyster beds were condemned, he retired on his savings and raised dahlias. He was a member of the Staten Island Horticultural Society, and his dahlias won medals at flower shows in Madison Square Garden. I've heard it said he was the first man on Staten Island to raise figs, and now there's fig bushes in back yards from one end of the island to the other. Joel Cooley had a brother named Obed Cooley who was very smart in school, and the Cooleys got together and sent him to college. They sent him to the University of Michigan, and he became a doctor. He practiced in Lexington, Kentucky, and he died in 1937, and he left a hundred thousand dollars. There used to be a lot of those old-fashioned names around here, Bible names. There was a Joel and an Obed and an Eben in the Cooley family, and there was an Ishmael and an Isaac and an Israel in the Purnell family. Speaking of names, come over here and look at this stone."

We stopped before a stone whose inscription read:

THOMAS WILLIAMS

AL MAJOR

1862–1928

"There used to be a rich old family down here named the Butlers," Mr. Hunter said. "They were old, old Staten Islanders, and they had a big estate over on the outside shore, between Prince's Bay and Tottenville, that they called Butler Manor. They even had a private race track. The last of the Butlers was Mr. Elmer T. Butler. Now, this fellow Thomas Williams was a Sandy Ground man who quit the oyster business and went to work for Mr. Elmer T. Butler. He worked for him many years, worked on the grounds, and Mr. Butler thought a lot of him. For some reason I never understood, Mr. Butler called him Al Major, a kind of nickname. And pretty soon everybody called him Al Major. In fact, as time went on and he got older, young people coming up took it for granted Al Major was his real name and called him Mr. Major. When he died, Mr. Butler buried him. And when he ordered the gravestone, he told the monument company to put both names on it, so there wouldn't be any confusion. Of course, in a few years he'll pass out of people's memory under both names—Thomas Williams, Al Major, it'll all be the same. To tell you the truth, I'm no great believer in gravestones. To a large extent, I think they come under the heading of what the old preacher called vanity—'vanity of vanities, all is vanity'—and by the old preacher I mean Ecclesiastes. There's stones in here that've only been up forty or fifty years, and you can't read a thing it says on them, and what difference does it make? God keeps His eye on those that are dead and buried the same as He does on those that are alive and walking. When the time comes the dead are raised, He won't need any directions where they're lying. Their bones may be turned to dust, and weeds may be growing out of their dust, but they aren't lost. He knows where they are; He knows the exact whereabouts of every speck of dust of every one of them. Stones rot the same as bones rot, and nothing endures but the spirit."

Mr. Hunter turned and looked back over the rows of graves.

"It's a small cemetery," he said, "and we've been burying in it a long time, and it's getting crowded, and there's generations yet to come, and it worries me. Since I'm the chairman of the board of trustees, I'm in charge of selling graves in here, graves and plots, and I always try to encourage families to bury two to a grave. That's perfectly legal, and a good many cemeteries are doing it nowadays. All the law says, it specifies that the top of the box containing the coffin shall be at least three feet below the level of the ground. To speak plainly, you dig the grave eight feet down, instead of six feet down, and that leaves room to lay a second coffin on top of the first. Let's go to the end of this path, and I'll show you my plot."

Mr. Hunter's plot was in the last row, next to the woods. There were only a few weeds on it. It was the cleanest plot in the cemetery.

"My mother's buried in the first grave," he said. "I never put up a stone for her. My first wife's father, Jacob Finney, is buried in this one, and I didn't put up a stone for him, either. He didn't own a grave, so we buried him in our plot. My son Billy is buried in this grave. And this is my first wife's grave. I put up a stone for her."

The stone was small and plain, and the inscription on it read:

HUNTER

1877 CELIA 1928

"I should've had her full name put on it—Celia Ann," Mr. Hunter said. "She was a little woman, and she had a low voice. She had the prettiest little hands; she wore size five-and-a-half gloves. She was little, but you'd be surprised at the work she done. Now, my second wife is buried over here, and I put up a stone for her, too. And I had my name carved on it, along with hers."

This stone was the same size and shape as the other, and the inscription on it read:

HUNTER
1877 EDITH 1938
1869 GEORGE

"It was my plan to be buried in the same grave with my second wife," Mr. Hunter said. "When she died, I was sick in bed, and the doctor wouldn't let me get up, even to go to the funeral, and I couldn't attend to things the way I wanted to. At that time, we had a gravedigger here named John Henman. He was an old man, an old oysterman. He's dead now himself. I called John Henman to my bedside, and I specifically told him to dig the grave eight feet down. I told him I wanted to be buried in the same grave. 'Go eight feet down,' I said to him, 'and that'll leave room for me, when the time comes.' And he promised to do so. And when I got well, and was up and about again, I ordered this stone and had it put up. Below my wife's name and dates I had them put my name and my birth year. When it came time, all they'd have to put on it would be my death year, and everything would be in order. Well, one day about a year later I was talking to John Henman, and something told me he hadn't done what he had promised to do, so I had another man come over here and sound the grave with a metal rod, and just as I had suspected, John Henman had crossed me up; he had only gone six feet down. He was a contrary old man, and set in his ways, and he had done the way he wanted, not the way I wanted. He had always dug graves six feet down, and he couldn't change. That didn't please me at all. It outraged me. So, I've got my name on the stone on this grave, and it'll look like I'm buried in this grave."

He took two long steps, and stood on the next grave in the plot.

"Instead of which," he said, "I'll be buried over here in this grave."

He stooped down, and pulled up a weed. Then he stood up, and shook the dirt off the roots of the weed, and tossed it aside.

"Ah, well," he said, "it won't make any difference."

(1956)

SECRETS OF THE MAGUS

T HE playwright David Mamet and the theatre director Gregory Mosher affirm that some years ago, late one night in the bar of the Ritz-Carlton Hotel in Chicago, this happened:

Ricky Jay, who is perhaps the most gifted sleight-of-hand artist alive, was performing magic with a deck of cards. Also present was a friend of Mamet and Mosher's named Christ Nogulich, the director of food and beverage at the hotel. After twenty minutes of disbelief-suspending manipulations, Jay spread the deck face up on the bar counter and asked Nogulich to concentrate on a specific card but not to reveal it. Jay then assembled the deck face down, shuffled, cut it into two piles, and asked Nogulich to point to one of the piles and name his card.

"Three of clubs," Nogulich said, and he was then instructed to turn over the top card.

He turned over the three of clubs.

Mosher, in what could be interpreted as a passive-aggressive act, quietly announced, "Ricky, you know, I also concentrated on a card."

After an interval of silence, Jay said, "That's interesting, Gregory, but I only do this for one person at a time."

Mosher persisted: "Well, Ricky, I really was thinking of a card."

Jay paused, frowned, stared at Mosher, and said, "This is a distinct change of procedure." A longer pause. "All right—what was the card?"

"Two of spades."

Jay nodded, and gestured toward the other pile, and Mosher turned over its top card.

The deuce of spades.

A small riot ensued.

Deborah Baron, a screenwriter in Los Angeles, where Jay lives, once invited him to a New Year's Eve dinner party at her home. About a dozen other people attended. Well past midnight, everyone gathered around a coffee table as Jay, at Baron's request, did closeup card magic. When he had performed several dazzling illusions and seemed ready to retire, a guest named Mort said, "Come on, Ricky. Why don't you do something truly amazing?"

Baron recalls that at that moment "the look in Ricky's eyes was, like, 'Mort—you have just fucked with the wrong person.' "

Jay told Mort to name a card, any card. Mort said, "The three of hearts." After shuffling, Jay gripped the deck in the palm of his right hand and sprung it, cascading all fifty-two cards so that they travelled the length of the table and pelted an open wine bottle.

"O.K., Mort, what was your card again?"

"The three of hearts."

"Look inside the bottle."

Mort discovered, curled inside the neck, the three of hearts. The party broke up immediately.

ONE morning last December, a few days before Christmas, Jay came to see me in my office. He wore a dark-gray suit and a black shirt that was open at the collar, and the colors seemed to match his mood. The most uplifting magic, Jay believes, has a spontaneous, improvisational vigor. Nevertheless, because he happened to be in New York we had made a date to get together, and I, invoking a journalistic imperative, had specifically requested that he come by my office and do some magic while I took notes. He hemmed and hawed and then, reluctantly, consented. Though I had no idea what was in store, I anticipated being completely fooled.

At that point, I had known Jay for two years, during which we had discussed his theories of magic, his relationships with and opinions of other practitioners of the art, his rigid opposition to public revelations of the techniques of magic, and his relentless passion for collecting rare books and manuscripts, art, and other artifacts connected to the history of magic, gambling, unusual entertainments, and frauds and confidence games. He has a skeptically friendly, mildly ironic conversational manner and a droll, filigreed prose style. Jay's collection functions as a working research library. He is the author of dozens of scholarly articles and also of two diverting and richly informative books, "Cards as Weapons" (1977) and "Learned Pigs & Fireproof Women" (1986). For the past several years, he has devoted his energies mainly to scholarship and to acting in and consulting on motion pictures. Though he loves to perform, he is extremely selective about venues and audiences. I've attended lectures and demonstrations by him before gatherings of East Coast under-graduates, West Coast students of the history of magic, and Midwestern bunco-squad detectives. Studying videotapes of him and observing at first hand some of his serendipitous microbursts of legerdemain have taught me how inappropriate it is to say that "Ricky Jay does card tricks"—a characteri-zation as inadequate as "Sonny Rollins plays tenor saxophone" or "Darci Kistler dances." None of my scrutinizing has yielded a shred of insight into how he does what he does. Every routine appears seamless, unparsable, sim-ply magical.

Before getting down to business in my office, we chatted about this and that: water spouters and armless origami artists and equestrian bee trainers, all sub-jects that Jay has written about. As we were talking, an editor friend and two other colleagues dropped by. I had introduced Jay and the editor once before and—presumptuously, it turned out—had mentioned earlier that morning that he would be coming by for a private performance. Politely but firmly, Jay made it plain that an audience of one was what he had in mind. There was an awkward moment after the others left. I apologized for the intrusion, and he apologized for not being more accommodating. He reassured me that he still had something to show me. My cluttered office didn't feel right, however, so we headed upstairs to a lunchroom, found that it was unoccupied, and seated our-selves in a corner booth, facing each other. He unzipped a black leather clutch that he had brought with him and removed a deck of red Bee playing cards im-printed with the logo of Harrah's Casino.

In "Cards as Weapons" Jay refers to Dai Vernon, who died last year, at ninety-eight, as "the greatest living contributor to the magical art," and he quotes Vernon's belief that "cards are like living, breathing human beings and should be treated accordingly." I was reminded of Vernon's dictum as Jay caressed the deck, as gently as if it were a newly hatched chick. He has small hands—just large enough so that a playing card fits within the plane of his palm. There is a slightly raised pad of flesh on the underside of the first joint of each finger. "Not the hands of a man who has done a lot of hard labor," Jay said—a completely disingenuous line, to which he added, "One of the best sleight-of-hand guys I know is a plumber."

Jay's hands seem out of scale with the rest of him. He is of average height but has a hefty, imposing build. During the seventies, he regularly toured with var-ious rock groups as an opening act and could easily have passed as foreman of the road crew; at the time, he had dark-brown hair that reached the middle of his back, and a dense, flowing beard. He now keeps his hair and beard neatly trimmed. He has a fleshy face, a high forehead, and dark eyes. His eyes light up and then crinkle when he laughs—a burst of what might or might not indicate pleasure, followed by a dry, wise-sounding chuckle that could mean anything. His inflection is New York with a Flatbush edge. In three of Mamet's films—"House of Games," "Things Change," and "Homicide"—Jay has been cast to type as a confidence man, a gangster, and an Israeli terrorist, respectively. In one scene of the play within a play of "House of Games," he portrays a menacing professional gambler.

"I'm always saying there's no correlation between gambling and magic," Jay said as he shuffle-cut the cards. "But this is a routine of actual gamblers' techniques within the context of a theatrical magic presentation."

He noticed me watching him shuffling, and asked softly, with deadpan sincerity, "Does that look fair?"

When I said it looked fair, he dealt two hands of five-card draw and told me to lay down my cards. Two pair. Then he laid down his. A straight.

"Was that fair?" he said. "I don't think so. Let's discuss the reason why that wasn't fair. Even though I shuffled openly and honestly, I didn't let you cut the cards. So let's do it again, and this time I'll let you cut the cards."

He shuffled again, I cut the cards, he dealt, and this time I had three tens.

"Ready to turn them over?"

My three-of-a-kind compared unfavorably with his diamond flush.

"Is that fair?" he said again. "I don't think so. Let's talk about why that might not be fair. Even though I shuffled the cards"—he was now reshuffling the deck—"and you cut the cards, you saw me pick up the cards after you cut them, and maybe you think there was some way for me to nullify the cut by sleight of hand. So this time I'll shuffle the cards and you shuffle the cards."

Jay shuffled the deck, I riffle-shuffled the deck and handed it back to him, and he said, "And I'll deal six hands of poker—one for myself and five for you. I'll let you choose any one of the five. And I'll beat you."

He dealt six hands. Instead of revealing only one of my five hands, I turned them all face up.

"Oh, oh," he said. "I see you want to turn them all over. I only intended for you to pick one—but, well, no, that's all right."

The best of my five hands was two pair.

Jay said, "Now, did that seem fair?"

I said yes.

Jay said, "I don't think so," and showed me his cards—four kings.

I rested my elbows on the table and massaged my forehead.

"Now, why might that be unfair?" he continued. "I'll tell you why. Because, even though you shuffled, I dealt the cards. That time, I also shuffled the cards. Now, this time you shuffle the cards and you deal the cards. And you pick the number of players. And you designate any hand for me and any hand for you."

After shuffling, I dealt four hands, arranged as the points of a square. I chose a hand for myself and selected one for him. My cards added up to nothing—king-high nothing.

"Is that fair?" Jay said, picking up his cards, waiting a beat, and returning them to the table, one by one—the coup de grâce. "I. Don't. Think. So." One, two, three, four aces.

· · ·

JAY has an anomalous memory, extraordinarily retentive but riddled with hard-to-account-for gaps. "I'm becoming quite worried about my memory," he said not long ago. "New information doesn't stay. I wonder if it's the Nutra-Sweet." As a child, he read avidly and could summon the title and the author of every book that had passed through his hands. Now he gets lost driving in his own neighborhood, where he has lived for several years—he has no idea how many. He once had a summer job tending bar and doing magic at a place called the Royal Palm, in Ithaca, New York. On a bet, he accepted a mnemonic challenge from a group of friendly patrons. A numbered list of a hundred arbitrary objects was drawn up: No. 3 was "paintbrush," No. 18 was "plush ottoman," No. 25 was "roaring lion," and so on. "Ricky! Sixty-five!" someone would demand, and he had ten seconds to respond correctly or lose a buck. He always won, and, to this day, still would. He is capable of leaving the house wearing his suit jacket but forgetting his pants. He can recite verbatim the rapid-fire spiel he delivered a quarter of a century ago, when he was briefly employed as a carnival barker: "See the magician; the fire 'manipulator'; the girl with the yellow e-e-elastic tissue. See Adam and Eve, boy and girl, brother and sister, all in one, one of the world's three living 'morphrodites.' And the e-e-electrode lady . . ." He can quote verse after verse of nineteenth-century Cockney rhyming slang. He says he cannot remember what age he was when his family moved from Brooklyn to the New Jersey suburbs. He cannot recall the year he entered college or the year he left. "If you ask me for specific dates, we're in trouble," he says.

Michael Weber, a fellow-magician and close friend, has said, "Basically, Ricky remembers nothing that happened after 1900."

Jay has many loyal friends, a protective circle that includes a lot of people with show-business and antiquarian-book-collecting connections and remarkably few with magic-world connections.

Marcus McCorison, a former president of the American Antiquarian Society, where Jay has lectured and performed, describes him as "a deeply serious scholar—I think he knows more about the history of American conjuring than anyone else."

Nicolas Barker, who recently retired as one of the deputy keepers of the British Library, says, "Ricky would say you can't be a good conjurer without knowing the history of your profession, because there are no new tricks under the sun, only variations. He's a superbly gifted conjurer, and he's an immensely scholarly person whose knowledge in his chosen field is gigantic, in a class by itself. And, like any other scholarly person, he has a very good working knowledge of fields outside his own."

The actor Steve Martin said not long ago, "I sort of think of Ricky as the intellectual élite of magicians. I've had experience with magicians my whole life. He's expertly able to perform and yet he knows the theory, history, literature of the field. Ricky's a master of his craft. You know how there are those teachers of creative writing who can't necessarily write but can teach? Well, Ricky can actually do everything."

A collector named Michael Zinman says, "He's instantly reachable, up to a limit." Those most familiar with his idiosyncrasies realize that there are at least three Ricky Jays: a public persona, a private persona, and a private persona within the private persona. Jay can remember his age—somewhere in his forties—but says that it is irrelevant. It is also irrelevant that Jay was not his surname at birth; it was his middle name. Janus Cercone, who wrote the screenplay for "Leap of Faith," a recent film that stars Steve Martin as a flim-flam faith healer and credits Jay as the "Cons and Frauds Consultant," told me, "I talk to Ricky three times a day. Other than my husband, he's my best friend. I think I know him as well as just about anyone does, and I know less about his background and his childhood than about those of anyone else I know."

Mamet and Jay have been friends for several years—a bond rooted, in part, in their shared fascination with the language, science, and art of cons and frauds.

"I'll call Ricky on the phone," Mamet says. "I'll ask him—say, for something I'm writing—'A guy's wandering through upstate New York in 1802 and he comes to a tavern and there's some sort of mountebank. What would the moun-tebank be doing?' And Ricky goes to his library and then sends me an entire de-scription of what the mountebank would be doing. Or I'll tell him I'm having a Fourth of July party and I want to do some sort of disappearance in the middle of the woods. He says, 'That's the most bizarre request I've ever heard. You want to do a disappearing effect in the woods? There's nothing like that in the litera-ture. I mean, there's this one 1760 pamphlet—"Jokes, Tricks, Ghosts and Diversions by Woodland, Stream and Campfire." But, other than that, I can't think of a thing.' He's unbelievably generous. Ricky's one of the world's great people. He's my hero. I've never seen anybody better at what he does."

I once asked Mamet whether Jay had ever shared with him details of his childhood.

Mamet replied, "I can't remember."

I said, "You can't remember whether you discussed it or you can't remember the details?"

He said, "I can't remember whether or not I know a better way to dissuade you from your reiteration of that question without seeming impolite."

Jay's condensed version of his early life goes like this: "I grew up like Athena—covered with playing cards instead of armor—and, at the age of seven, material-ized on a TV show, doing magic." Confronted with questions about his parents, he suggests a different topic. Whatever injuries were inflicted, his mother and his father were apparently equally guilty. Any enthusiasm he ever expressed they managed not to share. "I'm probably the only kid in history whose parents made him stop taking music lessons," he says. "They made me stop studying the accor-dion. And, I suppose, thank God." He loved to play basketball. There was a backboard above the garage of the family house, which had aluminum siding. "Don't dent the house!" his mother routinely warned. His father oiled his hair with Brylcreem and brushed his teeth with Colgate. "He kept his toothpaste in the medicine cabinet and the Brylcreem in a closet about a foot away," Jay recalls. "Once, when I was ten, I switched the tubes. All you need to know about my father is that after he brushed his teeth with Brylcreem he put the toothpaste in his hair."

Though Jay first performed in public at the age of four, he rejects the notion that magic—or, in any case, his mature style of magic—is suitable entertainment for children. Nor does he apologize for his lack of susceptibility to the charms of children themselves. I once drove with him from central Massachusetts to my home, near New York City. We had to catch a plane together the next day, and I had invited him to spend the night in a spare room, on a floor above and beyond earshot of my three sons. While acknowledging that they were Ricky Jay fans, I promised him that they would all be in bed by the time we arrived and off to school before he awoke the next morning. As it turned out, we had no sooner entered the house than I heard one of my six-year-old twins announce, "I think Ricky's here!" Before he could remove his coat, the three of them, all in their pajamas, had him cornered in the kitchen. My eleven-year-old son handed him a deck of cards. The other boys began parroting the monologue from one of his television appearances—patter from a stunt in which he tosses a playing card like a boomerang and during its return flight bisects it with a pair of giant scissors. Jay gave me the same look I imagine he gave Mort, the unfortunate New Year's Eve party guest. I immediately reached for the phone directory and found the number of a nearby motel.

Just as resolutely as he avoids children, Jay declines opportunities to perform for other magicians. This habit has earned him a reputation for aloofness, to which he pleads guilty-with-an-explanation. According to Michael Weber, he has a particular aversion to the "magic lumpen"—hoi polloi who congregate in magic clubs and at conventions, where they unabashedly seek to expropriate each other's secrets, meanwhile failing to grasp the critical distinction between doing tricks and creating a sense of wonder. One guy in a tuxedo producing doves can be magic, ten guys producing doves is a travesty. "Ricky won't perform for magicians at magic shows, because they're interested in things," Weber says. "They don't get it. They won't watch him and be inspired to make magic of their own. They'll be inspired to do that trick that belongs to Ricky. Magic is not about someone else sharing the newest secret. Magic is about working hard to discover a secret and making something out of it. You start with some small principle and you build a theatrical presentation out of it. You do something that's technically artistic that creates a small drama. There are two ways you can expand your knowledge—through books and by gaining the confidence of fellow-magicians who will explain these things. Ricky to a large degree gets his information from books—old books—and then when he performs for magicians they want to know, 'Where did that come from?' And he's appalled that they haven't read this stuff. So there's this large body of magic lumpen who really don't understand Ricky's legacy—his contribution to the art, his place in the art, his technical proficiency and creativity. They think he's an élitist and a snob."

Jay does not regard "amateur" as a pejorative. His two most trusted magician confidants are Persi Diaconis, a professor of mathematics at Harvard, and Steve Freeman, a corporate comptroller who lives in Ventura, California. Both are world-class sleight-of-hand artists, and neither ever performs for pay. Jay extolls them as "pure amateurs in the best sense." The distinction that matters to Jay is between "good" magic and "bad." Magic "gives me more pleasure and more pain than anything else I've ever dealt with," he says. "The pain is bad magicians ripping off good ones, doing magic badly, and making a mockery of the art." One specific locale that he steers clear of is the Hollywood Magic Castle, a club whose membership consists of both amateur and professional conjurers. On a given night, one can see a great performer at the Magic Castle, but all too often the club is a tepid swamp of gossip, self-congratulation, and artistic larceny—a place where audiences who don't know better are frequently fed a bland diet of purloined ineptitude. Many years ago, Jay had an encounter there that he describes as typical.

"A guy comes up and starts telling me he's a fan," he recalls. "I say thank you, that's nice to hear. He says he used to see me perform in Boulder, Colorado. That's nice, too, I say. Then he starts talking about this wonderful piece I did with a mechanical monkey—really one of the most bizarre routines I ever worked out—and I thank him, and he says, 'Yeah, I get a tremendous response when I do that. Audiences just love it.' And I say, 'Let me ask you something. Suppose I invite you over to my house for dinner. We have a pleasant meal, we talk about magic, it's an enjoyable evening. Then, as you're about to leave, you walk into my living room and you pick up my television and walk out with it. You steal my television set. Would you do that?' He says, 'Of course not.' And I say, 'But you already did.' He says, 'What are you talking about?' I say, 'You stole my television!' He says, 'How can you say that? I've never even been to your house.' This guy doesn't even know what a metaphor is. People ask me why I don't do lectures at magic conventions, and I say, 'Because I'm still learning.' Meanwhile, you've got people who have been doing magic for ten months and they are actually out there pontificating. It's absurd."

T. A. Waters, a mentalist and writer, who is the librarian at the Magic Castle, told me, "Some magicians, once they learn how to do a trick without dropping the prop on their foot, go ahead and perform in public. Ricky will work on a routine a couple of years before even showing anyone. One of the things that I love about Ricky is his continued amazement at how little magicians seem to care about the art. Intellectually, Ricky seems to understand this, but emotionally he can't accept it. He gets as upset about this problem today as he did twenty years ago."

At some point within the past twenty years, Jay asked Dai Vernon—a.k.a. the Professor—how he coped with affronts of this sort, and Vernon replied, "I forced myself not to care."

"Maybe that's how he lived to be ninety-eight years old," Jay says.

Jay's admirers invariably dwell upon his technical mastery—what is known in the trade as "chops." According to Diaconis, he is, "simply put, one of the half-dozen best card handlers in the world. Not maybe; everybody thinks so." Diaconis and Jay were casual acquaintances as kids on the New York magic scene during the fifties, then lost track of each other for several years, in part because Jay deliberately exiled himself from the mainstream magic world. They reëstablished contact twenty-odd years ago, after Diaconis caught one of Jay's appearances on the "Tonight Show." By then, Jay had honed an out-of-left-field brand of gonzo-hip comedy magic, a combination of chops and antic irreverence. Often, he would begin a performance by demonstrating a not easily marketable skill that eventually earned him a listing in the "Guinness Book of World Records": throwing a playing card for distance. A properly launched card would go ninety miles an hour. Unobstructed, it could travel a hundred and ninety feet. From ten paces, it could pierce the outer rind of a watermelon. After impaling the flesh of a watermelon with a card, Jay would rifle one card after another into the exact same spot. He also used a plastic chicken and windup toys as props and targets, often inflicting disabling injuries. His patter was voluble, embroidered with orotund, baroque locutions; he would describe the watermelon rind, for instance, as the "thick pachydermatous outer melon layer."

In a memorable routine, the "Laughing Card Trick," which involved no words at all, Jay showed his hands empty and then produced cards one at a time, along the way building suspense with cackling laughter. Each time he produced a card—somehow, it was always a jack of spades—he gripped it with his lips. After doing this maneuver four times, he removed the cards from his mouth and revealed that—voilà!—they had become the four aces. Next, he would do spirit-writing on a tortilla. Downshifting, he would segue to "The Four Queens," a minuetlike Victorian parable in which the four face cards representing "the feminine portion of the smart set" were "besieged" by "suitors from the lower orders." In other words, each of the four queens was grouped with three numbered cards. "Ladies and gentlemen," he would announce, "as you have seen, I have taken advantage of these tenderly nurtured and unsophisticated young ladies by placing them in positions extremely galling to their aristocratic sensibilities." Somehow, the queens must "find each other's company"—that is, transport themselves so that what remained would be three groups of four numbered cards and a quartet of queens. This Jay accomplished in a manner so simple, natural, and miraculous as to render prestidigitation invisible, thereby raising the strong possibility of divine intervention.

Jules Fisher, the theatrical-lighting designer and a friend of Jay's, told me, "Ricky will look into any effect and find the side of it that is inherently magical.

He doesn't present magic as a challenge—as a matter of 'Look, I can make this disappear and you can't.' Rather, he wraps it in a dramatic plot. In many of his tricks, there are stories. In 'The Four Queens,' the cards take on personas, which is much more impressive than the question of how that card disappeared."

Michael Weber has a vivid memory of seeing Jay execute "The Four Queens" fifteen years ago on a network-television special with Doug Henning as host. "It was a transcendent moment in popular magic," he says. "Ricky had attitude, presentation, humor, and chops. Everybody was talking about that show. It was one of those times when all the elements of his talent were so self-evidently on display that even the people who could never before get it finally got it." Dai Vernon once saw Jay perform "The Four Queens" live, during a lecture-demonstration at the William Andrews Clark Memorial Library, at the University of California at Los Angeles. Afterward, the Professor told his disciple that the entire performance "restored dignity to the art of magic."

"The magical aspect of Ricky is very strong," Diaconis says. "It's one thing to see someone who is very skillful with cards and quite another to witness an effect and have just no idea what happens. With Ricky, it's very hard to isolate technique from performance. I can sense when a sleight has happened and how it happened, but I still don't see it. I just feel it intellectually. When Ricky is doing one of his poetical pieces, he's working in his own unique venue. He's mixing disparate things—quirky scholarship, iconoclasm, technique, a good story—into some soup that works. Because he picks good, strong tricks and makes them come to life, in the end there's this basic simplicity about what he does. Before Ricky came along, there had been comedy magicians, but never ones who really fooled people. And you can see the consequence—there are a dozen people now working in night clubs doing Ricky Jay acts. But none of them are Ricky Jay."

IN "Learned Pigs & Fireproof Women" Jay devotes a chapter to "Max Malini: The Last of the Mountebanks." Malini, who was born in 1873, stood five feet two, had short arms and unusually small hands, dressed like a dandy, spoke English with a comically heavy Eastern European accent, and was celebrated as the most astonishing sleight-of-hand artist of his day. He performed all over the world, for Presidents, prime ministers, robber barons, emperors, kings, and Al Capone. Jay quotes Nate Leipzig, "a master exponent of pure magic technique" and a contemporary of Malini's: "I would give up everything I know in magic just to get the reaction Malini does from vanishing a single coin." At a dinner party where Dai Vernon was present, Malini borrowed a female guest's hat, spun a half-dollar on the table, and covered it with the hat, which he then lifted to reveal not the coin but a block of ice. Though Vernon knew ahead of time that this effect would be performed, he later reported that Malini, who had remained at the table throughout the meal, "fooled the hell out of me." Jay recounts this and other Malini anecdotes with a mixture of delight and wistfulness. In a just universe, he seems to imply, he himself would have been in Leipzig's and Vernon's shoes, playing to the same discerning audiences that witnessed Malini's exemplary talents. He writes, "Malini was rarely featured on music hall or theatre stages, even though he performed in the heyday of the great illusionists. Yet far more than Malini's contemporaries, the famous conjurers Herrmann, Kellar, Thurston, and Houdini, Malini was the embodiment of what a magician should be—not a performer who requires a fully equipped stage, elaborate apparatus, elephants, or handcuffs to accomplish his mysteries, but one who can stand a few inches from you and with a borrowed coin, a lemon, a knife, a tumbler, or a pack of cards convince you he performs miracles."

Jay feels connected to Malini not only out of veneration but by a strange coincidence. Malini, who was born in a small town on the Polish-Austrian border, had the given name of Max Katz (or, perhaps, Max Katz-Breit). Max Katz was also the name of Jay's maternal grandfather, a well-to-do accountant and, most important, the one member of the family who loved and appreciated Ricky and for whom Ricky in return felt love and gratitude. "My grandfather was an amateur acquisitor of skill and knowledge," Jay says. "He was interested in a lot of things—pool, chess, checkers, calligraphy, cryptography, origami, magic. His philosophy was to take lessons from the best available people and then proceed on his own. He was really a terrific teacher. And his greatest contribution was to expose me to the best. Because of him, I was able to see on a regular basis the finest closeup-magic people in the world. Unlike me, he actually liked to fraternize with magicians." At one time, Katz was president of the Society of American Magicians. When, at the age of four, Ricky did his first trick in front of an audience—he multiplied paper coffee creamers during a backyard barbecue for the Society of American Magicians—Dai Vernon was a witness.

Jay told me, "When we watched Vernon, my grandfather would say, 'Look at the Professor and study the naturalness with which he handles objects.' He introduced me to Slydini and to Francis Carlyle, two other great closeup illusionists. These were guys who were capable of doing magic—something beyond tricks—and the fact that they were stylistically so different from each other fascinated me. With Slydini, it was important to understand that he was the master of misdirection—drawing the spectator's attention away from the sleight. With Carlyle, the purpose was to absorb what my grandfather called the clarity of instruction—how Carlyle subtly guided the spectator in a way that enhanced the clarity of the effect. There was a period of several years when I took formal lessons with Slydini. In his stage appearances, which were infrequent, he used to perform in a toreador suit, and he made one for me. I wore it with my hair slicked back, and I had these fake sideburns pencilled in. I performed with doves. I did a piece called 'The

Floating Cane'—stage-illusion work, with no patter, that eventually made me realize I wanted to speak and I preferred closeup. An audition was arranged for me for 'The Ed Sullivan Show.' I wore my toreador suit and wanted to pretend I was Spanish, knowing it would increase my chances of getting on the show, but my parents wouldn't let me. By then, I had already done a lot of television. When I was five, I was supposed to appear on 'Startime Kids,' with Ed Herlihy, but I dozed during the dress rehearsal and slept through the show. I was on a program called 'Time for Pets' when I was seven. I was the youngest magician who had ever been on TV. I was awful. I was a kid. The only thing that's important is that I was very comfortable performing. I was supposed to produce a rabbit, but they couldn't find one, so I had to work with a guinea pig, which took a leak on my father's necktie. My father said, 'Perfect. You get all the glory and I get all the piss.' "

Weekends, Jay often made trips to Manhattan, first in the company of his grandfather and by adolescence often on his own. The cafeteria on the ground floor of the Wurlitzer Building, on West Forty-second Street, was to the magic demimonde what the White Horse Tavern was to literary pretenders. Jay also spent many contented hours at Al Flosso's magic shop, on West Thirty-fourth Street. He preferred Flosso's to the more popular Tannen's, which was then in Times Square, because, above all, he loved Flosso. Also, the marvellous clutter of old posters, handbills, and books appealed to him far more than the antiseptic ambience of Tannen's. "Early on, I knew I didn't want to do the kind of magic other people were doing," he says. "So I started buying old books to look for material." Flosso, in the guise of a sideshow pitchman from Coney Island, did wonderful comedy sleight of hand and had a flourishing career—in the big rooms at Grossinger's and the Concord, on the Sullivan show. When Ricky's parents asked what kind of bar-mitzvah celebration he wanted, he said he wanted Flosso to perform. "The thing that's significant about that event is that it's literally the only warm memory I have of my parents," he has said.

Prodded by Slydini and his grandfather, he entered several performing competitions at magic conventions. "I always won," he says. "But the whole thing soured me on the idea of competitions within an art." By the time he was fifteen, he had had enough of living at home. He moved in with a friend's family, moved back home again, moved to the resort town of Lake George, in upstate New York (where he discovered what it was like to support himself as a pro), and, before he turned eighteen, had left home for good. He either did or did not officially complete high school—another one of those elusive memories. Max Katz died around that time. At the funeral, Flosso ceremonially broke a wand and placed it in the casket—"the single most frightening thing I ever saw," Jay says. His grandfather's death marked the end of his relationship with his parents. (He remains on good terms with his younger sister, whom he says he admires tremendously.) By then, he was living in Illinois, having begun a peripatetic college career. Over a period of ten years, he attended five different colleges and "officially was never anything other than a freshman." At Cornell, he enrolled in the School of Hotel Management. "In case I had my own joint in Vegas, I thought I might be the only guy in the business who would know how to get around in both the casino and the kitchen," he likes to say. He and several friends formed an a-cappella doo-wop group called Chico and the Deaf Tones. The Deaf Tones were five guys named Tony plus a girl named Laura. Their big number was "Tell Laura I Love Her."

To pay tuition and otherwise make ends meet, he briefly sold encyclopedias, travelled with a carnival, worked on Wall Street as an accountant, tended bar, and, of course, did magic. From talking to Jay's friends, I gathered that there was a time when he played cards for a living. Boldly, I once raised this subject with him, and he pretended not to hear me.

"Would anybody play cards with you today?" I asked.

"Sure," he said. "Silly people."

Twice while he was still at Cornell, he appeared on the "Tonight Show." With Ithaca as his home base, he became nomadic. He performed frequently in Aspen and Lake George, did club and concert dates all over the country with various rock and jazz groups—Ike and Tina Turner, the Chambers Brothers, Leon Redbone, Al Jarreau, Emmylou Harris, Herbie Hancock, the Nitty Gritty Dirt Band. Sometimes he was the opening act, sometimes he was the headliner. Invitations to perform in Europe materialized. In the early seventies, he moved to Los Angeles and found plenty of work, first at a club in Santa Monica called McCabe's Guitar Shop and then at the Magic Castle. Tracy Newman, a television-comedy writer, who lived with him for a year, says she went to see him perform "probably seventeen times" before they started dating. Not long ago, she told me, "The thing Ricky had that I'd never before seen in a magician was charm. At McCabe's, he was doing improvisational patter. He had his stuff down so well he was just free. He had the guts to bring people onstage and really play with them, instead of having to be so careful that they might see something that would cause him to blow what he was trying to do. He was very casual, but his language had a Shakespearean feel. He was brutal with hecklers—not because it would throw him off. He just didn't like hecklers. He vaporized them."

In those days, Dai Vernon had a sinecure at the Magic Castle that entitled him to living quarters nearby. Vernon's presence was the main thing that had attracted Jay to Los Angeles. When he was not on the road, he sought out the Professor's company virtually every night. Wherever they started the evening—at the Castle or somewhere else—they would invariably wind up at Canter's Deli, on Fairfax Avenue, a shrine of vinyl and Formica and leaden matzo balls. There Vernon would hold forth until five or six in the morning. A few years ago, Jay wrote a magazine article in which he described one such session at Canter's, an occasion when he petitioned for practical counsel rather than the generous praise that Vernon typically dispensed:

"Professor," I protested, "I really want to know how I can improve my technique and performance. I want to take lessons from you. I really want advice."

Vernon smiled his patented half smile, and with a delicate movement of his eyes beckoned me closer. I leaned forward with anticipation, almost unable to contain my excitement, about to receive my benediction from the master. "You want advice, Ricky," he said. "I'll give you advice. Fuck as many different women as you can. Not the same one. Not the same one. Fuck many different women. Many different women."

Persi Diaconis ran away from his unhappy home at the age of fourteen and spent two years travelling with Vernon—an unsentimental education. "Life with Vernon was a challenge," Diaconis says. "Vernon would use secrecy as a way of torturing you. When he and I were on the road, he woke up one morning and said, 'You know, I've been thinking about sleight of hand my whole life, and I think I now know how to encapsulate it in one sentence.' And then, of course, he refused to tell me." Another friend of Vernon's once said, "I wouldn't have taken a million dollars not to have known him. But I'd give a million not to know another one like him."

Vernon was extroverted, insouciant, a winning combination of gentleman and rake. Though he perfectly fitted the role of guru, he was not the paternal mentor that Jay's grandfather had been. To the extent that anyone could fill that void, Charlie Miller did. "Learned Pigs & Fireproof Women," which Jay spent ten years writing, is dedicated "to my wonderful friend Charles Earle Miller, a unique, eccentric, and remarkable entertainer." Had Miller not been Vernon's contemporary, Jay believes, he would have been regarded as the greatest sleight-of-hand figure of his time. "For fifty or sixty years, Charlie lived in Vernon's shadow," he says. "And yet Vernon knew that Charlie was the best sleight-of-hand artist he'd ever seen." Vernon once described Miller as "unquestionably the most skillful exponent of the magic art it has ever been my pleasure to know." Miller was a shy, vulnerable man, for whom public performance was a bravura act. As a friend to Jay, Diaconis, Steve Freeman, and another accomplished magician, John Thompson—his four most reverent acolytes—he was emotionally much warmer than Vernon. "Vernon was very comfortable to be around," Freeman says. "But Charlie was your pal, Charlie was your uncle, Charlie cared about you." On the West Coast, he was the premier cruise-ship performer, and this arrangement suited his essentially rootless nature. (Jay himself worked very few cruise ships—a merciful policy, he says, because "the people who went on cruises had saved up their entire lives just to get on a boat and be away from people who looked like me.") For Vernon, Jay says, "making money was only a means of allowing him to sit in a hotel room and think about his art, about cups and balls and coins and cards." Charlie Miller was, if anything, more cerebral, even more obsessive.

"Charlie and Vernon were both magicians for magicians," says Robert Lund, the founder of the American Museum of Magic, in Marshall, Michigan. "Only magicians truly appreciated what Charlie was doing. Charlie knew more about why you do it this way instead of that way than anyone I've ever met in my life, including Ricky Jay. If there were a hundred ways of doing an effect—a card trick or sawing a lady in half—Charlie went through all hundred and analyzed each one, looking for the most natural way of doing it, the approach that would be the most palatable and acceptable to an audience."

More than any other magician Jay has known, Miller had an orthodox devotion to preserving the secrets of the art—a fundamental precept that Jay today shares with Diaconis and Freeman. To their dismay, Vernon wrote a series of instruction books. When these began to appear in print, Diaconis said to Vernon, "Why did you publish these, Professor? We don't want the animals using tools." As a palliative, they can speculate about the secrets that Miller took to the grave—an absolutism that, while perhaps depriving him of mundane celebrity, at least made the secrets themselves immortal. "Charlie would never tell anything to anybody who wasn't really on the inside," Diaconis says. "There's something called the Sprong shift. Sprong was a night watchman— he did that for a living so that he could spend his days practicing card handling. The Sprong shift is a certain way of reversing the cards so that a card that would be in the middle will end up on top. It's a move that has been passed down only orally. It's never been described or even hinted at in writing that such a thing existed. It got disseminated to three or five of us, and the one who does it beautifully is Ricky. Charlie had the capacity to watch Ricky practice it for several hours non-stop. He'd keep moving around the room to see it from every possible angle."

After both Vernon and Miller died, there were memorial services at the Magic Castle—events that Jay refused to attend, because, he said to Freeman, "most of those people didn't know anything about Vernon and Charlie."

"I now say that keeping secrets is my single most important contribution to magic," Diaconis says. "Listen, I have lots of things I won't tell Ricky about. It's pretty hard for us to fool each other. Several years ago, he borrowed my deck and had me pick a card. Then he told me to reach into my left trousers pocket and there was the card I'd picked. For half an hour, I was as badly fooled as I've ever been. In order for him to bring that about, he had to take dead aim at me. That's a phrase we use in discussing the big con: taking dead aim—deeply researching somebody's habits."

Jay once subjected Freeman to an equally unsettling experience. "I walked into Ricky's apartment one day, and I was wearing a shirt that Charlie Miller had given to Ricky and that Ricky had left at my house," Freeman says. "I was returning it, but, just for fun, I had put it on. I took the shirt off, and Ricky said, 'Oh, just leave it on the back of that chair.' Then we started talking for a while and he said he wanted to show me a new trick. He spread the deck face up and told me to point to a card. I did, and then I gathered and shuffled and dealt them face up. There were only fifty-one. I didn't see my card. And he said, 'Oh, well, go over and look in the pocket of that shirt over there.' And the card was in the shirt pocket. It takes a lot of knowledge about people to be able to do something like that. Ricky was enormously satisfied. Did I figure it out? Well, I was very fooled at the time. I felt stupid, but it was nice to be fooled. That's not a feeling we get to have very often anymore."

VICTORIA Dailey, who, along with her former husband, William Dailey, deals in rare books from a shop on Melrose Avenue, in Los Angeles, likes to refer to Jay as "our worst customer." She hastens to point out, "He could be our best customer. He wants everything but can hardly buy anything." Both Daileys regard Jay as "a true eccentric" in the English sense—part Bloomsbury, part Fawlty Towers. More than fifteen years ago, they sold Jay the first book for which he paid more than a hundred dollars. The first time he spent more than a thousand dollars for a book, and, again, when he reached the five-thousand-dollar threshold, the Daileys were also involved. The latter item was Jean Prévost's "La Première Partie des Subtiles et Plaisantes Inventions," the earliest known important conjuring book, printed in Lyons in 1584.

"I bought it unhesitatingly," recalls Jay, for whom possession of the Prévost is a bittersweet memory; uncharacteristically, he parted with it during a fiscal crisis. "I bought it and then, with remarkable rapidity, three particular jobs that I thought I had went sour. One was a Johnny Carson special on practical jokes that didn't pan out because of one of his divorces. Another was a tour of Australia that was cancelled by a natural disaster—in other words, by an act of God. This book was so fucking rare that people in the magic world just didn't know about it."

It is the Daileys' impression—a perception shared by other dealers in rare books and incunabula—that Jay spends a higher proportion of his disposable income on rare books and artifacts than anyone else they know. His friend Janus Cercone has described him as "an incunable romantic."

"Probably, no matter how much money he had, he would be overextended bibliomaniacally—or should the word be 'bibliographically'? Anyway, he'd be overextended," William Dailey has said. "The first time I met him, I recognized him as a complete bibliomaniac. He's not a complete monomaniac about books on magic, but within that field he is remarkably focussed. His connoisseurship is impeccable, in that he understands the entire context of a book's emergence. He's not just interested in the book's condition. He knows who printed it, and he knows the personal struggle the author went through to get it printed."

In 1971, during Jay's nomadic phase, he spent a lot of time in Boston hanging out with Diaconis, who had begun to assemble a library of rare magic books. Diaconis takes credit for explicating the rudiments of collecting to Jay and animating his academic interest. He now regards Jay as "ten standard deviations out, just the best in the world in his knowledge of the literature of conjuring." Jay's collection—several thousand volumes, plus hundreds of lithographs, playbills, pamphlets, broadsides, and miscellaneous ephemera—reflects his interest not only in magic but also in gambling, cheating, low life, and what he described in the subtitle of "Learned Pigs & Fireproof Women" as "unique, eccentric and amazing entertainers: stone eaters, mind readers, poison resisters, daredevils, singing mice, etc., etc., etc., etc." Though Jay abhors the notion of buying books as investments, his own collection, while it is not for sale and is therefore technically priceless, more or less represents his net worth. There was a time, within the past decade, when he seriously considered becoming a bookdealer himself. The main thing that dissuaded him, he says, is that "I wouldn't want to sell a book to a philistine, which is what every bookseller has to do." Unlike a lot of collectors, he actually reads and rereads the books and other materials he buys, and puts them to scholarly and performing use. Therefore, he has no trouble rationalizing why he, rather than someone else who might turn up at an auction or peruse a dealer's catalogue, is more worthy of owning, say, both variant editions of "A Synopsis of the Butchery of the Late Sir Washington Irving Bishop (Kamilimilianalani), a most worthy Mason of the thirty-second degree, the Mind Reader and philanthropist, by Eleanor Fletcher Bishop, His Broken Hearted Mother," Philadelphia, 1889 and 1890.

One day last spring, I got a phone call from Jay, who had just returned to Los Angeles from Florida, where he and Michael Weber spent several months doing "pyromagical effects" on a movie called "Wilder Napalm."

"There's a pile of mail on my desk," he said.

"I hope there are a few checks in it," I said.

"Yes, actually, there are. But, of course, I just spent it all on a book."

The book in question was Thomas Ady's "A Candle in the Dark: Or a Treatise Concerning the Nature of Witches and Witchcraft," which includes an important seventeenth-century account of an English magic performance. I had once heard Jay allude to "A Candle in the Dark" during a lecture at the Huntington Library, in San Marino, California. The Huntington owned a copy, and so did a few other institutions. Jay described it to me as "exceedingly rare—only one copy has been sold in my collecting lifetime," and said that he had acquired his from a New York dealer "after a long negotiation." On a subsequent visit to New York, he took me to meet the dealer, Steve Weissman, a preternaturally relaxed fellow, who was obviously quite fond of him.

"We have a common interest," Weissman, who does business out of an office on the East Side, said. "We do like the same kinds of books. I don't specialize in Ricky's area of interest—only Ricky does—but I find that I gravitate toward it. My stock is dominantly literary. And I like oddball subjects: slang dictionaries, magic, gambling, con games. The advantage for me with Ricky is that he's an enthusiast for a wide range of subjects. Most customers arrive and they're entering the dealer's world, my world. He walks in and I enter his world. The next customer through the door might be a Byron fanatic and I'll have to enter *his* world. It's not a unique situation, but with Ricky it's particularly gratifying, because of the kind of collector he is—passionate and knowledgeable. Ideally, I would also include rich in that equation, but he doesn't qualify."

Referring to "A Candle in the Dark," Weissman added, "I don't doubt that I could have sold it for more money to someone else. But it's more fun to sell it to Ricky."

A young man with a ponytail and peach-fuzzy sideburns and wearing a herringbone-tweed topcoat entered the shop. As he closed the door behind him, the doorknob fell off. He picked it up and handed it to Weissman's assistant and said, "I think this is yours."

Sotto voce, Jay said, "Who is that guy?"

"I think he's someone who's trying to swindle us into buying a Visa card, or something," Weissman said.

When the young man was ready to leave, a few minutes later, the doorknob had been reattached but would not turn. Twenty minutes elapsed before we were finally rescued by an upstairs neighbor who was able to open the door from the outside. While we waited, before our liberation seemed certain, Jay gestured at the wall-to-wall, floor-to-ceiling shelves of rare books and said, "To most people this would be hell. But to me it's just a holiday."

Several years ago, Weissman attended an auction at Christie's and, bidding on behalf of Jay and Nicolas Barker, of the British Library, bought a collection of rare engravings whose subject matter was calligraphy. Jay writes in a stylized calligraphic script, and Barker, having spent much of his professional life cataloguing and studying antiquarian manuscripts, confesses to being "passionately interested in the history of handwriting." There were more than thirty items in the auction lot, and Jay and Barker divided them according to a simple formula. "I kept all the images related to armless calligraphers," Jay says, "and Nicolas got all the calligraphers with arms."

In a chapter of "Learned Pigs" entitled "More Than the Sum of Their Parts," Jay recounts the skills and accomplishments of various men and women, all celebrated figures between the sixteenth and the early twentieth centuries, who lacked the usual complement of appendages—arms or legs or digits—and compensated in inspiring ways. He dotes especially on Matthew Buchinger, "The Wonderful Little Man of Nuremberg," who was born in 1674, died around 1740, and, in between, married four times, sired fourteen children, and "played more than a half dozen musical instruments, some of his own invention, and danced the hornpipe . . . amazed audiences with his skills at conjuring . . . was a marksman with the pistol and demonstrated trick shots at nine pins . . . was a fine penman; he drew portraits, landscapes, and coats of arms, and displayed remarkable calligraphic skills." Buchinger managed these transactions without the benefit of feet or thighs, and instead of arms he had "two fin-like excrescences growing from his shoulder blades." He stood, so to speak, only twenty-nine inches high. The Christie's auction enabled Jay to add significantly to his trove of Buchingeriana—playbills, engravings by and of the Wonderful Little Man, self-portraits, specimens of his calligraphy, and accounts of his performances as a conjurer.

Segueing from a passage about Carl Herman Unthan, who was armless, played the violin with his feet, toured in vaudeville as "Unthan, the Pedal Paganini," and "fired the rifle . . . with enough skill and accuracy to be compared with the great trick shot artists Ira Paine and Doc Carver," Jay writes, "Writers, scientists, and medical men have explored the psychologies and physiologies of these prodigies; they and the public alike are intrigued by the relationship between the horrific and miraculous."

This last phrase concisely expresses Jay's central preoccupation as a scholar and a performer. "Learned Pigs" contains only passing references to Houdini, whose tirelessness as a self-promoter was concomitant with his gifts as an illusionist. Jay has attempted to rescue from the margins of history performers who in their day were no less determined than Houdini to please their audiences. Here is an echt-Jay paragraph:

> As the novelty of fire-eating and -handling wore off, those performers not versatile enough to combine their talents into more diversified shows took to the streets. In 1861 Henry Mayhew, in Volume 3 of "London Labour and the London Poor," described one such salamander. After a fascinating and detailed account of a fire king learning his trade and preparing his demonstrations, we find the poor fellow has been reduced to catching rats with his teeth to earn enough money to survive.

The rest of the fire-handlers, geeks, acid-drinkers, bayonet-swallowers, mentalists, contortionists, illiterate savants, faith-healing charlatans, porcine-faced ladies, and noose-wearing high-divers who populate "Learned Pigs" routinely sacrifice their dignity, but they never lose their humanity. "I don't want to be seen as somebody who just writes about freaks," Jay says. "A lot of the people I write about were very famous in their day, and they were a great source of entertainment. Today, audiences are just as curious, just as willing to be amazed. But look at everything we're barraged with—it just doesn't lodge in the imagination the same way." His mission, in sum, is to reignite our collective sense of wonder.

Jay's fruitful combination of autodidacticism and free-lance scholarship is itself a wonderful phenomenon. Reviewing "Learned Pigs" in the *Times*, John Gross wrote, "One effect of Mr. Jay's scholarship is to make it clear that even among freaks and prodigies there is very little new under the sun. Show him a stone-eater or a human volcano or an enterologist and he will show you the same thing being done before, often hundreds of years earlier." In the Philadelphia *Inquirer* Carlin Romano wrote, " 'Learned Pigs & Fireproof Women' is a book so magnificently entertaining that if a promoter booked it into theatres and simply distributed a copy to each patron to read, he'd have the hit of the season." A blurb on the jacket from Penn and Teller says, "It's the coolest book . . . and probably the most brilliantly weird book ever." Jay wrote much of "Learned Pigs" while occupying a carrel in the rare-book stacks of the Clark Library, at U.C.L.A. At one point, Thomas Wright, a librarian at the Clark and a former professor of English literature, tried to persuade him to apply for a postdoctoral research fellowship. When Jay explained that he didn't have a doctorate, Wright said, "Maybe a master's degree would be sufficient."

"Thomas, I don't even have a B.A."

Wright replied, "Well, you know, Ricky, a Ph.D. is just a sign of docility."

AS Jay was completing the writing of "Learned Pigs," he received an offer, unexpected and irresistible, to become the curator of the Mulholland Library of Conjuring and the Allied Arts. John Mulholland, who died in 1970, was a distinguished magician, historian, and writer. He was also a close friend of Houdini, whom he befriended in his capacity as editor of *The Sphinx*, the leading magic journal of its time. Above all, he was an obsessively thorough collector of printed materials and artifacts relating to magic and other unusual performing arts. In other words, if Jay and Mulholland had got to know each other they would have become soul mates. Mulholland's collection comprised some ten thousand volumes, in twenty languages. In 1966, he moved it to The Players Club, on Gramercy Park, and until his death he remained its curator. In 1984, the club put it up for sale. The auction gallery that was handling the sale enlisted Jay to help catalogue the collection and advise on its dispersal. Jay feared that it would be broken up or sold overseas, and either outcome seemed perilously likely. At a late hour, however, a young Los Angeles attorney, businessman, and novice magician named Carl Rheuban—someone Jay had never heard of—turned up and bought the library intact, for five hundred and seventy-five thousand dollars.

Like a lot of promoters who floated extravagant fantasies during the profligate eighties, Rheuban knew friendly and indulgent bankers. As it happened, the friendliest of these bankers was Rheuban himself. In 1983, he founded the First Network Savings Bank, leased office space in Century City, offered high-interest rates to attract deposits from all over the country, and started investing the funds in complex and wishful real-estate ventures. By the spring of 1985, Jay had an office on the bank premises, where the collection was housed. Soon, he also had a steady salary, a staff of three assistants, a healthy acquisitions allowance, friendlier-than-ever relationships with dealers all over the world, and control of a superb research library. Plans were drafted for what Jay anticipated would be "a dream come true": the collection would be moved to a building in downtown Los Angeles, which would also accommodate a museum and a small theatre where he would regularly perform, as would other artists who appealed to his sensibilities. Edwin Dawes, a British historian of magic and a professor of biochemistry, who visited the library and regularly corresponded with Jay, has said, "It just seemed as if Ricky's fairy godmother had appeared to provide the environment in which to work and all the facilities to do the job." Even from the perspective of Jay, the inveterate skeptic, it was a nearly ideal situation. And, clearly, Rheuban, who was occupied with diverse enterprises, regarded him as the ideal overseer.

In April of 1990, however, First Network was abruptly closed by California banking regulators, and the Resolution Trust Corporation (R.T.C.), the federal agency created to cope with the nationwide savings-and-loan crisis, moved in to liquidate its assets. Rheuban soon filed for personal bankruptcy, and was reported to be the subject of a criminal-fraud investigation. With no forewarning, Jay discovered that he could not even gain access to his own office without first receiving permission from self-important bureaucrats who didn't know Malini from minestrone. The irony of this was unbearable. Had Ricky Jay, of all people, been victimized by a high-stakes con game?

If Rheuban did commit crimes, the government has yet to persuade a grand jury that they were transgressions worthy of an indictment. Nor does Jay at this point have a desire to know how, precisely, First Network came undone. Regardless of what was going on inside the bank, Jay had felt that his working arrangement with Rheuban was basically satisfactory. Though they have not spoken in almost two years, he expresses no bitterness toward his former employer and benefactor. For the functionaries of the R.T.C., however, he harbors deep contempt. Because Rheuban's personal insolvency was enmeshed with the bank's insolvency, the fate of the Mulholland Library was for many months suspended in legal limbo. Brian Walton, an attorney and friend of Jay's, who advised him during the fiasco, has said, "When you look at the question of the ownership of the library, the moral ownership was clearly in Ricky's hands. The financial ownership was obviously elsewhere. But, of course, artists will often become divorced from what they create. Every day, there would be one yahoo or another messing with what were, in a moral sense, Ricky's treasures. One day, Ricky came by the library and there were some government people videotaping the collection for inventory purposes. And they'd just placed their equipment wherever they felt like it. Ricky looked at one guy and said, 'Get your stuff off those posters.' And the guy said, 'I'm So-and-So, from the F.B.I.' And Ricky said, 'I don't care who the fuck you are. Get your crap off those posters.' "

The outlandishness of the situation was compounded by the fact that the Mulholland Library proved to be a splendid investment—the only asset in the First Network bankruptcy which had appreciated significantly. After a year and a half of what Jay regarded as neglect and mismanagement, the R.T.C. finally put it up for sale at auction. The day before the auction, which was to be presided over by a bankruptcy judge in a downtown courtroom, Jay gave me my first and last glimpse of the collection, which was still in Century City. In the building lobby, on our way to what had been First Network's offices, on the fifth floor, Jay pointed out that the bank's small retail operation was now occupied by a custom tailor shop. Upstairs, we walked through an empty anteroom that had once been lined with vitrines, then headed down a long beige-carpeted corridor. James Rust, a young R.T.C. employee, emerged from a corner office—formerly Rheuban's—and greeted us.

Our first stop was a large storage room filled with material from the collection of a German physician named Peter Hackhofer. "I bought different parts of this collection from Hackhofer in several crazy transactions," Jay said. "He used to lead me on incredible goose chases all over Germany. We'd end up doing business at three in the morning on the Autobahn, halfway between Cologne and Frankfurt. We'd be pulled over to the side of the road with theatrical posters spread out on the roof of his car. Once, I went all the way to Germany to buy a collection that Hackhofer was going to broker, only to find out that the owner refused to sell. Months later, in New York, I met Hackhofer at a hotel. He'd brought with him a hundred posters, which, because his room was so small, he spread out in the hallway. He had to restrain me from attacking a bellboy who rolled over some of them with a luggage cart." The storage room contained hundreds of books, in German and French, as well as a silk pistol, a billiard-ball stand, a vanishing and appearing alarm clock, a cube-shaped metal carrying case for a spirit bell, and a paper box with a ribbon on it, which was about the size of a lady's handbag, and which Jay said was "a Victorian production reticule." I knew that I could have happily occupied myself there for several hours, but he seemed eager to move on. We walked down another long corridor, past the erstwhile loan-servicing and accounting departments, and came to a locked door. As Rust unlocked it, Jay looked at me with a wry, I-will-now-have-my-liver-eaten-by-vultures sort of smile.

We stepped into a square room, perhaps thirty by thirty. Bookshelves and glass-enclosed cabinets lined the walls, and tables and flat files filled the interior. Separated from this room by a glass partition was a ten-by-twelve cubicle that had been Jay's office. It contained a desk, a wall of bookshelves, and a side table. Two automatons stood on the table. One, called "The Singing Lesson," was the creation of Jean-Eugène Robert-Houdin, the nineteenth-century watchmaker-turned-conjurer, who is considered the father of modern magic. The other was a Chinese cups-and-balls conjurer built by Robert-Houdin's father-in-law, Jacques Houdin. A large, framed color poster of Malini, advertising his "Round the World Tour," hung on the wall to the left of Jay's desk.

"I heard that that poster holds some sort of special significance for you, Ricky," James Rust said.

Jay responded with an opaque, querulous stare that said, in effect, "Hey, pal, everything in this place holds special significance for me."

Along the back wall of the main room were shelved bound volumes of *The Sphinx*, *The Wizard*, *The Conjurer's Monthly*, *The Linking Ring*, *The Magic Circular*,

Das Programm, La Prestidigitation, Ghost, The Magic Wand, The Gen, Mahatma, and other periodicals. I spent an hour and a half in the main room, exploring the contents of the file drawers, staring into the glass display cases, pulling books from shelves, admiring framed lithographs, and listening to Jay. Ultimately, the experience was disquieting. Connected to virtually every item was a piquant vignette—a comic oddity, a compilation of historical or biographical arcana—but each digression inevitably led to a plaintive anticlimax, because the tangible artifacts had now passed from Jay's care. I paged through the scrapbook of Edward Maro, "a Chautauqua-circuit magician who played the mandolin and did hand shadows." A Barnum & Bailey poster trumpeting automotive daredevils—"L'Auto Bolide Thrilling Dip of Death"—had been used by Jay when he was "writing a piece about crazy car acts for an automotive magazine." There was a lithograph of Emil Naucke, a corpulent charmer in a flesh-colored tutu, of whom Jay said, "He was a German wrestler in drag, he was a famous strongman, he had a theatre of varieties, and as part of his act he danced with a midget." A lithograph of Martini-Szeny depicted "a Hungarian Houdini imitator who wore chaps and a Mexican hat and used to have himself strapped to a cactus," Jay said. "I was going to write a book on Houdini imitators that I would call 'Houdini: Howdini, Oudini, Martini-Szeny, and Zucchini, Pretenders to the Throne.' And with these reference books over here I could look up and see exactly where Martini-Szeny performed in, say, February of 1918. I bought this entire collection from an old circus artist in Atlanta who did a barrel act."

We wandered back into Jay's former office at one point. To his obvious annoyance, Rust wound up the "Singing Lesson" automaton. While it was playing, Jay turned his attention to a book that had been sitting on his desk, a seventeenth-century copy of the first book on magic to be printed in Dutch. The front cover had become separated from the binding.

"That's nice," he said with sarcasm. "This was not detached."

Rust nodded in acknowledgment.

"That's creepy," Jay continued. "This was a really solid vellum binding. That's why I don't want people in here who don't know how to handle books."

"Do you know how many hands have been here, Ricky?"

"Yes, and it's really creepy."

When Rust left the room, Jay said to me, "You know, I never had any agreement with Carl. At the outset, he asked me, 'What do you want?' And I said, 'I want access to this collection for the rest of my life.' And he said, 'Fine.' After we moved in here, I unpacked every single book. We catalogued what we could, but, as with any active collection, you can never really catch up. In the five years I was here, I almost doubled the size of the collection. This was the only thing I ever did that I spoke of myself as doing into the indefinite future."

Shortly after eight o'clock the next morning, I picked Jay up in front of his apartment building, and we drove downtown to the courthouse, where the auction would take place. A couple of days earlier, he had said to me, "I've talked to a lot of people who say they might be bidding, and I can tell you that, without a single exception, they're utterly soulless. No one gets it, no one has a clue to what the collection is really about. There actually are people who are knowledgeable about this, but they're not the ones who are able to buy it." As it was, the disposition of the Mulholland Library now seemed a foregone conclusion. David Copperfield, a workaholic stage illusionist who spends several weeks each year performing in Las Vegas and the other weeks touring the world, had agreed to pay two million two hundred thousand dollars for it. The only thing that could alter this outcome would be a competing bidder—bids would be allowed in minimum increments of fifty thousand dollars—and none had materialized.

At the courthouse, we discovered that the bankruptcy-court clerk had altered the docket and we were more than an hour early. Jay and I retreated to a cafeteria, where we were soon joined by William Dailey, the bookdealer, and by Steve Freeman, Michael Weber, and Brian Walton. When we finally entered the courtroom, Copperfield was already seated in the front row of the spectator gallery, along with two attorneys, a personal assistant, and a couple of advisers, who were also acquaintances of Jay's. Twenty or so other people, among them several lawyers representing creditors in the Rheuban bankruptcy, were also present. Copperfield is a slender, almost gaunt man in his mid-thirties with thick black eyebrows, brown eyes, aquiline features, and leonine dark hair. He was dressed all in black: double-breasted suit, Comme des Garçons T-shirt, suède cowboy boots.

John Gaughan, a designer of stage illusions, who was seated with Copperfield, said to Jay, "Did you bring some cards?"

"Oh, yes," Jay replied. "When you feel your life threatened, you're always prepared." Then he asked Copperfield, "Where have you come from?"

"Atlantic City."

"Ah—from one gambling arena to another."

The judge, the Honorable Vincent P. Zurzolo, appeared briefly, only to learn that Katherine Warwick, the main lawyer for the R.T.C., had not yet arrived. Ten minutes later, she breezed in and, in a friendly, casual manner, distributed to the other lawyers present her reply to a motion objecting to the allocation of the proceeds. About half an hour of legalistic colloquy ensued—a debate over whether the auction could even take place and, if so, when. At last, the Judge asked a fifty-thousand-dollar question: "Is there anyone who is here to overbid the bidder who has made the initial offer?"

There was a minute of silence, broken in my corner of the spectator section by Jay muttering, "Unbelievable. Unbelievable."

And, with that, David Copperfield—a man who owned neither a home nor an automobile but was reported to be looking for a warehouse; a man whose stage presentations were once described to me as "resembling ‹ the way Velveeta resembles cheese"—had bought the Mulholla two million two hundred thousand dollars. Katherine Warw Copperfield's attorneys that he had fifteen days—until the end ol to remove the collection from Century City, because the R.T.C. was shutting down its operation there. There were handshakes among the Copperfield entourage, and then Copperfield approached Jay.

"Thank you for everything," he said, extending his hand.

"You'll enjoy it," Jay said. "I did."

"You know you'll be welcome any time."

"We'll speak again in the future, I'm sure," Jay said.

A friend of Jay's who also knew Copperfield said to me later, "David Copperfield buying the Mulholland Library is like an Elvis impersonator winding up with Graceland."

A few weeks ago, Copperfield arranged for Jay to be flown to Las Vegas to discuss the collection. A driver met Jay at the airport and delivered him to a warehouse. In front was an enormous neon sign advertising bras and girdles. It was Copperfield's conceit that the ideal way for a visitor to view the Mulholland Library would be to pass first through a storefront filled with lingerie-clad mannequins and display cases of intimate feminine apparel. With enthusiasm, Copperfield escorted Jay around the premises, insisting that he read each of the single-entendre slogans posted on the walls—"We Support Our Customers" and "Our Bras Will Never Let You Down"—and also the punning tributes inscribed on celebrity photographs from the likes of Debbie Reynolds, Jerry Lewis, and Buddy Hackett. When Copperfield pressed one of the red-nippled breasts of a nude mannequin, the electronic lock on a mirrored door deactivated, and he and Jay stepped into the main warehouse space. Construction work had recently been completed on an upper level. Jay followed Copperfield up a stairway and into a suite of rooms that included several offices, a bedroom, and a marble-tiled bathroom. The bathroom had two doors, one of which led to an unpartitioned expanse where the contents of the Mulholland Library—much of it shelved exactly as it had been in Century City, some of it on tables, some of it not yet unpacked—had been deposited.

Jay stayed an hour—long enough to register pleasure at seeing the collection once again and dismay at the context in which he was seeing it. When Copperfield asked whether he would be willing to work as a consultant on an occasional basis—"Basically, he wanted to know whether, whenever he needs me, I would drop whatever I'm doing and tell him what he'd bought"—Jay recognized an offer that he could easily resist.

After Jay returned to Los Angeles, he said, "As much as I love this collection, I didn't think I could handle going through Copperfield's bra-and-girdle emporium every time I went to see it."

CLEARLY, Jay has been more interested in the craft of magic than in the practical exigencies of promoting himself as a performer. His friend T. A. Waters has said, "Ricky has turned down far more work than most magicians get in a lifetime." Though he earns high fees whenever he does work, a devotion to art rather than a devotion to popular success places him from time to time in tenuous circumstances. At the moment, he is mobilizing a project that should reward him both artistically and financially. What he has in mind is a one-man show, on a stage somewhere in New York, to be billed as "Ricky Jay and His 52 Assistants"—an evening's entertainment with a deck of cards. He envisions an intimate setting.

"All I value as a performer is for people to want to see me," Jay says. "I mean people who have come just to see me—they're not going out to hear music, they're not out to get drunk or to pick up women. I'd much rather perform in a small theatre in front of a few people than in an enormous Las Vegas night club."

Provided that the right theatre and the right situation materialize, David Mamet has agreed to direct such a production. "I'm very honored to be asked," Mamet told me. "I regard Ricky as an example of the 'superior man,' according to the I Ching definition. He's the paradigm of what a philosopher should be: someone who's devoted his life to both the study and the practice of his chosen field."

Having directed Jay now in three films—and they are collaborating on the screenplay of another—Mamet holds him in high esteem as an actor. "Ricky's terrific," Mamet said. "He doesn't make anything up. He knows the difference between doing things and not doing things. The magician performs a task and the illusion is created in the mind of the audience. And that's what acting is about."

Jay now spends the greater part of his typical workdays alone in his Old Spanish–style Hollywood apartment. It is the repository of his collection, the research facility for his scholarly pursuits. Overloaded bookshelves line the living-room and bedroom walls, and stacks of books on the floors make navigation a challenge. Posters, playbills, and engravings decorate any available wall space—several Buchingers, Toby the Learned Pig (the most gifted of the sapient swine), Madame Girardelli (the fireproof woman), Houdini suspended upside down in a water-torture cell, Erno Acosta balancing a piano on his head, a three-sheet poster of Cinquevalli (the most famous juggler at the turn of the century). Jay sleeps beneath a huge color lithograph of an Asian-looking man billed as Okito, whom he described to me as "the fifth of six generations or the fourth of five generations—depending on whose story you want to believe—of a family of Dutch Jewish magicians, a twentieth-century performer whose real name was Theodore Bamberg." Between two books on a shelf in the corner of his kitchen is a photograph of Steve Martin, inscribed "To Ricky, Without you there would be no Flydini. Think about it, Steve." This refers to a comedy magic routine that Jay helped Martin develop a few years ago, a dumb-show piece that he has performed at charity events and on television. As the Great Flydini, Martin appears onstage dressed in tails, unzips his trousers, and smiles uncomfortably as an egg emerges from his fly, followed by another egg, a third egg, a lit cigarette, a puff of smoke, two more eggs, a ringing telephone, a bouquet of flowers, a glass of wine, a silk handkerchief that a pretty girl walks off with and drops, whereupon it flies back inside his trousers, a Pavarotti hand puppet, and soap bubbles.

The last time I visited Jay in his apartment, he was working simultaneously on more than half a dozen projects. Within the past year, he has begun to do his writing on a computer, rather than in longhand on a legal pad with a calligraphic pen. This has evidently not made the process any less daunting. "Writing is the only thing in my life that hasn't got easier," he said. "I can say that categorically. Right now, I'm finishing a magazine article that was supposed to be about human ingenuity, but somehow I've ended up writing about child prodigies. Here's my lead sentence: 'Solomon Stone, the midget lightning calculator, was an overachiever.' I go from Solomon Stone to the Infant Salambo. This was a child who was from a turn-of-the-century showbiz family. She was abandoned by them for several years, and when they turned up again they realized she had been neglected, had had absolutely no education. But within a year she was appearing onstage, having been reinvented as Salambo, the Infant Historian—get this—'absolutely the most clever and best-informed child the world has ever seen.' "

He showed me a prospectus for *Jay's Journal of Anomalies*, a letterpress-printed broadside for "a periodical devoted to the investigation of conjurers, cheats, hustlers, hoaxers, pranksters . . . arcana, esoterica, curiosa, varia . . . scholarly and entertaining . . . amusing and elucidating . . . iconographically stimulating . . ."

"I just finished a piece for *Jay's Journal* on performing dogs who stole the acts of other dogs," he said. "Next, I want to do a piece about crucifixion acts—you know, real crucifixions that were done as entertainment. The idea for this came to me one Easter Sunday. Bob Lund, from the American Museum of Magic, has just sent me a little book on Billy Rose's Theatre that contained one sentence he knew would interest me—about a woman who swung nude from a cross to the strains of Ravel's 'Boléro.' Her name was Faith Bacon. This was in the thirties. Unlike some of the other performers I've turned up, in her act she only simulated crucifixion. Anyway, I'm playing around with that."

Over the past few years, Jay has given a number of lectures on the origins of the confidence game, which he hopes to expand into a book-length history of cheating and deception. For the Whitney Museum's Artists and Writers series, he is writing a book to be illustrated by William Wegman and others. It is a history of trick magic books, which were first produced in the sixteenth century.

"I'm really intrigued with the concept of the book as both a subject and an object of mystery," he said.

Most afternoons, Jay spends a couple of hours in his office, on Sunset Boulevard, in a building owned by Andrew Solt, a television producer who three years ago collaborated with him on an hour-long CBS special entitled "Learned Pigs & Fireproof Women," which is the only prime-time network special ever hosted by a sleight-of-hand artist. He decided now to drop by the office, where he had to attend to some business involving a new venture that he has begun with Michael Weber—a consulting company called Deceptive Practices, Ltd., and offering "Arcane Knowledge on a Need to Know Basis." They are currently working on the new Mike Nichols film, "Wolf," starring Jack Nicholson. When Jay arrived at his office, he discovered that a parcel from a British dealer had been delivered in that day's mail.

"Oh my. Oh my. This is wonderful," he said as he examined an early-nineteenth-century chapbook that included a hand-colored engraving of its subject—Claude Seurat, the Living Skeleton. "Look," he said, pointing to some scratched numerals on the verso of the title page. "This shelf mark means this was in the library of Thomas Phillips, the most obsessive book-and-manuscript collector of the nineteenth century."

The mail had also brought a catalogue from another British dealer, who was offering, for a hundred and fifty pounds, an engraving and broadside of Ann Moore, the Fasting Woman of Tutbury. By the time we left the office, an idea for an issue of *Jay's Journal* had begun to percolate.

"I could do fasting impostors and living skeletons," Jay said. "Or what might really be interesting would be to do living skeletons and fat men. For instance, I could write about Seurat and Edward Bright, the Fat Man. Except I might prefer a contemporary of Seurat's, Daniel Lambert. He was even fatter than Bright, but he's been written about more. With Bright, the pleasure would be writing about the wager involving his waistcoat. When he died, the wager was that five men twenty-one years of age could fit into his waistcoat. As it happened, seven grown men could fit inside. I have an exquisite black-and-white engraving of Bright, from 1751. And I have a great hand-colored engraving of Bright and Lambert, from 1815, which has an inset of the seven men in the waistcoat."

Back at the apartment, Jay examined the Seurat book and brought out for comparison an 1827 eight-page French pamphlet on Seurat. I asked what other Seurat material he had, and he removed his shoes, stood on the arm of a sofa, and brought down from a shelf one of four volumes of the 1835 edition of "Hone's Every Day Book, and Table Book; or, Everlasting Calendar of Popular Amusements, Sports, Pastimes, Ceremonies, Manners, Customs, and Events, Incident to Each of the Three Hundred and Sixty-five Days, in Past and Present Times; forming a Complete History of the Year, Months, and Seasons, and a Perpetual Key to the Almanac." In it he immediately found two engrav-

ings of Seurat, alongside one of which he had written in pencil a page reference to a competing living skeleton. "Oh, yes, I remember this," he said. "I have
stuff on other living skeletons, too. I've got to show you this George Anderson
poster I bought at an auction in London in 1983."

We moved into the dining room, where there was a flat-file cabinet. He
opened the bottom drawer, which was filled to capacity with lithographs and
engravings, each one a Ricky Jay divagation: "T. Nelson Downs, the King of
Koins . . . Samri S. Baldwin, the White Mahatma . . . Holton the Cannonball
Catcher. I have a lot of stuff on cannonball catchers. . . . The Freeze Brothers,
blackfaced tambourine jugglers . . . Sylvester Schaffer, a great variety artist . . .
Josefa and Rosa Blazek, the Bohemian violin-playing Siamese twins. And here
are Daisy and Violet Hilton, the saxophone-playing Siamese twins from San
Antonio. . . . And here's Rastelli, perhaps the greatest juggler who ever lived. . . .
What's that? Oh, a poster for 'House of Games.' . . . I'm just trying to get to the
George Anderson piece that's sticking out at the end. . . . Oh, this is the Chevalier
D'Eon, a male fencer in drag. He used to be the French Ambassador to the Court
of St. James's. It's a great story but it takes too long."

Jay had reached and placed on the dining-room table the George Anderson
poster, a postbellum piece printed in New Hampshire using wooden type and a
large woodblock image of Anderson, who had made an art and livelihood of at-
tenuation. He appeared to be five and a half feet tall and to weigh about sixty-
five pounds.

"I know some people find this strange and weird," Jay said. "Actually, after
this life I've lived, I have no idea what is strange and weird and what isn't. I
don't know who else waxes poetic about the virtues of skeleton men, fasting
impostors, and cannonball catchers. And, to be honest, I don't really care. I
just think they're wonderful. I really do."

(1993)

ISADORA

L IKE a ghost from the grave Isadora Duncan is dancing again at Nice. A decade ago her art, animated by her extraordinary public personality, came as close to founding an esthetic renaissance as American morality would allow, and the provinces especially had a narrow escape. Today her body, whose Attic splendor once brought Greece to Kansas and Kalamazoo, is approaching its half-century mark. Her spirit is still green as a bay tree, but her flesh is worn, perhaps by the weight of laurels. She is the last of the trilogy of great female personalities our century produced. Two of them, Duse and Bernhardt, have gone to their elaborate national tombs. Only Isadora Duncan, the youngest, the American, remains wandering the European earth.

No one has taken Isadora's place in her own country and she is not missed. Of that fervor for the classic dance which she was the first to bring to a land bred on "Turkey in the Straw," beneficial signs remain from which she alone has not benefited. Eurythmic movements now appear in the curricula of girls' schools. Vestal virgins frieze about the altar fire of St. Marks-in-the-Bouwerie on Sabbath afternoons. As a cross between gymnasia and God, Greek dance camps flourish in the Catskills, where under the summer spruce, metaphysics and muscles are welded in an Ilissan hocus-pocus for the female young. Lisa, one of her first pupils, teaches in the studio of the Champs-Elysées. Isadora's sister Elizabeth, to whom Greek might still be Greek if it had not been for Isadora, has a toga school in Berlin. Her brother Raymond, who operates a modern craft-school in Paris, wears sandals and Socratic robes as if they were a family coat-of-arms. Isadora alone has neither sandals nor school. Most grandiose of all her influences, Diaghileff's Russian Ballet—which ironically owed its national rebirth to the inspiration of Isadora, then dancing with new terpsichorean ideals in Moscow—still seasons as an exotic spectacle in London and Monte Carlo. Only Isadora, animator of all these forces, has become obscure. Only she with her heroic sculptural movements has dropped by the wayside where she lies inert like one of those beautiful battered pagan tombs that still line the Sacred Road between Eleusis and the city of the Parthenon.

Isadora arrived in our plain and tasteless Republic before the era of the half-nude revue, before the discovery of what is now called our Native Literary School, even before the era of the celluloid sophistication of the cinema, which by its ubiquity does so much to unite the cosmopolisms of Terre Haute and New York. What America now has, and gorges on in the way of sophistication, it then hungered for. Repressed by generations of Puritanism, it longed for bright, visible and blatant beauty presented in a public form the simple citizenry could understand. Isadora appeared as a half-clothed Greek. . . . A Paris couturier recently said woman's modern freedom in dress is largely due to Isadora. She was the first artist to appear uncinctured, barefooted and free. She arrived like a glorious bounding Minerva in the midst of a cautious corseted decade. The clergy, hearing of (though supposedly without ever seeing) her bare calf, denounced it as violently as if it had been golden. Despite its longings, for a moment, America hesitated, Puritanism rather than poetry coupling lewd with nude in rhyme. But Isadora, originally from California and by then from Berlin, Paris and other points, arrived bearing her gifts as a Greek. She came like a figure from the Elgin marbles. The world over, and in America particularly, Greek sculpture was recognized to be almost notorious for its purity. The overpowering sentiment for Hellenic culture, even in the unschooled United States, silenced the outcries. Isadora had come as antique art and with such backing she became a cult.

THOSE were Isadora's great years. Not only in New York and Chicago but in the smaller, harder towns, when she moved across the stage, head reared, eyes mad, scarlet kirtle flying to the music of the "Marseillaise," she lifted from their seats people who had never left theatre seats before except to get up and go home. Whatever she danced to, whether it was France's revolutionary hymn, or the pure salon passion of Chopin's waltzes, or the unbearable heat of Brahms' German mode, she conspired to make the atmosphere Greek, fusing Zeitgeists and national sounds into one immortal Platonic pantomime.

Thus she inspired people who had never been inspired in their lives and to whom inspiration was exhilarating, useless and unbecoming. Exalted at the concert hall by her display of Greek beauty, limbs and drapes which though they were two thousand years old she seemed to make excitingly modern, her followers, dazzled, filled with Phidianisms, went home to Fords, big hats and the theory of Bull Moose, the more real items of their progressive age.

. . .

DANCING appeals less to the public than the other two original theatrical forms, drama and opera (unless, like the Russian Ballet, dancing manages to partake of all three). Nevertheless, Isadora not only danced but was demanded all over America and Europe. On the Continent she is more widely known today than any other American of our decade, including Woodrow Wilson and excepting only Chaplin and Fairbanks, both of whom, via a strip of celluloid, can penetrate to remote hamlets without ever leaving Hollywood. But Isadora has gone everywhere in the flesh. She has danced before kings and peasants. She has danced from the Pacific to London, from Petrograd to the Black Sea, from Athens to Paris and Berlin.

SHE penetrated to the Georgian States of the Caucasus, riding third-class amid fleas and disease, performing in obscure halls before yokels and princes whom she left astonished, slightly enlightened and somehow altered by the vision. For twenty years her life has been more exciting and fantastic than anything Zola or Defoe ever fabricated for their heroines. Her companions have been the great public talent of our generation—Duse, d'Annunzio, Bakst, Rodin, Bernhardt, Picabia, Brancusi, and so on. Her friends have run the gamut from starving poets down to millionaires. She has been prodigal of herself, her art, illusions, work, emotions and funds. She has spent fortunes. After the war her Sunday night suppers in the Rue de Pompe were banquets where guests strolled in, strolled out, and from low divans supped principally on champagne and strawberry tarts, while Isadora, barely clad in chiffon robes, rose when the spirit moved her to dance exquisitely. Week after week came people whose names she never knew. They were like moths. She once gave a house party that started in Paris, gathered force in Venice and culminated weeks later on a houseboat on the Nile.

IN order to promulgate her pedagogic theories of beauty and education for the young, she has legally adopted and supported some thirty or forty children during her life, one group being the little Slavs who are still dancing in Soviet Russia. During her famous season at the New York Century Theatre where she gave a classic Greek cycle, "Oedipus Rex," "Antigone," and the like, she bought up every Easter lily in Manhattan to decorate the theatre the night she opened in Berlioz' "L'Enfance du Christ," which was her Easter program. The lilies, whose perfume suffocated the spectators, cost two thousand dollars. Isadora had, at the moment, three thousand dollars to her name. And at midnight, long after all good lily-selling florists were in bed, she gave a champagne supper. It cost the other thousand.

Isadora, who has an un-American genius for art, for organizing love, maternity, politics and pedagogy on a great personal scale, had also an un-American genius for grandeur.

After the lilies faded, Isadora and her school sat amid their luggage on the pier where a ship was about to sail for France. They had neither tickets nor money. But they had a classic faith in fate and a determination to go back to Europe where art was understood. Just before the boat sailed, there appeared a school teacher. Isadora had never seen her before. The teacher gave Isadora the savings of years and Isadora sailed away. Herself grand, she could inspire grandeur in others, a tragic and tiring gift. There have always been school teachers and lilies in Isadora's life.

IN the three summer programs which Isadora recently gave in her studio at Nice, one with the concordance of Leo Tecktonius, the pianist, the other two with Jean Cocteau, French poet and *éphèbe*, who accompanied her dancing with his spoken verse, her art was seen to have changed. She treads the boards but little now, she stands almost immobile or in slow splendid steps with slow splendid arms moves to music, seeking, hunting, finding. Across her face, tilting this way and that, flee the mortal looks of tragedy, knowledge, love, scorn, pain. Posing through the works of Wagner, through tales of Dante, through the touching legend of St. Francis feeding crumbs and wisdom to his birds, Isadora is still great. By an economy (her first) she has arrived at elimination. As if the movements of dancing had become too redundant for her spirit, she has saved from dancing only its shape.

WHERE will she dance next? In one of her periodic fits of extravagant poverty and although needing the big sum offered, she once refused to dance in Wanamaker's Auditorium, disdaining for her art such a "scene of suspenders." She has refused other theatres because they contain restaurants. She has just refused to appear at the Champs-Elysées because it is a music-hall. She talks of giving some performances in Catalonia. She might dance in a castle in Spain.

There is also much ado about her now in the Paris journals because of the recent sale of her house in Neuilly, a sale she was forced to make to pay a debt of ten thousand francs, and her refusal of a legacy valued at 300,000 francs from her one-time husband, Yessenin, the Russian poet. The Neuilly house has just been repurchased by a group of friends who will make it into a school as a memorial to the dancer's two children so tragically drowned in Paris in 1913.

ALL her life Isadora has been a practical idealist. She has put into practice certain ideals of art, maternity and political liberty which people prefer to read as theories on paper. Her ideals of human liberty are not unsimilar to those of Plato, to those of Shelley, to those of Lord Byron which led him to die dramatically in Greece. All they gained for Isadora was the loss of her passport and the presence of the constabulary on the stage of the Indianapolis Opera House where the chief of police watched for sedition in the movement of Isadora's knees.

Denounced as a Russian "red" sympathizer, Isadora does not even receive a postal card from the Soviet Government to give her news of her school which she housed in its capital. For Isadora has had a fancy for facts. As she once told Boston it was tasteless and dull, so, when they were fêting her in triumph in Moscow, she told the Bolsheviks she found them bourgeois.

GREAT artists are tragic. Genius is too large; and it may have been grandeur that proved Isadora's undoing—the grandeur of temporary luxury, the grandeur of permanent ideals.

She is too expansive for personal salvation. She has had friends. What she needed was an entire government. She had checkbooks. Her scope called for a national treasury. It is not for nothing that she is hailed by her first name only as queens have been, were they great Catherines or Marie Antoinettes. Isadora is now writing her memoirs. Her private life, which always aroused public interest, is therein detailed. By her, the truth can then be told.

(1927)

THE SOLOIST

T is raining, and Mikhail Baryshnikov is standing in a courtyard in Riga, the capital of Latvia, pointing up at two corner windows of an old stucco building that was probably yellow once. With him are his companion, Lisa Rinehart, a former dancer with American Ballet Theatre, and two of his children—Peter, eight, and Aleksandra, or Shura, sixteen. He is showing them the house where he grew up. "It's Soviet communal apartment," he says to the children. "In one apartment, five families. Mother and Father have room at corner. See? Big window. Mother and Father sleep there, we eat there, table there. Then other little room, mostly just two beds, for half brother, Vladimir, and me. In other rooms, other people. For fifteen, sixteen people, one kitchen, one toilet, one bathroom, room with bathtub. But no hot water for bath. On Tuesday and Saturday, Vladimir and I go with Father to public bath."

I open the front door of the building and peer into the dark hallway. "Let's go up," I suggest. "No," he says. "I can't." It is more than a quarter century since he was here last.

AFTER his defection to the West, in 1974, Baryshnikov said again and again that he had no wish to return to the Soviet Union, or even to the former Soviet Union. Then, late last year, he accepted an invitation to dance at the Latvian National Opera, the stage on which he first set foot as a ballet dancer. Why he changed his mind is something of a mystery. Perhaps he just felt that it was time. (He will turn fifty next week.) Perhaps he wanted to show his children what he came from. To me all he said was "I am going to visit my mother's grave."

Baryshnikov, actually, is not a man for sentimental journeys. He is too resistant to falseness. Nor does he like being followed around by journalists. Interviews are torture to him: "You ask me what's happened in my life, why and how I did this and that. And I think and tell, but it's never true story, because everything is so much more complicated, and also I can't even remember how things happened. Whole process is boring. Also false, but mostly boring." He politely does not point out the journalist's role in this: how the questions are pitched, and the answers interpreted, according to already established ideas about the life in question—in this case, the life of a man who escaped from the Soviet Union at the age of twenty-six. It is hard to find an article on Baryshnikov that does not describe a look of melancholy in his eyes, supposedly the consequence of exile from his Russian homeland. This is the dominant theme of writings about him, but in his view it has nothing to do with him. He has lived in the United States for almost half his life. He is a United States citizen and regards this country as his home. He has lived with an American, Rinehart, for about ten years, and they have three children who speak no Russian.

Of course, when his return to Latvia was announced, the exile theme sounded with new force. The press in Riga was sown with sentimental formulas: the prodigal-son motif, the return-home motif, the ancestral-roots motif. He refused them all. For Russia, he says, he feels no nostalgia. Though his parents were Russian, he did not move to Russia until he was sixteen: "I was guest there, always." As for Latvia, it was his birthplace, but his parents were "occupiers" (his word) there. "The minute plane set down, the minute I stepped again on Latvian land, I realized this was never my home. My heart didn't even skip one beat."

WHAT has made Baryshnikov a paragon of late-twentieth-century dance is partly the purity of his ballet technique. In him the hidden meaning of ballet, and of classicism—that experience has order, that life can be understood—is clearer than in any other dancer on the stage today. Another part of his preëminence derives, of course, from his virtuosity, the lengths to which he was able to take ballet—the split leaps, the cyclonic pirouettes—without sacrificing purity. But what has made him an artist, and a popular artist, is the completeness of his performances: the level of concentration, the fullness of ambition, the sheer amount of detail, with the cast of the shoulder, the angle of the jaw, even the splay of the fingers, all deployed in the service of a single, pressing act of imagination. In him there is simply more to see than in most other dancers. No matter what role he is playing (and he has played some thankless ones), he always honors it completely, working every minute to make it a serious human story. In an interview prior to the Riga concerts, the Latvian theatre critic Normunds Naumanis asked him why he danced. He answered that he was not a religious person (quickly adding that his mother had been, and had had him secretly baptized) but that he thought he found onstage what people seek in religion: "some approximation to exaltation, inner purification, self-discovery." He may hate interviews, but once he is in one he tends to pour his heart out. (This may be why he hates them.)

Though Baryshnikov directs a company, the White Oak Dance Project, he went to Riga in October alone, as a solo dancer, and next week (January 21st–25th), at the City Center, in New York, he will again perform by himself— his first solo concerts, ever, in the United States. There is something fitting in this. The things he now seeks in dance—the exaltation, the self-discovery—are easier to find if one is not lifting another dancer at the same time. Furthermore, audiences these days don't want their view of him blocked by other people. But, basically, solo is his natural state, the condition that made him. The root-lessness of his childhood sent him into himself—made him a reader, a thinker, a mind—and the rule of force he worked under in the Soviet Union had the same effect: it made him cherish what could not be forced, his own thoughts. This became a way of dancing. It is not that when he is performing he is telling us who he is. Rather, he is telling us, as fully as he can, what truth he has found in the role, what he has thought about it. In many of his solos today, he seems to be giving us a portrait of thought itself—its bursts and hesitations, the neural firings—and this is something one must do solo.

IT was as a presenter of new work, not just as a dancer, that Baryshnikov re-turned to Riga. Most of the solos he brought were from his White Oak reper-tory—works by people like Mark Morris, Twyla Tharp, and Dana Reitz. These pieces were far removed from the earnest Soviet ballets that the Latvians had last seen him in and that some of them would probably have liked to see him in again. (The Reitz piece, "Unspoken Territory," has him, in a sarong, stalking around the stage in silence—no music—for twenty minutes.) In his mind, he was going to Riga not as he was then but as he is today.

To the Riga press, however, it was what he was then—the man who had been one of them and had left—that was important. Also, as usual in the Soviet Union, former or otherwise, politics came to greet him. There is considerable tension between Riga's Latvian and Russian populations. (Though Russians outnumber Latvians in the capital, Latvian independence has made the Russians the underdogs now: Russians must pass a Latvian-language test to get a job in the government.) The Russians wanted to know why Baryshnikov had come to Latvia, not to Russia, and why, if he gave only three interviews concerning his visit (he wanted no press, no questions), he gave them to Latvian, not to Russian, journalists.

To such problems Baryshnikov applied his usual remedy: work. The happiest I ever saw him in Riga was in a studio in his old school, rehearsing works for the upcoming program. Perched on a folding chair, watching him, was the director

of the school, Haralds Ritenbergs, who had been the leading danseur noble of
the Latvian state ballet company when Baryshnikov was a child. ("To us he
was like Rock Hudson," Baryshnikov says.) Next to Ritenbergs sat Juris
Kapralis, a handsome, bighearted Latvian whom Baryshnikov had as his ballet
teacher from age twelve to sixteen. What must these men have felt? Here was
the dear, small, hard-working boy they had known, now almost fifty years old
and the most famous dancer in the world, rehearsing before them steps such as
they had never seen. There should have been some shock, some acknowledgment of the break in history—of all the years when so many things had happened to him, and to them, to make their lives so different. But there was none
of that. What I saw was just three old pros working together. Baryshnikov
would perform the steps. Then he and the two older men would huddle together and, in the hand language that dancers use, discuss the choreography.
Yes, Baryshnikov said, this piece, no music. Yes, here I do arms this way, and he
demonstrated a stiff, right-angled arm, the opposite of what ballet dancers are
taught. I looked for raised eyebrows. There were none. The older men nodded,
watched, asked questions. To them, it seemed, he was still their hardworking
boy, and his business was their business, dancing. Baryshnikov showed them
his shoes—jazz shoes, Western shoes—and Ritenbergs and Kapralis unlaced
them, peered into them, poked the instep, flexed the sole. They were like two
veteran wine makers inspecting a new kind of cork. Whatever feelings passed
among the three men, they were all subsumed into work. Now, as had not happened when Baryshnikov showed me his old house or the hospital where he
was born, time vanished. He had returned home at last, but the home wasn't
Riga; it was ballet.

MIKHAIL Nikolaievich Baryshnikov was born in Riga eight years after
Latvia, in the midst of the Second World War, was forcibly annexed to the Soviet
Union. Once the war was over, Russian workers streamed into this tiny Baltic
country, the size of Vermont. Among them was Baryshnikov's father, Nikolai, a
high-ranking military officer who was sent to Riga to teach military topography
in the Air Force academy. With him came his new wife, Aleksandra, who had
lost her first husband in the war, and Vladimir, her son by that first marriage. By
Nikolai, she had Mikhail, eight years younger than Vladimir, in 1948. The parents' marriage was not happy. The father seems to have been a curt, cold man.
The mother, Aleksandra, was another matter, Baryshnikov says—"softer, interesting." She had had very little education but was a passionate theatregoer. She
went to drama, opera, and ballet, and she took Misha with her.
    Misha was one of those children who cannot sit still. Erika Vitina, a friend of
the family, says that when he ate at their house you could see his legs dancing
around under the glass-topped dinner table. He himself remembers movement
as an outlet for emotion. "One time I recall is when my mother first took me to

visit my grandmother, on the Volga River," he told me. "Volga, it's a long way up from Latvia. We took a train through Moscow, and Moscow to Gorky, plus then you drive another seventy miles. We took taxi, or some car delivered us. It was very early morning when we arrived—little village, and very simple house, and there was my grandmother. And I was in such anticipation, because I was like five or so, maybe six. My mother said to me, 'Mikhail, hug your grandmother.' But I was so overwhelmed that I couldn't run to her and hug her. So I just start to jump and jump, jump like crazy, around and around. It was embarrassing, but same time totally what I needed to do. Mother and Grandmother stood and looked until it was over."

When he was about nine, his mother became friends with a woman who had danced with the Bolshoi Ballet in Moscow and who now gave ballet lessons in Riga. "Mother was very excited by this friendship," Baryshnikov says. She enrolled him in her friend's class. When he was eleven, he moved over to the Riga School of Choreography, the state ballet academy. (One of his classmates there was Alexander Godunov, who would also defect, and dance at American Ballet Theatre under Baryshnikov's directorship.) Soon he showed extraordinary talent. Erika Vitina stresses the mother's involvement in Misha's ballet studies: "The father had no interest whatsoever in the ballet school. The mother brought him to the ballet school, put him there. All this happened physically, hand to hand."

"I was mama's boy in a way," Baryshnikov says. He remembers how beautiful she was. (In fact, in the one photograph I have seen of her she looks uncannily like him. It could be Baryshnikov with a wig on.) "My mother was a country girl from the Volga River," he said in a 1986 interview with Roman Polanski. "She spoke with a strong Volga accent. Very beautiful, very Russian—a one-hundred-per-cent pure Russian bride. But to tell the whole story of my mother, it's a long story." The end of the story is that during the summer when he was twelve she took him to the Volga to stay with her mother and then went back to Riga and hanged herself in the bathroom of the communal apartment. Vladimir found her. Baryshnikov never knew why she did it. "Father did not want to talk about it," he told me. Soon afterward, Vladimir left for the Army, and the father told Misha that now they would live together, just the two of them. The following year, Nikolai went away on a business trip and returned with a new wife, a new life. "I understood that I am not wanted," Baryshnikov said.

He looked for other families. He spent most summers with the family of Erika Vitina, and he stayed with them at other times as well. "Quite often," Vitina says, "he would ring our doorbell late at night, saying that he had run away. But a week later I would receive a call from the ballet school"—she, too, had a child enrolled there—"and would be told that unless I sent Misha home they would have to call the police. We spent two years in this manner. From time to time, he'd come to stay with me, and then his father would take him away again." Insofar as Baryshnikov has lived a life of exile, it had begun.

Erika Vitina recalls that his nights were often hard. Because he worried that he was too short to be a ballet dancer, he slept on a wooden plank—he had been told that this would help him grow faster (less traction)—and the blankets wouldn't stay tucked in. Before going to bed herself, Vitina would look in and cover him up again. Often, he would be calling out in his sleep, caught in a nightmare. But during the day, she says, he was "a happy, sunny boy." Now, looking back on those years, Baryshnikov is quick to dispel any atmosphere of pathos: "Children being left, it's not always like books of Charles Dickens. When you lose your parents in childhood, it's a fact of life, and, you know, human beings are extraordinary powerful survivors. My mother commit suicide. I was lucky it was not in front of me, O.K.? Which is truth, and Father was confused, and we never had any relationship, serious relationship. I never knew my father, in a way. But what? It's made me different? No. I mean, I blame for every fuckups in my life my parents? No."

"I got lucky," he adds. "I fell in love with dance." Every ounce of energy he had was now channelled into ballet. According to Juris Kapralis, who became his ballet teacher two months after his mother's death, he was a child workaholic: "Very serious boy. Perfectionist. Even in free time, go in corner and practice over and over again. Other boys playing, Misha studying. And not just steps, but artistic, as actor. He is thinking all the time what this role must be. I remember, once, 'Nutcracker.' He was thirteen, perhaps. I was prince, and he was toy soldier. After Mouse King dies, Misha relax his body. No longer stiff, like wooden soldier. Soft. Our ballet director ask him, 'Who say you should do this?' And he answer, 'When Mouse King dies, toys become human. Toys become boys. Movements must change.' He devise that himself. Small boy, but thinking."

I asked Baryshnikov recently whether, after his mother's death, ballet might have been a way for him to return to her. He paused for a long time and then said, "In Russia, dancing is part of happiness in groups. Groups at parties, people dancing in circle, and they push child to center, to dance. Child soon works up little routine. Can do a little this"—hand at the back of the neck—"a little this"—arms joined horizontally across the chest—"and soon make up some special steps, and learn to save them for end, to make big finale. This way, child gets attention from adults."

In the case of a child artist, and particularly one who has suffered a terrible loss, it is tempting to read artistic decisions as psychological decisions, because we assume that a child cannot really be an artist. But, as many people have said, children are probably more artistic than adults, bolder in imagination, more unashamedly fascinated with shape, line, detail. In Baryshnikov's case, the mother's devotion and then the loss of her can help to explain one thing: the *work* he put into ballet. For the rest—the physical gift, the fusion of steps with fantasy, the interest in making something true and complete ("Toys become boys"), all of which are as much a part of him today as they were when he was twelve—we must look to him alone.

. . .

IN 1964, the Latvian state ballet went on tour to Leningrad with a ballet in which Baryshnikov, now sixteen, had a small role, and a member of the company took him to Alexander Pushkin, a revered teacher at the Kirov Ballet's school, the Vaganova Choreographic Institute. Pushkin immediately asked the director of the school to admit the boy. By September, Baryshnikov had moved to Leningrad and was installed at the barre in Pushkin's class. Thereafter, he rarely went back to Riga.

Next to his mother, Pushkin was probably the most important person in Baryshnikov's early life. Pushkin had begun his own ballet training in the studio of Nikolai Legat, who had helped train Nijinsky. Later, he studied with other famous teachers. When Baryshnikov joined his class, Pushkin was fifty-seven, and past dancing, but he had performed with the Kirov for almost thirty years, mostly in secondary roles. "Pas de deux, pas de trois," Baryshnikov says. "Sometimes substitute for a principal, but he was not principal type. Not very handsome—big nose, long legs, short body—and not very expressive. But classical, classical. Old-school, traditional, square. Academician. Usually, it's those kind of people, people who dance twenty-five years the same parts, who know more about technique than people who are advancing and trying out other sort of areas. Twenty-five years you come back after summer vacation and tune your body into same routine, you figure out timing, you figure out method."

Pushkin had begun teaching early, at the age of twenty-five, and he soon specialized in men. His classroom manner was famously laconic. He rarely offered corrections, and when he did they were of the most elementary sort. (It was said at the school that he had two: "Don't fall" and "Get up.") Rather, as Baryshnikov explains it, what made Pushkin so effective was the *logic* of the step combinations he taught—the fact that they were true not just to classical ballet but also to human musculature. They seemed right to the body, and so you did them right. And the more you did them the more you became a classical dancer. Another thing about Pushkin, his students say, is that he was a developer of individuality. He steered the students toward themselves, helped them find out what kinds of dancers they were. "Plus," Baryshnikov says, "he was extraordinary patient and extraordinary kind person. Really, really kind." If there is a point in classical art where aesthetics meet morals—where beauty, by appearing plain and natural, gives us hope that we, too, can be beautiful— Pushkin seems to have stood at that point, and held out a hand to his pupils. In any case, he was a specialist in calming down teen age boys, getting them to work, and making them take themselves seriously. Out of his classroom in the fifties and sixties came the Kirov's finest male dancers—notably Nikita Dolgushin, Yuri Soloviev, and Rudolf Nureyev.

. . .

PUSHKIN took certain of his students very directly under his wing. The best-known example is Nureyev, who was ten years older than Baryshnikov. Nureyev had started studying ballet extremely late. "It was not until he was sixteen or seventeen that he came to Leningrad and put his leg in first position professionally," Baryshnikov says. "And he took this opportunity very— *errgghh*—like a tank. Very aggressive in terms of the education, in terms of the catch-up. And short temper. Sometimes in rehearsal, if he couldn't do certain steps he would just run out, crying, run home. Then, ten o'clock in the evening, he is back in studio working on the step till he will get it. People think he is oddball. And already his ambivalent sexuality was obvious, which in that conservative atmosphere was big problem. People were teasing him." So Pushkin and his wife, Xenia Jurgensen, another former Kirov dancer, took Nureyev into their home. He lived with them for a long time, not just while he was in school but also during his early years at the Kirov. The fact that Nureyev defected in 1961—that he was accomplished enough and brave enough to go—was probably due in large measure to them, though it broke their hearts. (When Baryshnikov first went to their house, he saw Nureyev's electric train, installed as a kind of relic, in their living room.) Sacred vessel of the Russian tradition, Pushkin bred dancers so good, so serious and ambitious, that they could not survive in Russia. Yuri Soloviev killed himself. Nikita Dolgushin was banished to the provinces. Nureyev and Baryshnikov defected.

PUSHKIN and Jurgensen took Baryshnikov in as they had taken in Nureyev. "I spent weeks, sometimes months, staying with them," he says. He also ate at their house almost every night. Jurgensen was a good cook. "Very upper-class Russian food," Baryshnikov says. "Winter food—veal, cream." Then Pushkin and his pupil would work together, sometimes for hours, often on arms: "Find my way of moving arms, coördination. Young dancers don't think about this, only think about feet." Then, very often, it was too late for Baryshnikov to return to the dormitory, so he slept on the Pushkins' couch.

Baryshnikov was still very worried about his height. Russian ballet companies follow a strict system, called *emploi*, whereby dancers are sorted by type into certain kinds of roles and remain there for the rest of their careers. Baryshnikov, though he was still growing (he eventually reached five feet seven), seemed too short for the danseur-noble roles, the grave, poetic leading-man roles. Not just his height but also his stage presence—he was boyish, vivacious, a personality—seemed to be pushing him toward demi-caractère roles, the quick, often comic supporting-actor roles. As he put it in his interview with Polanski, "I thought I would end up as a Joker or a Harlequin somewhere," and this was not what he wanted. But Pushkin believed that his pupil would be a danseur noble, and he got him just to go on working. In 1967, Baryshnikov graduated from the Vaganova school. At his graduation performance, in the "Corsaire" pas de deux, "the scene was unimaginable," his biographer Gennady Smakov writes. The crowd howled; the chandeliers shook. Baryshnikov was taken into the Kirov Ballet as a soloist, skipping the normal starting position in the corps de ballet, and now his troubles really began.

"I joined the company when it was falling apart," Baryshnikov told Smakov. In the late sixties and the seventies, the Kirov went through a period of repression from which it has never fully recovered. In part, this was due to a society-wide tightening up after the Khrushchev "thaw." But in the ballet world there was redoubled anxiety, the result of Nureyev's defection. Konstantin Sergeyev, the director of the Kirov, turned the company into a mini police state. The repertory consisted either of nineteenth-century classics, restaged by Sergeyev, or of socialist flag-wavers. (Sergeyev himself, in 1963, made a ballet, "The Distant Planet," inspired by Yuri Gagarin's spaceflight.) Any newly commissioned ballets were vetted to make sure they threatened neither government policy nor Sergeyev's primacy as company choreographer. The dancers were watched vigilantly for signs of insubordination. If they looked like defection risks—indeed, if they failed to attend company meetings or had the wrong friends—they were often barred from foreign tours, which were their only means of supplementing their tiny incomes. Typically, the list of who would be going on a tour was not posted until the day of departure. Shortly beforehand, meetings would be held at which the dancers were encouraged to denounce their colleagues, so that their own names, rather than their colleagues', would be on the list. Many coöperated. Coöperate or not, the dancers were brought to their knees. Righteous suffering can ruin you almost as fast as shame. Other privileges at the Kirov—roles, choice of partners, time onstage—were also awarded less on the basis of merit than according to one's history of coöperation. The careers of what were reportedly superb artists, people who were one in a thousand, and in whom ten years' training had been invested, were destroyed in this way.

Such were the circumstances in which Baryshnikov, nineteen years old and hungry to dance, found himself in 1967. He had to fight just to get onstage—at that time, even leading Kirov dancers performed only three to four times a month—and also to get the partners he wanted. Above all, he had to struggle over his casting. He was given danseur-noble roles eventually, but only eventually. (He waited six years to dance Albrecht in "Giselle," a part he desperately wanted.) Worse was the problem of getting a chance to perform in something other than the standard repertory. Baryshnikov wanted to dance new ballets, modern ballets, and some were being created at the Kirov, with excellent roles for him. But again and again such ballets were vetoed by the company's *art-soviet*, or artistic committee, and dropped after one or two performances. Baryshnikov was sent back to dancing "Don Quixote."

In 1970, midway into his seven-year career in Russia, things got a great deal worse, for in that year Natalia Makarova, the Kirov's rising young ballerina, defected while the company was performing in London. Baryshnikov was on this tour, and it was to him, not to Makarova, that the authorities devoted their special attention. As he sees it, they did not take Makarova seriously as a potential defector, because she was a woman: "They wouldn't think a woman would have guts to defect." Baryshnikov, on the other hand, sometimes had as many as three K.G.B. agents tailing him as he walked down the streets of London. He says that at that time he had no thoughts of defection. If he was closely confined at the Kirov, that was because he was greatly valued there. He was one of the company's leading dancers. "Also," he says, "the Kirov was a home to me, and I had unfinished business. I wanted to do *this* dance, with *these* people." Indeed, when he got the news about Makarova, who was a friend and also a former girlfriend of his, he was terribly worried for her: "I thought it will be difficult for her to survive in the West, that people will get advantage of her, that she will be sorry. Can you believe how stupid?"

But the events that led to his own defection were already accumulating. Four months before the London tour, Pushkin had died—of a heart attack, on a sidewalk—at the age of sixty-two. At that point, Baryshnikov later told an interviewer, "I realized that I was totally on my own." A second important development was the London tour itself. The audience and the critics went crazy over him. (If he thought it would be hard for a Soviet dancer to survive in the West, his London reviews may have given him reason to rethink that conclusion later.) But London gave him more than good reviews: "You cannot know what it meant to travel. Just to see how other people react to you, and to *measure* your ability as an artist, as a dancer. And to see what's supposed to be your *life*—that your life is not just in cocoon, that other people in other countries do have same emotions." He met Western dancers. He became friends with Margot Fonteyn. He attended rehearsals at the Royal Ballet. He went to modern-dance classes. He saw American Ballet Theatre, which was performing in London at the same time.

He also met Nureyev, who was now living in London and dancing with the Royal Ballet. Nureyev went to see the Kirov performances and managed to get a message to Baryshnikov. "A man we both knew came to me and said, 'Rudolf want to see you if you want to.'" So the next morning Baryshnikov gave the K.G.B. the slip and spent a whole day in Nureyev's big house, overlooking Richmond Park. They talked about ballet, he says: "Russian exercises, French exercises, teachers, class, how long barre—all technique, Rudolf's obsession." At lunch, Nureyev drank a whole bottle of wine by himself. (Baryshnikov couldn't drink. He was performing that night.) Then they went out and lay on the grass and talked about technique some more. "When I left, he gave me a couple of books—one with beautiful Michelangelo drawings—and some scarf he gave me. I was very touched by him." The two men remained friends until Nureyev's death, in 1993.

With Makarova's defection, the panic at the Kirov was even worse than it had been with Nureyev's. Sergeyev was removed from his post; a number of brief, fumbling directorships followed. Baryshnikov was watched more and more carefully. If Western dancers came to Leningrad and he went out to dinner with them, this was noted in his file, and the K.G.B. came to talk to him about it. When Western choreographers got in touch with the Kirov to see if he could work with them, they were told he was sick. He was also under pressure to go to political rallies, and privileges in the theatre were made contingent on his attendance: "They'd say, if not this, then not this. Blackmail, you know?"

IN 1974, Baryshnikov staged what was called a Creative Evening—a favor sometimes accorded leading dancers. The dancer would commission an evening's worth of short works, often from young choreographers. (Whatever nonconformist ballets made it onto the Kirov stage were usually part of a Creative Evening.) The dancer would also choose the casts, assemble the sets and costumes, and star in the program. Then, after this display of open-mindedness, the administration would normally shelve the ballets. For his Creative Evening, Baryshnikov hired two experimental (and therefore extra-Leningrad) choreographers—Georgi Alexidze, based in Tbilisi, and Mai Murdmaa, an Estonian. There followed several months of anguish as, faced with harassment from the administration and apathy from the demoralized dancers, Baryshnikov tried to get the new ballets onstage. Cast members dropped out; costume designs were argued over (too revealing). Shortly before the première, Baryshnikov was pulled out of rehearsals to go to Moscow for another political rally. After the first preview, he met with the *artsoviet*, and they told him how bad they thought the show was. It was allowed a few performances anyway—all the tickets were already sold—but afterward, at a cast banquet, Baryshnikov burst into tears while he was trying to make a speech to the dancers. "He was talking and crying," Nina Alovert reports in her 1984 book, "Baryshnikov in Russia." "Some people listened to him . . . while others continued to eat, scraping their plates with their forks."

The disappointments apart, Baryshnikov remembers Leningrad as a place of immense tedium: "The most interesting objects were people, saying what they would have done, if they could have. Which is what they talked about if they drank a little. But they didn't drink a little. They drank a lot." In a 1986 interview, Arlene Croce asked Baryshnikov's close friend Joseph Brodsky what would have become of the dancer if he had remained in Russia. "He'd be a ruin by now," Brodsky answered, "both physically and mentally. Physically because of the bottle. . . . Mentally because of that mixture of impotence and cynicism that corrodes everyone there—the stronger you are the worse it is."

Finally, he refused that fate. A few months after the Creative Evening, a group of dancers from the Bolshoi Ballet were leaving for a tour of Canada. The two Bolshoi veterans leading the tour, Raissa Struchkova and her husband,

Alexander Lapauri, asked the Kirov if Baryshnikov and his frequent partner Irina Kolpakova could join them, to add heft to the roster. The Kirov refused; at this point, the K.G.B. was barely letting Baryshnikov out of its sight. But Kolpakova intervened, and she was a well-placed person—not just the Kirov's leading ballerina but a former administrator of the company and a member of the Party, with excellent connections. She apparently guaranteed Baryshnikov's safe return, and therefore they were allowed to go. That was the tour from which Baryshnikov did not return. Kolpakova somehow survived as the leading ballerina at the Kirov, but Struchkova and Lapauri were forbidden ever to leave the Soviet Union again. The following year, Lapauri got drunk one night, drove his car into a lamppost, and died. By that time, Baryshnikov was the new sensation of Western ballet, and if, with his fame, he also had a sad look in his eyes the cause was probably not nostalgia for the Soviet Union.

BARYSHNIKOV'S career as a ballet dancer in the seventies and eighties has by now been the subject of hundreds of articles, and of half a dozen books as well. It had three stages: four years as the star of American Ballet Theatre (from 1974 to 1978), one year at George Balanchine's New York City Ballet (from 1978 to 1979), then nine years as the director of American Ballet Theatre (from 1980 to 1989). What he did during this time, above all, was acquire new repertory—the thing he had most wanted to do. In just his first two years in the West, he learned twenty-six new roles, more than he would have been given in a lifetime in the Soviet Union. And the process of working with new choreographers nudged his style in new directions.

Most important was his collaboration with Twyla Tharp. In the nineteen-seventies, Tharp was undergoing a transition from modern dance to ballet. Baryshnikov was also in transition, so he made a perfect subject for her. Starting with the hugely popular "Push Comes to Shove," in 1976, she created for him a series of ballets that seemed to be about the project facing them both: how to marry the Old World dance to the new—in particular, how to join ballet, so outward and perfect, to the inwardness, the ruminations, of jazz. In Tharp's works, Baryshnikov's dancing became more shaded, with more hitches and grace notes, more little thoughts, tucked in between one step and the next. And it was these—the transitions, the secret places between the steps—that seemed to give the dancing its meaning. The big ballet moves were still there, but they were thrown off casually, like something taken for granted. Suddenly, out of some low-down noodling, Baryshnikov would rise up into an utterly perfect leap, and then land and noodle some more. This was surprising, witty, but it also seemed philosophical: a meditation on history, a memory of innocence in a mind past innocence. Appropriately, Tharp had Baryshnikov do this kind of dancing alone. It influenced all his future work, affecting not just him but the choreographers who worked with him after Tharp. The more he became that kind of dancer—inward, alone—the more they made that kind of dance for him.

At the same time, what Tharp made of Baryshnikov was in him already. He *was* a transplant, and alone, and he combined an exquisitely schooled classical technique with what seemed, even before Tharp, an increasingly ruminative quality, a deep sort of cool. He danced that way not only in Tharp's ballets but also in "Giselle," and this gave him a special glamour. Soon he was more than an acclaimed ballet dancer: he was a celebrity, a dream-boat. Crucial to this development was the fact that in his hunger for new outlets he looked beyond live theatre. He made movies ("The Turning Point," in 1977; "White Nights," in 1985; "Dancers," in 1987), and television specials, too, and he turned out to be extremely filmable. Now you didn't have to live in New York to be a Baryshnikov fan, any more than you had to live in Hollywood to be a Sylvester Stallone fan. He was an electronic-media ballet star, the first one in history.

The movies, of course, made use not only of his dancing but of his sex appeal. In all three of his Hollywood films, he was cast as a roué, a heartbreaker. The newspapers, meanwhile, were doing what they could to cover his love life: his rocky affair with Gelsey Kirkland, the ballerina who had left New York City Ballet to become his partner at A.B.T.; his long liaison with Jessica Lange (which produced his first child, Aleksandra, named after his mother); his shorter stopovers with many others. "He goes through everybody, he doesn't miss anyone," the post-Baryshnikov Kirkland told a reporter. "I should have been so lucky," Baryshnikov says. But in a male ballet dancer even medium-level skirt-chasing makes good copy. Combined with all the other factors—his "exile," his famous melancholy, his tendency to flee interviewers, his hunger for new projects—it gave him a sort of Byronic profile, as a haunted man, a man of unfulfillable desires, unassuageable griefs. He did not fashion the image, but he fitted it, and nothing could have been more attractive. Posters of him hung in dorm rooms.

In 1979, only a year after he had made the switch from American Ballet Theatre to New York City Ballet, A.B.T. asked him to come back, this time as the head of the company, and he accepted. The story of Baryshnikov's nine-year directorship of A.B.T. is a long, messy, fascinating tale that has never been fully told. Briefly, he tried to modernize the company. He junked the star system and began promoting from within the ranks. He regalvanized the company's notoriously feckless corps de ballet. He brought in new repertory, including modern-dance pieces, plus crossover ballets by the most interesting American choreographers of the moment—people such as Tharp, David Gordon, and Mark Morris. Suddenly, the air began to circulate again at A.B.T. The corps moved with beauty and pride. The young soloists danced like demons. The new works were talked about, argued about. Before, what was interesting at A.B.T. was merely this or that performance, usually by a foreign star. Now, for the first time since the nineteen-fifties, the company itself was a serious subject, an art-producing organization.

Not all of Baryshnikov's reforms were successful, and when they did succeed they weren't necessarily popular. Stars left in huffs. Critics deplored many of the new works. People accused Baryshnikov of trying to turn A.B.T. into New York City Ballet, or into a modern-dance company, or, in any case, into something other than the plump, old-style, stars-and-classics institution that it had been, and which they still loved. The company's deficit swelled. The dancers went out on strike. There was constant friction between Baryshnikov and the board. He had ostensibly been hired as the company's artistic director, but the board also expected him to be its leading dancer and its No. 1 fund-raiser—roles that he declined. (He had repeated injuries; he could not dance as much. As for fund-raising, he loathed it. At parties for patrons, he was often the first person out the door.) And by insisting on a salary of a dollar a year as director—which, given his performance fees, he could afford—he felt he had given himself that right. But the wear on him was severe. In 1989, he gave notice that he would leave in 1990. A few months later, the administration went over his head and fired his second-in-command, Charles France. Baryshnikov resigned in a fury.

WHY had he taken the job in the first place? He is not a natural leader. He can't press the flesh, give the interviews, settle the quarrels, or not willingly. Yet at the time when it came, the offer of the A.B.T. directorship was something he could not refuse. Having seen at the Kirov how badly a ballet company could be directed, he was, of course, tempted to find out if he could run one well. At the same time, there was another factor—his year at New York City Ballet. It has often been claimed that Baryshnikov's experience there was a bitter disappointment to him because by the time he arrived Balanchine was already ill (he died within five years) and could not make new ballets for him. "That's nonsense, absolute nonsense," Baryshnikov says. "That one year was most interesting time in my American career." Part of the pleasure, again, was new repertory. In fifteen months at N.Y.C.B., he learned twenty-odd roles, and though he had trouble fitting into some of them—and not enough time—there were others, particularly Balanchine's "Apollo" and "Prodigal Son," that seemed to have been waiting all those years just for him. He was tremendous, utterly wrenching, as the Prodigal, and he was probably the best Apollo ever to inhabit that role. All the qualities needed to represent Balanchine's boy-god—childlikeness, aloneness, dignity, a sense of high mission—were already in him. He filled the ballet to its skin.

But Baryshnikov says that what was most important to him at N.Y.C.B. was his sense that he had found a home. Balanchine had gone to the same school and made his professional début at the same theatre that Baryshnikov had, and, like him, had decided that to be an artist he must leave Russia. (Baryshnikov defected fifty years, almost to the day, after Balanchine left.) Balanchine had then created in the West what, in Baryshnikov's view, Russian ballet would have become but for the Revolution: modernist classicism. "I am entering the ideal future of the Maryinsky Ballet," he told reporters when he announced his switch to N.Y.C.B. (The Maryinsky was the Kirov's pre-Revolutionary name.) Also, Balanchine seems to have treated him like a son: "He told me, 'I wish I could be a little younger, a little healthier, that we could work more on new pieces, but let's not waste time. Let's do "Harlequinade," let's do "Prodigal," let's do this, let's do that, and think—whatever you want to do.' He cared what I will do."

The story is terrible. The homeless boy found a home, the sonless master found a son, but it was very late. Then came the invitation from A.B.T. Curiously, it was in part because of the gifts Baryshnikov was given at N.Y.C.B. that he decided to leave. For one thing, Balanchine told him he could always come back. "I went to him and we talked for a long time," he recalls. "We talked for an hour one day, and he said, 'Come back tomorrow.' And he was very, sort of—not encouraging me, but said, 'If you can see what you want to do and can deal with people on the board and you have a clear vision, I think you should do it, take this chance.' He said, 'If it doesn't work, it doesn't work. You can come back, anytime. This is your home.' "

But it wasn't just the N.Y.C.B. safety net that emboldened Baryshnikov to go to A.B.T. It was also what he saw as the moral lesson of N.Y.C.B., as taught to him by Balanchine and Jerome Robbins, the company's second ballet master. "Working with Balanchine and Jerry every day—just to see their *dedication* to the institution, the company, the school. Their seriousness, the seriousness of the whole setup, everything about it. Very different from the world which I come from, government-supported company, or commercially set up company like Ballet Theatre. I learn so much. Something about dance ethics, about being a dancer, and the *quality* of the work. I learn how and why to respect choreographic vision and morale of theatre. And that was most important experience. On the surface I was just one of them, and that was fine. But deep inside I experienced extraordinary transformation, and I understand a lot of things, for my future work." Clearly, that was a major reason for his going to A.B.T. He felt he had learned something tremendous, and he wanted to use it. Those who accused him of trying to turn A.B.T. into N.Y.C.B. were partly right.

NEARLY ten years after Baryshnikov's departure from A.B.T., with the current administration trying desperately to restore the old stars-and-classics order, the company still reflects the changes he made: the corps still shows the verve he instilled in it, and the young soloist-level dancers still seem to dance with a sort of wild hope, as if they might actually be promoted. But these are things you can't discuss with Baryshnikov at present. The bitterness of the

A.B.T. years is still too keen. What he sees now as the "future work" to which he tried to carry the spirit of New York City Ballet is his present project: directing a modern-dance company. This troupe, the White Oak Dance Project, is a great curiosity. What is a Russian-trained ballet dancer doing directing an American modern-dance company? And why is a man who during the A.B.T. years repeatedly said that he wanted to retire from the stage—that he had had it, that his knee was killing him (it has now been operated on five times)—still performing intensively: an activity that requires him to undergo two hours of physical therapy every day, and, on days when he is performing, four additional hours of warmups and rehearsal, not to speak of the travelling and the room-service dinners? "Well," he said to me in 1990, at the time of White Oak's founding, "I thought there is maybe a couple of years left, for fun." The late philanthropist Howard Gilman, a friend of his, offered to build him a rehearsal studio at the Gilman Foundation's White Oak Plantation, in Florida—in gratitude, Baryshnikov named the troupe after the plantation—and operations were set up in such a way that, unlike A.B.T., the company would not be a noose around his neck. He hired seasoned dancers—people who would not develop eating disorders—and he engaged them on a tour-by-tour basis. The company was not a company; it was a "project." It could vanish at any time. It had no board, no grants, no deficit. Either it paid for itself or Baryshnikov wrote a check. In other words, he set up the least institutional institution he could possibly create—one in which, for the first time, he could present and perform dance without the thousand circumstances that in his experience had compromised those activities.

White Oak has now been in existence for seven years. It is small, usually eight to twelve dancers. It is classy. (It travels with its own five-piece chamber orchestra. No taped music.) It tours for about four months a year, and it has been all around the world. For its first three or four years, the repertory was mostly by "name" choreographers: Martha Graham, Paul Taylor, David Gordon, Twyla Tharp, Mark Morris. (Morris helped Baryshnikov set up the company.) But in the last few years White Oak has begun dangling from the treetops, offering works by avant-gardists almost unknown outside New York and also by beginners—people who are making only their second or third pieces but whom Baryshnikov finds interesting. Still, the concerts regularly sell out, because he is performing in them. Two years ago, I sat in the Kravis Center, in West Palm Beach, Florida, with two thousand Republicans as they watched a big, ambitious, confusing piece called "What a Beauty!," created by Kraig Patterson, a fledgling choreographer who is also a dancer with the Mark Morris Dance Group. The audience looked puzzled. But on this program there was also a solo for Baryshnikov; that is, the audience got to see, for perhaps twelve minutes, the most interesting dancer in the world today performing alone, and therefore they got their money's worth. In a sense, the situation is an artificial one. Baryshnikov probably knows this, but it doesn't seem to bother him. He is having an adventure, presenting new choreography. He is at last putting on his Creative Evening—night after night, with no *artsoviet* to tell him what they think—and if his fame can induce people to come and see it that is fine by him. Recently, I asked him the big question: In the West, had he got what he wanted? Had he found what he came for? "Oh, more than that, more than that," he said. "I never dreamt that I would work with so many extraordinary people." That was all he wanted, just to work with interesting people.

IN return for taking only a nominal fee in Riga, Baryshnikov had arranged for the state opera's general-admission prices to be lowered for his performances, but the tickets were still beyond the means of most of Riga's ballet people. (The average salary in Riga is five hundred dollars a month.) So he opened his first dress rehearsal to the staff and pensioners of the opera house and the ballet school, and before the rehearsal began he came out in front of the curtain and addressed them. It was a strange moment—packed with history, like the session in the studio—and in parts of the audience there was probably some resentment against the local boy who made good. The people in that auditorium represented an old tradition, the one that had bred him and from which he had fled. Now they would see the new kind of dancing that he had preferred to theirs. But as he spoke, it was to their world, not his, that he addressed himself. He told them how this solo concert was dedicated to the memory of his mother; how happy he was, after so many years, to perform again on the stage where he had first danced; how pleased he was to present these dances to his theatre colleagues. And he choked up—the first time I ever saw him do so—and had to stop and pause repeatedly before speaking again.

Later, he said to me, "All those people who were sitting there, they were veterans of this society, this space. All these people that I saw when I was young, they were some very good dancers or not that good dancers, some of them good actors, or some of them just beautiful women, or some of them were great character dancers, or some very enthusiastic performers. I knew them by name, I knew their history. Half of those people are dead already, but the other half, in their sixties or their eighties, are sitting in that audience. And they're all of them in me, in my body, in my brain. You know, you learn to dance when you're very young. And in subconsciousness you take pieces from every person. Even worst dancers have two moves, one move, and you say, 'What was that? How did he do that?' And already it's in you. That's why I—that's why it was very moving—because, you know, I owe them." So again he did have a family, but it was dancers. In his second concert, he shared the program with the Latvian state ballet and its school—he did two solos, they did various dances, including some that he had appeared in as a boy (the Garland Waltz from "The Sleeping Beauty," the "Corsaire" pas de deux)—and he donated the proceeds to his old school.

Both shows were a great success, but nothing was quite like the piece that Baryshnikov closed with on the last night. This was Tharp's "Pergolesi"—a smart choice, since, like the other pieces Tharp has made for Baryshnikov, it includes ballet, and so Baryshnikov was able to show the audience his old fireworks. Actually, though, "Pergolesi" includes just about everything: folk dance, eighteenth-century dance, quotes from famous ballets ("Le Spectre de la Rose," "La Sylphide," "Swan Lake"), shimmies, bugaloo, golf swings. He got a chance to do every kind of dance he knew—not just what he had learned in the West but also what he had been taught at the Riga School of Choreography. And I don't know what happened—maybe it was the bringing together of the two halves of his history, or maybe it was relief that this heavily freighted trip was nearly over, or maybe now, at the end, he just wanted to give these people everything he had—but he exploded. I have never seen him so happy onstage, or so wild. ("He's showing off!" said Lisa Rinehart, who was sitting next to me.) He gave them the double barrel turns, he gave them the triple pirouettes in attitude (and then he switched to the other leg and did two more). He rose like a piston; he landed like a lark. He took off like Jerry Lee Lewis; he finished like Jane Austen. From ledge to ledge of the dance he leapt, surefooted, unmindful, a man in love. The audience knew what they were seeing. The air in the theatre thickened almost visibly. Even the members of the orchestra, though their backs were to him, seemed to understand that something unusual was happening. Out of the pit, the beautiful introduction to Pergolesi's "Adriano in Siria" rose like a wave, and he rode it to the finish. By that time, we actually wanted him to stop, so that we could figure out what had happened to us. Latvians, I was told by the locals, almost never give standing ovations. And they never yell "Bravo!" in the theatre; they consider that vulgar. But they yelled "Bravo!" for him, and everyone stood, including the President of the Republic.

Baryshnikov took his curtain calls with the members of the Latvian National Opera Ballet, they in their dirndls and harem pants, he in his Isaac Mizrahi jerseys—messengers of the two worlds created when Europe broke in half. It will never wholly mend, any more than Baryshnikov, child of that break, was ever able to find an artistic home. But it is hard to regret his fate. Homelessness turned him inward, gave him to himself. Then dance, the substitute home, turned him outward, gave him to us.

(1998)

WOLCOTT GIBBS

TIME . . . FORTUNE . . . LIFE . . . LUCE

S AD-EYED last month was nimble, middle-sized *Life*-President Clair
Maxwell as he told newshawks of the sale of the fifty-three-year-old gag-
mag to *Time*. For celebrated name alone, price: $85,000.

Said he: "*Life* . . . introduced to the world the drawings . . . of such men as
Charles Dana Gibson, the verses of . . . James Whitcomb Riley and Oliver
Herford, such writers as John Kendrick Bangs. . . . Beginning next month the
magazine *Life* will embark on a new venture entirely unrelated to the old."

How unrelated to the world of the Gibson Girl is this new venture might have
been gathered at the time from a prospectus issued by enormous, Apollo-faced
C. D. Jackson, of Time, Inc.

"*Life*," wrote he, "will show us the Man-of-the-Week . . . his body clothed
and, if possible, nude." It will expose "the loves, scandals, and personal affairs
of the plain and fancy citizen . . . and write around them a light, good-
tempered 'colyumnist' review of these once-private lives."

29,000 die-hard subscribers to *Life*,* long accustomed to he-she jokes, many
ignorant of King of England's once-private life (*Time*, July 25 *et seq.*), will be
comforted for the balance of their subscription periods by familiar, innocent jo-
cosities of *Judge*. First issue of new publication went out last week to 250,000
readers, carried advertisements suggesting an annual revenue of $1,500,000,
pictured Russian peasants in the nude, the love life of the Black Widow spider,
referred inevitably to Mrs. Ernest Simpson.

Behind this latest, most incomprehensible Timenterprise looms, as usual,

*Peak of *Life* circulation (1921): 250,000.

ambitious, gimlet-eyed, Baby Tycoon Henry Robinson Luce, co-founder of *Time*, promulgator of *Fortune*, potent in associated radio & cinema ventures.

"HIGH-BUTTONED . . . BRILLIANT"

Headman Luce was born in Tengchowfu, China, on April 3, 1898, the son of Henry Winters & Elizabeth Middleton Luce, Presbyterian missionaries. Very unlike the novels of Pearl Buck were his early days. Under brows too beetling for a baby, young Luce grew up inside the compound, played with his two sisters, lisped first Chinese, dreamed much of the Occident. At 14, weary of poverty, already respecting wealth & power, he sailed alone for England, entered school at St. Albans. Restless again, he came to the United States, enrolled at Hotchkiss, met up & coming young Brooklynite Briton Hadden. Both even then were troubled with an itch to harass the public. Intoned Luce years later: "We reached the conclusion that most people were not well informed & that something should be done. . . ."

First publication to inform fellowman was *Hotchkiss Weekly Record;* next *Yale Daily News*, which they turned into a tabloid; fought to double hours of military training, fought alumni who wished to change tune of Yale song from *Die Wacht am Rhein.* Traditionally unshaven, wearing high-buttoned Brooks jackets, soft white collars, cordovan shoes, no garters, Luce & Hadden were Big Men on a campus then depleted of other, older Big Men by the war. Luce, pale, intense, nervous, was Skull & Bones, Alpha Delta Phi, Phi Beta Kappa, member of the Student Council, editor of the *News;* wrote sad poems, read the *New Republic*, studied political philosophy. As successful, less earnest, more convivial, Hadden collected china dogs, made jokes.* In 1920 the senior class voted Hadden Most Likely to Succeed, Luce Most Brilliant. Most Brilliant he, Luce sloped off to Christ Church, Oxford, there to study European conditions, take field trips into the churning Balkans.

BEST ADVICE: DON'T

Twenty months after commencement, in the city room of Paperkiller Frank Munsey's *Baltimore News*, met again Luce, Hadden. Newshawks by day, at night they wrangled over policies of the magazine they had been planning since Hotchkiss. Boasted the final prospectus: "*Time* will be free from cheap sensationalism . . . windy bias."

In May, 1922, began the long struggle to raise money to start *Time*. Skeptical at the outset proved Newton D. Baker, Nicholas Murray Butler, Herbert Bayard Swope, William Lyon Phelps. Pooh-poohed *Review of Reviews* Owner Charles

*Once, watching Luce going past, laden with cares & responsibilities, Hadden chuckled, upspoke: "Look out, Harry. You'll drop the college."

Lanier: "My best advice . . . don't do it." From studious, pint-sized Henry Seidel Canby, later editor of Lamont-backed *Saturday Review of Literature*, came only encouraging voice in this threnody.

Undismayed Luce & Hadden took the first of many offices in an old brownstone house at 9 East 17th Street, furnished it with a filing cabinet, four secondhand desks, a big brass bowl for cigarette stubs, sought backers.*

JPMorganapoleon H. P. Davison, Yale classmate of Luce, Hadden, great & good friend of both, in June contributed $4,000. Next to succumb: Mrs. David S. Ingalls, sister of Classmate William Hale Harkness; amount, $10,000. From Brother Bill, $5,000. Biggest early angel, Mrs. William Hale Harkness, mother of Brother Bill & Mrs. Ingalls, invested $20,000. Other original stockholders: Robert A. Chambers, Ward Cheney, F. Trubee Davison, E. Roland Harriman, Dwight W. Morrow, Harvey S. Firestone, Jr., Seymour H. Knox, William V. Griffin. By November Luce & Hadden had raised $86,000, decided to go to work on fellowman.

"SNAGGLE-TOOTHED . . . PIG-FACED"

Puny in spite of these preparations, prosy in spite of the contributions of Yale poets Archibald MacLeish & John Farrar, was the first issue of *Time* on March 3, 1923. Magazine went to 9,000 subscribers; readers learned that Uncle Joe Cannon had retired at 86, that there was a famine in Russia, that Thornton Wilder friend Tunney had defeated Greb.

---

*In return for $50 cash, original investors were given two shares 6% Preferred Stock with a par value of $25, one share Class A Common Stock without par value. 3,440 Preferred, 1,720 Class A Common were so sold.

170 shares of Class A Common, 8,000 shares of Class B Common, also without par value, not entitled to dividends until Preferred Shares had been retired, were issued to Briton Hadden, Henry R. Luce, who gave one-third to associates, divided remainder equally.

In 1925, authorized capital of Time, Inc., was increased to 19,000 shares; of which 8,000 were Preferred, 3,000 Class A; as before, 8,000 Class B.

In June, 1930 (if you are still following this), the Preferred Stock was retired in full & dividends were initiated for both Common Stocks. Corporation at this time had 2,400 shares Class A, 7,900 Class B outstanding.

By the spring of 1931 *Time* had begun to march, shares were nominally quoted at $1,000. Best financial minds advised splitting stock on basis of twenty shares for one. Outstanding after clever maneuver: 206,400 shares Common.

In 1933, outlook still gorgeous, each share of stock was reclassified into 1/10th share of $6.50 Dividend Cumulative Convertible Preferred Stock ($6.50 div. cum. con. pfd. stk.) and one share of New Common Stock. New div. cum. con. pfd. stk. was convertible into a share and a half of New Common Stock, then selling around $40 a share, now quoted at over $200.

Present number of shares outstanding, 238,000; paper value of shares, $47,000,000; conservative estimate of Luce holding, 102,300 shares; paper value, $20,460,000; conservative estimate of Luce income from *Time* stock (shares earned $9.74 in 1935, paid so far in 1936, $6.50; anticipated dividend for full year, $8), $818,400; reported Luce income from other investments, $100,000; reported Luce bagatelle as editor of Time, Inc., $45,000; reported total Lucemolument, $963,400.

Boy!

Yet to suggest itself as a rational method of communication, of infuriating readers into buying the magazine, was strange inverted Timestyle. It was months before Hadden's impish contempt for his readers,* his impatience with the English language, crystallized into gibberish. By the end of the first year, however, Timeditors were calling people able, potent, nimble; "Tycoon," most successful Timepithet, had been coined by Editor Laird Shields Goldsborough; so fascinated Hadden with "beady-eyed" that for months nobody was anything else. Timeworthy were deemed such designations as "Tom-tom" Heflin, "Body-lover" Macfadden.

"Great word! Great word!" would crow Hadden, coming upon "snaggle-toothed," "pig-faced." Appearing already were such maddening coagulations as "cinemaddict," "radiorator." Appearing also were first gratuitous invasions of privacy. Always mentioned as William Randolph Hearst's "great & good friend" was Cinemactress Marion Davies, stressed was the bastardy of Ramsay MacDonald, the "cozy hospitality" of Mae West. Backward ran sentences until reeled the mind.

By March, 1924, the circulation had doubled, has risen since then 40,000 a year, reaches now the gratifying peak of 640,000, is still growing. From four meagre pages in first issue, *Time* advertising has now come to eclipse that in *Satevepost*. Published *Time* in first six months of 1936, 1,590 pages; *Satevepost*, 1,480.

NO SLUGABED, HE . . .

Strongly contrasted from the outset of their venture were Hadden, Luce. Hadden, handsome, black-haired, eccentric, irritated his partner by playing baseball with the office boys, by making jokes, by lack of respect for autocratic business. Conformist Luce disapproved of heavy drinking, played hard, sensible game of tennis, said once: "I have no use for a man who lies in bed after nine o'clock in the morning," walked to work every morning, reproved a writer who asked for a desk for lack of "log-cabin spirit."

In 1925, when *Time* moved its offices to Cleveland, bored, rebellious was Editor Hadden; Luce, busy & social, lunched with local bigwigs, addressed Chamber of Commerce, subscribed to Symphony Orchestra, had neat house in the suburbs. Dismayed was Luce when Hadden met him on return from Europe with premature plans to move the magazine back to New York. In 1929, dying of a streptococcus infection, Hadden still opposed certain details of success-formula of *Fortune*, new, beloved Lucenterprise.

OATS, HOGS, CHEESE . . .

In January, 1930, first issue of *Fortune* was mailed to 30,000 subscribers, cost as now $1 a copy, contained articles on branch banking, hogs, glassblowing,

---

*Still framed at *Time* is Hadden's scrawled dictum: "Let Subscriber Goodkind mend his ways!"

how to live in Chicago on $25,000 a year. Latest issue (Nov., 1936) went to 130,000 subscribers, contained articles on bacon, tires, the New Deal, weighed as much as a good-sized flounder.*

Although in 1935 *Fortune* made a net profit of $500,000, vaguely dissatisfied was Editor Luce. Anxious to find & express "the technological significance of industry," he has been handicapped by the fact that his writers are often hostile to Big Business, prone to insert sneers, slithering insults. In an article on Bernard Baruch, the banker was described as calling President Hoover "old cheese-face." Protested Tycoon Baruch that he had said no such thing. Shotup of this was that Luce, embarrassed, printed a retraction; now often removes too-vivid phrasing from writers' copy.

Typical perhaps of Luce methods is *Fortune* system of getting material. Writers in first draft put down wild gossip, any figures that occur to them. This is sent to victim, who indignantly corrects the errors, inadvertently supplies facts he might otherwise have withheld.

March of Time in approximately its present form was first broadcast on March 6, 1931, paid the Columbia System for privilege, dropped from the air in February, 1932, with Luce attacking radio's "blatant claim to be a medium of education." Said he: "Should *Time* or any other business feel obliged to be the philanthropist of the air; to continue to pay for radio advertising it doesn't want in order to provide radio with something worthwhile?" So popular, so valuable to the studio was *March of Time* that it was restored in September of the same year, with Columbia donating its time & facilities. Since then *March of Time* has been sponsored by Remington-Rand typewriter company, by Wrigley's gum, by its own cinema *March of Time*, has made 400 broadcasts.† Apparently reconciled to philanthropy is Luce, because time for latest version will be bought & paid for by his organization.

No active connection now has Luce with the moving-picture edition of *March of Time*, which was first shown on February 1, 1935, appears thirteen times a year in over 6,000 theatres, has so far failed to make money, to repay $900,000 investment. Even less connection has he with *Time*'s only other unprofitable venture. Fifty-year-old *Architectural Forum*, acquired in 1932, loses still between $30,000 and $50,000 a year, circulates to 31,000.

Letters, five-cent fortnightly collection of *Time*'s correspondence with its indefatigable readers, was started in 1931, goes to 30,000, makes a little money.

For a time, Luce was on Board of Directors of Paramount Pictures. Hoped to learn something of cinema, heard nothing discussed but banking, resigned sadly.

---

*Two pounds, nine ounces.
†By some devious necromancy, statisticians have calculated that *March of Time* ranks just behind *Amos & Andy* as most popular of all radio programs; reaches between 8,000,000 and 9,000,000 newshungry addicts.

Net profits of Time, Inc., for the past nine years:

1927	3,860
1928	125,787
1929	325,412
1930	818,936
1931	847,447
1932	613,727*
1933	1,009,628
1934	1,773,094
1935	$2,249,823$^†^

In 1935 gross revenue of *Time-Fortune* was $8,621,170, of which the news-magazine brought in approximately $6,000,000. Outside investments netted $562,295. For rent, salaries, production & distribution, other expenses went $6,594,076. Other deductions: $41,397. Allowance for federal income tax: $298,169.

Time's books, according to Chicago Statisticians Gerwig & Gerwig, show total assets of $6,755,451. Liabilities, $3,101,584. These figures, conventionally allowing $1 for name, prestige of *Time*, come far from reflecting actual prosperity of Luce, his enterprises. Sitting pretty are the boys.

LUCE . . . MARCHES ON!

Transmogrified by this success are the offices, personnel of *Time-Fortune.* Last reliable report: *Time,* 308 employees; *Fortune,* 103; Cinemarch, 58; Radiomarch, 10; *Architectural Forum,* 40; *Life,* 47. In New York; total, 566. In Chicago, mailing, editorial, mechanical employees, 216. Grand total Timemployees on God's earth, 782. Average weekly recompense for informing fellowman, $45.67802.

From first single office, Timen have come to bulge to bursting six floors of spiked, shiny Chrysler Building, occupy 150 rooms, eat daily, many at famed Cloud Club, over 1,000 eggs, 500 cups of coffee, much bicarbonate of soda. Other offices: Cinemarch, 10th Avenue at 54th Street; Radiomarch, Columbia Broadcasting Building.

Ornamented with Yale, Harvard, Princeton diplomas, stuffed fish, terrestrial globes are offices of Luce & other headmen; bleak, uncarpeted the writer's dingy lair.

Heir apparent to mantle of Luce is dapper, tennis-playing, $35,000-a-year

---

*Hmm.

†Exceeded only by Curtis Publishing Co. (*Satevepost*): $5,329,900; Crowell Publishing Co. (*Collier's*): $2,399,600.

Roy Larsen, nimble in Radio- & Cinemarch, vice-president & second largest stockholder in Time, Inc. Stock income: $120,000.

Looming behind him is burly, able, tumbledown Yaleman Ralph McAllister Ingersoll, former Fortuneditor, now general manager of all Timenterprises, descendant of 400-famed Ward McAllister. Littered his desk with pills, unguents, Kleenex, Socialite Ingersoll is *Time*'s No. 1 hypochondriac, introduced ant palaces for study & emulation of employees, writes copious memoranda about filing systems, other trivia, seldom misses a Yale football game. His salary: $30,000; income from stock: $40,000.

Early in life Timeditor John Stuart Martin lost his left arm in an accident. Unhandicapped he, resentful of sympathy, Martin played par golf at Princeton, is a crack shot with a rifle or shotgun, holds a telephone with no hands, using shoulder & chin, chews paperclips. First cousin of Cofounder Hadden, joined in second marriage to daughter of Cunard Tycoon Sir Ashley Sparks, Timartin is managing editor of newsmagazine, has been nimble in Cinemarch, other Timenterprises, makes $25,000 a year salary, gets from stock $60,000.

$20,000 salary, $20,000 from stock gets shyest, least-known of all Timeditors, Harvardman John S. Billings, Jr., now under Luce in charge of revamped *Life*, once Washington correspondent for the Brooklyn *Eagle*, once National Affairs Editor for *Time*. Yclept "most important man in shop" by Colleague Martin, Billings, brother of famed muralist Henry Billings, is naïve, solemn, absent-minded, once printed same story twice, wanted to print, as news, story of van Gogh's self-mutilation, drives to office in car with liveried chauffeur, likes Jones Beach.

Fortuneditor Eric Hodgins is thin-haired, orbicular, no Big Three graduate. Formerly on *Redbook*, boy & girl informing *Youth's Companion*, Hodgins inherited Pill-Swallower Ingersoll's editorial job two years ago when latter was called to greater glory, higher usefulness, still writes much of content of magazine, is paid $15,000; from stock only $8,000.

Doomed to strict anonymity are *Time-Fortune* staff writers, but generally known in spite of this are former *Times* bookritic John Chamberlain, Meistersinger Archibald MacLeish. Both out of sympathy with domineering business, both irked by stylistic restrictions, thorns to Luce as well as jewels they. Reward for lack of fame: Chamberlain, $10,000; MacLeish, $15,000; each, two months' vacation.

Brisk beyond belief are carryings-on these days in Luce's chromium tower. *Time*, marching on more militantly than ever, is a shambles on Sundays & Mondays, when week's news is teletyped to Chicago printing plant; *Fortune*, energetic, dignified, its offices smelling comfortably of cookies, is ever astir with such stupefying projects as sending the entire staff to Japan; new whoopsheet *Life* so deep in organization that staff breakfasts are held to choose from 6,000 submitted photographs the Nude of the Week; so harried perpetually all editors that even interoffice memoranda are couched in familiar Time-style,* that an appointment to lunch with Editor Luce must be made three weeks in advance.

Caught up also in the whirlwind of progress are *Time*, *Fortune*'s 19 maiden checkers. Bryn Mawr, Wellesley, Vassar graduates they, each is assigned to a staff writer, checks every word he writes, works hard & late, is barred by magazine's anti-feminine policy from editorial advancement.

COLD, BAGGY, TEMPERATE . . .

At work today, Luce is efficient, humorless, revered by colleagues; arrives always at 9:15, leaves at 6, carrying armfuls of work, talks jerkily, carefully, avoiding visitor's eye; stutters in conversation, never in speechmaking. In early days kept standing at Luce desk like butlers were writers while he praised or blamed; now most business is done by time-saving memoranda called "Luce's bulls." Prone he to wave aside pleasantries, social preliminaries, to get at once to the matter in hand. Once to interviewer who said, "I hope I'm not disturbing you," snapped Luce, "Well, you are." To ladies full of gentle misinformation he is brusque, contradictory, hostile; says that his only hobby is "conversing with somebody who knows something," argues still that "names make news," that he would not hesitate to print a scandal involving his best friend.

Because of his Chinese birth, constantly besieged is Luce by visiting Orientals; he is polite, forbearing, seethes secretly. Lunch, usually in a private room at the Cloud Club, is eaten quickly, little attention paid to the food, much to business. He drinks not at all at midday, sparingly at all times, takes sometimes champagne at dinner, an occasional cocktail at parties. Embarrassed perhaps by reputation for unusual abstemiousness, he confesses proudly that he smokes too much.

Serious, ambitious Yale standards are still reflected in much of his conduct; in indiscriminate admiration for bustling success, in strong regard for conventional morality, in honest passion for accuracy; physically, in conservative, baggy clothes, white shirts with buttoned-down collars, solid-color ties. A budding joiner, in New York, Luce belongs to the Yale, Coffee House, Racquet & Tennis, Union, & Cloud Clubs; owns a box at the Metropolitan; is listed in *Who's Who & Social Register.*

Colder, more certain, more dignified than in the early days of the magazine, his prose style has grown less ebullient, resembles pontifical *Fortune* rather than chattering *Time.* Before some important body he makes now at least one speech a year, partly as a form of self-discipline, partly because he feels that his position as head of a national institution demands it. His interests wider, he likes to travel, meet &

---

*Sample Luce memorandum: "Let *Time*'s editors next week put thought on the Japanese beetle. H. R. L."

observe the Great. Five or six times in Europe, he has observed many Great & Near Great. Of a twenty-minute conversation with King Edward, then Prince of Wales, says only "Very interesting." Returning from such trips, he always provides staff members with 10 & 12-page memoranda carefully explaining conditions.

Orated recently of conditions in this country: "Without the aristocratic principle no society can endure. . . . What slowly deadened our aristocratic sense was the expanding frontier, but more the expanding machine. . . . But the aristocratic principle persisted in the United States in our fetish of comparative success. . . . We got a plutocracy without any common sense of dignity and obligation. Money became more and more the only mark of success, but still we insisted that the rich man was no better than the poor man—and the rich man accepted the verdict. And so let me make it plain, the triumph of the mass mind is nowhere more apparent than in the frustration of the upper classes." Also remarked in conversation: "Trouble is—great anti-social development— is the automobile trailer. Greatest failure of this country is that it hasn't provided good homes for its people. Trailer shows that."

MILESTONES

Good-naturedly amused by Luce tycoon ambitions was Lila Hotz, of Chicago, whom he married there on Dec. 22, 1923. In 1935, the father of two boys, Luce was divorced by her in Reno on Oct. 5. Married in Old Greenwich, Conn., without attendants, on Nov. 23, 1935, were Luce, Novelist-Playwright Clare Boothe Brokaw, described once by Anglo-aesthete Cecil Beaton as "most drenchingly beautiful," former wife of elderly Pantycoon George Tuttle Brokaw.

Two days before ceremony, "Abide with Me," by new, beautiful Mrs. Luce, was produced at the Ritz Theatre. Play dealt with young woman married to sadistic drunkard, was unfavorably reviewed by all newspaper critics.*

In a quandary was Bridegroom Luce when *Time*'s own critic submitted a review suggesting play had some merit. Said he: "Show isn't that good. . . . Go back. . . . Write what you thought." Seven times, however, struggled the writer before achieving an acceptable compromise between criticism, tact.

A MILLION ROOMS, A THOUSAND BATHS . . .

Long accustomed to being entertained, entertaining, is Mrs. Luce, intimate of Mr. & Mrs. A. Coster Schermerhorn, Bernard M. Baruch, Jock Whitney, glis-

*Of it said Richard Watts, blue-shirted, moon-faced *Tribune* dramappraiser:
"One almost forgave 'Abide with Me' its faults when its lovely playwright, who must have been crouched in the wings for a sprinter's start as the final curtain mercifully descended, heard a cry of 'author,' which was not audible in my vicinity, and arrived onstage to accept the audience's applause just as the actors, who had a head-start on her, were properly lined up and smoothed out to receive their customary adulation."

tening stage & literary stars. Many were invited last summer to 30-acre estate in Stamford to play tennis, croquet, swim; many more will be when Mrs. Luce has finished her new play, "The Women,"* when *Life*'s problems, budding policies have been settled by Luce.

Many, too, will come to 7,000-acre, $100,000 Luce plantation, near Charleston, S. C.; will sleep there in four streamlined, prefabricated guest cottages. Given to first Mrs. Luce in divorce settlement, along with $500,000 in cash & securities, was French Manoir at Gladstone, N. J., where Luce once planned to raise Black Angus cows, to become gentleman farmer.

Described too modestly by him to Newyorkereporter as "smallest apartment in River House,"† Luce duplex at 435 East 52nd Street contains 15 rooms, 5 baths, a lavatory; was leased furnished from Mrs. Bodrero Macy for $7,300 annually, contains many valuable French, English, Italian antiques, looks north and east on the river. In décor, Mrs. Luce prefers the modern; evasive is Luce. Says he: "Just like things convenient & sensible." Says also: "Whatever furniture or houses we buy in the future will be my wife's buying, not mine."

WHITHER, WHITHER?

Accused by many of Fascist leanings, of soaring journalistic ambition, much & conflicting is the evidence on Luce political faith, future plans. By tradition a Tory, in 1928 he voted for Alfred E. Smith, in 1932 for Herbert Hoover, this year for Alfred M. Landon. Long at outs with William Randolph Hearst, it was rumored that a visit last spring to California included a truce with ruthless, shifting publisher. Close friend for years of Thomas Lamont, Henry P. Davison, the late Dwight Morrow, it has been hinted that an official connection with the House of Morgan in the future is not impossible. Vehemently denies this Luce, denies any personal political ambition, admits only that he would like eventually to own a daily newspaper in New York.

Most persistent, most fantastic rumor, however, declares that Yaleman Luce already has a wistful eye on the White House. Reported this recently Chicago's *Ringmaster*; added: "A legally-minded friend . . . told him that his Chinese birth made him ineligible. Luce dashed to another lawyer to check. Relief! He was born of American parents and properly registered at the Consulate."

Whatever the facts in that matter, indicative of Luce consciousness of budding greatness, of responsibility to whole nation, was his report to *Time*'s Board of Directors on March 19, 1936. Declaimed he: "The expansion of your company has brought it to a point beyond which it will cease to be even a big Small Business and become a small Big Business. . . . The problem of public relations

---

*Among backers are sad, ramshackle George S. Kaufman, high-domed furbearing Moss Hart.
†Smallest apartment in River House has six rooms, one bath.

also arises. *Time*, the Weekly Newsmagazine, has been, and still is, its own adequate apologist. Ditto, *Fortune*. But with a motion-picture journal, a nightly radio broadcast, and with four magazines, the public interpretation of your company's alleged viewpoint or viewpoints must be taken with great seriousness." Certainly to be taken with seriousness is Luce at thirty-eight, his fellowman already informed up to his ears, the shadow of his enterprises long across the land, his future plans impossible to imagine, staggering to contemplate. Where it all will end, knows God!

(1936)

NOBODY BETTER,

BETTER THAN NOBODY

PONCÉ Cruse Evans, the woman who writes "Hints from Heloise," the syndicated household-hints column that appears in more than five hundred newspapers in twenty countries, has a cute nose and a cute smile and a strong chin that precedes her into confrontations with people who smoke in elevators and dry cleaners who ruin good silk blouses. On television (she often appears on talk shows, and forty-seven TV stations around the country use her minute-long household-hints tapes), her luxuriant head of completely gray hair catches the eye. She is only thirty-one years old. Her hair started turning gray when she was twelve, and she thinks that worry about her mother, who had many illnesses and died in 1977, made it turn grayer faster. Her gray hair and young face add to the confusion of people who expect her to be older and who are also not clear on the difference between her and her mother. Poncé's mother, Heloise, founded the column in 1959. Poncé began to write for the column occasionally under the name Heloise II in 1975, took over the column in 1977, and dropped the "II" in 1978. Her full name is Poncé Kiah Marchelle Heloise Cruse Evans. Poncé (pronounced *Pahn*-see) was the nickname of her paternal grandmother, Florence; it does not appear in the Dictionary of Common English First Names. Kiah is short for Hezekiah, a name of several uncles on her father's side. Marchelle comes from her father's first name, which is Marshal. Heloise is from her mother. Cruse was Poncé's last name before she married. Evans comes from her husband of two years, David Evans, a plumbing contractor.

When Poncé tells a story about a phone call between her and Joseph D'Angelo, the president of King Features Syndicate (her column makes more money than any other at King Features), she holds her right hand to her ear with index, middle, and ring finger bent and little finger and thumb extended, to represent a telephone. When she wants to express strong aversion, she closes her eyes, raises her thick, dark eyebrows, and turns the corners of her mouth down. When she describes how wonderful certain recipes are, she presses both hands to her breastbone, fingers spread. When she is mortified with embarrassment, she flops her head over onto the arm of the chair she is sitting in and stays like that for a minute or so. When she is having trouble with a door that is supposed to open inward but is stuck, she gives it a solid shot with her hip, like a basketball player throwing a hip check. When she realizes that someone she has just met is attempting a joke at an unexpected point in the conversation, she does a mild double take and then looks at the person as if the person were a common household object suddenly revealing a new and different use. Her regard is unusual, because whatever she looks at she looks at with one eye at a time.

"I'm an alternator," Poncé says. "That means I see with alternate eyes. I have no binocular vision and very little depth perception. Sometimes it freaks people out who ride with me, because I stay so far away from other cars, just to be on the safe side. I was born with severe astigmatism. I'm talking about *kabongas!* My eyes were so crossed all you could see were the whites. When I was born, my mother was in labor for thirty-two hours, and the doctors said that maybe the pressure on my skull was what caused the condition. I had six operations to correct it. My mother promised God that if my astigmatism was cured she'd tithe her income to the blind, and He must've liked the deal, because the operations worked. Even today, ten to fifteen per cent of the income from her estate goes to purchase Braille typewriters for children who cannot afford them. When I was on my book tour in Washington last April, I passed the hospital where I had the operations. I will always remember being in that hospital with my eyes bandaged shut, feeling totally vulnerable. When someone comes into the room, you don't know whether they've come to give you a shot, take your temperature, or give you ice cream. Listening to the hospital sounds—the cart rolling down the hall, cla-*klunk* cla-*klunk;* the bottles on the cart rattling; squeaky nurses' shoes; the sound effects of the cartoons on TV, like that weird bongo noise feet make when the guy runs; the sound of scissors cutting away tape. In the movies, they always show the doctors and nurses standing around the bed when they cut the bandage from the patient's eyes, but to be on the inside is really worse. It's probably because of that that I've had such acute hearing my whole life."

Poncé imitates sounds all the time when she talks. For example:

kneehhh—Her hair dryer stuck on its lowest speed when she has just washed her hair and has to go on TV in half an hour.

sploof!—Baking soda coming out of the box all at once.

swt swt swt—Her mother making an abstract oil painting, applying the paint with clips from her hair.

ch-ch-ch-ch-ch-ch—Chinese people chopping vegetables.

chop chop chop—Americans chopping vegetables.

klonk! klonk!—Her father, six-two and two hundred pounds, taking a shower in a tiny shower stall with metal sides.

plunk!—Her pet macaw, Rocky, after being sprayed with a hose, falling from a tree where he had flown in an escape attempt.

ghhich!—Her father when he realized that the pilot of the plane he was boarding was a five-foot-tall woman.

Poncé lives outside San Antonio, Texas, and not long ago I drove down to see her and her husband. From Chicago to San Antonio, the road is basically one big strip. In Illinois, I passed a motor home with a large metal nameplate on the back saying "The Humberts." When the combined Interstates 55 and 70 cross into Missouri at St. Louis, there is no sign on the bridge identifying the river underneath as the Mississippi. In Muskogee, Oklahoma—"a place where even squares can have a ball," according to Merle Haggard—I saw a Taco Hut, a Taco Bell, and a Taco Tico.

I drove around San Antonio for a long time looking for a motel. I wanted a locally owned one—the kind of motel that was built in the days when people thought owning a motel was a good way to get rich. Loop 410, the freeway that goes around San Antonio, is a circuit of more than fifty miles. The only motels I saw were the ones you usually see. Finally, driving around the side streets of a neighborhood sliced through with freeways near the center of the city, I saw out of the corner of my eye a motel that I will call the Miramar Motor Inn. I had seen no signs advertising it. It was on a street that dead-ended at a fence along a freeway. On one side of the street it had many rooms in cinder-block buildings surrounding a large parking lot, and on the other side of the street it had other buildings and more rooms. I went in and registered, and after the woman behind the counter took my money she asked, "How did you find out about this motel?"

I had not been in Texas long before I started having millions of insights about the difference between Texas and the rest of America. I was going to write these insights down, but then I thought—Nahhh.

PONCÉ'S mother, Heloise, was born in Fort Worth, Texas, on May 4, 1919, to Mr. and Mrs. Charles Bowles. She and her sister Louise were identical twins. Heloise's mother was herself an identical twin, and the day on which her daughters were born also happened to be her own birthday. As a girl, Heloise liked to rub empty spools on the soap when she was in the bath, and blow bubbles from the hole in the center of the spool. She was interested in the Orient— an interest encouraged and shared by her mother, who gave Heloise and Louise matching Chinese cedar chests for their sixteenth birthday. Heloise went to public school in Fort Worth, and she was the only girl in her high school to take shop class, and she got an A in it. She also took private lessons in smoking, to learn how to smoke a cigarette glamorously. She attended the Texas School of Fine Arts in 1938, and in 1939 she graduated from the Felt and Tarrent Business College and also from Draughn's Business College. In 1940, she married Adolph Risky, an Air Corps pilot. After two miscarriages, she thought that she could not have children, so she and her husband adopted a son, Louis. She and her son stayed in Texas when her husband went off to war. In 1943, he was shot down over Europe. Heloise received a flag and his medals in the mail, but she did not have enough money to go to Cambridge, England, where he was buried. (Thirty years later, on her only trip to Europe, she did visit the grave.)

In 1946, at a party in Fort Worth, Heloise met Marshal (Mike) Cruse, a captain in the Army Air Forces. He asked her out, and on their first date they went target shooting. They were married three weeks later, and they honeymooned in Mexico. Early in 1948, she and Louis went to join her husband in China, where he had been stationed. First, they lived in Shanghai and then they lived in Nanking. Heloise was both thrilled and horrified by China. In her book "Heloise in China," written in 1948 (published in 1971), she said, "There are no words in the dictionary to describe this country and its people." She visited Peking, which she thought was the most beautiful and mysterious city in the world. Outside the wall of the Forbidden City, she saw many Communist students machine-gunned by Chinese Nationalist troops. She managed a household without a stove or heat or running water. She used rice water for starch, beet juice to dye clothes, and cabbage to clean rugs. She shot a .22 rifle to scare away Chinese people who broke down the bamboo fence around her house and began stealing clothes off the clothesline. She and her husband became friends with their upstairs neighbors, Major Les Garrigus and his wife, Helen, who were also from Texas. One day, Helen and Heloise made one huge Texas state flag and two smaller ones and hung them on the house, causing people to wonder what new embassy that might be. Another time, Helen and Heloise were going shopping and they saw a Chinese man raping a goat. This became a running joke between the couples, and in later years whenever they called each other long-distance they began the conversation by saying "Baa-baa-baa."

The Cruses left China in 1948, before the Communists took over, and moved to Waco, Texas, near where Captain Cruse was stationed. In the first five years of her second marriage, Heloise became pregnant five times. She always knew she was pregnant when she felt a strong urge to go out in the yard and suck rocks. All those five pregnancies ended in miscarriages. Finally, after a difficult pregnancy and a difficult labor, she gave birth to Poncé on April 15, 1951. The Cruses moved from Waco to Arlington, Virginia, in 1953, and in 1958 they moved to Hawaii. In 1958, Heloise and her husband went to a party of Air Force people where everyone outranked them. The conversation turned to different ways to supplement service pensions after retirement. Heloise said that she would like to write a column in a newspaper to help housewives. A colonel laughed in her face and bet her a hundred to one she couldn't get a job on a newspaper. Heloise had some engraved calling cards made, and then she dressed in her best suit, with matching purse, hat, shoes, and gloves, and she went to the office of the Honolulu *Advertiser* when she knew the editor was out to lunch. She made sure she created quite a stir, and she left her card. Two days later, she went back, and this time a secretary gave her an appointment to see the editor. Heloise often dyed her hair off-beat colors; for the appointment she sprayed her hair silver. The editor asked her if she could type, and she said no. She told him her idea for a column and offered to work for free for thirty days. The editor decided to give her a chance, and she soon began a column called "Readers' Exchange."

At first, the column offered both practical and personal advice, but after a while the household hints that the column printed attracted the most attention. Once, Heloise printed a hint from a reader which said that Sanford's X-it, an ink eradicator, would remove banana-leaf stains, and all the Sanford's X-it in Hawaii sold out and a fresh planeload had to be flown in. Another time, she said that Hershey's cocoa butter was good for soothing rough hands, and the same thing happened. After the Honolulu *Advertiser* had been running the "Readers' Exchange" for less than three years, its circulation was up forty per cent, and the editor said that it was mostly because of her. *Time* printed an article on her and her column in June of 1961, and Elwin Thompson, the editor at King Features Syndicate, saw the article and suggested to Heloise that she go into syndication. In September of 1961, King Features began to distribute "Hints from Heloise" nationally, and by April of 1962 the column was appearing in a hundred and fifty-eight papers. Her readership was so enthusiastic that when she offered free to anyone who asked for it a booklet about laundry that she had written she received two hundred thousand requests—the largest delivery of mail to an individual in the history of Hawaii. In November of 1962, she published her first book, "Heloise's Housekeeping Hints." Early in 1963, the Cruses moved back to Arlington, Virginia. In October of 1963, Heloise published her second book, "Heloise's Kitchen Hints." In 1964, at the Waldorf-Astoria Hotel, she received the Silver Lady award from an association of communications executives called the Banshees, in recognition of her achievements as a columnist. By the end of 1964, her column was appearing in five hundred and ninety-three newspapers, in America and foreign countries. The colonel who had laughed at her at the party in Hawaii wrote to her and asked how he could get a job.

For a long time, Heloise and her husband had been looking for a place to move after he retired. They wrote to chambers of commerce and considered many cities all over the country. They wanted a place with a good climate, low cost of living, good military hospitals, and good mail service. San Antonio won out, and in 1966 the Cruses moved into a five-room apartment on Broadway, eighty blocks from downtown. They also rented an adjoining two-bedroom apartment, converted it into an office, and knocked out a wall in a closet so Heloise could go back and forth easily. The San Antonio *Light*, a newspaper that carried Heloise's column, sent a reporter named Marjorie Clapp to do a story about Heloise soon after the Cruses moved. Marjorie Clapp mainly wrote stories about medical science, and she was unhappy to be assigned to a celebrity interview. When she arrived at Heloise's apartment, she noticed that Heloise was barefoot and had blacked out several of her teeth with some kind of black gum. She also noticed that the closet that led to Heloise's office still had clothes hanging in it, and to get through she had to push the clothes aside. Marjorie Clapp was not surprised by Heloise's strange appearance or bowled over by Heloise's celebrity, and that pleased Heloise, and the two went on to become close friends. Not long after the Cruses moved to San Antonio, Heloise and her husband divorced. In December of 1970, Heloise remarried; her third husband was A. L. Reese, a Houston businessman and widower, whom she met while doing volunteer work with the Optimist Club. Heloise did not want to move to Houston, and Mr. Reese did not want to move to San Antonio, and so they divorced, and Heloise went back to calling herself Heloise Bowles, her maiden name.

Heloise had health problems her whole life. In addition to having seven miscarriages, she had a growth in her stomach (it was successfully removed), a disease of the heart carried by pigeons, tic douloureux (a nervous disease involving severe facial twitching and pain, sometimes leading to loss of consciousness), arteriosclerosis, and a cracked vertebra, suffered when a car she was riding in was struck by a drunk driver. (After the accident, Heloise sent state legislators letters printed on little Japanese fans saying that they should pass stricter laws against drunk drivers.) At one point when Heloise was very sick, Dr. Denton Cooley, the famous Houston heart specialist, told her he could help her if she agreed to stop smoking, and she said she just couldn't, and he said, "Then I can't help you," and walked out of the room. She planned her funeral over several years, with the help of Mr. and Mrs. Lelon Cude, a couple she met at a party. They visited many cemeteries shopping for burial plots. The Cudes (who owned a funeral parlor themselves) later remembered that at one cemetery she told the director in detail how to get rid of the anthills. She had picked a site, and had a tombstone carved and set up, by 1975. The tombstone read "Heloise, Every Housewife's Friend." She died December 28, 1977, and was buried in a red silk Japanese wedding robe, which she had always worn on New Year's Eve. At her funeral, each mourner was given a long-stemmed red carnation, and a friend, Mrs. Paul Loomis, sang "There Are No Phones to Heaven"—a song written and copyrighted by Heloise. Several obituaries recalled that she had liked unusual hair coloring, and these ended with a quotation taken from an official biography distributed by King Features Syndicate: "I just can't abide a dreary look, and when I wear a blue dress and blue shoes, why I'm going to have blue hair."

PONCÉ told me how to get to her house: "Come out San Pedro past the airport, which you can't miss because the planes land practically right on top of your car, get off at the Bitters Road exit, go left under the overpass, go straight through the light (if it's green, of course) . . ." I liked the last instruction, because it reminded me of the generous specificity of many of her household hints. For example, a hint telling how to polish sterling-silver bracelets by rubbing them on wool carpeting begins, "Remove the bracelets from your arm." Before I went, I put on a new pair of socks. These socks came on a sock hanger. This sock hanger was a single piece of molded silver plastic, about three and a half inches long and an inch and a half high. Essentially, it was a little clip with teeth to grip the socks and a hook at the top so the socks could hang on display at the store. It looked somehow special to me. I put it in my pocket and took it with me. When I was sitting in Poncé's living room talking to her, I remembered I had it, and I showed it to her.

She reacted like an Audubon Society member spotting an indigo bunting at her bird feeder. "Aren't those *neat?* You can do lots of things with those. They make great tie hangers or clothespins for dainty items like lingerie or clips to keep potato-chip bags shut after opening. You can clip matching socks together when you dry them (on medium heat), and that saves having to match socks later. Kids like 'em for clothes hangers for Barbie Doll clothes. This is the good kind, too—the teethy kind."

The good kind. Poncé knows that there are sock hangers without teeth, sock hangers of light-gauge plastic which break easily, sock hangers that are only a plastic ring with a tab that goes through the socks. She knows that the heavier-gauge sock hangers with the teeth—functional, eye-pleasing in design—are the good kind. Poncé knows about sock hangers because it is her job to know. Poncé's mother believed that homemakers were "the precious backbone of the world," and she saw significance in the smallest detail of a homemaker's life. Her vision, as she expressed it in her column, was so powerful that it gave her name a status bordering on the official. To many people, Heloise is a name like Aunt Jemima or Betty Crocker, and they are surprised to find out that there was an actual woman named Heloise. Poncé inherited not only her mother's name and her mother's column but also the vision that her mother shared with millions of readers. For most of the history of the column, about eighty per cent of the hints have been ones submitted by readers (and tested by the "Hints from Heloise" staff). So many people participate in the column that the question of authorship is fuzzy: some hints readers send in, some Poncé thinks of, some her mother first came up with twenty years ago. But every hint is like another facet on the same crystal: "Hints from Heloise" will pick one item from the stream that sluices through our lives and then spotlight it, put it on a dais, examine its essence. A rubber crutch tip; a back scratcher; a skin-diving mask and snorkel; toy handcuffs; rubber fruit-jar rings; a shish-kebab skewer; a birthday-candle holder; a bowling-shoe bag; a nylon pastry brush; a Worcestershire-sauce bottle; a toy carpet sweeper; the skinny jar that olives come in; aquarium paint; a glass-doored china hutch; a thick book; a dresser scarf; the little piece of cork inside a soda-pop bottle cap; the square piece of sticky paper that covers the holes on a can of cleanser; a long-handled snow brush; a baby-food jar with a screw-type cap; a wire bicycle basket; a spice-bottle top; half a yardstick; the little circles of paper made by a hole puncher; a toy wagon. "Hints from Heloise" shows that these items are other than they appear. A back scratcher is perfect for cleaning the crevices behind the lint trap in an electric clothes dryer. Two rubber fruit-jar rings placed under an ice tray will prevent the tray from sticking to the bottom of the freezer compartment. Toy handcuffs can keep the cabinets under the kitchen sink shut, so crawling infants won't get into them. Thick books can weight down a towel blotting a stain from a carpet. If you wear a skin-diving face mask and snorkel when you peel onions, you won't cry.

When people complain that a hint in "Hints from Heloise" is sometimes more trouble than the problem it is intended to solve, they forget that just by naming the problem Heloise already has the battle practically won. Before "Hints from Heloise" noticed it, the problem of rump-sprung knit suits existed in the limbo of real but unnamed things. The problems of soiled artificial flowers, soggy undercrust, leaky milk cartons, sour dishrags, girdle stays jabbing, meringue weeping, soda straws sticking out of bag lunches, shower curtains flapping out of the tub, creases in the middle of the tablecloth sticking up, wet boxes in the laundry room, roach eggs in the refrigerator motor, shiny seam marks on the front of recently ironed ties, flyspecks on chandeliers, film on bathroom tiles, steam on bathroom mirrors, rust in Formica drainboards, road film on windshields—all were acknowledged and certified, probably for the first time ever, in "Hints from Heloise." Heloise was the first to call attention to the problem of unevenly distributed curtain gathers. Heloise observed that some things stick: zippers; car doors; bureau drawers; gum in kids' hair; toast in the toaster; plastic placemats to the tabletop; pieces of bacon to one another; one drinking glass inside another; envelopes to one another in humid weather. Other things slide: clothes to one end of the clothesline; purses and bags of groceries off car seats; devilled eggs to one end of the serving tray; quilts off the bed; honeydew melons off the plate; sewing-machine foot controls across the floor; dog bowls across waxed kitchen floors; slipcovers off chair arms; sofa sections apart. "Hints from Heloise" noticed places that no one had officially noticed before: behind the radiator; under the bottom of the blender; between the door runners of sliding glass shower doors; between the little ridges on the bathroom scale; between the washing machine and the wall; between the stove and the countertop; where the grout meets the bathtub; where the carpeting meets the baseboard.

The intelligence at work in "Hints from Heloise" is confident. It likes to begin sentences with "Never," or sometimes with "*Never*" or "Never ever" or "Never, never, never" or "Don't ever, and I mean ever": "Never put any hot food into your freezer. . . . Never take anyone with you when shopping if you can possibly help it. . . . *Never* make one piecrust at a time. . . . Never walk down a long hall more often than necessary. . . . *Never* clean a closet or drawer when you are not angry or in the throwing-away mood. . . . Never walk into a room you are going to clean without a paper sack. . . . Never buy cheap paint for the kitchen. . . . *Never* wash windows when the sun is shining on them. . . . *Never* soak clothes over ten minutes. . . . Never iron a dish towel. . . . Never use bleach on treated cottons. . . . Never use scouring powders or bleaches on plastic cups. . . . *Never* sit, lie, or stretch out on concrete (that's cement) in any type of elasticized bathing suit. . . . Never buy shoes in the morning, because your feet *can* stretch as much as a half size by the afternoon. . . . Never put a rubber band around silverware. . . . Never use a perfume spray near silver, as perfume can mark it. . . . Never use ammonia on a mustard stain. . . . Never, never over-water a philodendron. . . . Never fill a dish to capacity. . . . Don't ever, and I mean ever, put hot grease down your sink drain. . . . Never, never, never use liquid dishwashing detergent in your clothes-washing machine. . . . Never run out of potatoes."

Although Heloise may congratulate herself and her readers for being "real smarties," she never wants to be mistaken for an intellectual. "I am no great brain, just a neighbor and friend," Heloise says. Sometimes the mathematics in the column seem to consist of one, two, three, four, five, six, seven, eight, nine, ten, eleven, a dozen, a bunch, two dozen, a whole bunch, oodles, umpteen, and a zillion. (Poncé, a business minor and a math major in college, once did a physics project on the rate of water loss from a dripping faucet and its effect on water bills. She is in fact very comfortable with numbers.) With its fondness for words like "thingamajig" and "doohickey," the column sometimes seems like the bright girl in class who hides her intelligence so people won't resent her; and, also like the bright girl, the column occasionally slips and uses a precise and abstruse word. Usually, it's a word that has to do with sewing, like selvage (the little strip at the edge of a piece of fabric which is of a different weave to prevent ravelling) or rickrack (a flat braid woven in zigzags and used as a trimming) or flatfelled (sewn by placing one folded raw edge over the other and stitching on the wrong side, like the inside seam of a bluejean leg) or gimp (the round cord used as trimming on furniture).

Time has many rewards for regular readers of "Hints from Heloise." One year, Heloise discovers that a soap-filled steel-wool pad kept completely underwater will not rust for as long as two weeks. Several years later, with an intuitive leap, she discovers that rust on the cut side of lettuce leaves can be prevented the same way. One year, Heloise has a hint for "those of you troubled with 'lines' on husband's shirt collars" or for "women who complain about nylon slips clinging to their bodies." Years later, the problems of "ring around the collar" and "static cling" turn up on television. Heloise's readers never know when a simple one-paragraph hint in the column will predict a multimillion-dollar project involving soap-company executives, advertising writers, and TV-commercial directors, technicians, and actors.

In its early days, the column combined its hints with many encouraging words for housewives. Heloise not only noticed her readers' problems but also believed that her readers' husbands and children probably did not. She sometimes called her readers "my precious ladybugs," and she often ended the column "God bless you." Occasionally, out of the blue, she would say something that admitted how unrewarding the life of a housewife can be. She ended one hint about spring-cleaning with the observation "All the furniture polish in the world won't put a gleam in your husband's eye!" When Poncé took over the column, she figured that homemakers were no longer only housewives but might also be men, grandparents, or even children, and she enlarged the column's focus to include them. "My precious ladybugs" disappeared. As if to compensate for the loss of that old camaraderie, Poncé made the column much more down-home and folksy. Expressions like "Golly whoopers" and "Doggone and heck a mile" multiplied. She also put more emphasis on consumer advocacy and consumer safety. Poncé is less shy than her mother was, and she decided, with newspapers folding under her at an unpleasant rate, that it might be a good idea to be on television. Over all, though, the column under Poncé and the column under her mother have been alike in more ways than they have differed. Nylon net—the product for which the first Heloise found so many uses that it is closely linked with her in the minds of many people—continues to divulge new applications. So does baking soda. So does vinegar—a substance that Poncé feels so strongly about that she flew to San Francisco to address the Vinegar Institute three days after her wedding. Poncé's mother thought that nylon net, baking soda, vinegar, and kerosene were the most important household aids of all. Poncé agrees, although she might replace kerosene with prewash laundry spray, since kerosene is now hard to find and prewash spray, a recent product, has a large number of uses, from removing bumper stickers to cleaning Naugahyde. She thinks she may write a book called "Nylon Net, Baking Soda, Vinegar, and Prewash Spray."

After the first Heloise realized how powerful her column could be, she decided never to mention brand names. The second Heloise follows this rule. She calls Kleenex "facial tissue," Scotchgard "spray-type soil repellent," Clorox "a common household bleach," Kitty Litter "cat-box deodorizer," and Frisbees "flying-saucer-shaped toys." Not mentioning brand names is a good idea, because a really apt hint in "Hints from Heloise" provides an aesthetic thrill that, for a second, makes a person feel like more than just a shopper.

WHAT actually happened was I got hardly any sleep at my motel, because someone kept slamming a door right next to my room all night, and then I got up in the morning and took my shirt off the hanger and a large cockroach jumped out of the shirt pocket and landed on the floor with a strangled cockroach yell. I drove out to David and Poncé's, and Poncé and I sat around and talked for a while, and then David said, "Let's eat." Poncé and I got in her Datsun 280 ZX, and David and Tom Carey, a partner in David's plumbing business, whose sister Sue was Poncé's college roommate and maid of honor, got in David's half-ton Ford pickup. We drove to a nearby restaurant called El Jarro, owned by Arthur Hernandez, whose uncle was married to Poncé's grandfather's sister and whose cousin was Poncé's mother's doctor. It was happy hour at El Jarro, where you got two drinks for every one you ordered, so the table was quickly covered with margarita glasses. Tom Carey said that sometimes when Poncé and David got into arguments he, Tom, would referee, and would jump in and yell, "Time out!" He asked me where I was staying and I said the Miramar and he'd never heard of it. Poncé said that she had had a dream the night before that she made David ten color-coördinated bibs with little clips on them like the clips on a dentist's bib, and she was so sure the dream was real that when she woke up she went looking for the bibs. I ordered the cabrito, which is goat, and a Carta Blanca beer, and they brought me two Carta Blanca beers. Poncé said, "Did you know that the Chinese have different sweat glands than we do?"

After lunch, Poncé picked up the check, and we went into the parking lot, which was very bright, and got in the car, whose seats were hot, and we drove back to Poncé and David's. Tom Carey got in his car and went somewhere, and I got in my van, and Poncé got in David's truck. I followed them into San Antonio on the freeway—everybody passed me because I was going only sixty—and at a stoplight David leaned over and lifted Poncé's sunglasses and looked at her. We went to a restaurant-bar named Yvan, where it was also happy hour. Poncé said, "Did you see they've invented a pill that you take and it tans you? Turns you kind of orange. Only problem is, it turns your palms orange, too." The bar filled with people, and Tom Carey showed up again. Poncé said, "Did you see that they've invented a flyswatter that looks like a little gun and the swatter shoots out and comes back?" Then the owner of the bar came over and talked to us. Tom Carey went somewhere again. Poncé said, "Do you *really* believe the Egyptians built the pyramids with wooden rollers?" Some guy with a beard came up to Poncé and asked her where she worked, and she said, "I'm a writer." He said, "You work for Ryder Trucks?" There was a lingerie show taking place in the bar, and models in nighties were walking around describing what they were wearing and how much the nighties cost. David said, "I don't like wishy-washy broads who say, 'Gee, maybe I will if you will, maybe I won't if you won't, oh, gee, I don't know.' Poncé isn't like that—she's not an easy woman." Then a model in a mostly see-through garment came up to David and said, "Hi, my name is Terri and I work for A Touch of Class Models and I'm wearing an apron-type baby-doll negligee from Shirlee of Hollywood and it just comes in red and the panties come with it and it ties in the back and it sells for thirty-nine dollars." David said, "I'm not interested in your body, I'm interested in your mind." Then we ate dinner and I don't remember what I had.

Next we drove to a place named Fuddruckers, and there was only about a parking space and a half left in the lot, and David pulled his truck in and I backed my van really fast right next to him. We stood in the back room, at a bar that was a replica of an old Mexican tequila bar. When we came out into the parking lot, we were surprised to see there was only about a quarter inch between our vehicles. Then we drove to a place called Maggie's, which had an electric train on rails running above the bar. Then we went to a place that had a good-sized tree growing right through the middle of it and out the ceiling. Then we went to a place called the S. K. Stampede, which was a dance bar in a shopping mall called the Central Park Mall. David and Poncé left and went on home, and I tried to talk to a girl who was standing holding two drinks, and I bounced off as if she had an invisible shield around her. Everybody on the dance floor was dancing one huge synchronized Western dance, and I decided to go back to the motel. I walked out a door that I thought led to the parking lot but in fact led into the mall, which by this time was closed and empty and dimly lit. The door back to the bar had locked behind me, and all the racket in the bar was just a tiny noise through the door. I walked around the mall until I found a door to the parking lot, but the door was locked, so I walked to another door, but it was also locked. I sat down on the cool floor for a while. Then I stood up and examined the sliding security grate over a store window, and I noticed that the store had for sale a digital wristwatch with an alarm that played "The Yellow Rose of Texas." I thought about spending the night in the mall, and then I walked around some more. Down a corridor I heard voices, which turned out to belong to two janitors, and one of them said he would take me to someone who had a key. He took me down another corridor and down a narrow hall that was completely dark and through a door into a carpeted, track-lit office with paintings on the wall, and he left. A member of the Bexar County Sheriff's Department was in the office, and he asked me for my driver's license. I told him how I came out of the wrong door of the bar, and he again asked for my license. I said all I wanted to do was get out of the mall, and he told me to give him my license and sit down and shut up or he'd throw my ass in jail for public intoxication. I told him I hadn't seen much else but public intoxication in San Antonio that night, and his handcuffs made a cricketlike sound as he took them off his belt. I gave him my license. He asked me my birthday and I told him. I looked several times at his name tag, which said "Vela," and he asked me why I kept looking at his name tag, and what I was thinking was, I thought white people beat up on Mexicans in Texas, not the other way around, but I didn't say that. Then I sat there for forty minutes while he checked my I.D. with the police computer, and when it didn't turn up any criminal record he took me to a door to the parking lot and told me that if it had been anyone but him I'd be in the Bexar County jail right now. I took a big roll of cash out of my pocket and said, "You think I'm some kind of vagrant, but I've got over a thousand dollars there." He said, "What motel are you staying at?" I said the Miramar. He said, "Well, you better not go flashing that money around the Miramar if you want to hang on to it." Then I got in my van and drove away.

THE house that Poncé and David live in is a hundred and eighty feet long. It is a contemporary-style ranch house, and Poncé and David designed and built it before they were married. It has two driveways. From the outside, at certain angles, it looks like acres and acres of blue clay-tile roof. At one end of the house, David and Poncé and Poncé's assistants have their offices. David runs his plumbing business from his office. The card catalogue in Poncé's assistants' office lists over fifty thousand household hints, with over two thousand cards just for nylon net. At the other end of the house is Poncé's bathroom, with a special deep drawer for electric curlers and hair dryers in the counter under the sink, and a scale set into the floor through the carpeting (because a scale won't weigh right if there's carpet under it), and a mirror with light bulbs around it, and a sunken marble bathtub with taps that look like golden shells, from which Poncé can look out the window and see the grove of cedar trees where her Chihuahua, Tequila, is buried. The other rooms in the house are a conference room next to her office, where Poncé can talk to people she doesn't want to bring into any other part of her home, and two guest bedrooms, a workroom, a den, four bathrooms, a dining room, a living room, a kitchen, a walk-in pantry, several walk-in closets, the master bedroom, a sauna, and a wine cellar. The wine cellar is a climate-controlled room, not a cellar. One of the guest rooms has a miniature bar in it. The living room is decorated with antique Chinese works of art—cloisonné incense burners, a temple table, an ivory ship with ivory figurines representing a Chinese version of the Atlantis story, and a folding screen with an ivory bas-relief of horses, which Poncé always liked as a little girl because one of the horses near the bottom of the screen has his legs backward. On one wall, there are opium bags embroidered with a tiny stitch called the blind stitch. Poncé said she'd heard that the blind stitch got its name because women went blind doing it, and that the Communist government made the stitch illegal when it took over. The living-room windows sometimes have feathery, sketchy body and wing prints made by Poncé's cockatiel, Fussy, when he gets out of his cage and flies around the house. These prints look pretty when the sun is right, and Poncé does not wash them off. In the hall by the living room hang two of Poncé's mother's paintings, "Euphoria" and "The Death of the Arizona." The kitchen is futuristically spare, with vacant expanses of butcher block. Its simplicity is refined, like the simplicity of the ideal gentleman. It is latent with appliances; there is an electric trash compactor under the counter, and a microwave oven, two ranges, and two infrared food-warming lights. A blender and a toaster oven sit back against the wall, under quilted dustcovers. There is an extra spigot, and the water that comes out of it is a hundred and sixty degrees. The decades that Poncé and her mother spent thinking about kitchens are palpable here. By the kitchen are sliding glass doors—with decals at both human and dog eye level to prevent collisions (a hint from years ago)—leading to the back-yard patio. In the patio are two Japanese pinball machines and a swimming pool.

Poncé: "I just love to sit by the pool and watch the roadrunners tease my little schnauzer, Zinfandel. They come up onto the patio as close as they dare, and when Zin can't stand it anymore she runs after them, yapping like mad, and the roadrunners take off, and then Zin gives up, and then pretty soon the roadrunners are back."

David: "That pool's just sitting there growing algae. I put half a gallon of muriatic acid in it and nothing happened. The problem was, a guy who worked for me left the filter on recycle instead of clean for four days, and we had a big rainstorm. Now I think we've got a kind of algae nothing will kill."

The San Antonio *Light,* in a front-page story about Poncé and David's wedding, said that a wedding guest said, "I've been in a lot of houses in Texas, but this is the first one that's in two time zones." The house feels that way not just because it's big. The sunlight ricocheting off the white driveways and the spicy breath of Mexico freshened through air-conditioning make most of the house feel like midafternoon in San Antonio, but the five or six hundred "Dear Heloise" letters that come to the office every day from all over the world bring that end of the house a much more dislocated sense of time. When the phone rings—with a discreet, understated, low-pitched ring that is somehow more compelling than a loud one—the call is often from New York, where it's an hour later, or Los Angeles, where it's two hours earlier. Poncé carries the phone with her on a long cord all over the house, and wherever the phone is, the feeling of abstract, average time floats above it. Poncé often answers the phone; when her assistants answer it, they tell her over the intercom who it is.

(ring)

"Poncé, a disc jockey from a station in Spokane, Washington, has a question for Heloise. He says the President of the United States is coming over to your house in five minutes, what do you do?"

"The President is coming in five minutes? Here?"

"No, no—he wants to know *what if* the President were coming over in five minutes, what would you do."

"My God, I thought he was coming here. O.K. . . . Hello. . . . Uh-huh. . . . Well, I would say first, pick up the big chunks. Hide the shoes. Stuff the dishes in the dishwasher, or put 'em in a tub and hide 'em in the oven. Open drawers and shove everything in off the countertops. Clean the bathroom mirror, make the bed. Then the house looks at least halfway decent. Then sprinkle some cinnamon in a pan and put it on a burner on low. By the time the President gets there, the whole house will smell nice, like cinnamon rolls."

(ring)

"Poncé, a newspaper writer from New Jersey says she's doing an article on freezers, and she wants to know what you have in yours."

"O.K., thanks, Hazel. . . . Hello. . . . I know there's all kinds of things you can keep in your freezer, like sprinkled clothes before you iron them, or valuable papers so they won't burn up in a fire (in plastic bags, of course, so they won't get wet), or homemade labelled TV dinners in foil, or vegetable scraps to make stock, or popcorn so it'll stay fresh, or candles so they won't drip when they burn, or girdles so they'll go on easier and be cool in the summer, but, to be perfectly honest with you, what I've got in my freezer right now is just some old rolls to feed the birds, a couple cans of coffee, a few frozen pizzas, and something all wrapped in freezer paper that I don't even know what it is."

(ring)

"Poncé, a man from *Parade* magazine says he's doing an article on pet peeves, and he wants to know what Heloise's are."

"O.K. . . . Hello. . . . Well, let's see. People who come in and drop their purse and shoes in the living room. It only would take a second to put them away. Drivers who don't use their blinkers when they turn, or who keep their blinkers on after they turn. People who put out cigarettes in their food. Oh—you know what really drives me crazy? Wax for no-wax floors. Here somebody saves their money to buy a no-wax floor, and the next thing they know someone comes along and tells them that not only do they need wax for their no-wax floor, they need a special kind of wax. I think that's really a crock of cranberries."

Since being a homemaker and ordinary citizen is Poncé's profession, she can turn from Poncé into Heloise at any second. "I never realized what Heloise was," she says. "I've always made a point of being Poncé. To me, Mother was always just Mother. The first time she left Hawaii on business, I couldn't understand it. It made me physically sick. I was in third grade. I cried and cried. She said, 'I'm not leaving you.' Suddenly—boom!—she was gone. Now I realize how much it must have hurt *her*, and I realize how gutsy she was back when women were not. When she became Heloise, she had something to do most of the time—there were always fourteen jars of something she was testing on the kitchen table—so I learned how to take care of myself. That was good experience for what I do now. I started helping on the column when I was ten or eleven. One time, she and some neighbors and I baked two hundred loaves of bread about two hundred different ways to see which way of baking kept the tops the softest. I helped in her office, too, some summers. Other summers, I got summer jobs. Baskin-Robbins trained me for a week so I could scoop ice cream to just a certain number of ounces. I worked there for about two months and gained ten pounds and quit. Don't ever believe it when they say you'll get tired of the ice cream if you work there. Then after high school—I went to Alamo Heights High School, which was and is known as the snob school in San Antonio—Chris Geppert, who is now Christopher Cross, who's won four Grammys, was in my class—anyway, for a graduation present I got to go to

Virginia, and from there some friends invited me to Ocean City, Maryland. One of those friends was Susan Dredge, who's now Susan Johnson, who lives in Hawaii, who invited us for a visit last fall. Anyway, in Ocean City I got a job in a Best Western hotel washing sheets and towels. When I went in for the job, the man there told me I was too short to fold the sheets without having them drag on the floor, so I went and found a wooden soda carton and told him I could stand on that, and he hired me. I got my best pair of cutoffs at that job—a maid found them in a room and gave them to me and they fit perfectly. The laundry room had no air-conditioning and very little ventilation and two commercial-size washers and one commercial-size dryer. I made seventy dollars for a seven-day week, and I learned quite a bit. My friends and I had a cabin across from the ocean near Phillips Crab House, which was always full of four hundred people knocking on crabs. I thought that was so barbaric. I also hated Maryland, because they had a state income tax. Mother kept writing and calling, telling me to come home, but I didn't want to. Finally, she said she was going to send the police after me, and I knew she would do it. So she flew to Washington and I went and met her at her hotel, which happened to be the Watergate, and we flew back to San Antonio. That was the first time I was ever out of the state of Texas by myself.

"After I got back, I decided to go to Southwest Texas State University, at San Marcos—L.B.J.'s alma mater. I wasn't a sorority type. I don't need a sorority. I know that they're very beneficial, I just don't need them. I lived in a private dorm off campus with Sue Carey and two other girls. Sue and I have been best friends since high school. We never worried about stealing each other's men. We could wear each other's clothes—each other's tops, actually. I had a purple VW that was so neat, and I also rode a motor scooter and neither of my parents knew. Once, my motor scooter fell over and I couldn't get it back up, and I decided it was time to get rid of it. When it was my turn to do the shopping, I'd drive twenty-two miles to the Air Force commissary and shop there, because that was cheaper than driving all over town to five different stores. When people came over, they always opened the refrigerator and said, 'Gosh, this looks like my mother's refrigerator.' For my college-graduation present, I went to Russia with Daddy. Someone had put the wrong entry date on our passports, so the Russians locked us up at the airport for a day until they could find someone with the authority to change the date. I stopped eating beef after I went to Russia—it was like junior-high roast beef. Over the next five years, I worked on the column, I took fencing lessons, I went to Europe three times, I went on a wine cruise, I went to China with Daddy. I would not trade my Russia or China experience for anything. I got a grasp of what it was to be an adult in an adult world. At the time, I would have traded it for a Thrifty Scot Motel. On January 8, 1977, when I was on a date with somebody else, I met David Evans at a friend's apartment, and then the next day, Super Bowl Sunday—the Raiders were playing the Vikings—I watched the game with him. Later, we went out to a bar, and David played 'Kaw-Liga,' that song about the wooden Indian, by Hank Williams, on the jukebox. That's when I knew David was a real San Antonio boy. I had several big arguments with Mother that year, because she was getting sicker and sicker and she kept right on smoking, but finally I accepted that smoking was what she wanted to do. Toward the end of 1977, Mother's health really declined. The day before Christmas, David and I kept trying to get her to go to the hospital, and she said, 'I am not going into the hospital on Christmas. I am not going to ruin your Christmas and I'm not going to ruin Dr. Hernandez's Christmas.' So David said, 'If you won't go, I'll carry you.' Well, Mother slept with a .32 revolver under the bed, and she pulled that revolver and she said, 'You lay a hand on me and I'll shoot holes in the ceiling.' "

(David: "I backed out of that bedroom pretty damn quick.")

"So she didn't go into the hospital until the day after Christmas, and two days after that she died. We were at the hospital. I cried and I hugged David and I hugged the Doctor, and then I went and made phone calls. When I got home, I called Mother's friends at King Features."

PONCÉ believes that everyone is created equal. One of the first things she ever said to me was "There's nobody better than me, I'm no better than anybody else." Her mother believed that, too. She used to tell her readers, "There is no one who will ever come into your home who is more important and loved any more than your own family," and "I hope you will want to accept the facts and tell yourself that you are just one of the multitude. I am!" The readers knew that Heloise was sincere in offering each of them a share in the column, and that is probably why they sent in hints so willingly. For Poncé, the only problem with this egalitarian attitude is that, although she may be no better than anybody, she is both smarter and richer than most people. Her mother spent almost none of the income from the column, preferring to keep herself within the limits of her husband's service pay and pension. The column has been one of the most widely syndicated columns in the world for over twenty years. Now Poncé is in the same situation as a comedian who has become so famous making jokes about how girls put him down that he attracts all the girls anyone could want. She has been so successful understanding the life of the average homemaker that she is no longer an average homemaker—she is probably a millionaire. Poncé's mother solved the problem by slipping away from the name Heloise, as if it were a too crowded party in her honor. Poncé's mother's middle name was Kathy, and after Heloise became a well-known name she began to call herself Kathy. She had many friends—particularly at a vacation spot in the Texas hill country where she had a cabin—who knew her only as Kathy and had no idea of her other identity. Maybe she anticipated that one day Poncé would have a similar problem, and that's why she gave Poncé so many names—so that she would have plenty of extras in case any one name became too famous.

. . .

WHEN I was in San Antonio, I met several people besides Tom Carey and Officer Vela. I met Barry Byrne, Anne Cravens, Hazel Bolton, Anne Mundy, Bruce Lynxwiler, Milton Willmann, John Kungle, and Judy Hill. Barry Byrne is a pilot who met Poncé and David at a balloon meet. (Ballooning is a hobby that the three share.) Barry works for Mexicans who own private planes, and he was staying at the house while his plane was fitted with new radar equipment. Anne Cravens is a friend of Barry's who teaches deaf children in elementary school. She had just bought a new house in San Antonio, and her new next-door neighbor was harassing her at all hours by opening his windows and blowing an automobile horn that he had set up inside his house. Hazel Bolton and Anne Mundy are mother and daughter. They are Poncé's assistants. Bruce Lynxwiler is a handyman who at the time was doing some work for David. Milton Willmann is a well-groomed local policeman with heavy dark-rimmed glasses who stopped by Poncé and David's one afternoon on a social call. John Kungle is a police officer in Poncé's township who stopped me one night because the light over my rear license plate was burned out. Judy Hill knows Poncé from college, when she was one of her roommates senior year, and she came by when I was there. She grew up in Del Rio, Texas, and is a social worker for the state's Department of Human Resources.

I was talking to Poncé and David and I said something funny, and David looked at Poncé and said, "You know, we should get him together with James Reveley." James Reveley and his wife are good friends of theirs. James Reveley is a well-built, snub-nosed man with brown hair and a red beard who holds his elbow to his side when he talks and illustrates points with compact hand gestures. He has two professions—dentist and undertaker. As a dentist, he occasionally makes scary or funny-looking sets of false teeth for his friends. As an undertaker, he is something of a maverick. Other undertakers do not like it that he favors funerals that cost no more than five hundred dollars—a cause he once went on the "Tomorrow" show to espouse. He wears a beeper on his belt. We met him and his wife at Maggie's, the place with the electric train above the bar. We had some drinks, and then we decided to go to a restaurant called Texan Seafoods North. James Reveley said we should all go in his truck. His truck was a Chevy Suburban with dark-tinted side and rear windows. He and his wife got in front. David opened the back door, and we saw a cot inside.

"I think we'll take my truck," David said.

"C'mon, climb in," James Reveley said.

"What if you get a call on your beeper when we're at the restaurant? If we don't have David's truck, we'll be stranded," Poncé said.

"Nobody wants to ride with me," said James Reveley.

Poncé and David and I went in David's truck. "I hurt his feelings," David said. "I feel bad about that. But I couldn't sit on that cot."

"What if he got a call while we were at the restaurant? We'd be stranded," Poncé said.

Texan Seafoods North had a salad bar set up in the hull of a twelve-foot sailboat. "That's nothing," said James Reveley, who had quickly let bygones be bygones. "I was in a restaurant last week where they had a salad bar in a red M.G." We sat at the seafood bar and ordered shrimp and raw oysters. James Reveley called them "aw-sters." James Reveley asked me if the seafood wasn't better than they had in New York, and I agreed that it was very good. The restaurant owner came by (as owners tend to do when Poncé eats out). "We've got a man here from New York," James Reveley told the owner, "and he's been sittin' here just eatin' the hell out of these aw-sters."

Then he said, "You know, this part of Texas—Dallas–Fort Worth, San Antonio, Houston—it's got everything you could want. All over the country, people are starting to refer to this area as the Third Coast." He turned to me. "What motel are you staying at?" he asked.

I told him I was staying at the Miramar.

"The *Mira*-mar?" he said. "The *Mira*-mar?! You're *staying*—at—the—*MIRA*-mar?" (He gave the name an inflection unrepresented by any typeface.) "I cannot believe it! Don't you know about the Miramar? Haven't you ever heard about the Miramar?" He grabbed his wife. "Dear, this man is staying at the Miramar!"

"The *Mira*-mar!" she said. The two of them began to laugh so hard that they had to hold on to each other.

"My God!" James Reveley said. "The Miramar is the biggest damn rut hut in San Antonio!"

"Haven't you noticed all the traffic? Haven't you noticed the hookers all over the place?" asked his wife.

"Why, that's the busiest motel in town at lunch hour," said James Reveley. "You want to find a lawyer in San Antonio at lunch hour, go to the Miramar. There's a little barbecue place around the corner from the Miramar where they have great ribs, and if you ask a girl at lunch if she wants to go get some ribs most of them know that's just a code word for going to the Miramar, which is just a code word for shackin' up."

"The *Mira*-mar!" his wife said.

"I've got a macabre sense of humor," said James Reveley, "and there was a time when a buddy of mine and I used to put on dark suits and ties and sit in his black Plymouth on Miramar Street and scare the hell out of all the guys, who thought we were plainclothes cops. Those johns would start slinking around, we'd laugh to death. Listen, when you check out, don't turn in your key. A key from the Miramar—now, that's a real San Antonio keepsake."

Off and on for the rest of the evening, James Reveley or his wife would say "The *Mira*-mar!" and then all of us would laugh.

. . .

ON Saturdays, Poncé's assistants don't come in to the office. The phone does not ring very much. Many of the rooms of the house are filled with the kind of midday twilight that goes well with the sound of someone vacuuming or the sound of a soap opera on TV. On a particular Saturday, Poncé woke up and exercised on the mini-trampoline in her bedroom. She made scrambled eggs and bacon and English muffins for herself and David. David asked her if she wanted to go to the big chili cook-off, the Chilympiad, up in San Marcos. She poured herself a Tab. I came over. We discussed the chili cook-off. Poncé said that the Chilympiad was interesting but in the last few years it had got so big that it was also a little sickening. Poncé poured me a root beer. David said he wanted to go up to Medina Lake and take his boat out, even though the wind was high and the lake was probably rougher than a cob. Poncé said she just wanted to stay around the house. She poured herself another Tab. David went to the lake. Poncé was walking around barefoot—the way she is most of the time when she's at home. She went out in the front yard to get the mail and play with her dog. She walked to the garage behind the house to show me the white 1972 Thunderbird her mother used to drive. It had only twenty thousand miles on it. She poured herself another Tab. She took an empty one-litre Coke bottle, soaked it in hot water, and removed the reinforced black plastic bottom. She punched some holes in the black plastic bottom with an icepick, put some potting soil in, and then used it to repot a several-month-old avocado plant. She washed her hands and fixed herself a cup of tea. She went to the workroom and caught her pet ferret, Fred. In the kitchen, she gave him a baking-soda bath, which she does often, because he is an albino and shows the dirt. She poured sploofs of baking soda on him and then brushed the baking soda out of his fur with an old, soft hairbrush. He lay quietly on his back during this. Then she tied a red ribbon around his neck and set him on the floor. She swept up the baking soda with a whisk broom. She washed her hands again. She made lunch—a tuna-fish sandwich, Fritos, and a root beer for me, tuna-fish salad on lettuce and tea for her. She put the mayonnaise back in the refrigerator and then asked me if I'd like a pickle. I said yes, and she went to open the refrigerator. Her refrigerator is the kind that closes with a hiss as the rubber vacuum seal around the door sucks it shut, and then won't let go for thirty seconds, so that it is impossible to shut the door and immediately reopen it.

"Shoot," she said, and stood by the refrigerator door. The wasted seconds were almost visible, expiring in the air around her.

"Isn't there some kind of hint that would solve that problem?" I asked.

"No," she said. "There is absolutely nothing you can do about this at all."

(1983)

THE MOUNTAINS OF PI

G REGORY Volfovich Chudnovsky recently built a supercomputer in his apartment from mail-order parts. Gregory Chudnovsky is a number theorist. His apartment is situated near the top floor of a run-down building on the West Side of Manhattan, in a neighborhood near Columbia University. Not long ago, a human corpse was found dumped at the end of the block. The world's most powerful supercomputers include the Cray Y-MP C90, the Thinking Machines CM-5, the Hitachi S-820/80, the nCube, the Fujitsu parallel machine, the Kendall Square Research parallel machine, the NEC SX-3, the Touchstone Delta, and Gregory Chudnovsky's apartment. The apartment seems to be a kind of container for the supercomputer at least as much as it is a container for people.

Gregory Chudnovsky's partner in the design and construction of the supercomputer was his older brother, David Volfovich Chudnovsky, who is also a mathematician, and who lives five blocks away from Gregory. The Chudnovsky brothers call their machine m zero. It occupies the former living room of Gregory's apartment, and its tentacles reach into other rooms. The brothers claim that m zero is a "true, general-purpose supercomputer," and that it is as fast and powerful as a somewhat older Cray Y-MP, but it is not as fast as the latest of the Y-MP machines, the C90, an advanced supercomputer made by Cray Research. A Cray Y-MP C90 costs more than thirty million dollars. It is a black monolith, seven feet tall and eight feet across, in the shape of a squat cylinder, and is cooled by liquid freon. So far, the brothers have spent around seventy thousand dollars on parts for their supercomputer, and much of the money has come out of their wives' pockets.

Gregory Chudnovsky is thirty-nine years old, and he has a spare frame and a bony, handsome face. He has a long beard, streaked with gray, and dark, unruly hair, a wide forehead, and wide-spaced brown eyes. He walks in a slow, dragging shuffle, leaning on a bentwood cane, while his brother, David, typically holds him under one arm, to prevent him from toppling over. He has severe myasthenia gravis, an auto-immune disorder of the muscles. The symptoms, in his case, are muscular weakness and difficulty in breathing. "I have to lie in bed most of the time," Gregory once told me. His condition doesn't seem to be getting better, and doesn't seem to be getting worse. He developed the disease when he was twelve years old, in the city of Kiev, Ukraine, where he and David grew up. He spends his days sitting or lying on a bed heaped with pillows, in a bedroom down the hall from the room that houses the supercomputer. Gregory's bedroom is filled with paper; it contains at least a ton of paper. He calls the place his junk yard. The room faces east, and would be full of sunlight in the morning if he ever raised the shades, but he keeps them lowered, because light hurts his eyes.

You almost never meet one of the Chudnovsky brothers without the other. You often find the brothers conjoined, like Siamese twins, David holding Gregory by the arm or under the armpits. They complete each other's sentences and interrupt each other, but they don't look alike. While Gregory is thin and bearded, David has a stout body and a plump, clean-shaven face. He is in his early forties. Black-and-gray curly hair grows thickly on top of David's head, and he has heavy-lidded deep-blue eyes. He always wears a starched white shirt and, usually, a gray silk necktie in a foulard print. His tie rests on a bulging stomach.

The Chudnovskian supercomputer, m zero, burns two thousand watts of power, and it runs day and night. The brothers don't dare shut it down; if they did, it might die. At least twenty-five fans blow air through the machine to keep it cool; otherwise something might melt. Waste heat permeates Gregory's apartment, and the room that contains m zero climbs to a hundred degrees Fahrenheit in summer. The brothers keep the apartment's lights turned off as much as possible. If they switched on too many lights while m zero was running, they might blow the apartment's wiring. Gregory can't breathe city air without developing lung trouble, so he keeps the apartment's windows closed all the time, with air-conditioners running in them during the summer, but that doesn't seem to reduce the heat, and as the temperature rises inside the apartment the place can smell of cooking circuit boards, a sign that m zero is not well. A steady stream of boxes arrives by Federal Express, and an opposing stream of boxes flows back to mail-order houses, containing parts that have bombed, along with letters from the brothers demanding an exchange or their money back. The building superintendent doesn't know that the Chudnovsky brothers have been using a supercomputer in Gregory's apartment, and the brothers haven't expressed an eagerness to tell him.

The Chudnovskys, between them, have published a hundred and fifty-four papers and twelve books, mostly in collaboration with each other, and mostly on the subject of number theory or mathematical physics. They work together so closely that it is possible to argue that they are a single mathematician— anyway, it's what they claim. The brothers lived in Kiev until 1977, when they left the Soviet Union and, accompanied by their parents, went to France. The family lived there for six months, then emigrated to the United States and set- tled in New York; they have become American citizens.

The brothers enjoy an official relationship with Columbia University: Colum- bia calls them senior research scientists in the Department of Mathematics, but they don't have tenure and they don't teach students. They are really lone inventors, operating out of Gregory's apartment in what you might call the old-fashioned Russo-Yankee style. Their wives are doing well. Gregory's wife, Christine Pardo Chudnovsky, is an attorney with a midtown law firm. David's wife, Nicole Lannegrace, is a political-affairs officer at the United Nations. It is their salaries that help cover the funding needs of the brothers' supercom- puting complex in Gregory and Christine's apartment. Malka Benjaminovna Chudnovsky, a retired engineer, who is Gregory and David's mother, lives in Gregory's apartment. David spends his days in Gregory's apartment, taking care of his brother, their mother, and m zero.

When the Chudnovskys applied to leave the Soviet Union, the fact that they are Jewish and mathematical attracted at least a dozen K.G.B. agents to their case. The brothers' father, Volf Grigorevich Chudnovsky, who was severely beaten by the K.G.B. in 1977, died of heart failure in 1985. Volf Chudnovsky was a professor of civil engineering at the Kiev Architectural Institute, and he specialized in the structural stability of buildings, towers, and bridges. He died in America, and not long before he died he constructed in Gregory's apartment a maze of bookshelves, his last work of civil engineering. The bookshelves ex- tend into every corner of the apartment, and today they are packed with liter- ature and computer books and books and papers on the subject of numbers. Since almost all numbers run to infinity (in digits) and are totally unexplored, an apartmentful of thoughts about numbers holds hardly any thoughts at all, even with a supercomputer on the premises to advance the work.

The brothers say that the "m" in "m zero" stands for "machine," and that they use a small letter to imply that the machine is a work in progress. They represent the name typographically as "m0." The "zero" stands for success. It implies a dark history of failure—three duds (in Gregory's apartment) that the brothers now refer to as negative three, negative two, and negative one. The brothers broke up the negative machines for scrap, got on the telephone, and waited for Federal Express to bring more parts.

M zero is a parallel supercomputer, a type of machine that has lately come to dominate the avant-garde in supercomputer architecture, because the design of- fers succulent possibilities for speed in solving problems. In a parallel machine, anywhere from half a dozen to thousands of processors work simultaneously on a problem, whereas in a so-called serial machine—a normal computer—the problem is solved one step at a time. "A serial machine is bound to be very slow, because the speed of the machine will be limited by the slowest part of it," Gregory said. "In a parallel machine, many circuits take on many parts of the problem at the same time." As of last week, m zero contained sixteen parallel processors, which ruminate around the clock on the Chudnovskys' problems.

The brothers' mail-order supercomputer makes their lives more convenient: m zero performs inhumanly difficult algebra, finding roots of gigantic systems of equations, and it has constructed colored images of the interior of Gregory Chudnovsky's body. According to the Chudnovskys, it could model the weather or make pictures of air flowing over a wing, if the brothers cared about weather or wings. What they care about is numbers. To them, numbers are more beautiful, more nearly perfect, possibly more complicated, and arguably more real than anything in the world of physical matter.

The brothers have lately been using m zero to explore the number pi. Pi, which is denoted by the Greek letter π, is the most famous ratio in mathematics, and is one of the most ancient numbers known to humanity. Pi is approximately 3.14—the number of times that a circle's diameter will fit around the circle. Here is a circle, with its diameter:

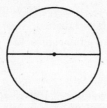

Pi goes on forever, and can't be calculated to perfect precision: 3.14-15926535897932384626433832795028841971693993751.... This is known as the decimal expansion of pi. It is a bloody mess. No apparent pattern emerges in the succession of digits. The digits of pi march to infinity in a predestined yet unfathomable code: they do not repeat periodically, seeming to pop up by blind chance, lacking any perceivable order, rule, reason, or design— "random" integers, ad infinitum. If a deep and beautiful design hides in the digits of pi, no one knows what it is, and no one has ever been able to see it by staring at the digits. Among mathematicians, there is a nearly universal feeling that it will never be possible, in principle, for an inhabitant of our finite universe to discover the system in the digits of pi. But for the present, if you want to attempt it, you need a supercomputer to probe the endless scrap of leftover pi.

Before the Chudnovsky brothers built m zero, Gregory had to derive pi over the telephone network while lying in bed. It was inconvenient. Tapping at a small keyboard, which he sets on the blankets of his bed, he stares at a computer display screen on one of the bookshelves beside his bed. The keyboard and the screen are connected to Internet, a network that leads Gregory through cyberspace into the heart of a Cray somewhere else in the United States. He calls up a Cray through Internet and programs the machine to make an approximation of pi. The job begins to run, the Cray trying to esti-mate the number of times that the diameter of a circle goes around the pe-riphery, and Gregory sits back on his pillows and waits, watching messages from the Cray flow across his display screen. He eats dinner with his wife and his mother and then, back in bed, he takes up a legal pad and a red felt-tip pen and plays with number theory, trying to discover hidden properties of num-bers. Meanwhile, the Cray is reaching toward pi at a rate of a hundred million operations per second. Gregory dozes beside his computer screen. Once in a while, he asks the Cray how things are going, and the Cray replies that the job is still active. Night passes, the Cray running deep toward pi. Unfortunately, since the exact ratio of the circle's circumference to its diameter dwells at in-finity, the Cray has not even begun to pinpoint pi. Abruptly, a message appears on Gregory's screen:

LINE IS
DISCONNECTED.

"What the hell is going on?" Gregory exclaims. It seems that the Cray has hung up the phone, and may have crashed. Once again, pi has demonstrated its ability to give a supercomputer a heart attack.

"MYASTHENIA Gravis is a funny thing," Gregory Chudnovsky said one day from his bed in the junk yard. "In a sense, I'm very lucky, because I'm alive, and I'm alive after so many years." He has a resonant voice and a Russian ac-cent. "There is no standard prognosis. It sometimes strikes young women and older women. I wonder if it is some kind of sluggish virus."

It was a cold afternoon, and rain pelted the windows; the shades were drawn, as always. He lay against a heap of pillows, with his legs folded under him. He wore a tattered gray lamb's-wool sweater that had multiple patches on the el-bows, and a starched white shirt, and baggy blue sweatpants, and a pair of hand-made socks. I had never seen socks like Gregory's. They were two-tone socks, wrinkled and floppy, hand-sewn from pieces of dark-blue and pale-blue cloth, and they looked comfortable. They were the work of Malka Benjaminovna, his mother. Lines of computer code flickered on the screen beside his bed.

This was an apartment built for long voyages. The paper in the room was jammed into the bookshelves, from floor to ceiling. The brothers had wedged the paper, sheet by sheet, into manila folders, until the folders had grown as fat as melons. The paper also flooded two freestanding bookshelves (placed strategically around Gregory's bed), five chairs (three of them in a row beside his bed), two steamer trunks, and a folding cocktail table. I moved carefully around the room, fearful of triggering a paperslide, and sat on the room's one empty chair, facing the foot of Gregory's bed, my knees touching the blanket. The paper was piled in three-foot stacks on the chairs. It guarded his bed like the flanking towers of a fortress, and his bed sat at the center of the keep. I sensed a profound happiness in Gregory Chudnovsky's bedroom. His happiness, it occurred to me later, sprang from the delicious melancholy of a life chained to a bed in a disordered world that breaks open through the portals of mathematics into vistas beyond time or decay.

"The system of this paper is archeological," he said. "By looking at a slice, I know the year. This slice is 1986. Over here is some 1985. What you see in this room is our working papers, as well as the papers we used as references for them. Some of the references we pull out once in a while to look at, and then we leave them somewhere else, in another pile. Once, we had to make a Xerox copy of a book three times, and we put it in three different places in the piles, so we would be sure to find it when we needed it. Unfortunately, once we put a book into one of these piles we almost never go back to look for it. There are books in there by Kipling and Macaulay. Actually, when we want to find a book it's easier to go back to the library. Eh, this place is a mess. Eventually, these papers or my wife will turn me out of the house."

Much of the paper consists of legal pads covered with Gregory's handwriting. His holograph is dense and careful, a flawless minuscule written with a red felt-tip pen—a mixture of theorems, calculations, proofs, and conjectures concerning numbers. He uses a felt-tip pen because he doesn't have enough strength in his hand to press a pencil on paper. Mathematicians who have visited Gregory Chudnovsky's bedroom have come away dizzy, wondering what secrets the scriptorium may hold. Some say he has published most of his work, while others wonder if his bedroom holds unpublished discoveries. He cautiously refers to his steamer trunks as valises. They are filled to the lids with compressed paper. When Gregory and David used to fly to Europe to speak at conferences, they took both "valises" with them, in case they needed to refer to a theorem, and the baggage particularly annoyed the Belgians. "The Belgians were always fining us for being overweight," Gregory said.

Pi is by no means the only unexplored number in the Chudnovskys' inventory, but it is one that interests them very much. They wonder whether the digits contain a hidden rule, an as yet unseen architecture, close to the mind of God. A subtle and fantastic order may appear in the digits of pi way out there somewhere; no one knows. No one has ever proved, for example, that pi does not turn into nothing but nines and zeros, spattered to infinity in some peculiar arrangement. If we were to explore the digits of pi far enough, they might resolve into a breathtaking numerical pattern, as knotty as "The Book of Kells," and it might mean something. It might be a small but interesting message from

God, hidden in the crypt of the circle, awaiting notice by a mathematician. On the other hand, the digits of pi may ramble forever in a hideous cacophony, which is a kind of absolute perfection to a mathematician like Gregory Chudnovsky. Pi looks "monstrous" to him. "We know absolutely *nothing* about pi," he declared from his bed. "What the hell does it mean? The definition of pi is really very simple—it's just the ratio of the circumference to the diameter— but the complexity of the sequence it spits out in digits is really unbelievable. We have a sequence of digits that looks like gibberish."

"Maybe in the eyes of God pi looks perfect," David said, standing in a corner of the room, his head and shoulders visible above towers of paper.

Pi, or π, has had various names through the ages, and all of them are either words or abstract symbols, since pi is a number that can't be shown completely and exactly in any finite form of representation. Pi is a transcendental number. A transcendental number is a number that exists but can't be expressed in any finite series of either arithmetical or algebraic operations. For example, if you try to express pi as the solution to an equation you will find that the equation goes on forever. Expressed in digits, pi extends into the distance as far as the eye can see, and the digits never repeat periodically, as do the digits of a rational number. Pi slips away from all rational methods used to locate it. Pi is a tran-scendental number because it transcends the power of algebra to display it in its totality. Ferdinand Lindemann, a German mathematician, proved the tran-scendence of pi in 1882; he proved, in effect, that pi can't be written on a piece of paper, not even on a piece of paper as big as the universe. In a manner of speaking, pi is indescribable and can't be found.

Pi possibly first entered human consciousness in Egypt. The earliest known reference to pi occurs in a Middle Kingdom papyrus scroll, written around 1650 B.C. by a scribe named Ahmes. Showing a restrained appreciation for his own work that is not uncommon in a mathematician, Ahmes began his scroll with the words "The Entrance Into the Knowledge of All Existing Things." He remarked in passing that he composed the scroll "in likeness to writings made of old," and then he led his readers through various mathematical problems and their solutions, along several feet of papyrus, and toward the end of the scroll he found the area of a circle, using a rough sort of pi.

Around 200 B.C., Archimedes of Syracuse found that pi is somewhere be-tween $3\frac{10}{71}$ and $3\frac{1}{7}$—that's about 3.14. (The Greeks didn't use decimals.) Archimedes had no special term for pi, calling it "the perimeter to the diame-ter." By in effect approximating pi to two places after the decimal point, Archimedes narrowed the known value of pi to one part in a hundred. There knowledge of pi bogged down until the seventeenth century, when new formu-las for approximating pi were discovered. Pi then came to be called the Ludolphian number, after Ludolph van Ceulen, a German mathematician who approximated it to thirty-five decimal places, or one part in a hundred million billion billion billion—a calculation that took Ludolph most of his life to accomplish, and gave him such satisfaction that he had the digits engraved on his tombstone, at the Ladies' Church in Leiden, in the Netherlands. Ludolph and his tombstone were later moved to Peter's Church in Leiden, to be installed in a special graveyard for professors, and from there the stone vanished, possibly to be turned into a sidewalk slab. Somewhere in Leiden, people may be walking over Ludolph's digits. The Germans still call pi the Ludolphian number. In the eighteenth century, Leonhard Euler, mathematician to Catherine the Great, called it p or c. The first person to use the Greek letter π for the number was William Jones, an English mathematician, who coined it in 1706 for his book "A New Introduction to the Mathematics." Euler read the book and switched to using the symbol π, and the number has remained π ever since. Jones probably meant π to stand for the English word "periphery."

Physicists have noted the ubiquity of pi in nature. Pi is obvious in the disks of the moon and the sun. The double helix of DNA revolves around pi. Pi hides in the rainbow, and sits in the pupil of the eye, and when a raindrop falls into water pi emerges in the spreading rings. Pi can be found in waves and ripples and spectra of all kinds, and therefore pi occurs in colors and music. Pi has lately turned up in superstrings, the hypothetical loops of energy vibrating inside subatomic particles. Pi occurs naturally in tables of death, in what is known as a Gaussian distribution of deaths in a population; that is, when a person dies, the event "feels" the Ludolphian number.

It is one of the great mysteries why nature seems to know mathematics. No one can suggest why this necessarily has to be so. Eugene Wigner, the physicist, once said, "The miracle of the appropriateness of the language of mathematics for the formulation of the laws of physics is a wonderful gift which we neither understand nor deserve." We may not understand pi or deserve it, but nature at least seems to be aware of it, as Captain O. C. Fox learned while he was recovering in a hospital from a wound sustained in the American Civil War. Having nothing better to do with his time than lie in bed and derive pi, Captain Fox spent a few weeks tossing pieces of fine steel wire onto a wooden board ruled with parallel lines. The wires fell randomly across the lines in such a way that pi emerged in the statistics. After throwing his wires eleven hundred times, Captain Fox was able to derive pi to two places after the decimal point, to 3.14. If he had had a thousand years to recover from his wound, he might have derived pi to perhaps another decimal place. To go deeper into pi, you need a powerful machine.

The race toward pi happens in cyberspace, inside supercomputers. In 1949, George Reitwiesner, at the Ballistic Research Laboratory, in Maryland, derived pi to two thousand and thirty-seven decimal places with the ENIAC, the first general-purpose electronic digital computer. Working at the same laboratory, John von Neumann (one of the inventors of the ENIAC) searched those digits for signs of order, but found nothing he could put his finger on. A decade later, Daniel Shanks and John W. Wrench, Jr., approximated pi to a hundred thousand decimal places with an I.B.M. 7090 mainframe computer, and saw nothing. The race continued desultorily, through hundreds of thousands of digits, until 1981, when Yasumasa Kanada, the head of a team of computer scientists at Tokyo University, used a NEC supercomputer, a Japanese machine, to compute two million digits of pi. People were astonished that anyone would bother to do it, but that was only the beginning of the affair. In 1984, Kanada and his team got sixteen million digits of pi, noticing nothing remarkable. A year later, William Gosper, a mathematician and distinguished hacker employed at Symbolics, Inc., in Sunnyvale, California, computed pi to seventeen and a half million decimal places with a Symbolics workstation, beating Kanada's team by a million digits. Gosper saw nothing of interest.

The next year, David H. Bailey, at the National Aeronautics and Space Administration, used a Cray 2 supercomputer and a formula discovered by two brothers, Jonathan and Peter Borwein, to scoop twenty-nine million digits of pi. Bailey found nothing unusual. A year after that, in 1987, Yasumasa Kanada and his team got a hundred and thirty-four million digits of pi, using a NEC SX-2 supercomputer. They saw nothing of interest. In 1988, Kanada kept going, past two hundred million digits, and saw further amounts of nothing. Then, in the spring of 1989, the Chudnovsky brothers (who had not previously been known to have any interest in calculating pi) suddenly announced that they had obtained four hundred and eighty million digits of pi—a world record—using supercomputers at two sites in the United States, and had seen nothing. Kanada and his team were a little surprised to learn of unknown competition operating in American cyberspace, and they got on a Hitachi supercomputer and ripped through five hundred and thirty-six million digits, beating the Chudnovksys, setting a new world record, and seeing nothing. The brothers kept calculating and soon cracked a billion digits, but Kanada's restless boys and their Hitachi then nosed into a little *more* than a billion digits. The Chudnovskys pressed onward, too, and by the fall of 1989 they had squeaked past Kanada again, having computed pi to one billion one hundred and thirty million one hundred and sixty thousand six hundred and sixty-four decimal places, without finding anything special. It was another world record. At that point, the brothers gave up, out of boredom.

If a billion decimals of pi were printed in ordinary type, they would stretch from New York City to the middle of Kansas. This notion raises the question: What is the point of computing pi from New York to Kansas? The question has indeed been asked among mathematicians, since an expansion of pi to only forty-seven decimal places would be sufficiently precise to inscribe a circle around the visible universe that doesn't deviate from perfect circularity by more than the distance across a single proton. A billion decimals of pi go so far beyond that kind of precision, into such a lunacy of exactitude, that physicists will never need to use the quantity in any experiment—at least, not for any physics we know of today—and the thought of a billion decimals of pi op-

presses even some mathematicians, who declare the Chudnovskys' effort trivial. I once asked Gregory if a certain impression I had of mathematicians was
true, that they spent immoderate amounts of time declaring each other's work
trivial. "It is true," he admitted. "There is actually a reason for this. Because
once you know the solution to a problem it usually is trivial."

Gregory did the calculation from his bed in New York, working through
cyberspace on a Cray 2 at the Minnesota Supercomputer Center, in Minnea-
polis, and on an I.B.M. 3090-VF supercomputer at the I.B.M. Thomas J.
Watson Research Center, in Yorktown Heights, New York. The calculation triggered some dramatic crashes, and took half a year, because the brothers could
get time on the supercomputers only in bits and pieces, usually during holidays
and in the dead of night. It was also quite expensive—the use of the Cray cost
them seven hundred and fifty dollars an hour, and the money came from the
National Science Foundation. By the time of this agony, the brothers had concluded that it would be cheaper and more convenient to build a supercomputer
in Gregory's apartment. Then they could crash their own machine all they
wanted, while they opened doors in the house of numbers. The brothers
planned to compute *two* billion digits of pi on their new machine—to try to
double their old world record. They thought it would be a good way to test their
supercomputer: a maiden voyage into pi would put a terrible strain on their
machine, might blow it up. Presuming that their machine wouldn't overheat
or strangle on digits, they planned to search the huge resulting string of pi for
signs of hidden order. If what the Chudnovsky brothers have seen in the
Ludolphian number is a message from God, the brothers aren't sure what God
is trying to say.

ON a cold winter day, when the Chudnovskys were about to begin their two-
billion-digit expedition into pi, I rang the bell of Gregory Chudnovsky's apartment, and David answered the door. He pulled the door open a few inches, and
then it stopped, jammed against an empty cardboard box and a wad of hanging coats. He nudged the box out of the way with his foot. "Look, don't worry,"
he said. "Nothing *unpleasant* will happen to you. We will not turn *you* into digits." A Mini Mag-Lite flashlight protruded from his shirt pocket.

We were standing in a long, dark hallway. The lights were off, and it was hard
to see anything. To try to find something in Gregory's apartment is like
spelunking; that was the reason for David's flashlight. The hall is lined on both
sides with bookshelves, and they hold a mixture of paper and books. The
shelves leave a passage about two feet wide down the length of the hallway. At
the end of the hallway is a French door, its mullioned glass covered with
translucent paper, and it glowed.

The apartment's rooms are strung out along the hallway. We passed a bathroom and a bedroom. The bedroom belonged to Malka Benjaminovna Chud-

novsky. We passed a cave of paper, Gregory's junk yard. We passed a small kitchen, our feet rolling on computer cables. David opened the French door, and we entered the room of the supercomputer. A bare light bulb burned in a ceiling fixture. The room contained seven display screens: two of them were filled with numbers; the others were turned off. The windows were closed and the shades were drawn. Gregory Chudnovsky sat on a chair facing the screens. He wore the usual outfit—a tattered and patched lamb's-wool sweater, a starched white shirt, blue sweatpants, and the hand-stitched two-tone socks. From his toes trailed a pair of heelless leather slippers. His cane was hooked over his shoulder, hung there for convenience. I shook his hand. "Our first goal is to compute pi," he said. "For that we have to build our own computer."

"We are a full-service company," David said. "Of course, you know what 'full-service' means in New York. It means 'You want it? You do it yourself.' "

A steel frame stood in the center of the room, screwed together with bolts. It held split shells of mail-order personal computers—cheap P.C. clones, knocked wide open, like cracked walnuts, their meat spilling all over the place. The brothers had crammed special logic boards inside the personal computers. Red lights on the boards blinked. The floor was a quagmire of cables.

The brothers had also managed to fit into the room masses of empty cardboard boxes, and lots of books (Russian classics, with Cyrillic lettering on their spines), and screwdrivers, and data-storage tapes, and software manuals by the cubic yard, and stalagmites of obscure trade magazines, and a twenty-thousand-dollar computer workstation that the brothers no longer used. ("We use it as a place to stack paper," Gregory said.) From an oval photograph on the wall, the face of their late father—a robust man, squinting thoughtfully—looked down on the scene. The walls and the French door were covered with sheets of drafting paper showing circuit diagrams. They resembled cities seen from the air: the brothers had big plans for m zero. Computer disk drives stood around the room. The drives hummed, and there was a continuous whirr of fans, and a strong warmth emanated from the equipment, as if a steam radiator were going in the room. The brothers heat their apartment largely with chips.

Gregory said, "Our knowledge of pi was barely in the millions of digits—"

"We need many billions of digits," David said. "Even a billion digits is a drop in the bucket. Would you like a Coca-Cola?" He went into the kitchen, and there was a horrible crash. "Never mind, I broke a glass," he called. "Look, it's not a problem." He came out of the kitchen carrying a glass of Coca-Cola on a tray, with a paper napkin under the glass, and as he handed it to me he urged me to hold it tightly, because a Coca-Cola spilled into— He didn't want to think about it; it would set back the project by months. He said, "Galileo had to build his telescope—"

"Because he couldn't afford the Dutch model," Gregory said.

"And we have to build our machine, because we have—"

"No money," Gregory said. "When people let us use their computer, it's always done as a kindness." He grinned and pinched his finger and thumb together. "They say, 'You can use it as long as nobody *complains.*' "

I asked the brothers when they planned to build their supercomputer.

They burst out laughing. "You are sitting inside it!" David roared.

"Tell us how a supercomputer should look," Gregory said.

I started to describe a Cray to the brothers.

David turned to his brother and said, "The interviewer answers our questions. It's Pirandello! The interviewer becomes a person in the story." David turned to me and said, "The problem is, you should change your thinking. If I were to put inside this Cray a chopped-meat machine, you wouldn't know it was a meat chopper."

"Unless you saw chopped meat coming out of it. Then you'd suspect it wasn't a Cray," Gregory said, and the brothers cackled.

"In ten years, a Cray will fit in your pocket," David said.

Supercomputers are evolving incredibly fast. The notion of what a supercomputer is and what it can do changes from year to year, if not from month to month, as new machines arise. The definition of a supercomputer is simply this: one of the fastest and most powerful scientific computers in the world, for its time. The power of a supercomputer is revealed, generally speaking, in its ability to solve tough problems. A Cray Y-MP8, running at its peak working speed, can perform more than two billion floating-point operations per second. Floating-point operations—or flops, as they are called—are a standard measure of speed. Since a Cray Y-MP8 can hit two and a half billion flops, it is considered to be a gigaflop supercomputer. Giga (from the Greek for "giant") means a billion. Like all supercomputers, a Cray often cruises along significantly below its peak working speed. (There is a heated controversy in the supercomputer industry over how to measure the typical working performance of any given supercomputer, and there are many claims and counterclaims.) A Cray is a so-called vector-processing machine, but that design is going out of fashion. Cray Research has announced that next year it will begin selling an even more powerful parallel machine.

"Our machine is a gigaflop supercomputer," David Chudnovsky told me. "The working speed of our machine is from two hundred million flops to two gigaflops—roughly in the range of a Cray Y-MP8. We can probably go faster than a Y-MP8, but we don't want to get too specific about it."

M zero is not the only ultrapowerful silicon engine to gleam in the Chudnovskian œuvre. The brothers recently fielded a supercomputer named Little Fermat, which they designed with Monty Denneau, an I.B.M. supercomputer architect, and Saed Younis, a graduate student at the Massachusetts Institute of Technology. Younis did the grunt work: he mapped out circuits containing more than fifteen thousand connections and personally plugged in some five thousand chips. Little Fermat is seven feet tall, and sits inside a steel frame in a laboratory at M.I.T., where it considers numbers.

What m zero consists of is a group of high-speed processors linked by cables (which cover the floor of the room). The cables form a network of connections among the processors—a web. Gregory sketched on a piece of paper the layout of the machine. He drew a box and put an "x" through it, to show the web, or network, and he attached some processors to the web:

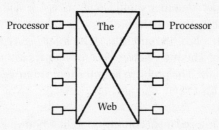

"Each processor is connected to a high-speed switching network that connects it to all the others," he said. "It's like a telephone network—everybody is talking to everybody else. As far as I know, no one except us has built a machine that has this type of web. In other parallel machines, the processors are connected only to near neighbors, while they have to talk to more distant processors through intervening processors. Think of a phone system: it wouldn't be very pleasant if you had to talk to distant people by sending them messages through your neighbors. But the truth is that nobody really knows how the hell parallel machines should perform, or the best design for them. Right now we have eight processors. We plan to have two hundred and fifty-six processors. We will be able to fit them into the apartment."

He said that each processor had its own memory attached to it, so that each processor was in fact a separate computer. After a processor was fed some data and had got a result, it could send the result through the web to another processor. The brothers wrote the machine's application software in FOR-TRAN, a programming language that is "a dinosaur from the late fifties," Gregory said, adding, "There is always new life in this dinosaur." The software can break a problem into pieces, sending the pieces to the machine's different processors. "It's the principle of divide and conquer," Gregory said. He said that it was very hard to know what exactly was happening in the web when the machine was running—that the web seemed to have a life of its own.

"Our machine is mostly made of connections," David said. "About ninety per cent of its volume is cables. Your brain is the same way. It is mostly made of connections. If I may say so, your brain is a liquid-cooled parallel supercomputer." He pointed to his nose. "This is the fan."

The design of the web is the key element in the Chudnovskian architecture. Behind the web hide several new findings in number theory, which the Chudnovskys have not yet published. The brothers would not disclose to me the exact shape of the web, or the discoveries behind it, claiming that they needed to protect their competitive edge in a worldwide race to develop faster supercomputers. "Anyone with a hundred million dollars and brains could be our competitor," David said dryly.

The Chudnovskys have formidable competitors. Thinking Machines Corporation, in Cambridge, Massachusetts, sells massively parallel supercomputers. The price of the latest model, the CM-5, starts at one million four hundred thousand dollars and goes up from there. If you had a hundred million dollars, you could order a CM-5 that would be an array of black monoliths the size of a Burger King, and it would burn enough electricity to light up a neighborhood. Seymour Cray is another competitor of the brothers, as it were. He invented the original Cray series of supercomputers, and is now the head of the Cray Computer Corporation, a spinoff from Cray Research. Seymour Cray has been working to develop his Cray 3 for several years. His company's effort has recently been troubled by engineering delays and defections of potential customers, but if the machine ever is released to customers it may be an octagon about four feet tall and four feet across, and it will burn more than two hundred thousand watts. It would melt instantly if its cooling system were to fail.

Then, there's the Intel Corporation. Intel, together with a consortium of federal agencies, has invested more than twenty-seven million dollars in the Touchstone Delta, a five-foot-high, fifteen-foot-long parallel supercomputer that sits in a computer room at Caltech. The machine consumes twenty-five thousand watts of power, and is kept from overheating by chilled air flowing through its core. One day, I called Paul Messina, a Caltech research scientist, who is the head of the Touchstone Delta project, to get his opinion of the Chudnovsky brothers. It turned out that Messina hadn't heard of them. As for their claim to have built a pi-computing gigaflop supercomputer out of mail-order parts for around seventy thousand dollars, he flatly believed it. "It can be done, definitely," Messina said. "Of course, seventy thousand dollars is just the cost of the components. The Chudnovskys are counting very little of their human time."

Yasumasa Kanada, the brothers' pi rival at Tokyo University, uses a Hitachi S-820/80 supercomputer that is believed to be considerably faster than a Cray Y-MP8, and it burns close to half a million watts—half a megawatt, practically enough power to melt steel. The Chudnovsky brothers particularly hoped to leave Kanada and his Hitachi in the dust with their mail-order funny car.

"We want to test our hardware," Gregory said.

"Pi is the best stress test for a supercomputer," David said.

"We also want to find out what makes pi different from other numbers. It's a business."

"Galileo saw the moons of Jupiter through his telescope, and he tried to figure out the laws of gravity by looking at the moons, but he couldn't," David said. "With pi, we are at the stage of looking at the moons of Jupiter." He pulled his Mini Mag-Lite flashlight out of his pocket and shone it into a bookshelf, rooted through some file folders, and handed me a color photograph of pi.

"This is a pi-scape," he said. The photograph showed a mountain range in cyberspace: bony peaks and ridges cut by valleys. The mountains and valleys were splashed with colors—yellow, green, orange, violet, and blue. It was the first eight million digits of pi, mapped as a fractal landscape by an I.B.M. GF-11 supercomputer at Yorktown Heights, which Gregory had programmed from his bed. Apart from its vivid colors, pi looks like the Himalayas.

Gregory thought that the mountains of pi seemed to contain structure. "I see something systematic in this landscape, but it may be just an attempt by the brain to translate some random visual pattern into order," he said. As he gazed into the nature beyond nature, he wondered if he stood close to a revelation about the circle and its diameter. "Any very high hill in this picture, or any flat plateau, or deep valley, would be a sign of *something* in pi," he said. "There are slight variations from randomness in this landscape. There are fewer peaks and valleys than you would expect if pi were truly random, and the peaks and valleys tend to stay high or low a little longer than you'd expect." In a manner of speaking, the mountains of pi looked to him as if they'd been molded by the hand of the Nameless One, *Deus absconditus* (the hidden God), but he couldn't really express in words what he thought he saw and, to his great frustration, he couldn't express it in the language of mathematics, either.

"Exploring pi is like exploring the universe," David remarked.

"It's more like exploring underwater," Gregory said. "You are in the mud, and everything looks the same. You need a flashlight. Our computer is the flashlight."

David said, "Gregory—I think, really—you are getting tired."

A fax machine in a corner beeped and emitted paper. It was a message from a hardware dealer in Atlanta. David tore off the paper and stared at it. "They didn't ship it! I'm going to kill them! This a service economy. Of course, you know what that means—the service is terrible."

"We collect price quotes by fax," Gregory said.

"It's a horrible thing. Window-shopping in supercomputerland. We can't buy everything—"

"Because everything won't *exist*," Gregory said.

"We only want to build a machine to compute a few transcendental numbers—"

"Because we are not licensed for transcendental meditation," Gregory said.

"Look, we are getting nutty," David said.

"We are not the only ones," Gregory said. "We are getting an average of one letter a month from someone or other who is trying to prove Fermat's Last Theorem."

I asked the brothers if they had published any of their digits of pi in a book.

Gregory said that he didn't know how many trees you would have to grind up in order to publish a billion digits of pi in a book. The brothers' pi had been published on fifteen hundred microfiche cards stored somewhere in Gregory's apartment. The cards held three hundred thousand pages of data, a slug of information much bigger than the Encylopædia Britannica, and containing but one entry, "Pi." David offered to find the cards for me; they had to be around here somewhere. He switched on the lights in the hallway and began to shift boxes. Gregory rifled bookshelves.

"Please sit down, Gregory," David said. Finally, the brothers confessed that they had temporarily lost their pi. "Look, it's not a problem," David said. "We keep it in different places." He reached inside m zero and pulled out a metal box. It was a naked hard-disk drive, studded with chips. He handed me the object. "There's pi stored on this drive." It hummed gently. "You are holding some pi in your hand. It weighs six pounds."

MONTHS passed before I visited the Chudnovskys again. The brothers had been tinkering with their machine and getting it ready to go for two billion digits of pi, when Gregory developed an abnormality related to one of his kidneys. He went to the hospital and had some CAT scans made of his torso, to see what things looked like, but the brothers were disappointed in the pictures, and persuaded the doctors to give them the CAT data on a magnetic tape. They took the tape home, processed it in m zero, and got spectacular color images of Gregory's torso. The images showed cross-sectional slices of his body, viewed through different angles, and they were far more detailed than any image from a CAT scanner. Gregory wrote the imaging software. It took him a few weeks. "There's a lot of interesting mathematics in the problem of imaging a body," he remarked. For the moment, it was more interesting than pi, and it delayed the brothers' probe into the Ludolphian number.

Spring came, and Federal Express was active at the Chudnovskys' building. Then the brothers began to calculate pi, slowly at first, more intensely as they gained confidence in their machine, but in May the weather warmed up and Con Edison betrayed the brothers. A heat wave caused a brownout in New York City, and as it struck, m zero automatically shut itself down, to protect its circuits, and died. Afterward, the brothers couldn't get electricity running properly through the machine. They spent two weeks restarting it, piece by piece.

Then, on Memorial Day weekend, as the calculation was beginning to progress, Malka Benjaminovna suffered a heart attack. Gregory was alone with his mother in the apartment. He gave her chest compressions and breathed air into her lungs, although David later couldn't understand how his brother didn't kill himself saving her. An ambulance rushed her to St. Luke's Hospital. The brothers were terrified that they would lose her, and the strain almost killed David. One day, he fainted in his mother's hospital room and threw up blood. He had developed a bleeding ulcer. "Look, it's not a problem," he said later. After Malka Benjaminovna had been moved out of intensive care, Gregory rented a laptop computer, plugged it into the telephone line in her hospital room, and talked to m zero at night through cyberspace, driving the supercomputer toward pi and watching his mother's blood pressure at the same time.

Malka Benjaminovna improved slowly. When St. Luke's released her, the brothers settled her in her room in Gregory's apartment and hired a nurse to look after her. I visited them shortly after that, on a hot day in early summer. David answered the door. There were blue half circles under his eyes, and he had lost weight. He smiled weakly and greeted me by saying, "I believe it was Oliver Heaviside, the English physicist, who once said, 'In order to know soup, it is not necessary to climb into a pot and be boiled.' But, look, if you want to be boiled you are welcome to come inside." He led me down the dark hallway. Malka Benjaminovna was asleep in her bedroom, and the nurse was sitting beside her. Her room was lined with bookshelves, packed with paper—it was an overflow repository.

"Theoretically, the best way to cool a supercomputer is to submerge it in water," Gregory said, from his bed in the junk yard.

"Then we could add goldfish," David said.

"That would solve all our problems."

"We are not good plumbers, Gregory. As long as I am alive, we will not cool a machine with water."

"What is the temperature in there?" Gregory asked, nodding toward m zero's room.

"It grows to thirty-four degrees Celsius. Above ninety Fahrenheit. This is not good. Things begin to fry."

David took Gregory under the arm, and we passed through the French door into gloom and pestilential heat. The shades were drawn, the lights were off, and an air-conditioner in a window ran in vain. Sweat immediately began to pour down my body. "I don't like to go into this room," Gregory said. The steel frame in the center of the room—the heart of m zero—had acquired more logic boards, and more red lights blinked inside the machine. I could hear disk drives murmuring. The drives were copying and recopying segments of transcendental numbers, to check the digits for perfect accuracy. Gregory knelt on the floor, facing the steel frame.

David opened a cardboard box and removed an electronic board. He began to fit it into m zero. I noticed that his hands were marked with small cuts, which he had got from reaching inside the machine.

"David, could you give me the flashlight?" Gregory said.

David pulled the Mini Mag-Lite from his shirt pocket and handed it to Gregory. The brothers knelt beside each other, Gregory shining the flashlight into the supercomputer. David reached inside with his fingers and palpated a logic board.

"Don't!" Gregory said. "O.K., look. No! No!" They muttered to each other in Russian. "It's too small," Gregory said.

David adjusted an electric fan. "We bought it at a hardware store down the street," he said to me. "We buy our fans in the winter. It saves money." He pointed to a gauge that had a dial on it. "Here we have a meat thermometer."

The brothers had thrust the thermometer between two circuit boards in order to look for hot spots inside m zero. The thermometer's dial was marked "Beef Rare—Ham—Beef Med—Pork."

"You want to keep the machine below 'Pork,' " Gregory remarked. He lifted a keyboard out of the steel frame and typed something on it, staring at a display screen. Numbers filled the screen. "The machine is checking its memory," he said. A buzzer sounded. "It shut down!" he said. "It's a disk-drive controller. The stupid thing obviously has problems."

"It's mentally deficient," David commented. He went over to a bookshelf and picked up a hunting knife. I thought he was going to plunge it into the super-computer, but he used it to rip open a cardboard box. "We're going to ship the part back to the manufacturer," he said to me. "You had better send it in the original box or you may not get your money back. Now you know the reason this apartment is full of empty boxes. We have to save them. Gregory, I wonder if you are tired."

"If I stand up now, I will fall down," Gregory said, from the floor. "Therefore, I will sit in my center of gravity. I will maintain my center of gravity. Let me see, meanwhile, what is happening with this machine." He typed something on his keyboard. "You won't believe it, Dave, but the controller now seems to work."

"We need to buy a new one," David said.

"Try Nevada."

David dialled a mail-order house in Nevada that here will be called Searchlight Computers. He said loudly, in a thick Russian accent, "Hi, Searchlight. I need a fifteen-forty controller. . . . No! No! No! I don't need any-thing else! Just the controller! Just a naked unit! Naked! How much you charge? . . . Two hundred and fifty-seven dollars?"

Gregory glanced at his brother and shrugged. "Eh."

"Look, Searchlight, can you ship it to me Federal Express? For tomorrow morning. How much? . . . *Thirty-nine dollars* for Fed Ex? Come on! What about afternoon delivery? . . . *Twenty*-nine dollars before 3 P.M.? *Relax*. What is your name? . . . Bob. Fine. O.K. So it's two hundred and fifty-seven dollars plus twenty-nine dollars for Federal Express?"

"Twenty-nine dollars for Fed Ex!" Gregory burst out. "It should be fifteen." He pulled a second keyboard out of the steel frame and tapped the keys. Another display screen came alive and filled with numbers.

"Tell me this," David said to Bob in Nevada. "Do you have thirty-day money-back guarantee? . . . No? Come on! Look, any device might not work."

"Of course, a part *might* work," Gregory muttered to his brother. "But it usu-ally doesn't."

"Question Number Two: The Fed Ex should not cost twenty-nine bucks,"

David said to Bob. "No, nothing! I'm just asking." David hung up the phone. "I'm going to call A.K.," he said. "Hi, A.K., this is David Chudnovsky, calling from New York. A.K., I need another controller, like the one you sent. Can you send it today Fed Ex? . . . How much you charge? . . . Naked! I want a naked unit! Not in a shoebox, nothing!"

A rhythmic clicking sound came from one of the disk drives. Gregory remarked to me, "We are calculating pi right now."

"Do you want my MasterCard? Look, it's really imperative that I get my unit tomorrow. A.K., please, I really need my unit bad." David hung up the telephone and sighed. "This is what has happened to a pure mathematician."

"GREGORY and David are both extremely childlike, but I don't mean childish at all," Gregory's wife, Christine Pardo Chudnovsky, said one muggy summer day, at the dining-room table. "There is a certain amount of play in everything they do, a certain amount of fooling around between two brothers." She is six years younger than Gregory; she was an undergraduate at Barnard College when she first met him. "I fell in love with Gregory immediately. His illness came with the package." She is still in love with him, even if at times they fight over his heaps of paper. ("I don't have room to put my things down," she says to him.) As we talked, though, pyramids of boxes and stacks of paper leaned against the dining-room windows, pressing against the glass and blocking daylight, and a smell of hot electrical gear crept through the room. "This house is an example of mathematics in family life," she said. At night, she dreams that she is dancing from room to room through an empty apartment that has parquet floors.

David brought his mother out of her bedroom, settled her at the table, and kissed her on the cheek. Malka Benjaminovna seemed frail but alert. She is a small, white-haired woman with a fresh face and clear blue eyes, who speaks limited English. A mathematician once described Malka Benjaminovna as the glue that holds the Chudnovsky family together. She was an engineer during the Second World War, when she designed buildings, laboratories, and proving grounds in the Urals for testing the Katyusha rocket; later, she taught engineering at schools around Kiev. She handed me plates of roast chicken, kasha, pickles, cream cheese, brown bread, and little wedges of The Laughing Cow cheese in foil. "Mother thinks you aren't getting enough to eat," Christine said. Malka Benjaminovna slid a jug of Gatorade across the table at me.

After lunch, and fortified with Gatorade, the brothers and I went into the chamber of m zero, into a pool of thick heat. The room enveloped us like noon on the Amazon, and it teemed with hidden activity. The disk drives clicked, the red lights flashed, the air-conditioner hummed, and you could hear dozens of whispering fans. Gregory leaned on his cane and contemplated the machine. "It's doing many jobs at the moment," he said. "Frankly, I don't know what it's doing. It's doing some algebra, and I think it's also backing up some pieces of pi."

"Sit down, Gregory, or you will fall," David said.

"What is it doing now, Dave?"

"It's blinking."

"It will die soon."

"Gregory, I heard a funny noise."

"You really heard it? Oh, God, it's going to be like the last time—"

"That's it!"

"We are dead! It crashed!"

"Sit down, Gregory, for God's sake!"

Gregory sat on a stool and tugged at his beard. "What was I doing before the system crashed? With God's help, I will remember." He jotted a few notes in a laboratory notebook. David slashed open a cardboard box with his hunting knife and lifted out a board studded with chips, for making color images on a display screen, and plugged it into m zero. Gregory crawled under a table. "Oh, shit," he said, from beneath the table.

"Gregory, you killed the system again!"

"Dave, Dave, can you get me a flashlight?"

David handed his Mini Mag-Lite under the table. Gregory joined some cables together and stood up. "Whoo! Very uncomfortable. David, boot it up."

"Sit down for a moment."

Gregory slumped into a chair.

"This monster is going on the blink," David said, tapping a keyboard.

"It will be all right."

On a screen, m zero declared, "The system is ready."

"Ah," David said.

The drives began to click, and the parallel processors silently multiplied and conjoined huge numbers. Gregory headed for bed, David holding him by the arm.

In the junk yard, his nest, his paper-lined oubliette, Gregory kicked off his gentleman's slippers, lay down on the bed, and predicted the future. He said, "The gigaflop supercomputers of today are almost useless. What is needed is a teraflop machine. That's a machine that can run at a trillion flops, a trillion floating-point operations per second, or roughly a thousand times as fast as a Cray Y-MP8. One such design for a teraflop machine, by Monty Denneau, at I.B.M., will be a parallel supercomputer in the form of a twelve-foot-wide box. You want to have at least sixty-four thousand processors in the machine, each of which has the power of a Cray. And the processors will be joined by a network that has the total switching capacity of the entire telephone network in the United States. I think a teraflop machine will exist by 1993. Now, a better machine is a petaflop machine. A petaflop is a quadrillion flops, a quadrillion floating-point operations per second, so a petaflop machine is a thousand times as fast as a teraflop machine, or a million times as fast as a Cray Y-MP8. The petaflop machine will exist by the year 2000, or soon afterward. It will fit into a sphere less than a hundred feet in diameter. It will use light and mirrors—the machine's network will consist of optical cables rather than copper wires. By that time, a gigaflop 'supercomputer' will be a single chip. I think that the petaflop machine will be used mainly to simulate machines like itself, so that we can begin to design some *real* machines."

IN the nineteenth century, mathematicians attacked pi with the help of human computers. The most powerful of these was Johann Martin Zacharias Dase, a prodigy from Hamburg. Dase could multiply large numbers in his head, and he made a living exhibiting himself to crowds in Germany, Denmark, and England, and hiring himself out to mathematicians. A mathematician once asked Dase to multiply 79,532,853 by 93,758,479, and Dase gave the right answer in fifty-four seconds. Dase extracted the square root of a hundred-digit number in fifty-two minutes, and he was able to multiply a couple of hundred-digit numbers in his head during a period of eight and three-quarters hours. Dase could do this kind of thing for weeks on end, running as an unattended supercomputer. He would break off a calculation at bedtime, store everything in his memory for the night, and resume calculation in the morning. Occasionally, Dase had a system crash. In 1845, he bombed while trying to demonstrate his powers to a mathematician and astronomer named Heinrich Christian Schumacher, reckoning wrongly every multiplication that he attempted. He explained to Schumacher that he had a headache. Schumacher also noted that Dase did not in the least understand theoretical mathematics. A mathematician named Julius Petersen once tried in vain for six weeks to teach Dase the rudiments of Euclidean geometry, but they absolutely baffled Dase. Large numbers Dase could handle, and in 1844 L. K. Schulz von Strassnitsky hired him to compute pi. Dase ran the job for almost two months in his brain, and at the end of the time he wrote down pi correctly to the first two hundred decimal places—then a world record.

To many mathematicians, mathematical objects such as the number pi seem to exist in an external, objective reality. Numbers seem to exist apart from time or the world; numbers seem to transcend the universe; numbers might exist even if the universe did not. I suspect that in their hearts most working mathematicians are Platonists, in that they take it as a matter of unassailable if unprovable fact that mathematical reality stands apart from the world, and is at least as real as the world, and possibly gives shape to the world, as Plato suggested. Most mathematicians would probably agree that the ratio of the circle to its diameter exists brilliantly in the nature beyond nature, and would exist even if the human mind was not aware of it, and might exist even if God had not bothered to create it. One could imagine that pi existed before the universe came into being and will exist after the universe is gone. Pi may even exist apart from God, in the opinion of some mathematicians, for while there is reason to doubt the existence of God, by their way of thinking there is no good reason to doubt the existence of the circle.

"To an extent, pi is more real than the machine that is computing it," Gregory remarked to me one day. "Plato was right. I am a Platonist. Of course pi is a natural object. Since pi is there, it exists. What we are doing is really close to experimental physics—we are 'observing pi.' Since we can observe pi, I prefer to think of pi as a natural object. Observing pi is easier than studying physical phenomena, because you can prove things in mathematics, whereas you can't prove anything in physics. And, unfortunately, the laws of physics change once every generation."

"Is mathematics a form of art?" I asked.

"Mathematics is partially an art, even though it is a natural science," he said. "Everything in mathematics does exist now. It's a matter of *naming* it. The thing doesn't arrive from God in a fixed form; it's a matter of representing it with symbols. You put it through your mind in order to make sense of it."

Mathematicians have sorted numbers into classes in order to make sense of them. One class of numbers is that of the rational numbers. A rational number is a fraction composed of integers (whole numbers): ⅟₁, ⅓, ⅗, ¹⁰⁄₇₁, and so on. Every rational number, when it is expressed in decimal form, repeats periodically: ⅓, for example, becomes .333. . . . Next, we come to the irrational numbers. An irrational number can't be expressed as a fraction composed of whole numbers, and, furthermore, its digits go to infinity without repeating periodically.

The square root of two ($\sqrt{2}$) is an irrational number. There is simply no way to represent any irrational number as the ratio of two whole numbers; it can't be done. Hippasus of Metapontum supposedly made this discovery in the fifth century B.C., while travelling in a boat with some mathematicians who were followers of Pythagoras. The Pythagoreans believed that everything in nature could be reduced to a ratio of two whole numbers, and they threw Hippasus overboard for his discovery, since he had wrecked their universe. Expanded as a decimal, the square root of two begins 1.41421 . . . and runs in "random" digits forever. It looks exactly like pi in its decimal expansion; it is a hopeless jumble, showing no obvious system or design. The square root of two is not a transcendental number, because it can be found with an equation. It is the solution (root) of an equation. The equation is $x^2 = 2$, and a solution is the square root of two. Such numbers are called algebraic.

While pi is indeed an irrational number—it can't be expressed as a fraction made of whole numbers—more important, it can't be expressed with finite algebra. Pi is therefore said to be a transcendental number, because it transcends algebra. Simply and generally speaking, a transcendental number can't be pinpointed through an equation built from a finite number of integers. There is no finite algebraic equation built from whole numbers that will give an exact value for pi. The statement can be turned around this way: pi is not the solution to any equation built from a less than infinite series of whole numbers. If equations are trains threading the landscape of numbers, then no train stops at pi.

Pi is elusive, and can be approached only through rational approximations. The approximations hover around the number, closing in on it, but do not touch it. Any formula that heads toward pi will consist of a chain of operations that never ends. It is an infinite series. In 1674, Gottfried Wilhelm Leibniz (the co-inventor of the calculus, along with Isaac Newton) noticed an extraordinary pattern of numbers buried in the circle. The Leibniz series for pi has been called one of the most beautiful mathematical discoveries of the seventeenth century:

$$\frac{\pi}{4} = \frac{1}{1} - \frac{1}{3} + \frac{1}{5} - \frac{1}{7} + \frac{1}{9} - \cdots.$$

In English: pi over four equals one minus a third plus a fifth minus a seventh plus a ninth—and so on. You follow the odd numbers out to infinity, and when you arrive there and sum the terms, you get pi. But since you never arrive at infinity you never get pi. Mathematicians find it deeply mysterious that a chain of discrete rational numbers can connect so easily to geometry, to the smooth and continuous circle.

As an experiment in "observing pi," as Gregory Chudnovsky puts it, I computed the Leibniz series on a pocket calculator. It was easy, and I got results that did seem to wander slowly toward pi. As the series progresses, the answers touch on 2.66, 3.46, 2.89, and 3.34, in that order. The answers land higher than pi and lower than pi, skipping back and forth across pi, and gradually closing in on pi. A mathematician would say that the series "converges on pi." It converges on pi forever, playing hopscotch over pi but never landing on pi.

You can take the Leibniz series out a long distance—you can even dramatically speed up its movement toward pi by adding a few corrections to it—but no matter how far you take the Leibniz series, and no matter how many corrections you hammer into it, when you stop the operation and sum the terms, you will get a *rational* number that is somewhere around pi but is not pi, and you will be damned if you can put your hands on pi.

Transcendental numbers continue forever, as an endless non-repeating string, in whatever rational form you choose to display them, whether as digits or as an equation. The Leibniz series is a beautiful way to represent pi, and it is finally mysterious, because it doesn't tell us much about pi. Looking at the Leibniz series, you feel the independence of mathematics from human culture. Surely, on any world that knows pi the Leibniz series will also be known. Leibniz wasn't the first mathematician to discover the Leibniz series. Nilakantha, an astronomer, grammarian, and mathematician who lived on the Kerala coast of India, described the formula in Sanskrit poetry around the year 1500.

It is worth thinking about what a decimal place means. Each decimal place of pi is a range that shows the *approximate* location of pi to an accuracy ten times as great as the previous range. But as you compute the next decimal place you have no idea where pi will appear in the range. It could pop up in 3, or just as easily in 9, or in 2. The apparent movement of pi as you narrow the range is known as the random walk of pi.

Pi does not move; pi is a fixed point. The algebra wobbles around pi. There is no such thing as a formula that is steady enough or sharp enough to stick a pin into pi. Mathematicians have discovered formulas that converge on pi very fast (that is, they skip around pi with rapidly increasing accuracy), but they do not and cannot hit pi. The Chudnovsky brothers discovered their own formula in 1984, and it attacks pi with great ferocity and elegance. The Chudnovsky formula is the fastest series for pi ever found which uses rational numbers. Various other series for pi, which use irrational numbers, have also been found, and they converge on pi faster than the Chudnovsky formula, but in practice they run more slowly on a computer, because irrational numbers are harder to compute. The Chudnovsky formula for pi is thought to be "extremely beautiful" by persons who have a good feel for numbers, and it is based on a torus (a doughnut), rather than on a circle. It uses large assemblages of whole numbers to hunt for pi, and it owes much to an earlier formula for pi worked out in 1914 by Srinivasa Ramanujan, a mathematician from Madras, who was a number theorist of unsurpassed genius. Gregory says that the Chudnovsky formula "is in the style of Ramanujan," and that it "is really very simple, and can be programmed into a computer with a few lines of code."

In 1873, Georg Cantor, a Russian-born mathematician who was one of the towering intellectual figures of the nineteenth century, proved that the set of transcendental numbers is infinitely more extensive than the set of algebraic numbers. That is, finite algebra can't find or describe most numbers. To put it another way, most numbers are infinitely long and non-repeating in any rational form of representation. In this respect, most numbers are like pi.

Cantor's proof was a disturbing piece of news, for at that time very few transcendental numbers were actually known. (Not until nearly a decade later did Ferdinand Lindemann finally prove the transcendence of pi; before that, mathematicians had only conjectured that pi was transcendental.) Perhaps even more disturbing, Cantor offered no clue, in his proof, to what a transcendental number might look like, or how to construct such a beast. Cantor's celebrated proof of the existence of uncountable multitudes of transcendental numbers resembled a proof that the world is packed with microscopic angels—a proof, however, that does not tell us what the angels look like or where they can be found; it merely proves that they *exist* in uncountable multitudes. While Cantor's proof lacked any specific description of a transcendental number, it showed that algebraic numbers (such as the square root of two) are few and far between: they poke up like marker buoys through the sea of transcendental numbers.

Cantor's proof disturbed some mathematicians because, in the first place, it suggested that they had not yet discovered *most* numbers, which were transcendentals, and in the second place that they lacked any tools or methods that would determine whether a given number was transcendental or not. Leopold Kronecker, an influential older mathematician, rejected Cantor's proof, and resisted the whole notion of "discovering" a number. (He once said, in a famous remark, "God made the integers, all else is the work of man.") Cantor's proof has withstood such attacks, and today the debate over whether transcendental numbers are a work of God or man has subsided, mathematicians having decided to work with transcendental numbers no matter who made them.

The Chudnovsky brothers claim that the digits of pi form the most nearly perfect random sequence of digits that has ever been discovered. They say that nothing known to humanity appears to be more deeply unpredictable than the succession of digits in pi, except, perhaps, the haphazard clicks of a Geiger counter as it detects the decay of radioactive nuclei. But pi is not random. The fact that pi can be produced by a relatively simple formula means that pi is orderly. Pi looks random only because the pattern in the digits is fantastically complex. The Ludolphian number is fixed in eternity—not a digit out of place, all characters in their proper order, an endless sentence written to the end of the world by the division of the circle's diameter into its circumference. Various simple methods of approximation will always yield the same succession of digits in the same order. If a single digit in pi were to be changed anywhere between here and infinity, the resulting number would no longer be pi; it would be "garbage," in David's word, because to change a single digit in pi is to throw all the following digits out of whack and miles from pi.

"Pi is a damned good fake of a random number," Gregory said. "I just wish it were not as good a fake. It would make our lives a lot easier."

Around the three-hundred-millionth decimal place of pi, the digits go 88888888—eight eights pop up in a row. Does this mean anything? It appears to be random noise. Later, ten sixes erupt: 6666666666. What does this mean? Apparently nothing, only more noise. Somewhere past the half-billion mark appears the string 123456789. It's an accident, as it were. "We do not have a good, clear, crystallized idea of randomness," Gregory said. "It cannot be that pi is truly random. Actually, a truly random sequence of numbers has not yet been discovered."

No one knows what happens to the digits of pi in the deeper regions, as the number is resolved toward infinity. Do the digits turn into nothing but eights and fives, say? Do they show a predominance of sevens? Similarly, no one knows if a digit stops appearing in pi. This conjecture says that after a certain point in the sequence a digit drops out completely. For example, no more fives appear in pi—something like that. Almost certainly, pi does not do such things, Gregory Chudnovsky thinks, because it would be stupid, and nature isn't stupid. Nevertheless, no one has ever been able to prove or disprove a certain basic conjecture about pi: that every digit has an equal chance of appearing in pi. This is known as the normality conjecture for pi. The normality conjecture says that, on average, there is no more or less of any digit in pi: for example, there is no excess of sevens in pi. If all digits do appear with the same average frequency in pi, then pi is a "normal" number—"normal" by the narrow mathematical definition of the word. "This is the simplest possible conjecture about pi," Gregory said. "There is absolutely no doubt that pi is a 'normal' number. Yet we can't prove it. We don't even know how to *try* to prove it. We know very little about transcendental numbers, and, what is worse, the number of conjectures about them isn't growing." No one knows even how to tell the difference between the square root of two and pi merely by looking at long strings of their digits, though the two numbers have completely distinct mathematical properties, one being algebraic and the other transcendental.

Even if the brothers couldn't prove anything about the digits of pi, they felt that by looking at them through the window of their machine they might at least see something that could lead to an important conjecture about pi or about transcendental numbers as a class. You can learn a lot about all cats by looking closely at one of them. So if you wanted to look closely at pi how much of it could you see with a very large supercomputer? What if you turned the universe into a supercomputer? What then? How much pi could you see? Naturally, the brothers had considered this project. They had imagined a computer built from the universe. Here's how they estimated the machine's size. It has been calculated that there are about 10^{79} electrons and protons in the observable universe; this is the so-called Eddington number of the universe. (Sir Arthur Stanley Eddington, the astrophysicist, first came up with the number.) The Eddington number is the digit 1 followed by seventy-nine zeros: 10,000,000,000,000,000,000,000,000,000,000,000,000,000,000,000,000, 000,000,000,000,000,000,000,000,000,000,000. Ten vigintsextillion. The Eddington number. It declares the power of the Eddington machine.

The Eddington machine would be the universal supercomputer. It would be made of all the atoms in the universe. The Eddington machine would contain ten vigintsextillion parts, and if the Chudnovsky brothers could figure out how to program it with FORTRAN they might make it churn toward pi. "In order to study the sequence of pi, you have to store it in the Eddington machine's memory," Gregory said. To be realistic, the brothers thought that a practical Eddington machine wouldn't be able to store pi much beyond 10^{77} digits—a number that is only a hundredth of the Eddington number. Now, what if the digits of pi only begin to show regularity beyond 10^{77} digits? Suppose, for example, that pi manifests a regularity starting at 10^{100} decimal places? That number is known as a googol. If the design in pi appears only after a googol of digits, then not even the Eddington machine will see any system in pi; pi will look totally disordered to the universe, even if pi contains a slow, vast, delicate structure. A mere googol of pi might be only the first knot at the corner of a kind of limitless Persian rug, which is woven into increasingly elaborate diamonds, cross-stars, gardens, and cosmogonies. It may never be possible, in principle, to see the order in the digits of pi. Not even nature itself may know the nature of pi.

"If pi doesn't show systematic behavior until more than ten to the seventy-seven decimal places, it would really be a disaster," Gregory said. "It would be actually horrifying."

"I wouldn't give up," David said. "There might be some other way of leaping over the barrier—"

"And of attacking the son of a bitch," Gregory said.

THE brothers first came in contact with the membrane that divides the dream-like earth from mathematical reality when they were boys, growing up in Kiev, and their father gave David a book entitled "What Is Mathematics?," by two mathematicians named Richard Courant and Herbert Robbins. The book is a classic—millions of copies of it have been printed in unauthorized Russian and Chinese editions alone—and after the brothers finished reading "Robbins," as the book is called in Russia, David decided to become a mathematician, and Gregory soon followed his brother's footsteps into the nature beyond nature. Gregory's first publication, in the journal *Soviet Mathematics—Doklady,* came when he was sixteen years old: "Some Results in the Theory of Infinitely Long Expressions." Already you can see where he was headed. David, sensing his younger brother's power, encouraged him to grapple with central problems in mathematics. Gregory made his first major discovery at the age of seventeen, when he solved Hilbert's Tenth Problem. (It was one of twenty-three great problems posed by David Hilbert in 1900.) To solve a Hilbert problem would be an achievement for a lifetime; Gregory was a high-school student who had read a few books on mathematics. Strangely, a young Russian mathematician named Yuri Matyasevich had just solved Hilbert's Tenth Problem, and the brothers hadn't heard the news. Matyasevich has recently said that the Chudnovsky method is the preferred way to solve Hilbert's Tenth Problem.

The brothers enrolled at Kiev State University, and both graduated summa cum laude. They took their Ph.D.s at the Institute of Mathematics at the Ukrainian Academy of Sciences. At first, they published their papers separately, but by the mid-nineteen-seventies they were collaborating on much of their work. They lived with their parents in Kiev until the family decided to try to take Gregory abroad for treatment, and in 1976 Volf and Malka Chudnovsky applied to the government to emigrate. Volf was immediately fired from his job.

The K.G.B. began tailing the brothers. "Gregory would not believe me until it became totally obvious," David said. "I had twelve K.G.B. agents on my tail. No, look, I'm not kidding! They shadowed me around the clock in two cars, six agents in each car. Three in the front seat and three in the back seat. That was how the K.G.B. operated." One day, in 1976, David was walking down the street when K.G.B. officers attacked him, breaking his skull. He went home and nearly died, but didn't go to the hospital. "If I had gone to the hospital, I would have died for sure," he told me. "The hospital is run by the state. I would forget to breathe."

On July 22, 1977, plainclothesmen from the K.G.B. accosted Volf and Malka on a street in Kiev and beat them up. They broke Malka's arm and fractured her skull. David took his mother to the hospital. "The doctor in the emergency room said there was no fracture," David said.

Gregory, at home in bed, was not so vulnerable. Also, he was conspicuous in the West. Edwin Hewitt, a mathematician at the University of Washington, in Seattle, had visited Kiev in 1976 and collaborated with Gregory on a paper, and later, when Hewitt learned that the Chudnovsky family was in trouble, he persuaded Senator Henry M. Jackson, the powerful member of the Senate Armed Services Committee, to take up the Chudnovskys' case. Jackson put pressure on the Soviets to let the family leave the country. Just before the K.G.B. attacked the parents, two members of a French parliamentary delegation that was in Kiev made an unofficial visit to the Chudnovskys to see what was going on. One of the visitors, a staff member of the delegation, was Nicole Lannegrace, who married David in 1983. Andrei Sakharov also helped to draw attention to the Chudnovskys' increasingly desperate situation. Two months after the parents were attacked, the Soviet government unexpectedly let the family go. "That summer when I was getting killed by the K.G.B., I could never have imagined that the next year I would be in Paris or that I would wind up in New York, married to a beautiful Frenchwoman," David said. The Chudnovsky family settled in New York, near Columbia University.

IF pi is truly random, then at times pi will appear to be ordered. Therefore, if pi is random it contains accidental order. For example, somewhere in pi a sequence may run 07070707070707 for as many decimal places as there are, say, hydrogen atoms in the sun. It's just an accident. Somewhere else the same sequence of zeros and sevens may appear, only this time interrupted by a single occurrence of the digit 3. Another accident. Those and all other "accidental" arrangements of digits almost certainly erupt in pi, but their presence has never been proved. "Even if pi is not truly random, you can still assume that you get *every* string of digits in pi," Gregory said.

If you were to assign letters of the alphabet to combinations of digits, and were to do this for all human alphabets, syllabaries, and ideograms, then you could fit any written character in any language to a combination of digits in pi. According to this system, pi could be turned into literature. Then, if you could look far enough into pi, you would probably find the expression "See the U.S.A. in a Chevrolet!" a billion times in a row. Elsewhere, you would find Christ's Sermon on the Mount in His native Aramaic tongue, and you would find versions of the Sermon on the Mount that are pure blasphemy. Also, you would find a dictionary of Yanomamo curses. A guide to the pawnshops of Lubbock. The book about the sea which James Joyce supposedly declared he would write after he finished "Finnegans Wake." The collected transcripts of "The Tonight Show" rendered into Etruscan. "Knowledge of All Existing Things," by Ahmes the Egyptian scribe. Each occurrence of an apparently ordered string in pi, such as the words "Ruin hath taught me thus to ruminate/That Time will come and take my love away," is followed by unimaginable deserts of babble. No book and none but the shortest poems will ever be seen in pi, since it is infinitesimally unlikely that even as brief a text as an English sonnet will appear in the first 10^{77} digits of pi, which is the longest piece of pi that can be calculated in this universe.

Anything that can be produced by a simple method is by definition orderly. Pi can be produced by various simple methods of rational approximation, and those methods yield the same digits in a fixed order forever. Therefore, pi is orderly in the extreme. Pi may also be a powerful random-number generator, spinning out any and all possible combinations of digits. We see that the distinction between chance and fixity dissolves in pi. The deep connection between disorder and order, between cacophony and harmony, in the most famous ratio in mathematics fascinated Gregory and David Chudnovsky. They wondered if the digits of pi had a personality.

"We are looking for the appearance of some rules that will distinguish the digits of pi from other numbers," Gregory explained. "It's like studying writers by studying their use of words, their grammar. If you see a Russian sentence that extends for a whole page, with hardly a comma, it is definitely Tolstoy. If someone were to give you a million digits from somewhere in pi, could you tell it was from pi? We don't really look for patterns; we look for rules. Think of games for children. If I give you the sequence one, two, three, four, five, can you tell me what the next digit is? Even a child can do it; the next digit is six. How about this game? Three, one, four, one, five, nine. Just by looking at that sequence, can you tell me the next digit? What if I gave you a sequence of a million digits from pi? Could you tell me the next digit just by looking at the sequence? Why does pi look like a totally unpredictable sequence with the highest complexity? We need to find out the rules that govern this game. For all we know, we may never find a rule in pi."

HERBERT Robbins, the co-author of "What Is Mathematics?," is an emeritus professor of mathematical statistics at Columbia University. For the past six years, he has been teaching at Rutgers. The Chudnovskys call him once in a while to get his advice on how to use statistical tools to search for signs of order in pi. Robbins lives in a rectilinear house that has a lot of glass in it, in the woods on the outskirts of Princeton. Some of the twentieth century's most creative and powerful discoveries in statistics and probability theory happened inside his head. Robbins is a tall, restless man in his seventies, with a loud voice, furrowed cheeks, and penetrating eyes. One recent day, he stretched himself out on a daybed in a garden room in his house and played with a rubber band, making a harp across his fingertips.

"It is a very difficult philosophical question, the question of what 'random' is," he said. He plucked the rubber band with his thumb, *boink, boink.* "Everyone knows the famous remark of Albert Einstein, that God does not throw dice. Einstein just would not believe that there is an element of randomness in the construction of the world. The question of whether the universe is a random process or is determined in some way is a basic philosophical question that has nothing to do with mathematics. The question is important. People consider it when they decide what to do with their lives. It concerns religion. It is the question of whether our fate will be revealed or whether we live by blind chance. My God, how many people have been murdered over an answer to that question! Mathematics is a lesser activity than religion in the sense that we've agreed not to kill each other but to discuss things."

Robbins got up from the daybed and sat in an armchair. Then he stood up and paced the room, and sat at a table in the room, and sat on a couch, and went back to the table, and finally returned to the daybed. The man was in constant motion. It looked random to me, but it may have been systematic. It was the random walk of Herbert Robbins.

"Mathematics is broken into tiny specialties today, but Gregory Chudnovsky is a generalist who knows the whole of mathematics as well as anyone," he said as he moved around. "You have to go back a hundred years, to David Hilbert, to find a mathematician as broadly knowledgeable as Gregory Chudnovsky. He's like Mozart: he's the last of his breed. I happen to think the brothers' pi project is a will-o'-the-wisp, and is one of the least interesting things they've ever done. But what do I know? Gregory seems to be asking questions that can't be answered. To ask for the system in pi is like asking 'Is there life after death?' When you die, you'll find out. Most mathematicians are not interested in the digits of pi, because the question is of no practical importance. In order for a mathematician to become interested in a problem, there has to be a possibility of solving it. If you are an athlete, you ask yourself if you can jump thirty feet. Gregory likes to ask if he can jump around the world. He likes to do things that are impossible."

At some point after the brothers settled in New York, it became obvious that Columbia University was not going to be able to invite them to become full-fledged members of the faculty. Since then, the brothers have always enjoyed cordial personal relationships with various members of the faculty, but as an institution the Mathematics Department has been unable to create permanent faculty positions for them. Robbins and a couple of fellow-mathematicians— Lipman Bers and the late Mark Kac—once tried to raise money from private sources for an endowed chair at Columbia to be shared by the brothers, but the effort failed. Then the John D. and Catherine T. MacArthur Foundation awarded Gregory Chudnovsky a "genius" fellowship; that happened in 1981, the first year the awards were given, as if to suggest that Gregory is a person for whom the MacArthur prize was invented. The brothers can exhibit other fashionable paper—a Prix Peccot-Vimont, a couple of Guggenheims, a Doctor of Science *honoris causa* from Bard College, the Moscow Mathematical Society Prize—but there is one defect in their résumé, which is the fact that Gregory has to lie in bed most of the day. The ugly truth is that Gregory Chudnovsky can't get a permanent job at any American institution of higher learning because he is physically disabled. But there are other, more perplexing reasons that have led the Chudnovsky brothers to pursue their work in solitude, outside the normal academic hierarchy, since the day they arrived in the United States.

Columbia University has awarded each brother the title of senior research scientist in the Department of Mathematics. Their position at Columbia is ambiguous. The university officially considers them to be members of the faculty, but they don't have tenure, and Columbia doesn't spend its own funds to pay their salaries or to support their research. However, Columbia does give them health-insurance benefits and a housing subsidy.

The brothers have been living on modest grants from the National Science Foundation and various other research agencies, which are funnelled through Columbia and have to be applied for regularly. Nicole Lannegrace and Christine Chudnovsky financed m zero out of their paychecks. Christine's father, Gonzalo Pardo, who is a professor of dentistry at the State University of New York at Stony Brook, built the steel frame for m zero in his basement during a few weekends, using a wrench and a hacksaw.

The brothers' mode of existence has come to be known among mathematicians as the Chudnovsky Problem. Herbert Robbins eventually decided that it was time to ask the entire American mathematics profession why it could not solve the Chudnovsky Problem. Robbins is a member of the National Academy of Sciences, and in 1986 he sent a letter to all of the mathematicians in the academy:

> I fear that unless a decent and honorable position in the American educational and research system is found for the brothers soon, a personal and scientific tragedy will take place for which all American mathematicians will share responsibility. . . .
> I have asked many of my colleagues why this situation exists, and what can be done to put an end to what I regard as a national disgrace. I have never received an answer that satisfies me. . . . I am asking you, then, as one of the leaders of American mathematics, to tell me what you are prepared to do to acquaint yourselves with their present circumstances, and if you are convinced of the merits of their case, to find a suitable position somewhere in the country for them as a pair.

There wasn't much of a response. Robbins says that he received three written replies to his letter. One, from a faculty member at a well-known East Coast university, complained about David Chudnovsky's personality. He remarked that "when David learns to be less overbearing" the brothers might have better luck. He also did not fully understand the tone of Robbins' letter: while he agreed that some resolution to the Chudnovsky Problem must be found, he thought that Herb Robbins ought to approach the subject realistically and with more candor. ("More candor? How could I have been more candid?" Robbins asked.) Another letter came from a faculty member at Princeton University, who offered to put in a good word with the National Science Foundation to help the brothers get their grants, but did not mention a job at Princeton or any-where else. The most thoughtful response came from a faculty member at M.I.T., who remarked, "It does seem odd that they have not been more sought after." He wondered if in some part this might be a consequence of their breadth. "A specialist appears as a safer investment to a cautious academic ad-ministrator. I'm sorry I have nothing more effective to propose."

An emotional reaction to Robbins' campaign on behalf of the Chudnovskys came a bit later from Edwin Hewitt, the mathematician who had helped get the family out of the Soviet Union, and one of the few Americans who has ever worked with Gregory Chudnovsky. Hewitt wrote to colleagues, "I have collabo-rated with many excellent mathematicians . . . but with no one else have I wit-nessed an outpouring of mathematics like that from Gregory. He simply KNOWS what is true and what is not." In another letter, Hewitt wrote:

> The Chudnovsky situation is a national disgrace. Everyone says, "Oh, what a crying shame" & then suggests that they be placed at *somebody else's institu-tion.* No one seems to want the admittedly burdensome task of caring for the Chudnovsky family. I imagine it would be a full-time, if not an impossible, job. We may remember that both Mozart and Beethoven were disagreeable people, to say nothing of Gauss.

The brothers would have to be hired as a pair. Gregory won't take any job un-less David gets one, and vice versa. Physically and intellectually commingled, like two trees that have grown together at the root and bole, the brothers claim that they can't be separated without becoming deadfalls and crashing to the ground. To hire the Chudnovsky pair, a department would have to create a joint opening for them. Gregory can't teach classes in the normal way, because he is more or less confined to bed. It would require a small degree of flexibility in a department to allow Gregory to concentrate on research, while David han-dled the teaching. The problem is that Gregory might still have the pleasure of working with a few brilliant graduate students—a privilege that might not go down well in an American academic department.

"They are prototypical Russians," Robbins said. "They combine a rather grandiose vision of themselves with an ability to live on scraps rather than compromise their principles. These are people the world is not able to cope with, and they are not making it any easier for the world. I don't see that the world is particularly trying to keep Gregory Chudnovsky alive. The tragedy—

the *disgrace*, so to speak—is that the American scientific and educational establishment is not benefitting from the Chudnovskys' assistance. Thirteen years have gone by since the Chudnovskys arrived here, and where are all the graduate students who would have worked with the brothers? How many truly great mathematicians have you ever heard of who couldn't get a job? I think the Chudnovskys are the only example in history. This vast educational system of ours has poured the Chudnovskys out on the sand, to waste. Yet Gregory is one of the remarkable personalities of our time. When I go up to that apartment and sit by his bed, I think, My God, when I was a student at Harvard I was in contact with people far less interesting than this. What happens to me in Gregory's room is like that line in the Gerard Manley Hopkins poem: 'Margaret, are you grieving/Over Golden-grove unleaving?' I'm grieving, and I guess it's me I'm grieving for."

"TWO billion digits of pi? Where do they keep them?" Samuel Eilenberg said to me. Eilenberg is a gifted and distinguished topologist, and an emeritus professor of mathematics at Columbia University. He was the chairman of the department when the question of hiring the brothers first became troublesome to Columbia. "There is an element of fatigue in the Chudnovsky Problem," he said. "In the academic world, we have to be careful who our colleagues are. David is a pain in the neck. He interrupts people, and he is not interested in anything except what concerns him and his brother. He is a nudnick! Gregory is certainly unusual, but he is not great. You can spend all your life computing digits. What for? You know in advance that you can't see any regularity in pi. It's about as interesting as going to the beach and counting sand. I wouldn't be caught dead doing that kind of work! Most mathematicians probably feel this way. An important ingredient in mathematics is taste. Mathematics is mostly about giving pleasure. The ultimate criterion of mathematics is aesthetic, and to calculate the two-billionth digit of pi is to me abhorrent."

"Abhorrent—yes, most mathematicians would probably agree with that," said Dale Brownawell, a respected number theorist at Penn State. "Tastes change, though. If something were to begin to show up in the digits of pi, it would boggle everyone's mind." Brownawell met the Chudnovskys at the Vienna airport when they escaped from the Soviet Union. "They didn't bring much with them, just a pile of bags and boxes. David would walk through a wall to do what is right for his brother. In the situation they are in, how else can they survive? To see the Chudnovskys carrying on science at such a high level with such meagre support is awe-inspiring."

Richard Askey, a prominent mathematician at the University of Wisconsin at Madison, occasionally flies to New York to sit at the foot of Gregory Chudnovsky's bed and learn about mathematics. "David Chudnovsky is a very good mathematician," Askey said to me. "Gregory is one of the few great mathematicians of our time. Gregory is so much better than I am that it is impossible for me to say how good he really is. Is he the best in the world, or one of the three best? I feel uncomfortable evaluating people at that level. The brothers' pi stuff is just a small part of their work. They are really trying to find out what the word 'random' means. I've heard some people say that the brothers are wasting their time with that machine, but Gregory Chudnovsky is a very intelligent man, who has his head screwed on straight, and I wouldn't begin to question his priorities. The tragedy is that Gregory has had hardly any students. If he dies without having passed on not only his knowledge but his whole way of thinking, then it will be a great tragedy. Rather than blame Columbia University, I would prefer to say that the blame lies with all American mathematicians. Gregory Chudnovsky is a national problem."

"IT looks like kvetching," Gregory said from his bed. "It looks cheap, and it is cheap. We are here in the United States by our own choice. I don't think we were somehow wronged. I really can't teach. So what does one want to do about it? Attempts to change the system are very expensive and time-consuming and largely a waste of time. We barely have time to do the things we want to do."

"To reform the system?" David said, playing his flashlight across the ceiling. "In this country? Look. Come on. It's much easier to reform a totalitarian system."

"Yes, you just make a decree," Gregory said. "Anyway, this sort of talk moves into philosophical questions. What is life, and where does the money come from?" He shrugged.

Toward the end of the summer of 1991, the brothers halted their probe into pi. They had surveyed pi to two billion two hundred and sixty million three hundred and twenty-one thousand three hundred and thirty-six digits. It was a world record, doubling the record that the Chudnovskys had set in 1989. If the digits were printed in ordinary type, they would stretch from New York to Southern California. The brothers had temporarily ditched their chief competitor, Yasumasa Kanada—a pleasing development when the brothers considered that Kanada had access to a half-megawatt Hitachi monster that was supposed to be faster than a Cray. Kanada reacted gracefully to the Chudnovskys' achievement, and he told *Science News* that he might be able to get at least a billion and a half digits of pi if he could obtain enough time on a Japanese supercomputer.

"You see the advantage to being truly poor. We had to build our machine, but now we get to use it, too," Gregory said.

The Chudnovskys' machine had spent its time both calculating pi and checking the result. The job had taken about two hundred and fifty hours on m zero. The machine had spent most of its time checking the answer, to make sure each digit was correct, rather than doing the fundamental computation of pi.

"We have done our tests for patterns, and there is nothing," Gregory said. "It would be rather stupid if there were something in a few billion digits. There are the usual things. The digit three is repeated nine times in a row, and we didn't see that before. Unfortunately, we still don't have enough computer power to see anything in pi."

Such was their scientific conclusion, and yet the brothers felt that they may have noticed something in pi. It hovered out of reach, but it seemed a little closer now. It was a slight sign of order—a possible sign—and it had to do with the running average of the digits. You can take an average of any string of digits in pi. It is like getting a batting average, an average height, an average weight. The average of the digits in pi should be 4.5. That's the average of the decimal digits zero through nine. The brothers noticed that the average seems to be slightly skewed. It stays a little high through most of the first billion digits, and then it stays a little low through the next billion digits. The running average of pi looks like a tide that rises and retreats through two billion digits, as if a distant moon were passing over a sea of digits, pulling them up and down. It may or may not be a hint of a rule in pi. "It's unfortunately not statistically significant yet," Gregory said. "It's close to the edge of significance." The brothers may have glimpsed only their desire for order. The tide that seems to flow through pi may be nothing but aimless gabble, but what if it is a wave rippling through pi? What if the wave begins to show a weird and complicated pulsation as you go deeper in pi? You could become obsessive thinking about things like this. You might have to build more machines. "We need a trillion digits," David said. A trillion digits printed in ordinary type would stretch from here to the moon and back, twice. The brothers thought that if they didn't get bored with pi and move on to other problems they would easily collect a trillion digits in a few years, with the help of increasingly powerful supercomputing equipment. They would orbit the moon in digits, and head for Alpha Centauri, and if they lived and their machines held, perhaps someday they would begin to see the true nature of pi.

Gregory is lying in bed in the junk yard, a keyboard on his lap. He offers to show me a few digits of pi, and taps at the keys.

On the screen beside his bed, m zero responds: "Please, give the beginning of the decimal digit to look."

Gregory types a command, and suddenly the whole screen fills with the raw Ludolphian number, moving like Niagara Falls. We observe pi in silence for quite a while, until it ends with:

... 18820 54573 01261 27678 17413 87779 66981 15311 24707
34258 41235 99801 92693 52561 92393 53870 24377 10069 16106
22971 02523 30027 49528 06378 64067 12852 77857 42344 28836
88521 72435 85924 57786 36741 32845 66266 96498 68308 59920
06168 63376 85976 35341 52906 04621 44710 52106 99079 33563

54625 71001 37490 77872 43403 57690 01699 82447 20059 93533
82919 46119 87044 02125 12329 11964 10087 41341 42633 88249
48948 31198 27787 03802 08989 05316 75375 43242 20100 43326
74069 33751 86349 40467 52687 79749 68922 29914 46047 47109
31678 05219 48702 00877 32383 87446 91871 49136 90837 88525
51575 35790 83982 20710 59298 41193 81740 92975 31.

"It showed the last digits we've found," Gregory says. "The last shall be first."
"Thanks for asking," m zero remarks, on the screen.

(1992)

COVERING THE COPS

IN the newsroom of the Miami *Herald*, there is some disagreement about which of Edna Buchanan's first paragraphs stands as the classic Edna lead. I line up with the fried-chicken faction. The fried-chicken story was about a rowdy ex-con named Gary Robinson, who late one Sunday night lurched drunkenly into a Church's outlet, shoved his way to the front of the line, and ordered a three-piece box of fried chicken. Persuaded to wait his turn, he reached the counter again five or ten minutes later, only to be told that Church's had run out of fried chicken. The young woman at the counter suggested that he might like chicken nuggets instead. Robinson responded to the suggestion by slugging her in the head. That set off a chain of events that ended with Robinson's being shot dead by a security guard. Edna Buchanan covered the murder for the *Herald*—there are policemen in Miami who say that it wouldn't be a murder without her—and her story began with what the fried-chicken faction still regards as the classic Edna lead: "Gary Robinson died hungry."

All connoisseurs would agree, I think, that the classic Edna lead would have to include one staple of crime reporting—the simple, matter-of-fact statement that registers with a jolt. The question is where the jolt should be. There's a lot to be said for starting right out with it. I'm rather partial to the Edna lead on a story last year about a woman about to go on trial for a murder conspiracy: "Bad things happen to the husbands of Widow Elkin." On the other hand, I can understand the preference that others have for the device of beginning a crime story with a more or less conventional sentence or two, then snapping the reader back in his chair with an abbreviated sentence that is used like a blunt instrument. One student of the form at the *Herald* refers to that device as the

Miller Chop. The reference is to Gene Miller, now a *Herald* editor, who, in a re-markable reporting career that concentrated on the felonious, won the Pulitzer Prize twice for stories that resulted in the release of people in prison for murder. Miller likes short sentences in general—it is sometimes said at the *Herald* that he writes as if he were paid by the period—and he particularly likes to use a short sentence after a couple of rather long ones. Some years ago, Gene Miller and Edna Buchanan did a story together on the murder of a high-living Miami lawyer who was shot to death on a day he had planned to while away on the golf course of La Gorce Country Club, and the lead said, ". . . he had his golf clubs in the trunk of his Cadillac. Wednesday looked like an easy day. He figured he might pick up a game later with Eddie Arcaro, the jockey. He didn't."

These days, Miller sometimes edits the longer pieces that Edna Buchanan does for the *Herald*, and she often uses the Miller Chop—as in a piece about a lovers' spat: "The man she loved slapped her face. Furious, she says she told him never, ever to do that again. 'What are you going to do, kill me?' he asked, and handed her a gun. 'Here, kill me,' he challenged. She did."

Now that I think of it, that may be the classic Edna lead.

THERE is no dispute about the classic Edna telephone call to a homicide detective or a desk sergeant she knows: "Hi. This is Edna. What's going on over there?" There are those at the *Herald* who like to think that Edna Buchanan knows every policeman and policewoman in the area—even though Dade County has twenty-seven separate police forces, with a total strength of more than forty-five hundred officers. "I asked her if by any chance she happened to know this sergeant," a *Herald* reporter once told me. "And she looked at her watch and said, 'Yeah, but he got off his shift twenty minutes ago.' " She does not in fact know all the police officers in the area, but they know her. If the desk sergeant who picks up the phone is someone Edna has never heard of, she gives her full name and the name of her paper. But even if she said, "This is Edna," there aren't many cops who would say, "Edna who?" In Miami, a few figures are regularly discussed by first name among people they have never actually met. One of them is Fidel. Another is Edna.

It's an old-fashioned name. Whoever picks up the phone at homicide when Edna Buchanan calls probably doesn't know any Ednas he might confuse her with. Edna is, as it happens, a rather old-fashioned person. "She should have been working in the twenties or thirties," a detective who has known her for years told me. "She'd have been happy if she had a little press card in her hat." She sometimes says the same sort of thing about herself. She laments the replacement of typewriters at the *Herald* with word processors. She would like to think of her clips stored in a place called a morgue rather than a place called an editorial reference library. She's nostalgic about old-fashioned criminals. As a girl growing up around Paterson, New Jersey, she used to read the New York tabloids out loud to her grandmother—a Polish grandmother, who didn't read English—and she still likes to roll out the names of the memorable felons in those stories: names like George Metesky, the Mad Bomber, and Willie Sutton, the man who robbed banks because that's where the money was. She even has a period look about her—something that recalls the period around 1961. She is a very thin woman in her forties who tends to dress in slacks and silk shirts and high heels. She wears her hair in a heavy blond shoulder-length fall. Her eyes are wide, and her brow is often furrowed in concern. She seems almost permanently anxious about one thing or another. Did she neglect to try the one final approach that would have persuaded the suspect's mother to open the door and have a chat? Will a stray cat that she spotted in the neighborhood meet an unpleasant end? Did she forget to put a quarter in the meter? Despite many years spent among people who often find themselves resorting to rough language—hookers, cocaine cowboys, policemen, newspaper reporters—her own conversation tends to sound like that of a rather demure secretary circa 1952. Her own cats—she has five of them—have names like Misty Blue Eyes and Baby Dear. When she is particularly impressed by a bit of news, she is likely to describe it as "real neat." When she discovers, say, a gruesome turn in a tale that might be pretty gruesome already, she may say, "That's interesting as heck!"

Among newspaper people, Edna's line of work is considered a bit old-fashioned. Daily police reporting—what is sometimes known in the trade as covering the cops—is still associated with that old-timer who had a desk in the station house and didn't have to be told by the sergeant in charge which part of the evening's activities to leave out of the story and thought of himself as more or less a member of the department. Covering the cops is often something a reporter does early in his career—an assignment that can provide him with enough war stories in six months to last him through years on the business page or the city desk. Even Gene Miller, a man with a fondness for illegalities of all kinds, turned rather quickly from covering the cops to doing longer pieces. The *Herald*, which regularly shows up on lists of the country's most distinguished dailies, does take a certain amount of pride in providing the sort of crime coverage that is not typical of newspapers on such lists, but it does not have the sort of single-minded interest in juicy felonies that characterized the New York tabloids Edna used to read to her grandmother. When Edna Buchanan began covering the cops for the *Herald*, in 1973, there hadn't been anyone assigned full time to the beat in several years.

In the dozen years since, Edna has herself broken the routine now and then to do a long crime piece or a series. But she invariably returns to the daily beat. She still dresses every morning to the sound of a police scanner. Unless she already has a story to do, she still drops by the Miami Beach department and the Miami municipal department and the Metro-Dade department on the way to work. She still flips through the previous night's crime reports and the log. She still calls police officers and says, "Hi. This is Edna. What's going on over there?"

. . .

LIKE a lot of old-fashioned reporters, Edna Buchanan seems to operate on the assumption that there are always going to be any number of people who, for perverse and inexplicable reasons of their own, will try to impede her in gathering a story that is rightfully hers and delivering it to where God meant it to be—on the front page of the Miami *Herald,* and preferably the front page of the Miami *Herald* on a Sunday, when the circulation is at its highest. There are shy witnesses who insist that they don't want to get involved. There are lawyers who advise their clients to hang up if Edna Buchanan calls to ask whether they really did it. (It could be libellous for a newspaper to call someone a suspect, but the paper can get the same idea across by quoting his denial of guilt.) There are closemouthed policemen. There are television reporters who require equipment that gets in the way and who ask the sort of question that makes Edna impatient. (In her view, television reporters on a murder story are concerned almost exclusively with whether they're going to be able to get a picture of the authorities removing the body from the premises, the only other question that truly engages them being whether they're going to get the picture in time for the six-o'clock news.) There are editors who want to cut a story even though it was virtually ordained to run at least sixteen inches. There are editors—often the same editors—who will try to take an interesting detail out of the story simply because the detail happens to horrify or appall them. "One of them kept saying that people read this paper at *breakfast,*" I was told by Edna, whose own idea of a successful lead is one that might cause a reader who is having breakfast with his wife to "spit out his coffee, clutch his chest, and say, 'My God, Martha! Did you read this!' " When Edna went to Fort Lauderdale not long ago to talk about police reporting with some of the young reporters in the *Herald*'s Broward County bureau, she said, "For sanity and survival, there are three cardinal rules in the newsroom: Never trust an editor, never trust an editor, and never trust an editor."

Edna likes and admires a lot of policemen, but, listening to her talk about policemen, you can get the impression that they spend most of their energy trying to deny her access to information that she is meant to have. Police officers insist on roping off crime scenes. ("The police department has too much yellow rope—they want to rope off the world.") Entire departments switch over to computerized crime reports, which don't accommodate the sort of detailed narrative that Edna used to comb through in the old written reports. Investigators sometimes decline to talk about the case they're working on. (Edna distinguishes degrees of reticence among policemen with remarks like "He wasn't *quite* as paranoid as the other guy.") Some years ago, the man who was then chief of the Metro-Dade department blocked off the homicide squad with a buzzer-controlled entrance whose function was so apparent that it was commonly referred to as "the Edna Buchanan door." Homicide investigators who arrive at a scene and spot Edna talking intently with someone assume that she has found an eyewitness, and they often snatch him away with cautioning words about the errors of talking to the press rather than to the legally constituted authorities. Edna discusses the prevalence of witnessnapping among police detectives in the tone of voice a member of the Citizens Commission on Crime might reserve for talking about an alarming increase in multiple murders.

ONCE the police arrive at a crime scene in force, Edna often finds it more effective to return to the *Herald* and work by telephone. The alternative could be simply standing behind the yellow rope—an activity she considers fit for television reporters. She may try calling the snatched witness. With a cross-indexed directory, she can phone neighbors who might have seen what happened and then ducked back into their own house for a bolstering drink. She will try to phone the victim's next of kin. "I thought you'd like to say something," she'll say to someone's bereaved wife or daughter. "People care what he was like." Most reporters would sooner cover thirty weeks of water-board hearings than call a murder victim's next of kin, but Edna tries to look on the positive side. "For some people, it's like a catharsis," she told me one day. "They want to talk about what kind of person their husband was, or their father. Also, it's probably the only time his name is going to be in the paper. It's their last shot. They want to give him a good sendoff."

There are people, of course, who are willing to forgo the sendoff just to be left alone. Some of them respond to Edna's call by shouting at her for having the gall to trouble them at such a time, and then slamming down the telephone. Edna has a standard procedure for dealing with that. She waits sixty seconds and then phones back. "This is Edna Buchanan at the Miami *Herald*," she says, using her full name and identification for civilians. "I think we were cut off." In sixty seconds, she figures, whoever answered the phone might reconsider. Someone else in the room might say, "You should have talked to that reporter." Someone else in the room might decide to spare the upset party the pain of answering the phone the next time it rings, and might be a person who is more willing to talk. A couple of years ago, Edna called the home of a TV-repair-shop operator in his sixties who had been killed in a robbery attempt—a crime she had already managed to separate from the run-of-the-mill armed-robbery murder. ("On New Year's Eve Charles Curzio stayed later than planned at his small TV repair shop to make sure customers would have their sets in time to watch the King Orange Jamboree Parade," Edna's lead began. "His kindness cost his life.") One of Curzio's sons answered, and, upon learning who it was, angrily hung up. "Boy, did I hate dialling the second time," Edna told me. "But if I hadn't I might have lost them for good." This time, the phone was answered by another of Curzio's sons, and he was willing to talk. He had some eloquent things to say about his father and about capital punishment. ("My father got no trial, no stay of execution, no Supreme Court hearing, nothing. Just some maniac who smashed his brains in with a rifle butt.") If the second call hadn't

COVERING THE COPS 151

been productive, Edna told me, she would have given up: "The third call would be harassment."

WHEN Edna is looking for information, slamming down the phone must sometimes seem the only way of ending the conversation. She is not an easy person to say goodbye to. Once she begins asking questions, she may pause occasionally, as if the interrogation were finally over, but then, in the sort of silence that in conventional conversations is ended with someone's saying "Well, O.K." or "Well, thanks for your help," she asks another question. The questioning may not even concern a story she's working on. I was once present when Edna began chatting with a Metro-Dade homicide detective about an old murder case that he had never managed to solve—the apparently motiveless shooting of a restaurant proprietor and his wife, both along in years, as they were about to enter their house. Edna would ask a question and the detective would shake his head, explaining that he had checked out that angle without result. Then, after a pause long enough to make me think that they were about to go on to another case, she would ask another question. Could it have been a mistake in the address? Did homicide check out the people who lived in the equivalent house on the next block? Did the restaurant have any connection with the mob? How about an ex-employee? What about a bad son-in-law? Over the years, Edna has come across any number of bad sons-in-law.

Earlier in the day, I had heard her use the same tone to question a young policewoman who was watching over the front desk at Miami Beach headquarters. "What do you think the rest of Bo's secret is?" Edna said as she skimmed log notations about policemen being called to a loud party or to the scene of a robbery or to a vandalized garage. "Is Kimberly going to get an abortion?" At first, I thought the questions were about cases she was reminded of by the log reports. They turned out to be about "Days of Our Lives," a soap opera that both Edna and the policewoman are devoted to. Fifteen minutes later, long after I thought the subject had been dropped, Edna was saying, "So is this new character going to be a friend of Jennifer's—the one in the car wreck?"

Bob Swift, a *Herald* columnist who was once Edna's editor at a paper called the Miami Beach *Sun*, told me that he arrived at the *Sun*'s office one day fuming about the fact that somebody had stolen his garbage cans. "I was really mad," he said. "I was saying, 'Who would want to steal two garbage cans!' All of a sudden, I heard Edna say, in that breathless voice, 'Were they empty or full?' "

"NOBODY loves a police reporter," Edna sometimes says in speeches. She has been vilified and shouted at and threatened. Perhaps because a female police reporter was something of a rarity when she began, some policemen took pleasure in showing her, say, the corpse of someone who had met a particularly

nasty end. ("Sometimes they try to gross you out, but when you're really curious you don't get grossed out. I'm always saying, 'What's this? What's that?' ")
When Edna was asked by David Finkel, who did a story about her for the St.
Petersburg *Times*, why she endured the rigors of covering the cops, she replied,
"It's better than working in a coat factory in Paterson, New Jersey." Working
in the coat factory was one of several part-time jobs that she had as a school-
girl to help her mother out. Aside from the pleasures Edna associates with
reading crime stories to her Polish grandmother, she doesn't have many happy
memories of Paterson. Her other grandmother—her mother's mother—was a
member of the Daughters of the American Revolution; Edna still has the
membership certificate to prove it. That grandmother, in the view of her D.A.R.
family, married beneath her—her husband was a Paterson schoolteacher—
and her own daughter, Edna's mother, did even worse. She married a Polish
factory worker who apparently had some local renown as a drinker and
carouser, and he walked out when Edna was seven. As soon as Edna finished
high school, an institution she loathed, she joined her mother in wiring switchboards at the Western Electric plant. Eventually, she transferred to an office job
at Western Electric—still hardly the career path that normally leads to a reporting job on the Miami *Herald*.

The enormous change in Edna's life came partly because a clotheshorse
friend who wanted to take a course in millinery design persuaded her to come
along to evening classes at Montclair State Teachers College. Edna, who had
been interested in writing as a child, decided to take a course in creative writing.
She remembers the instructor as a thin, poetic-looking man who travelled to
New Jersey every week from Greenwich Village. He may have had a limp—a war
wound, perhaps. She is much clearer about what happened when he handed
back the first short stories the students had written. First, he described one he
had particularly liked, and it was Edna's—a sort of psychological thriller about
a young woman who thought she was being followed. Edna can still recall what
the teacher said about the story—about what a rare pleasure it was for a teacher
to come across such writing, about how one section reminded him of early
Tennessee Williams. It was the one radiant New Jersey moment. The teacher
told her about writers she should read. He told her about paragraphing; the first
story she turned in was "just one long paragraph." She decided that she could
be a writer. Years later, a novelist who had been hanging around with Edna for
a while to learn about crime reporting recognized the teacher from Edna's description and provided his telephone number. She phoned him to tell him how
much his encouragement had meant to her. He was pleasant enough, Edna told
me, but he didn't remember her or her short story.

Not long after the writing course, Edna and her mother decided to take their
vacation in Miami Beach, and Edna says that as she walked off the plane she
knew she was not going to spend the rest of her life in Paterson, New Jersey.
"The instant I breathed the air, it was like coming home," she told me. "I loved

it. I absolutely loved it. I had been wandering around in a daze up there, like a displaced person. I was always a misfit." Edna and her mother tried to get jobs at the Western Electric plant in South Florida; when they couldn't arrange that, they moved anyway. While taking a course in writing, Edna heard that the Miami Beach *Sun* was looking for reporters. The *Sun,* which is now defunct, was the sort of newspaper that hired people without any reporting experience and gave them a lot of it quickly. Edna wrote society news and local political stories and crime stories and celebrity interviews and movie reviews and, on occasion, the letters to the editor.

Now, years later, Edna Buchanan may be the best-known newspaper reporter in Miami, but sometimes she still sounds as if she can't quite believe that she doesn't work in a factory and doesn't live in Paterson, New Jersey. "I've lived here more than twenty years," she said recently. "And every day I see the palm trees and the water and the beach, and I'm thrilled with how beautiful it is. I'm really lucky, coming from a place like Paterson, New Jersey. I live on a waterway. I have a house. I almost feel, My God, it's like I'm an impostor!"

When Edna says such things, she sounds grateful—a state that an old newspaper hand would tell you is about as common among reporters as a prolonged, religiously inspired commitment to the temperance movement. Edna can even sound grateful for the opportunity to work the police beat—although in the next sentence she may be talking about how tired she is of hearing policemen gripe or how irritated she gets at editors who live to pulverize her copy. She seems completely lacking in the black humor or irony that reporters often use to cope with even a short hitch covering the cops. When she says something is interesting as heck, she means that it is interesting as heck.

Some years ago, she almost went over to the enemy. A Miami television station offered her a hundred and thirty-seven dollars more a week than she was making at the *Herald,* and she had just about decided to take it. She had some ideas about how crime could be covered on television in a way that did not lean so heavily on pictures of the body being removed from the premises. At the last moment, though, she decided not to accept the offer. One reason, she now says, is that she faced the fact that crime could never be covered on local television with the details and the subtleties possible in a newspaper story. Also, she couldn't quite bring herself to leave the *Herald.* "If I had been eighteen, maybe I would have done it," she says. "But the *Herald* is the only security I ever had."

EVEN before the appearance of "Miami Vice," Miami was the setting of choice for tales of flashy violence. Any number of people, some of them current or former *Herald* reporters, have portrayed Miami crime in mystery novels or television shows or Hollywood movies. Some of the show-business types might have been attracted mainly by the palm trees and the beach and the exotica of the Latin drug industry: the opening shots of each "Miami Vice" episode are so glamorous that some local tourist-development people have been quoted in the *Herald* as saying that the overall impact of the series is positive. But the volume and the variety of real crime in Miami have in fact been of an order to make any police reporter feel the way a stockbroker might feel at a medical convention: opportunities abound. Like most police reporters, Edna specializes in murder, and, as she might express it in a Miller Chop at the end of the first paragraph, so does Miami.

When Edna began as a reporter, a murder in Miami was an occasion. A woman who worked with Edna at the Miami Beach *Sun* in the days when it was sometimes known as "Bob Swift and his all-girl newspaper" has recalled the stir in the *Sun* newsroom when a body washed up on the beach: "I had a camera, because my husband had given it to me for Christmas. The managing editor said, 'Go take a picture of the body.' I said, 'I'm not taking a picture of a washed-up body!' Then I heard a voice from the other end of the room saying, 'I'll do it, I'll do it.' It was Edna."

In the late seventies, Miami, like other American cities, had a steady increase in the sort of murders that occur when, say, an armed man panics while he is robbing a convenience store. It also had some political bombings and some shooting between outfits that were, depending on your point of view, either running drugs to raise money for fighting Fidel or using the fight against Fidel as a cover for running drugs. At the end of the decade, Dade County's murder rate took an astonishing upturn. Around that time, the Colombians who manufactured the drugs being distributed in Miami by Cubans decided to eliminate the middleman, and, given a peculiar viciousness in the way they customarily operated, that sometimes meant eliminating the middleman's wife and whoever else happened to be around. Within a couple of years after the Colombians began their campaign to reduce overhead, Miami was hit with the Mariel-boat-lift refugees. In 1977, there were two hundred and eleven murders in Dade County. By 1981, the high point of Dade murder, there were six hundred and twenty-one. That meant, according to one homicide detective I spoke to, that Miami experienced the greatest increase in murders per capita that any city had ever recorded. It also meant that Miami had the highest murder rate in the country. It also meant that a police reporter could drive to work in the morning knowing that there would almost certainly be at least one murder to write about.

"A personal question," one of the Broward-bureau reporters said after Edna had finished her talk in Fort Lauderdale. "I hope not to embarrass you, but I've always heard a rumor that you carried a gun. Is that true?"

"I don't carry a gun," Edna said. "I own a gun or two." She keeps one in the house and one in the car—which seems only sensible, she told the reporters, for someone who lives alone and is often driving through unpleasant neighborhoods late at night. It also seems only sensible to spend some time on the shooting range, which she happens to enjoy. ("They let me shoot an Uzi the other day," she once told me. "It was interesting as heck.") A lot of what Edna says about her life seems only sensible, but a lot of it turns out to have something to do with violence or crime, the stuff of an Edna story. Talking about her paternal grandfather, she'll say that he was supposed to have killed or maimed someone in a barroom brawl and that his children were so frightened of his drunken rages that the first sign of an eruption would send some of them leaping out of second-floor windows to escape. As an example of her nearsightedness, she'll mention some revelations in Paterson that seemed to indicate that she had been followed for months by a notorious sex criminal without realizing it. When Edna talks about places where she has lived in Miami, she is likely to identify neighbors with observations like "He lived right across the street from this big dope dealer" or "He was indicted for Medicare fraud but he beat it."

Edna's first marriage, to someone she met while she was working at the Miami Beach *Sun*, could provide any number of classic Edna leads. James Buchanan had some dealings with the anti-Castro community, and was close to Frank Sturgis, one of the Watergate burglars. Edna says that for some time she thought her husband was simply a reporter on the Fort Lauderdale *Sun-Sentinel* who seemed to be out of town more than absolutely necessary. The story she sometimes tells of how she discovered otherwise could be written with an Edna lead: "James Buchanan seemed to make a lot of unexplained trips. Yesterday, at the supermarket, his wife found out why. Mrs. Buchanan, accompanied by a bag boy who was carrying a large load of groceries, emerged from the supermarket and opened the trunk of her car. It was full of machine guns. 'Just put the groceries in the back seat,' she said."

Edna tried a cop the next time, but that didn't seem to have much effect on the duration or quality of the marriage. Her second husband, Emmett Miller, was on the Miami Beach force for years, and was eventually appointed chief. By that time, though, he had another wife, his fifth—a wife who, it turned out, was part owner of what the *Herald* described as "an X-rated Biscayne Boulevard motel and a Beach restaurant alleged to be a center of illegal gambling." The appointment was approved by the Miami Beach City Commission anyway, although one commissioner, who stated that the police chief ought to be "above suspicion," did say, "I don't think we're putting our city in an enviable position when we overlook this."

Since the breakup of her marriage to Miller, Edna has almost never been seen at parties or *Herald* hangouts. "I love to be alone," she says. One of the people closest to her is still her mother, who lives not far from Edna and seems to produce ceramic animals even faster than she once turned out fully wired switchboards. Edna's house is a menagerie of ceramic animals. She also has ceramic planters and a ceramic umbrella holder and a ceramic lighthouse—not to speak of a watercolor and a sketch by Jack (Murph the Surf) Murphy, the Miami beachboy who in 1964 helped steal the Star of India sapphire and the

deLong Star Ruby from the American Museum of Natural History—but ceramic animals are the predominant design element. She has penguins and turtles and horses and seagulls and flamingos and swans and fish and a rabbit and
a pelican. She has a ceramic dog that is nearly life-size. She has cats in practically every conceivable pose—a cat with nursing kittens, a cat carrying a kit-
ten in its mouth, a curled-up cat. Edna is fond of some of the ceramic animals,
but the fact that her mother's productivity seems to be increasing rather than
waning with the passing of the years has given her pause.

All of Edna's live animals are strays. Besides the cats, she has a dog whose
best trick is to fall to the floor when Edna points an imaginary gun at him and
says, "Bang! You're dead!" Some colleagues at the *Herald* think that a stray animal is about the only thing that can distract Edna from her coverage of the
cops. It is assumed at the *Herald* that she takes Mondays and Tuesdays off because the weekend is traditionally a high-crime period. (Edna says that the
beaches are less crowded during the week, and that working weekends gives
her a better chance at the Sunday paper.) Around the *Herald* newsroom, Edna
is known for being fiercely proprietary about stories she considers hers—any
number of *Herald* reporters, running into her at the scene of some multiple
murder or major disaster, have been greeted with an icy "What are *you* doing
here?"—and so combative about her copy that a few of the less resilient editors
have been reduced almost to the state in which they would fall to the floor if
Edna pointed an imaginary gun at them and said, "Bang! You're dead!" Edna's
colleagues tend to speak of her not as a pal but as a phenomenon. Their Edna
stories are likely to concern her tenacity or her superstitions or the remarkable
intensity she maintains after all these years of covering a beat that quickly
strikes many reporters as unbearably horrifying or depressing. They often
mention the astonishing contrast between her apparent imperviousness to the
grisly sights on the police beat and her overwhelming concern for animals.
While I was in Miami, two or three *Herald* reporters suggested that I look up
some articles in which, as they remembered it, Edna hammered away so intensely at a retired French-Canadian priest who had put to death some stray
cats that the poor man was run out of the country. When I later told one of the
reporters that I had read the *Herald*'s coverage of the incident and that almost
none of it had been done by Edna, he said, "I'm not surprised. Probably didn't
trust herself. Too emotionally involved."

POLICEMEN, Edna told the young reporters in Fort Lauderdale, have an in-
stinctive mistrust of outsiders—"an 'us-and-them' attitude." Edna can never
be certain which category she's in. Any police reporter these days is likely to
have a less comfortable relationship with the police than the one enjoyed by the
old-fashioned station-house reporter who could be counted on to be looking
the other way if the suspect met with an accident while he was being taken into

custody. Since Watergate, reporters all over the country have been under pressure to cast a more suspicious eye on any institution they cover. Partly because of the availability of staggering amounts of drug money, both the Miami and the Metro-Dade departments have had serious scandals in recent years, making them particularly sensitive to inspection by critical outsiders. The *Herald* has covered police misconduct prominently, and it has used Florida's public-records act aggressively in court to gain access to police documents—even documents involved in Internal Affairs investigations. A lot of policemen regard the *Herald* as their adversary and see Edna Buchanan as the embodiment of the *Herald*.

Edna says that she makes every effort to portray cops as human beings—writing about a police officer who has been charged with misconduct, she usually manages to find some past commendations to mention—but it has never occurred to anybody that she might look the other way. Edna broke the story of an attempted coverup involving a black insurance man named Arthur McDuffie, who died as a result of injuries suffered in an encounter with some Metro-Dade policemen—policemen whose acquittal on manslaughter charges some months later touched off three nights of rioting in Miami's black community. There are moments when Edna seems to be "us" and "them" at the same time. Keeping the picture and the press release sent when someone is named Officer of the Month may give Edna one extra positive sentence to write about a policeman the next time she mentions him; also, as it happens, it is difficult to come by a picture of a cop who gets in trouble, and over the years Edna has found that a cop who gets in trouble and a cop who was named Officer of the Month are often the same person.

"There's a love-hate relationship between the police and the press," Mike Gonzalez, one of Edna's best friends on the Miami municipal force, says. A case that Edna covers prominently is likely to get a lot of attention in the department, which means that someone whose name is attached to it might become a hero or might, as one detective I spoke to put it, "end up in the complaint room of the property bureau." Edna says that the way a reporter is received at police headquarters can depend on "what you wrote the day before—or their perception of what you wrote the day before."

Some police officers in Dade County won't talk to Edna Buchanan about the case they're working on. Some of those who do give her tips—not just on their own cases but on cases being handled by other people, or even other departments—won't admit it. (According to Dr. Joseph Davis, the medical examiner of Dade County, "Every police agency thinks she has a direct pipeline into someone else's agency.") Cops who become known as friends and sources of Edna's are likely to be accused by other cops of showboating or of trying to further their careers through the newspaper. When I mentioned Mike Gonzalez to a Metro-Dade lieutenant I was talking to in Miami, he said, "What Howard Cosell did for Cassius Clay, Edna Buchanan did for Mike Gonzalez."

Gonzalez is aware of such talk, and doesn't show much sign of caring about it. He thinks most policemen are nervous about the press because they aren't confident that they can reveal precisely what they find it useful to reveal and no more. Edna's admirers among police investigators—people like Gonzalez and Lloyd Hough, a Metro-Dade homicide detective—tend to admire her for her skill and independence as an investigator. "I'd take her any time as a partner," Hough told me. "Let's put it like this: If I had done something, I wouldn't want Edna investigating me. Internal Affairs I don't care about, but Edna . . ." They also admire her persistence, maddening as it may sometimes be. Hough nearly had her arrested once when she persisted in coming under the yellow rope into a crime scene. "She knows when she's pushed you to the limit, and she'll do that often," Hough told me. "And I say that with the greatest admiration."

A police detective and a police reporter may sound alike as they stand around talking about past cases—recalling the airline pilot who killed the other airline pilot over the stewardess, or exchanging anecdotes about the ag-grieved bag boy who cleared a Publix supermarket in a hurry by holding a re-volver to the head of the manager—but their interests in a murder case are not necessarily the same. If an armed robber kills a convenience-store clerk, the po-lice are interested in catching him; Edna is interested in distinguishing what happened from other killings of other convenience-store clerks. To write about any murder, Edna is likely to need details that wouldn't help an investigator close the case. "I want to know what movie they saw before they got gunned down," she has said. "What were they wearing? What did they have in their pockets? What was cooking on the stove? What song was playing on the juke-box?" Mike Gonzalez just sighs when he talks about Edna's appetite for irrele-vant detail. "It infuriates Mike," Edna says. "I always ask what the dog's name is, what the cat's name is." Edna told me that Gonzalez now advises rookie de-tectives that they might as well gather such details, because otherwise "you're just going to feel stupid when Edna asks you."

THERE are times when Edna finds herself longing for simpler times on the po-lice beat. When she began, the murders she covered tended to be conventional love triangles or armed robberies. She was often dealing with "an up-front per-son who happened to have bludgeoned his wife to death." These days, the mur-ders are likely to be Latin drug murders, and a lot fewer of them produce a suspect. Trying to gather information from Cubans and Central Americans, Edna has a problem that goes beyond the language barrier. "They have a Latin love of intrigue," she says. "I had a Cuban informant, and I found that he would sometimes lie to me just to make it more interesting." It is also true that even for a police reporter there can be too many murders. Edna says that she was "a little shell-shocked" four or five years ago, when Dade murders hit their peak. She found that she barely had time to make her rounds in a thorough way. "I used to like to stop at the jail," she has said. "I used to like to browse in the morgue. To make sure who's there."

Edna found that the sheer number of murders overwhelmed each individual murder as the big story. "Dade's murder rate hit new heights this week as a wave of unrelated violence left 14 people dead and five critically hurt within five days," a story bylined Edna Buchanan began in June of 1980. After a couple of paragraphs comparing the current murder figures with those of previous years, the story went on, "In the latest wave of violence, a teenager's throat was cut and her body dumped in a canal. A former airline stewardess was garroted and left with a pair of scissors stuck between her shoulder blades. Four innocent by-standers were shot in a barroom gun battle. An 80-year-old man surprised a burglar who battered him fatally with a hammer. An angry young woman who 'felt used' beat her date to death with the dumbbells he used to keep fit. And an apparent robbery victim was shot dead as he ran away from the robbers." The murder rate has levelled off since 1981, but Edna still sometimes writes what amount to murder-roundup stories. "I feel bad, and even a little guilty, that a murder no longer gets a story, just a paragraph," she says. "It dehumanizes it." A paragraph in a roundup piece is not Edna's idea of a sendoff.

On a day I was making the rounds with Edna, there was a police report say-ing that two Marielitos had begun arguing on the street and the argument had ended with one shooting the other dead. That sounded like a paragraph at most. But Edna had a tip that the victim and the killer had known each other in Cuba and the shooting was actually the settling of an old prison score. That sounded to me more like a murder that stood out a bit from the crowd. Edna thought so, too, but her enthusiasm was limited. "We've already had a couple of those," she told me. Edna has covered a few thousand murders by now, and she's seen a couple of most things. She has done stories about a man who was stabbed to death because he stepped on somebody's toes on his way to a seat in a movie theatre and about a two-year-old somebody tried to frame for the mur-der of a playmate and about an eighty-nine-year-old man who was arrested for beating his former wife to death and about a little boy killed by a crocodile. She has done stories about a woman who committed suicide because she couldn't get her leaky roof fixed and about a newspaper deliveryman who committed suicide because during a petroleum shortage he couldn't get enough gasoline. She has done stories about a man who managed to commit suicide by stabbing himself in the heart *twice* and about a man who threw a severed head at a po-lice officer twice. She has done a story about two brothers who killed a third brother because he interrupted a checkers game. ("I thought I had the best-raised children in the world," their mother said.) She has done a story about a father being killed at the surprise birthday party given for him by his thirty children. She has done a story about a man who died because fourteen of the eighty-two double-wrapped condom packages of cocaine he tried to carry into the country inside his stomach began to leak. ("His last meal was worth

$30,000 and it killed him.") She has done any number of stories about bodies being discovered in the bay by beachcombers or fishermen or University of Miami scientists doing marine research. (" 'It's kind of a nuisance when you plan your day to do research on the reef,' fumed Professor Peter Glynn, of the university's Rosenstiel School of Marine and Atmospheric Science.") Talking to Edna one day about murder cases they had worked on, a Metro-Dade homicide detective said, "In Dade County, there are no surprises left."

Edna would agree that surprises are harder to find in Dade County these days. Still, she finds them. Flipping through page after page of routine police logs, talking to her sources on the telephone, chatting with a homicide detective, she'll come across, say, a shopping-mall murder that might have been done against the background of a new kind of high-school gang, or a murderer who seemed to have been imprisoned with his victim for a time by a sophisticated burglar-gate system. Then, a look of concern still on her face, she'll say, "That's interesting as heck."

(1986)

TRAVELS IN GEORGIA

I ASKED for the gorp. Carol passed it to me. Breakfast had been heavy with cathead biscuits, sausage, boiled eggs, Familia, and chicory coffee, but that was an hour ago and I was again hungry. Sam said, "The little Yankee bastard wants the gorp, Carol. Shall we give him some?" Sam's voice was as soft as sphagnum, with inflections of piedmont Georgia.

"The little Yankee bastard can have all he wants this morning," Carol said. "It's such a beautiful day."

Although Sam was working for the state, he was driving his own Chevrolet. He was doing seventy. In a reverberation of rubber, he crossed Hunger and Hardship Creek and headed into the sun on the Swainsboro Road. I took a ration of gorp—soybeans, sunflower seeds, oats, pretzels, Wheat Chex, raisins, and kelp—and poured another ration into Carol's hand. At just about that moment, a snapping turtle was hit on the road a couple of miles ahead of us, who knows by what sort of vehicle, a car, a pickup; run over like a manhole cover, probably with much the same sound, and not crushed, but gravely wounded. It remained still. It appeared to be dead on the road.

Sam, as we approached, was the first to see it. "D.O.R.," he said. "Man, that is a big snapper." Carol and I both sat forward. Sam pressed hard on the brakes. Even so, he was going fifty when he passed the turtle.

Carol said, "He's not dead. He didn't look dead."

Sam reversed. He drove backward rapidly, fast as the car would go. He stopped on the shoulder, and we all got out. There was a pond beyond the turtle. The big, broad head was shining with blood, but there was, as yet, very little blood on the road. The big jaws struck as we came near, opened and closed bloodily—not the kind of strike that, minutes ago, could have cut off a finger, but still a strike with power. The turtle was about fourteen inches long and a shining horn-brown. The bright spots on its marginal scutes were like light bulbs around a mirror. The neck lunged out. Carol urged the turtle, with her foot, toward the side of the road. "I know, big man," she said to it. "I know it's bad. We're not tormenting you. Honest we're not." Sam asked her if she thought it had a chance to live and she said she was sure it had no chance at all. A car, coming west, braked down and stopped. The driver got out, with some effort and a big paunch. He looked at the turtle and said, "Fifty years old if he's a day." That was the whole of what the man had to say. He got into his car and drove on. Carol nudged the snapper, but it was too hurt to move. It could only strike the air. Now, in a screech of brakes, another car came onto the scene. It went by us, then spun around with squealing tires and pulled up on the far shoulder. It was a two-tone, high-speed, dome-lighted Ford, and in it was the sheriff of Laurens County. He got out and walked toward us, all Technicolor in his uniform, legs striped like a pine-barrens tree frog's, plastic plate on his chest, name of Wade.

"Good morning," Sam said to him.

"How y'all?" said Sheriff Wade.

Carol said, "Would you mind shooting this turtle for us, please?"

"Surely, Ma'am," said the sheriff, and he drew his .38. He extended his arm and took aim.

"Uh, Sheriff," I said. "If you don't mind . . ." And I asked him if he would kindly shoot the turtle over soil and not over concrete. The sheriff paused and looked slowly, with new interest, from one of us to another: a woman in her twenties, good-looking, with long tawny hair, no accent (that he could hear), barefoot, and wearing a gray sweatshirt and brown dungarees with a hunting knife in the belt; a man (Sam) around forty, in weathered khaki, also without an accent, and with a full black beard divided by a short white patch at the chin—an authentic, natural split beard; and then this incongruous little Yankee bastard telling him not to shoot the road. Carol picked up the turtle by its long, serrated tail and carried it, underside toward her leg, beyond the shoulder of the highway, where she set it down on a patch of grass. The sheriff followed with his .38. He again took aim. He steadied the muzzle of the pistol twelve inches from the turtle. He fired, and missed. The gun made an absurdly light sound, like a screen door shutting. He fired again. He missed. He fired again. The third shot killed the turtle. The pistol smoked. The sheriff blew the smoke away, and smiled, apparently at himself. He shook his head a little. "He should be good," he said, with a nod at the turtle. The sheriff crossed the road and got into his car. "Y'all be careful," he said. With a great screech of tires, he wheeled around and headed on west.

Carol guessed that the turtle was about ten years old. By the tail, she carried it down to the edge of the pond, like a heavy suitcase with a broken strap. Sam fetched plastic bags from the car. I found a long two-by-ten plank and carried it to the edge of the water. Carol placed the snapper upside down on the plank. Kneeling, she unsheathed her hunting knife and began, in a practiced and professional way, to slice around the crescents in the plastron, until the flesh of the legs—in thick steaks of red meat—came free. Her knife was very sharp. She put the steaks into a plastic bag. All the while, she talked to the dead turtle, soothingly, reassuringly, nurse to patient, doctor to child, and when she reached in under the plastron and found an ovary, she shifted genders with a grunt of surprise. She pulled out some globate yellow fat and tossed it into the pond. Hundreds of mosquito fish came darting through the water, sank their teeth, shook their heads, worried the fat. Carol began to remove eggs from the turtle's body. The eggs were like ping-pong balls in size, shape, and color, and how they all fitted into the turtle was more than I could comprehend, for there were fifty-six of them in there, fully finished, and a number that had not quite taken their ultimate form. "Look at those eggs. Aren't they beautiful?" Carol said. "Oh, that's sad. You were just about to do your thing, weren't you, girl?" That was why the snapper had gone out of the pond and up onto the road. She was going to bury her eggs in some place she knew, perhaps drawn by an atavistic attachment to the place where she herself had hatched out and where many generations of her forebears had been born when there was no road at all. The turtle twitched. Its neck moved. Its nerves were still working, though its life was gone. The nails on the ends of the claws were each an inch long. The turtle draped one of these talons over one of Carol's fingers. Carol withdrew more fat and threw a huge hunk into the pond. "Wouldn't it be fun to analyze *that* for pesticides?" she said. "You're fat as a pig, Mama. You sure lived high off the hog." Finishing the job—it took forty minutes—Carol found frog bones in the turtle. She put more red meat into plastic sacks and divided the eggs. She kept half for us to eat. With her knife she carefully buried the remaining eggs, twenty-eight or so, in a sandbank, much as the mother turtle might have been doing at just that time. Carol picked away some leeches from between her fingers. The leeches had come off the turtle's shell. She tied the sacks and said, "All right. That's all we can say grace over. Let's send her back whence she came." Picking up the inedible parts—plastron, carapace, neck, claws—she heaved them into the pond. They hit with a slap and sank without bubbles.

AS we moved east, pine trees kept giving us messages—small, handpainted signs nailed into the loblollies. "HAVE YOU WHAT IT TAKES TO MEET JESUS WHEN HE RETURNS?" Sam said he was certain he did not. "JESUS WILL NEVER FAIL YOU." City limits, Adrian, Georgia. Swainsboro, Georgia. Portal, Georgia. Towns on the long, straight roads of the coastal plain. White-painted, tin-roofed bungalows. Awnings shading the fronts of stores—prepared for heat and glare. Red earth. Sand roads. Houses on short stilts. Sloping verandas. Unpainted boards.

"D.O.R.," said Carol.

"What do you suppose that was?"

"I don't know. I didn't see. It could have been a squirrel."

Sam backed up to the D.O.R. It was a brown thrasher. Carol looked it over, and felt it. Sam picked it up. "Throw him far off the road," Carol said. "So a possum won't get killed while eating him." Sam threw the bird far off the road. A stop for a D.O.R. always brought the landscape into detailed focus. Pitch coming out of a pine. Clustered sows behind a fence. An automobile wrapped in vines. A mailbox. "Donald Foskey." His home. Beyond the mailbox, a set of cinder blocks, and on the cinder blocks a mobile home. As Sam regathered speed, Carol turned on the radio and moved the dial. If she could find some Johnny Cash, it would elevate her day. Some Johnny Cash was not hard to find in the airwaves of Georgia. There he was now, resonantly singing about his Mississippi Delta land, where, on a sharecropping farm, he grew up. Carol smiled and closed her eyes. In her ears—pierced ears—were gold maple leaves that seemed to move under the influence of the music.

"D.O.R. possum," Sam said, stopping again. "Two! A grown one and a baby." They had been killed probably ten minutes before. Carol carried the adult to the side of the road and left it there. She kept the baby. He was seven inches long. He was half tail. Although dead, he seemed virtually undamaged. We moved on. Carol had a clipboard she used for making occasional notes and sketches. She put the little possum on the clipboard and rested the clipboard on her knees. "Oh, you sweet little angel. How could anybody run over *you*?" she said. "Oh, I just love possums. I've raised so many of them. This is a great age. They are the neatest little animals. They love you so much. They crawl on your shoulder and hang in your hair. How people can dislike them I don't understand." Carol reached into the back seat and put the little opossum into a container of formaldehyde. After a while, she said, "What mystifies me is: that big possum back there was a male."

Bethel Primitive Baptist Church. Old Canoochee Primitive Baptist Church. "THE CHURCH HAS NO INDULGENCES." A town every ten miles, a church—so it seemed—every two. Carol said she frequently slept in church graveyards. They were, for one thing, quiet, and, for another, private. Graham Memorial Church of the Nazarene.

Sam and Carol both sat forward at the same moment, alert, excited. "D.O.R. Wow! That was something special. It had a long yellow belly and brown fur or feathers! Hurry, Sam. It's a good one." Sam backed up at forty miles an hour and strained the Chevrolet.

"What is it? What is it?"

"It's a piece of bark. Fell off a pulpwood truck."

The approach to Pembroke was made with a sense of infiltration—Pembroke, seat of Bryan County. "Remember, now, we're interested in frogs," Sam said, and we went up the steps of Bryan County Courthouse. "We understand there is a stream-channelization project going on near here. Could you tell us where? We're collecting frogs." It is hard to say what the clerks in the courthouse thought of this group—the spokesman with the black-and-white beard, the shoeless young woman, and their silent companion. They looked at us—they in their pumps and print dresses—from the other side of a distance. The last thing they might have imagined was that two of the three of us were representing the state government in Atlanta. The clerks did not know where the channelization was going on but they knew who might—a woman in town who knew everything. We went to see her. A chicken ran out of her house when she opened the screen door. No, she was not sure just where we should go, but try a man named Miller in Lanier. He'd know. He knew everything. Lanier was five miles down the track—literally so. The Seaboard Coast Line ran beside the road. Miller was a thickset man with unbelievably long, sharp fingernails, a driver of oil trucks. It seemed wonderful that he could get his hands around the wheel without cutting himself, that he could deliver oil without cutting the hose. He said, "Do you mind my asking why you're interested in stream channelization?"

"We're interested in frogs," Sam said. "Snakes and frogs. We thought the project might be stirring some up."

Miller said, "I don't mind the frog, but I want no part of the snake."

His directions were perfect—through pine forests, a right, two lefts, to where a dirt road crossed a tributary of the Ogeechee. A wooden bridge there had been replaced by a culvert. The stream now flowed through big pipes in the culvert. Upriver, far as the eye could see, a riparian swath had been cut by chain saws. Back from the banks, about fifty feet on each side, the overstory and the understory—every tree, bush, and sapling—had been cut down. The river was under revision. It had been freed of meanders. It was now two yards wide between vertical six-foot banks; and it was now as straight as a ditch. It had, in fact, become a ditch—in it a stream of thin mud, flowing. An immense yellow machine, slowly backing upstream, had in effect eaten this river. It was at work now, grunting and belching, two hundred yards from the culvert. We tried to walk toward it along the bank but sank to our shins in black ooze. The stumps of the cut trees were all but covered with mud from the bottom of the river. We crossed the ditch. The dredged mud was somewhat firmer on the other side. Sam and I walked there. Carol waded upcurrent in the stream. The machine was an American dragline crane. The word "American" stood out on its cab in letters more than a foot high. Its boom reached up a hundred feet. Its bucket took six-foot bites. As we approached, the bucket kept eating the riverbed, then swinging up and out of the channel and disgorging tons of mud to either side. Carol began to take pictures. She took more and more pictures as she waded on upstream. When she was fifty feet away from the dragline, its engine coughed down and stopped. The sudden serenity was oddly disturbing. The operator stepped out of the cab and onto the catwalk. One hand on the flank of his crane, he inclined his head somewhat forward and stared down at Carol. He was a stocky man with an open shirt and an open face, deeply tanned. He said, "Howdy."

"Howdy," said Carol.

"You're taking some pictures," he said.

"I sure am. I'm taking some pictures. I'm interested in the range extension of river frogs, and the places they live. I bet you turn up some interesting things."

"I see some frogs," the man said. "I see lots of frogs."

"You sure know what you're doing with that machine," Carol said. The man shifted his weight. "That's a *big* thing," she went on. "How much does it weigh?"

"Eighty-two tons."

"Eighty-two *tons?*"

"Eighty-two tons."

"Wow! How far can you dig in one day?"

"Five hundred feet."

"A mile every ten days," Sam said, shaking his head with awe.

"Sometimes I do better than that."

"You live around here?"

"No. My home's near Baxley. I go where I'm sent. All over the state."

"Well, sorry. Didn't mean to interrupt you."

"Not 't all. Take all the pictures you want."

"Thanks. What did you say your name was?"

"Chap," he said. "Chap Causey."

We walked around the dragline, went upstream a short way, and sat down on the trunk of a large oak, felled by the chain saws, to eat our lunch—sardines, chocolate, crackers, and wine. Causey at work was the entertainment, pulling his levers, swinging his bucket, having at the stream.

If he had been at first wary, he no doubt had had experience that made him so. All over the United States, but particularly in the Southeast, his occupation had become a raw issue. He was working for the Soil Conservation Service, a subdivision of the United States Department of Agriculture, making a "water-resource channel improvement"—generally known as stream channelization, or reaming a river. Behind his dragline, despite the clear-cutting of the riverine trees, was a free-flowing natural stream, descending toward the Ogeechee in bends and eddies, riffles and deeps—in appearance somewhere between a trout stream and a bass river, and still handsomely so, even though it was shaved and ready for its operation. At the dragline, the recognizable river disappeared, and below the big machine was a kind of reverse irrigation ditch, engineered to re-move water rapidly from the immediate watershed. "How could anyone even conceive of this idea?" Sam said. "Not just to do it, but even to *conceive* of it?"

The purpose of such projects was to anticipate and eliminate floods, to drain swamps, to increase cropland, to channel water toward freshly created reser-voirs serving and attracting new industries and new housing developments.

Water sports would flourish on the new reservoirs, hatchery fish would proliferate below the surface: new pulsations in the life of the rural South. The Soil Conservation Service was annually spending about fifteen million dollars on stream-channelization projects, providing, among other things, newly arable land to farmers who already had land in the Soil Bank. The Department of Agriculture could not do enough for the Southern farmer, whose only problem was bookkeeping. He got money for keeping his front forty idle. His bottomland went up in value when the swamps were drained, and then more money came for not farming the drained land. Years earlier, when a conservationist had been someone who plowed land along natural contours, the Soil Conservation Service had been the epicenter of the conservation movement, decorated for its victories over erosion of the land. Now, to a new generation that had discovered ecology, the S.C.S. was the enemy. Its drainage programs tampered with river mechanics, upsetting the relationships between bass and otter, frog and owl. The Soil Conservation Service had grown over the years into a bureau of fifteen thousand people, and all the way down at the working point, the cutting edge of things, was Chap Causey, in the cab of his American dragline, hearing nothing but the pounding of his big Jimmy diesel while he eliminated a river, eradicated a swamp.

After heaving up a half-dozen buckets of mud, Causey moved backward several feet. The broad steel shoes of the crane were resting on oak beams that were bound together in pairs with cables. There were twelve beams in all. Collectively, they were called "mats." Under the crane, they made a temporary bridge over the river. As Causey moved backward and off the front pair of beams, he would reach down out of the sky with a hook from his boom and snare a loop of the cable that held the beams. He snatched them up—they weighed at least half a ton—and whipped them around to the back. The beams dropped perfectly into place, adding a yard to Causey's platform on the upstream side. Near the tree line beyond one bank, he had a fuel tank large enough to bury under a gas station, and every so often he would reach out with his hook and his hundred-foot arm and, without groping, lift the tank and move it on in the direction he was going. With his levers, his cables, his bucket, and hook, he handled his mats and his tank and his hunks of the riverbed as if he were dribbling a basketball through his legs and behind his back. He was deft. He was world class. "I bet he could put on a baby's diapers with that thing," Sam said.

Carol said, "See that three-foot stump? I sure would like to see him pull *that* out." She gestured toward the rooted remains of a tree that must have stood, a week earlier, a hundred and fifty feet high. Causey, out of the corner of his eye, must have seen the gesture. Perhaps he just read her mind. He was much aware that he was being watched, and now he reached around behind him, grabbed the stump in his bucket, and ripped it out of the earth like a molar. He set it at Carol's feet. It towered over her.

After a modest interval, a few more buckets of streambed, Causey shut off the dragline and stopped for an adulation break. Carol told him he was fabulous. And she meant it. He was. She asked him what the name of the stream was. He said, "To tell you the truth, Ma'am, I don't rightly know."

CAROL said, "Do you see many snakes?"

"Oh, yes, I see lots of snakes," Causey said, and he looked at her carefully.

"What kinds of snakes?"

"Moccasins, mainly. They climb up here on the mats. They don't run. They never run. They're not afraid. I got a canoe paddle in the cab there. I kill them with the paddle. One day, I killed thirty-five moccasins. People come along sometimes, like you, visitors, come up here curious to see the digging, and they see the dead snakes lying on the mats, and they freeze. They refuse to move. They refuse to walk back where they came from."

If Causey was trying to frighten Carol, to impress her by frightening her, he had picked the wrong person. He might have sent a shot or two of adrenalin through me, but not through Carol. I once saw her reach into a semi-submerged hollow stump in a man-made lake where she knew a water snake lived, and she had felt around in there, underwater, with her hands on the coils of the snake, trying to figure out which end was the front. Standing thigh-deep in the water, she was wearing a two-piece bathing suit. Her appearance did not suggest old Roger Conant on a field trip. She was trim and supple and tan from a life in the open. Her hair, in a ponytail, had fallen across one shoulder, while her hands, down inside the stump, kept moving slowly, gently along the body of the snake. This snake was her friend, she said, and she wanted Sam and me to see him. "Easy there, fellow, it's only Carol. I sure wish I could find your head. Here we go. We're coming to the end. Oh, damn. I've got his tail." There was nothing to do but turn around. She felt her way all four feet to the other end. "At last," she said. "How are you, old fellow?" And she lifted her arms up out of the water. In them was something like a piece of television cable moving with great vigor. She held on tight and carried her friend out of the lake and onto the shore.

At Carol's house, Sam and I one night slept in sleeping bags on the floor of her study beside Zebra, her rattlesnake. He was an eastern diamondback, and he had light lines, parallel, on his dark face. He was young and less than three feet long. He lived among rocks and leaves in a big glass jar. "As a pet, he's ideal," Carol told us. "I've never had a diamondback like him before. Anytime you get uptight about anything, just look at him. He just sits there. He's so great. He doesn't complain. He just waits. It's as if he's saying, 'I've got all the time in the world. I'll outwait you, you son of a bitch.' "

"He shows you what patience is," Sam said. "He's like a deer. Deer will wait two hours before they move into a field to eat."

In Carol's kitchen was the skin of a mature diamondback, about six feet long, that Sam and Carol had eaten in southwest Georgia, roasting him on a stick like a big hot dog, beside the Muckalee Creek. The snake, when they came upon him, had just been hit and was still alive. The men who had mortally wounded the snake were standing over it, watching it die. A dump truck full of gravel was coming toward the scene, and Carol, imagining the truck running over and crushing the diamondback, ran up to the men standing over it and said, "Do you want it?" Surprised, they said no. "No, *Ma'am!*" So she picked up the stricken snake, carried it off the road and back to the car, where she coiled it on the floor between her feet. "Later, in a gas station, we didn't worry about leaving the car unlocked. Oh, that was funny. We do have some fun. We ate him that night."

"What did he taste like?" I asked her.

"Taste like? You know, like rattlesnake. Maybe a cross between a chicken and a squirrel."

Carol's house, in Atlanta, consisted of four small rooms, each about ten feet square—kitchen, study, storage room, bedroom. They were divided by walls of tongue-and-groove boards, nailed horizontally onto the studs. A bathroom and vestibule were more or less stuck onto one side of the building. She lived alone there. An oak with a three-foot bole stood over the house like an umbrella and was so close to it that it virtually blocked the front door. An old refrigerator sat on the stoop. Around it were the skulls of a porpoise, a horse, a cow, and a pig. White columns adorned the façade. They were made of two-inch iron pipe. Paint peeled from the clapboard. The front yard was hard red clay, and it had some vestigial grasses in it (someone having once tried a lawn) that had not been mowed for possibly a decade. Carol had set out some tomatoes among the weeds. The house stood on fairly steep ground that sloped through woods to a creek. The basement was completely above grade at the rear, and a door there led into a dim room where Carol's red-tailed hawk lived. He was high in one corner, standing on a pipe. I had never been in the immediate presence of a red-tailed hawk, and at sight of him I was not sure whether to run or to kneel. At any rate, I could not have taken one step nearer. He was two feet tall. His look was incendiary. Slowly, angrily, he lifted and spread his wings, reached out a yard and a half. His talons could have hooked tuna. His name was Big Man. His spread-winged posture revealed all there was to know about him: his beauty— the snowy chest, the rufous tail; his power; his affliction. One of his wings was broken. Carol had brought him back from near death. Now she walked over to him and stood by him and stroked his chest. "Come on, Big Man," she said. "It's not so bad. Come on, Big Man." Slowly, ever so slowly—over a period of a minute or two—the wide wings came down, folded together, while Carol stroked his chest. Fear departed, but nothing much changed in his eyes.

"What will he ever do?" I asked her.

She said, "Nothing, I guess. Just be someone's friend."

Outside the basement door was a covered pen that housed a rooster and a seagull. The rooster had been on his way to Colonel Sanders' when he fell off a truck and broke a drumstick. Someone called Carol, as people often do, and she took the rooster into her care. He was hard of moving, but she had hopes for him. He was so new there he did not even have a name. The seagull, on the other hand, had been with her for years. He had one wing. She had picked him up on a beach three hundred miles away. His name was Garbage Belly.

Carol had about fifteen ecosystems going on at once in her twenty-by-twenty house. In the study, a colony of dermestid beetles was eating flesh off the pelvis of an alligator. The beetles lived in a big can that had once held forty pounds of mincemeat. Dermestids clean bones. They do thorough work. They all but simonize the bones. Carol had obtained her original colony from the Smithsonian Institution. One of her vaulting ambitions was to be able to identify on sight any bone that she happened to pick up. Also in the can were the skulls of a water turkey, a possum, and a coon.

The beetles ate and were eaten. Carol reached into the colony, pulled out a beetle, and gave it to her black-widow spider. The black widow lived in a commercial mayonnaise jar. Carol had found her in the basement while cleaning it up for Big Man. The spider's egg was getting ready to hatch, and when it did thousands like her would emerge into the jar. Efficiently, the black widow encased the beetle in filament gauze that flowed from her spinnerets.

Carol then fed dermestids to her turtles. She had three galvanized tubs full of cooters and sliders, under a sunlamp. "They need sun, you know. Vitamin D." She fed dermestids to her spotted salamander, and to her gray tree frog. Yellow spots, polka dots, on black, the salamander's coloring was so simple and contrasting that he appeared to be a knickknack from a gift shop, a salamander made in Japan. The tree frog lived in a giant brandy snifter, furnished with rocks and dry leaves. With his latex body and his webbed and gummy oversize hands, he could walk right up the inside of his brandy snifter, even after its shape began to tilt him backward, then lay a mitt over the rim and haul himself after and walk down the outside. He could walk straight up a wall; and he did that, while digesting his beetle. He had been with Carol three years. He was a star there in her house. No mayonnaise jar for him. He had the brandy snifter. It was all his and would be as long as he lived.

Notebooks were open on Carol's desk, a heavy, kneehole desk, covered with pens, Magic Markers, brushes, pencils, drawing materials. The notebooks had spiral bindings and were, in part, diaries.

17 April. Okefenokee. Caught two banded water snakes, one skink. . . .

18 April. To King's Landing. Set three line traps baited with peanut butter, caught a rather small moccasin AGKISTRODON coming from under shed. Put out ninety-five set hooks baited with pork liner. To gator hole. Tried to use shocker, after putting up seines across exit. No luck!

19 April. D.O.R. *Natrix rigida*, glossy water snake; *Farancia abacura*, mud snake; *Elaphe guttata guttata*, corn snake. . . .

21 April. S.W. Georgia. D.O.R. vulture, ½ mi. E. Leary, Hwy 62, Calhoun Country. Fresh. Possum D.O.R. nearby. . . .

The notebooks were also, in part, ledgers of her general interests.

Dissolve mouse in nitric acid and put him through spectrophotometer—can tell every element.

A starving snake can gain weight on water.

Gray whales are born with their bellies up and weigh a ton, and when they are grown they swim five thousand miles to breed in shallow lagoons and eat sand and stand on their tails and gravity-feed on pelagic crabs.

And the notebooks were, in part, filled with maps and sketches. Making a drawing of something—a mermaid weed, the hind foot of an opossum, the egg case of a spotted salamander, a cutaway of a deer's heart—was her way of printing it into her memory. The maps implied stories. They were of places too specific—too eccentric, wild, and minute—to show up as much of anything on other maps, including a topographical quadrangle. They were of places that Carol wanted to remember and, frequently enough, to find again.

12 May. Caught *Natrix erythrogaster flavigaster*, red-bellied water snake 9:30 A.M. Saw quite a large gator at 9:35. Ten feet. Swarm of honeybees 25 feet up cypress at edge of creek. Large—six-foot—gray rat snake in oak tree over water. *Elaphe obsoleta spiloides.* Tried unsuccessfully to knock it into canoe. Finally climbed tree but snake had gone into hole in limb. . . .

26 June. Sleep on nest where loggerhead laid eggs Cumberland Island, to protect eggs from feral hogs. Return later find that hog has eaten eggs. Shoot hog. . . .

27 August. Oconee River. Saw *Natrix* wrestling with a catfish in water. *Natrix* was trying to pull fish out on bank. Snake about 2½ feet. Fish 8 inches. Snake finally won. Didn't have heart to collect snake as he was so proud of fish and wouldn't let go even when touched. Camped by railroad bridge. Many trains. Found catfish on set hook, smoked him for supper. . . .

The rods of the vertebrate eye provide scotopic vision—sight in dim light. Nocturnal animals that also go out in daylight need slit eyes to protect the rods. Crocodiles. Seals. Rattlesnakes. Cottonmouths.

13 June. North Georgia. Oh, most glorious night. The fireflies are truly in competition with the stars! At the tops of the ridges it is impossible to tell them apart. As of old, I wished for a human companion. On the banks of a road, a round worm was glowing, giving off light. What a wonderful thing it is. It allows us to see in the darkness.

Above the desk, tacked to a wall, was the skin of a bobcat—D.O.R. two miles west of Baxley, Highway 341. "I was excited out of my mind when we found him," Carol said. "He was the best D.O.R. ever. It was late afternoon. January. He was stiff, but less than a day old. Bobcats move mostly at night. He was un-bloody, three feet long, and weighed twenty-one pounds. I was amazed how small his testicles were. I skinned him here at home. I tanned his hide—salt, alum, then neat's-foot oil. He had a thigh like a goat's—so big, so much beauti-ful meat. I boiled him. He tasted good—you know, the wild taste. Strong. But not as strong as a strong coon."

Zebra lifted his head, flashed his fangs, and yawned a pink yawn. This was the first time in at least a day that Zebra had moved. Carol said the yawn meant he was hungry. Zebra had had his most recent meal seven weeks before. Carol went over to the gerbil bin to select a meal for Zebra. "Snakes just don't eat that much," she said, shaking her head in dismay over the exploding population of gerbils. She tossed one to a cat. She picked up another one, a small one, for Zebra. "Zebra eats every month or two," she went on. "That's all he needs. He doesn't do anything. He just sits there." She lifted the lid of Zebra's jar and dropped the gerbil inside. The gerbil stood still, among the dry leaves, looking. Zebra did not move. "I'm going to let him go soon. He's been a good friend. He really has. You sometimes forget they're deadly, you know. I've had my hand down inside the jar, cleaning it out, and suddenly realized, with cold sweat, that he's poisonous. Ordinarily, when you see a rattlesnake you are on guard immediately. But with him in the house all the time I tend to forget how deadly he is. The younger the snake, the more concentrated the venom."

The gerbil began to walk around the bottom of the big glass jar. Zebra, whose body was arranged in a loose coil, gave no sign that he was aware of the gerbil's presence. Under a leaf, over a rock, sniffing, the gerbil explored the periphery of Zebra's domain. Eventually, the gerbil stepped up onto Zebra's back. Still Zebra did not move. Zebra had been known to refuse a meal, and perhaps that would happen now. The gerbil walked along the snake's back, stepped down, and con-tinued along the boundary of the base of the jar, still exploring. Another leaf, an-other stone, the strike came when the gerbil was perhaps eight inches from Zebra's head. The strike was so fast, the strike and the recovery, that it could not really be followed by the eye. Zebra lanced across the distance, hit the gerbil in the heart, and, all in the same instant, was back where he had started, same loose coil, head resting just where it had been resting before. The gerbil took three steps forward and fell dead, so dead it did not even quiver, tail out straight behind.

Sam had once told me how clumsy he thought rattlesnakes were, advising me never to walk through a palmetto stand third in a line, because a rat-tlesnake, said Sam, takes aim at the first person, strikes at the second, and hits the third. After watching Zebra, though, I decided to go tenth in line, if at all. Carol seemed thoughtful. "I've had copperheads," she said. "But I'm not really that much on snakes. I'm always worrying that someday I'll come home and find the jar turned over and several dead cats lying around on the floor." That night, on the floor in my sleeping bag, I began to doze off and then imagined rolling over and knocking Zebra out of his jar. The same thought came to me when I started to doze off again. I spent most of the night with my chin in my hands, watching him through the glass.

There was a baby hawk in a box in the kitchen, and early in the morning he began to scream. Nothing was going to quiet him except food. Carol got up, took a rabbit out of the refrigerator, and cut it up with a pair of scissors. It had been a rabbit D.O.R. The rabbit was twice the size of the hawk, but the hawk ate most of the rabbit. There followed silence, bought and paid for. In the freezer, Carol had frogs' legs, trout, bream, nighthawk, possum, squirrel, quail, turtle, and what she called trash fish. The trash fish were for Garbage Belly. The destiny of the other items was indistinct. They were for the consumption of the various occupants of the house, the whole food chain—bird, amphibian, beast and beetle, reptile, arachnid, man. A sign over the kitchen sink said "EAT MORE POSSUM," black on Chinese red.

In the bedroom was a deerskin. "I saw blood on the trail," Carol said. "I knew a deer wouldn't go uphill shot, so I went down. I found it. It wasn't a spike buck, it was a slickhead. It had been poached. I poached it from the poacher." On the walls were watercolors and oils she had done of natural scenes, and three blown-up photographs of Johnny Cash. A half-finished papier-mâché head of Johnny Cash was in her bedroom as well, and other pieces of her sculpture, including "Earth Stars," a relief of mushrooms. Carol looked reverently at the photographs and said that whenever she had had depressing and difficult times she had turned to Johnny Cash, to the reassurances in the timbre of his voice, to the philosophy in his lyrics, to his approach to life. She said he had more than once pulled her through.

Carol grew up in Rochester, New York, until she was twelve, after that in Atlanta. Her father, Earl Ruckdeschel, worked for Eastman Kodak and managed the Atlanta processing plant. She was an only child. Animals were *non grata* at home, so she went to them. "You have to turn to something. There was a lot of comfort out there in those woods. Wild creatures were my brothers and sisters. That is why I'm more interested in mammals than anything else. They're warm-blooded. Fish are cold-blooded. You can't snuggle up with a fish." Her parents mortally feared snakes, but she never did. Her father once made her a snake stick. Her mother told her, many times a month and year, that it was not ladylike to be interested in snakes and toads. Carol went to Northside High in Atlanta. After high school, for five years, she worked at odd jobs—she fixed car radios, she wandered. Then she went to Georgia State University, studied biology, and married a biologist there. He was an authority on river swamps, an ecologist—a tall, prognathous, slow-speaking scientific man. His subspecialty was cottonmouths. He had found an island in the Gulf that had a cottonmouth under every palmetto, and he lived for a time among them. He weighed and measured them one by one. He was a lot older than Carol. She had taken his course in vertebrate zoology. The marriage did not really come apart. It evaporated. Carol kept going on field trips with him, and she stayed on at Georgia State as a biological researcher. The little house she moved into could not have been better: low rent, no class, high privacy, woods, a creek. And it was all her own. A cemetery was across the street. She could sleep there if she wanted to get out of the house. On Mother's Day, or whenever else she needed flowers, she collected bouquets from among the graves. From time to time, she wandered away. She had a white pickup truck and a German shepherd. His name was Catfish, and he was "all mouth and no brains." Carol and Catfish slept on a bale of hay in the back of the truck, and they went all over, from the mountains to the sea. They fished in the mountains, hunted in the sand hills, set traps in the Okefenokee Swamp. She began collecting specimens for the Georgia State University research collection. Most she found dead on the road. Occasionally, she brought new specimens into the collection, filling in gaps, but mainly she replenished exhausted supplies—worn-out pelts and skulls. There was always a need. An animal's skin has a better chance against a Goodyear tire than it does against the paws of a college student. She had no exclusive specialty. She wanted to do everything. Any plant or creature, dead or alive, attracted her eye.

She volunteered, as well, for service with the Georgia Natural Areas Council, a small office of the state government that had been established to take an inventory of wild places in Georgia worth preserving, proclaiming, and defending. While she travelled around Georgia picking up usable D.O.R.s for the university, she appraised the landscape for the state, detouring now and again into river swamps to check the range of frogs. Sam Candler, who also worked for the Natural Areas Council, generally went with her. Rarely, they flew in his plane. For the most part, they were on the road. Sam had a farm in Coweta County. He had also spent much of his life in the seclusion of Cumberland Island, off the Georgia coast. He was a great-grandson of the pharmacist who developed and at one time wholly owned the Coca-Cola Company, so he could have been a rampant lion in social Atlanta, but he would have preferred to wade blindfolded through an alligator swamp with chunks of horsemeat trussed to his legs. He wanted to live, as he put it, "close to the earth." He knew wilderness, he had been in it so much, and his own outlook on the world seemed to have been formed and directed by his observations of the creatures that ranged in wild places, some human, some not. Sam had no formal zoological or ecological training. What he brought to his work was mainly a sense of what he wanted for the region where he had lived his life. He had grown up around Atlanta, had gone to Druid Hills Grammar School and to Emory University and on into the Air Force. He had lived ever since on the island and the farm. His wife and their four children seemed to share with him a lack of interest in urban events. The Natural Areas Council had been effective. It had the weight of the government behind it. Georgia was as advanced in this respect as, say, Indiana, Illinois, Iowa, and New Jersey, where important conservancy work was also being accomplished on the state-government level, and far more advanced than most other states. There was much to evaluate. Georgia was, after all, the largest state east of the Mississippi River, and a great deal of it was still wild. Georgia forests, mountains, swamps, islands, and rivers—a long list of sites of special interest or value—had become Registered Natural Areas. Sam and Carol had done the basic work—exploring the state, following leads, assessing terrain, considering vegetation and wildlife, choosing sites, and persuading owners to register lands for preservation.

Sam had been a friend of mine for some years, and when he wrote to say that he was now travelling around the state collecting skulls and pelts, eating rattlesnakes, preserving natural areas, and charting the ranges of river frogs, I could not wait until I could go down there and see. I had to wait more than a year, though, while finishing up some work. I live in Princeton, New Jersey, so I flew from Newark when the day came, and I nearly missed the plane. Automobiles that morning were backed up at least a mile from the Newark Airport tollbooths (fourteen tollbooths, fourteen lanes), and the jam was just as thick on the paid side as it was on the unpaid side—thousands and thousands of murmuring cars, moving nowhere, nowhere to move, shaking, vibrating, stinking, rattling, *Homo sapiens* D.O.R. I got out of my car and left it there, left it, shamefully, with a high-school student who was accepting money to drive it home, and began to make my way overland to the terminal. I climbed up on bumpers and over corrugated fences and ducked under huge green signs. I went around tractor trailers and in front of buses. Fortunately, Sam had told me to bring a backpack. Carrying a suitcase through that milieu would have been like carrying a suitcase up the Matterhorn. Occasionally, I lost direction, and once I had to crawl under a mastodonic truck, but I did get through, and I ran down the cattle-pen corridors of the airport and, with a minute to go, up the steps and into the plane—relieved beyond measure to be out of that ruck and off to high ground and sweet air, taking my chances on the food. Sam and Carol met me, and we went straight to the mountains, stopping all the way for D.O.R.s. That night, we ate a weasel.

IN a valley in north Georgia, Carol had a cabin that was made of peeled logs, had a stone fireplace, and stood beside a cold stream. We stayed there on the first night of a journey that eventually meandered through eleven hundred miles of the state—a great loop, down out of the river gorges and ravine forests of the mountains, across the granitic piedmont and over the sand hills and the red hills to the river swamps and pine flatwoods of the coastal plain. Sam had a canoe on the top of the car. We slept in swamps and beside a lake and streams. Made, in part, in the name of the government, it was a journey that tended to mock the idea of a state—as an unnatural subdivision of the globe, as a metaphor of the human ego sketched on paper and framed in straight lines and

in riparian boundaries behind an unalterable coast. Georgia. A state? Really a
core sample of a continent, a plug in the melon, a piece of North America. Pull
it out and wildcats would spill off the high edges. Alligators off the low ones.
The terrain was crisscrossed with geological boundaries, mammalian boundaries, amphibian boundaries—the range of the river frogs. The range of the
wildcat was the wildcat's natural state, overlaying segments of tens of thousands of other states, one of which was Georgia. The State of Georgia.
Governor Jimmy Carter in the mansion in Atlanta.

The first thing Sam and Carol wanted to assess on this trip was a sphagnum
bog in Rabun County, off the north side of the Rabun Bald (4,696 feet). The
place seemed marginal to me, full of muck and trout lilies, with swamp pinks in
blossom under fringe trees and smooth alders, but Sam and Carol thought it
ought to be registered, and they sought out the owner, a heavy woman, greatly
slow of speech, with a Sears, Roebuck tape measure around her neck. She
stood under a big white pine by the concrete front porch of her shingled house
on a flinty mountain farm. Sam outlined the value of registering a natural area
for preservation beyond one's years. She looked at him with no expression and
said, "We treasure the bog." He gave her an application. ("Being aware of the
high responsibility to the State that goes with the ownership and use of a property which has outstanding value in illustrating the natural history of Georgia,
we morally agree to continue to protect and use this site for purposes consistent
with the preservation of its natural integrity.") Perhaps she could consider it
with her husband and his brothers and nephews when they came home. One
day soon, he would stop back to talk again. She said, "We likes to hunt arrow-
heads. We treasure the bog."

The D.O.R.s that first day included a fan belt Sam took for a blacksnake—
jammed on his brakes, backed up to see—and a banana peel that Carol identified, at first glimpse, as a jumping mouse. Eager was the word for them. They
were so much on the hunt. "It is rare for specimens to be collected this way,"
Carol said. "Most people are too lazy. Or they're hung up on just frogs or just
salamanders, or whatever, and they don't care about other things. Watching
for D.O.R.s makes travelling a lot more interesting. I mean, can you imagine
just *going* down the road?"

We went around a bend in a mountain highway and the road presented
Carol with the find of the day. "D.O.R.!" she said. "That was a good one. That
was a *good* one! Sam, hurry back. That was a weasel!"

Sam hurried back. It was no banana peel. It was exactly what Carol said it
was: *Mustela frenata,* the long-tailed weasel, dead on the road. It was fresh-
killed, and—from the point of view of Georgia State University—in fine condition. Carol was so excited she jumped. The weasel was a handsome thing,
minklike, his long body a tube roughly ten by two, his neck long and slender.
His fur was white and yellow on the underside and dark brown on his back.
"What a magnificent animal!" Carol said. "And hard as hell to trap. Smell his

musk. The scent glands are back here by the tail." While backing up after seeing him, she had hoped against hope that he would be a least weasel—smallest
of all carnivores. She had never seen one. The least weasel diets almost exclusively on tiny, selected mice. This one would have eaten almost anything warm,
up to and including a rabbit twice his size. Carol put him in an iced cooler that
was on the back seat. The cooler was not airtight. Musk permeated the interior
of the car. It was not disturbing. It was merely powerful. Carol said they had
once collected a skunk D.O.R. They had put it in a plastic bag within a plastic
bag within four additional plastic bags. The perfume still came through.

Carol's valley resisted visitors. It was seven miles from a paved road. It was
rimmed with mountains. It was the coldest valley in Georgia. A trout stream
cascaded out of the south end. Ridges pressed in from east and west. The north
was interrupted by a fifty-five-hundred-foot mountain called Standing Indian.
Standing Indian stood in North Carolina, showing Georgia where to stop. The
valley was prize enough. Its floor was flat and green with pastureland and
shoots of new corn. Its brooks were clear. Now, in May, there would be frost
across the fields in the morning, heavy and bright, but blossoms were appearing on the dogwoods and leaves on the big hardwoods—only so far up the
mountains, though; it was still winter on Standing Indian, stick-figure forests
to the top. Sam had flown over this whole area, minutely, in his Cessna—Mt.
Oglethorpe to the Chattooga River, Black Rock Mountain to the Brasstown
Bald. He said there was no valley in Georgia like this one in beauty or remoteness. It was about two miles long and a half mile wide. Its year-round population was twelve. Someone else, somewhere else, would have called it by another
name, but not here. Lyrical in its effrontery to fact, the name of the valley was
Tate City. On our way in, we stopped to see Arthur and Mammy Young, its senior residents. Their house, until recently, had had so many preserves stacked
on boards among the rafters that the roof sagged. Their outhouse straddled a
stream. Their house, made of logs, burned to the ground one day when they
were in town, eighteen miles away. Now they lived in a cinder-block hut with a
pickup truck outside, fragments of machinery lying on the ground, hound
dogs barking. The Youngs were approaching old age, apparently with opposite
metabolisms, he sinewy, she more than ample, after sixty years of cathead biscuits. Inside, Arthur rolled himself a cigarette and sat down to smoke it beside
his wood-burning stove. Near him was a fiddle. Sam said that Arthur was a
champion fiddler. Arthur went on smoking and did not reach for the fiddle. He
exchanged news with Carol. Christ looked down on us from pictures on each
wall. The room had two kerosene lanterns, and its windows were patched with
tape. "I always wished I had power, so I could iron," Mammy said. "When I had
kids. Now I don't care." Dusk was near and Carol wanted time in the light, so
we left soon and went on up the valley, a mile or so, to her log cabin.

A wooden deck reached out from the cabin on stilts toward the stream. The
place had been cut out of woods—hemlock, ironwood, oak, alder, dogwood,

rhododendron. A golden birch was standing in a hole in the center of the deck. Carol got out the weasel and set him, paws up, on the deck. Sam unpacked his things and set a bottle of The Glenlivet near the weasel, with three silver cups. I added a bottle of Talisker. Sam was no bourbon colonel. He liked pure Highland malt Scotch whisky. Carol measured the weasel. She traced him on paper and fondled his ears. His skull and his skin would go into the university's research collection. She broke a double-edged Gillette blade in half the long way. "Weasels are hard to come by, hard to scent, hard to bait," she said. "We've tried to trap a least weasel. We don't even have one. I hate to catch animals, though. With D.O.R.s, I feel great. We've got the specimen and we're making use of it. The skull is the most important thing. The study skin shows the color pattern."

With a simple slice, she brought out a testicle; she placed it on a sheet of paper and measured it. Three-quarters of an inch. Slicing smoothly through the weasel's fur, she began to remove the pelt. Surely, she worked the skin away from the long neck. The flesh inside the pelt looked like a segment of veal tenderloin. "I lived on squirrel last winter," she said. "Every time you'd come to a turn in the road, there was another squirrel. I stopped buying meat. I haven't bought any meat in a year, except for some tongue. I do love tongue." While she talked, the blade moved in light, definite touches. "Isn't he in perfect shape?" she said. "He was hardly touched. You really lose your orientation when you start skinning an animal that's been run over by a Mack truck." From time to time, she stopped for a taste of The Glenlivet, her hand, brown from sun and flecked with patches of the weasel's blood, reaching for the silver cup. "You've got to be careful where you buy meat anyway. They inject some animals with an enzyme, a meat tenderizer, before they kill them. *That* isn't any good for you." Where the going was difficult, she moistened the skin with water. At last it came away entire, like a rubber glove. She now had the weasel disassembled, laid out on the deck in cleanly dissected parts. "I used to love to take clocks apart," she said. "To see how they were built. This is the same thing. I like plants and animals and their relationship to the land and us. I like the vertebrates especially." The weasel's tailbone was still in the skin. She tugged at it with her teeth. Pausing for a sip, she said that sometimes you just had to use your mouth in her line of work, as once when she was catching cricket frogs. She had a frog in each hand and saw another frog, so she put one frog into her mouth while she caught the third. Gradually, the weasel's tailbone came free. She held it in her hand and admired it. "Some bones are real neat," she said. "In the heart of a deer, there's a bone. And not between the ventricles, where you'd expect it. Some animals have bones in their penises—raccoons, for example, and weasels." She removed the bone from the weasel's penis. It was long, proportionately speaking, with a hook at the penetrating end. It was called a baculum, she said, which meant "rod" in Latin. She would save it. Its dimensions were one way to tell the weasel's age. Baculums are also involved in keying dif-

ferences in species. Sam said he kept a raccoon's baculum in his wallet because
it made a great toothpick. He got out his wallet and displayed his great toothpick. Carol turned the pelt inside out and folded the forepaws in an X, standard
procedure with a study skin. She covered it with a deep layer of salt and packed
it away.

The dusk was deep then. Carol had finished working almost in the dark. The
air was cold. It was on its way to thirty. Sam had a fire going, inside, already disintegrating into coals. The smell of burning oak was sweet. We went into the
cabin. Carol put the weasel on the tines of a long fork and roasted it over the
coals.

"How do you like your weasel?" Sam asked me.

"Extremely well done," I said.

Carol sniffed the aroma of the roast. "It has a wild odor," she said. "You *know*
it's not cow. The first time I had bear, people said, 'Cut the fat off. That's where
the bad taste is.' I did, and the bear tasted just like cow. The next bear, I left the
fat on."

The taste of the weasel was strong and not unpleasant. It lingered in the
mouth after dinner. The meat was fibrous and dark. "It just goes to show you
how good everything is," said Carol. "People who only eat cows, pigs, sheep,
chickens—boy, have those people got blinders on! Is that tunnelization! There's
one poisonous mammal in the United States: the short-tailed shrew. And you
can even eat that."

Sam built up the fire.

"How can you be sure that something is not too old?" I asked.

"My God, if you can't tell if it's bad, what's the difference?" said Carol.

Sam said, "If it tastes good, don't knock it."

"People don't make sense," Carol said. "They hunt squirrels, but they
wouldn't consider eating a squirrel killed on the road. Only once have I ever
had competition for a D.O.R. A man wanted a squirrel for his black servant, and
we had a set-to in the road."

There were double-deck bunks in the corners of the room. The corners were
cold. We pulled three mattresses off the bunks and put them down side by side
before the fire. We unrolled our three sleeping bags. It had been a big day; we
were tired, and slept without stirring. Sam dreamed in the night that he was
eating his own beard.

WITH a load of honey and cathead biscuits, gifts of Mammy Young, we went
down out of the valley in the morning, mile after mile on a dirt road that ran
beside and frequently crossed the outlet stream, which was the beginnings of
the Tallulah River. Some twenty miles on down, the river had cut a gorge, in
hard quartzite, six hundred feet deep. Warner Brothers had chosen the gorge
as the site for the filming of a scene from James Dickey's novel, "Deliverance."

This mountain land in general was being referred to around the state as " 'Deliverance' country." The novel seemed to have been the most elaborate literary event in Georgia since "Gone with the Wind." "Deliverance" was so talked about that people had, for conversational convenience, labelled its every part ("the owl scene," "the guitar scene"). It was a gothic novel, a metaphysical terror novel, the structural center of which involved four men going through the rapids of a mountain river in canoes. They were attacked. The action climax occurred when one of the canoemen scaled the wall of a fantastically sheer gorge to establish an ambush and kill a mountain man. He killed him with a bow and arrow. Carol and Sam, like half the people in Atlanta and a couple of dozen in Hollywood, called this "the climb-out scene," and they took me to see where Warners would shoot. The six-hundred-foot gorge was a wonder indeed, clefting narrowly and giddily down through the quartzite to the bed of the river that had done the cutting. Remarkably, though, no river was there. A few still pools. A trickle of water. Graffiti adorned the rock walls beside the pools. There was a dam nearby, and, in 1913, the river had been detoured through a hydropower tunnel. Steel towers stood on opposite lips of the chasm, supported by guy wires. A cable connected the towers. They had been built for performances of wire walkers, the Flying Wallendas. Nearby was the Cliffhanger Café. A sign said, "Enjoy Coca-Cola. See it here, free. Tallulah Gorge. 1200 feet deep." The Georgia Natural Areas Council looked on. Too late to register that one. The eye of the Warner Brothers camera would, however, register just what it wanted to select and see, and it would move up that wall in an unfailing evocation of wilderness. I was awed by the power of Dickey. In writing his novel, he had assembled " 'Deliverance' country" from such fragments, restored and heightened in the chambers of his imagination. The canoes in his novel dived at steep angles down breathtaking cataracts and shot like javelins through white torrents among blockading monoliths. If a canoe were ten inches long and had men in it three inches high, they might find such conditions in a trout stream, steeply inclined, with cataracts and plunge pools and rushing bright water falling over ledges and splaying through gardens of rock. Dickey must have imagined something like that and then enlarged the picture until the trout stream became a gothic nightmare for men in full-size canoes. A geologically maturer, less V-shaped stream would not have served. No actual river anywhere could have served his artistic purpose—not the Snake, not the Upper Hudson, not even the Colorado— and least of all a river in Georgia, whose wild Chattooga, best of the state's white-water rivers, has modest rapids: a bouncing run, much pleasure, no particular danger. The people of the "Deliverance" mountains were malevolent, opaque, and sinister. Arthur and Mammy Young.

There were records of the presence of isolated cottonmouths on Dry Fork Creek, in wild, forested piedmont country east of Athens. Dry Fork Creek, a tributary of a tributary of the Savannah River, was about halfway between

Vesta and Rayle, the beginning and the end of nowhere. We searched the woods along the creek. It would not have been at all unusual had we found the highland moccasin (the copperhead) there, for this was his terrain—*Agkistrodon contortrix contortrix*. What we were looking for, though, was the water moccasin (the cottonmouth), inexplicably out of his range. Cottonmouths belong in the coastal plain, in the rice fields, in the slow-moving rivers—*Agkistrodon piscivorus piscivorus*. Seeing a cottonmouth in a place like this would be a rare experience, and Carol fairly leaped into the woods. For my part, I regretted that I lacked aluminum boots. Carol was wearing green tennis shoes. Sam's feet were covered with moccasins. Carol rolled every log. She lifted anything that could have sheltered a newt, let alone a snake. By the stream, she ran her eye over every flat rock and projecting branch. Always disappointed, she quickly moved on. Sam sauntered beside her. The flood plain was beautiful under big sycamores, water oaks, maples: light filtering down in motes, wet leaves on the ground, cold water moving quietly in the stream. But the variety of tracks she found was disturbingly incomplete. "There, on that sandbar—those are possum tracks. Possums and coons go together, but that's just possum right there, no way about it. And that is not right. There shouldn't be a bar like that with no coon tracks on it, even if the water goes up and down every night. Possums can live anywhere. Coons can't. Coon tracks signify a healthy place. I don't much like this place. It's been cut over. There are no big dead trees." One big dead tree with a cottonmouth under it would have changed that, would have glorified Dry Fork Creek for Carol, coons or no coons—*piscivorus piscivorus* caught poaching, out of his territory, off the edge of his map, beyond his range. I felt her disappointment and was sorry the snakes were not there. "Don't be disappointed," she said. "When we go down the Cemocheckobee, cottonmouths will show us the way."

Buffalo disappeared from Georgia in early Colonial time. William Bartram noted this when he visited the colony and wrote "Travels in Georgia and Florida, 1773–74." Bartram, from Philadelphia, was the first naturalist to describe in detail the American subtropics. After his book reached London, sedentary English poets cribbed from his descriptions (Wordsworth, for example, and Coleridge). Ten miles south of Dry Fork Creek, Sam, Carol, and I crossed Bartram's path. In Bartram's words, "We came into an open Forest of Pines, Scrub white Oaks, Black Jacks, Plumb, Hicory, Grapes Vines, Rising a sort of Ridge, come to a flat levill Plain, and at the upper side of this, levell at the foot of the hills of the great Ridge, is the great Buffiloe Lick, which are vast Pits, licked in the Clay, formerly by the Buffiloes, and now kept smoothe and open by Cattle, deer, and horses, that resort here constantly to lick the clay, which is a greesey Marle of various colours, Red, Yellow & white, & has a sweetish taste, but nothing saltish that I could perceive." Bartram was describing what is now Philomath, Georgia 30659—a one-street town consisting of thirty houses and a buffalo lick. Philomath was established, early in the nineteenth century, as a seat of learning—hence the name. The town was the address of an academy whose students, in time, vanished like the buffalo. Now it was a place of pre-eminent silence under big oaks, and as we glided into town we were the only thing that moved. Ninety blacks, fifty whites lived there, but no one was out in the midday shade. The almost idling engine was the only sound. In an L-shaped elegant clapboard house, built in 1795, lived Dorothy Daniel Wright. Sam and Carol, having read Bartram's description and having determined that the buffalo lick was still intact, wanted to see it and, they hoped, to register it as a Georgia Natural Area. Miss Wright was the person to see. It was her lick. She was in her upper sixties. Her hair was white and swept upward, and crowned with a braided gold bun. Her welcome was warm. She showed us the lick. Cattle and deer had licked it slick all through her girlhood, she said. Now it was covered with grass, some hawthorn and sumac, and dominated by an immense, outreaching laurel oak. Carol squatted flat-footed, knees high, and dug with her hands for various colors of clay. She ate some blue clay, and handed pieces to me and Sam. It was sweet, bland, alkaline, slightly chewy. "My first thought was 'soapy,' " she said. "I expected it to get stronger, but it didn't. The final thought was 'sweetness.' " She put a bit more in her mouth and ate it contemplatively. There was, apparently, no sodium chloride in this ground. Phosphate, sodium, and calcium are what the buffalo licked. Where did they get their salt? "Twelve miles away there was salt," Miss Wright said. "Twelve miles is nothin' to a buffalo roamin' around. Between the two licks, they got all the minerals they needed for their bovine metabolism." Miss Wright had taught biology and chemistry in various high schools for forty-three years. She was eager to register the Great Buffalo Lick Natural Area, which had once been a boundary-line landmark separating the Georgia colony from the territory of the Creeks and Cherokees. She took us home to a lunch of salad and saltines. Into the salad went mushrooms, violets, and trout lilies that Carol had gathered in the mountains the day before.

Leaving Philomath, heading south, Sam commented how easy and pleasant that experience had been and how tense such encounters could sometimes be. He talked about a redneck peanut farmer in south Georgia, owner of a potential Natural Area. This redneck had taken one look at Sam's beard and had seemed ready to kill him then and there.

"What is a redneck, Sam?"

"You know what a redneck is, you little Yankee bastard."

"I want to hear your definition."

"A redneck is a fat slob in a pickup truck with a rifle across the back. He hates 'niggers.' He would rather have his kids ignorant than go to school with colored. I guess I don't like rednecks. I guess I've known some."

"Some of my best friends are rednecks," Carol said.

D.O.R. blacksnake, five miles south of Irwinton—old and bloated. "I'll just get it off the road, so its body won't be further humiliated," Carol said. Across a fence, a big sow was grunting. Carol carried the snake to the fence. She said, "Here, piggy-poo, look what I've got for you." She tossed the snake across the fence. The sow bit off the snake's head and ate it like an apple.

"Interesting," Carol said, "that we can feed a rotten snake to something we in turn will eat."

I said I would rather eat the buffalo lick.

Carol said, "I'll tell you the truth, I've had better clay."

We were out of the piedmont and down on the coastal plain, into the north of south Georgia. The roadside ads were riddled with bullet holes.

"PREPARE TO MEET JESUS CHRIST THE LORD." "WE WANT TO WIPE OUT CANCER IN YOUR LIFETIME." "WE CANNOT ACCEPT TIRES THAT HAVE BEEN CAPPED AS TRADE-INS."

Johnny Cash was back. Indians were now his theme. He was singing about a dam that was going to flood Seneca land, although the Senecas had been promised title to their land "as long as the moon shall rise." Cash's voice was deeper than ever. He sounded as if he were smoking a peace pipe through an oboe. Carol hugged herself. "As long . . . as the moon . . . shall rise . . . As long . . . as the rivers . . . flow."

"DON'T LOSE YOUR SOUL BY THE MARK OF THE BEAST."

We ate muskrat that night in a campsite on flat ground beside Big Sandy Creek, in Wilkinson County, innermost Georgia—muskrat with beans, chili powder, onions, tomatoes, and kelp. "I have one terrible handicap," Carol said. "I cannot follow a recipe." The muskrat, though, was very good. Carol had parboiled it for twenty minutes and then put it through a meat grinder, medium grind. Firewood was scarce, because the area was much used by fishermen who were prone to build fires and fish all night. Carol went up a tall spruce pine, and when she was forty feet or so above the ground she began to break off dead limbs and throw them down. She had to throw them like spears to clear the living branches of the tree. Pine burns oily, but that would not matter tonight. The muskrat was in a pot. Sam and I built up the fire. He pitched a tent.

To pass time before dinner, I put the canoe into the river and paddled slowly downstream. Carol called to me from the tree, "Watch for snakes. They'll be overhead, in the limbs of trees." She was not warning me; she was trying to raise the pleasure of the ride. "If you don't see the snake, you can tell by the splash," she went on. "A frog splash is a concentrated splash. A snake splash is a long splat." Gliding, watching, I went a quarter of a mile without a splash or a splat. It was dusk. The water was growing dark. I heard the hoot of a barred owl. Going back against the current, I worked up an appetite for muskrat.

After dinner, in moonlight, Sam and Carol and I got into the canoe and went up the river. A bend to the left, a bend to the right, and we penetrated the intense darkness of a river swamp that seemed to reach out unendingly. We could only guess at its dimensions. Upland swamps occur in areas between streams. River swamps are in the flood plains of rivers, and nearly all the streams in the Georgia coastal plain have them. They can be as much as six miles wide, and when the swamps of two or more big rivers connect, the result can be a vast and separate world. The darkness in there was so rich it felt warm. It was not total, for bars and slats of moonlight occasionally came through, touched a root or a patch of water. Essentially, however, everything was black: black water, black vegetation—water-standing maples, cypress—black on black. Columnar trunks were all around us, and we knew the channel only by the feel of the current, which sometimes seemed to be coming through from more than one direction. Here the black water sucked and bubbled, roiled by, splashed through the roots of the trees. Farther on, it was silent again. Silent ourselves, we pushed on into the black. Carol moved a flashlight beam among the roots of trees. She held the flashlight to her nose, because the eye can see much more if the line of sight is closely parallel to the beam. She inspected minutely the knobby waterlines of the trees. Something like a sonic boom cracked in our ears. "Jesus, what was that?"

"Beaver."

The next two slaps were even louder than the first. Carol ignored the beaver, and continued to move the light. It stopped. Out there in the obsidian was a single blue eye.

"A blue single eye is a spider," she said. "Two eyes is a frog. Two eyes almost touching is a snake. An alligator's eyes are blood red."

Two tiny coins now came up in her light. "Move in there," she said. "I want that one."

With a throw of her hand, she snatched up a frog. It was a leopard frog, and she let him go. He was much within his range. Carol was looking for river frogs, pig frogs, carpenter frogs, whose range peripheries we were stalking. She saw another pair of eyes. The canoe moved in. Her hand swept out unseen and made a perfect tackle, thighs to knees. This was a bronze frog, home on the range. Another pair of eyes, another catch, another disappointment—a bullfrog. Now another shattering slap on the water. Another. The beaver slapped only when the canoe was moving upstream. The frog chorus, filling the background, varied in pitch and intensity, rose and fell. Repeatedly came the hoot of the barred owl.

Sam dipped a cup and had a drink. "I feel better about drinking water out of swamps than out of most rivers," he said. "It's filtered. No one ever says a good word for a swamp. The whole feeling up to now has been 'Fill it in—it's too wet to plow, too dry to fish.' Most people stay out of swamps. I love them. I like the water, the reptiles, the amphibians. There is so much life in a swamp. The sounds are so different. Frogs, owls, birds, beavers. Birds sound different in swamps."

"You see a coon in here and you realize it's his whole world," Carol said.

"It's a beautiful home with thousands of creatures," Sam said.

With all this ecological intoxication, I thought they were going to fall out of the canoe.

"Life came out of the swamps," Sam said. "And now swamps are among the last truly wild places left."

We went back downstream. Tobacco smoke was in the air over the river. Occasionally, on the bank, we saw an orange-red glow, momentarily illuminating a black face. Fishing lines, slanting into the stream, were visible against the light of small fires. The canoe moved soundlessly by, and on into the darkness. "The groids sure love to fish," Sam murmured. The moon was low. It was midnight.

NOW, at noon, a hundred miles or so to the southeast and by another stream, we were sitting on the big felled oak, pouring out the last of the wine, with Chap Causey moving toward us a foot at a time in his American dragline crane. He swung a pair of mats around behind him and backed up a bit more, and as he went on gutting the streambed the oak began to tremble. It must have weighed two or three tons, but it was trembling and felt like an earthquake—time to move. Carol picked up a piece of dry otter scat. She bounced it in the palm of her hand and looked upcurrent at the unaltered stream and downcurrent into the new ditch. She said, "You can talk about coons' being able to go off into the woods and eat nuts and berries, because they're omnivores. But not this otter. He's finished." She broke open the scat. Inside it were fishbones and hair—hair of a mouse or hair of a young rabbit. There were fish otoliths as well, two of them, like small stones. She flung it all into the stream. "He's done for," she said, and waved good-bye to Chap Causey.

On down the dirt road from the stream-channelization project, we saw ahead a D.O.R.

"Looks like a bad one," Carol said.

Sam stopped. "Yes, it's a bad one," he said. "Canebrake. Do you want to eat him?"

Carol leaned over and looked. "He's too old. Throw him out of the road, the poor darlin'. What gets me is that some bastard is proud of having run over him. When I die, I don't want to be humiliated like that."

Sam threw the rattlesnake out of the road. Then we headed southwest through underdeveloped country, almost innocent of towns—Alma, Douglas, Adel, Moultrie, a hundred miles from Alma to Moultrie.

D.O.R. king snake, blue jay, sparrow hawk, wood thrush, raccoon, catbird, cotton rat. The poor darlin's. Threw them out of the road.

A.O.R. hobo—man with a dog. "Oh, there's a good guy," Carol said as we passed him. "He has a dog and a bedroll. What else do you need?"

D.O.R. opossum. Cook County. Three miles east of Adel. Carol spoke admiringly of the creature flexibility of the opossum. Among the oldest of mammals, the possum goes all the way back to Cretaceous time, she said, and, like people, it has never specialized, in a biological sense. "You can specialize yourself out of existence. Drain the home of the otter. The otter dies. The opossum, though, can walk away from an ecological disaster. So much for that. Try something else. He eats anything. He lives almost anywhere. That's why the possum is not extinct. That's why the possum has been so successful." One place this particular possum was never going to walk away from was Georgia Highway 76. Technology, for him the ultimate ecological disaster, had clouted him at seventy miles an hour.

Between Moultrie and Doerun, in the watershed of the Ochlockonee, was a lake in a pine grove surrounded by fifty acres of pitcher plants. They belonged to a couple named Barber, from Moultrie, who had read about the Natural Areas Council and had offered their pitcher plants to posterity. Sam and Carol, posterity, would accept. This was the largest colony of pitcher plants any of us was ever likely to see. Bright-green leaves, ruddy blooms, they glistened in the sun and nodded in the breeze and reached out from the lakeshore like tulips from a Dutch canal. Barber cut one off at the base and held up a leaf—folded upon itself like a narrow goblet, half full of water. The interior was lined with bristles, pointing downward. In the water were dozens of winged creatures, some still moving, most not. Barber had interrupted a handsome meal. His pitcher plants, in aggregate, could probably eat a ton of bugs a day. Sam said he sure was pleased to be able to make the pitcher plants a Georgia Natural Area. Carol saw a tiny water snake. She picked it up. It coiled in her hand and snapped at her. She talked gently to it until it settled down. "Are you going to be good now?" she said. She opened her hand, and the snake sat there, placidly, on her palm. The Barbers did not seem charmed. They said nothing and did not move. Carol set down the snake. It departed, and so did the Barbers. They went back to Moultrie in their air-conditioned car, leaving us their lake, their pines, their pitcher plants.

We jumped into the lake with a bar of soap and scrubbed ourselves up for dinner. In places, the lake was warm from the sun and in places cold from springs. We set up the tent and built a fire. The breeze was cool in the evening in the pines. Carol's stomach growled like a mastiff. She said that when she was hungry she could make her stomach growl on cue. It growled again. She had a tape recorder in the car. Sam got it and recorded the growls, which seemed marketable. He said they could scare away burglars. We fried beefsteaks and turtle steaks under a gibbous moon. We buried the fossils of pleasure: three cow bones and a bottle that had held The Glenlivet. Frogs were hooting. There were no owls. We slept like bears.

At six in the morning, we got into the canoe and moved slowly around the lake. Sam cast for bass. He could flick his lure seventy feet and drop it on a pine needle. He could lay it under stumps with the delicacy of an eyedropper, or drive it, if he wanted to, halfway down the lake. He caught two bass. One wrapped itself hopelessly into a big waterlogged multiple branch. We pulled the branch up out of the water. The bass had himself woven into it like a bird in a cage. Under blue sky and star-burst clusters of longleaf pine—pitcher plants far as you could see, the lake blue and cool—we cooked the bass in butter and ate it with fried turtle eggs. Then we fried salt-risen bread in the bass butter with more turtle eggs and poured Tate City honey over the bread. Chicory coffee with milk and honey. Fish-crackling off the bottom of the pan.

The yolk of a turtle egg cooks readily to a soft, mushy yellow. The albumen, though, pops and bubbles and jumps around the pan, and will not congeal. No matter how blazing the heat beneath it may be, the white of the egg of the snapping turtle will not turn milky and set. It will jump like a frog and bounce and dance and skitter all over the pan until your patience snaps or the fire dies. So you give up trying to cook it. You swallow it hot and raw.

D.O.R. cat. D.O.R. dog. Near the Mitchell County line. Carol sighed, but no move was made to stop. We were heading west on 37 to check out a river that the Natural Areas Council had been told was like no other in Georgia. Florida was only forty miles away. The terrain was flat and serene between the quiet towns—Camilla, Newton, Elmodel. Cattle stood on light-green grassland under groves of dark pecans. Sometimes the road was a corridor walled with pines. Sometimes the margins opened out into farms, then closed down toward small cabins, more palisades of pine.

D.O.R. gray squirrel. "We could eat him," Carol said.

"We've got enough food," said Sam.

More pines, more pecans, more farms, a mild morning under a blue-and-white sky. Out of the sky came country music—the Carter Sisters, Johnny Cash, philosophy falling like hail: "It's not easy to be all alone, but time goes by and life goes on . . . for after night there comes a dawn. Yes, time goes by and life goes on."

D.O.R. fox squirrel. Baker County. He was as warm as in life, and he was in perfect shape. Kneeling in the road, Carol held out his long, feathery silver-gray tail so that it caught the sunlight. "There aren't many things prettier than that," she said. "Makes a human being sort of jealous not to have a pretty tail like that." Gently, she brushed the squirrel and daubed blood from his head. He looked alive in her hands. She put him in a plastic bag. The ice was low. We stopped at the next icehouse and bought twenty-five pounds.

D.O.R. nighthawk, fresh as the squirrel. Carol kept the hawk for a while in her lap, just to look at him. He could have been an Aztec emblem—wings half spread, head in profile, feathers patterned in blacks and browns and patches of white. Around the mouth were stiff bristles, fanned out like a radar screen, adapted for catching insects.

D.O.R. box turtle.

D.O.R. loggerhead shrike.

D.O.R. gas station. It was abandoned, its old pumps rusting; beside the pumps, a twenty-year-old Dodge with four flat tires.

D.O.R. cottonmouth. Three miles east of Bluffton. Clay County. Finding him there was exciting to Carol. We were nearing the Cemocheckobee, the river we had come to see, and the presence of one cottonmouth here on the road implied crowded colonies along the river. There was no traffic, no point in moving him immediately off the road. Carol knelt beside him. "He was getting ready to shed. He would have been a lot prettier when he had," she said. The skin was dull olive. Carol felt along the spine to a point about three-quarters of the way back and squeezed. The dead snake coiled. "That is what really frightens some people," she said. She lifted the head and turned it so that we could see, between the mouth and the nostrils, the deep pits, sensory organs, through which the striking snake had homed on his targets. Slowly, Carol opened the creature's mouth. The manuals of herpetology tell you not to do that, tell you, in fact, not to touch a dead cottonmouth, because through reflex action a dead one can strike and kill a human being. Now a fang was visible—a short brown needle projecting down from the upper jaw. "You have to be very careful not to scratch your finger on one of those," Carol said. She pressed with her fingertips behind the eyes, directly on the poison sacs, and a drop of milky fluid fell onto a stick she held in her other hand. Four more drops followed, forming a dome of venom. "That amount could kill you," she said, and she pressed out another drop. "Did you know that this is where they got the idea for the hypodermic syringe?" Another drop. "It has to get into the bloodstream. You could drink all you want and it wouldn't hurt you." She placed the cottonmouth off the road. Carol once milked honeysuckle until she had about two ounces, which she then drank. The fluid was so concentratedly sweet it almost made her sick.

Carol's purse fell open as we got back into the car, and out of it spilled a .22-calibre revolver in a case that looked much like a compact. Also in the purse was a Big Brother tear-gas gun, flashlight bulbs, chapstick, shampoo, suntan lotion, and several headbands. Once, when she was off in a swamp frogging and salamandering, a state trooper came upon the car and—thinking it might be an abandoned vehicle—rummaged through it. He found the purse and opened it. He discovered the pistol, the chapstick, the shampoo, et cetera, and a pink garter belt and black net stockings. He might have sent out a five-state alert, but Carol just then emerged from the swamp. She was on her way, she told him, to make a call on Kimberly-Clark executives in an attempt to get them to register some forest and riverbank land with the Natural Areas Council, and for that mission the black net stockings would be as useful as the pistol might be in a swamp or the chapstick in a blistering sun. "Yes, Ma'am." The visit to the Kleenex people was successful, as it happened, and the result was the Griffin's Landing Registered Natural Area, fifty acres—a series of fossil beds on the Savannah River containing by the many thousands *Crassostrea gigantissima*, forty-million-year-old oysters, the largest that ever lived.

Down a dirt road, across a railroad track, and on through woods that scraped the car on both sides, Sam worked his way as far as he could toward the river's edge. We took down the canoe, and carried it to the water. The Cemocheckobee was a rejuvenated stream. Widening its valley, long ago, it had formed relaxed meanders, and now, apparently, the land was rising beneath it, and the river had speeded up and was cutting deeply into the meanders. The current was strong—nothing spectacular, nothing white, but forceful and swift. It ran beneath a jungle of overhanging trees. The river was compact and intimate. The distance from bank to bank was only about thirty feet, so there could be no getting away from the trees. "I'd venture to say we'll see our share of snakes today," Carol exulted. "Let's go! This is cottonmouth country!" Carol shoved up the sleeves of her sweatshirt over her elbows. Sam went to the car and got a snakebite kit.

I had thought I might be apprehensive about this part of the journey. I didn't see how I could help but be. Now I realized that I was having difficulty walking toward the river. "Sam," I said, "wouldn't you prefer that I paddle in the stern?" I had put in many more hours than he had in canoes on rivers, so it seemed only correct to me that Sam should sit up in the bow and fend off branches and cottonmouths while I guided the canoe from the commanding position in the rear.

"I'll go in the stern," said Sam. "Carol will go in the middle to collect snakes. You go in the bow." So much for that. It was his canoe. I got in and moved to the bow. They got in, and we shoved off.

The canoe found the current, accelerated, went downstream fifty feet, and smashed into a magnolia branch. I expected cottonmouths to strike me in both shoulders and the groin. But the magnolia proved to be snakeless. We shot on through and downriver. We could not avoid the overhanging branches. The current was too fast and there were too many of them. Once or twice a minute, we punched through the leafy twigs reaching down from a horizontal limb. But I began to settle down. There weren't any snakes, after all—not in the first mile, anyway. And things Carol was saying made a difference. She said, for example, that snakes plop off branches long before the canoe gets to them. She also said that cottonmouths rarely go out onto branches. They stay back at the river's edge and in the swamps. Snakes on branches are, in the main, as harmless as licorice. Bands of tension loosened and began to drop away. I looked ahead. At the next bend, the river was veiled in a curtain of water oak. I was actually hoping to see a snake hit the surface, but none did. We slipped through and into the clear.

This was heavy current for a river with no white water, and when we rested the river gave us a fast drift. Scenes quickly changed, within the steep banks, the incised meanders, against backgrounds of beech and laurel, white oak, spruce pine, Venus maidenhair, and resurrection fern. We came upon a young coon at the foot of a tree. He looked at us with no apparent fear. We pulled in to the bank. "Hey, there, you high-stepper, you," Carol said. "Get up that tree!" The coon put a paw on the tree and went up a foot or two and looked around. "Why aren't you afraid?" Carol went on. "Are you O.K., cooner?" The raccoon's trouble—probably—was that he had never seen a human. He was insufficiently afraid, and Carol began to worry about him. So she got out of the canoe and went after him. The coon moved up the tree fifteen feet. The tree was a slender maple. Carol started up it like a rope climber. The coon stayed where he was. Carol said, "I'm not climbing the tree to make him jump out. I'll just go high enough to let him know he ought to be afraid of people." When she got near him, the coon scrambled to the high branches, where he hung on to one and swayed. Carol stopped about twenty feet up. "Hey, coon! We're no good. Don't you know that?" she called to him. Then she slid on down. "Let that be a lesson to you!" she called from the bottom.

We moved on downstream, passing blue-tailed skinks and salamanders, animal tracks on every flat. A pair of beavers dived into the water and went around slapping the surface, firing blanks. Carol saw the mouth of their den, and she got out of the canoe, climbed the bank, and stuck her head inside. She regretted that she had not brought a flashlight with her. We moved on. We passed a banded snake sitting on a limb. He produced mild interest. Fear was gone from me. It had gone off with the flow of the river. There was a light splash to the right—as if from a slide, not a dive. No one saw what made it. "Otter," Carol said. "Pull in to the opposite bank—over there. Quickly!" We stopped the canoe, and held on to bush stems of the riverbank and waited. Nothing happened. The quiet grew. "The otter will come up and look at us," Carol said. We waited. Smooth, the river moved—never the same, always the same. No otter. "He is an extraordinarily intelligent and curious animal," Carol said. "He could go off somewhere, if he wanted to, just to breathe. But he wants to see us. He will not be able to stand it much longer. He will have to come up." Up came a face, chin on the water—dark bright eyes in a dark-brown head, small ears, wide snout: otter. His gaze was direct and unflinching. He looked at us until he had seen his fill; then he went back under. "Wouldn't you like to live in this creek?" Carol said. "You'd never get lonely. Wouldn't you like to play with the otter?"

A waterfall, about twelve feet high, poured into the river from the left. Two hundred yards downstream, another fall dropped into the river from the right. The feeder streams of the Cemocheckobee were not cutting down as fast as the river itself, and these hanging tributaries poured in from above, all the way down. We now moved through stands of royal fern under big sycamores and big beeches, and past another waterfall. "This is otter, beaver, coon heaven," Carol said. Her only disappointment was the unexpected scarcity of snakes. She said she had seen more than her share of "magnolia-leaf snakes" that day. Her imagination, charged with hope and anticipation, could, and frequently did, turn magnolia leaves into snakes, green upon the branches. I found myself feeling disappointed, too. Only one lousy banded snake. The day was incomplete.

Sam said the threat to this river was the lumber industry. Logging was going on in the forests on both sides, and he would try to persuade the lumbermen to register the river—and its marginal lands—before the day came when it would be too late. While he was speaking, I saw a snake on a log at the water's edge, and pointed to it, interrupting him.

"Is that a banded snake?"

"That is not a banded snake," Carol said.

"Is it a bad one?"

"It's a bad one, friend."

"Well, at last. Where have you been all day?"

He had been right there, of course, in his own shaft of sun, and the sight of a shining aluminum canoe with three figures in it was not going to cause him to move. Moving back was not in his character. He would stay where he was, or go toward something that seemed to threaten him. Whatever else he might be, he was not afraid. He was a cottonmouth, a water moccasin. Carol was closer to him than I was, and I felt no fear at all. Sam, in the stern, was closest of all, because we were backing up toward the snake. I remember thinking, as we moved closer, that I preferred that they not bring the thing into the canoe, but that was the sum of my concern; we were ten miles downstream from where we had begun. The moccasin did not move. We were now right next to it. Sam reached toward it with his paddle.

"Rough him up a little to teach him to beware of humans," Carol said. "But don't hurt him."

Under the snake Sam slipped the paddle, and worked it a bit, like a spatula, so that the snake came up onto the blade. Sam lifted the cottonmouth into the air. Sam rocked the paddle. "Come on," he said. "Come on, there. Open your mouth so John can see the cotton."

"Isn't he magnificent?" Carol said. "Set him down, Sam. He isn't going to open his mouth."

Sam returned the moccasin to the log. The canoe moved on into a gorge. The walls of the gorge were a hundred feet high.

THE Cemocheckobee was itself a feeder stream, ending in the Chattahoochee, there in southwestern Georgia, at the Alabama line. An appointment elsewhere with the Chattahoochee—a red-letter one for Sam and Carol—drew us back north. The Chattahoochee is Georgia's most prodigious river. Atlanta developed where railheads met the river. The Chattahoochee rises off the slopes of the Brasstown Bald, Georgia's highest mountain, seven miles from North Carolina, and flows to Florida, where its name changes at the frontier. It is thereafter called the Appalachicola. In all its four hundred Georgia miles, what seems most remarkable about this river is that it flows into Atlanta nearly wild. Through a series of rapids between high forested bluffs, it enters the city clear and clean. From parts of the Chattahoochee within the city of Atlanta, no structures are visible—just water, sky, and woodland. The circumstance is nostalgic, archaic, and unimaginable. It is as if an unbefouled Willamette were to flow wild into Portland—Salt into Phoenix, Missouri into Omaha, Charles into Boston, Hudson into New York, Delaware into Philadelphia, James into Richmond, Cuyahoga into Cleveland (the Cuyahoga caught fire one day, and fire engines had to come put out the blazing river). Atlanta deserves little credit for the clear Chattahoochee, though, because the Chattahoochee is killed before it leaves the city. It dies between Marietta Boulevard and South Cobb Drive, just below the Atlanta Water Intake, at the point where thirty-five million gallons of partially treated sewage and forty million gallons of raw sewage are poured into the river every day. A short distance below that stand two enormous power plants, whose effluent pipes raise the temperature of the river. A seven-pound brown trout was caught recently not far above the Water Intake. It is difficult to imagine what sort of fin-rotted, five-legged, uranium-gilled, web-mouthed monster could live in the river by Georgia Power. Seen from the air (Sam showed it to me once in his plane), the spoiling of the Chattahoochee is instant, from river-water blue to sewer ochre-brown, as if a pair of colored ribbons had been sewn together there by the city.

Now a sewer line was projected to run upstream beside the river to fresh subdivisions that would bloom beyond the city's perimeter highway. The sewer would not actually be in the water, but, unless it could be tunnelled or not built at all, it would cause the clear-cutting of every tree in a sixty-foot swath many miles long. A segment of the sewer was already under construction. The Georgia Natural Areas Council was among the leadership in an effort to put down this specific project and at the same time to urge a bill through the legislature that would protect permanently the river and its overview. Sam had asked Jimmy Carter to come get into a canoe and shoot the metropolitan rapids and see for himself the value and the vulnerability of the river. Carter was willing. So, in three canoes, six of us put in under the perimeter highway, I-285, and paddled into Atlanta.

Sam had Carter in his bow. Carter might be governor of Georgia but not of Sam's canoe. Carol and I had the second canoe. In the third was a state trooper, who had a pistol on his hip that could have sunk a frigate. In the stern was James Morrison, of the federal government, the Bureau of Outdoor Recreation's man in Atlanta. He wore wet-suit bootees and rubber kneepads and seemed to be ready to go down the Colorado in an acorn.

The current was strong. The canoes moved smartly downstream. Carter was a lithe man, an athletic man in his forties—at home, obviously enough, in boats. He was wearing a tan windbreaker, khaki trousers, and white basketball shoes. He had a shock of wind-tossed sandy hair. In the course of the day, he mentioned that he had grown up in Archery, Georgia, by a swamp of the Kinchafoonee and the Choctawhatchee. He and his friend A. D. Davis, who was black, had built a twelve-foot bateau. "When it rained and we couldn't work in the fields, we went down to the creek and set out set hooks for catfish and eels, and we drifted downstream in the bateau hunting ducks with a shotgun. We fished for bass and redbellies, and we waded for jack. The bateau weighed eighty pounds. I could pick it up." Archery was three miles west of Plains, a crossroads with a short row of stores and less than a thousand people. Sam, Carol, and I had passed through Plains—in fifteen seconds—on our way north. An enormous red-lettered sign over the stores said, "PLAINS, GEORGIA, HOME OF JIMMY CARTER." Carter had played basketball at Plains High School, had gone on to Annapolis and into nuclear submarines, and had come back to Plains in 1953 to farm peanuts and to market them for himself and others, businesses he continued as he went on into the legislature and upward to become governor. The career of his boyhood friend had been quite different. The last Carter had heard of A. D. Davis, Davis was in jail for manslaughter.

Now, on the Chattahoochee, the Governor said, "We're lucky here in Georgia that the environment thing has risen nationally, because Georgia is less developed than some states and still has much to save." With that, he and Sam went into the largest set of rapids in the city of Atlanta. The rip was about a hundred yards long, full of Vs confusing to the choice, broad ledges, haystacks, eddies, and tumbling water. They were good rapids, noisy and alive, and strong enough to flip a canoe that might hit a rock and swing broadside.

In the shadow of a two-hundred-foot bluff, we pulled out on a small island to survey the scene. Carol said the bluff was a gneiss and was full of garnets. The Governor had binoculars. With them, he discovered a muskrat far out in the river. The muskrat was gnawing on a branch that had been stopped by a boulder. "He's sniffin' around that little old limb on top of that rock," Carter said. "Maybe he's eating the lichens off it. Look, there's another. Who owns the land here?"

"Various people," Morrison said. "Some are speculators. A lot of it is owned by Alfred Kennedy."

"Kennedy?"

"A director of the First National Bank," Carol said.

"Is he a good guy, so far as conservancy goes?"

"From what I hear, he's too busy making money."

"Sometimes it's better to slip up on people like that," Carter told her. "Rather than make an issue of it right away." He spoke in a low voice, almost shyly. There was a touch of melancholy in his face that disappeared, as it did frequently, when he grinned. A trillium caught his eye. He asked her what it was, and she told him. "And what's that?" he said.

"Dog hobble," Carol said. "*Leucothoë.* Look here." She pointed at the ground. "A coon track."

The canoes moved on, and the next stop was a visit with a fisherman who was casting from the bank. He was middle-aged and weathered, a classical, prototype fisherman, many years on the river. He was wreathed in smiles at sight of the Governor. I looked hard at Sam, but nothing in his face indicated that he had planted the man there. The fisherman, Ron Sturdevant, showed the Governor a Kodacolor print of a twenty-three-inch rainbow he had recently caught right here under this bluff. "I guess I'm glad I met you," Sturdevant said. "I'm glad you're taking this trip. I'm worried about the river."

"I hope we can keep it this way," Carter said.

We climbed from the river through a deep wood of oaks and big pines to a cave in which families of Cherokees had once lived. It was about a hundred feet up. The view swept the river, no structures visible. "Who owns this place?"

Sam said, "Alfred Kennedy."

"And he hasn't even slept here," said Carol.

"Have you slept here, Carol?" the Governor asked her.

"Many times," she told him. "With a dog named Catfish."

Morrison said, "There's gold here, around the Indian cave. It's never been mined."

"That would be a good way to keep this place undisturbed," Carter said. "To announce that there was gold up here."

Back on the river, he used his binoculars while Sam paddled. He saw four more muskrats and an automobile, upside down in the water, near the far bank. He also saw a turtle.

"What kind is it?" Carol asked him.

"If I knew what kind it was, I could tell you." He handed the binoculars across to her, too late.

"I've been down through here and seen fifteen turtles with bullet holes in their shells," Carol told him.

"What kind?" Carter said.

"Cooters and sliders."

There was a racket of engines. Out of nowhere came two motorcyclists riding *in* the river. A mile or so later, we took out, beside an iron bridge. Carol said she had washed her hair any number of times under that bridge.

The Governor invited us home for lunch. The mansion was new—a million-dollar neo-Palladian Xanadu, formal as a wedding cake, and exquisitely landscaped. Carol and Sam and I were ropy from a thousand miles of mountains, rivers, and swamps. None of us had changed clothes in nearly a week, but we would soon be eating grilled cheese sandwiches at a twenty-foot table under a crystal chandelier. The Governor, for that matter, did not look laundered anymore—mud on his trousers, mud on his basketball shoes. We parked in back of the mansion. A backboard, hoop, and net were mounted there. A ball sat on the pavement. Before going in, we shot baskets for a while.

"The river is just great," the Governor said, laying one in. "And it ought to be kept the way it is. It's almost heartbreaking to feel that the river is in danger of destruction. I guess I'll write a letter to all the landowners and say, 'If you'll use some self-restraint, it'll decrease the amount of legal restraint put on you in the future.' I don't think people want to incur the permanent wrath of the governor or the legislature."

"I've tried to talk to property owners," Carol said. "To get them to register their land with the Natural Areas Council. But they wouldn't even talk to me."

The Governor said, "To be blunt about it, Carol, why would they?"

The Governor had the ball and was dribbling in place, as if contemplating a property owner in front of him, one-on-one. He went to the basket, shot, and missed. Carol got the rebound and fed the ball to Sam. He shot. He missed, too.

(1973)

THE MAN WHO WALKS ON AIR

F ROM the departure point, the void hits you like a thunderclap. It is sixteen hundred feet down, straight down, to the meandering bed of the Little Colorado River. The distance across, to the isolated mesa on the other side, which Philippe Petit will walk to on his cable, is twelve hundred feet. Several million years of geological time are on view in that perpendicular rockface, with its tan, purple, and reddish-ochre layers. Petit has photographed and mapped every inch of it. He has given names to certain areas, to help him identify the forty-six anchor points for the twenty-three cavalletti, or guy lines, that are needed to stabilize the cable. "You see that circle there?" he says, pointing to a patch of lighter tan near the top. "I call it the Clock. If you imagine a clock's hands there, I will arrive at noon."

Philippe Petit, the only living high-wire artist who performs in the world at large, outside the circus, has been planning his Canyon Walk for years. He put a cable across in 1988, but then Jacques Chirac, the mayor of Paris, gave him permission to do his Eiffel Tower walk for the Bicentennial of the French Revolution, and that and other projects intervened. The old cable, recently severed, hangs down the cliff face from the departure point; it will be removed before Petit and his crew of riggers install the new one. Standing too close to the edge, jauntily pointing out other spots he has named on the sheer rockface—"giant's foot," "shopping list," "living room," "stovepipe"—Petit is the focal point in this harsh, tremendous landscape. He is five feet seven inches tall, slim but sturdy, with red-brown hair and large, powerful-looking hands. He talks fast, in French-accented but confident English. He is forty-nine years old. It is twenty-five years since he secretly stretched a cable between the twin towers of the World Trade Center and electrified New York by performing on it for nearly an hour. He has made seventy high-wire walks, all over the world. Most of them have been legal, unlike the World Trade Center caper, and each one, in his mind and in the eyes of thousands of spectators, has been a work of art—not a daredevil stunt but a complex and intricately choreographed theatrical performance.

After the World Trade Center crossing, in 1974, American admirers kept telling Petit that he should "do" the Grand Canyon, so eventually he went to see it. "I found it almost ugly or boring," he recalls. "Two rims twelve miles apart— for four hours I would be a little dot in the sky, and break a record for distance. I'm sorry, that doesn't interest me." Looking at the map, though, he noticed that about fifteen miles east of Grand Canyon National Park, where the tourists congregate, a tributary of the Colorado River narrowed and ran through a vast tract called the Navajo Tribal Lands. Petit and Kathy O'Donnell, who is his companion and since 1987 has been the producer of his high-wire spectacles, spent two weeks driving around this area with a Navajo guide. "I didn't know what I was looking for except that it should be something that will stop my heart in the landscape," Petit told me. "We saw many magnificent canyons, but essentially boring canyons, until the very last day, when we rented a small plane. We had no more money, we could not have bought one more hour of air time, but then, from the airplane, I saw a site that had profundity, that had mystery, that was stopping my heart. In a bend of the Little Colorado River gorge I saw a rim that was like a *presqu'ile*—an almost island—and across from it a solitary mesa, a tower of gigantic proportions. Here was a site, I realized, where I could walk from the known to the unknown, from civilization to a place where man had never set foot. I made a quick sketch from the air, and the next day I came back and explored that place on foot, and then it became the only place."

Canyon Walk, Petit says, will be his masterpiece. In a written statement whose cadences simultaneously echo and mock the circus hyperbole that he detests, he calls it "the greatest show of my life, the most arduous crossing, the most fragile, the most astonishing, the most icy, the most shared, the most intimate, the most radiant, the most imposing, the most celestial. Like all the others, past and future." It is scheduled to take place in September, 2000, and it will be telecast, live, for a global audience that is expected to be in the millions. Although his Eiffel Tower walk, in 1989, was much longer than this one—more than two thousand feet, on an inclined cable stretching from ground level, at the Place du Trocadéro, to a point near the tower's second-stage landing— Canyon Walk is the highest: the cable here will be three hundred feet higher than the one at the World Trade Center. The combination of length and height and the exposed nature of the site, which offers no protection from the wind, makes this the most demanding and, of course, the most dangerous of his walks, but danger is not an element that figures in Petit's calculations. As he often says, he takes no risks. What he means is that he prepares so thoroughly for each walk—learning everything there is to learn about the site (weather, wind patterns, history, geological or architectural features, etc.), rigging his cable and cavalletti according to ultra-conservative safety factors, and trusting his own phenomenal powers of concentration to rule out any misstep—that the danger, although real and present, is subject to his control.

"I prepare by reducing the unknown to nothing," he tells me, up there on that cliff, "but also by knowing my limits. If I think I am a hero who is invincible, I will pay for it with my life. Anyone you bring here will be slapped in the face by the immensity of the site. How arrogant of me to dare to put a wire across and say I will walk! I have to be very respectful of the space. The space is something I will never conquer or master. But if I walk it with artistry, with poetry, with meaning, as a piece of theatre, or an opera, which is what I call this walk, then maybe it can inspire you. I would never have attempted this walk thirty years ago. It has taken me a lifetime of serious confrontation."

THE history of walking on ropes has not yet been written. Petit plans to do that when he finds time. He has been gathering material for it since he began wire walking, at the age of sixteen, and in "Funambule," one of four books he has written and published, he devotes a section to historical notes on the practice. Ropewalking, he tells us, had its origins in ancient Greece. It spread to Rome in the time of Marcus Aurelius and became hugely popular during the Middle Ages, when acrobats danced and performed high above the heads of spectators at major public events, or ascended and descended inclined ropes attached to the bell towers of cathedrals and other high places. The immense popularity of these spectacles eventually led to their being shut down by the clergy, and in the seventeenth and eighteenth centuries the art of ropedancing, as it had come to be called, was confined to small theatres in Paris and a few other cities. Open-air "ascensions" reëmerged after the Revolution, and master funambulists—from the Latin *funis* ("rope") and *ambulare* ("to walk")—became the toast of Paris. Pierre Forioso (the "incomparable") walked on a rope from the Pont de la Concorde to the Pont des Tuileries to celebrate Napoleon's birthday in 1807. Mme. Saqui, née Marguerite-Antoinette Lalanne, so captivated the susceptible Bonaparte with her ascensions and her dramatic evocations, at great heights, of the Battle of Wagram and the crossing of the Great St. Bernard pass that he named her Première Acrobate de Sa Majesté l'Empereur et Roi and sent her off to perform for his troops.

The most famous *funambule* of the last century, however, was Jean-François Gravelet, known as Blondin, "whose dangerous and difficult leaps," Petit writes, "were executed with a precision and assurance that exceeded anything done before him." Having conquered his native France and the rest of Europe, Blondin laid claim to America by walking over Niagara Falls, in 1859. Not the falls itself, as Petit points out: he put his manila rope across a narrow gorge some distance below the falls and enthralled thousands of spectators with his daring maneuvers; on one crossing he cooked and ate an omelette. Petit, playing the role of Blondin, re-created his Niagara crossing for a 1986 IMAX film called "Niagara: Miracles, Myths & Magic." The film, he says, was "historically ridiculous." His unfulfilled ambition is to make films—films conceived, written, directed, produced, starred in, and maybe even distributed by him. There is a certain arrogance in this, but then, as Petit says in more ebullient and playful moments, he has earned the right to be arrogant.

GROWING up in the suburbs of Paris, an absurdly rebellious middle child (older sister, younger brother) in a bourgeois family, Petit taught himself to walk on a rope by stretching several ropes between two trees in a meadow on the family's country estate and then taking them away one at a time. Other passions competed in those years—magic, juggling, classical equitation, fencing, theatre, drawing, bullfighting. All played havoc with his education (he was kicked out of five schools) and tried the patience of his father, Edmond Petit, a French Army pilot and an author. (His "World History of Aviation" is currently in its ninth printing.) The wire won out, but when Rudolf Omankowsky, the leader of a famous troupe of touring wire walkers called Les Diables Blancs, offered to train Petit as a circus performer. Petit declined. He paid Papa Rudy to show him the techniques of rigging and securing wire cables, and learned the rest on his own. Petit swears that he has no special athletic abilities or sense of balance. "It is not difficult to walk on a tightrope," he assured me. "But you need to have passion, and you have to work madly, to practice all day long. Within one year, I taught myself to do all the things you could do on a wire. I learned the backward somersault, the front somersault, the unicycle, the bicycle, the chair on the wire, jumping through hoops. But I thought, What is the big deal here? It looks almost ugly. So I started to discard those tricks and to reinvent my art."

Because no circus would hire Petit, who demanded to be allowed to perform in his own style, he became a street juggler. He developed a character (nonverbal, black-clad, intensely concentrated) and a brief performance that included some magic, some juggling, and much subtle and humorous interaction with the spectators; it usually ended with a few minutes on a length of rope strung between improvised supports. He would perform three or four times a day, creating his own stage by drawing a circle in white chalk on some chosen spot (for years he worked outside the Café les Deux Magots, in Saint-Germain des Près), and, in spite of more than five hundred arrests (by his own count), he never went hungry.

He lived in a tiny room on the Rue Laplace. From that Left Bank neighborhood he could just see the towers of the Cathedral of Notre-Dame. "One day," he recalls, "I decide that I am going to put a wire there, and surprise Paris, surprise the world." It took him three years and countless visits in the guise of a tourist to prepare this first, clandestine "coup," which took place on June 26, 1971. The day before, using subterfuges and techniques that he later adapted for the World Trade Center walk, Petit and two volunteer assistants smuggled in several hundred pounds of cable and other equipment, hid until dark, and passed the cable across from one tower to the other by throwing a rubber ball with a fishing line attached to it. At ten o'clock the next morning, Petit emerged from his hiding place, picked up his long balancing pole, and stepped out onto the wire. He crossed and recrossed between the towers, knelt on the wire, lay down on it, put aside his pole and juggled three Indian clubs, and held the city of Paris in a delirium of suspense and delight. It was the beginning of his real life as a high-wire walker and the end, in a sense, of his life as a Frenchman. Deeply wounded by what he felt to be the short-lived enthusiasm of his countrymen—he was arrested, released, lionized for a day or so, and then quickly forgotten by the French news media—he packed up and took his street-juggling act to the South of France and then to other countries: to Russia; to Australia, where he pulled off another clandestine walk, on a cable between the pylons of the Sydney Harbour Bridge; and eventually to New York, where, without money and knowing no one, he achieved the almost unimaginable feat of investing the World Trade Center, those two slabs of architectural ennui, with a thrilling and terrible beauty.

The offers poured in after that, of course—from Arrow Shirts and Burger King and a dozen other commercial franchises. He rejected them all. Instead, with certain misgivings, he joined the circus. Ringling Brothers and Barnum & Bailey Circus made him a featured performer, and he toured the United States in that capacity for nearly a year—an experience he describes as "a dream and a nightmare combined." He disliked doing the same twelve-minute routine two or sometimes three times a day, so he improvised freely. Performing without a net, he did all the circus tricks that were expected—the forward and backward somersaults and the unicycle and the stick-and-ball balanced on his forehead—but he refused to play to the audience in the "vulgar" way that a circus walker does, by making the tricks look more difficult than they are, or pretending to lose his balance so the crowd will scream. Petit fell once, from a forty-five-foot-high wire, during that year with Ringling Brothers. It was the only serious fall he has ever had—he broke several ribs, and sustained internal injuries as well—but because it happened while he was practicing, rather than performing, he insists that it doesn't count. He made a rapid recovery, and finished out his contract with Ringling Brothers. He has been on his own ever since.

"Some wire walkers in the circus are technically much better than I am," Petit told me. "They perform every day, and they do things I never do—human pyramids, somersaults from a bicycle. But I am a better wire walker because I have something they will never have. There is nothing more beautiful or essential in the world of wire walking than simply walking on the wire, but in circus school no high-wire walker is learning that. They don't walk beautifully, or elegantly, because they don't love it enough. They are not inhabited by the wire."

ST. John the Divine is the largest Gothic cathedral in the world. The church, its ancillary structures, and its garden occupy three blocks from Amsterdam Avenue to Morningside Drive, between 110th and 113th Streets. Philippe Petit has been an artist-in-residence there since 1980. He fell in love with the place when James Parks Morton, the cathedral's charismatic and somewhat unorthodox dean, invited the fledgling Big Apple Circus, with which Petit had appeared once or twice as a guest artist, to use the Synod House as its circus school for a few weeks. Petit told Morton he would like to do a high-wire walk inside the cathedral. Morton, who knew about the association of cathedrals and tightrope walking in the Middle Ages, was all for it, but his trustees said no. (What if he fell?) Petit put up a cable anyway and did his walk. When he came down, the police arrested him for trespassing. They were taking him away in handcuffs when Dean Morton, who hadn't witnessed the walk, appeared and told them to release the culprit. "He wasn't trespassing," Morton told the cops. "He is an artist of this cathedral." Afterward, it seemed like such a good idea that Morton and Petit made it official.

Petit has his "office" high up in the triforium, a narrow balcony over the nave. He has built shelves, cabinets, and workspaces there; everything is organized cleverly and meticulously, as on a ship. He and I stood on his balcony at five o'clock one Sunday afternoon, listening to a choir rehearsing for Vespers far below us. "I am not a man of belief, but I really belong in this cathedral," Petit said quietly. "When you think about it, wire walking is very close to what religion is. 'Religion' is from the Latin *religare*, which means to link something, people or places. And to know, before you take your first step on a wire, that you are going to do the last one—this is a kind of faith." Dean Morton had told me that Petit is one of the most religious people he knows. "Sometimes very unusual people turn out to be the most religious," the Dean said. "I think of this as God's joke."

Since his unauthorized 1980 walk, Petit has done six authorized walks in St. John the Divine, the last one in honor of Dean Morton's retirement, in 1996. He has a practice cable installed in the Synod House, and one evening last winter I went there with a small group of his friends to see him walk. "This is not a show," he explained to us at the outset. "Just cooking." He stripped down to a black T-shirt and black knee-length tights, which gave him a sort of rough-and-ready, working-class look, and put a tape of classical guitar music on his portable tape player. Before getting on the wire, he did some juggling to warm up. Petit, who readily admits that he is not a great juggler, seemed rusty at first. Every time he got six rings in the air at once, one or two of them would clatter to the floor. Two teen-age girls in our group started to giggle. Petit's movements were quick, fluid, and a little impatient. After ten minutes of this, he got on the wire, which was stretched fifty feet between the balconies on either side of the room and guyed by two cavalletti anchored to the hardwood floor, about eighteen feet below.

He looked entirely different to me up there—lighter, taller, aristocratic. He walked barefoot, in a smooth, steady rhythm, his head held high. His eighteen-foot-long balancing pole nearly brushed the chandeliers when he made his turn and started back. After several crossings, he stepped off the wire, put on a pair of ballet slippers, and changed the tape from guitar music to jazz. Back on the wire, he moved in a different style, which I recognized, from his writings, as his *marche de torero.*

There are an infinite number of walks on the wire, Petit tells us in "On the High Wire," the only one of his books available in English. (The translation is by the novelist Paul Auster, who is a friend of his.) "There is the walk that glides, like that of a bullfighter who slowly approaches his adversary, the presence of danger growing with each new step, his body arched outrageously, hypnotized." Petit, who spent a year of his youth as an apprentice torero in France and Spain, slid one foot along the wire and then the other, his body projecting a sinuous arrogance. By this time, I had lost any sense that he could fall. He knelt down on the wire, and then reclined on his back, stretching his legs until one lay along the wire and the other hung down; he rested the balancing pole on his stomach, and let his arms hang free.

After another sequence of linked crossings, he put the balancing pole down on one balcony and crossed back and forth without it, using his arms for balance. He walked quickly, in a sort of running dance step. He picked up three Indian clubs and juggled them, expertly this time—no misses. Leaving the wire again, he signalled to Evelyne Crochet, a concert pianist who has worked with him on a number of his performances. She left our group and walked across to a piano at the far end of the room. As she began a meditative rendering of "The Well-Tempered Clavier," Petit slung his balancing pole over one shoulder and demonstrated another of his favorite walks, a casual and relaxed stroll, eyes turned upward, free arm swinging at his side. It is what he calls "the solid walk of a man of the earth returning home, a tool over his shoulder, satisfied with the day's work."

Afterward, over dinner at a nearby Indian restaurant, Petit told me that he likes to work without a balancing pole. He has done many short walks that way, including several on an inclined wire. (Inclined wires are no more difficult to walk on than straight ones, he says. He has even walked on them blindfolded. In circus parlance, the blindfolded walk on an inclined wire is a "death walk," and it is always referred to as an "attempt.") "I want one day to do a big walk without a balancing pole," Petit said. "It has never been done, in the history of acrobatics. And, since I am a man of the theatre, I have invented a dramatic way of introducing that. I turn the pole until it is almost vertical and then throw it out, so that it does not bang on the wire. I would love to present the image of a human being leaving the crowd and becoming part of the sky, with no balancing pole."

IN the living room of a small, cozy farmhouse near Woodstock, in upstate New York, Petit shows me "The Book" for Canyon Walk, a bulging album filled with eleven years of accumulated data: handwritten notes; drawings and photographs; engineering specifications; geological surveys; maps; weather records from Grand Canyon Village going back fifteen years; information on Navajo customs, dress, music, art, history, and mythology; and technical information on cables, state-of-the-art polypropylene ropes (for the cavalletti), clamps, shackles, rock drills, bits, pulleys, anchors, block and tackles, counterweights. In an office in his basement are file cabinets and plastic cartons filled with more data, all splendidly organized. This represents the enormous effort of reducing the unknown to nothing, and Petit does it himself, without a secretary or a computer.

Kathy O'Donnell handles the computer work, the telephone, the fax machine. As Petit's producer and working partner, she makes it possible for him to do what he does. "I'm the bitch in the organization," she tells me, laughing easily. "I'm much tougher than he is, and I don't suffer fools gladly. It was always easy for me to talk to people about Philippe, because I got what he was trying to do. When you have a man who won't do commercials, and who is as uncompromising about his work and his life as Philippe is, it is pretty clear that he is not going to give us cheap thrills. But a lot of people just don't get it." O'Donnell grew up in Manhattan. Her father was the executive vice-president of Doubleday, and she worked in the book business herself until 1987, when, having met Petit and helped out on a couple of his walks, she quit her job to help produce Walking the Harp/A Bridge for Peace, a high-wire performance on a cable linking the Jewish and the Arab quarters of Jerusalem. She has been the producer of all his projects since then, and he depends on her for many things. She helped him survive the death of Gypsy, a daughter he had with his previous companion, Elaine Fasula. A lovely and spirited child, Gypsy died of a cerebral hemorrhage in 1992, when she was nine and a half years old. Her ashes were placed in the columbarium at St. John the Divine.

Across the driveway from the house, Petit is building an eighteenth-century barn. He has worked on it since 1993, off and on, using only the methods and the tools that were available to builders then: no nails, no power saws. "I actually dislike pretty much the world in which we live," he told me. "If I could choose, I would probably live in the Renaissance or the Middle Ages." Since the World Trade Center walk, he has lived mostly in this country. "I love many things in France—the wine, the cheese, the bread, the art, the architecture, the history—but there is a lot I dislike in the French system," he confided. "Do I like America? Not really. I have nothing to do with money, with power, with success. I didn't choose this country, I chose the twin towers, and I stay here one week, one month, one year, and now it's twenty-five years. But I live in my own world. I could be anywhere."

Petit's intransigent nature and his drive to control every aspect and detail of his strange calling make Kathy O'Donnell's job difficult at times. But Petit can be gregarious, funny, charming, and mesmerizingly persuasive. "Philippe has never been bored in his life," according to O'Donnell, "and there has never been a moment when he didn't know what he wanted to do." In spite of having no interest in money or success, he loves good food and good wine, and he is on friendly terms with the owners of some superlative restaurants, including Taillevent, in Paris, and Chanterelle, in New York. Petit designed a menu for Chanterelle some years back, a talent for drawing being another in his seemingly endless repertoire of skills. A number of artists in other fields are in awe of him. Mikhail Baryshnikov, who engineered the crucial meeting between Petit and Jacques Chirac which led to the permission for Petit's Eiffel Tower walk, vividly remembers a night in a Copenhagen restaurant when Petit invited a young woman who was dining alone to join their table and then managed to get her watch off her wrist and on his own without her noticing it. "What's impressive about Philippe is the purpose, the idea, the complexity of his work," Baryshnikov said recently. "There is always a certain quest, which is noble."

Canyon Walk will cost three and a half million dollars to produce. O'Donnell had hoped that a large part of this would come from the sale of television rights, but none of the networks would commit themselves to a live telecast (Petit insists that the walk be shown live) because of the perennial "what-if factor"— not what if he falls but what if somebody's four-year-old sees him fall and the parents sue the network for traumatizing their child. At the moment, O'Donnell is working out a deal with a pay-per-view provider, to do a live ninety-minute telecast of the walk, with interlinear footage on Petit and his career, and on the Navajos. Meanwhile, a young German management consultant named Thomas Ring volunteered to raise the front money for the walk. Ring had heard Petit lecture at a symposium on creativity and motivation, in Zermatt; hugely impressed, he arranged to meet him and asked what he could do to help. O'Donnell, who had been skeptical at first, was eventually won over by Ring's dedication and enterprise, and he ended up raising the necessary funds. Petit and O'Donnell are cautiously hopeful that the global telecast of Canyon Walk will be a watershed event in his career, one that will make future projects easier to produce. "It may change my life, don't you think?" he asked me, half kidding. "If not, I am going to kill myself."

THREE months before Canyon Walk, Petit and O'Donnell will move out to Flagstaff, Arizona, for the final preparations. A new cable will be stretched across in June, and Petit and his team of riggers, who are also experienced rock

climbers, will spend eight weeks anchoring and installing the twenty-three cavalletti. Petit usually depends on this hard and highly specialized work to get him
in shape for a performance, but during the countdown to Canyon Walk he will
also work out in a gym adjacent to their motel, and, not far from the walk site,
set up a practice cable about twelve feet off the ground and three hundred and
fifty feet longer than the real one. "It has the same orientation, so I will receive
the same winds," he told me. "And I will practice sometimes under the worst
conditions: at dusk, when I can hardly see, with a balancing pole that is too
heavy, without cavalletti. I will do it with friends banging on the cable. I will do
it in the strongest wind, to the point where maybe I will have to grab the wire. I
will do it in the rain, and with the sun in my eyes, and when I am too tired to do
it. That will put me in a very aggressive frame of mind, so that when I find myself on the real wire, on a beautiful calm, sunny day, it will seem like a nice
promenade."

Cables for industrial use have grease worked into them during the manufac-
turing process (wire walkers must clean them carefully), but Diepa, the German
firm that is making Petit's cable for Canyon Walk, agreed to do it without grease.
This meant shutting down the machinery that weaves the wires into cables,
scouring away all the accumulated grease, and forming the cable very slowly, to
keep it from getting too hot. Petit's cable will be able to sustain a load of a hundred tons. To Petit, it is a live entity, like an animal. "To become a good wire
walker, you should understand the wire, its construction, its tension, its vibration," he says. "It has many moods that you can accord yourself with—by controlling your breathing, by controlling the way you shift your weight. The cable
has three movements. There is the vertical, up-and-down movement. There is
also a swinging movement; even with cavalletti, the whole system is going to
swing. And then there is a very treacherous movement, which is inside the
cable—a kind of torque, with the cable moving on itself. These three movements
do not occur in a predictable way but in a completely surprise way."

Since Canyon Walk will take place in the Navajo Tribal Lands, Petit and
O'Donnell have spent a lot of time talking with various Navajo groups and organizations, and negotiating with them for the necessary permits. From the
start, the Navajos have been impressed by Petit's respectful attitude and by his
wanting to make them part of his "opera." Although Petit is reluctant to divulge the scenario of his performance in advance, he plans to begin it with a
ceremony involving Navajos in tribal dress and traditional flute and drum
music. He has also engaged a Spanish flamenco singer, who will be stationed on
the riverbank at the bottom of the canyon. Petit wants him to perform the vocal
exercise that flamenco singers use in preparing themselves for the extremes of
flamenco sound, "a sort of howling," and then, a little later, he wants him to
improvise a song about the walker while he is on the wire.

There are to be just a few hundred invited spectators, sitting on bleachers
about fifty yards back from the canyon's edge, and they will not be able to hear

or see the singer. Canyon Walk was conceived as a television performance; there will be at least fifteen cameras in use, and the best place to watch the performance, Petit tells everyone, is at home, on your TV screen. O'Donnell has arranged for tight security at the site, with a police checkpoint at the turnoff to the dirt road that Petit put in to provide access to his site, and a number of black-belt karate masters (friends of O'Donnell's, who have helped out on other productions) to discourage gate-crashers. Petit expects the walk itself to take about thirty-five minutes. He will pause at intervals on the wire to perform movements and gestures that he has prepared, along with others he may improvise, but there will be no return trip. The scenario calls for him to cross from the known to the unknown, and then, metaphorically speaking, to vanish into the territory of myth. (Off camera, a helicopter will pick him up and bring him back.) The only thing that could delay his journey at this point is the weather. Wind is the wire walker's nightmare. Just before Petit began a walk in Frankfurt, in 1994, the wind was blowing so hard that O'Donnell and others begged him to wait. He waited for twenty-five minutes and then went ahead anyway, unwilling to disappoint five hundred thousand spectators assembled in the square below, but there was a scary moment when a gust caught the long cloak that was part of his costume and almost lifted him off the wire. This time, if it's too windy, he has said he'll agree to postpone the walk until the following day.

"It is a terrifying walk, but you won't be terrified," he assured me. That may be true. Paul Auster, who has known Petit for twenty years, believes that the exhilaration we feel in watching him on the high wire comes from his taking us up there with him and conquering our fear in the process. "Obviously, it requires tremendous skill, and practice, and courage, but he makes it look so easy," Auster said. "He wants to inspire that sense of participation." Seeing him work out on the practice wire convinced me that Auster was right. And yet there is no denying that for both the artist and the spectator Petit's art is conditioned by the knowledge that he is risking his life.

"I have the patience of those who have fallen once," Petit wrote in "On the High Wire," "and whenever someone tells me of a high-wire walker who fell to the ground and was crushed, I answer: 'He got what he deserved.' " Petit knows that this will not happen to him. "I am not a death-wish person," he said to me. "I want to live very old. It is true that death is part of the frame—that it frames such activities as bullfighting and tightrope walking. My world is a dangerous world, sure, but I am very safe in knowing my limits. I am not playing with words when I say I don't take risks. The danger becomes so narrow that it is a novel companion with whom you travel. It is not an enemy."

(1999)

GEOFFREY HELLMAN

A HOUSE ON GRAMERCY PARK

B ENJAMIN Sonnenberg, a bouncy, indefatigable publicity man and public-relations counsellor, whose clients include Philip Morris, the Sperry Corporation, E. R. Squibb & Sons, the Beech-Nut Packing Company, Pepperidge Farm Bread, the Federated Department Stores, the American Export Lines, the Columbia Broadcasting System, and the American branch of Lever Brothers, has for years been a prime topic of conversation in Manhattan. The people who talk about him generally ignore his professional activities, which are somewhat arcane, and concentrate on his house and clothes, which are not. Sonnenberg's private movie theatre has succeeded the late Thomas Fortune Ryan's private chapel as one of the domestic wonders of New York. As a colloquial gambit, his collection of brass has replaced the eleven identical mirrors in the ballroom of the old Peter Cooper house. His suits and shirts are today almost as widely discussed as were the Beaux-Arts Ball costumes of Mrs. S. Stanwood Menken. The Sonnenberg house is on Gramercy Park South. It is thirty-two feet by sixty, has five stories and thirty-seven rooms, and is air-conditioned throughout. It was built in 1831 for Stuyvesant Fish. Several years ago, Sonnenberg spent three hundred and fifty thousand dollars to remodel and redecorate it. It is probably the busiest private house in New York. During eight or nine months of the year, it is, every few days, the scene of a party attended by from twenty to two hundred guests. It is run by a staff of six, who live next door, in a house Sonnenberg also owns. It contains so many brass urns, samovars, pitchers, charcoal burners, mugs, cups, lamps, candlesticks, candelabra, boxes, plates, andirons, teakettles, coal buckets, mortars, pestles, mirror frames, ferneries, wall sconces, bowls, beakers, salvers, and canisters that the polishing of these items constitutes the principal occupation of the Sonnenberg houseman. For parties, the permanent staff is assisted by an auxiliary body of tailcoated door-openers, coat-checkers, and waiters engaged for the occasion. These are lean times when it comes to gracious and capacious living, though. The Sonnenberg house, much talked about as it is, is innocent of ballroom, squash court, organ, gymnasium, Turkish bath, and conservatory. It cannot compare with the old Schwab, Carnegie, Frick, Kahn, Vanderbilt, Blumenthal, Schiff, Speyer, Warburg, Bishop, James, Pratt, Duke, and Astor town houses. However, since these mansions and most of their peers and runners-up have been torn down or taken over by institutions, or are now rarely occupied, it stands out, perhaps uniquely among local homes, as a robust, arresting anachronism.

Sonnenberg's wardrobe also runs counter to the trend. His suits—at last count he had sixty-seven—are built to his specifications by Bernard Weatherill: dark colors, four-button single-breasted coats, outside change pocket, no vest, double vent in back. His dinner jackets are cut more or less like his daytime coats. He carries twenty-eight-inch-square handkerchiefs that Tripler's imports for him from Switzerland, and he wears custom shirts with dickey bosoms, stiff collars, and starched cuffs; cuff links made of large Roman or Hapsburg coins; solid-color or small-figured wool ties in winter and white linen ones in summer; bowlers or black Homburgs in winter and boaters in summer. He is a short, rotund man, and he believes that the costumes he affects make him more noticeable than he would be otherwise. He has increased the individuality of his appearance by cultivating a walrus mustache. This frames, fitfully, a vivacious and selective smile. His façade is a calculated business asset. The construction of it was well along in 1926, when, at twenty-five, he became a full-time publicity man. In the early years, he wanted to look older than his clients, and he thought that his nineteen-hundredish clothes and the mustache gave him a mature and reassuring air. "I have always felt that in my business I am a lay psychoanalyst," he recently told a friend, "and that the transference would take place more readily from son to father than from father to son. Do you understand what I am talking about?" His conversational style verges on the grandiloquent, and he sometimes wonders whether it is getting across.

Sonnenberg's house, clothes, and career as a host reflect the goal he set for himself in 1922. He was then only a few years removed from Grand Street, where his father, a Russian immigrant, had a clothing stand. His capital was a few hundred dollars saved from his salary as a social worker. "I resolved to become a cross between Condé Nast and Otto Kahn," he has said. It is his view that he has gone a long way toward fulfilling his ambition. He pursues his Nast-and-Kahn-like activities not only on Gramercy Park but in eight fashionable restaurants he goes to constantly—Voisin, "21," Robert, the Colony, the Oak Rooms of the Ritz and the Plaza, the Cub Room of the Stork Club, and the

Champagne Room of El Morocco—and in commodious pleasure domes, generally on Long Island, which he rents summers. Against these imposing backgrounds, he plies guests—most of whom are listed in a four-thousand-name card file he keeps—with a practically uninterrupted procession of meals, hot and cold canapés, sandwiches, and drinks. In addition, he occasionally presides, on behalf of clients, at really large parties of three or four hundred guests. For these gatherings, he rents the main room of the Stork Club, the Maisonette of the St. Regis, or a hotel ballroom suite. He gives a number of headwaiters a hundred dollars at Christmas, and he hasn't had to wait for a table anywhere in years.

Perhaps because his profession is such a modern one and, in his opinion, so intangible ("I'm the builder of bridges into posterity," he once said when pressed for a definition of what he does for his clients. "I supply the Listerine to the commercial dandruff on the shoulders of corporations"), Sonnenberg likes to surround himself with solid appurtenances of the past. "I may gross five or six hundred thousand dollars a year, but to the public the business I'm in still seems a flimflam, fly-by-night business," he says. "I want my house and office to convey an impression of stability and to give myself a dimension, background, and tradition that go back to the Nile." He hasn't entirely realized this aim, but the fact that some of Mrs. Fish's social triumphs and Harry Lehr's shenanigans took place in what is now his dining room strikes him as proof that he has made strides in the right direction. He likes to identify himself, however peripherally, with history and with bygone stateliness, and he is willing to settle for the eighteenth, the nineteenth, or even the early twentieth century. His offices, at 247 Park Avenue, are decorated with wallpaper bearing London scenes in the time of Dickens. He is driven to them in a 1942 Rollston-body Packard by a chauffeur named James, whom he hired away from a funeral establishment sixteen years ago. He takes pleasure in telling friends that his steward, Walter Blanchard, used to be with Ambassador David K. E. Bruce, and before that with Ambassador Myron T. Herrick, and that it was a pair of Blanchard's pajamas—and not, as commonly believed, a pair of Herrick's— that Lindbergh wore while putting up at the American Embassy in Paris after his celebrated solo flight. Even Sonnenberg's part-time retainers are, for the most part, old family servants. "They represent the super-duper echelon of service today," he says. "You no longer find them in the great houses, which don't exist, but in the private dining rooms of banks. The man who at lunch served Sloan Colt at the Bankers Trust or Winthrop Aldrich at the Chase shows up at my place in the evening. It's a kind of inner coterie—the last remnant of the permanent butlers, now, alas, a thing of the past." A few months ago, a Sonnenberg guest, seventeen years a married woman, was relieved of her coat at the door by a servitor who greeted her by her maiden name. She remembered that he had been the butler in the Arthur Curtiss James house. She had last dined there, with her parents, in 1930. Advised of the episode, Sonnenberg was enchanted. He instructed Blanchard, who hires the rest of the household help, to place this distinguished factotum at the head of his free-lance list. For a couple of years, Sonnenberg had a full-time butler-valet named Mears, who came to him from the Duke of Windsor. This circumstance tickled Sonnenberg. "Mears regales me with all kinds of stories about the Duke," he used to tell friends during this well-connected period. Once, as he was having his dessert at lunchtime, he said, "Mears, you must be in love."

"Why, sir?" asked Mears.

"You have failed to remove the salt," his employer said.

"Not customary to remove it at lunch, sir. Only at dinner, sir," said Mears.

Sonnenberg pulled at his mustache and settled back to think it over. He did not venture any further technical remarks to Mears for several days.

SONNENBERG'S guests have included such competent talkers as Somerset Maugham, Rebecca West, Dorothy Thompson, Norman Cousins, Max Lerner, Cecil Brown, Quentin Reynolds, Senator Brien McMahon, Thurman Arnold, Thomas K. Finletter, Morris Ernst, Irwin Edman, Alfred de Laigre, Jr., Geoffrey Parsons, Leonard Lyons, Samuel Grafton, Fannie Hurst, Miriam Hopkins, Max Lincoln Schuster, Fredric March, Florence Eldridge, and Walter Duranty, but he doesn't trust the people he entertains to keep themselves amused very long. He likes best to have twenty people to dinner. Generally, they include his wife, an unpretentious lady with a useful sense of humor, who has been known to duck her husband's parties and attend a movie with a friend. On such occasions, the dinner is served by three men in the candlelit dining room on the street floor. Scarcely have the diners finished with their brandy inhalers when thirty after-dinner guests arrive. Usually, all hands, in clumps, take an elevator upstairs for the evening's film, a picture that has not yet been shown publicly. The movie theater occupies the entire top floor. It has enough red plush divans and arm-chairs to accommodate an audience of fifty. Roast beef sandwiches and high-balls served by footmen in the candlelit second-floor living room round out the evening. Sonnenberg has a low opinion of scrambled eggs, chicken à la king, lobster Newburg, and anything with bones in it. "I think that when you enter-tain there should be a minimum of clutter and fuss," he says. "I don't like the fuss about bones and all that kind of business. I don't go in for whipped cream on my sliced pineapples. There is no goo at my dinners."

Sonnenberg deals professionally with the heads of large corporations, most of which pay him an annual fee of between twenty-five thousand and fifty thousand dollars. He figures that his activities as a host are a business asset in that they indicate that he leads a life as expansive as, if not more expansive than, the men who hire him, and that it would be infra dig for him to confer with a No. 2 or No. 3 man in their companies. Once they have seen his movie theatre and his collection of brass, he feels, they realize that they are in the presence of a person with whom haggling over a fee would be indelicate, as well as probably useless. In his makeup, candor is pleasingly mixed with shrewdness. "No question about it, I've become very adroit at this thing," he says. "I deal only with the head men, and in general I confine myself to corporations rather than individuals. I have a *couvert*. Twenty-five or fifty thousand dollars is a drop in the bucket for a company that spends seven million a year on advertising. A company can hire me for a *year* for the price of a double-spread ad in *Life*! I deal mostly with hundred-thousand-a-year men, and when they come to my house, they know I make more than that myself."

Although Sonnenberg's gooless soirées are usually held, and their personnel is chosen, for practical reasons, he is, in the conventional social sense, a disinterested host, since he doesn't care much whether his guests invite him back. "I love to *own* things," he says. "Being a host is part of ownership, since, in a way, you own your guests. I hate being a guest myself. I like to control the menu, both as to food and people. I suppose it's the philosophy of a man of property," Sonnenberg's guests often *do* ask him back, and he often accepts their invitations, but he is apt to take precautions. Once, invited to dinner by a newspaper-feature writer he had entertained, he climbed five flights of stairs to his host's apartment and fooled around uncomplainingly with a chicken leg and some gooey dessert. The doorbell rang, and Sonnenberg's chauffeur presently appeared with a box of Cuban cigars. Another time, Sonnenberg telephoned a man who had invited him to dinner and asked his host if he might contribute a birthday cake. He had learned, he said, that one of the other guests was to be Richard de Rochemont, producer of "The March of Time," and that it was de Rochemont's birthday; he felt that a cake would be in order. This attempt at extraterritorial menu control didn't work out very well. The host's cook had already baked a mince pie, and she insisted on serving it before a couple of Sonnenberg's staff carried in the cake, which turned out to be big enough for a convention. Sonnenberg occasionally contributes guests as well as provisions when he dines out. A friend who was expecting him for an informal buffet supper was mystified when, as the party was getting under way, a man with a black satchel came in and said, "I'm Mr. Currie." The host then recollected that he had been having trouble with his telephone, and supposed that he notified the phone company, though he couldn't recall having done so, and that this was one of its repairmen. He motioned the visitor to the back room where the instrument was. Twenty minutes later, Sonnenberg bustled in. "Where's Currie?" he asked. The stranger was Lauchlin Currie, one of President Roosevelt's administrative assistants. Sonnenberg had invited him to the party.

A few weeks ago, a new acquaintance who had been invited to Sonnenberg's house for a cocktail party expressed great interest in his surroundings. Sonnenberg told him to wander around. The visitor explored the house, whose contents, he learned later, have been appraised at $340,619.80. He admired, among other things, the brass collection, most of which Sonnenberg has picked up in the neighborhood of Allen Street; sixteen antique clocks, which Sonnenberg pays a man from Morriss & Sasek, Madison Avenue clockmakers, eight dollars a month to wind up; a day bed and a settee—in a den known as the Scottish Room—covered with the tartan of the clan Macpherson; and a dozen English eighteenth-century cabinets and credenzas, ranging in value from $425 up to $2,800. He peeked in various closets and at various shelves containing most of the household's roster of chinaware, worth $3,525.50, glassware worth $6,510.80, silverware worth $9,998, two hundred and eighty-three bath towels, a hundred and twenty of them monogrammed, seventy-two washcloths (thirty-two monogrammed), forty bathmats (twenty monogrammed), fifty-four linen or damask tablecloths, six hundred and twenty-four napkins, a hundred and seventy-two sheets, and a hundred and thirty-eight pillowcases. He strolled around Sonnenberg's bedroom, a hive of Chippendale and Sheraton whose furnishings, among them a $2,200 eighteenth-century sideboard and an $1,800 marble-manteled fireplace, have been valued at $19,956.80, and he poked around in Sonnenberg's bathroom, where he was transfixed by the sight of a black-and-gold marble-topped washbasin that cost $2,555, a built-in slate seat in the shower stall, and Sonnenberg's dressing room, containing clothes that are insured for $9,000 and include three hundred neckties. He examined the antique furniture, mirrors, and so forth, worth $14,973, in Mrs. Sonnenberg's bedroom suite; the furnishings, worth $6,132, in the room occupied by the Sonnenberg daughter, Helen, a recent Vassar graduate; and the relatively monastic sleeping quarters of the Sonnenbergs' thirteen-year-old son, whom his father dynastically named Benjamin Sonnenberg II and who does his homework for the Collegiate School in a $2,199 bedroom. The guest wound up his tour in the movie theatre and rejoined his host with a bad case of museum fatigue.

Sonnenberg, touched by his new friend's exclamations of wonder, urged him to stay on for a quiet supper. He explained that he felt it was advisable to let guests troop over his house examining its treasures, since such courtesies contributed to his reputation as a character, which is good for business. After dinner, over the brandy and cigars, his visitor asked him to expatiate on his philosophy as a host, and he obligingly embarked on a considerable disquisition. "I work while I play, and I play while I work," he said. "I feel that entertaining is helpful to my general reputation, and I also enjoy it. I don't have to drink the wine—I just like to hear it gurgle. I like to mix people up. I think a really good dinner party should consist of an archbishop, an authoress, a lady of easy virtue, a tycoon, and a Powers model. Actually, the people you ask at night need not have a virile daytime point of view. When you have as many celebrities among your friends as I have, it is important not to subject them to people who are rubbernecks, autograph hunters, or inquisitive about the movie star's final scene in some eight-year-old picture, because to him it was only an assignment and he doesn't remember it and he didn't like the picture in the first place. There is a certain common language that famous people talk. There is a certain recognition that they afford one another. As a matter of fact, famous people are themselves careful where they go, because they know that their personality is often not as well expressed in private as it is when they have their makeup on and they are on location and the film is cut so that only the best frames are preserved. There is another thing that you find very often: There are some people who are really only meant to come to cocktail parties, and some people who are really only meant to come to dinner parties, and you have to exercise certain selective qualities as a host, because in my book it is as great a mistake to mix the wrong people as it is to mix the wrong drinks, and when I say you should not mix the wrong people, I don't mean that they have to be all of the same set—quite the contrary. I would like to say the following: If you are a host, remember that you don't have to gratuitously invite a couple of people who hate the living bloody guts of each other and after thirty years of friendship have finally parted company, and if you happen to know that So-and-So is suing So-and-So, and that they were just in court this morning on account of something, you don't have to ask them. However, you don't always know. Here is the trick: The smaller the party, the more careful you have to be. If you have only six people at your dinner, you have to be more careful than if you have twenty-six, or two hundred and six. So I generally give large parties, where people who used to be married to each other can go to different floors."

Sonnenberg's friend asked him how he happened to get started as a big-scale host.

"In my early days," said Sonnenberg, "I resolved never to entertain at home in a formal way until I could give guests the same kind of food and the same service I could get them at a topnotch restaurant. I started to go to Voisin about twenty years ago, almost at the very inception of my career, for the following reason: I like Voisin, as against a Broadway restaurant. I abhor the sound of a drum or a clarinet in my ear when I am dining, unless the people are inordinately boring. Today I can entertain as well in my house as in any restaurant. I like to get the illusion that my dining table has merely moved down thirty or forty blocks. My house, in a way, is simply an extension of the Perroquet Suite of the Waldorf." He paused to reflect. "Don't get the idea that this is a hotel," he said. "I like my privacy. I stay home alone with my family two or three nights a week. I read. I peruse, I scrutinize, I scan hundreds of magazines and newspapers. I also read books with hard covers. I am a great fan of the Laurence Sterne–Dr. Johnson period, and I kind of know what goes on. I am a great reader of biographies, because they give me a tincture of reality as to the notions of people who made out O.K. in other periods, and how. I am not awed by big shots, because I know that a man could be No. 1 on the Hooperating and still have all the insecurity and unsureness that is not resident in the heart of a bellboy who takes his girl to a ten-cent movie. I am a kind of worldly-wise gent."

SONNENBERG achieved his worldly wisdom despite a family background and early youth of Old World innocence and poverty. He is convinced that the reason he has sixty-seven suits, three hundred neckties, and enough credenzas to start a credenza store is that when he was a child he never knew luxury, or, for that matter, more than the barest comfort. Even today, he thinks he may be living in a dream. "There are compensations about having lots of shirts and ties," he says, "because they are insurance against the day when it might all stop, and you want to anticipate living a long time, wearing those things. It goes back to your days of deprivation." Sonnenberg was born in 1901, in Brest Litovsk, in Russia, the only son of Harry Zonnenberg. He had two sisters, one older and one younger. Mr. Zonnenberg, a clothing merchant, came here in 1905 to improve his fortunes. He acquired a clothing stand and a flat on Grand Street, changed the spelling of his name, and in 1910 sent for his wife and three children. Benjamin was then a precocious nine. "Here is the phenomenon of a young immigrant," he has said, employing the rather ornate autobiographical style of which he is a master, "who, while he willy-nilly is dumped on the Eastern seaboard of the United States, through a process of experiences becomes more American than Coca-Cola and assimilates himself to the point of knowing the latest boogie-woogie beat in the propaganda of his times. I could have sold rugs in Stamboul, but I became a ballyhoo artist. I was meant to operate from Bagdad to Trafalgar Square. I brought to America a kind of freshness but assimilated America's Coca-Cola idiom. It's as though a Paderewski became a Joe DiMaggio, or a Rachmaninoff took to chewing gum on the stage and twirling a lasso, the way Will Rogers did."

This metamorphosis got under way while its subject was attending Public School No. 62. He later went to DeWitt Clinton High School. The elder Sonnenberg continued to run his clothing stand on Grand Street, his income rarely rising above twenty dollars a week. Summers, Benjamin was a stock boy in Gimbel's and other stores. He got most of his recreation at the Henry Street Settlement House, where he took part in dramatics, forensics, and dances. He made such a model-boy impression on Lillian D. Wald, the organization's founder and director, that when he was in his late teens she gave him board and lodging there in exchange for his services as a boys'-club leader. She also helped him get a scholarship at Columbia, which he entered in 1919. He stayed on at the settlement. He raised money for his textbooks and his lunches by covering Columbia sports events for the Brooklyn *Eagle*. His classes bored him. After his freshman year, he decided to go to work. In the summer of 1920, by answering an ad in the *Times*, he got a job at ten dollars a week, plus commissions, with the Chicago Portrait Company. This entailed travelling around the Middle West and calling on people in their homes to try to persuade them to have their photographs tinted, enlarged, and framed. He shipped any such pictures to the company. After a couple of months of this, he ended up in Bay City, Michigan, with forty or fifty dollars and an uncontrollable desire to better himself. He mailed his resignation and a final photograph to his employers and hitchhiked to Flint, where, at twenty-five dollars a week, he became a reporter and the movie critic of the *Daily Journal.* He found Flint provincial, and in the winter of 1921 returned to New York.

Here, Sonnenberg became a paid worker for the Joint Distribution Committee, a charitable outfit that was raising funds for European and Near East war sufferers. Its chairman was Felix M. Warburg. One of Sonnenberg's duties was to call on businessmen and try to sign them up for fifty-dollar-a-plate war-relief dinners. He sometimes mentioned Warburg's name, which he regarded as a talisman. Having beat his way into the office of Herbert N. Straus, one of the owners of Macy's, he urged Straus to buy tickets to a do-good banquet. The merchant hesitated. "Mr. Warburg sent me," said Sonnenberg. "I'm talking for Mr. Warburg." "What's the matter with Mr. Warburg?" asked Straus, an old friend of the banker. "Can't he come to see me himself?" Sonnenberg had never met Warburg, and he came away from this interview with a feeling that he could act with more authority if he had. He persuaded an associate to introduce him to Warburg at the charity headquarters. The Henry Street Settlement House had been heavily supported by Jacob H. Schiff, Warburg's father-in-law. Sonnenberg told Warburg what a splendid place it was, and the banker gave him a friendly nod. Sonnenberg pursued his war-relief activities with renewed confidence.

In 1922, Lewis L. Strauss, a former secretary to Herbert Hoover and a director of the American Relief Administration, an organization formed by Hoover in 1919 to get food and medical assistance to the famine regions of the Ukraine and other parts of Europe, asked Lillian Wald to recommend a young man to do field work for this project. She recommended Sonnenberg, and Strauss, after an interview, recruited him. (Sonnenberg's subsequent career has given Strauss, who until recently was a member of the Atomic Energy Commission, a great regard for him. "He is one of the outstanding examples in our generation of the success of Operation Bootstrap," Strauss has said.) Sonnenberg spent six months in the Ukraine. His inclination for his present ample way of life stems from this period. Social work brought him in contact with the fleshpots and enabled him to steep himself, if briefly, in gracious living. "Incongruous as it was, my cohorts and I lived in a villa outside Odessa with a chef and five other servants," he says. "We were driven around in chauffeured Cadillacs. I got a salary of two hundred dollars a month and a per-diem allowance of six dollars. Practically all our expenses were taken care of, so I was able to save a couple of thousand dollars. After my mission was completed, I went to Rome, and later, in the fall of 1923, to Paris, and then to London. You could live like a lord in Europe for thirty or forty dollars

a week then. I stayed at first-class hotels, bought books, went to the theatre and
the ballet, had some suits made to order, and acquired a cane, a black Homburg,
and a Burberry. The significance of having a man draw your bath and lay out
your clothes burst upon me like a revelation. I realized for the first time what it
was to be rich. I took a tintype in my mind of the way I wanted to be—a bon vi-
vant, a patron of the arts, a man who could mix Picasso with Dun & Bradstreet.
I think it was while feeding the people in Odessa, paradoxically, that I first decided
to become a cross between Condé Nast and Otto Kahn."

SONNENBERG came back to New York in the winter of 1923. Most of his
savings were gone, but his Bond Street wardrobe was intact, and his clothes
began to cause the faint murmurs that were to grow into a mighty diapason
two decades later. He took a room in the Village, did some publicity work for
Jewish-charity and Salvation Army drives, and, early in 1924, married Hilda
Caplan, a girl he had met at a Henry Street Settlement dance when he was sixteen. "The next couple of years were hard sledding but enjoyable," he says. "I
did some free-lance press-agent jobs for theatrical shows and night-club
dancers. I sported my cane, my Homburg, and my Burberry, and hung around
with a bunch that included Konrad Bercovici, Floyd Dell, Louise Bryant, Harry
Kemp, Rockwell Kent, Elinor Wylie, Harold Loeb, and George Luks. I tried to
write for *Smart Set* but was unsuccessful. I recall having tea at Henry Seidel
Canby's. The economic heat was always on me."

In 1926, Sonnenberg began to cool himself off economically. One day in the
summer of that year, twirling his cane, he walked into the Fifth Avenue Hotel,
which had just been completed, and talked the manager, Oscar Wintrab, into
giving him fifty dollars a week, plus meals, an office, and an entertainment allowance, to act as the hotel's press agent. His duties, as he saw them, involved
publicizing some of the more celebrated guests. One of these was Trader Horn,
a bearded septuagenarian African adventurer who was the purported author
of a best-seller. Sonnenberg borrowed a touring car from the Studebaker people, got Trader Horn in it, and drove up Fifth Avenue while his passenger wag-
gled his beard at the populace, who had been alerted about the journey by
newspaper stories planted by Sonnenberg. Another hotel guest was Prince
Georges Matchabelli, a Georgian émigré who had become a perfume manufacturer a short time before. Sonnenberg brought the Prince's colorful personality
to the notice of editors, reporters, and columnists. The result, a spate of feature
articles, some of them widely syndicated, caused Matchabelli to hire him in
1928 as press agent for his perfume company, at two hundred dollars a month.
This fee was eventually raised to a thousand. Sonnenberg speedily took advantage of the fact that one thing leads to another. A major Matchabelli outlet was
Bergdorf Goodman. Sonnenberg saw to it that his releases on the Prince contained mention of this circumstance. Whenever a newspaper or magazine arti-

cle on Matchabelli contained a reference to Bergdorf Goodman, Sonnenberg would clip it, circle the store's name with red crayon, and send it to Edwin Goodman, the establishment's head, whom he had met through Matchabelli. At the end of 1928, Mr. Goodman, peering gratefully at a mound of these clippings, signed a ten-thousand-dollar-a-year contract with Sonnenberg.

Still operating out of the Fifth Avenue Hotel, Sonnenberg was now extolling the virtues of several other hotels, including the White, on Lexington Avenue, and the Half Moon, in Coney Island, both of which were under Wintrab's supervision. Wintrab, a Viennese, recognized in his press agent a congenial fellow-Continental. He introduced him to Joel Hillman, owner of the about-to-open Georges V, in Paris. Sonnenberg added this hotel to his portfolio. He advised celebrities of stage and screen, whom he had begun to cultivate, that the Georges V was the place for them to stay at in Paris, and added that if they ever wanted a dinner in bracing local surroundings, they had but to mention his name at the Half Moon and the meal would be on the house. One personage he courted was a fairly well-known actor who, with his wife, had run into Sonnenberg at a couple of cocktail parties. One Friday afternoon, when the actor's wife had gone to New England to visit her mother, he collected an acquiescent young woman and suggested that they repair to the Half Moon for the weekend. "No one will see us there," he said. At dinner, the headwaiter recognized him and called up Sonnenberg, who had instructed him to relay the names of any distinguished guests. "Send some champagne to their table with my compliments," said Sonnenberg. An hour later, a bunch of American Beauties in his arms, he appeared in the hotel dining room. His acquaintance, already shaken by the champagne, looked up from his brandy in horror as Sonnenberg skated across the room, thrust the roses at the girl, and, before he realized who she was, or wasn't, said, "Welcome to the Half Moon, darling." Sonnenberg, who had twenty-twenty vision in those days, immediately discovered his error. He sat down and chatted suavely for a few moments, like a man of the world, then said something generally reassuring to the couple, ordered another bottle of champagne, took the subway home, and tore up a short newspaper release he had written. The actor remained for the weekend and was unable to extract a bill from the management. "It was an early example of Ben's urbanity," a man privy to the facts has stated.

One of Sonnenberg's first retainers came from Major E. P. Dalmasse, manager of the Park Lexington Corporation, which then owned the office building at 247 Park Avenue. In 1929, Sonnenberg rented an office on the second floor of this building and installed a secretary. Presently, he added a writer, and began to farm out some writing assignments. He, too, did a certain amount of writing, sometimes, in those days, turning out two versions of the same release—one, perhaps florid and overflattering to the client, to be sent to the client; the other, more matter-of-fact, to be sent to the press. (He long ago gave up writing releases, even in a single version, himself.) Sonnenberg cleared twenty-five thousand dollars in 1929, thirty thousand in 1930, and thirty-five thousand in 1931. He then ran into a few bad years, because, he believes, he overexpanded his office force. He cured this by expanding still further and getting a bigger bag of clients, at higher fees. In 1934, he borrowed money and moved into a larger office, on the top floor of 247 Park. Since then, his fees have never amounted to less than $250,000 a year, and since 1942 never less than a half million.

DURING the early thirties, Sonnenberg represented, among others, Delman Shoes; the Hygrade Food Products Corporation; Aris Gloves; the Book-of-the-Month Club; Viking Press; Ely Culbertson; Morris Gest; J. David Stern, publisher of the Philadelphia *Record;* Russeks; I. Miller; Charles V. Paterno, the real-estate operator; Colette d'Arville, a singer; Paul Whiteman; William Bloom, a wholesale haberdasher and blouse manufacturer; John Cavanagh, the hat man; Bollinger Champagne; Elizabeth Arden; and Helena Rubinstein. Some of his business relationships were short-lived; others went on for years. He usually managed to replace an outgoing account with an incoming one, and sometimes with two. He made extraordinary efforts to please, and did not confine himself to the orthodox publicity services of providing and placing handouts. For clients who wanted them, he arranged for theatre tickets down in front, hotel suites, reservations in caste-conscious restaurants, and other worldly accommodations. He was on call at all hours of the day and night. In 1927, he retired his father, who has since died, from the clothing stand; he still supports his mother on Riverside Drive. He has been an affectionate husband and father, but his home life has been as spotty as a fire engine's. "Ben used to be the slave of his clients," a friend has said. "He never forgot his early poverty and his resolve to become rich. He was willing to sacrifice his time, his privacy, and his personal relationships to be successful and to stay successful. Today he's more relaxed; he sometimes associates with people simply because they amuse him, and he sometimes promotes artists he likes without charging them a fee, but in his early days he cultivated only those who were useful to him, or who he thought might be useful to him. Of course, his conception of usefulness is very broad. But to all the others, including people whose period of usefulness seemed to him to be at an end, he was as inaccessible as the Pope."

Sonnenberg's papal attributes became really noticeable in 1934. In 1933, he had done some publicity to help the Union Bag & Paper Corporation float a new stock issue. He next acquired as clients Cyrus Eaton and Edward Wellington Backus, the spearheads of two proxy fights, involving, respectively, the B. F. Goodrich Co. and the Ontario & Minnesota Power Co. These jobs were necessarily brief, but they opened his eyes to the potentialities of big business. He cast about for more lasting attachments in this field. Through an advertising agent, he met the managements of Beech-Nut and of Squibb. He persuaded them to sign him up. His next conquest was the Texas Company. These firms started him out at fees ranging from one thousand to two thousand dollars a month. He came to the conclusion that it was just as easy to earn two thousand dollars a month from a large corporate client as two hundred from a small one or from an individual. He began to divest himself of his singers, haberdashers, and modest-sized companies and to replace them with the solid, national industries that are now his chief source of income. In 1935, Walter S. Marvin, a stockbroker who handles Sonnenberg's investments, introduced him to Thomas A. Morgan, then president of the Sperry Corporation and now chairman of its board. Sonnenberg added Sperry to his stable. Later, Morgan introduced him to Juan Trippe, president of Pan American Airways. Sonnenberg got the Pan American account and kept it ten years. "I left the minnow pond for waters where whales abounded," he has said of his transitional period.

In the past decade, Sonnenberg has, with rare exceptions, confined himself to corporate accounts. "I think the sponsor is better able to pay than the actor," he said the other day, "and also that he is sure for the pay, and for a longer period of time. I now work only on a very high level. I am an economic snob. As a rule, I won't accept personalities as clients. I might boost Fred Allen or Bob Hope, but only if they were appearing on the radio or television for one of my clients." One personality he has represented since he left the minnow pond is Samuel Goldwyn, whom Sonnenberg regards, even in his non-corporate aspect, as a whale. Sonnenberg's job on Goldwyn is the sort of thing that is thought of in the profession as public relations rather than mere publicity. He once dictated its case history to a stenographer, as follows:

In the case of Goldwyn, Sam Goldwyn had been catapulted to fame and pyramided into a Number One movie-mogul position, albeit on the carpet of ridicule, woven by Alva Johnston in a very telling series in the *Saturday Evening Post*, which made Goldwyn the Number One Mr. Malaprop of the contemporary scene. These malapropisms were planted after a while—it became a kind of convenient Dorothy Parker trick to attribute to him even the things that he did not say. Well, for a while he liked it, and then he grew to statesmanlike stature, and began to worry about it. Then, when he entered or approached his sixties, and saw the possibility of entering Valhalla, he wanted to straighten out this somewhat twisted, albeit powerful, shillelagh. His reputation was powerful, but, like a shillelagh, it had carbuncles on it. So he engaged me, and he was entirely different from what I expected him to be. My job was to convince the rest of the United States that what I saw was true. I proceeded to assess his reputation on the basis of performance, and on the real contribution that he made as a fighting and stormy petrel independent in a business that was growing more and more monopolistic. I proceeded to add a measure of statesmanship, maturity, and seasoning to what he did, so that he later appeared at Oxford University and received accolades by the dozen, and today he is taken seriously.

Public relations, as distinguished from publicity, has taken up more and more of Sonnenberg's time in recent years, since the heads of the companies employing him constantly turn to him for personal as well as corporate advice. In general, he has counselled them to pursue liberal labor policies and to avoid strikes. He often encourages them to head charity drives and, in one or two instances, has recommended a flyer into public service, on the theory that it would make a good impression not only on the stockholders and directors of their companies, thus helping consolidate their position, but on the public, thus helping sales. Moreover, he has tried to create a climate favorable to public-service appointments—by hints dropped into influential ears (he has been received at the White House and he has dined with Mrs. Mesta), by planting useful rumors and humanizing anecdotes in popular columns, and by providing his candidates with socially conscious ideas appropriate to certain speeches that they are to deliver, and to magazine articles, signed by them, that are intended for thoughtful magazines. He realizes that businessmen are sometimes humdrum, and he has done his best to alleviate this situation. By feeding material to the public prints, radio, and television, he has managed to invest some of the men whose companies have retained him with characters more colorful than the facts warrant. "Ben is a frustrated artist," a man who has known him twenty years says. "He paints with a bold brush. Not all the men he has boosted have quite been able to live up to his portrayal of them."

The synthetic portraits that public-relations practitioners occasionally impose on a gullible public through a gullible or laissez-faire press have given pause to some students of contemporary civilization, but Sonnenberg sees no cause for anxiety. His attitude toward his profession is pragmatic. Last fall, a young man who was thinking of going into the public-relations business came to him for counsel. The young man was the nephew of a prominent brewer, and Sonnenberg put himself out. He took his interlocutor—as well as a journalist friend of his—to the Oak Room of the Ritz, where, according to the best recollection of the journalist, he said, "In the matter of giving people advice, this is what operates: First, almost without fail, people who need advice are myopic and astigmatic about their own problems and what to do. That is almost axiomatic. Second, by and large, people look for assurance and reassurance, and they want the additional strength that they get out of sound advice and out of someone, like myself, who represents operational effectiveness. I represent the doer. I don't know much about the symbolism of my business, but I know the know-how and the politics the way Jim Farley knows how to deliver the third ward in Cook County, in Illinois. Do you understand? I am as good a persuader as you will ever find in your life. Do you understand? I am probably the best telephone salesman you ever met. I can sing 'Mammy,' exhort, beseech, cajole, plead, and understand, and over the telephone I ooze more of the fluid that makes people want to do things for me than any guy you will ever meet. I know how to alkalize antipathy. Most people think that a problem that is wrong must be handled in an electric-push-button way to be righted. My procedure is that when I find that a problem is wrong, I first bring it to Greenwich time, instead of dead center, and I neutralize it, and then I plus it. Do you follow what I mean?"

The young man nodded uncertainly, and Sonnenberg continued, "Public relations is the practice of popular persuasion. Its method is to make the planned seem spontaneous, accidental, natural, instead of poised. The most important ingredient in public relations is timing. What is heroic in one hour may be villainous in the next, and yet an hour later may again prove heroic. Do you get me? Look. In the olden days, your only forum was a courtroom. At the present time, you are tried in the press or in other public media; you are tried before the bar of public opinion. A man's whole career can be ruined, because of the media of mass communication, by innuendo. The law can't catch up with that. The result is that as a man or even a corporation is more and more dependent on public opinion, it is necessary to practice preventive medicine in publicity and to initiate counterattacks. Sometimes you have to make your client change, so that the charges which may have been true at one time cease to be true and he really does become a public benefactor. It is no longer enough merely for a man to sell his wares at a profit. He must take time out to express a feeling of social responsibility. It is important what he does with the money after he makes his profit, how large that profit is, and whether or not he is at all times behaving in the public interest. Because, by and large, the people that I work for can survive only by the consent of the consumer, and by the consent of the multitudes, you understand, and they are not the sort to listen to William H. Vanderbilt's philosophy of 'The public be damned!' The public-relations man sees to it that his client puts the best foot forward in the corporate equation. It makes a lot of difference, goodwill-wise, whether the company is run by Alfred Sloan, of General Motors, or Tom Morgan, of Sperry, or by some anti-social or pugnacious character. Is there anything else you want to know?"

"How do you get new accounts?" the young man asked.

"Oh," said Sonnenberg as a waiter brought him his favorite drink, a tall glass of hot tea with lemon, "I gravitate naturally to the seats of power. I roam around in the lanes of traffic, where you are most likely to be hit. The idea is you have a better chance to get knocked down by a car if you stand in the middle of Broadway and Forty-second Street than in the meadows of Fairfield, Connecticut." He paused to ask for the check. "I *did* once pick up an account while summering in Fairfield," he said. "Pepperidge Farm bread. It belonged to some neighbors. I now own a small block of its stock, and I wouldn't take four hundred thousand dollars for it."

ACTUALLY, Sonnenberg does very little roaming in Times Square, though he was once knocked down by a new account, a prominent lawyer with political ambitions, in the St. Régis (he brought the profitable accident on himself by shouting at the lawyer "I thought you were dead"). However, he has managed to have the traffic lanes converge in his own house and office. His working day begins at eight, when his chauffeur, who has already picked up his early-morning office mail, brings it to the house, along with six newspapers, including the *Wall Street Journal.* Munching his breakfast in his mahogany Chippendale bed, Sonnenberg looks through the newspapers for material relevant to his clients' progress, makes a few telephone calls to other influential early-birds, and answers his mail by dictating to a stenographer. He may then prepare a list of fifteen or twenty people for his secretary to call when he gets uptown, which he does around nine-thirty. He works in a large room with a marble fireplace, sitting at an enormous mahogany desk that used to belong to Harry Payne Whitney. He employs eight or nine writers, a dozen secretaries, and one policy assistant. He also hires outside writers for certain jobs, and he has a representative in Hollywood, whose chief duties are to funnel material to West Coast newspapers and to publicize the radio shows put on by Philip Morris and Lever Brothers. His office day, spent at the telephone, in relaying ideas to his writing staff, in dictation, and lunch with clients, potential clients, journalists, or radio and television people, ends around four. He may then drive to Central Park and walk around the Reservoir, or stop at an antique shop, or, if he is giving a party, go home, undress, turn off the four telephones in his bedroom, and sleep for two hours. He has lived in the Gramercy Park house since 1931. He rented it at first and sublet the two upper floors. In 1936, he bought it and took possession of the whole thing, along with the house next door, on Irving Place.

At some of Sonnenberg's larger functions, his friends sometimes bring *their* friends along. Occasionally, in the crush, not everyone gets a chance to meet the host and hostess. A few weeks ago, Mrs. Sonnenberg found herself sitting next to a young man who seemed out of sorts.

"Who's that fellow with the walrus mustache?" he asked, pointing to the far end of the room.

"That's Ben Sonnenberg," she said.

"Well, I don't like his mustache, and somebody ought to talk to his tailor," said the young man.

Mrs. Sonnenberg reported the incident to her husband, and he appeared delighted. "I'm surprised he didn't recognize me," he said, fingering his mustache. "But at least he was aware of me."

(1950)

HOW DO YOU LIKE IT NOW,

GENTLEMEN?

E RNEST Hemingway, who may well be the greatest living American novelist and short-story writer, rarely comes to New York. He spends most of his time on a farm, the Finca Vigia, nine miles outside Havana, with his wife, a domestic staff of nine, fifty-two cats, sixteen dogs, a couple of hundred pigeons, and three cows. When he does come to New York, it is only because he has to pass through it on his way somewhere else. Not long ago, on his way to Europe, he stopped in New York for a few days. I had written to him asking if I might see him when he came to town, and he had sent me a typewritten letter saying that would be fine and suggesting that I meet his plane at the airport. "I don't want to see anybody I don't like, nor have publicity, nor be tied up all the time," he went on. "Want to go to the Bronx Zoo, Metropolitan Museum, Museum of Modern Art, ditto of Natural History, and see a fight. Want to see the good Breughel at the Met, the one, no two, fine Goyas and Mr. El Greco's Toledo. Don't want to go to Toots Shor's. Am going to try to get into town and out without having to shoot my mouth off. I want to give the joints a miss. Not seeing news people is not a pose. It is only to have time to see your friends." In pencil, he added, "Time is the least thing we have of."

TIME did not seem to be pressing Hemingway the day he flew in from Havana. He was to arrive at Idlewild late in the afternoon, and I went out to meet him. His plane had landed by the time I got there, and I found him standing at a gate waiting for his luggage and for his wife, who had gone to attend to it. He had one arm around a scuffed, dilapidated briefcase pasted up with travel stickers. He had the other around a wiry little man whose forehead was covered with enormous beads of perspiration. Hemingway was wearing a red plaid wool shirt, a figured wool necktie, a tan wool sweater-vest, a brown tweed jacket tight across the back and with sleeves too short for his arms, gray flannel slacks, Argyle socks, and loafers, and he looked bearish, cordial, and constricted. His hair, which was very long in back, was gray, except at the temples, where it was white; his mustache was white, and he had a ragged, half-inch full white beard. There was a bump about the size of a walnut over his left eye. He was wearing steel-rimmed spectacles, with a piece of paper under the nose-piece. He was in no hurry to get into Manhattan. He crooked the arm around the briefcase into a tight hug and said that it contained the unfinished manuscript of his new book, "Across the River and into the Trees." He crooked the arm around the wiry little man into a tight hug and said he had been his seat companion on the flight. The man's name, as I got it in a mumbled introduction, was Myers, and he was returning from a business trip to Cuba. Myers made a slight attempt to dislodge himself from the embrace, but Hemingway held on to him affectionately.

"He read book all way up on plane," Hemingway said. He spoke with a perceptible Midwestern accent, despite the Indian talk. "He like book, I think," he added, giving Myers a little shake and beaming down at him.

"Whew!" said Myers.

"Book too much for him," Hemingway said. "Book start slow, then increase in pace till it becomes impossible to stand. I bring emotion up to where you can't stand it, then we level off, so we won't have to provide oxygen tents for the readers. Book is like engine. We have to slack her off gradually."

"Whew!" said Myers.

Hemingway released him. "Not trying for no-hit game in book," he said. "Going to win maybe twelve to nothing or maybe twelve to eleven."

Myers looked puzzled.

"She's better book than 'Farewell,' " Hemingway said. "I think this is best one, but you are always prejudiced, I guess. Especially if you want to be champion." He shook Myers' hand. "Much thanks for reading book," he said.

"Pleasure," Myers said, and walked off unsteadily.

Hemingway watched him go, and then turned to me. "After you finish a book, you know, you're dead," he said moodily. "But no one knows you're dead. All they see is the irresponsibility that comes in after the terrible responsibility of writing." He said he felt tired but was in good shape physically; he had brought his weight down to two hundred and eight, and his blood pressure was down too. He had considerable rewriting to do on his book, and he was determined to keep at it until he was absolutely satisfied. "They can't yank novelist like they can pitcher," he said. "Novelist has to go the full nine, even if it kills him."

We were joined by Hemingway's wife, Mary, a small, energetic, cheerful woman with close-cropped blond hair, who was wearing a long, belted mink coat. A porter pushing a cart heaped with luggage followed her. "Papa, everything is here," she said to Hemingway. "Now we ought to get going, Papa." He assumed the air of a man who was not going to be rushed. Slowly, he counted the pieces of luggage. There were fourteen, half of them, Mrs. Hemingway told me, extra-large Valpaks designed by her husband and bearing his coat of arms, also designed by him—a geometric design. When Hemingway had finished counting, his wife suggested that he tell the porter where to put the luggage. Hemingway told the porter to stay right there and watch it; then he turned to his wife and said, "Let's not crowd, honey. Order of the day is to have a drink first."

We went into the airport cocktail lounge and stood at the bar. Hemingway put his briefcase down on a chromium stool and pulled it close to him. He ordered bourbon and water. Mrs. Hemingway said she would have the same, and I ordered a cup of coffee. Hemingway told the bartender to bring double bourbons. He waited for the drinks with impatience, holding on to the bar with both hands and humming an unrecognizable tune. Mrs. Hemingway said she hoped it wouldn't be dark by the time they got to New York. Hemingway said it wouldn't make any difference to him, because New York was a rough town, a phony town, a town that was the same in the dark as it was in the light, and he was not exactly overjoyed to be going there anyway. What he was looking forward to, he said, was Venice. "Where I like it is out West in Wyoming, Montana, and Idaho, and I like Cuba and Paris and around Venice," he said. "Westport gives me the horrors." Mrs. Hemingway lit a cigarette and handed me the pack. I passed it along to him, but he said he didn't smoke. Smoking ruins his sense of smell, a sense he finds completely indispensable for hunting. "Cigarettes smell so awful to you when you have a nose that can truly smell," he said, and laughed, hunching his shoulders and raising the back of his fist to his face, as though he expected somebody to hit him. Then he enumerated elk, deer, possum, and coon as some of the things he can truly smell.

The bartender brought the drinks. Hemingway took several large swallows and said he gets along fine with animals, sometimes better than with human beings. In Montana, once, he lived with a bear, and the bear slept with him, got drunk with him, and was a close friend. He asked me whether there were still bears at the Bronx Zoo, and I said I didn't know, but I was pretty sure there were bears at the Central Park Zoo. "I always used to go to the Bronx Zoo with Granny Rice," he said. "I love to go to the zoo. But not on Sunday. I don't like to see the people making fun of the animals, when it should be the other way around." Mrs. Hemingway took a small notebook out of her purse and opened it; she told me she had made a list of chores she and her husband had to do before their boat sailed. They included buying a hot-water-bottle cover, an elementary Italian grammar, a short history of Italy, and, for Hemingway, four

woollen undershirts, four cotton underpants, two woollen underpants, bedroom slippers, a belt, and a coat. "Papa has never had a coat," she said. "We've
got to buy Papa a coat." Hemingway grunted and leaned against the bar. "A
nice, rainproof coat," Mrs. Hemingway said. "And he's got to get his glasses
fixed. He needs some good soft padding for the nosepiece. It cuts him up brutally. He's had that same piece of paper under the nosepiece for weeks. When he
really wants to get cleaned up, he changes the paper." Hemingway grunted
again.

The bartender came up, and Hemingway asked him to bring another round
of drinks. Then he said, "First thing we do, Mary, as soon as we hit hotel, is call
up the Kraut." "The Kraut," he told me, with that same fist-to-the-face laugh,
is his affectionate term for Marlene Dietrich, an old friend, and is part of a large
vocabulary of special code terms and speech mannerisms indigenous to the
Finca Vigia. "We have a lot of fun talking a sort of joke language," he said.

"First we call Marlene, and then we order caviar and champagne, Papa,"
Mrs. Hemingway said. "I've been waiting months for that caviar and champagne."

"The Kraut, caviar, and champagne," Hemingway said slowly, as though he
were memorizing a difficult set of military orders. He finished his drink and
gave the bartender a repeat nod, and then he turned to me. "You want to go
with me to buy coat?" he asked.

"Buy coat and get glasses fixed," Mrs. Hemingway said.

I said I would be happy to help him do both, and then I reminded him that he
had said he wanted to see a fight. The only fight that week, I had learned from
a friend who knows all about fights, was at the St. Nicholas Arena that night. I
said that my friend had four tickets and would like to take all of us. Hemingway
wanted to know who was fighting. When I told him, he said they were bums.
Bums, Mrs. Hemingway repeated, and added that they had better fighters in
Cuba. Hemingway gave me a long, reproachful look. "Daughter, you've got to
learn that a bad fight is worse than no fight," he said. We would all go to a fight
when he got back from Europe, he said, because it was absolutely necessary to
go to several good fights a year. "If you quit going for too long a time, then you
never go near them," he said. "That would be very dangerous." He was interrupted by a brief fit of coughing. "Finally," he concluded, "you end up in one
room and won't move."

AFTER dallying at the bar a while longer, the Hemingways asked me to go
along with them to their hotel. Hemingway ordered the luggage loaded into
one taxi, and the three of us got into another. It was dark now. As we drove
along the boulevard, Hemingway watched the road carefully. Mrs. Hemingway
told me that he always watches the road, usually from the front seat. It is a
habit he got into during the First World War. I asked them what they planned

to do in Europe. They said they were going to stay a week or so in Paris, and then drive to Venice.

"I love to go back to Paris," Hemingway said, his eyes still fixed on the road. "Am going in the back door and have no interviews and no publicity and never get a haircut, like in the old days. Want to go to cafés where I know no one but one waiter and his replacement, see all the new pictures and the old ones, go to the bike races and the fights, and see the new riders and fighters. Find good, cheap restaurants where you can keep your own napkin. Walk over all the town and see where we made our mistakes and where we had our few bright ideas. And learn the form and try and pick winners in the blue, smoky after-noons, and then go out the next day to play them at Auteuil and Enghien."

"Papa is a good handicapper," Mrs. Hemingway said.

"When I know the form," he said.

We were crossing the Queensboro Bridge, and we had a good view of the Manhattan skyline. The lights were on in the tall office buildings. Hemingway did not seem to be impressed. "This ain't my town," he said. "It's a town you come to for a short time. It's murder." Paris is like another home to him, he said. "I am as lonesome and as happy as I can be in that town we lived in and worked and learned and grew up in, and then fought our way back into." Venice is another of his home towns. The last time he and his wife were in Italy, they lived for four months in Venice and the Cortina Valley, and he went hunt-ing, and now he had put the locale and some of the people in the book he was writing. "Italy was so damned wonderful," he said. "It was sort of like having died and gone to Heaven, a place you'd figured never to see."

Mrs. Hemingway said that she had broken her right ankle skiing there but that she planned to go skiing there again. Hemingway was hospitalized in Padua with an eye infection, which developed into erysipelas, but he wanted to go back to Italy and wanted to see his many good friends there. He was looking forward to seeing the gondoliers on a windy day, the Gritti Palace hotel, where they stayed during their last visit, and the Locanda Cipriani, an old inn on Torcello, an island in the lagoon northeast of Venice on which some of the orig-inal Venetians lived before they built Venice. About seventy people live on Torcello, and the men are professional duck hunters. While there, Hemingway went duck-hunting a lot with the gardener of the old inn. "We'd go around through the canals and jump-shoot, and I'd walk the prairies at low tide for snipe," he said. "It was a big fly route for ducks that came all the way down from the Pripet Marshes. I shot good and thus became a respected local character. They have some sort of little bird that comes through, after eating grapes in the north, on his way to eat grapes in the south. The local characters sometimes shot them sitting, and I occasionally shot them flying. Once, I shot two high doubles, rights and lefts, in a row, and the gardener cried with emotion. Coming home, I shot a high duck against the rising moon and dropped him in the canal. That precipitated an emotional crisis I thought I would never get him out of but did, with about a pint of Chianti. We each took a pint out with us. I drank mine to keep warm coming home. He drank his when overcome by emotion." We were silent for a while, and then Hemingway said, "Venice was lovely."

THE Hemingways were stopping at the Sherry-Netherland. Hemingway registered and told the room clerk that he did not want any announcement made of his arrival and did not want any visitors, or any telephone calls either, except from Miss Dietrich. Then we went up to the suite—living room, bedroom, and serving pantry—that had been reserved for them. Hemingway paused at the entrance and scouted the living room. It was large, decorated in garish colors, and furnished with imitation Chippendale furniture and an imitation fireplace containing imitation coals.

"Joint looks O.K.," he said. "Guess they call this the Chinese Gothic Room." He moved in and took the room.

Mrs. Hemingway went over to a bookcase and held up a sample of its contents. "Look, Papa," she said. "They're phony. They're pasteboard backs, Papa. They're not real books."

Hemingway put his briefcase down on a bright-red couch and advanced on the bookcase, then slowly, with expression, read the titles aloud—"Elementary Economics," "Government of the United States," "Sweden, the Land and the People," and "Sleep in Peace," by Phyllis Bentley. "I think we are an outfit headed for extinction," he said, starting to take off his necktie.

After getting his necktie off, and then his jacket, Hemingway handed them to his wife, who went into the bedroom, saying she was going to unpack. He unbuttoned his collar and went over to the telephone. "Got to call the Kraut," he said. He telephoned the Plaza and asked for Miss Dietrich. She was out, and he left word for her to come over for supper. Then he called room service and ordered caviar and a couple of bottles of Perrier-Jouët, *brut*.

Hemingway went back to the bookcase and stood there stiffly, as though he could not decide what to do with himself. He looked at the pasteboard backs again and said, "Phony, just like the town." I said that there was a tremendous amount of talk about him these days in literary circles—that the critics seemed to be talking and writing definitively not only about the work he had done but about the work he was going to do. He said that of all the people he did not wish to see in New York, the people he wished least to see were the critics. "They are like those people who go to ball games and can't tell the players without a score card," he said. "I am not worried about what anybody I do not like might do. What the hell! If they can do you harm, let them do it. It is like being a third baseman and protesting because they hit line drives to you. Line drives are regrettable, but to be expected." The closest competitors of the critics among those he wished least to see, he said, were certain writers who wrote books about the war when they had not seen anything of war at first hand. "They are just like an outfielder who will drop a fly on you when you have pitched to have the batter hit a high fly to that outfielder, or when they're pitching they try to strike everybody out." When he pitched, he said, he never struck out anybody, except under extreme necessity. "I knew I had only so many fast balls in that arm," he said. "Would make them pop to short instead, or fly out, or hit it on the ground, bouncing."

A waiter arrived with the caviar and champagne, and Hemingway told him to open one of the bottles. Mrs. Hemingway came in from the bedroom and said she couldn't find his toothbrush. He said that he didn't know where it was but that he could easily buy another. Mrs. Hemingway said all right, and went back into the bedroom. Hemingway poured two glasses of champagne, gave one to me, and picked up the other one and took a sip. The waiter watched him anxiously. Hemingway hunched his shoulders and said something in Spanish to the waiter. They both laughed, and the waiter left. Hemingway took his glass over to the red couch and sat down, and I sat in a chair opposite him.

"I can remember feeling so awful about the first war that I couldn't write about it for ten years," he said, suddenly very angry. "The wound combat makes in you, as a writer, is a very slow-healing one. I wrote three stories about it in the old days—'In Another Country,' 'A Way You'll Never Be,' and 'Now I Lay Me.' " He mentioned a war writer who, he said, was apparently thinking of himself as Tolstoy, but who'd be able to play Tolstoy only on the Bryn Mawr field-hockey team. "He never hears a shot fired in anger, and he sets out to beat who? Tolstoy, an artillery officer who fought at Sevastopol, who knew his stuff, who was a hell of a man anywhere you put him—bed, bar, in an empty room where he had to think. I started out very quiet and I beat Mr. Turgenev. Then I trained hard and I beat Mr. de Maupassant. I've fought two draws with Mr. Stendhal, and I think I had an edge in the last one. But nobody's going to get me in any ring with Mr. Tolstoy unless I'm crazy or I keep getting better."

He began his new book as a short story. "Then I couldn't stop it. It went straight on into a novel," he said. "That's the way all my novels got started. When I was twenty-five, I read novels by Somersault Maugham and Stephen St. Vixen Benét." He laughed hoarsely. "They had written novels, and I was ashamed because I had not written any novels. So I wrote 'The Sun' when I was twenty-seven, and I wrote it in six weeks, starting on my birthday, July 21st, in Valencia, and finishing it September 6th, in Paris. But it was really lousy and the rewriting took nearly five months. Maybe that will encourage young writers so they won't have to go get advice from their psychoanalysts. Analyst once wrote me, What did I learn from psychoanalysts? I answered, Very little but hope they had learned as much as they were able to understand from my published works. You never saw a counter-puncher who was punchy. Never lead against a hitter unless you can outhit him. Crowd a boxer, and take everything he has, to get inside. Duck a swing. Block a hook. And counter a jab with everything you own. Papa's delivery of hard-learned facts of life."

Hemingway poured himself another glass of champagne. He always wrote in longhand, he said, but he recently bought a tape recorder and was trying to get up the courage to use it. "I'd like to learn talk machine," he said. "You just tell talk machine anything you want and get secretary to type it out." He writes without facility, except for dialogue. "When the people are talking, I can hardly write it fast enough or keep up with it, but with an almost unbearable high manifold pleasure. I put more inches on than she will take, and then fly her as near as I know to how she should be flown, only flying as crazy as really good pilots fly crazy sometimes. Most of the time flying conservatively but with an awfully fast airplane that makes up for the conservatism. That way, you live longer. I mean your writing lives longer. How do you like it now, gentlemen?" The question seemed to have some special significance for him, but he did not bother to explain it.

I wanted to know whether, in his opinion, the new book was different from his others, and he gave me another long, reproachful look. "What do you think?" he said after a moment. "You don't expect me to write 'The Farewell to Arms Boys in Addis Ababa,' do you? Or 'The Farewell to Arms Boys Take a Gunboat'?" The book is about the command level in the Second World War. "I am not interested in the G.I. who wasn't one," he said, suddenly angry again. "Or the injustices done to *me*, with a capital 'M.' I am interested in the goddam sad science of war." The new novel has a good deal of profanity in it. "That's be-cause in war they talk profane, although I always try to talk gently," he said, sounding like a man who is trying to believe what he is saying. "I think I've got 'Farewell' beat in this one," he went on. He touched his briefcase. "It hasn't got the youth and the ignorance." Then he asked wearily, "How do you like it now, gentlemen?"

THERE was a knock at the door, and Hemingway got up quickly and opened it. It was Miss Dietrich. Their reunion was a happy one. Mrs. Hemingway came out of the bedroom and greeted the guest enthusiastically. Miss Dietrich stood back from Hemingway and looked at him with approval. "Papa, you look won-derful," she said slowly.

"I sure missed you, daughter," said Hemingway. He raised his fist to his face, and his shoulders shook as he laughed silently.

Miss Dietrich was wearing a mink coat. She sighed loudly, took off the coat, and handed it to Mrs. Hemingway. Then she sighed again and sat down in an overstuffed chair. Hemingway poured a glass of champagne, brought it to her, and refilled the other glasses.

"The Kraut's the best that ever came into the ring," he said as he handed me my glass. Then he pulled a chair up beside Miss Dietrich's, and they compared notes on friends and on themselves. They talked about theatre and motion-picture people, one of whom, a man, Hemingway referred to as a "sea heel."

Miss Dietrich wanted to know what a "sea heel" was.

"The sea is bigger than the land," he told her.

Mrs. Hemingway went into the serving pantry and came out in a few minutes with caviar spread on toast.

"Mary, I am telling Papa how I have to behave because I am a grandmother," Miss Dietrich said, taking a piece of toast. "I have to think always of the children. You know, Papa?"

Hemingway gave a sympathetic grunt, and Miss Dietrich took from her purse some snapshots of her grandson and passed them around. He was eighteen months old, she told us. Hemingway said he looked like a winner, and that he would be proud to own a piece of him if he ever got into the ring.

Miss Dietrich said that her daughter was going to have another child soon. "I'll be a grandmother *again*, Papa," she said.

Hemingway gave her a bleak look. "I'm going to be a grandfather in a few months," he said. "My son Bumby's wife."

Mrs. Hemingway told me that Bumby is the nickname of her husband's eldest son, John, an Army captain stationed in Berlin. His two other sons, she said, are Patrick, known as Mouse, who is a twenty-one-year-old sophomore at Harvard, and is planning to get married in June, and Gregory, known as Gigi, who is eighteen and a freshman at St. John's, at Annapolis. In addition to the present Mrs. Hemingway, Patrick is going to invite to his wedding his and Gigi's mother Pauline Pfeiffer, who was Hemingway's second wife. Bumby's mother and Hemingway's first wife was Hadley Richardson, who is now Mrs. Paul Scott Mowrer, and Hemingway's third wife was Martha Gellhorn.

"Everything you do, you do for the sake of the children," Miss Dietrich said.

"Everything for the children," Hemingway said. He refilled Miss Dietrich's glass.

"Thank you, Papa," she said, and sighed. She lives at the Plaza, she told him, but spends a good deal of her time at the apartment of her daughter, who lives on Third Avenue. "Papa, you should see me when they go out," she said, and took a sip of champagne. "I'm the baby-sitter. As soon as they leave the house, I go around and look in all the corners and straighten the drawers and clean up. I can't stand a house that isn't neat and clean. I go around in all the corners with towels I bring with me from the Plaza, and I clean up the whole house. Then they come home at one or two in the morning, and I take the dirty towels and some of the baby's things that need washing, and, with my bundle over my shoulder, I go out and get a taxi, and the driver, he thinks I am this old washerwoman from Third Avenue, and he takes me in the taxi and talks to me with sympathy, so I am afraid to let him take me to the Plaza. I get out a block away from the Plaza and I walk home with my bundle and I wash the baby's things, and then I go to sleep."

"Daughter, you're hitting them with the bases loaded," Hemingway said earnestly.

There was a ring at the door, and a bellboy brought in a florist's box. Mrs. Hemingway opened it and took out some green orchids and read the card: "Love from Adeline." "Who the hell is Adeline?" she asked. Nobody knew. Mrs. Hemingway put the flowers in a vase and said it was time to order supper.

As we ate, the Hemingways and Miss Dietrich talked about the war. All three had seen it at first hand. Mrs. Hemingway, who, as Mary Welsh, was a *Time* correspondent in London, met Hemingway there during the war, and both saw a good deal of Miss Dietrich there and, later on, in Paris. Miss Dietrich was a U.S.O. entertainer, and performed on almost every front in the European the-atre. She grew a little sad as she talked about the war. She had loved entertain-ing the troops, and the spirit overseas, she said, was the best she had ever found in people anywhere. "Everybody was the way people should be all the time," she continued. "Not mean and afraid but good to each other."

Hemingway raised his glass in a toast to her.

"I've finally figured out why Papa sometimes gets mean now that the war is over," Mrs. Hemingway said. "It's because there is no occasion for him to be valorous in peacetime."

"It was different in the war," Miss Dietrich said. "People were not so selfish and they helped each other."

Hemingway asked her about some recordings she had made, during the war, of popular American songs with lyrics translated into German, and said he'd like to have them. "I'll give you manuscript of new book for recordings if you want to trade even, daughter," he told her.

"Papa, I don't trade with you. I love you," said Miss Dietrich.

"You're the best that ever came into the ring," Hemingway said.

Mrs. Hemingway said, "Who the hell is Adeline?"

LATE the next morning, I was awakened by a telephone call from Hem-ingway, who asked me to come right over to the hotel. He sounded urgent. I had a fast cup of coffee, and when I turned up at the suite, I found the door open and walked in. Hemingway was talking on the telephone. He was wearing an orange plaid bathrobe that looked too small for him and he had a glass of champagne in one hand. His beard looked more scraggly than it had the day before. "My boy Patrick is coming down from Harvard and I'd like to reserve a room for him," he was saying into the telephone. " 'P,' as in 'Patrick.' " He paused and took a sip of champagne. "Much obliged. He'll be down from Harvard."

Hemingway hung up, and from his bathrobe pocket took a box of pills. He shook two of them into the palm of his hand, and downed them with a mouth-ful of champagne. He told me that he had been up since six, that his wife was still asleep, and that he had done enough work for that morning and wanted to talk, an activity he finds relaxing. He always wakes at daybreak, he explained, because his eyelids are especially thin and his eyes especially sensitive to light. "I have seen all the sunrises there have been in my life, and that's half a hundred years," he said. He had done considerable revision that morning on the manuscript. "I wake up in the morning and my mind starts making sentences, and I have to get rid of them fast—talk them or write them down," he said. "How did you like the Kraut?"

Very much, I said.

"I love the Kraut and I love Ingrid," he said. "If I weren't married to Miss Mary and didn't love Miss Mary, I would try to hook up with either of them. Each one has what the other hasn't. And what each has, I love very much." For a moment, he looked bewildered, and then he said quickly, "Would never marry an actress, on account they have their careers and they work bad hours."

I asked him whether he still wanted to buy a coat, and he said sure but he didn't want to be rushed or crowded and it was cold outside. He went over to the vase of green orchids and looked at the card, which was still attached to them. Adeline, he said, was the name of nobody he knew or ever would know, if he could help it. On a serving table near the couch were two champagne coolers, each containing ice and a bottle. He carried his glass over there and held up one of the bottles and squinted at it. It was empty. He put it back in the cooler, head down. Then he opened the other bottle, and as he poured some champagne into his glass, he sang, " 'So feed me am-mu-nition, keep me in the Third Division, your dog-face soldier boy's O.K.' " Breaking off, he said, "Song of the Third Infantry Division. I like this song when I need music inside myself to go on. I love all music, even opera. But I have no talent for it and cannot sing. I have a perfect goddam ear for music, but I can't play any instrument by ear, not even the piano. My mother used to make me play the cello. She took me out of school one year to learn the cello, when I wanted to be out in the fresh air playing football. She wanted to have chamber music in the house."

His briefcase was lying open on a chair near the desk, and the manuscript pages were protruding from it; someone seemed to have stuffed them into the briefcase without much care. Hemingway told me that he had been cutting the manuscript. "The test of a book is how much good stuff you can throw away," he said. "When I'm writing it, I'm just as proud as a goddam lion. I use the oldest words in the English language. People think I'm an ignorant bastard who doesn't know the ten-dollar words. I know the ten-dollar words. There are older and better words which if you arrange them in the proper combination you make it stick. Remember, anybody who pulls his erudition or education on you hasn't any. Also, daughter, remember that I never carried Teddy bears to bed with me since I was four. Now, with seventy-eight-year-old grandmothers taking advantage of loopholes in the G.I. Bill of Rights whereby a gold-star mother can receive her son's education, I thought of establishing a scholarship and sending myself to Harvard, because my Aunt Arabelle has always felt very bad that I am the only Hemingway boy that never went to college. But I have been so busy I have not got around to it. I only went to high school and a couple of military cram courses, and never took French. I began to learn to read French by reading the A.P. story in the French paper after reading the American A.P. story, and finally learned to read it by reading accounts of things I had seen—*les événements sportifs*—and from that and *les crimes* it was only a jump to Dr. de Maupassant, who wrote about things I had seen or could understand. Dumas, Daudet, Stendhal, who when I read him I knew that was the way I wanted to be able to write. Mr. Flaubert, who always threw them perfectly straight, hard, high, and inside. Then Mr. Baudelaire, that I learned my knuckle ball from, and Mr. Rimbaud, who never threw a fast ball in his life. Mr. Gide and Mr. Valéry I couldn't learn from. I think Mr. Valéry was too smart for me. Like Jack Britton and Benny Leonard."

Jack Britton, he continued, was a fighter he admired very much. "Jack Britton kept on his toes and moved around and never let them hit him solid," he said. "I like to keep on my toes and never let them hit me solid. Never lead against a hitter unless you can outhit him. Crowd a boxer," he said, assuming a boxing stance and holding his right hand, which was grasping the champagne glass, close to his chest. With his left hand, he punched at the air, saying, "Remember. Duck a swing. Block a hook. And counter a jab with everything you own." He straightened up and looked thoughtfully at his glass. Then he said, "One time, I asked Jack, speaking of a fight with Benny Leonard, 'How did you handle Benny so easy, Jack?' 'Ernie,' he said, 'Benny is an awfully smart boxer. All the time he's boxing, he's thinking. All the time he was thinking, I was hitting him.' " Hemingway gave a hoarse laugh, as though he had heard the story for the first time. "Jack moved very geometrically pure, never one-hundredth of an inch too much. No one ever got a solid shot at him. Wasn't anybody he couldn't hit any time he wanted to." He laughed again. " 'All the time he was thinking, I was hitting him.' " The anecdote, he told me, had been in the original version of his short story "Fifty Grand," but Scott Fitzgerald had persuaded him to take it out. "Scott thought everybody knew about it, when only Jack Britton and I knew about it, because Jack told it to me," he said. "So Scott told me to take it out. I didn't want to, but Scott was a successful writer and a writer I respected, so I listened to him and took it out."

Hemingway sat down on the couch and nodded his head up and down sharply a couple of times to get my attention. "As you get older, it is harder to have heroes, but it is sort of necessary," he said. "I have a cat named Boise, who wants to be a human being," he went on slowly, lowering his voice to a kind of grumble. "So Boise eats everything that human beings eat. He chews Vitamin B Complex capsules, which are as bitter as aloes. He thinks I am holding out on him because I won't give him blood-pressure tablets, and because I let him go to sleep without Seconal." He gave a short, rumbling laugh. "I am a strange old man," he said. "How do you like it now, gentlemen?"

Fifty, Hemingway said, on reconsideration, is not supposed to be old. "It is sort of fun to be fifty and feel you are going to defend the title again," he said. "I won it in the twenties and defended it in the thirties and the forties, and I don't mind at all defending it in the fifties."

After a while, Mrs. Hemingway came into the room. She was wearing gray flannel slacks and a white blouse, and she said she felt wonderful, because she had had her first hot bath in six months. She walked over to the green orchids and looked at the card. "Who *is* Adeline?" she asked. Then she abandoned the problem and said she was going out to do her errands, and suggested that Hemingway get dressed and go out and do his. He said that it was lunchtime and that if they went out then, they would have to stop someplace for lunch, whereas if they had lunch sent up to the room, they might save time. Mrs. Hemingway said she would order lunch while he got dressed. Still holding his glass, he reluctantly got up from the couch. Then he finished his drink and went into the bedroom. By the time he came out—wearing the same outfit as the day before, except for a blue shirt with a button-down collar—a waiter had set the table for our lunch. We couldn't have lunch without a bottle of Tavel, Hemingway said, and we waited until the waiter had brought it before starting to eat.

Hemingway began with oysters, and he chewed each one very thoroughly. "Eat good and digest good," he told us.

"Papa, please get glasses fixed," Mrs. Hemingway said.

He nodded. Then he nodded a few times at me—a repetition of the sign for attention. "What I want to be when I am old is a wise old man who won't bore," he said, then paused while the waiter set a plate of asparagus and an artichoke before him and poured the Tavel. Hemingway tasted the wine and gave the waiter a nod. "I'd like to see all the new fighters, horses, ballets, bike riders, dames, bullfighters, painters, airplanes, sons of bitches, café characters, big international whores, restaurants, years of wine, newsreels, and never have to write a line about any of it," he said. "I'd like to write lots of letters to my friends and get back letters. Would like to be able to make love good until I was eighty-five, the way Clemenceau could. And what I would like to be is not Bernie Baruch. I wouldn't sit on park benches, although I might go around the park once in a while to feed the pigeons, and also I wouldn't have any long beard, so there could be an old man didn't look like Shaw." He stopped and ran the back of his hand along his beard, and looked around the room reflectively. "Have never met Mr. Shaw," he said. "Never been to Niagara Falls, either. Anyway, I would take up harness racing. You aren't up near the top at that until you're over seventy-five. Then I could get me a good young ball club, maybe, like Mr. Mack. Only I wouldn't signal with a program—so as to break the pattern. Haven't figured out yet what I would signal with. And when that's over, I'll make the prettiest corpse since Pretty Boy Floyd. Only suckers worry about saving their souls. Who the hell should care about saving his soul when it is a man's duty to lose it intelligently, the way you would sell a position you were defending, if you could not hold it, as expensively as possible, trying to make it the most expensive position that was ever sold. It isn't hard to die." He opened his mouth and laughed, at first soundlessly and then loudly. "No more worries," he said. With his fingers, he picked up a long spear of asparagus and looked at it without enthusiasm. "It takes a pretty good man to make any sense when he's dying," he said.

Mrs. Hemingway had finished eating, and she quickly finished her wine. Hemingway slowly finished his. I looked at my wristwatch, and found that it was almost three. The waiter started clearing the table, and we all got up. Hemingway stood looking sadly at the bottle of champagne, which was not yet empty. Mrs. Hemingway put on her coat, and I put on mine.

"The half bottle of champagne is the enemy of man," Hemingway said. We all sat down again.

"If I have any money, I can't think of any better way of spending money than on champagne," Hemingway said, pouring some.

When the champagne was gone, we left the suite. Downstairs, Mrs. Hemingway told us to remember to get glasses fixed, and scooted away.

HEMINGWAY balked for a moment in front of the hotel. It was a cool, cloudy day. This was not good weather for him to be out in, he said sulkily, adding that his throat felt kind of sore. I asked him if he wanted to see a doctor. He said no. "I never trust a doctor I have to pay," he said, and started across Fifth Avenue. A flock of pigeons flew by. He stopped, looked up, and aimed an imaginary rifle at them. He pulled the trigger, and then looked disappointed. "Very difficult shot," he said. He turned quickly and pretended to shoot again. "Easy shot," he said. "Look!" He pointed to a spot on the pavement. He seemed to be feeling better, but not much better.

I asked him if he wanted to stop first at his optician's. He said no. I mentioned the coat. He shrugged. Mrs. Hemingway had suggested that he look for a coat at Abercrombie & Fitch, so I mentioned Abercrombie & Fitch. He shrugged again and lumbered slowly over to a taxi, and we started down Fifth Avenue in the afternoon traffic. At the corner of Fifty-fourth, we stopped on a signal from the traffic cop. Hemingway growled. "I love to see an Irish cop being cold," he said. "Give you eight to one he was an M.P. in the war. Very skillful cop. Feints and fakes good. Cops are not like they are in the Hellinger movies. Only once in a while." We started up again, and he showed me where he once walked across Fifth Avenue with Scott Fitzgerald. "Scott wasn't at Princeton any more, but he was still talking football," he said, without animation. "The ambition of Scott's life was to be on the football team. I said, 'Scott, why don't you cut out this football?' I said, 'Come on, boy.' He said, 'You're crazy.' That's the end of that story.

If you can't get through traffic, how the hell are you gonna get through the line? But I am not Thomas Mann," he added. "Get another opinion."

By the time we reached Abercrombie's, Hemingway was moody again. He got out of the taxi reluctantly and reluctantly entered the store. I asked him whether he wanted to look at a coat first or something else.

"Coat," he said unhappily.

In the elevator, Hemingway looked even bigger and bulkier than he had before, and his face had the expression of a man who is being forcibly subjected to the worst kind of misery. A middle-aged woman standing next to him stared at his scraggly white beard with obvious alarm and disapproval. "Good Christ!" Hemingway said suddenly, in the silence of the elevator, and the middle-aged woman looked down at her feet.

The doors opened at our floor, and we got out and headed for a rack of top-coats. A tall, dapper clerk approached us, and Hemingway shoved his hands into his pants pockets and crouched forward. "I think I still have credit in this joint," he said to the clerk.

The clerk cleared his throat. "Yes, sir," he said.

"Want to see coat," Hemingway said menacingly.

"Yes, sir," said the clerk. "What kind of coat did you wish to see, sir?"

"That one." He pointed to a straight-hanging, beltless tan gabardine coat on the rack. The clerk helped him into it, and gently drew him over to a full-length mirror. "Hangs like a shroud," Hemingway said, tearing the coat off. "I'm tall on top. Got any other coat?" he asked, as though he expected the answer to be no. He edged impatiently toward the elevators.

"How about this one, sir, with a removable lining, sir?" the clerk said. This one had a belt. Hemingway tried it on, studied himself in the mirror, and then raised his arms as though he were aiming a rifle. "You going to use it for *shooting*, sir?" the clerk asked. Hemingway grunted, and said he would take the coat. He gave the clerk his name, and the clerk snapped his fingers. "Of course!" he said. "There was *something*—" Hemingway looked embarrassed and said to send the coat to him at the Sherry-Netherland, and then said he'd like to look at a belt.

"What kind of belt, Mr. Hemingway?" the clerk asked.

"Guess a brown one," Hemingway said.

We moved over to the belt counter, and another clerk appeared.

"Will you show Mr. Hemingway a belt?" the first clerk said, and stepped back and thoughtfully watched Hemingway.

The second clerk took a tape measure from his pocket, saying he thought Hemingway was a size 44 or 46.

"Wanta bet?" Hemingway asked. He took the clerk's hand and punched himself in the stomach with it.

"Gee, he's got a hard tummy," the belt clerk said. He measured Hemingway's waistline. "Thirty-eight!" he reported. "Small waist for your size. What do you do—a lot of exercise?"

Hemingway hunched his shoulders, feinted, laughed, and looked happy for the first time since we'd left the hotel. He punched himself in the stomach with his own fist.

"Where you going—to Spain again?" the belt clerk asked.

"To Italy," Hemingway said, and punched himself in the stomach again. After Hemingway had decided on a brown calf belt, the clerk asked him whether he wanted a money belt. He said no—he kept his money in a checkbook.

Our next stop was the shoe department, and there Hemingway asked a clerk for some folding bedroom slippers.

"Pullman slippers," the clerk said. "What size?"

"'Levens," Hemingway said bashfully. The slippers were produced, and he told the clerk he would take them. "I'll put them in my pocket," he said. "Just mark them, so they won't think I'm a shoplifter."

"You'd be surprised what's taken from the store," said the clerk, who was very small and very old. "Why, the other morning, someone on the first floor went off with a big roulette wheel. Just picked it up and—"

Hemingway was not listening. "Wolfie!" he shouted at a man who seemed almost seven feet tall and whose back was to us.

The man turned around. He had a big, square red face, and at the sight of Hemingway it registered extreme joy. "Papa!" he shouted.

The big man and Hemingway embraced and pounded each other on the back for quite some time. It was Winston Guest. Mr. Guest told us he was going upstairs to pick up a gun and proposed that we come along. Hemingway asked what kind of gun, and Guest said a ten-gauge magnum.

"Beautiful gun," Hemingway said, taking his bedroom slippers from the clerk and stuffing them into his pocket.

In the elevator, Hemingway and Guest checked with each other on how much weight they had lost. Guest said he was now down to two hundred and thirty-five, after a good deal of galloping around on polo ponies. Hemingway said he was down to two hundred and eight, after shooting ducks in Cuba and working on his book.

"How's the book now, Papa?" Guest asked, as we got out of the elevator.

Hemingway gave his fist-to-the-face laugh and said he was going to defend his title once more. "Wolfie, all of a sudden I found I could write wonderful again, instead of just biting on the nail," he said slowly. "I think it took a while for my head to get rebuilt inside. You should not, ideally, break a writer's head open or give him seven concussions in two years or break six ribs on him when he is forty-seven or push a rearview-mirror support through the front of his skull opposite the pituitary gland or, really, shoot at him too much. On the other hand, Wolfie, leave the sons of bitches alone and they are liable to start crawling back into the womb or somewhere if you drop a porkpie hat." He exploded into laughter.

Guest's huge frame shook with almost uncontrollable laughter. "God, Papa!" he said. "I still have your shooting clothes out at the island. When are you coming out to shoot, Papa?"

Hemingway laughed again and pounded him on the back. "Wolfie, you're so damn big!" he said.

Guest arranged to have his gun delivered, and then we all got into the elevator, the two of them talking about a man who caught a black marlin last year that weighed a thousand and six pounds.

"How do you like it now, gentlemen?" Hemingway asked.

"God, Papa!" said Guest.

On the ground floor, Guest pointed to a mounted elephant head on the wall. "Pygmy elephant, Papa," he said.

"Miserable elephant," said Hemingway.

Their arms around each other, they went out to the street. I said that I had to leave, and Hemingway told me to be sure to come over to the hotel early the next morning so that I could go with him and Patrick to the Metropolitan Museum. As I walked off, I heard Guest say, "God, Papa, I'm not ashamed of anything I've ever done."

"Nor, oddly enough, am I," said Hemingway.

I looked around. They were punching each other in the stomach and laughing raucously.

THE following morning, the door of the Hemingway suite was opened for me by Patrick, a shy young man of medium height, with large eyes and a sensitive face. He was wearing gray flannel slacks, a white shirt open at the collar, Argyle socks, and loafers. Mrs. Hemingway was writing a letter at the desk. As I came in, she looked up and said, "As soon as Papa has finished dressing, we're going to look at pictures." She went back to her letter.

Patrick told me that he'd just as soon spend the whole day looking at pictures, and that he had done a bit of painting himself. "Papa has to be back here for lunch with Mr. Scribner," he said, and added that he himself was going to stay in town until the next morning, when the Hemingways sailed. The telephone rang and he answered it. "Papa, I think it's Gigi calling you!" he shouted to the bedroom.

Hemingway emerged, in shirtsleeves, and went to the phone. "How are you, kid?" he said into it, then asked Gigi to come down to the Finca for his next vacation. "You're welcome down there, Gigi," he said. "You know that cat you liked? The one you named Smelly? We renamed him Ecstasy. Every one of our cats knows his own name." After hanging up, he told me that Gigi was a wonderful shot—that when he was eleven he had won second place in the shoot championship of Cuba. "Isn't that the true gen, Mouse?" he asked.

"That's right, Papa," said Patrick.

I wanted to know what "true gen" means, and Hemingway explained that it is British slang for "information," from "intelligence." "It's divided into three classes—gen; the true gen, which is as true as you can state it; and the really true gen, which you can operate on," he said. He looked at the green orchids and asked whether anybody had found out who Adeline was.

"I forgot to tell you, Papa," said Mrs. Hemingway. "It's Mother. Adeline is *Mother.*" She turned to me and said that her mother and father are in their late seventies, that they live in Chicago, and that they always remember to do exactly the right thing at the right time.

"My mother never sent *me* any flowers," Hemingway said. His mother is now about eighty, he said, and lives in River Forest, Illinois. His father, who was a physician, has been dead for many years; he shot himself when Ernest was a boy. "Let's get going if we're going to see the pictures," he said. "I told Charlie Scribner to meet me here at one. Excuse me while I wash. In big city, I guess you wash your neck." He went back into the bedroom. While he was gone, Mrs. Hemingway told me that Ernest was the second of six children—Marcelline, then Ernest, Ursula, Madelaine, Carol, and the youngest, his only brother, Leicester. All the sisters were named after saints. Every one of the children is married now; Leicester is living in Bogotá, Colombia, where he is attached to the U.S. Embassy.

Hemingway came out in a little while, wearing his new coat. Mrs. Hemingway and Patrick put on their coats, and we went downstairs. It was raining, and we hurried into a taxi. On the way to the Metropolitan, Hemingway said very little; he just hummed to himself and watched the street. Mrs. Hemingway told me that he was usually unhappy in taxis, because he could not sit in the front seat to watch the road ahead. He looked out the window and pointed to a flock of birds flying across the sky. "In this town, birds fly, but they're not serious about it," he said. "New York birds don't climb."

When we drew up at the Museum entrance, a line of school children was moving in slowly. Hemingway impatiently led us past them. In the lobby, he paused, pulled a silver flask from one of his coat pockets, unscrewed its top, and took a long drink. Putting the flask back in his pocket, he asked Mrs. Hemingway whether she wanted to see the Goyas first or the Breughels. She said the Breughels.

"I learned to write by looking at paintings in the Luxembourg Museum in Paris," he said. "I never went past high school. When you've got a hungry gut and the museum is free, you go to the museum. Look," he said, stopping before "Portrait of a Man," which has been attributed to both Titian and Giorgione. "They were old Venice boys, too."

"Here's what I like, Papa," Patrick said, and Hemingway joined his son in front of "Portrait of Federigo Gonzaga (1500–1540)," by Francesco Francia. It shows, against a landscape, a small boy with long hair and a cloak.

"This is what we try to do when we write, Mousie," Hemingway said, pointing to the trees in the background. "We always have this in when we write."

Mrs. Hemingway called to us. She was looking at "Portrait of the Artist," by Van Dyck. Hemingway looked at it, nodded approval, and said, "In Spain, we had a fighter pilot named Whitey Dahl, so Whitey came to me one time and said, 'Mr. Hemingway, is Van Dyck a good painter?' I said, 'Yes, he is.' He said, 'Well, I'm glad, because I have one in my room and I like it very much, and I'm glad he's a good painter because I like him.' The next day, Whitey was shot down."

We all walked over to Rubens' "The Triumph of Christ Over Sin and Death." Christ is shown surrounded by snakes and angels and is being watched by a figure in a cloud. Mrs. Hemingway and Patrick said they thought it didn't look like the usual Rubens.

"Yeah, he did that all right," Hemingway said authoritatively. "You can tell the real just as a bird dog can tell. Smell them. Or from having lived with very poor but very good painters."

That settled that, and we went on to the Breughel room. It was closed, we discovered. The door bore a sign that read, "NOW UNDERTAKING REPAIRS."

"They have our indulgence," Hemingway said, and took another drink from his flask. "I sure miss the good Breughel," he said as we moved along. "It's the great one, of the harvesters. It is a lot of people cutting grain, but he uses the grain geometrically, to make an emotion that is so strong for me that I can hardly take it." We came to El Greco's green "View of Toledo" and stood looking at it a long time. "This is the best picture in the Museum for me, and Christ knows there are some lovely ones," Hemingway said.

Patrick admired several paintings Hemingway didn't approve of. Every time this happened, Hemingway got into an involved, technical discussion with his son about it. Patrick would shake his head and laugh and say he respected Hemingway's opinions. He didn't argue much. "What the hell!" Hemingway said suddenly. "I don't want to be an art critic. I just want to look at pictures and be happy with them and learn from them. Now, this for me is a damn good picture." He stood back and peered at a Reynolds entitled "Colonel George Coussmaker," which shows the Colonel leaning against a tree and holding his horse's bridle. "Now, this Colonel is a son of a bitch who was willing to pay money to the best portrait painter of his day just to have himself painted," Hemingway said, and gave a short laugh. "Look at the man's arrogance and the strength in the neck of the horse and the way the man's legs hang. He's so arrogant he can afford to lean against a tree."

We separated for a while and looked at paintings individually, and then Hemingway called us over and pointed to a picture labelled, in large letters, "Catharine Lorillard Wolfe" and, in small ones, "By Cabanel." "This is where I got confused as a kid, in Chicago," he said. "My favorite painters for a long time were Bunte and Ryerson, two of the biggest and wealthiest families in Chicago. I always thought the names in big letters were the painters."

After we reached the Cézannes and Degases and the other Impressionists, Hemingway became more and more excited, and discoursed on what each artist could do and how and what he had learned from each. Patrick listened respectfully and didn't seem to want to talk about painting techniques any more. Hemingway spent several minutes looking at Cézanne's "Rocks—Forest of Fontainebleau." "This is what we try to do in writing, this and this, and the woods, and the rocks we have to climb over," he said. "Cézanne is my painter, after the early painters. Wonder, wonder painter. Degas was another wonder painter. I've never seen a bad Degas. You know what he did with the bad Degases? He burned them."

Hemingway took another long drink from his flask. We came to Manet's pastel portrait of Mlle. Valtesse de la Bigne, a young woman with blond hair coiled on the top of her head. Hemingway was silent for a while, looking at it; finally he turned away. "Manet could show the bloom people have when they're still innocent and before they've been disillusioned," he said.

As we walked along, Hemingway said to me, "I can make a landscape like Mr. Paul Cézanne. I learned how to make a landscape from Mr. Paul Cézanne by walking through the Luxembourg Museum a thousand times with an empty gut, and I am pretty sure that if Mr. Paul was around, he would like the way I make them and be happy that I learned it from him." He had learned a lot from Mr. Johann Sebastian Bach, too. "In the first paragraphs of 'Farewell,' I used the word 'and' consciously over and over the way Mr. Johann Sebastian Bach used a note in music when he was emitting counterpoint. I can almost write like Mr. Johann sometimes—or, anyway, so he would like it. All such people are easy to deal with, because we all know you have to learn."

"Papa, look at this," Patrick said. He was looking at "Meditation on the Passion," by Carpaccio. Patrick said it had a lot of strange animals in it for a religious painting.

"Huh!" Hemingway said. "Those painters always put the sacred scenes in the part of Italy they liked the best or where they came from or where their girls came from. They made their girls the Madonnas. This is supposed to be Palestine, and Palestine is a long way off, he figures. So he puts in a red parrot, and he puts in deer and a leopard. And then he thinks, This is the Far East and it's far away. So he puts in the Moors, the traditional enemy of the Venetians." He paused and looked to see what else the painter had put in his picture. "Then he gets hungry, so he puts in rabbits," he said. "Goddam, Mouse, we saw a lot of good pictures. Mouse, don't you think two hours is a long time looking at pictures?"

Everybody agreed that two hours was a long time looking at pictures, so Hemingway said that we would skip the Goyas, and that we would all go to the Museum again when they returned from Europe.

It was still raining when we came out of the Museum. "Goddam, I hate to go out in the rain," Hemingway said. "Goddam, I hate to get wet."

. . .

CHARLES Scribner was waiting in the lobby of the hotel. "Ernest," he said, shaking Hemingway's hand. He is a dignified, solemn, slow-speaking gentleman with silvery hair.

"We've been looking at pictures, Charlie," Hemingway said as we went up in the elevator. "They have some pretty good pictures now, Charlie."

Scribner nodded and said, "Yuh, yuh."

"Was fun for country boy like me," Hemingway said.

"Yuh, yuh," said Scribner.

We went into the suite and took off our coats, and Hemingway said we would have lunch right there. He called room service and Mrs. Hemingway sat down at the desk to finish her letter. Hemingway sat down on the couch with Mr. Scribner and began telling him that he had been jamming, like a rider in a six-day bike race, and Patrick sat quietly in a corner and watched his father. The waiter came in and passed out menus. Scribner said he was going to order the most expensive item on the menu, because Hemingway was paying for it. He laughed tentatively, and Patrick laughed to keep him company. The waiter retired with our orders, and Scribner and Hemingway talked business for a while. Scribner wanted to know whether Hemingway had the letters he had written to him.

Hemingway said, "I carry them every place I go, Charlie, together with a copy of the poems of Robert Browning."

Scribner nodded, and from the inner pocket of his jacket took some papers—copies of the contract for the new book, he said. The contract provided for an advance of twenty-five thousand dollars against royalties, beginning at fifteen per cent.

Hemingway signed the contract, and got up from the couch. Then he said, "Never ran as no genius, but I'll defend the title again against all the good young new ones." He lowered his head, put his left foot forward, and jabbed at the air with a left and a right. "Never let them hit you solid," he said.

Scribner wanted to know where Hemingway could be reached in Europe. Care of the Guaranty Trust Company in Paris, Hemingway told him. "When we took Paris, I tried to take that bank and got smacked back," he said, and laughed a shy laugh. "I thought it would be awfully nice if I could take my own bank."

"Yuh, yuh," Scribner said. "What are you planning to do in Italy, Ernest?"

Hemingway said he would work in the mornings and see his Italian friends and go duck-hunting in the afternoons. "We shot three hundred and thirty-one ducks to six guns there one afternoon," he said. "Mary shot good, too."

Mrs. Hemingway looked up. "Any girl who marries Papa has to learn how to carry a gun," she said, and returned to her letter-writing.

"I went hunting once in Suffolk, England," Scribner said. Everyone waited politely for him to continue. "I remember they gave me goose eggs to eat for breakfast in Suffolk. Then we went out to shoot. I didn't know how to get my gun off safety."

"Hunting is sort of a good life," Hemingway said. "Better than Westport or Bronxville, I think."

"After I learned how to get my gun off safety, I couldn't hit anything," Scribner said.

"I'd like to make the big Monte Carlo shoot and the Championship of the World at San Remo," Hemingway said. "I'm in pretty good shape to shoot either one. It's not a spectator sport at all. But exciting to do and wonderful to manage. I used to handle Wolfie in big shoots. He is a great shot. It was like handling a great horse."

"I finally got one," Scribner said timidly.

"Got what?" asked Hemingway.

"A rabbit," Scribner said. "I shot this rabbit."

"They haven't held the big Monte Carlo shoot since 1939," Hemingway said. "Only two Americans ever won it in seventy-four years. Shooting gives me a good feeling. A lot of it is being together and friendly instead of feeling you are in some place where everybody hates you and wishes you ill. It is faster than baseball, and you are out on one strike."

The telephone rang, and Hemingway picked it up, listened, said a few words, and then turned to us and said that an outfit called Endorsements, Inc., had offered him four thousand dollars to pose as a Man of Distinction. "I told them I wouldn't drink the stuff for four thousand dollars," he said. "I told them I was a champagne man. Am trying to be a good guy, but it's a difficult trade. What you win in Boston, you lose in Chicago."

(1950)

THE EDUCATION OF A PRINCE

HIS Imperial Highness, the Prince Michael Alexandrovitch Dmitry Obolensky Romanoff, who was deported from America this May and placed in jail at Grasse, France, for swindling American tourists, may never take rank in history with the great impostors. Perkin Warbeck and Lambert Simnel played for the throne of England; Marina Mniszek married three husbands and tried to palm off all three as the lost Czar Dmitry; Romanoff squandered his genius on petty objectives. Some of his greatest strokes were planned merely to finance himself over the weekend.

In the number and quality of his victims, however, Prince Michael (Harry F. Gerguson, in the New York orphan-asylum and police records) has no rival at the present time. The Prince had a glittering career in New York, Boston, Newport, on Long Island, in high-caste settlements along the Hudson, and among the aristocracies of a dozen American cities. Twice he swept over Hollywood in a confetti shower of bad checks. He was repeatedly exposed, but exposure does not embarrass him greatly. He is widely admired today, not for his title but for his own sake. He has convinced a fairly large public that a good impostor is preferable to the average prince. Some of those who have been victimized by Romanoff treasure the experience. Some, who know him to be a fraud, a confidence man, and a pilferer, consider him the salt of the earth.

Romanoff has won admiration by his physical courage, demonstrated in fist and White Rock bottle combats against heavy odds. He is respected for his noble bearing in melodramatic unmasking scenes. Again and again these crises have ended with Prince Michael cool, amused, triumphant; his exposers crushed, ridiculous, speechless. Mike never looks so much like a true prince as when he is being exposed as a false one. His freedom from small virtues is another source of his popularity. He has no thrift, no prudence, no thought of the future. The revenues from his frauds are scattered with an imperial hand. In the intervals between streaks of prosperity, he has slept in doorways and on park benches. No man starves more gracefully than the Prince. Disappointments, unmaskings, hunger, cold, head injuries inflicted by policemen and landladies, jail and deportation—these are only the starting points for Romanoff's fresh campaigns to carve a place for himself in an unfriendly economic and social order.

MIKE, in his rise from problem child to prince, overcame great handicaps. The soul of a *grand seignior* had found lodgment in a regrettable exterior. Undersized and ill-favored, he often makes an unfortunate first impression. He has, however, a rare power of attracting attention and sympathy, a power strongly manifested in his childhood, when, under his real name of Harry Gerguson, he was the celebrated bad boy of the six New York orphan homes to which he was successively committed. Thirty years ago, visitors at asylums were fascinated by the wicked Gerguson boy. Frequently, when a charitable lady decided to brighten up the life of an orphan, she decided to brighten up the life of the little Gerguson monster. Even when he was the terror of public institutions, Mike was weekending in stately residences and country places. His whole life became a struggle to parade in handsome settings and mingle with distinguished personages. The orphan's talent for touching deep chords of sympathy, for establishing a sudden and strong bond between himself and another human being, was improved by constant practice.

Scotland Yard described the Prince as a "rogue of uncertain nationality." The United States immigration authorities describe him as a Russian, insisting that Mike was born in Vilna in 1890 and that at the age of six years he came to this country with his parents. Prince Michael insists that he is an American citizen, born in New York City. E. K. Tonkonogy, who represented the Prince this spring as a lawyer and friend, held that the evidence favored American citizenship and that Mike could have lawfully entered this country if he had not confused the issue by his sensational escape from Ellis Island this May.

Mike's orphanage career began in New York when he was picked up as a runaway boy at the age of eight years. For the next ten years he shuttled from institution to institution. The Hebrew Orphan Asylum gave him up as an Incorrigible Case. Judge Mayo gave the boy into the custody of an uncle, Joseph Blomberg, of 28 Monroe Street. Blomberg sent Mike back to the Judge, who placed him in another institution. Mike remained long enough with his uncle, however, to master the rudiments of buttonhole-making, a trade which he followed occasionally up to the time when he became a Romanoff. The S.P.C.C., the Children's Aid Society, the Protestant Orphan Asylum, the New York Juvenile Asylum, and the United Hebrew Charities executed a series of remarkable plays on Mike in the style of Tinker to Evers to Chance. He finally settled down for a long stay at The Children's Village near Dobbs Ferry, where he met nice people of the Hudson River set. At the age of seventeen, he was shipped West with a carload of orphans. Judge Kronk of Hillsboro, Ill., obtained Mike, but Mike ran away from the Judge's farm because of chores. He slept for a time in the churchyard at Hillsboro. The sympathy of the community became aroused, and Mike was soon installed in one of the best homes, that of F. L. McDavid, vice-president of the Montgomery Loan & Trust Company, who wrote in a letter this May: "Then, as now, he was one of the most convincing liars you can imagine and his development from a boy who was not housebroke to Prince Romanoff was some step." Mike moved on to Litchfield, Ill., found a new patron, and started to school, but a rebellion of the teachers caused him to be sent back to New York. This time the child-care authorities shipped him further West to a farm near Bullard, Smith County, Tex. Mike ran away again. He obtained a new patron in former Congressman Gordon Russell of Tyler, Tex., but they soon parted company. The boy had now found his true vocation, that of being the protégé of wealthy persons. Much of his subsequent life has been spent in discovering rich patrons and living on their bounty.

Mike was nineteen years old when he made his first journey to England, travelling on a cattleship. He returned to America as Arthur Wellesley, Willoughby de Burke, William A. Wellington, Arthur Edward Willoughby, Count Gladstone, and others. Under the name of Count Gladstone he had trouble with the St. Louis police. In recent years, Mike has cultivated an infinite contempt for the lower aristocracy. He despises most of all the title of Count. Mike's self-possession is almost perfect, ordinary abuse cannot ruffle him; but he becomes visibly moved when addressed as "Count."

THE period from 1914 to 1918 is a dark era in the Prince's history. That part of his life, he boasts, is known only to himself. The Schindler, Pinkerton, and other private agencies, the police, probation officers, and immigration authorities, have made researches into Romanoff's past, but the 1914–1918 period remains a blank. According to Mike's declarations at a variety of official inquisitions, he spent this time in solitary confinement for killing a German nobleman in a duel; spent it on the Western front as a British lieutenant; spent it on the Eastern front as a Cossack colonel; was in the Foreign Legion and with Allenby in Palestine. Mike always wore a Legion of Honor ribbon and held it sacred. He flattened a man in a speakeasy once for insulting it. "They may do what they will with Romanoff," he said, "but they cannot touch that ribbon." This, however, is no proof that Mike is entitled to wear the ribbon. Through years of imposture, he has developed a childlike faith in some of his fictions.

However Mike spent the blank years in the chronicle, he gained a choice Oxford accent, a British upper-class mood and manner, much knowledge of the world, and some minute information about Eton, Oxford, and Cambridge. One legend is that Mike was the valet of an American student in Oxford; another that he was employed in the shop of an Oxford tailor; a third that he was shut up in an institution for harmless lunatics near Oxford and allowed to wander freely. There is Scotland Yard authority for the statement that Mike worked for a time as a buttonhole-maker in London. There is, however, no reliable account of the transformation of the incorrigible New York orphan into a cultured Briton. It seems possible, in view of his other achievements, that he may have, for brief periods, attended Eton, Oxford, Cambridge, and perhaps Heidelberg. In those days, the whole science of life with Mike was that of getting millionaires to send him to college. He went to Yale and Harvard by that method; he was also, briefly, a Princetonian. With his resourcefulness, Mike could walk through entrance requirements like cobwebs. It would be strange if he hadn't attended Eton, Cambridge, Oxford, and Heidelberg. In his later life in New York, when Mike had obtained a unique social importance by his fame as an impostor, efforts were made to expose him as a fake Etonian and Oxonian. At a dinner, arranged to trap him, Oxford was made the subject of conversation. Mike recalled the follies of various dons and provosts, and talked learnedly of the ale houses. Henry Rogers, an Oxford man and grandson of the Standard Oil Rogers, thought Mike's Oxford knowledge thin in spots and doubted that Mike had been there as a student. Another Oxford man, one of the Guinnesses of Dublin Stout lineage, talked Oxford with Mike on another occasion. "He knows more about the place than I do," said Guinness. Others found the Prince a storehouse of anecdote and legend about Eton. Altogether, it seems probable that Mike is the only living Eton-Oxford-Cambridge-Heidelberg-Yale-Harvard-Princeton man.

Another conjecture is that Mike absorbed his Mayfair manner during the war years by acting as an officer's batman or waiting on table at some staff headquarters, but there is an audacity and independence about the Prince that seems inconsistent with prolonged menial service. It may have been in a prison for alien enemies, in England or elsewhere, that the maladjusted boy completed his transformation into a cultivated man of the world. At any rate, Mike entered the postwar period with the outlook, prejudices, interests, passions, and foibles of a spoiled youth of rank and privilege. He had the unaffected dignity, the easy, unassertive assurance of the man born to have his way. He had nearly everything that a prince needs except his high birth and demesnes.

BEFORE the war, Mike had tried out several British titles without much success, and he saw no future in being a British nobleman. He could not hope, in a world honeycombed with British consuls, to rise above the rank of Earl. So in 1919, attracted by the vacancies in the Romanoff household, Mike turned

Slav. He established himself in Paris as Prince Michael Romanoff, son of Alexander III and brother of the late Czar. At the Ritz bar he later became the son of the man who killed Rasputin.

Americans in Paris, by winning Mike's confidence with small loans, were able to badger out of him the story of his defense of the Winter Palace and the crimson epic of his flight from Moscow; how it had been necessary for him to carve his way out of Russia because his identity was betrayed at every turn by his unforgettable Romanoff features. Mike lived in Paris chiefly on loans secured against millions of dollars' worth of Romanoff treasures which were expected to arrive any day by way of the Baltic. In 1920 and 1921, he made several dashes across the Channel. British tailors, outfitters, bootmakers, jewellers, and tobacconists had him arrested four times in those years on charges of fraud. Mike pleaded that it was the practice of Russian nobles to settle their accounts with tradespeople but once a year. The records indicate that the magistrates were puzzled. One suspended sentence, another put Mike in the madhouse, a third gave him one day in jail, a fourth released him on the stipulation that he sail immediately for Guatemala. Mike was later arrested a fifth time in London for stealing a dress shirt from a man's room. For that he was "bound over" for two years.

In 1922, a Russian prince was somebody. That was before the novelty had been taken off by the importation, for the Hollywood trade, of shiploads of husbands from the Caucasus, where the title of Prince is roughly equivalent to our title of Mister. Mike was in great demand in Paris, not only because he was a Romanoff but because he was entertaining. There is, however, a difference of opinion about just how amusing he really is, some holding that Mike is pleasing for about half an hour, after which his animal spirits grow oppressive. Mike entered the grand phase of his career in 1922, when he returned to New York after many years of absence. He landed on November 28, 1922, on the "repatriation ship" President Adams, which carried stranded soldiers and war workers back to America. Mike had obtained passage through the American consulate and the American Aid Society in Paris. He carried letters of introduction, which made him known in the best circles as Prince Michael Romanoff, but he presented himself to the immigration authorities as Harry Gerguson. It did not embarrass the Prince to be both Romanoff and Gerguson.

As a routine matter, Mike was detained at Ellis Island for verification of his American citizenship. He was vague about the details of his early life. He said that his memory had not been the same since his six years in solitary confinement for killing the German baron. The immigration authorities were baffled. While they were still puzzling over his case, the Prince escaped from the Island on December 23, 1922.

Seventeen days after his disappearance from Ellis Island, Mike, using his subtitle of Prince Obolensky, granted an interview to the American press at the Hotel Belmont. A sort of duel has been carried on for years between Mike and

American journalism. It stands about a draw; Mike has victimized American papers nearly as often as they have exposed him. The *Times*, for instance, ridiculed Mike's Ellis Island story; six weeks later, it printed the Hotel Belmont interview. The *Times* unmasked Mike in 1924; then it gave him the place of honor at the head of the passenger list when he sailed for Europe in 1925. In the Hotel Belmont interview, the Prince said he had a grievance against America. He came over to this country to work, he was laden with letters of introduction to New York commercial and financial houses, but he could convince no one that a young man who had formerly enjoyed pocket money of a hundred thousand dollars a year could be sincere in demanding a chance to sweep floors, operate a lift, or perch, ink-stained, on a high stool. His Highness desired to know whether there was no room in this great country for one whose only fault was illustrious origin. The *Times* traced Mike's ancestry back to 1365 and added that he spoke six languages fluently, although the fact is that Mike's great handicap is that he knows no language except English. He has barely enough French to abuse a wine steward. The Hotel Belmont interview brought Mike many friends. He lectured at Pelham Manor and elsewhere on "Russia, Past and Present." During his brief career as a lecturer, Mike demanded a police bodyguard because of threats against his life by the local Bolsheviki.

The Prince had one great disappointment in New York in 1922. It arose from the fact that he was a great pipe-smoker and had cultivated a taste for Royal Yacht, which costs ten dollars a pound and is said to be the most expensive mixture in the world. Back in London, in 1921, the Prince had placed an enormous order with Dunhill's for Royal Yacht. The manager, S. J. Ballinger, strolled by. "Cash!" he hissed into the clerk's ear. That blighted the whole transaction. But a few weeks thereafter, Mike dropped into the shop again when Ballinger was on his vacation and acquired a seventy-five-dollar cigarette case on credit. On his return, Ballinger became Mike's nemesis. He twice led the procession of merchants who appeared against Mike in the London courts. More than a year passed. Then, a day or two after his escape from Ellis Island, Mike entered Dunhill's, on Fifth Avenue. He had just started to lay in a winter's supply of Royal Yacht when his eye fell on Ballinger. The manager had been transferred from the London shop to the New York shop, just before Mike crossed the Atlantic. "It's good to see you, old man," exclaimed the Prince in his deep, baying Oxford accent. "This is a pleasant encounter, indeed." Mike changed his order to a pocket-sized tin of tobacco, paid cash, and departed. Following his custom of winning the friendship of complaining witnesses, victims, and denouncers, Mike was soon on good terms with Ballinger. In the past ten years, Mike has boosted the sales of the ten-dollar tobacco tremendously; in order to have this shredded gold available for his own use, Mike made addicts of his friends, and helped himself from their supplies. He had acquired his expensive taste, he explained, when he was Master of the Hounds of the Bullingdon Club at Oxford, where he contracted the Royal Yacht habit from David, as Mike and George V call the Prince of Wales.

. . .

EARLY in 1923, Prince Michael Romanoff saw reason to leave New York. In Pittsburgh he visited the family of the late James McCrea, vice-president of the Pennsylvania Railroad. A few days later, young Jim McCrea, one of Mike's Paris friends, received a letter from home reproaching him for neglecting to tell the family about his friendship with the charming Prince. A week later, young McCrea, who was then in Tulsa, Okla., received another letter from home, saying that the Prince had left for the oil fields, after accidentally writing a check for one hundred dollars on the wrong bank. A few days later, McCrea, Jr., received a telephone call from the Prince. A hotel man in a small oil town had demanded that Romanoff pay his bill in cash. The Prince wanted to take the outrage up with the State Department. McCrea settled the matter quietly, but the Prince abandoned the oil fields in a huff. He proceeded to St. Paul, Minn., where he was welcomed by some of the leading families, including the empire-building Hills and the great lumber house of Weyerhaeuser. The Prince had a vision of uniting the Romanoffs and Hills in a matrimonial alliance, but he was unexpectedly exposed as an impostor. This did not wholly spoil St. Paul for him. One of the Weyerhaeusers, discerning the spark of genius in Mike, offered to educate him for a profession, if Mike would turn straight.

Hence there appeared on the Harvard campus in March, 1923, a sawed-off youth wearing a monocle, top hat, morning coat, and sponge-bag trousers. He was temporarily put up at the Harvard Union in a bed in which President Roosevelt once had slept. Later he stopped for a time at the Phoenix Club. Specialists in the Prince's Harvard career say that he brushed aside the matter of entrance requirements by describing to President Lowell, in a personal interview, how his papers had been destroyed when the Reds burned the Winter Palace. Mike was enrolled as a student of engineering in the Graduate School of Arts and Sciences. One of his intimates at Harvard was Henri de Castellane. Mike had introduced himself. "Old man," he said, "I find we are cousins." Mike gained many other interesting friends, some of whom are still his friends, but he was not entirely popular. Some of the students complained that his face had a Near-Eastern cast. Cases of champagne and buckets of caviar, which Mike opened when funds arrived from the Northwest, won over many from the anti-Romanoff faction. The news spread with magical rapidity through the ancient seat of learning that a new and important "green pea," or inexhaustible spender, had been discovered. The greatest of Mike's parties at the Copley-Plaza was attended by representatives of many feudal houses of Boston. The Prince put a sudden stop to his grandiose hospitality in order to punish the hotel for presenting a bill. "This is most presumptuous," said Mike. "My people are accustomed to receive annual statements only. I shall never patronize your hostelry again."

Mike quit the hotel. In November, 1923, he quit Harvard. He had been summoned to the University office, where many documents were laid before him.

These indicated that he was not a Romanoff, that his current name was unknown at Eton or Oxford, and that he had bilked many students, professors,
and tradespeople. "Gentlemen," replied Mike, "I must decline to discuss the
matter."

MIKE headed for the midlands—the Interior, as he usually called it. The
newspapers of Wichita, Kan., soon announced that Wichita was harboring
royalty. An imperial Russian, exiled and impoverished, had been discovered
working as a floorwalker in a Wichita department store. Mike left Wichita after
inviting everybody to look him up in New York at the Racquet & Tennis Club.
He circulated swiftly through other Middle-Western cities, while clerks back in
New York were wearing out their "No funds" stamps on Mike's checks. He was
annoyed by the police in Kansas City. He found himself obliged to request an
amende honorable from the city authorities because a police official had hailed
him coarsely, saying: "Hello, Prince. Where are the crown jewels?" Mike's career in the midlands, however, was cut short in January, 1924, when Harry
Leslie, an agent of the Department of Justice, seized him for having escaped
from Ellis Island.

Under questioning at Ellis Island, Mike said that he had escaped from the
Island thirteen months before by swimming to the Battery, holding between his
teeth a walking-stick to which was attached an oilskin bag containing his most
precious belongings. Lily-painters added later that the Prince wore a top hat
when he made the swim, but this does not appear in the transcript of his testimony. Arriving exhausted at the Battery, the Prince said, he had been helped over
the sea wall by a policeman. "Too many cocktails," Mike explained. The policeman made an entry in his notebook and walked off. Mike's swim from Ellis Island
grew into a legend, like Casanova's escape from the Leads. Years afterward, at the
opening of Rockwell Kent's outdoor swimming pool at Ausable Forks, sensational aquatic feats were expected of the Prince. The guests grew impatient when
he did nothing but parade up and down in his bathing suit. Somebody shoved
him in. He sank to the bottom like a rock. He was hauled out half-drowned. "Too
many cocktails" was the explanation. Mike could, in fact, swim a little when
sober, but he did not escape from Ellis Island by swimming. The investigation by
H. H. Curran, Immigration Commissioner at the time, indicated that Mike had
made his escape by stowing away on a ferryboat. At the Ellis Island hearing, Mike
could not prove that he was born in this country, but the immigration authorities
could not prove their claim that he was born in Russia. He could not be deported
to Russia anyway, because the United States has no diplomatic relations with
Russia; so the Prince was liberated. Like most others who came in contact with
Mike, Commissioner Curran took a friendly interest in him. Later he met Mike at
a social gathering. Mike was very cold. He made it plain that it was impossible for
him to know immigration commissioners socially.

Mike left Ellis Island a free man, on April 3, 1924, but he was arrested the moment he set foot on Manhattan, and was lodged in a jail in Cambridge, Mass., on the following day, charged with defrauding a Harvard student. The Cambridge jail was practically turned into a Romanoff palace, and the guards and turnkeys became members of the imperial household. At Cambridge, the minor instruments of justice still wear seventeenth-century costumes; functionaries in cocked hats and robin's-egg-blue breeches rushed about to do the Prince's bidding. Acquaintances who had in happier days engulfed Mike's sturgeon eggs at the Copley-Plaza called on the prisoner. "You must all," said Mike, "be with me in the hunting season on my Galician estate." He asked forgiveness because they would find no wild boar; the war had driven them from his preserves.

On Mike's appearance in court, the clerk called for his full name. "Prince Michael Alexandrovitch Dmitry Obolensky Romanoff" was the reply. Mike dwelt enthusiastically on every syllable. The clerk called for the complaining witness. There was no answer. Mike was discharged from custody. The absent witness was a Harvard man of a famous New York family, and one of Mike's closest friends. Mike had obtained one hundred and fifty dollars from him under false pretences. This had not disturbed their friendship. The landlady of the victim, however, put in her oar. "Young man," she said, "do you want to be a target for scamps all the rest of your life? Have him arrested. That will serve notice on everybody that you are not an easy mark." As a matter of policy, therefore, the victim finally made the complaint against Mike, but he was in Scandinavia when the case was called. A year later the two men met on Fifth Avenue, exchanged forgiveness, and resumed their friendship.

Through some of his Harvard admirers, after his release from jail, Mike had a fairly successful season in Newport. This required careful management, because at the time Bailey's Beach was black with genuine Russian émigrés. Important business suddenly called Mike away from one houseparty when his hostess, intending to make things pleasant and homelike for him, told him that she was having Prince Serge Gagarin over just to provide him with Slavic company. One of the documents found in Mike's trunk this May, when it was sold for storage charges, was an invitation to Prince Michael Romanoff to a *bal costumé* given by Mr. and Mrs. Reginald Claypoole Vanderbilt at Newport.

IT was about this time that Mike began to frequent the genteel speakeasies of Manhattan. One of them became his headquarters, and there Mike formed a large collection of fashionable friendships, living for about a year on borrowed money and bad checks. Finally, the Romanoff credit collapsed, and he was forced into new fields.

The Prince's connection with the Woodstock art colony began in 1925 and has continued to the present, some of the Woodstock set having given him aid and comfort after his escape from Ellis Island this spring. Mike became a favorite

of the late "Sheriff Bob" Chanler, a regal character, and gained the friendship of
many artists and of the *atelier* mob—dealers, connoisseurs, interior decorators,
collectors, critics, and crackpots. He learned to cock a malignant monocle at an
Old Master and to talk the language of Ming and Sung, Picasso and Matisse. In
the first place, Mike had crashed the Woodstock art colony by a masterpiece of
his own art. Having temporarily exhausted the possibilities of Manhattan, Mike
had donned knapsack, puttees, and the rest of an English hiking costume, and
entered Woodstock on foot, without friends, money, or letters of introduction. It
was not Mike's strategy to charge at the first big house he saw; he held back until
he found conditions suitable for his peculiar attack. He located a handsome residence in which he felt that he could be comfortable. Seated on the lawn under
the trees was a small group of women; the Lord had delivered Woodstock into
his hands. Mike presented himself with his easy audacity, announced cheerily
in rich Oxford that he was broke and hungry, and proposed that he mow the
lawn for a meal. Without waiting for an answer, he became eloquent on the natural beauty of the place, which he compared unhesitatingly to choice country-
sides in Surrey, Normandy, and the lower Urals. Mike aroused curiosity; he was
cross-examined and forced to confess his royal lineage. Mike made light of his titles and asked to be regarded merely as an itinerant nature-lover. He moved in,
stayed for a month, and mowed no lawns.

Mike became widely known in the fine-estate section along the Hudson near
Woodstock. His status in the past few years was that of an acceptable impostor
rather than that of a prince, though friends of the real Prince Obolensky, who
is the husband of the former Muriel Astor, and who has an estate on the
Hudson at Rhinebeck, always considered it a nuisance to have a fake prince in
the same region. In 1929, through the courtesy of Ashley Chanler, Mike had
the use for several weeks of the Chanler estate at Red Hook, one of the aristocratic Hudson River communities. As a token of the brotherhood between the
Protestant Episcopal Church and the Greek Orthodox and as a gesture in the direction of church unity, Prince Michael was asked to read the lesson one
Sunday at Christ Church in Red Hook, which he did in an unctuous rumbling
voice, with the broadest of Oxford "a"s.

At one time during his first visit at Woodstock, suspicion was aroused
against Mike. His hostess took the precaution of telegraphing to distinguished
persons, who, according to the Prince, had previously entertained him. Each
reply confirmed Mike's statement. Later, however, there was a new whispering
campaign against Mike. A Russian was summoned to Woodstock to put Mike to
further tests. When the newcomer spoke in Russian, the Prince replied calmly:
"For reasons of my own, I would prefer to converse with you in the English language." Mike's manner was convincing, but the incident undermined his
standing to some extent. Mike repaired the damage partially by receiving a series of cablegrams signed "Zenia," "Cyril," "Mother," and "Boris." At the close
of the first Woodstock sojourn, he left a puzzled art colony behind him. Even

after it became definitely known that he was a fraud, Mike continued to be *persona grata* in several homes in Woodstock.

Mike's ignorance of Russian was his greatest handicap. His enemies, intent on showing him up, and his friends, bent on having a little fun, kept introducing Russians to Mike. Usually, at the sound of the Russian language, Mike became a stricken man; the mother tongue conjured up tragic pictures which caused him to bury his face in his hands. When Prince Yussupoff addressed him in Russian, Mike said: "Never speak Russian in an American speakeasy. You will soon learn why." To another Russian, Mike said: "Let's talk English. Isn't it discourteous to our American friends to talk Russian?" An art dealer found himself in a dilemma when the Prince, claiming to be art advisor to George Eastman, sought to carry off some valuable art objects on approval. The dealer did not want to lose a sale, but he doubted that Mike was a Romanoff. To test the Prince, a Russian porter was directed to open a conversation with him in Russian. Mike, furious at the menial's presumption, gave him a look which froze the Slav consonants in his throat.

BY living the Prince Michael rôle for years, Mike developed a Romanoff psychology. He was not a lunatic on the subject, like the Napoleons in the asylums. He could shed the Romanoff identity and assume other aliases, and he could, in order to pass through Ellis Island, stoop to be the low-life Harry Gerguson that he really is. Nevertheless, Mike had steeped himself to the depths of his personality in the imperial purple; his very soul was emblazoned with Romanoff heraldry. When he had a room of his own, it became a gallery of Romanoff photographs. Showing a blurred spot in a picture of the family group, he would say: "This is I." Mike caused the dynasty's coat-of-arms to be emblazoned on the doors of a topless Ford touring car with red wire wheels, in which he drove about New York, wearing a top hat, monocle, and white gloves, and maintaining a regal dignity, even when hooted at from Fifth Avenue buses. "Chuck this Romanoff business," a friend once advised him. "With your talent you can become rich in any legitimate line." "But," replied Mike, "I *am* a Romanoff." Even Mike's wit had an imperial tinge. In a New York night club, someone told him that a button was missing from his coat sleeve. "Oh, these souvenir-hunters!" he exclaimed. When another Russian prince once left a table at which Mike was sitting, Mike was asked if the man was a genuine prince. "Yes, after a fashion," said Mike. "He's one of those Georgian princes. Everybody who owns four cows is a prince in Georgia." Mike's opinion was asked about Mme. Tschaikowsky, who claims to be Anastasia, daughter of the murdered Czar. "Confidentially, old man," said Mike, "a colossal fraud."

Mike had certain traits that go with the sceptre. He loved to reward merit. Once, on a night shortly before Christmas, after witnessing some gallant rescues by firemen in an apartment-house fire, Mike lifted a holly wreath from a peddler's stand and presented it to the battalion chief. "With the Mayor's compliments," said Mike. It pleased the Romanoff in him to exercise absolute power. Once, during Grover Whalen's commissionership, the Prince, immaculately dressed, with a gardenia in his buttonhole, walked briskly along in front of Police Headquarters and summoned several policemen with his walking-stick. "Have those removed," directed Mike, pointing his stick at a row of wooden stands on which Centre Street merchants were displaying lathes, drills, vices, and other second-hand machinery. The policemen hesitated for a moment, and then, as the Prince's brow darkened, went to work with a will. The proprietors came rushing out, claiming the stands were there by legal authority. "Remove them," commanded Mike. As the hardware clanked on the sidewalk and the stands were detached from the storefronts, Mike cried: "Good work, my men," and started north in a taxicab. Another time, holding the Jews responsible for the misfortunes of the Romanoffs, Mike started a crusade against them, and spent ten days in the workhouse for mounting a soapbox at Fourteenth Street and Avenue A and making an anti-Semitic speech to a Jewish audience. One of Mike's bloodiest fights was fought for the honor of the dynasty; he battled a delicatessen keeper and two waiters because they tried to palm off whitefish eggs on him as Romanoff caviar. Mike was locked up for a few hours in the East Side prison, but the matter was arbitrated, the tradesman accepting a promissory note for fifty dollars from Mike to cover the damages. When the man asked payment, Mike said: "Lock that note away in your safe and forget it. Some day that autograph will be worth many times fifty dollars." But one incident shows more vividly than all the rest how thoroughly the Romanoff idea had worked itself into Mike's brain. At dawn one day, Mike was put to bed in the Great Northern Hotel. Mike rarely drank too much, but this time he was in a bad way, and he wanted milk to straighten him out. At that hour, the nearby restaurants were closed, and a bellboy was sent out in search of milk. The bottle finally arrived. Friends propped Mike up in bed. His eyes fell on the label. He smashed the bottle against the wall. "What the hell!" he cried. "Grade B milk for a Romanoff!"

IT was probably as a result of his contact with art at Woodstock that Prince Michael Romanoff, the graduate of six New York orphanages, developed the Romanoff Collection. He began receiving mysterious cablegrams from his secret agents concerning his Old Masters. Great obstacles were encountered in smuggling them into America, but Mike was able to borrow small sums on his descriptions of the imperial masterpieces. As a side line, he earned a few commissions as a broker in works of art. He kept getting into scrapes, however, and had to shift from hotel to hotel. Circumstances obliged him to grow a beard and take lodgings on Eleventh Avenue. Shaving, he emerged late in 1925 to take charge of an Oriental-rug booth at a charity bazaar in the Grand Central

Palace. Here he was harassed by blackmailers, who exposed him after he refused to pay hush money, and was arrested as an alien unlawfully in this country, but the police at the East Fifty-first Street station were informed by the Ellis Island authorities that Mike was free to live in America. A few days after the charity bazaar, Mike was having a sandwich in an automat when he had a feeling that hostile eyes were focussing on his back. Mike hurried out and took a taxicab. He changed cabs twice as traffic halted at the red signal. At Tenth Street and Broadway, he jumped out of his cab and legged it. After a chase of three blocks, he was caught by a Pinkerton and locked up in the Tombs on charges of grand larceny.

One of the charges on which he was held was that of swindling Pirie MacDonald, the photographer. MacDonald has made camera portraits of sixty thousand persons. After scrutinizing the Romanoff features, the artist stepped into the next room and said to his secretary: "Let the gentleman pay cash." The photographer explained later that he took this precaution because he detected prevaricating wrinkles in Mike's countenance when Mike was describing some of the Oxford escapades of himself and Cousin David, heir to the British throne. "Send the pictures over to my hotel," Mike telephoned a few days later. The secretary explained that that was against the rules. Mike then appeared and started to write out a check. "I am sorry, but we would greatly prefer cash," said the secretary. "Certainly," said Mike. The secretary, who had been dreading a scene with the visiting potentate, was greatly relieved; so much so that she was caught off her guard as Mike went on writing the check and said: "I have just looked at my bank account and I find there is ample cash to cover this." He placed the check in her hand and took the photographs. It was a sort of psychological Japanese wrestling trick, of which the Prince was a master. Before the secretary had recovered from her momentary loss of vigilance, Mike was gone. A few months later, Pirie MacDonald visited the studio of Notman, a Montreal photographer. A camera study of Prince Romanoff hung on the wall. "How much did he sting you?" asked MacDonald. "He didn't sting me," said Notman. "Of course, people like that are slow pay." "He's a fraud," said MacDonald. "That cannot be," said Notman. "He came to Montreal in the Prince of Wales' entourage."

Another charge against Mike was that of swindling H. Michaelyan, tapestry and rug dealer, who had been an intimate of Mike at the art colony at Woodstock. He had carried off a twenty-five-hundred-dollar tapestry of Michaelyan to sell on commission to the widow of a famous theatrical producer. Mike, however, sold it to a stockbroker for five hundred dollars and kept the money.

MIKE was in the Tombs from December, 1925, until April, 1926. He is still remembered there as the only prisoner who ever carried a walking-stick during the exercise hour. Mike never let down the dynasty; the Romanoff manner clung to him in the Tombs corridor as in Peacock Alley. The Prince was placed in a tier with some tough members of society. Ordinarily, they would not take kindly to the presence of an undersized, cane-carrying boulevardier; but with his power of winning esteem under any circumstances, Mike gained the favor of his fellow-prisoners and guards. Probation officers liked him and became strong advocates of leniency.

Friends came to his support. E. W. Marland, the oil man, took an interest in Mike. Alexander Hadden of the Hotel Plaza, a wealthy New Yorker known as the Friend of the Prisoners because of his charitable work in New York jails, regarded Mike as one of the finds of his career. Seeking to interest the Russian colony in their fellow-émigré, Mr. Hadden took Prince Serge Gagarin to the Tombs. Mike received him coldly and declined to converse in Russian. He explained later that the Romanoffs and Gagarins had not been on good terms for centuries.

For a brief period, Mike lost his optimism. He went through the motions of committing suicide in modified Petronius fashion. A guard found him lying on his cot, bleeding from his left wrist and holding a cigarette to his lips with his right hand. The scar that resulted, together with other scars, received when he was hurled through a glass case filled with Bismarck herring and pickled salmon in a battle in a delicatessen shop, became the souvenirs of Bolshevik bayonets, mementos of the day when, almost single-handed, he defended the Winter Palace against the rabble.

Mike received a suspended sentence of two years and left the Tombs after affectionate farewell scenes. He called immediately on Michaelyan, from whom he had stolen the tapestry, and asked to be reëmployed in the tapestry department. The Prince was stunned on meeting with a refusal, but recovered quickly and applied for a small loan. He said the du Ponts were holding a place open for him, but that he lacked the fare to Wilmington. Michaelyan refused to give Mike cash, but bought him a ticket to Wilmington. It was a bad investment, as the Prince failed to hit it off with the du Ponts and was soon back in New York; but Michaelyan, like so many of Romanoff's victims, is still one of his admirers. "He is not a criminal," said Michaelyan, "he is a remarkable man. I believe he will go down in history. Perhaps my name will go down in history with him."

After his release from the Tombs, Mike was on probation for two years. He gave a revised history of his life to the probation officers. Skeletonized, it is as follows:

Born in Moscow, son of the late Czar's uncle and an actress; born in modified wedlock, fifty per cent legitimate; reared in the Czar's household; student at Oxford; quit Oxford to enlist; fought four years in France as officer in crack Lancashire regiment; had ill-fated love affair with wife of French general; buried self in Foreign Legion; fought the Riff; invalided back to France; slew German nobleman in friendly duel at Heidelberg; fled to France, then to America.

Edmund C. Collins, now an assistant attorney-general and then a supervisor of probation officers, became inquisitive and sent Mike's fingerprints all over the world. He received many interesting replies. Collins placed before Mike the documents covering Mike's record as the incorrigible orphan, Harry Gerguson, in New York asylums; arrests as impostor, thief, and bad-check man in America; dress-shirt theft and other crimes in England; his deportations from England and short stays in British jails and lunatic asylums. Mike glanced at the papers with amusement.

"You cannot imagine," he said, "that that person is I."

"You know it is, Mike," said Collins. "Why not tell me the truth? I am your friend. You are out of jail. You have paid your debt. Why keep up this pretence?"

"I'll explain," said Mike, after a pause. "Have you ever been in a bare room in a new house with a view overlooking a park? You look at the park and it is marvellous. You look at the bare walls, and you find them absolutely repulsive. They cry for adornment. That is I. I don't lie because I desire to be a crook and a thief, but because I wish to associate with persons whose lives I believe to be adorned. Frankly, I will lie to you as long as you know me. If I told you the truth, I would feel like a bare wall."

Perceiving that it was futile to urge Mike to go straight, Collins urged him to go literary. "You have a gift for brilliant characterization and you could make a name for yourself as a writer," said the probation official. Mike promised to consider the matter, but the advice went against the grain. The Prince divided all mankind into two classes: charming people who do nothing, and the dromedaries. It was his studied opinion that a man who worked was a pack animal. He was not yet prepared to become one.

LUCKILY for the Prince, he had not become a great newspaper celebrity by 1926, and the tapestry incident was hardly mentioned in the press. The Tombs, in Mike's account of his absence from his old haunts, became Venice, Capri, and the Riviera. But it was steadily growing more difficult for him to live in princely style in New York. The tapestry incident and similar affairs impeded his career as a broker in objects of art. Barriers of unpaid bills and bad checks interposed themselves between him and the more brilliant night life. Many of his old friends were still faithful, and Mike still had his unequalled equipment for grappling new comrades to his soul: the tie of a common Alma Mater linked him to Yale, Harvard, Princeton, Oxford, Cambridge, and Heidelberg men; he had fought the war on every front and could establish brotherhood-in-arms from any angle; and he still had the Romanoff snob appeal for strangers, though he had long ceased to be anything but Mike to insiders. He could still find hospitality and money, but not on the old scale. The Prince could not forgo an imperial gesture; he had fixed himself in the mind not only of hotel managers and restaurateurs but of their entire staffs by settling enormous bills with bad checks and then by scattering a kingly largess of bad checks to headwaiters, waiters, chefs, busboys, hat-check girls, and doormen. Mike's scale of tipping was a phony two-dollar check to the headwaiter, a phony ten-dollar check to the chef, and a phony five-dollar check to the others. Now and then, when a new place opened or when Mike discovered an old place previously overlooked, he dined in Lucullan fashion. After he had stopped up the entrances of most of the best establishments with bad checks, Mike invaded a Sixteenth Street restaurant with two handsome women. The three ate twenty-seven dollars' worth. Mike tendered a fifty-dollar check and called for twenty-three dollars in change. The proprietor said he would accept Mike's check for the dinner, but that it was against the rules to give change. "In that case," said Mike, "bring a magnum of champagne. I never wrote a check for less than fifty dollars in my life."

Mike maintained two or three favorite speakeasies as a last line of retreat and never cashed bad checks there except on new customers. He earned a little money at cards, being now and then accused of cheating. He won drinks and a little money playing chess. Mike was an unsound but brilliant player. Experts could beat him because of his recklessness, but they admired his capacity for carrying a long series of future moves in his head. During fits of plutocracy, Mike would get his clothes out of hock, pay a few debts of honor, and order champagne all around. During intervals of bad luck, so much of his wardrobe was posted as collateral that he was reduced to the hardship of mingling in horsy circles at the Central Park Casino in a fox-hunting costume when fashion dictated a riding habit. The food and lodging problems gradually became acute. Mike solved them at times by accepting invitations months or years old. Once, without a cent in his pocket for telephone, railroad, or taxicab fare, he visited a friend in Connecticut. He met the telephone difficulty by telephoning to the country place from the friend's New York office; he took an express train which made its first stop at Stamford, Conn., so that he could not be thrown off prematurely; gave the conductor a Prince Romanoff card and an explanation in lieu of a ticket; and arrived at the country place shouting: "I say, William, let me have two dollars for the driver!"

Mike loved sumptuous fare and luxurious surroundings, but he was ready to starve or go thirsty rather than accept drink in circumstances which impaired his dignity. In convivial company, he has whispered: "Lend me five dollars, old man. I must hold up my end. This round is on me, you know." But he preferred cheating a man to borrowing from him. His pride rose geometrically with his poverty. Once, when the Prince had fallen on evil days, an old friend noticed his hungry face and emaciated frame and invited him to dinner. In a time of prosperity, Mike would have accepted at once; this time, he said: "Sorry, old man, I have just had a hearty dinner. But I'll sit down and drink a liqueur with you while you eat." During a cold snap in the winter of 1926, Jim Moriarity, the clubman, discovered that Mike had been sleeping in subways and going without food. He forced a loan of fifteen dollars on the Prince. The next day, Moriarity accidentally met the proprietor of the Hotel Élysée, who said: "Mike is in funds. He came into my place last night and treated himself to a pheasant." Mike had dined in solitary state at the Élysée. He ran up a thirteen-dollar bill and left a two-dollar tip. Calling the headwaiter, he said: "Delicious dinner. Delightful dinner. Very pleasant. Thanks very much." He deplored the fact that the law did not permit him to wash it down with a rare Burgundy. In lieu thereof, he lifted a glass of water and drank a toast. "Here's to you, Romanoff, you bastard." Then he walked out, penniless and homeless again, in freezing weather.

FOR a time, Mike slept on the floor in the room of a young reporter on the *Herald Tribune*. He made a visit to that newspaper and read with pleasure the clippings relating to his impostures. He refused to be introduced to anybody but the proprietor. "If Ogden Reid is here, I would like to meet him," said Mike. "Never mind the others." In January, 1927, the Prince's distress reached an acute stage. He was suffering not only from hunger but from mental anguish. The date of the Beaux-Arts Ball was January 28. Mike had no costume and no ticket. To keep Mike away from the Beaux-Arts Ball was like barring a bishop from his own cathedral on Easter morning or locking up the toast of the waterfront on Fleet Day. Early on the evening of the ball, Mike was in his favorite speakeasy receiving satirical condolences on his plight. "Gentlemen," said Mike, "when the clock strikes one, I shall be there in the most magnificent costume of all." At one o'clock, Mike entered the ballroom in a gorgeous Louis Seize costume. Mike had borrowed it from R. H. Waegen of Jacques Seligmann & Company, who recovered it later on payment of ten dollars to a pawnbroker. How Mike obtained his ticket on this occasion is not known, but he had a special technique for meeting the ticket problem. Wearing evening clothes, he would linger near the entrance of a ballroom with his right hand negligently extended. Guests mistook him for the doorkeeper and placed invitation cards in his hand. On at least one occasion, when penniless, Mike collected enough tickets not only to attend the ball but to bring along a party of friends.

The day after the Beaux-Arts Ball, Mike disappeared. As he frequently vanished for weeks at a time, sometimes returning with pockets stuffed with money, Mike's disappearance caused no general concern. But he was still on probation, and his failure to report disturbed the probation officers. They made a search and found Mike hovering between life and death in Bellevue Hospital. On the afternoon after the Beaux-Arts Ball, he had collapsed on the sidewalk. His complaint was diagnosed as starvation. Weeks of careful feeding were necessary before the Prince could leave the hospital.

PRINCE Michael's first expedition to Hollywood took place in March, 1927. It was strange that Mike had not visited Hollywood earlier. His career had been one long series of movie gags. A graduate of the New York Hebrew and other orphanages, dauntlessly sticking to the Romanoff imposture in spite of countless exposures, Mike was constantly entangled in new complications from which he escaped by inventing new climaxes. Few men have lived so much farce and melodrama. His qualifications for the cinema also included wit, humor, and imagination.

Mike was discovered for the screen by Mal St. Clair, Adolphe Menjou, Harry D'Arrast, Richard Dix, Tom Moore, and other movie celebrities who used to meet him when they dropped into the late Dan Moriarity's place on East Fifty-eighth Street on the route to the Paramount studio in Astoria. A collection was taken, and a nontransferable, irredeemable one-way ticket to Los Angeles purchased for Mike. He was vexed and rebellious when he learned that the newspapers had been invited to send photographers around to the Grand Central to picture the late Czar's relative who had hearkened to the call of Hollywood. No cameramen appeared, however, and just before the train started, Mike began to shout from the rear platform: "Where are those damn photographers? Where are those damn photographers?" Mike left New York in an upper berth. The legend is that he arrived in Hollywood in a newly-acquired friend's private car. This is in character, but caution is necessary, because some of the Romanoff enthusiasts try to improve on the sacred truth about their hero.

Southern California lay before Mike as Italy before Napoleon. He arrived without funds, moved into the Hotel Ambassador, and entertained lavishly. The region abounds in wealthy widows, Mike's specialty. He placed himself on a sound financial basis at the expense of the widow of a Western meatpacker. One of the first things the Prince did in Hollywood was to give himself two promotions: he rose to be half-brother of the late Czar, instead of cousin; he became the man who killed Rasputin, instead of the son of the man who killed Rasputin. Mike's nearness to the Russian throne varies as the square of the ignorance of the community he is in. At Harvard, he was five removes from the Czardom; in New York, three removes; in Hollywood, one remove; in Tijuana, he was the rightful Czar himself. Mike was welcomed in the highest Hollywood circles. He summoned Los Angeles reporters and gave the imperial impressions of America. He rode horseback as a guest of the Hollywood Breakfast Club and broadcast from the club's radio station, uttering, among other things, a warning that synthetic gin was an enemy to the complexion of women.

WARNER Brothers were in search of an authority on British military life in the Sudan. Mike recalled that he had been a British army officer in the Sudan. He produced a photograph of a caravan crossing a desert. He pointed to a faint blur in one corner, saying: "This is I." Mike was engaged as technical director for the picture called "The Desired Woman," and he travelled into the Arizona desert to help make it. It was a good picture. Mordaunt Hall, a former British officer, said, however, in a review in the *Times,* that it embodied grave misconceptions of British military life in the Sudan. Mike later sold a scenario. It was said to be a powerful thing, but was not picturized, because it was found that Mike's idea had been plagiarized from him twenty years earlier by John Galsworthy. Mike was decoyed from Warner's by Fox. Altogether, he worked in several studios. His last employment was as technical director of a film dealing with pre-war Russian life. Mike made a hit with his superiors. Heavy expense was incurred in preparing thousands of photographs and thrilling newspaper releases featuring "His Imperial Highness the Prince Michael Alexandrovitch Dmitry Obolensky Romanoff of Russia." In his capacity as technical director of the picture, however, Mike had to direct many real Russians. They found him aloof and unapproachable. Theodor Lodijensky, a former Russian general, felt himself insulted when Mike refused to talk to him in Russian, and hired a detective agency to investigate Mike. The agency's report traced Mike through many orphanages, jails, and various stages of his career, and Mike was summoned to the offices of the studio. He listened to the charges, inspecting General Lodijensky with princely amusement.

"I think I remember you," said Mike. "Were you not a restaurateur in New York?"

The General admitted it.

"I think you had a place in Fifty-seventh Street known as the Russian Eagle?"

The General admitted that, too.

"I believe I used to buy my liquor of you," said Mike. The General protested vehemently against being put in the light of a bootlegger.

"Gentlemen," said Mike, quietly, informatively, "a Romanoff never degrades himself by having a controversy with an inferior."

Mike bowed and made a splendid exit. The General, however, was not through. He turned his documents over to the Los Angeles *Examiner,* which printed a full-page exposure of Mike. The Prince was hurt to find that this made an unfavorable impression. In New York, his friends never noticed such things. There is a touch of real Americanism in the New York attitude: here it is considered more creditable for a man to be a Romanoff by his own efforts than by accident of birth. The exposure, however, flustered Hollywood's immature aristocracy. Mike's dupes hung their heads. His first Hollywood campaign was over. He could no longer finance himself; the "No funds" stamps of Mike's New York banks had a rest. The Prince was soon sleeping in the open air.

MIKE'S return to New York was a typical Romanoff *coup d'état.* A friend in Los Angeles lent him fifty dollars; Mike got his trunk with his wardrobe out of hock and expressed it to the Hotel Langdon, off Fifth Avenue. Bearded, bronzed, travel-stained by three thousand miles on the brake-beams, Mike arrived in New York a few weeks later. Borrowing a few dollars at his old speakeasy headquarters, he had a shine, shave, and haircut; bought a new shirt and put it on in the back room of the haberdasher's, leaving the old one; sat in undress reading the papers in a tailor shop while his suit was being freed from dust and train oil, patched, and pressed; walked a few blocks to get rid of the gasoline fumes; registered at the Fifth Avenue hostelry, had his trunk sent up to his suite, and remained there two weeks on credit. He had entered the speakeasy at four P.M. a hobo; he reëntered at eight P.M. in top hat and tails.

Mike had a glorious welcome, but he still found it difficult to finance himself in Manhattan. After a round of joyous reunions, he disappeared again, but returned in a short time quilted with money. He seized a Tom Collins that a friend was drinking, poured it out, and ordered champagne. "I have sold a patent on a new color process to the Eastman Company at Rochester," explained Mike. It soon came to light that Mike actually had been in Rochester: he spent two days in a Rochester jail for non-payment of a hotel bill. He had, however, made his money in Cleveland, where he sold a municipally-owned Old Master that hung on the wall of the Cleveland Museum of Art to an elderly Cleveland lady for fifteen hundred dollars. Mike had told her that it was one of the items of his Romanoff Collection and that he had been allowed to hang it there by the courtesy of the Chamber of Commerce and the City Commission, but that the Shylocks would rob him of the old family heirloom if he failed to raise fifteen hundred dollars at once. The lady and her chauffeur later narrowly escaped arrest at the hands of a museum guard when they were caught trying to remove the canvas from the wall. On other occasions, Mike returned, temporarily wealthy, from dashes into what he called the Interior. The details of these raids are seldom aired in court, as Mike enjoys an almost magical immunity from prosecution, an immunity often due to the fact that publicity about his escapades would embarrass distinguished persons.

HIS genius for meeting uncommon situations was put to a severe test on the morning of January 27, 1928, in a suite at the Hotel Astor where a party was held by B. W. Morris, Jr., in connection with the Beaux-Arts Ball of that year. A lady complained that she had missed her gold cigarette-lighter and several other gold objects from her toilet-case. A guest of giant stature seized the diminutive Romanoff, turned him upside down, and shook him by the ankles. The missing articles rolled on the floor. Mike scrambled to his feet roaring with laughter. "You planted those on me," he cried. Pointing the finger of suspicion at one after another, he laughed himself into tears.

The Prince at this period was increasingly afflicted by his chronic trouble: lack of suitable revenues. He had outgrown his old vocation of finding new papas and mammas. Up to the age of thirty-five, he had been a perpetual promising child, adopting new parents from time to time, but alienating them by his strange capers. Now, verging on forty, he was getting somewhat old and stringy to be a little jewel to brighten new foster-homes. His credit was in a bad state; prejudice had developed against his promissory notes. Finally, Mike's morale broke; he decided to work. As America's greatest industrial centre, Pittsburgh received the preference. Mike had made a brief trip to Pittsburgh the year before as the guest of Paul Mellon, son of the Ambassador to England. Young Mellon had taken the Prince there for the wedding of David K. E. Bruce and Ailsa Mellon on May 29, 1926. At the last minute, however, Paul Mellon asked Mike to absent himself from the wedding. The Prince was angry and humiliated at first, but he restored his self-respect by stealing Mellon's suitcase. On his return to New York, Mike summoned his friends to his room to see his magnificent gold military brushes. "What does the 'P. M.' stand for?" he was asked. "Prince Michael, of course," replied Mike.

Revisiting Pittsburgh, Mike looked over the industrial opportunities and accepted a position as laborer in a construction gang. A few months later he arrived in New York a shadow of his former self. He was making a poor convalescence from fractured ribs and internal injuries. Friends sent him to a hospital, where he slowly regained his health. He explained that he had risen meteorically from common laborer to foreman by voluntarily working overtime to impress his superiors. One day when, from pure ambition, he kept on working after the bell, a scoop shovel opened, he said, and dropped tons of débris on him. Mike said that he had saved six hundred dollars and it all went to pay doctors and nurses. When he sought workman's compensation, his claim was denied, he said, on the ground that he had been wantonly working after hours and that the company was therefore in no way liable.

Rockwell Kent sent Mike to the Kent place at Ausable Forks, N.Y., to complete his recovery. Kent knew that Mike was no prince but believed that he had been an officer in the Cossacks. Mike was expected to be invaluable about the Kent stables, but it became quickly apparent that the Prince was grossly deficient in hippology. He was promoted to the position of "factor," a high office of obscure duties, in the Kent ménage. He showed no special talent until Kent started to build a tennis court. Then the Prince displayed an unlooked-for knowledge of masonry. He chipped stones well.

Mike was profoundly influenced by Kent. He imitated Kent's mannerisms and began to dress like him—exactly like him, for he had access to Kent's wardrobe. He tried to write and draw like Kent. He became as good as Kent in one form of writing, the writing of Kent's signature. He began to drop in at bookshops in Syracuse, Binghamton, and elsewhere, saying "I'm Kent," collecting acclaim and hospitality and running up small bills with the tradespeople. For a time, the Kent and Romanoff identities struggled for the possession of Mike's personality.

BOSWELL wrote five volumes about Dr. Johnson before he could bring himself to state that the great man had not always been virtuous. In similar fashion, it must now be conceded that there are some dark spots on Mike's record. Once, at least, he acted as a trapper for a detective agency; and once, at least, after swindling a wealthy benefactress, he stopped prosecution by hinting she had been his mistress; for a brief period in 1929, he was a customers' man for a bond house.

The blackest chapter in Mike's history came later, when he was hired to create statutory grounds for divorce. A wealthy industrialist desired his freedom and felt obliged to obtain evidence against his wife. The Prince was selected to decoy her and a series of traps were laid that might have ensnared Diana. First a stranger named Legrand called on the unsuspecting wife, saying that he had a letter of introduction from a friend of hers living in Paris. He called a second time and took her to dinner. That was the last she saw of Legrand. However, before he had passed out of her life, Legrand had presented one Willie Harris. Willie took her to dinner and then vanished in his turn, but not until he had introduced a Mrs. Grace Wilkins. Grace vanished in her turn, but not until she had introduced Prince Michael Romanoff. Legrand, Willie, and Grace had merely set the stage for the entrance of the imperial Russian. Mike thereupon started briskly to work to win the heart of the industrialist's wife.

Mike was put on an expense account as he courted his victim. He took a suite at a Fifth Avenue hotel, sent out for tubs of caviar and cases of champagne, and summoned all his friends. "Go right up," said the hotel clerk when a guest asked to be announced. "The Prince is expecting everybody." In the intervals between his cocktail parties, Mike paced the floor dictating to two stenographers. He was a statesman one minute, a playwright the next. He had an order, he said, to turn "The Brothers Karamazov" into a drama in seven days, and he was engaged at the same time in mighty negotiations pertaining to the reënthronement of the Romanoffs. He barked dialogue and stage directions from one corner of his mouth, world politics and dynastic schemes from the other. Now and then he took a cavalry revolver out of a bureau drawer and assured himself that it was well oiled.

The victim of the divorce conspiracy was impressed with the greatness of the Prince, although she complained later in an affidavit that his clothes were baggy and he was somewhat dirty. He took her to teas and dinners. Finally— after putting knockout drops into her coffee, according to the victim—Mike delivered her at an apartment which had been provided. A mammoth raiding party led by the husband crashed the love nest. As the door was smashed, Mike is said to have cried: "Who enters the bedchamber of Romanoff?"

The industrialist started his divorce action. The wife hired a lawyer and fought the suit. A library of material on Romanoff was gathered by the Schindler detective agency. The conspiracy was so thoroughly exposed that the divorce suit was dropped. The wife then started suit against her husband and Romanoff for a million dollars. The trial of the civil suit would have revealed grounds for criminal proceedings. There was only one legal method of halting the suit, and that method was adopted. The husband proclaimed that he was insane and for that reason could not be sued. A jury trial was later held to determine whether he was sane or insane. The jury rendered a verdict that he was sane. The husband is now appealing the verdict.

Mike's presence in New York became a peril. He had repented and tearfully begged the lady's pardon. There was great danger that he would tell all. To avert this danger, the Prince was provided with funds and placed on a westbound train.

WHAT started as Prince Michael Romanoff's flight from New York, because of his too intimate connection with the divorce conspiracy case, ended as a raid on the West. Mike's 1931 tour was one of his greater successes. It was on this trip that he obtained a loan of thirty-two dollars from a pawnbroker on his trunk, sight unseen. After two minutes with the Prince, the pawnbroker handed over the thirty-two dollars for the baggage check. With an audience of one person, Mike was always a Patrick Henry; the pawnbroker incident was his masterpiece of tête-à-tête eloquence. On Mike's failure to redeem the trunk, the pawnbroker opened it and the Kansas City press published the contents. One item was a dead man's registration certificate which Mike had used in travelling abroad. There was a quantity of stationery engraved with several aliases, enabling Mike, if one of his identities got into hot water, to shift quickly to another. There was also a volume of tender correspondence and a list of one hundred and fifty well-to-do widows, fourteen of whom lived on Park Avenue.

Mike abandoned an empty wallet in Kansas City and put in a claim against the Santa Fe Railroad for the loss of a wallet containing three hundred and fifty dollars. This was disallowed. With the thirty-two dollars taken from the dazzled pawnbroker, Mike went to Phoenix, Ariz. Arriving there travel-stained, penniless, baggageless, he installed himself in the Westward Ho Hotel. He lacked funds to buy a clean shirt and collar, but the haberdashery problem solved itself. Heaven had directed a Peck & Peck salesman to Phoenix; by special appointment, he became purveyor to His Highness. Mike took a large stock of the salesman's samples for immediate use, gave an immense order for future delivery, and paid for both with one bad check.

Mike was overwhelmed with hospitality at Phoenix. Riding horses and racing cars were placed at his disposal, and parties held in his honor. For refusing to cash a large check, Mike arraigned the manager of the Westward Ho in the hotel lobby before a crowd and transferred his patronage to the Arizona-Biltmore. Mike's Phoenix friends did not doubt his authenticity until after Mike's sudden departure, which fell on the date when his checks were due to come loping back from New York.

The Prince steered a careful course through the Southwest. He had ravaged it several times before, leaving large areas seared and scarred. He was in danger anywhere within a five-hundred-mile radius of Tulsa, Okla., which he had visited some years before. Mike had put up at the Tulsa University Club, which he entertained with the sagas of the love-lives of kings and queens, his cousins.

Evasive at first about the assassination of Rasputin, Mike came clean when bluntly accused. Not since Coronado had any visitor caused such excitement among the natives.

FROM Phoenix, however, Mike had an uneventful trip West, and was soon started on his second Hollywood campaign. Four years before, the Los Angeles papers had exposed him in front-page stories and Mike had departed on the brake-beams, but now he worked the same region more successfully than before. He registered at his old hotel, the Ambassador, and put up in a detached Ambassador bungalow, formerly occupied by John McCormack. He gathered a brilliant retinue and did the night clubs again on a wild spending tour. He was unmasked in Henry's restaurant. The manager spotted Mike as the fake prince of four years before and presented him with a fifty-dollar check of 1927 marked "No funds." Mike loudly blamed his secretary and bankers. He settled the matter on the spot by writing another bad check for fifty dollars in favor of Henry's. Then he paid for his meal with another bad check and left.

Mike split himself three ways for his West Coast campaign of 1931. He was Rockwell Kent, Romanoff, and Captain Chitterin of the British Army. There is nothing startling about this, as seventeen aliases have been traced to Mike. But there is something unique, there is something peculiarly Romanoff, in the fact that Mike had a dog that had an alias. When Mike was Rockwell Kent, his collie was Sport; when Mike was Romanoff, his collie was Michael. There is a gap in the chronicle; it has not been established to what name the dog answered when Mike was Captain Chitterin. Mike shifted rôles and hotels rapidly. Besides living on a grand scale at the Hotel Ambassador, he had run up a tremendous Los Angeles-to-New York telephone bill, and a hotel detective mounted guard in front of his bungalow. Mike abandoned most of his baggage and departed with a suitcase through a hedge in the rear.

Dressed in a Paisley shirt and orange tie, the Prince dropped in at the Hollywood Book Store. The shop had a register or visitors' album, and Mike did a perfect Rockwell Kent signature. O. B. Stade, manager of the store, had seen Kent's autograph on limited editions and welcomed the author-artist to his store. The bookseller had Mike to dinner to meet Robert and Katharine Barrett, who had been writing "A Yankee in Patagonia." Mike volunteered not only to illustrate the book but to write a preface for it. The Barretts wired the good news to Houghton Mifflin & Company, who announced it to the press. (Later, when the hoax became known, the publishers made good by hiring the real Rockwell Kent to do the work.) Mike was widely entertained in Hollywood as Kent. With his usual complaisance, he consented to sit in the bookstore from one till two every day, autographing Kent books. "My books never had such a run in southern California before," said the real Kent later. Finally, at a party in his honor, Mike was exposed. He handled himself with such dignity that the guests were about evenly divided as to whether a great artist had been insulted or a great impostor had been exposed.

THE Los Angeles *Examiner* had a scoop on the exposure of Mike in 1927. It had a scoop on his return in 1931. "Hollywood's entertaining royalty unawares," stated the scoop of 1931. "On the modest register of the Hotel Warwick appears this name: 'Michael Romanoff, 216 East Fifty-second Street, New York City.'

"Mr. Romanoff, as he insists on being called, is no less a person than His Royal Highness, Prince Michael Alexevitch of Russia, first cousin to the late Tsar Nicholas." In the interview, Mike said he was just a dirt farmer in New York and was trying to forget his greatness. The article raved about Mike's diffidence and about "his cunning canine pal, Michael." That was on February 25, 1931. On March 19, 1931, the Los Angeles *Examiner* had another scoop: its second great exposure of Mike. He was unmasked by Theodor Lodijensky, the former Russian general, who had unmasked him in 1927. General Lodijensky, who is six feet three inches tall, does many of the dignified old-régime Russian nobles in the films. He had told people that the fake Romanoff had permanently embittered his life. Further than that, General Lodijensky was at this time suffering intense pain from a Kleig eye. He was pacing the floor with his hands on his bandaged head when a caller arrived at his house and said: "General Lodijensky, a man calling himself Prince Michael Romanoff has given us your name as a reference." The General let out a howl, waved his long arms, and acted like a madman. He rushed into his study and came back with an armful of documents relating to Mike. A Los Angeles *Examiner* reporter was summoned at once, but Michael had left southern California before the exposure was printed. The "No funds" stamps of his New York banks were pounding away at Romanoff checks, which came pouring in from San Diego, Tijuana, Reno, and elsewhere. He was finally caught at Salt Lake City, and locked up because of a Reno check for $386. It was like incarcerating a ghost. Mike walks through stone walls and iron bars. In a few days, he was hurrying East, the charge withdrawn.

Mike has been in jail countless times in America. His arrest is normally followed by a huddle at Police Headquarters, another in the prosecutor's office, another in the judge's chambers, and Mike goes free. With the Pacific Slope papered by Mike's bad checks, he was released by the intercession of New York friends. The penal systems of the world break down before the Prince. Five times he was convicted of crimes in England, and the longest term he served, according to the Scotland Yard record, was one month. Even in France, a country which fails to see the droll side of a bad check, Mike has been fairly lucky. When he is in trouble in America, mysterious benefactors pay back the stolen funds, or the victim himself intercedes for Mike, or the witnesses vanish, or Mike talks his way out. In this instance, the mysterious protectors of the Prince not only settled the pending case but guaranteed payment of future bad checks of Romanoff that might turn up in Salt Lake City.

FROM Salt Lake City, the Prince travelled incognito to New York, his favorite principality, where he patronized cheap hotels, disguised himself by shaving his mustache and wearing college-cut clothes, though occasionally changing at night to tails and a top hat. After a quiet period in Manhattan, he went abroad. On his last crossing, Mike had stowed away on the Olympic, mingling with the first-class passengers but going ashore at Southampton by the service gangplank, wearing a steward's coat and staggering under a load of soiled linen. This time Mike stowed away on the De Grasse of the French Line, carrying a letter addressed "To Whom It May Concern" and stating that the bearer had been authorized to stow away in order to write his adventures; that he was not to be annoyed or inconvenienced. The document bore the signature of a well-known writer. Mike did not find it necessary to intimidate anybody with this paper.

On his arrival at the Ritz bar in Paris, Mike was presented with a bill, dated 1922. "You cannot enter, Prince," he was told, "until this is settled." "Nonsense," replied Mike. "Don't you know that all bills are outlawed in France after seven years?" The hotel people bowed to Mike's legal knowledge. Mike passed on to the Riviera, where several New Yorkers found him holding court on the beach. A young American girl to whom the Prince was attentive resented the advice to lock up her costly bracelets. One night at Cannes, Mike leaped from poverty to riches, recruited a large party, and footed all bills. "Money, I'll have none of it!" he shouted, tossing paper and silver into the air, but picking it up again. A few days later he was arrested for stealing express checks from an American. Handcuffs were clapped on the Prince as he sat with friends in front of the Café Miramar. Between two gendarmes, he walked away puffing leisurely at his pipe and wearing the handcuffs like accessories dictated by fashion. After a brief stay in jail at Cannes he was released. Later he defeated one charge against him by telling the judge that he had been slightly intoxicated, that there had been an uncommon run on his autograph, that he had carelessly dashed off signatures right and left for the milling and struggling autograph fiends, and that certain rogues had inserted blank checks under his scurrying pen.

Mike was entertained for a time by an American couple in a decrepit château at Tours. They found him invaluable in fixing the plumbing and the other weak spots of a château; but they had to get rid of the Prince because their servants spent too much of their time waiting on him. Mike franked himself back to Paris by railroad; he never paid railroad fare, travelling gratis by hiding here and there, switching from car to car and train to train. In Paris he lived well for a while by borrowing from Americans to finance a trip to America. Having no passport, he could not buy a ticket, but he obtained loans on the pretext that he had to bribe ship's officers. Mike found it easier to borrow money when he said he had a crooked use for it. One American loaned two hundred dollars to help Mike to America and received a wire two days later for twenty-five dollars to help Mike back from Havre to Paris. Later Mike recorded his gratitude by writing a note in the friend's album, saying that this obligation would remain "a secret debt which I am glad to think I can never possibly repay." When he found a new American, Mike prospered, but in the intervals between Americans, times were hard. He tided himself over one period of distress by cashing at Manny's Cozy Bar in Montmartre a substantial check which he signed "William Rockefeller."

In April of this year, the Prince decided in earnest to reëmbark for America. His worldly circumstances at the time were not good, but not bad; he was penniless, but part of his baggage was out of hock. His great problem in stowing away on the Île-de-France this spring was that of managing two suitcases. On the boat train, Mike made himself delightful to a young couple sailing for America. "I'll throw myself on your mercy," said Mike, and with his power of capturing sympathy, he told a story that inspired them with that old burning zeal to aid the Prince which he has kindled in thousands. They carried his bags aboard and placed them in their cabins. Mike was soon amusing many of the important ones on the ship. In fact, Mike became the victim of his own charm. His popularity betrayed him. A passenger, searching for him to put life into a cocktail party, asked the purser the number of Romanoff's cabin. "There is no Romanoff on board," said the purser. "I've been with him every day," said the passenger. "He's Prince Romanoff, but he likes to be called plain Mister." They searched the passenger list in vain and concluded that the Prince must be travelling incognito. At about the same time, another passenger told Captain Blancart of the well-turned compliments which Prince Romanoff had paid him. "He's my favorite skipper," Mike had said. The Captain expressed a desire to know Romanoff. In the meantime, the chatter of the cabin stewards was weaving a net about Mike. By comparing notes, they found that the liveliest, most ubiquitous, most conspicuous passenger on the ship belonged to no steward. Three lines of inquiry—the purser's, captain's, and stewards'—converged on Mike just before the Île-de-France reached New York. Mike had his landing card ready. He had entered the purser's office on the pretext of writing some letters, stolen a landing card, and forged the appropriate signatures and countersignatures. Almost to the last, the minor ship's officers were afraid to beard the Prince because he was always in the company of distinguished patrons of the line. At last, however, the purser demanded the number of Mike's cabin. "The whole ship is my cabin," said Mike. He refused to name his accomplices and said that he had slept in some of the finest unoccupied cabins on the ship, though officials of the line asserted that Mike had headquartered for a time in the dog kennels on the top deck. The Prince was held a prisoner and on April 24 turned over to the Ellis Island authorities.

Mike was exposed again, this time at great length, in the New York press. The fact that he was an impostor was old news to thousands of acquaintances, but those who had known Mike as a convivial nobleman, an accomplished citizen of the world, or even as a charming crook, could not credit the statement that he had spent eight or nine years in orphans' homes, never heretofore ranked with Groton and Eton as polishing and refining academies. But Mike's orphanage experience is the true key to his career. His psychology and accomplishments are intelligible only in the light of his early days as a problem child and an incorrigible case. An orphan is painstakingly coached to make a good impression and win a foster-home. Child-care specialists become highly skilled in training children in the knack of winning hearts. A born actor, Mike had mastered all the tricks of the trade and was a professional interesting child before he was in his teens. Under all his titles and disguises, under his polish, under his wealth of criminal experience, Mike is still the appealing, sympathy-capturing orphan. He escaped from Ellis Island in 1922 by winning the sympathy of members of the hospital staff. In spite of his record of escapes, stowaways, and larcenies, he was able to cast the old magic over Ellis Island again in 1932. Minor officials on the Island were simply unable to refuse Mike when he asked permission to visit Manhattan in order to obtain clothes which he said he had in storage. An immigration guard was assigned as his escort. The quest for Mike's wardrobe rapidly changed into a tour of speakeasies. Mike and his aide visited all his old haunts. "Who is that with you?" asked one speakeasy proprietor who was an old friend. "My travelling companion," said Mike. The guard was overwhelmed at meeting the celebrities who hastened to welcome Prince Michael home. At one place, Mike said "I must pay off that taxi," and stepped outside, dismissed the taxi, and returned. The guard, in the heat of his excitement, had not even noticed Mike's absence.

ITwas a return from Elba for Mike. He was joyously received everywhere in the dollar-a-drink belt. Small sums of money were pressed on him. He was egged on to escape. "I can't," said Mike. "I have given my *parole d'honneur* not to escape." "Escape anyway," he was advised. Mike didn't escape, as a matter of fact. A time arrived when the guard was physically unable to accompany him. It was an abandonment rather than a flight. Some time after Mike had forsaken his slumbering companion, the guard roused himself and started a frenzied pursuit. They nearly met at one bar. "I have committed the first despicable act of my life," said the Prince, "I have violated my *parole d'honneur.*" He drank up and left. A moment later, the guard came in crying: "Where is that little cockroach?" The Prince, as he came out of his alcoholic daze, asked advice as to his next step. "I think I must go into the Interior," he said. "By the way, what is in season in the Interior?" On the following day, Mike telephoned to Ellis Island to inquire after the health of the guard and to assure the immigration authorities that the guard was in no way to blame for what had happened.

The dignity of the United States was hurt by all this. An expeditionary force, roughly comparable to that which chased Villa, was sent after Mike. The Federals swarmed into the most august joints in Manhattan. One of Mike's old friends drove him through the Holland Tunnel to start him on the westward journey, but Mike doubled on his trail to make one last tour of the speakeasies. On the next day, a Park Avenue friend equipped him with clothes and money and started him on the way to Canada. Again Mike doubled on his trail. This time he was bagged by the Federal hosts.

Mike was returned to Ellis Island and shipped for France two days later on the De Grasse. At Ellis Island, Mike declined an offer of one hundred dollars from the New York *Journal* for the story of his escape. "Damn their insolence!" exclaimed Mike later, in talking to callers. "Offering me only fifteen hundred dollars for my story!" Shortly before he sailed, Mike agreed to devote his time in French prisons to writing his memoirs for a New York publishing house. The Prince was furious with America because the government people had refused to let him recover his walking-stick, which he had left in a speakeasy.

At Havre, Mike was sent to jail for two months for stowing away. Mike denied in an interview that he had stowed away on the Île-de-France. He went to the boat, he said, to see friends off, fell asleep, and awakened to find the liner far out at sea. "Who," demanded Mike, "would stow away for that country? Miserable America!"

FROM Havre, the Prince was taken early in July to Grasse, in the south of France, where he was imprisoned for stealing an American's passport. He feigned insanity, hoping to be removed to a hospital, from which escape would be easier than from a jail. This trick, an old one with the Prince, failed, and he served out his term. Released in September, he hitched and trolleyed from Grasse to Marseille. On his title alone, he borrowed three hundred francs from the *concierge* of the Hôtel de Marseille and hastened to Paris, where he attached himself to the American colony of St.-Germain-des-Prés and started to organize conspiracies to restore himself to America. He lived by collecting subscriptions for a fund of one thousand francs to hire a Calais fisherman to take him across the Channel. During part of this time, Mike, with his usual generosity, shared his room with an American prizefight-promoter in worse straits than himself. Mike formed another plan to enter England without a passport; he was to tell the British immigration authorities that he was a rich American living in France and that he carried no papers because he wanted to stay in England only long enough to complete the purchase of a shooting place. Mike believed that, by exhibiting bogus checks of enormous size, he could bewilder British officials long enough for him to escape. His plots were temporarily disorganized, however, and Mike was forced into hiding because the Paris police wanted him for beating an employee of the Brasserie Lipp. Mike had been growing irritable; he did not carry his liquor as well as formerly, and he imagined that people failed to treat him with proper respect. One day his fortunes took an upturn. An American woman of means took him in hand, interrogated him closely about his past, broke him down, and obtained a confession. Analyzing this confession, she found that the Prince was an innocent victim of circumstances. She began to pull wires to get him a League of Nations passport and in the meantime appointed him tutor to her son. But she lost an American Express check for one hundred dollars. Tracings of her signature were found and the police gave Mike forty-eight hours in which to leave France. On his failure to disappear, he was arrested and sentenced to a month in jail. He is in jail in Paris now; his friends do not expect him over here much before the night of the Beaux-Arts Ball.

(1932)

WHITE LIKE ME

IN 1982, an investment banker named Richard Grand-Jean took a summer's lease on an eighteenth-century farmhouse in Fairfield, Connecticut; its owner, Anatole Broyard, spent his summers in Martha's Vineyard. The house was handsomely furnished with period antiques, and the surrounding acreage included a swimming pool and a pond. But the property had another attraction, too. Grand-Jean, a managing director of Salomon Brothers, was an avid reader, and he took satisfaction in renting from so illustrious a figure. Anatole Broyard had by then been a daily book reviewer for the *Times* for more than a decade, and that meant that he was one of literary America's foremost gatekeepers. Grand-Jean might turn to the business pages of the *Times* first, out of professional obligation, but he turned to the book page next, out of a sense of self. In his Walter Mittyish moments, he sometimes imagined what it might be like to be someone who read and wrote about books for a living— someone to whom millions of readers looked for guidance.

Broyard's columns were suffused with both worldliness and high culture. Wry, mandarin, even self-amused at times, he wrote like a man about town, but one who just happened to have all of Western literature at his fingertips. Always, he radiated an air of soigné self-confidence: he could be amiable in his opinions or waspish, but he never betrayed a flicker of doubt about what he thought. This was a man who knew that his judgment would never falter and his sentences never fail him.

Grand-Jean knew little about Broyard's earlier career, but as he rummaged through Broyard's bookshelves he came across old copies of intellectual journals like *Partisan Review* and *Commentary*, to which Broyard had contributed a few pieces in the late forties and early fifties. One day, Grand-Jean found himself leafing through a magazine that contained an early article by Broyard. What caught his eye, though, was the contributor's note for the article—or, rather, its absence. It had been neatly cut out, as if with a razor.

A few years later, Grand-Jean happened on another copy of that magazine, and decided to look up the Broyard article again. This time, the note on the contributor was intact. It offered a few humdrum details—that Broyard was born in New Orleans, attended Brooklyn College and the New School for Social Research, and taught at New York University's Division of General Education. It also offered a less humdrum one: the situation of the American Negro, the note asserted, was a subject that the author "knows at first hand." It was an elliptical formulation, to be sure, but for Anatole Broyard it may not have been elliptical enough.

BROYARD was born black and became white, and his story is compounded of equal parts pragmatism and principle. He knew that the world was filled with such snippets and scraps of paper, all conspiring to reduce him to an identity that other people had invented and he had no say in. Broyard responded with X-Acto knives and evasions, with distance and denials and half denials and cunning half-truths. Over the years, he became a virtuoso of ambiguity and equivocation. Some of his acquaintances knew the truth; many more had heard rumors about "distant" black ancestry (wasn't there a grandfather who was black? a great-grandfather?). But most were entirely unaware, and that was as he preferred it. He kept the truth even from his own children. Society had decreed race to be a matter of natural law, but he wanted race to be an elective affinity, and it was never going to be a fair fight. A penalty was exacted. He shed a past and an identity to become a writer—a writer who wrote endlessly about the act of shedding a past and an identity.

Anatole Paul Broyard was born on July 16, 1920, in New Orleans to Paul Broyard and Edna Miller. His father was a carpenter and worked as a builder, along with his brothers; neither parent had graduated from elementary school. Anatole spent his early years in a modest house on St. Ann Street, in a colored neighborhood in the French Quarter. Documents in the Louisiana state archives show all Anatole's ancestors, on both sides, to have been Negroes, at least since the late eighteenth century. The rumor about a distant black ancestor was, in a sense, the reverse of the truth: he may have had one distant white ancestor. Of course, the conventions of color stratification within black America—nowhere more pronounced than in New Orleans— meant that light-skinned blacks often intermarried with other light-skinned blacks, and this was the case with Paul and his "high yellow" wife, Edna. Anatole was the second of three children; he and his sister Lorraine, two years older, were light-skinned, while Shirley, two years younger, was not so light-skinned. (The inheritance of melanin is an uneven business.) In any event, the family was identified as Negro, and identified itself as Negro. It was not the most interesting thing about them. But in America it was not a negligible social fact. The year before Anatole's birth, for example, close to a hundred blacks were lynched in the South and anti-black race riots claimed the lives of hundreds more.

While Anatole was still a child, the family moved to the Bedford-Stuyvesant area of Brooklyn, thus joining the great migration that took hundreds of thousands of Southern blacks to Northern cities during the twenties. In the French Quarter, Paul Broyard had been a legendary dancer, beau, and *galant;* in the French Quarter, the Broyards—Paul was one of ten siblings—were known for their craftsmanship. Brooklyn was a less welcoming environment. "He should never have left New Orleans, but my mother nagged him into it," Broyard recalled years later. Though Paul Broyard arrived there a master carpenter, he soon discovered that the carpenters' union was not favorably inclined toward colored applicants. A stranger in a strange city, Paul decided to pass as white in order to join the union and get work. It was strictly a professional decision, which affected his work and nothing else.

For Paul, being colored was a banal fact of life, which might be disguised when convenient; it was not a creed or something to take pride in. Paul did take pride in his craft, and he liked to boast of rescuing projects from know-nothing architects. He filled his home with furniture he had made himself—flawlessly professional, if a little too sturdily built to be stylish. He also took pride in his long legs and his dance-hall agility (an agility Anatole would share). It was a challenge to be a Brooklyn *galant,* but he did his best.

"Family life was very congenial, it was nice and warm and cozy, but we just didn't have any sort of cultural or intellectual nourishment at home," Shirley, who was the only member of the family to graduate from college, recalls. "My parents had no idea even what *The New York Times* was, let alone being able to imagine that Anatole might write for it." She says, "Anatole was different from the beginning." There was a sense, early on, that Anatole Broyard—or Buddy, as he was called then—was not entirely comfortable being a Broyard.

Shirley has a photograph, taken when Anatole was around four or five, of a family visit back to New Orleans. In it you can see Edna and her two daughters, and you can make out Anatole, down the street, facing in the opposite direction. The configuration was, Shirley says, pretty representative.

After graduating from Boys High School, in the late thirties, he enrolled in Brooklyn College. Already, he had a passion for modern culture—for European cinema and European literature. The idea that meaning could operate on several levels seemed to appeal to him. Shirley recalls exasperating conversations along those lines: "He'd ask me about a Kafka story I'd read or a French film I'd seen and say, 'Well, you see that on more than one level, don't you?' I felt like saying 'Oh, get off it.' Brothers don't say that to their sisters."

Just after the war began, he got married, to a black Puerto Rican woman, Aida, and they soon had a daughter. (He named her Gala, after Salvador Dali's wife.) Shirley recalls, "He got married and had a child on purpose—the purpose being to stay out of the Army. Then Anatole goes in the Army anyway, in spite of this child." And his wife and child moved in with the Broyard family.

Though his military records were apparently destroyed in a fire, some people who knew him at this time say that he entered the segregated Army as a white man. If so, he must have relished the irony that after attending officers' training school he was made the captain of an all-black stevedore battalion. Even then, his thoughts were not far from the new life he envisioned for himself. He said that he joined the Army with a copy of Wallace Stevens in his back pocket; now he was sending money home to his wife and asking her to save it so that he could open a bookstore in the Village when he got back. "She had other ideas," Shirley notes. "She wanted him to get a nice job, nine to five."

Between Aida and the allure of a literary life there was not much competition. Soon after his discharge from the Army, at war's end, he found an apartment in the Village, and he took advantage of the G.I. Bill to attend evening classes at the New School for Social Research, on Twelfth Street. His new life had no room for Aida and Gala. (Aida, with the child, later moved to California and remarried.) He left other things behind, too. The black scholar and dramatist W. F. Lucas, who knew Buddy Broyard from Bed-Stuy, says, "He was black when he got into the subway in Brooklyn, but as soon as he got out at West Fourth Street he became white."

He told his sister Lorraine that he had resolved to pass so that he could be a writer, rather than a Negro writer. His darker-skinned younger sister, Shirley, represented a possible snag, of course, but then he and Shirley had never been particularly close, and anyway she was busy with her own life and her own friends. (Shirley graduated Phi Beta Kappa from Hunter College, and went on to marry Franklin Williams, who helped organize the Peace Corps and served as Ambassador to Ghana.) They had drifted apart: it was just a matter of drifting farther apart. Besides, wasn't that why everybody came to New York—to run away from the confines of family, from places where people thought they knew who and what you were? Whose family *wasn't* in some way unsuitable? In a *Times* column in 1979 Broyard wrote, "My mother and father were too folksy for me, too colorful. . . . Eventually, I ran away to Greenwich Village, where no one had been born of a mother and father, where the people I met had sprung from their own brows, or from the pages of a bad novel. . . . Orphans of the avant-garde, we outdistanced our history and our humanity." Like so much of what he wrote in this vein, it meant more than it said; like the modernist culture he loved, it had levels.

IN the Village, where Broyard started a bookstore on Cornelia Street, the salient thing about him wasn't that he was black but that he was beautiful, charming, and erudite. In those days, the Village was crowded with ambitious and talented young writers and artists, and Broyard—known for calling men "Sport" and girls "Slim"—was never more at home. He could hang out at the San Remo bar with Dwight Macdonald and Delmore Schwartz, and with a younger set who yearned to be the next Macdonalds and the next Schwartzes. Vincent Livelli, a friend of Broyard's since Brooklyn College days, recalls, "Everybody was so brilliant around us—we kept duelling with each other. But he was the guy that set the pace in the Village." His conversation sparkled—everybody said so. The sentences came out perfectly formed, festooned with the most apposite literary allusions. His high-beam charm could inspire worship but also resentment. Livelli says, "Anatole had a sort of dancing attitude toward life—he'd dance away from you. He had people understand that he was brilliant and therefore you couldn't hold him if you weren't worthy of his attention."

The novelist and editor Gordon Lish says, "Photographs don't suggest in any wise the enormous power he had in person. No part of him was ever for a moment at rest." He adds, "I adored him as a man. I mean, he was really in a league with Neal Cassady as a kind of presence." But there was, he says, a fundamental difference between Broyard and Kerouac's inspiration and muse: "Unlike Cassady, who was out of control, Anatole was *exorbitantly* in control. He was fastidious about managing things."

Except, perhaps, the sorts of things you're supposed to manage. His bookstore provided him with entrée to Village intellectuals—and them with entrée to Anatole—yet it was not run as a business, exactly. Its offerings were few but choice: Céline, Kafka, other hard-to-find translations. The critic Richard Gilman, who was one of its patrons, recalls that Broyard had a hard time parting with the inventory: "He had these books on the shelf, and someone would want to buy one, and he would snatch it back."

Around 1948, Broyard started to attract notice not merely for his charm, his looks, and his conversation but for his published writings. The early pieces, as often as not, were about a subject to which he had privileged access: blacks and black culture. *Commentary*, in his third appearance in its pages, dubbed him an "anatomist of the Negro personality in a white world." But was he merely an anthropologist or was he a native informant? It wasn't an ambiguity that he was in any hurry to resolve. Still, if all criticism is a form of autobiography (as Oscar Wilde would have it), one might look to these pieces for clues to his preoccupations at the time. In a 1950 *Commentary* article entitled "Portrait of the Inauthentic Negro," he wrote that the Negro's embarrassment over blackness should be banished by the realization that "thousands of Negroes with 'typical' features are accepted as whites merely because of light complexion." He continued:

The inauthentic Negro is not only estranged from whites—he is also estranged from his own group and from himself. Since his companions are a mirror in which he sees himself as ugly, he must reject them; and since his own self is mainly a tension between an accusation and a denial, he can hardly find it, much less live in it. . . . He is adrift without a role in a world predicated on roles.

A year later, in "Keep Cool, Man: The Negro Rejection of Jazz," he wrote, just as despairingly, that the Negro's

contact with white society has opened new vistas, new ideals in his imagination, and these he defends by repression, freezing up against the desire to be white, to have normal social intercourse with whites, to behave like them. . . . But in coolness he evades the issue . . . he becomes a pacifist in the struggle between social groups—not a conscientious objector, but a draft-dodger.

These are words that could be read as self-indictment, if anybody chose to do so. Certainly they reveal a ticklish sense of the perplexities he found himself in, and a degree of self-interrogation (as opposed to self-examination) he seldom displayed again.

In 1950, in a bar near Sheridan Square, Broyard met Anne Bernays, a Barnard junior and the daughter of Edward L. Bernays, who is considered the father of public relations. "There was this guy who was the handsomest man I have ever seen in my life, and I fell madly in love with him," Bernays, who is best known for such novels as "Growing Up Rich" and "Professor Romeo," recalls. "He was physically irresistible, and he had this dominating personality, and I guess I needed to be dominated. His hair was so short that you couldn't tell whether it was curly or straight. He had high cheekbones and very smooth skin." She knew that he was black, through a mutual friend, the poet and Blake scholar Milton Klonsky. (Years later, in a sort of epiphany, she recognized Anatole's loping walk as an African-American cultural style: "It was almost as if this were inside him dying to get out and express itself, but he felt he couldn't do it.")

After graduation, she got a job as an editor at the literary semiannual *Discovery.* She persuaded Broyard to submit his work, and in 1954 the magazine ran a short story entitled "What the Cystoscope Said"—an extraordinary account of his father's terminal illness:

I didn't recognize him at first, he was so bad. His mouth was open and his breathing was hungry. They had removed his false teeth, and his cheeks were so thin that his mouth looked like a keyhole. I leaned over his bed and brought my face before his eyes. "Hello darlin'," he whispered, and he smiled. His voice, faint as it was, was full of love, and it bristled the hairs on the nape of my neck and raised goose flesh on my forearms. I couldn't speak, so I kissed him. His cheek smelled like wax.

Overnight, Broyard's renown was raised to a higher level. "Broyard knocked people flat with 'What the Cystoscope Said,' " Lish recalls. One of those people was Burt Britton, a bookseller who later co-founded Books & Co. In the fifties, he says, he read the works of young American writers religiously: "Now, if writing were a horse race, which God knows it's not, I would have gone out and put my two bucks down on Broyard." In "Advertisements for Myself," Norman Mailer wrote that he'd buy a novel by Broyard the day it appeared. Indeed, Bernays recalls, on the basis of that story the Atlantic Monthly Press offered Broyard a twenty-thousand-dollar advance—then a staggeringly large sum for a literary work by an unknown—for a novel of which "Cystoscope" would be a chapter. "The whole literary world was waiting with bated breath for this great novelist who was about to arrive," Michael Vincent Miller, a friend of Broyard's since the late fifties, recalls. "Some feelings of expectation lasted for years."

Rumor surrounded Broyard like a gentle murmur, and sometimes it became a din. Being an orphan of the avant-garde was hard work. Among the black literati, certainly, his ancestry was a topic of speculation, and when a picture of Broyard accompanied a 1958 *Time* review of a Beat anthology it was closely scrutinized. Arna Bontemps wrote to Langston Hughes, "His picture . . . makes him look Negroid. If so, he is the only spade among the Beat Generation." Charlie Parker spied Broyard in Washington Square Park one day and told a companion, "He's one of us, but he doesn't want to admit he's one of us." Richard Gilman recalls an awkwardness that ensued when he stumbled across Anatole with his dark-skinned wife and child: "I just happened to come upon them in a restaurant that was not near our usual stomping grounds. He introduced me, and it was fine, but my sense was that he would rather not have had anyone he knew meet them." He adds, "I remember thinking at the time that he had the look of an octoroon or a quadroon, one of those—which he strenuously denied. He got into very great disputes with people."

One of those disputes was with Chandler Brossard, who had been a close friend: Broyard was the best man at Brossard's wedding. There was a falling out, and Brossard produced an unflattering portrait of Broyard as the hustler and opportunist Henry Porter in his 1952 novel, "Who Walk in Darkness." Brossard knew just where Broyard was most vulnerable, and he pushed hard. His novel originally began, "People said Henry Porter was a Negro," and the version published in France still does. Apparently fearing legal action, however, Brossard's American publisher, New Directions, sent it to Broyard in galley form before it was published.

Anne Bernays was with Broyard when the galleys arrived. Broyard explained to her, "They asked me to read it because they are afraid I am going to sue." But why would he sue, she wanted to know. "Because it says I'm a Negro," he replied grimly. "Then," Bernays recalls, "I said, 'What are you going to do?' He said, 'I am going to make them change it.' And he did."

The novel went on to be celebrated as a groundbreaking chronicle of Village hipsters; it also—as a result of the legal redactions—reads rather oddly in places. Henry Porter, the Broyard character, is rumored to be not a Negro but merely "an illegitimate":

> I suspect [the rumor] was supposed to explain the difference between the way he behaved and the way the rest of us behaved. Porter did not show that he knew people were talking about him this way. I must give him credit for maintaining a front of indifference that was really remarkable.
>
> Someone both Porter and I knew quite well once told me the next time he saw Porter he was going to ask him if he was or was not an illegitimate. He said it was the only way to clear the air. Maybe so. But I said I would not think of doing it. . . . I felt that if Porter ever wanted the stories about himself cleared up, publicly, he would one day do so. I was willing to wait.

And that, after all, is the nature of such secrets: they are not what cannot be known but what cannot be acknowledged.

Another trip wire seems to have landed Broyard in one of the masterpieces of twentieth-century American fiction, William Gaddis's "The Recognitions." Livelli explains, "Now, around 1947 or '48, William Gaddis and Anatole were in love with the same gal, Sheri Martinelli. They were rivals, almost at each other's throats. And Willie was such a sweetheart that he had a mild approach to everything, and Anatole was sort of a stabber: he injected words like poison into conversations." When "The Recognitions" came out, in 1955, "Anatole caught on to it right away, and he was kind of angry over it." The Broyard character is named Max, and Gaddis wrote that he "always looked the same, always the same age, his hair always the same short length," seemingly "a parody on the moment, as his clothes caricatured a past at eastern colleges where he had never been." Worse is his "unconscionable smile," which intimates "that the wearer knew all of the dismal secrets of some evil jungle whence he had just come."

Broyard's own account of these years—published in 1993 as "Kafka Was the Rage"—is fuelled by the intertwined themes of writing and women. Gaddis says, "His eyes were these great pools—soft, gentle pools. It was girls, girls, girls: a kind of intoxication of its own. I always thought, frankly, that that's where his career went, his creative energies."

Anne Bernays maintains, "If you leave the sex part out, you're only telling half the story. With women, he was just like an alcoholic with booze." She stopped seeing him in 1952, at her therapist's urging. "It was like going cold turkey off a drug," she says, remembering how crushing the experience was, and she adds, "I think most women have an Anatole in their lives."

Indeed, not a few of them had Anatole. "He was a pussy gangster, really," Lucas, a former professor of comparative literature, says with Bed-Stuy bluntness. Gilman recalls being in Bergdorf Goodman and coming across

Broyard putting the moves on a salesgirl. "I hid behind a pillar—otherwise he'd know that I'd seen him—and watched him go through every stage of seduction: 'What do you think? Can I put this against you? Oh, it looks great against your skin. You have the most wonderful skin.' And then he quoted Baudelaire."

Quoting Baudelaire turns out to be key. Broyard's great friend Ernest van den Haag recalls trolling the Village with Broyard in those days: "We obviously quite often compared our modus operandi, and what I observed about Anatole is that when he liked a girl he could speak to her brilliantly about all kinds of things which the girl didn't in the least understand, because Anatole was really vastly erudite. The girl had no idea what he was talking about, but she loved it, because she was under the impression, rightly so, that she was listening to something very interesting and important. His was a solipsistic discourse, in some ways." Indeed, the narrator of "What the Cystoscope Said" tells of seducing his ailing father's young and ingenuous nurse in a similar manner:

> "Listen," I said, borrowing a tone of urgency from another source, "I want to give you a book. A book that was written for you, a book that belongs to you as much as your diary, that's dedicated to you like your nurse's certificate." . . . My apartment was four blocks away, so I bridged the distance with talk, raving about *Journey to the End of the Night*, the book she needed like she needed a hole in her head.

Broyard recognized that seduction was a matter not only of talking but of listening, too, and he knew how to pay attention with an engulfing level of concentration. The writer Ellen Schwamm, who met Broyard in the late fifties, says, "You show me a man who talks, and I'll show you a thousand women who hurl themselves at his feet. I don't mean just talk, I mean dialogues. He *listened*, and he was willing to speak of things that most men are not interested in: literature and its effect on life." But she also saw another side to Broyard's relentless need to seduce. She invokes a formulation made by her husband, the late Harold Brodkey: "Harold used to say that a lot of men steal from women. They steal bits of their souls, bits of their personalities, to construct an emotional life, which many men don't have. And I think that Anatole needed something of that sort."

It's an image of self-assemblage which is very much in keeping with Broyard's own accounts of himself. Starting in 1946, and continuing at intervals for the rest of his life, he underwent analysis. Yet the word "analysis" is misleading: what he wanted was to be refashioned—or, as he told his first analyst, to be *transfigured*. "When I came out with the word, I was like someone who sneezes into a handkerchief and finds it full of blood," he wrote in the 1993 memoir. "I wanted to discuss my life with him not as a patient talking to

an analyst but as if we were two literary critics discussing a novel. . . . I had a
literature rather than a personality, a set of fictions about myself." He lived a lie
because he didn't want to live a larger lie: and Anatole Broyard, Negro writer,
was that larger lie.

ALEXANDRA Nelson, known as Sandy, met Broyard in January of 1961.
Broyard was forty, teaching the odd course at the New School and supporting
himself by freelancing: promotional copy for publishers, liner notes for
Columbia jazz records, blurbs for the Book-of-the-Month Club. Sandy was
twenty-three and a dancer, and Broyard had always loved dancers. Of
Norwegian descent, she was strikingly beautiful, and strikingly intelligent.
Michael Miller recalls, "She represented a certain kind of blonde, a certain kind
of sophisticated carriage and a way of moving through the world with a sense
of the good things. They both had marvellous taste."

It was as if a sorcerer had made a list of everything Broyard loved and had
given it life. At long last, the conqueror was conquered: in less than a year,
Broyard and Sandy were married. Sandy remembers his aura in those days:
"Anatole was very hip. It wasn't a pose—it was in his sinew, in his bones. And,
when he was talking to you, you just felt that you were receiving all this radiance from him." (Van den Haag says, "I do think it's not without significance
that Anatole married a blonde, and about as white as you can get. He may have
feared a little bit that the children might turn out black. He must have been
pleased that they didn't.")

While they were still dating, two of Broyard's friends told Sandy that he was
black, in what seemed to be a clumsy attempt to scare her off. "I think they
really weren't happy to lose him, to see him get into a serious relationship," she
says. "They were losing a playmate, in a way." Whatever the cultural sanc-
tions, she was unfazed. But she says that when she asked Broyard about it he
proved evasive: "He claimed that he wasn't black, but he talked about 'island
influences,' or said that he had a grandmother who used to live in a tree on
some island in the Caribbean. Anatole was like that—he was very slippery."
Sandy didn't force the issue, and the succeeding years only fortified his sense of
reserve. "Anatole was very strong," she says. "And he said about certain things,
'Just keep out. This is the deal if you get mixed up with me.' " The life that
Broyard chose to live meant that the children did not meet their Aunt Shirley
until after his death—nor, except for a couple of brief visits in the sixties, was
there any contact even with Broyard's light-skinned mother and older sister. It
was a matter of respecting the ground rules. "I would try to poke in those
areas, but the message was very direct and strong," Sandy explains. "Oh, when
I got angry at him, you know, one always pushes the tender points. But over
time you grow up about these things and realize you do what you can do and
there are certain things you can't."

In 1963, just before their first child, Todd, was born, Anatole shocked his friends by another big move—to Connecticut. Not only was he moving to Connecticut but he was going to be commuting to work: for the first time in his life, he would be a company man. "I think one of his claims to fame was that he hadn't had an office job—somehow, he'd escaped that," Sandy says. "There had been no real need for him to grow up." But after Todd was born—a daughter, Bliss, followed in 1966—Anatole spent seven years working full-time as a copywriter at the Manhattan advertising agency Wunderman Ricotta & Kline.

Over the next quarter century, the family lived in a series of eighteenth-century houses, sometimes bought on impulse, in places like Fairfield, Redding, Greens Farms, and Southport. Here, in a land of leaf-blowers and lawnmowers, Bed-Stuy must have seemed almost comically remote. Many of Broyard's intimates from the late forties knew about his family; the intimates he acquired in the sixties did not, or else had heard only rumors. Each year, the number of people who knew Buddy from Bed-Stuy dwindled; each year, the rumors grew more nebulous; each year, he left his past further behind. Miller says, "Anatole was a master at what Erving Goffman calls 'impression management.' " The writer Evelyn Toynton says, "I remember once going to a party with Sandy and him in Connecticut. There were these rather dull people there, stockbrokers and the usual sorts of people, and Anatole just knocked himself out to charm every single person in the room. I said to him, 'Anatole, can't you ever *not* be charming?' " Miller observes, "He was a wonderful host. He could take people from different walks of life—the president of Stanley Tools or a vice-president of Merrill Lynch, say, and some bohemian type from the Village—and keep the whole scene flowing beautifully. He had perfect pitch for the social encounter, like Jay Gatsby."

It was as if, wedded to an ideal of American self-fashioning, he sought to put himself to the ultimate test. It was one thing to be accepted in the Village, amid the Beats and hipsters and émigrés, but to gain acceptance in Cheever territory was an achievement of a higher order. "Anatole, when he left the Village and went to Connecticut, was able not only to pass but even to be a kind of influential presence in that world of rich white Wasps," Miller says. "Maybe that was a shallower part of the passing—to be accepted by Connecticut gentry."

Broyard's feat raised eyebrows among some of his literary admirers: something borrowed, something new. Daphne Merkin, another longtime friend, detected "a 'country-squire' tendency—a complicated tendency to want to establish a sort of safety through bourgeoisness. It was like a Galsworthy quality."

Even in Arcadia, however, there could be no relaxation of vigilance: in his most intimate relationships, there were guardrails. Broyard once wrote that Michael Miller was one of the people he liked best in the world, and Miller is candid about Broyard's profound influence on him. Today, Miller is a psychotherapist, based in Cambridge, and the author, most recently, of "Intimate

Terrorism." From the time they met until his death, Broyard read to him the first draft of almost every piece he wrote. Yet a thirty-year friendship of unusual intimacy was circumscribed by a subject that they never discussed. "First of all, I didn't *know*," Miller says. "I just had intuitions and had heard intimations. It was some years before I'd even put together some intuition and little rumblings—nothing ever emerged clearly. There was a certain tacit understanding between us to accept certain pathways as our best selves, and not challenge that too much." It was perhaps, he says a little sadly, a limitation on the relationship.

IN the late sixties, Broyard wrote several front-page reviews for the *Times Book Review.* "They were brilliant, absolutely sensational," the novelist Charles Simmons, who was then an assistant editor there, says. In 1971, the *Times* was casting about for a new daily reviewer, and Simmons was among those who suggested Anatole Broyard. It wasn't a tough sell. Arthur Gelb, at the time the paper's cultural editor, recalls, "Anatole was among the first critics I brought to the paper. He was very funny, and he also had that special knack for penetrating hypocrisy. I don't think he was capable of uttering a boring sentence."

You could say that his arrival was a sign of the times. Imagine: Anatole Broyard, downtown flaneur and apostle of sex and high modernism, ensconced in what was, literarily speaking, the ultimate establishment perch. "There had been an awful lot of very tame, very conventional people at the *Times,* and Broyard came in as a sort of ambassador from the Village and Village sophistication," Alfred Kazin recalls. Broyard had a highly developed appreciation of the paper's institutional power, and he even managed to use it to avenge wrongs done him in his Village days. Just before he started his job at the daily, he published a review in the *Times Book Review* of a new novel by one Chandler Brossard. The review began, "Here's a book so transcendently bad it makes us fear not only for the condition of the novel in this country, but for the country itself."

Broyard's reviews were published in alternation with those of Christopher Lehmann-Haupt, who has now been a daily reviewer at the *Times* for more than a quarter century, and who readily admits that Broyard's appointment did not gladden his heart. They hadn't got along particularly well when Lehmann-Haupt was an editor at the *Times Book Review,* nor did Lehmann-Haupt entirely approve of Broyard's status as a fabled libertine. So when A. M. Rosenthal, the paper's managing editor, was considering hiring him, Lehmann-Haupt expressed reservations. He recalls, "Rosenthal was saying, 'Give me five reasons why not.' And I thoughtlessly blurted out, 'Well, first of all, he is the biggest ass man in town.' And Rosenthal rose up from his desk and said, 'If that were a disqualification for working for *The New York Times*'—and he waved—'this place would be empty!' "

Broyard got off to an impressive start. Lehmann-Haupt says, "He had a wonderful way of setting a tone, and a wonderful way of talking himself through a review. He had good, tough instincts when it came to fiction. He had taste." And the jovial Herbert Mitgang, who served a stint as a daily reviewer himself, says, "I always thought he was the most literary of the reviewers. There would be something like a little essay in his daily reviews."

Occasionally, his acerbic opinions got him in trouble. There was, for example, the storm that attended an uncharitable review of a novel by Christy Brown, an Irish writer who was born with severe cerebral palsy. The review concluded:

> It is unfortunate that the author of "A Shadow on Summer" is an almost total spastic—he is said to have typed his highly regarded first novel, "Down All the Days," with his left foot—but I don't see how the badness of his second novel can be blamed on that. Any man who can learn to type with his left foot can learn to write better than he has here.

Then, there was the controversial review of James Baldwin's piously sentimental novel of black suffering, "If Beale Street Could Talk." Broyard wrote:

> If I have to read one more description of the garbage piled up in the streets of Harlem, I may just throw protocol to the winds and ask whose garbage is it? I would like to remind Mr. Baldwin that the City Health Code stipulates that garbage must be put out in proper containers, not indiscriminately "piled."

No one could accuse Broyard of proselytizing for progressive causes. Jason Epstein, for one, was quick to detect a neoconservative air in his reviews, and Broyard's old friend Ernest van den Haag, a longtime contributing editor at *National Review*, volunteers that he was available to set Broyard straight on the issues when the need arose. Broyard could be mischievous, and he could be tendentious. It did not escape notice that he was consistently hostile to feminist writers. "Perhaps it's naïve of me to expect people to write reasonable books about emotionally charged subjects," one such review began, irritably. "But when you have to read and review two or three books each week, you do get tired of 'understanding' so much personal bias. You reach a point where it no longer matters that the author's mistakes are well meant. You don't care that he or she is on the side of the angels: you just want them to tell the truth."

Nor did relations between the two daily reviewers ever become altogether cordial. Lehmann-Haupt tells of a time in 1974 when Broyard said that he was sick and couldn't deliver a review. Lehmann-Haupt had to write an extra review in less than a day, so that he could get to the Ali-Frazier fight the next night, where he had ringside seats. Later, when they discussed the match, Broyard seemed suspiciously knowledgeable about its particulars; he claimed that a friend of his had been invited by a television executive to watch it on closed-circuit TV. "I waited about six months, because one of the charming things about Anatole was that he never remembered his lies," Lehmann-Haupt says, laughing. "And I said, 'Did you see that fight?' And he said, 'Oh, yeah—I was there as a guest of this television executive.' *That's* why he couldn't write the review!"

BROYARD had been teaching off and on at the New School since the late fifties, and now his reputation as a writing teacher began to soar. Certainly his fluent prose style, with its combination of grace and clarity, was a considerable recommendation. He was charismatic and magisterial, and, because he was sometimes brutal about students' work, they found it all the more gratifying when he was complimentary. Among his students were Paul Breslow, Robert Olen Butler, Daphne Merkin, and Hilma Wolitzer. Ellen Schwamm, who took a workshop with him in the early seventies, says, "He had a gourmet's taste for literature and for language, and he was really able to convey that: it was a very sensual experience."

These were years of heady success and, at the same time, of a rising sense of failure. An arbiter of American writing, Broyard was racked by his inability to write his own magnum opus. In the fifties, the Atlantic Monthly Press had contracted for an autobiographical novel—the novel that was supposed to secure Broyard's fame, his place in contemporary literature—but, all these years later, he had made no progress. It wasn't for lack of trying. Lehmann-Haupt recalls his taking a lengthy vacation in order to get the book written. "I remember talking to him—he was up in Vermont, where somebody had lent him a house—and he was in agony. He banished himself from the Vineyard, was clearly suffering, and he just couldn't do it." John Updike, who knew Broyard slightly from the Vineyard, was reminded of the anticipation surrounding Ellison's second novel: "The most famous non-book around was the one that Broyard was not writing." (The two non-book writers were in fact quite friendly: Broyard admired Ellison not only as a writer but as a dancer—a high tribute from such an adept as Broyard.)

Surrounded by analysts and psychotherapists—Sandy Broyard had become a therapist herself by this time—Broyard had no shortage of explanations for his inability to write his book. "He did have a total writer's block," van den Haag says, "and he was analyzed by various persons, but it didn't fully overcome the writer's block. I couldn't prevent him from going back to 'The Cystoscope' and trying to improve it. He made it, of course, not better but worse." Broyard's fluency as an essayist and a reviewer wasn't quite compensation. Charles Simmons says, "He had produced all this charming criticism, but the one thing that mattered to him was the one thing he hadn't managed to do."

As the seventies wore on, Miller discussed the matter of blockage with his best friend in relatively abstract terms: he suggested that there might be something in Broyard's relationship to his family background that was holding him back. In the eighties, he referred Broyard to his own chief mentor in gestalt therapy, Isador From, and From became perhaps Broyard's most important therapist in his later years. "In gestalt therapy, we talk a lot about 'unfinished business': anything that's incomplete, unfinished, haunts the whole personality and tends, at some level, to create inhibition or blockage," Miller says. "You're stuck there at a certain point. It's like living with a partly full bladder all your life."

Some people speculated that the reason Broyard couldn't write his novel was that he was living it—that race loomed larger in his life because it was unacknowledged, that he couldn't put it behind him because he had put it beneath him. If he had been a different sort of writer, it might not have mattered so much. But Merkin points out, "Anatole's subject, even in fiction, was essentially himself. I think that ultimately he would have had to deal with more than he wanted to deal with."

Broyard may have been the picture of serene self-mastery, but there was one subject that could reliably fluster him. Gordon Lish recalls an occasion in the mid-seventies when Burt Britton (who was married to a black woman) alluded to Anatole's racial ancestry. Lish says, "Anatole became inflamed, and he left the room. He snapped, like a dog snapping—he *barked* at Britton. It was an ugly moment." To people who knew nothing about the matter, Broyard's sensitivities were at times simply perplexing. The critic Judith Dunford used to go to lunch with Broyard in the eighties. One day, Broyard mentioned his sister Shirley, and Dunford, idly making conversation, asked him what she looked like. Suddenly, she saw an extremely worried expression on his face. Very carefully, he replied, "Darker than me."

There was, finally, no sanctuary. "When the children were older, I began, every eighteen months or so, to bring up the issue of how they needed to know at some point," Sandy Broyard says. "And then he would totally shut down and go into a rage. He'd say that at some point he would tell them, but he would not tell them now." He was the Scheherazade of racial imposture, seeking and securing one deferral after another. It must have made things not easier but harder. In the modern era, children are supposed to come out to their parents: it works better that way around. For children, we know, can judge their parents harshly—above all, for what they understand as failures of candor. His children would see the world in terms of authenticity; he saw the world in terms of self-creation. Would they think that he had made a Faustian bargain? Would they speculate about what else he had not told them—about the limits of self-invention? Broyard's resistance is not hard to fathom. He must have wondered when the past would learn its place, and stay past.

Anatole Broyard had confessed enough in his time to know that confession did nothing for the soul. He preferred to communicate his truths on higher frequencies. As if in exorcism, Broyard's personal essays deal regularly with the necessary, guilt-ridden endeavor of escaping family history: and yet the feelings involved are well-nigh universal. The thematic elements of passing— fragmentation, alienation, liminality, self-fashioning—echo the great themes of modernism. As a result, he could prepare the way for exposure without ever risking it. Miller observes, "If you look at the writing closely enough, and listen to the intonations, there's something there that is like no writer from the completely white world. Freud talked about the repetition compulsion. With Anatole, it's interesting that he was constantly hiding it and in some ways constantly revealing it."

Sandy speaks of these matters in calmly analytic tones; perhaps because she is a therapist, her love is tempered by an almost professional dispassion. She says, "I think his own personal history continued to be painful to him," and she adds, "In passing, you cause your family great anguish, but I also think, conversely, do we look at the anguish it causes the person who is passing? Or the anguish that it was born out of?"

IT may be tempting to describe Broyard's self-positioning as arising from a tortured allegiance to some liberal-humanist creed. In fact, the liberal pieties of the day were not much to his taste. "It wasn't about an ideal of racelessness but something much more complex and interesting," Miller says. "He was actually quite anti-black," Evelyn Toynton says. She tells of a time when she was walking with him on a street in New York and a drunken black man came up to him and asked for a dollar. Broyard seethed. Afterward, he remarked to her; "I look around New York, and I think to myself, If there were no blacks in New York, would it really be any loss?"

No doubt this is a calculation that whites, even white liberals, sometimes find themselves idly working out: How many black muggers is one Thelonious Monk worth? How many Willie Hortons does Gwendolyn Brooks redeem? In 1970, Ellison published his classic essay "What America Would Be Like Without Blacks," in *Time*; and one reason it is a classic essay is that it addresses a question that lingers in the American political unconscious. Commanding as Ellison's arguments are, there remains a whit of defensiveness in the very exercise. It's a burdensome thing to refute a fantasy.

And a burdensome thing to be privy to it. Ellen Schwamm recalls that one of the houses Broyard had in Connecticut had a black jockey on the lawn, and that "he used to tell me that Jimmy Baldwin had said to him, 'I can't come and see you with this crap on your lawn.' " (Sandy remembers the lawn jockey—an antique—as having come with the house; she also recalls that it was stolen one day.) Charles Simmons says that the writer Herbert Gold, before introducing him to Broyard, warned him that Broyard was prone to make comments about "spades," and Broyard did make a few such comments. "He personally, on a deeper level, was not enamored of blacks," van den Haag says. "He avoided blacks. There is no question he did." Sandy is gingerly in alluding to this subject. "He was very short-tempered with the behavior of black people, the sort of behavior that was shown in the news. He had paid the price to be at liberty to say things that, if you didn't know he was black, you would misunderstand. I think it made him ironical."

EVERY once in a while, however, Broyard's irony would slacken, and he would speak of the thing with an unaccustomed and halting forthrightness. Toynton says that after they'd known each other for several years he told her there was a "C" (actually, "col," for "colored") on his birth certificate. "And then another time he told me that his sister was black and that she was married to a black man." The circumlocutions are striking: not that *he* was black but that his birth certificate was; not that *he* was black but that his family was. Perhaps this was a matter less of evasiveness than of precision.

"Some shrink had said to him that the reason he didn't like brown-haired women or dark women was that he was afraid of his own shit," Toynton continues. "And I said, 'Anatole, it's as plain as plain can be that it has to do with being black.' And he just stopped and said, 'You don't know what it was like. It was horrible.' He told me once that he didn't like to see his sisters, because they reminded him of his unhappy childhood." (Shirley's account suggests that this unhappy childhood may have had more to do with the child than with the hood.)

Ellen Schwamm remembers one occasion when Broyard visited her and Harold Brodkey at their apartment, and read them part of the memoir he was working on. She says that the passages seemed stilted and distant, and that Brodkey said to him, "You're not telling the truth, and if you try to write lies or evade the truth this is what you get. What's the real story?" She says, "Anatole took a deep breath and said, 'The real story is that I'm not who I seem. I'm a black.' I said, 'Well, Anatole, it's no great shock, because this rumor has been around for years and years and years, and everyone assumes there's a small percentage of you that's black, if that's what you're trying to say.' And he said, 'No, that's not what I'm trying to say. My father could pass, but in fact my mother's black, too. We're black as far back as I know.' We never said a word of it to anybody, because he asked us not to."

Schwamm also says that she begged him to write about his history: it seemed to her excellent material for a book. But he explained that he didn't want notoriety based on his race—on his revealing himself to be black—rather than on his talent. As Toynton puts it, Broyard felt that he had to make a choice between being an aesthete and being a Negro. "He felt that once he said, 'I'm a

Negro writer,' he would have to write about black issues, and Anatole was such an aesthete."

All the same, Schwamm was impressed by a paradox: the man wanted to be appreciated not for being black but for being a writer, even though his pretending not to be black was stopping him from writing. It was one of the very few ironies that Broyard, the master ironist, was ill equipped to appreciate.

BESIDES, there was always his day job to attend to. Broyard might suffer through a midnight of the soul in Vermont; but he was also a working journalist, and when it came to filing his copy he nearly always met his deadlines. In the late seventies, he also began publishing brief personal essays in the *Times*. They are among the finest work he did—easeful, witty, perfectly poised between surface and depth. In them he perfected the feat of being self-revelatory without revealing anything. He wrote about his current life, in Connecticut: "People in New York City have psychotherapists, and people in the suburbs have handymen. While anxiety in the city is existential, in the country it is structural." And he wrote about his earlier life, in the city: "There was a kind of jazz in my father's movements, a rhythm compounded of economy and flourishes, functional and decorative. He had a blues song in his blood, a wistful jauntiness he brought with him from New Orleans." (Wistful, and even worrisome: "I half-expected him to break into the Camel Walk, the Shimmy Shewobble, the Black Bottom or the Mess Around.") In a 1979 essay he wrote about how much he dreaded family excursions:

> To me, they were like a suicide pact. Didn't my parents know that the world was just waiting for a chance to come between us?
> Inside, we were a family, but outside we were immigrants, bizarre in our differences. I thought that people stared at us, and my face grew hot. At any moment, I expected my father and mother to expose their tribal rites, their eccentric anthropology, to the gape of strangers.
> Anyone who saw me with my family knew too much about me.

These were the themes he returned to in many of his personal essays, seemingly marking out the threshold he would not cross. And if some of his colleagues at the *Times* knew too much about him, or had heard the rumors, they wouldn't have dreamed of saying anything. Abe Rosenthal (who did know about him) says that the subject never arose. "What was there to talk about? I didn't really consider it my business. I didn't think it was proper or polite, nor did I want him to think I was prejudiced, or anything."

But most people knew nothing about it. C. Gerald Fraser, a reporter and an editor at the *Times* from 1967 until 1991, was friendly with Broyard's brother-in-law Ambassador Franklin Williams. Fraser, who is black, recalls that one day Williams asked him how many black journalists there were at the *Times*. "I listed them," he says, "and he said, 'You forgot one.' I went over the list again, and I said, 'What do you mean?' He said, 'Shirley's brother, Anatole Broyard.' I was dumbstruck, because I'd never heard it mentioned at the *Times* that he was black, or that the paper had a black critic."

In any event, Broyard's colleagues did not have to know what he was to have reservations about *who* he was. He cultivated his image as a trickster—someone who would bend the rules, finesse the system—and that image only intensified his detractors' ire. "A good book review is an act of seduction, and when he did it there was nobody better," John Leonard says, but he feels that Broyard's best was not always offered. "I considered him to be one of the laziest book reviewers to come down the pike." Soon a running joke was that Broyard would review only novels shorter than two hundred pages. In the introduction to "Aroused by Books," a collection of the reviews he published in the early seventies, Broyard wrote that he tried to choose books for review that were "closest to [his] feelings." Lehmann-Haupt says dryly, "We began to suspect that he often picked the books according to the attractiveness of the young female novelists who had written them." Rosenthal had shamed him for voicing his disquiet about Broyard's reputation as a Don Juan, but before long Rosenthal himself changed his tune. "Maybe five or six years later," Lehmann-Haupt recalls, "Rosenthal comes up to me, jabbing me in the chest with a stiffened index finger and saying, 'The trouble with Broyard is that he writes with his cock!' I bit my tongue."

Gradually, a measure of discontent with Broyard's reviews began to make itself felt among the paper's cultural commissars. Harvey Shapiro, the editor of the *Book Review* from 1975 to 1983, recalls conversations with Rosenthal in which "he would tell me that all his friends hated Anatole's essays, and I would tell him that all my friends loved Anatole's essays, and that would be the end of the conversation." In 1984, Broyard was removed from the daily *Times* and given a column in the *Book Review*.

Mitchel Levitas, the editor of the *Book Review* from 1983 to 1989, edited Broyard's column himself. He says, "It was a tough time for him, you see, because he had come off the daily book review, where he was out there in the public eye twice a week. That was a major change in his public role." In addition to writing his column, he was put to work as an editor at the *Book Review*. The office environment was perhaps not altogether congenial to a man of his temperament. Kazin recalls, "He complained to me constantly about being on the *Book Review*, because he had to check people's quotations and such. I think he thought that he was superior to the job."

Then, too, it was an era in which the very notion of passing was beginning to seem less plangent than preposterous. Certainly Broyard's skittishness around the subject wasn't to everyone's liking. Brent Staples, who is black, was an editor at the *Book Review* at the time Broyard was there. "Anatole had it both ways," Staples says. "He would give you a kind of burlesque wink that seemed to indicate he was ready to accept the fact of your knowing that he was a black person. It was a real ambiguity, tacit and sort of recessed. He jived around and played with it a lot, but never made it express the fact that he was black." It was a game that tried Staples' patience. "When Anatole came anywhere near me, for example, his whole style, demeanor, and tone would change," he recalls. "I took that as him conveying to me, 'Yes, I am like you. But I'm relating this to you on a kind of recondite channel.' Over all, it made me angry. Here was a guy who was, for a long period of time, probably one of the two or three most important critical voices on literature in the United States. How could you, actively or passively, have this fact hidden?"

Staples pauses, then says, "You know, he turned it into a joke. And when you change something basic about yourself into a joke, it spreads, it metastasizes, and so his whole presentation of self became completely ironic. *Everything* about him was ironic."

There were some people who came to have a professional interest in achieving a measure of clarity on the topic. Not long before Broyard retired from the *Times*, in 1989, Daphne Merkin, as an editor at Harcourt Brace Jovanovich, gave him an advance of a hundred thousand dollars for his memoirs. (The completed portion was ultimately published, as "Kafka Was the Rage," by Crown.) Merkin learned that "he was, in some ways, opaque to himself," and her disquiet grew when the early chapters arrived. "I said, 'Anatole, there's something odd here. Within the memoir, you have your family moving to a black neighborhood in Brooklyn. I find that strange—unless they're black.' I said, 'You can do many things if you're writing a memoir. But if you squelch stuff that seems to be crucial about you, and pretend it doesn't exist . . .'" She observes that he was much attached to aspects of his childhood, but "in a clouded way."

WHEN Broyard retired from the *Times*, he was nearly sixty-nine. To Sandy, it was a source of some anguish that their children still did not know the truth about him. Yet what was that truth? Broyard was a critic—a critic who specialized in European and American fiction. And what was race but a European and American fiction? If he was passing for white, perhaps he understood that the alternative was passing for black. "But if some people are light enough to live like white, mother, why should there be such a fuss?" a girl asks her mother in "Near-White," a 1931 story by the Harlem Renaissance author Claude McKay. "Why should they live colored when they could be happier living white?" Why, indeed? One could concede that the passing of Anatole Broyard involved dishonesty; but is it so very clear that the dishonesty was mostly Broyard's?

To pass is to sin against authenticity, and "authenticity" is among the founding lies of the modern age. The philosopher Charles Taylor summarizes its ideology thus: "There is a certain way of being human that is *my* way. I am called upon to live my life in this way, and not in imitation of anyone else's life. But this notion gives a new importance to being true to myself. If I am not, I miss the point of my life; I miss what being human is for *me*." And the Romantic fallacy of authenticity is only compounded when it is collectivized: when the putative real me gives way to the real us. You can say that Anatole Broyard was (by any juridical reckoning) "really" a Negro, without conceding that a Negro is a thing you can really be. The vagaries of racial identity were increased by what anthropologists call the rule of "hypodescent"—the one-drop rule. When those of mixed ancestry—and the majority of blacks are of mixed ancestry—disappear into the white majority, they are traditionally accused of running from their "blackness." Yet why isn't the alternative a matter of running from their "whiteness"? To emphasize these perversities, however, is a distraction from a larger perversity. You can't get race "right" by refining the boundary conditions.

The act of razoring out your contributor's note may be quixotic, but it is not mad. The mistake is to assume that birth certificates and biographical sketches and all the other documents generated by the modern bureaucratic state reveal an anterior truth—that they are merely signs of an independently existing identity. But in fact they constitute it. The social meaning of race is established by these identity papers—by tracts and treatises and certificates and pamphlets and all the other verbal artifacts that proclaim race to be real and, by that proclamation, make it so.

So here is a man who passed for white because he wanted to be a writer, and he did not want to be a Negro writer. It is a crass disjunction, but it is not his crassness or his disjunction. His perception was perfectly correct. He *would* have had to be a Negro writer, which was something he did not want to be. In his terms, he did not want to write about black love, black passion, black suffering, black joy; he wanted to write about love and passion and suffering and joy. We give lip service to the idea of the writer who happens to be black, but had anyone, in the postwar era, ever seen such a thing?

Broyard's friend Richard A. Shweder, an anthropologist and a theorist of culture, says, "I think he believed that reality is constituted by style," and ascribes to Broyard a "deeply romantic view of the intimate connection between style and reality." Broyard passed not because he thought that race wasn't important but because he knew that it was. The durable social facts of race were beyond reason, and, like Paul Broyard's furniture, their strength came at the expense of style. Anatole Broyard lived in a world where race had, indeed, become a trope for indelibility, for permanence. "All I *have* to do," a black folk saying has it, "is stay black and die."

Broyard was a connoisseur of the liminal—of crossing over and, in the familiar phrase, getting over. But the ideologies of modernity have a kicker, which is that they permit no exit. Racial recusal is a forlorn hope. In a system where whiteness is the default, racelessness is never a possibility. You cannot opt out; you can only opt in. In a scathing review of a now forgotten black author, Broyard announced that it was time to reconsider the assumption of many black writers that " 'whitey' will never let you forget you're black." For his part, he wasn't taking any chances. At a certain point, he seems to have decided that all he had to do was stay white and die.

IN 1989, Broyard resolved that he and his wife would change their life once more. With both their children grown, they could do what they pleased. And what they pleased—what he pleased, anyway—was to move to Cambridge, Massachusetts. They would be near Harvard, and so part of an intellectual community. He had a vision of walking through Harvard Square, bumping into people like the sociologist Daniel Bell, and having conversations about ideas in the street. Besides, his close friend Michael Miller was living in the area. Anne Bernays, also a Cambridge resident, says, "I remember his calling several times and asking me about neighborhoods. It was important for him to get that right. I think he was a little disappointed when he moved that it wasn't to a fancy neighborhood like Brattle or Channing Street. He was on Wendell Street, where there's a tennis court across the street and an apartment building and the houses are fairly close together." It wasn't a matter of passing so much as of positioning.

Sandy says that they had another the-children-must-be-told conversation shortly before the move. "We were driving to Michael's fiftieth-birthday party—I used to plan to bring up the subject in a place where he couldn't walk out. I brought it up then because at that point our son was out of college and our daughter had just graduated, and my feeling was that they just absolutely needed to know, as adults." She pauses. "And we had words. He would just bring down this gate." Sandy surmises, again, that he may have wanted to protect them from what he had experienced as a child. "Also," she says, "I think he needed still to protect himself." The day after they moved into their house on Wendell Street, Broyard learned that he had prostate cancer, and that it was inoperable.

BROYARD spent much of the time before his death, fourteen months later, making a study of the literature of illness and death, and publishing a number of essays on the subject. Despite the occasion, they were imbued with an almost dandyish, even jokey sense of incongruity: "My urologist, who is quite famous, wanted to cut off my testicles. . . . Speaking as a surgeon, he said that it was the surest, quickest, neatest solution. Too neat, I said, picturing myself with no balls. I knew that such a solution would depress me, and I was sure that depression is bad medicine." He had attracted notice in 1954 with the account of his father's death from a similar cancer; now he recharged his writing career as a chronicler of his own progress toward death. He thought about calling his collection of writings on the subject "Critically Ill." It was a pun he delighted in.

Soon after the diagnosis was made, he was told that he might have "in the neighborhood of years." Eight months later, it became clear that this prognosis was too optimistic. Richard Shweder, the anthropologist, talks about a trip to France that he and his wife made with Anatole and Sandy not long before Anatole's death. One day, the two men were left alone. Shweder says, "And what did he want to do? He wanted to throw a ball. The two of us just played catch, back and forth." The moment, he believes, captures Broyard's athleticism, his love of physical grace.

Broyard spent the last five weeks of his life at the Dana Farber Cancer Institute, in Boston. In therapy sessions, the need to set things straight before the end had come up again—the need to deal with unfinished business and, most of all, with his secret. He appeared willing, if reluctant, to do so. But by now he was in almost constant pain, and the two children lived in different places, so the opportunities to have the discussion as a family were limited. "Anatole was in such physical pain that I don't think he had the wherewithal," Sandy says. "So he missed the opportunity to tell the children himself." She speaks of the expense of spirit, of psychic energy, that would have been required. The challenge would have been to explain why it had remained a secret. And no doubt the old anxieties were not easily dispelled: would it have been condemned as a Faustian bargain or understood as a case of personality overspilling, or rebelling against, the reign of category?

It pains Sandy even now that the children never had the chance to have an open discussion with their father. In the event, she felt that they needed to know before he died, and, for the first time, she took it upon herself to declare what her husband could not. It was an early afternoon, ten days before his death, when she sat down with her two children on a patch of grass across the street from the institute. "They knew there was a family secret, and they wanted to know what their father had to tell them. And I told them."

The stillness of the afternoon was undisturbed. She says carefully, "Their first reaction was relief that it was only this, and not an event or circumstance of larger proportions. Only following their father's death did they begin to feel the loss of not having known. And of having to reformulate who it was that they understood their father—and themselves—to be."

At this stage of his illness, Anatole was moving in and out of lucidity, but in his room Sandy and the children talked with humor and irony about secrets and about this particular secret. Even if Anatole could not participate in the conversation, he could at least listen to it. "The nurses said that hearing was the last sense to go," Sandy says.

It was not as she would have planned it. She says, gently, "Anatole always found his own way through things."

The writer Leslie Garis, a friend of the Broyards' from Connecticut, was in Broyard's room during the last weekend of September, 1990, and recorded much of what he said on his last day of something like sentience. He weighed perhaps seventy pounds, she guessed, and she describes his jaundice-clouded eyes as having the permanently startled look born of emaciation. He was partly lucid, mostly not. There are glimpses of his usual wit, but in a mode more aleatoric than logical. He spoke of Robert Graves, of Sheri Martinelli, of John Hawkes interpreting Miles Davis. He told Sandy that he needed to find a place to go where he could "protect his irony." As if, having been protected by irony throughout his life, it was now time to return the favor.

"I think friends are coming, so I think we ought to order some food," he announced hours before he lapsed into his final coma. "We'll want cheese and crackers, and Faust."

"Faust?" Sandy asked.

Anatole explained, "He's the kind of guy who makes the Faustian bargain, and who can be happy only when the thing is revealed."

A memorial service, held at a Congregationalist church in Connecticut, featured august figures from literary New York, colleagues from the *Times*, and neighbors and friends from the Village and the Vineyard. Charles Simmons told me that he was surprised at how hard he took Broyard's death. "You felt that you were going to have him forever, the way you feel about your own child," he said. "There was something wrong about his dying, and that was the reason." Speaking of the memorial service, he says, marvelling, "You think that you're the close friend, you know? And then I realized that there were twenty people ahead of me. And that his genius was for close friends."

Indeed, six years after Broyard's death many of his friends seem to be still mourning his loss. For them he was plainly a vital principle, a dancer and romancer, a seducer of men and women. (He considered seduction, he wrote, "the most heartfelt literature of the self.") Sandy tells me, simply, "You felt more alive in his presence," and I've heard almost precisely the same words from a great many others. They felt that he lived more intensely than other men. They loved him—perhaps his male friends especially, or, anyway, more volubly—and they admired him. They speak of a limber beauty, of agelessness, of a radiance. They also speak of his excesses and his penchant for poses. Perhaps, as the bard has it, Broyard was "much more the better for being a little bad."

And if his presence in American fiction was pretty much limited to other people's novels, that is no small tribute to his personal vibrancy. You find him reflected and refracted in the books of his peers, like Anne Bernays (she says there is a Broyard character in every novel she's written) and Brossard and Gaddis, of course, but also in those of his students. His own great gift was as a feuilletonist. The personal essays collected in "Men, Women and Other Anticlimaxes" can put you in mind of "The Autocrat of the Breakfast-Table," by Oliver Wendell Holmes, Sr. They are brief impromptus, tonally flawless. To read them is to feel that you are in the company of someone who is thinking things through. The essays are often urbane and sophisticated, but not unbearably so, and they can be unexpectedly moving. Literary culture still fetishizes the novel, and there he was perhaps out of step with his times. Sandy says, "In the seventies and eighties, the trend, in literature and film, was to get sparer, and the flourish of Anatole's voice was dependent on the luxuriance of his language." Richard Shweder says, "It does seem that Anatole's strength was the brief, witty remark. It was aphoristic. It was the critical review. He was brilliant in a thousand or two thousand words." Perhaps he wasn't destined to be a novelist, but what of it? Broyard was a Negro who wanted to be something other than a Negro, a critic who wanted to be something other than a critic. Broyard, you might say, wanted to be something other than Broyard. He very nearly succeeded.

SHIRLEY Broyard Williams came to his memorial service, and many of his friends—including Alfred Kazin, who delivered one of the eulogies—remember being puzzled and then astonished as they realized that Anatole Broyard was black. For Todd and Bliss, however, meeting Aunt Shirley was, at last, a flesh-and-blood confirmation of what they had been told. Shirley is sorry that they didn't meet sooner, and she remains baffled about her brother's decision. But she isn't bitter about it; her attitude is that she has had a full and eventful life of her own—husband, kids, friends—and that if her brother wanted to keep himself aloof she respected his decision. She describes the conversations they had when they did speak: "They always had to be focussed on something, like a movie, because you couldn't afford to be very intimate. There had to be something that would get in the way of the intimacy." And when she phoned him during his illness it was the same way. "He never gave that up," she says, sounding more wistful than reproachful. "He never learned how to be comfortable with me." So it has been a trying set of circumstances all around. "The hypocrisy that surrounds this issue is so thick you could chew it," Shirley says wearily.

Shirley's husband died several months before Anatole, and I think she must have found it cheering to be able to meet family members who had been sequestered from her. She says that she wants to get to know her nephew and her niece—that there's a lot of time to make up. "I've been encouraging Bliss to come and talk, and we had lunch, and she calls me on the phone. She's really responded very well. Considering that it's sort of last minute."

Years earlier, in an essay entitled "Growing Up Irrational," Anatole Broyard wrote, "I *descended* from my mother and father. I was *extracted* from them." His parents were "a conspiracy, a plot against society," as he saw it, but also a source of profound embarrassment. "Like every great tradition, my family had to die before I could understand how much I missed them and what they meant to me. When they went into the flames at the crematorium, all my letters of introduction went with them." Now that he had a wife and family of his own, he had started to worry about whether his children's feelings about him would reprise his feelings about his parents: "Am I an embarrassment to them, or an accepted part of the human comedy? Have they joined my conspiracy, or are they just pretending? Do they understand that, after all those years of running away from home, I am still trying to get back?"

(1996)

WUNDERKIND

ONE of the greatest men I ever knew was the celebrated middleweight Philadelphia Jack O'Brien—"Philadelphia Jack O'Brien from Americaw" was the way he liked best to hear it, and he would say it that way aloud to cheer himself up when his spirits flagged. "That was how they introduced me at the National Sporting Club in London," he would explain, "and the sonorousness of the effect compensates the redundancy." The "Philadelphia" was to distinguish him from the numerous other O'Briens and pseudo-O'Briens active in the American ring in his era. (The current edition of Nat Fleischer's record book, "The Ring," lists only three O'Briens; the Irish are in a professional decline.) The agility of Mr. O'Brien's mind exceeded even that of his footwork, which was the most spectacular of his generation. Once, in his robust, athletic middle years, which coincided with the depression, he was shy the rent for a gymnasium he conducted atop a Broadway building. He therefore invited the landlord, a dropsical old German gentleman, to a free boxing lesson, in the course of which he pretended that the old fellow had knocked him out. The landlord, fearing a damage suit, avoided O'Brien for months, and never bothered him about the rent.

This, however, is what my (and, during O'Brien's life, his) friend Colonel John R. Stingo would call a labyrinthian digression. What enshrined O'Brien in the memory of millions who never enjoyed the privilege of his personal acquaintance was that in March, 1909, he was knocked into a cerebral hiatus, unique for him, in the last five seconds of a ten-round bout with a less deservedly eminent contemporary called Stanley Ketchel, the Michigan Assassin, after he, O'Brien, had won six or seven rounds of the fight. Because the bell interrupted the referee's count, there was no knockout, and under the present rules of the New York State Athletic Commission this would have entitled him to the decision, even though prostrate. The state law then forbade decisions of any kind, and fellows in barrooms have been arguing intermittently ever since over who won the fight. Both O'Brien and Ketchel, according to all qualified observers, were great middleweights, but I sometimes wonder whether their encounter wouldn't be remembered as just a pretty good fight, instead of an epic, if it hadn't ended the way it did.

What made me think of the O'Brien-Ketchel fight was the fact that in the *last* second of the final round of a run-of-the-mill fight at Madison Square Garden a week ago, I saw a young colored light heavyweight named Floyd Patterson knock his opponent through the ropes with a punch that would surely have been a knockout if the final bell hadn't sounded just as the victim fell. It's the only time I've seen this happen in what must be several hundred fights I've watched. (I started going to them in about 1920, and while I've never attended more than about a dozen cards in a year, they begin to mount up.) Since this was an eight-round bout, the mathematical odds against the thing's coming off in the last second were 1,439 to 1. Another odd feature of the bout was that it was limited to eight rounds to protect Patterson, who is not yet twenty and therefore, in the eyes of the Athletic Commission, too tender a vessel for a longer course. If there had been a ninth round, the other fellow wouldn't have been able to come up for it.

Fight snobs will consider my analogy with O'Brien and Ketchel sacrilegious, because, as I have said, this Garden bout wasn't much of a fight. Patterson is a couple of years away, as the connoisseurs have it, and Joe Gannon, the fellow he hit, shouldn't be in feature bouts at all. Moreover, it developed later that Gannon wasn't leading on points in the opinions of the judges, the referee, the newspapermen, or the people watching the show on television. He was walking a tightrope from the first round on. But for two friends of Gannon's who sat behind me he had run up a bigger lead than old Philadelphia Jack enjoyed when Ketchel caught him. I went to the fight because I wanted to see how far Patterson had progressed since turning professional in 1952, and I suppose that the same curiosity brought out most of the rest of the small crowd. Among the exceptions were half a hundred Occidentals wearing Chinese lampshade hats, whom I took to be delegates to some convention of Shriners or Red Men of the World. I learned later they were Philadelphia rooters for a lightweight named Jimmy Soo, whose father runs a Chinese restaurant down there. Soo was fighting in the semifinal.

MY interest in Patterson goes back to the summer of 1952, when he was a member of the United States boxing team at the Olympic Games in Helsinki, which I attended. There was no boxing ring at Olympic Village, on the outskirts of Helsinki, and the American boxers used to go into town by bus every morning to train in the gymnasium of a workingmen's club in Häkäniemi, the proletarian quarter of town. The club, in a great granite building known as the People's House, stood on a small square, in the center of which was a statue of a completely naked boxer. The daily bus trip gave the American boxers a closer contact with Helsinki and its residents than most of the other athletes got; every morning, a knot of admiring, towheaded small boys and not-so-small girls would wait for the American bus to draw up at the curb outside the People's House, and they would all be there again an hour later to see the boxers leave. The trip made excellent counterpropaganda to the Communist legend of the Land of Lynching, for eleven of the fourteen members of the boxing squad were Negroes. They looked very sharp in their American sports clothes, and the girls quite evidently thought they were beautiful.

There was one working coach with the squad, a jolly, sagacious fellow named Pete Mello, who is head coach of the Catholic Youth Organization boxing team in New York; he had as colleagues a couple of free riders in blue blazers and white buckskin shoes, who stayed far from sweat and Vaseline. On the first morning I met the team, Mello tipped me off to Patterson, who was seventeen and entered in the hundred-and-sixty-five-pound class. Mello picked him as the surest winner for the United States, although the rest of the team included boys who had been amateur stars for years and had won enough watches to stock three hock shops on Sixth Avenue.

Patterson was having no trouble making the weight; he was a tall, straight stick of a boy, slender except for big shoulders. He had a long, straight nose and wore long sideburns; there was something humorously dandified about his appearance. Outside the ring, his favorite position was horizontal. If he saw a bench, he would lie on it rather than sit on it. Inside the ring, he fought with a wild exuberance. He would begin from a crouch, with shoulders and forearms protecting his head, and then would start to wing punches, being as likely to lead with a right as with a left. His style was crude, but his reflexes were so fast he got away with it. His leverage was perfect—his blows hurt, and after throwing one he was almost always in position to hit again. Furthermore, he liked to fight, and was as strong as a snake, grabbing his sparring partners and whirling them off balance—an unconventional and technically illegal maneuver that draws only a warning from referees here but is likely to lead to disqualification by the more precise European judges. Mello's one worry about Patterson was that this would happen, and he kept cautioning the boy on the subject. All Patterson's hard fights in Helsinki were in the training ring, against heavier teammates. We had a huge heavyweight there named Ed Sanders, who was a football player from Idaho State College, and an alternate named Norvel Lee, who weighed a bit over a hundred and eighty and had won dozens of amateur titles. Lee, who was twenty-eight, was a law-school man heading for the F.B.I., and he knew about as much about boxing as an amateur can know. There was a hundred-and-seventy-eight-pound class in the Olympics, and Lee decided to aim for that. Patterson and Lee liked to fight each other, and Lee, even with his extra twenty pounds and his big edge in experience, couldn't quite hold Patterson even.

There was nothing much to Patterson's Olympic bouts themselves. In the hundred-and-sixty-five-pound final, Patterson met a Rumanian. The fellow was frightened, as well he might have been, and Patterson clowned a bit. He whirled the Rumanian clean around once, and I could imagine Mello blanching. The crowd booed, although he hadn't done anything to harm the fellow— it was a mere *pas de danse.* The judges didn't disqualify him, however, and since the boo had warned him to get down to work, he hit the Rumanian once and knocked him out. After that, there was "the Olympic ceremony." Three portable platforms were moved into the ring. Patterson stood on the highest, with the resuscitated Rumanian at his right, on a lower level, and a Finn, the winner of third honors, at his left. A girl in Finnish national costume had handed Patterson a big bouquet, and he held it in his left hand. A band played the Olympic fanfare and then "The Star-Spangled Banner," and, tucking his right forearm into his belly, Patterson made a deep, dancing-school bow.

Later, Lee won the hundred-and-seventy-eight-pound final, and got a special cup for being the most skillful boxer in the Olympics. He has a classic, stand-up style that goes over big with Europeans. Sanders won the heavyweight title; he was so big that his final opponent, a Swede, simply ran away. The judges disqualified the Swede, who said afterward that it had suddenly occurred to him he might be killed. The American boxers won five first places out of a possible ten. The mass of unofficial points the Americans picked up in the boxing competition went so far to offset the unofficial points the Russians scored in gymnastics that in the unofficial point score covering all events the United States won a psychologically important unofficial victory. And that was the last time I had seen Patterson in the flesh before I went to the Garden the night he fought Gannon.

In the meanwhile, I knew, Patterson had been doing well, without being rushed unduly. In any art, the prodigy presents a problem. Given too easy a program, he goes slack, but asked too hard a question early, he becomes discouraged. Finding a middle course is particularly difficult in the prize ring; in comparison, the management of juvenile orchestra conductors, mathematicians, and billiardists is simple. The fighter must be confirmed in the belief that he can lick anybody in the world and at the same time be restrained from testing this belief on a subject too advanced for his attainments. The trick lies in keeping the fellow entertained while enriching his curriculum. In my young manhood, there were two *Wunderkinder* in the light-heavyweight class whose handlers failed to bring it off; one, Young Stribling, was made overcautious by doting parents, and the other, Jimmy Slattery, was made overconfident by adulation. Slattery, like Icarus, made a great splash, though. He was a boy Mozart, a honeydew melon.

In the two years following his return from Finland, Patterson had had seventeen professional fights. Of these, the first thirteen had been with opponents of progressively diminishing unimportance, each picked to contribute something to his education. From the beginning, Patterson was a fair television attraction, because of his Olympic fame, and his TV fees served as a kind of scholarship for him. Almost all his fights were on Monday nights—television nights—at a club called the Eastern Parkway Arena, in Brooklyn. His graduation exercises took place last June, when he went eight televised Eastern Parkway rounds with Joey Maxim, a former light-heavyweight champion of the world, who is still tough and a great cutie, or opportunist. Maxim was never a great hitter, though, so he didn't figure to knock Patterson out. I watched the fight from a stool in the Palace Bar & Grill, on West Forty-fifth Street, and what impressed me was that Maxim couldn't make Patterson look foolish except at infrequent intervals, and then only for a second or two. He would have handled the Helsinki Patterson the way a rodeo clown handles a bull. In the Olympics, Patterson had wasted much time in aimless body-weaving, and had often launched himself through the air like a man trying to get through a closing subway door before the train pulls out. Against Maxim, he held himself together better and hit more often, with shorter, quicker blows. Also, he had got pretty cute himself. His greater vigor more than made up for Maxim's slight margin in acuity, I thought, and when the ex-champion got the decision, I agreed with the other patrons of the Palace that Patterson had been robbed. The newspaper writers the next morning were of the same opinion, but the chief significance of the bout was that Patterson had proved he could no longer be considered an undergraduate. After the commencement exercises, he knocked out a fellow named Tommy Harrison, who should have given him a good fight, and then polished off a couple of light summer snacks while waiting for the rodeo to get out of Madison Square Garden.

Gannon, the fellow chosen for Patterson's début on the Garden's Friday-night television program, which pays four thousand dollars an appearance, figured no better than most of the twenty-nine-hundred-dollar opponents Patterson had been meeting on Monday nights, although he was, of course, considerably superior to a Rumanian amateur. The simplest reason for the match that I could think of was that the International Boxing Club feared Patterson might suffer from stagefright in his first Eighth Avenue appearance. Gannon was a fighter calculated to get him over any initial nervousness. Another reason, I supposed, was that Gannon is managed by Al Weill, who also manages Rocky Marciano. Weill is a man of weight and profundity; when he makes a match for one of his fighters, it often turns out that he has had in view some chink in the armor of the adversary party. If I hadn't seen Gannon fight a couple of times this summer, I might have thought that Weill thought that he had a chance. Unfortunately, however, Weill had got him preliminary engagements on both the Charles-Marciano shows, and I had been forced to watch him twice. He is an old-looking young man with a serious, puggy face and a heavy beard, which shows through his white skin like Senator Joe McCarthy's. According to the program notes, Gannon is twenty-seven, which indicates that he must have been something of a prodigy himself in his time. He was national amateur welterweight champion in 1944, when, if the program was right, he was seventeen. Subsequently, however, he renounced his art to become a policeman in Washington, and during his resumed career under Mr. Weill's guidance he has retained a coppish gloom. Sitting in his corner, he frequently looks as though he were counting the number of places he lost on the sergeant's list through his truancy. He is a pretty good conventional boxer, but even the slow-moving hooker he fought both times I saw him managed to hit him fairly often, so I couldn't imagine his staying ahead of Patterson. After Maxim, Gannon would be a refresher course in the rudiments.

THE purpose of going to a fight isn't always to see a close contest. A great many close fights are hardly worth looking at, while the development of an interesting performer is always an attraction; Native Dancer and Man o' War were drawing cards when they were 1–100 to win. Since I anticipated no strong emotions from the main bout, I went to the Garden early, hoping to see a good preliminary. The small-club atmosphere that has prevailed since television was evident. Perhaps fifteen hundred fans huddled around the ring; the galleries and the mezzanine were empty. By lowering the price of admission to that of a movie theatre, the I.B.C. might attract a few more customers, but it is possible that the television sponsor would object. A fight seen on television has the appeal of being something for nothing, and this appeal is increased by the notion that it is something expensive for nothing. It might even help sell beer or razor blades if the I.B.C. made the price for ringside seats fifty dollars instead of eight dollars. Only the elfin Orientals from Philadelphia were animated as a couple of better-than-average colored welterweights fought a hard, skillful eight-rounder. "Stop that bloody fight!" one yelled roguishly as the boys slugged away. This insensitivity to what is going on before their eyes is one of the weirdest characteristics of fight crowds. One oaf having suggested that the welterweights were not fighting hard, his companions tried to outdo him in cynicism. They stamped, clapped, and whistled while the welters worked out their tense little problem. One fighter, a light-tan boy, worked in from his opponent's flanks, throwing wide hooks and uppercuts, moving around his man. The other, bitter-chocolate and grim, worked the inside lines, moving forward, punching shorter and straighter. He took the first round, and then the flashier boy won the next four, anticipating his opponent's blows and hitting him with some notable left hooks to his solidly attached head. In the sixth, the dark boy came on, his mathematically superior strategy of the inner lines paying off and his steady hitting taking some of the steam out of the tan fellow. In the last round, the enveloper rallied with what I judged to be his last strength, but he was too late, and the straight-mover got the decision. There was nothing theatrical in either performance—just a good professional fight.

Next, Jimmy Soo, whom the Philadelphians had come to root for, went on with a lad named Jimmy Wilde, billed as "a rough, tough lightweight from the Bronx." I learned from my program that Soo, an "undefeated lightweight of Chinese-Irish descent, is colorful, flashy, and talented." He proved to be all that—at least, far too talented for Wilde—but the rough, tough lightweight kept on coming in for more. The bout was scheduled for eight rounds but was stopped after the sixth, because it was by then ten o'clock and the main bout had to go on for television. Wilde and I were both relieved. Soo got the decision, of course; he should soon be a television star in his own right.

FINALLY, the main fight went on. Joe Gannon came into the ring—white-skinned, spindly, and determined, knobby of knee and elbow, bristly jowled, and wearing the expression of a ventriloquist's dummy who knows a secret and won't tell. He looks less durable than he is; I have seen him take a few very solid punches and come back gaily. One of the seconds in his corner was Al Colombo, from Brockton, Massachusetts, who is Marciano's best friend and home-town sidekick. Gannon has worked as a Marciano sparring partner. Weill himself wasn't there, though, and neither was Charles Goldman, who is the Weill boxers' chief trainer. Patterson came in next, looking about as he had in Helsinki—dark, dandified, and grave. His handlers wore jerseys with "Floyd Patterson" embroidered on their backs—he had made it; he was an institution. Patterson had not filled out noticeably, and this must be a disappointment to his backers; when you have a seventeen-year-old fighter who is six feet tall, it is only human to hope that he will grow into a real heavyweight. His weight was announced as a hundred and seventy and a half, but he had boxed at the old hundred and sixty-five only a month or two earlier, and he would have had slight trouble making it again. Gannon weighed a hundred and seventy-four and a half, but his arms were pipestems compared to Patterson's. He walked out bravely at the bell, as if resolved to make an arrest.

At first, I didn't realize what a close fight it was. All I saw was Patterson moving in and Gannon sticking out his left, as if to halt traffic, and then stepping away rapidly—but all too often not rapidly enough. Patterson wasn't exactly killing him, but he was landing three punches for one, throwing them in quick, sharp sequences and driving Gannon in front of him. It was a voice from directly behind my right ear that apprised me of what was actually happening. "Come on, Joe!" the voice howled. "You got him wobbling!"

"I wonder if he can reckernize our voice?" a voice behind my left ear said, and then, before I could roll my head, came, "In da breadbasket, Joe! He don't like dem deah!"

Gannon's mouth was at that moment open, as he stared, glassy-eyed, over Patterson's back while the Negro pounded his belly. "You got him holding now, Joe!" the right-ear voice bellowed.

When the round ended, the left-ear voice said, "He's doing good."

From then on, I attended two fights—the one I saw and the one I heard. With my eyes I apprehended poor Gannon—astonishingly brave and astonishingly persistent—sticking and hopping, holding in close for dear life, and taking a beating without ever changing that Boston-terrier expression. Patterson, more patient than in his amateur days, stalked him and outboxed him, nailing him with flurries of blows but never getting him with the one big punch. Sometimes I thought that a spark of his amateur recklessness would help, since Gannon was no hitter. Once Gannon staggered away and Patterson did jump after him. "You got him hopping now, Joe!" my right-ear voice yelled. And as the grim assault continued, the two enthusiasts convinced each other that their friend was far ahead on points.

"He looks good," left-ear voice said after the fifth round. Gannon had lost four, according to all the officials, and five by my count.

"But he gotta knock him out," said right-ear voice. "If he don't knock him out, they'll give it to Patterson. Joe gotta use his right." Joe was already using it, to protect his poor, battered noggin, but left-ear voice and right-ear voice were relentless.

"Hey, Joe, trow your right, huh?" yelled right-ear voice.

"Connect wit' one, Joe, will ya?" concurred left ear.

And they began to chorus, "Trow your right, Joe! Trow your right!"

The sixth round was more of the same. When Patterson, reverting for a moment to his old habit, whirled around in a clinch and, in throwing Gannon out of it, turned his back on him for a split second, right-ear voice yelled disconsolately, "Joe! You din't take avantage!" But Joe, disregarding their incitements to murder, continued to box correctly—feinting, though Patterson didn't follow; jabbing, though it didn't throw Patterson off balance; taking each smack on the chops unblinking; and holding his right high to pick off punches, which usually arrived from another direction. It was such a one-sided fight that Patterson's problem, patently, was to end it with a flourish. Gannon's mere survival would be a reflection on the *Wunderkind*'s Eastern Parkway education.

Then, in the seventh, Joe reckernized the voices, or else had got bad advice in his corner. He trun rights. Unhappily, one of them connected. Maybe several of them did, but they were of a force incommensurate with their purpose. Patterson reacted with acerbity. He is a vain fellow—a great asset in a fighting man. (Abe Attell, the illustrious featherweight champion turned boulevardier, once said to a man I know, "I never seen a good fighter who wasn't a conceited son of a bitch.") His temperament is not evil, but he craves admiration. As long as Gannon acted like a man trying to avoid destruction, Patterson had difficulty igniting what Colonel Stingo calls the driving inflatus. Live conspicuously and let live inconspicuously is Patterson's motto. He accepts the fact that others raise their hands against him, but when a fellow like Gannon raises his *right* hand, a fellow like Patterson feels himself belittled. He went straight after Gannon, and Gannon, intoxicated by success or else knocked silly already, disdained to get back on his motorcycle. At the end of the round, right-ear voice was ecstatic. "I tol' him trow da right!" he thundered. "He's *got* um!" howled left-ear.

The eighth was a case of assaulting an officer. Patterson was punching for keeps, raising the tempo to the point at which he used to fight in the gymnasium in the People's House. It is safe to assume that his handlers have been teaching him to pace himself, but with only three minutes left he didn't have to think about that. Poor Gannon moved like a gull on a wave. Now he was in that distressful state when every evasive move brings new disaster, until it seems to the boxer and his public that he is ducking into fists, circling into fists, slipping into fists. His nose was a red circle on his face. But one row behind me he was still winning. "Trow da right, Joe!" the voices were yelling in chorus. "You're in front!" I looked, at shorter and shorter intervals, at the clock dial on which a hand indicates the progress of the round. For the ex-cop's sake, I was glad it was nearly over. Then, as I turned from the clock for one last look at the ring, Patterson hit Gannon with a left hook, and, following him as he staggered across the ring, hit him with five more punches, of which the last, a blow with all the finesse of a pickaxe, smashed into Gannon's face as he stood straight up with his back to the ropes, where the preceding volley had carried him. Gannon came right on through the ropes, landing flat on his back on the ring apron, out, and the bell rang.

Right-ear voice said, "Well, howdaya like that?"

Left-ear voice said, "It's all over, huh?"

And a minute later, when I turned around, the seats behind me were empty.

(1954)

KENNETH TYNAN

FIFTEEN YEARS

OF THE SALTO MORTALE

JULY 14, 1977: There is a dinner party tonight at the Beverly Hills home of
Irving Lazar, doyen of agents and agent of doyens. The host is a diminutive
potentate, as bald as a doorknob, who was likened by the late screenwriter
Harry Kurnitz to "a very expensive rubber beach toy." He has represented
many of the top-grossing movie directors and best-selling novelists of the past
four decades, not always with their prior knowledge, since speed is of the
essence in such transactions; and Lazar's flair for fleet-footed deal-clinching—
sometimes on behalf of people who had never met him—has earned him the
nickname of Swifty. On this occasion, at his behest and that of his wife, Mary
(a sleek and catlike sorceress, deceptively demure, who could pass for her husband's ward), some fifty friends have gathered to mourn the departure of Fred
de Cordova, who has been the producer of NBC's "Tonight Show" since 1970;
he is about to leave for Europe on two weeks' vacation. A flimsy pretext, you
may think, for a wingding; but, according to Beverly Hills protocol, anyone
who quits the state of California for more than a long weekend qualifies for a
farewell party, unless he is going to Las Vegas or New York, each of which
counts as a colonial suburb of Los Angeles. Most of the Lazars' guests tonight
are theatre and/or movie people; e.g., Elizabeth Ashley, Tony Curtis, Gregory
Peck, Sammy Cahn, Ray Stark, Richard Brooks. And even Fred de Cordova
spent twenty years working for the Shuberts, Warner Brothers, and Universal
before he moved into television. The senior media still take social precedence
in the upper and elder reaches of these costly hills.

One of the rare exceptions to this rule is the male latecomer who now enters, lean and dapper in an indigo blazer, white slacks, and a pale-blue open-

necked shirt. Apart from two months in the late nineteen-fifties (when he re-placed Tom Ewell in a Broadway comedy called "The Tunnel of Love"), Johnny Carson has never been seen on the legitimate stage; and, despite a multitude of offers, he has yet to appear in his first film. He does not, in fact, much like appearing *anywhere* except (a) in the audience at the Wimbledon tennis championships, which he and his wife recently attended, (b) at his home in Bel Air, and (c) before the NBC cameras in Burbank, which act on him like an addictive and galvanic drug. Just how the drug works is not known to science, but its effect is witnessed—ninety minutes per night, four nights per week, thirty-seven weeks per year—by upward of fourteen million viewers; and it provoked the actor Robert Blake, while he was being inter-viewed by Carson on the "Tonight Show" in 1976, to describe him with hon-est adulation as "the ace comedian top-dog talk artist of the universe." I once asked a bright young Manhattan journalist whether he could define in a sin-gle word what made television different from theatre or cinema. "For good or ill," he said, "Carson."

This pure and archetypal product of the box shuns large parties. Invitations from the Lazars are among the few he accepts. Tonight, he arrives alone (his wife, Joanna, has stopped off in New York for a few days' shopping), greets his host with the familiar smile, cordially wry, and scans the assembly, his eyes twinkling like icicles. Hard to believe, despite the pewter-colored hair, that he is fifty-one: he holds himself like the midshipman he once was, chin well tucked in, back as straight as a poker. (Carson claims to be five feet ten and a half inches in height. His pedantic insistence on that extra half inch betokens a man who suspects he looks small.) In repose, he resembles a king-sized ventril-oquist's dummy. After winking impassively at de Cordova, he threads his way across the crowded living room and out through the ceiling-high sliding win-dows to the deserted swimming pool. Heads discreetly turn. Even in this posh peer group, Carson has cynosure status. Arms folded, he surveys Los Angeles by night—"glittering jewel of the Southland, gossamer web of loveliness," as Abe Burrows ironically called it. A waiter brings him a soft drink. "He looks like Gatsby," a young actress whispers to me. On the face of it, this is nonsense. Fitzgerald's hero suffers from star-crossed love, his wealth has criminal origins, and he loves to give flamboyant parties. But the simile is not without elements of truth. Gatsby, like Carson, is a Midwesterner, a self-made millionaire, and a habitual loner, armored against all attempts to invade his emotional privacy. "He had come a long way to this blue lawn," Fitzgerald wrote of Gatsby—as far as Carson has come to these blue pools, from which steam rises on even the warmest nights.

"He doesn't drink now." I turn to find Lazar beside me, also peeking at the man outside. He continues, "But I remember Johnny when he was a *blackout* drunk." That was before the "Tonight Show" moved from New York to Los Angeles, in 1972. "A couple of drinks was all it took. He could get very hostile."

I point out to Lazar that Carson's family tree has deep Irish roots on the maternal side. Was there something atavistic in his drinking? Or am I glibly casting him as an ethnic ("black Irish") stereotype? At all events, I now begin to see in him—still immobile by the pool—the lineaments of a magnified leprechaun.

"Like a lot of people in our business," Lazar goes on, "he's a mixture of extreme ego and extreme cowardice." In Lazar's lexicon, a coward is one who turns down starring roles suggested to him by Lazar.

Since Carson already does what nobody has ever done better, I reply, why should he risk his reputation by plunging into movies or TV specials?

Lazar concedes that I may be right. "But I'll tell you something else about him," he says, with italicized wonder. *"He's celibate."* He means "chaste." "In his position, he could have all the girls he wants. It wouldn't be difficult. But he never cheats."

It is thirty minutes later. Carson is sitting at a table by the pool, where four or five people have joined him. He chats with impersonal affability, making no effort to dominate, charm, or amuse. I recall something that George Axelrod, the dramatist and screenwriter, once said to me about him: "Socially, he doesn't exist. The reason is that there are no television cameras in living rooms. If human beings had little red lights in the middle of their foreheads, Carson would be the greatest conversationalist on earth."

One of the guests is a girl whose hobby is numerology. Taking Carson as her subject, she works out a series of arcane sums and then offers her interpretation of his character. "You are an enormously mercurial person," she says, "who swings between very high highs and very low lows."

His eyebrows rise, the corners of his lips turn down: this is the mock-affronted expression he presents to the camera when a baby armadillo from some local zoo declines to respond to his caresses. "This girl is great," he says to de Cordova. "She makes me sound like a cross between Spring Byington and Adolf Hitler."

Before long, he departs as unobtrusively as he came.

MEETING him a few days afterward, I inquire what he thought of the party. He half grins, half winces. "Torturous?" he says.

Within a month, however, I note that he is back in the same torture chamber. Characteristically, although he is surrounded by the likes of Jack Lemmon, Roger Vadim, Michael Caine, James Stewart, and Gene Kelly, he spends most of the evening locked in NBC shoptalk with Fred de Cordova. De Cordova has just returned from his European safari, which has taken him through four countries in half as many weeks. The high point of the trip, de Cordova tells me, was a visit to Munich, where his old friend Billy Wilder was making a film. This brings to mind a recent conversation I had with Wilder in this very living room. He is a master of acerbic put-downs who has little time for TV pseudostars, and when I mentioned the name of Carson I expected Wilder to dismiss him with a mordant one-liner. What he actually said surprised me. It evolved in the form of a speech. "By the simple law of survival, Carson is the best," he said. "He enchants the invalids and the insomniacs as well as the people who have to get up at dawn. He is the Valium and the Nembutal of a nation. No matter what kind of dead-asses are on the show, he has to make them funny and exciting. He has to be their nurse and their surgeon. He has no conceit. He does his work and he comes prepared. If he's talking to an author, he has read the book. Even his rehearsed routines sound improvised. He's the cream of middle-class elegance, yet he's not a mannequin. He has captivated the American bourgeoisie without ever offending the highbrows, and he has never said anything that wasn't liberal or progressive. Every night, in front of millions of people, he has to do the *salto mortale*"—circus parlance for an aerial somersault performed on the tightrope. "What's more"—and here Wilder leaned forward, tapping my knee for emphasis—"he does it without a net. No rewrites. No retakes. The jokes must work tonight."

SINCE a good deal of what follows consists of excerpts from the journal of a Carson-watcher, I feel bound to declare a financial interest, and to admit that I have derived pecuniary benefit from his activities. During the nineteen-sixties, I was twice interviewed on the "Tonight Show." For each appearance I received three hundred and twenty dollars, which was then the minimum payment authorized by AFTRA, the TV and radio performers' union. (The figure has since risen to four hundred and twenty-seven dollars.) No guest on the show, even if he or she does a solo spot in addition to just chatting, is paid more than the basement-level fee. On two vertiginous occasions, therefore, my earning power has equalled that of Frank Sinatra, who in November, 1976, occupied the hot seat on Carson's right for the first time. (A strange and revealing encounter, to which we'll return.) Actually, "hot" is a misnomer. To judge from my own experience, "glacial" would be nearer the mark. The other talk shows in which I have taken part were all saunas by comparison with Carson's. Merv Griffin is the most disarming of ego strokers; Mike Douglas runs him a close second in the ingratiation stakes; and Dick Cavett creates the illusion that *he* is *your* guest, enjoying a slightly subversive private chat. Carson, on the other hand, operates on a level of high, freewheeling, centrifugal banter that is well above the snow line. Which is not to say that he is hostile. Carson treats you with deference and genuine curiosity. But the air is chill; you are definitely on probation.

Mort Sahl, who was last seen on the "Tonight Show" in 1968, described to me not long ago what happens when a guest fails to deliver the goods. "The producer is crouching just off camera," he said, "and he holds up a card that says, 'Go to commercial.' So Carson goes to a commercial, and the whole team rushes up to his desk to discuss what went wrong. It's like a pit stop at Le Mans.

Then the next guest comes in, and—I promise you this is true—she's a girl who says straight out that she's a practicing lesbian. The card goes up again, only this time it means, 'Come in at once, your right rear wheel is on fire.' So we go to another commercial. . . ." Sahl is one of the few performers who are willing to be quoted in dispraise of Carson. Except for a handful of really big names, people in show business need Carson more than he needs them; they hate to jeopardize their chance of appearing on the program that pays greater dividends in publicity than any other. "Carson's assumption is that the audience is dumb, so you mustn't do difficult things," Sahl continued. "He never takes serious risks. His staff will only book people who'll make him look artistically potent. They won't give him anyone who'll take him for fifteen rounds. The whole operation has got lazy."

When an interviewer from *Playboy* asked Robert Blake whether he enjoyed doing the "Tonight Show," he gave a vivid account of how it feels to face Carson. He began by confessing that "there's a certain enjoyment in facing death, periodically." He went on:

> There's no experience I can describe to you that would compare with doin' the "Tonight Show" when *he's* on it. It is so wired, and so hyped, and so up. It's like Broadway on opening night. There's nothing casual about it. And it's not a talk show. It's some other kind of show. I mean, he has such energy, you got like six minutes to do your thing. . . . And you better be good. Or they'll go to the commercial after two minutes. . . . They are highly professional, highly successful, highly dedicated people. . . . The producer, all the *federales* are sittin' like six feet away from that couch. And they're right on top of you, man, just watchin' ya. And when they go to a break, they get on the phone. They talk upstairs, they talk to—Christ, who knows? They talk all over the place about how this person's going over, how that person's going over. They whisper in John's ear. John gets on the phone and he talks. And you're sittin' there watchin', thinkin', What, are they gonna hang somebody? . . . And then the camera comes back again. And John will ask you somethin' else or he'll say, "Our next guest is . . ."

Carson's office suite at Burbank is above the studio in which, between 5:30 and 7 P.M., the show is taped. Except for his secretary, the rest of the production team occupies a crowded bungalow more than two hundred yards away, outside the main building. "In the past couple of months," a receptionist in the bungalow said to me not long ago, "I've seen Mr. Carson in here just once." Thus the king keeps his distance—not merely from his colleagues but from his guests, with whom he never fraternizes either before or after the taping. Or hardly ever: he may decide, if a major celebrity is on hand, to bend the rule and grant him or her the supreme privilege of prior contact. But such occasions are rare. As Orson Welles said to me, "he's the only invisible talk host." A Carson guest of long standing, Welles continued, "Once, before the show, he put his head into my dressing room and said hello. The effect was cataclysmic. The production staff behaved the way the stagehands did at the St. James's Theatre in London twenty-five years ago when Princess Margaret came backstage to visit me. They were in awe! One of Carson's people stared at me and said, 'He actually came to *see* you!' " (Gust of Wellesian laughter.) Newcomers like me are interviewed several days in advance by one of Carson's "talent coördinators," who makes a list of the subjects on which you are likely to be eloquent or funny. This list is in Carson's head as you plunge through the rainbow-hued curtains, take a sharp right turn, and just avoid tripping over the cunningly placed step that leads up to the desk where you meet, for the first time, your host, interrogator, and judge. The studio is his native habitat. Like a character in a Harold Pinter play, or any living creature in a Robert Ardrey book, you have invaded his territory. Once you are on Carson's turf, the onus is on you to demonstrate your right to stay there; if you fail, you will decorously get the boot. You feel like the tourist who on entering the Uffizi Gallery, in Florence, was greeted by a guide with the minatory remark "Remember, Signore, that here it is not the pictures that are on trial." Other talk hosts flatter their visitors with artificial guffaws; Carson laughs only when he is amused. All I recall of my first exposure to the Carson ordeal is that (a) I had come to discuss a controversial play about Winston Churchill, (b) the act I had to follow was the TV début of Tiny Tim, who sang "Tip Toe Through the Tulips," (c) Carson froze my marrow by suddenly asking my opinion not of Churchill but of General de Gaulle, and (d) from that moment on, fear robbed me of saliva, so that my lips clove to my gums, rendering coherent speech impossible. The fault was mine, for not being the sort of person who can rise to Carson's challenge—i.e., a professional performer. There is abundant evidence that comedians, when they are spurred by Carson, take off and fly as they cannot in any other company. David Brenner, who has been a regular Carson guest since 1971, speaks for many young entertainers when he says, "Nowhere is where I'd be without the 'Tonight Show.' It's a necessary ingredient. . . . TV excels in two areas—sports and Carson. The show made my career."

OCTOBER 1, 1977, marked Carson's fifteenth anniversary as the star of a program he recently called "NBC's answer to foreplay." For purposes of comparison, it may be noted that Steve Allen, who was the show's host when it was launched, in September, 1954, lasted only two years and four months. The mercurial and thin-skinned Jack (Slugger) Paar took over from Allen in the summer of 1957, after a six-month interregnum during which doomed attempts were made to turn the "Tonight Show" into a nocturnal TV magazine, held together by live contributions from journalists in New York, Chicago, and Los Angeles. Paar's tenure of office seems in retrospect longer than it was, perhaps because of the emotional outbursts that kept his name constantly in the headlines; it actually ended after four years and eight months. On March 29, 1962, having resigned for positively the last time, he took his final bow on the program, his face a cascade of tears. *"Après le déluge, moi"* is the thought that should have passed through Carson's mind, though there is no evidence that it did. He was then in his fifth year as m.c. of "Who Do You Trust?," an ABC quiz show that had become, largely because of his verbal dexterity, the hottest item on daytime television. A few months before Paar's farewell, Carson had turned down a firm offer from NBC to replace its top banana. The gulf between chatting with unknown contestants for half an hour every afternoon and matching wits with celebrities for what was then an hour and forty-five minutes every night seemed unnervingly wide, and he doubted his ability to bridge it. However, when the job had been rejected by a number of possible candidates—among them Bob Newhart, Jackie Gleason, Joey Bishop, and Groucho Marx—either because they wanted too much money or because they were chary of following Paar, NBC came back in desperation to Carson. This time, he asked for two weeks to consider the proposition. Coolly, he weighed the size of his talent against the size of his ambition, decided that the scales approximately balanced, and told NBC that his answer was yes. The only snag was that his contract with ABC did not run out until September. Undismayed, NBC agreed to keep the "Tonight Show" supplied with guest hosts (they included Merv Griffin, Mort Sahl, and Groucho) throughout the summer. On October 1, 1962, Carson took command. His announcer and second banana, transplanted from "Who Do You Trust?," was Ed McMahon, who was already in great demand as the owner of the most robust and contagious laugh in television. The guests were Rudy Vallée, Tony Bennett, Mel Brooks (then a mere comedy writer, though he nowadays insists that he gave a dazzling impersonation of Fred Astaire on that October evening), and Joan Crawford.

Any qualms that NBC may have had about its new acquisition were soon allayed. Star performers lined up to appear with Carson. Even his fellow-comedians, a notoriously paranoid species, found that working with him was a stimulus rather than a threat. "He loves it when you score," Woody Allen said, "and he's witty enough to score himself." Mel Brooks has explained to me, "From the word go, Carson could tell when you'd hit comic gold, and he'd help you to mine it. He always knew pay dirt when he saw it. The guys on other talk shows didn't." There were one or two dissenters. Jackie Mason enjoyed his first session with Carson but reported that during his second appearance he was treated with "undisguised alienation and contempt," and went on to say, "I'd never go back again, even if he asked me." The press reaction to Carson was enthusiastic, except for a blast of puritanism from John Horn, of the *Herald Tribune,* who wrote of Carson, "He exhibits all the charm of a snickering small boy scribbling graffiti on a public wall." He added, in one of those phrases that return to haunt critics in their declining years, that Carson had "no apparent gift for the performing arts."

With the public, Carson's triumph was immediate and nonpareil. Under the Paar regime, the show had very seldom been seen by more than seven and a half million viewers. (One such occasion was March 7, 1960, when the unruly star came back to his post after walking out in a fit of pique, brought on by the network's decision to delete a mildly scatological joke and protracted for several well-publicized weeks.) Under Carson, the program *averaged* seven million four hundred and fifty-eight thousand viewers per night during its first six months. The comparable figure for the same period in 1971–72 was eleven million four hundred and forty-one thousand, and it is currently being seen by seventeen million three hundred thousand. Over fifteen years, therefore, Carson has more than doubled his audience—a feat that, in its blend of staying power and mounting popularity, is without precedent in the history of television. (Between April and September, the numbers dip, but this reflects a seasonal pattern by which all TV shows are affected. A top NBC executive explained to me, with heartless candor, "People who can afford vacations go away in the summer. It's only the poor people who watch us all the year round.") By network standards, the ultimate test is not so much the size of the audience as the share it represents of the total viewing public in the show's time slot. Here, after some early ups and downs, the Carson trend has been consistently upward; for example, from twenty-eight per cent in the third quarter of 1976 to thirty per cent in the second quarter of 1977. Moreover, his percentage seems to rise with the temperature; for example, in the four weeks that ended on July 15, 1977—a period during which guest hosts frequently stood in for Carson, whose absence from the show normally cuts the audience by about one-sixth—NBC chalked up thirty-two per cent of the late-night viewers, against twenty-four per cent registered by CBS and twenty-three per cent by ABC. These, of course, are national figures. The happiness of Fred de Cordova, as producer, is incomplete unless Carson not only leads the field nationwide but beats the combined opposition (ABC plus CBS) in the big cities, especially New York and Los Angeles. He is seldom unhappy for long. On peak nights, when Carson rakes in a percentage of fifty or more from the key urban centers, de Cordova is said to emit an unearthly glow, visible clear across the Burbank parking lot.

For his first year on the show, making five appearances per week, Carson was paid just over a hundred thousand dollars. His present contract (the latest of many), which comes into force this spring, guarantees him an annual salary of two and a half million dollars. For twenty-five weeks of the year, his performances, which were long since reduced from five to four, will further dwindle, to three; and his vacation period will stay at fifteen weeks—its duration under several previous contracts. These details, which were announced by NBC last December, leave no doubt that Carson qualifies for admission to what the late Lucius Beebe called "the mink-dust-cloth set." Whether they tell the whole story is less certain. Carson's earlier agreements with NBC contained clauses that both parties were forbidden to disclose, reportedly relating to such additional rewards as large holdings in RCA stock and a million-dollar life-insurance policy at the network's expense. Concerning Carson's total earnings, I cannot do better than quote from one of his employers, who told me, months before the new contract was signed, "If someone were to say in print that Johnny takes home around four million a year, I doubt whether anyone at NBC would feel an overpowering urge to issue a statement denying it." And even this figure excludes the vast amounts he makes from appearances at resort centers—preëminently Las Vegas—and from Johnny Carson Apparel, Inc., a thriving menswear business, founded in 1970, whose products he models on the show. David Tebet, the senior vice-president of NBC, who is revered in the trade as a finder, keeper, and cosseter of talent, and is described in his publicity handout as being "solely in charge of the Johnny Carson show," said to me recently, "For the past four or five years, Johnny has made more money per annum than any other television performer ever has. And he has also made more money per *week* than anyone else—except, maybe, for a very rare case like Sinatra, where you can't be sure, because Sinatra will sell you a special through his own company and you don't know how much he's personally taking out of the deal." Despite the high cost of Carson, he remains a bargain. The network's yearly income from the show is at present between fifty and sixty million dollars. "As a money-maker," de Cordova says, "there's nothing in television close to it." In 1975, a sixty-second commercial on the program cost twenty-six thousand dollars. In 1977, that sum had risen by half.

I dwell on these statistics because they are unique in show business. Yet there is a weird disproportion between the facts and figures of Carson's success and the kind of fame he enjoys. To illustrate what I mean, let me cite a few analogies. Star tennis players are renowned in every country on earth outside China, and the same is true of top heavyweight boxers. (A probably exception in the latter category is Muhammad Ali, who must surely be known inside China as well.) At least fifty living cricketers are household names throughout the United Kingdom, the West Indies, Australia, South Africa, India, and Pakistan. Movie stars and pop singers command international celebrity; and Kojak, Starsky, Hutch, Columbo, and dozens more are acclaimed (or, at any rate, recognized) wherever the TV programs that bear their names are bought and transmitted. Outside North America, by contrast, Johnny Carson is a nonentity: the general public has never heard of him. The reason for his obscurity is that the job at which he excels is virtually unexportable. (O. J. Simpson is a parallel case, illustrious at home and *nada* abroad; and if the empire of baseball had not reached out and annexed Japan, Reggie Jackson would be in the same plight.) The TV talk show as it is practiced by Carson is topical in subject matter and local in appeal. To watch it is like dropping in on a nightly family party, a conversational serial, full of private jokes, in which a relatively small and regularly rotated cast of characters, drawn mainly from show business, turn up to air their egos, but which has absolutely no plot. Sometimes the visitors sing. Sometimes, though less often nowadays than in the past, they are people of such worldwide distinction that their slightest hiccup is riveting. But otherwise most of what happens on the show would be incomprehensible or irrelevant to foreign audiences, even if they were English-speaking. This drives yet another nail into the coffin lid, already well hammered down, of Marshall McLuhan's theory that TV has transformed the world into a global village. (Radio is, as it has long been, the only medium that gives us immediate access to what the rest of the planet is doing and thinking, simply because every country of any size operates a foreign-language service.) Only for such events as moon landings and Olympiads does TV provide live coverage that spans the globe. The rest of the time, it is obstinately provincial, addressing itself to a village no bigger than a nation. Carson, in his own way, is what Gertrude Stein called Ezra Pound—a village explainer.

He has spent almost all his life confined, like his fame, to his country of origin. He served in the Navy for three years, beginning in 1943, and was shipped as far west as Guam. Thereafter, his travels abroad indicate no overwhelming curiosity about the world outside his homeland. Apart from brief vacations in Mexico, and a flying visit to London in 1961, when he appeared in a TV special starring Paul Anka, he has left the United States only on three trips: in 1975, to the ultrasmart Hôtel du Cap in Antibes (at the instigation of his wife, Joanna, who had been there before); in 1976, to see the tennis at Wimbledon; and in 1977, when he threw caution to the winds and went to both Wimbledon *and* the Hôtel du Cap. He was recognized in neither place, except by a handful of fellow-Americans. This, of course, was the purpose of the exercise. Carson goes to foreign parts for the solace of anonymity. But enough is enough: he is soon impatient to return to the cavernous Burbank studio, where his personality burgeons in high definition, and where he publicly discloses as much of his private self as he has ever revealed to anyone, except (I assume, though even here I would not care to bet) his parents, siblings, sons, and wives.

"Johnny Carson on TV," one of his colleagues confided to me, "is the visible eighth of an iceberg called Johnny Carson." The remark took me back to something that Carson said of himself ten years ago, when, in the course of a question-and-answer session with viewers, he was asked, "What made you a star?" He replied, "I started out in a gaseous state, and then I cooled." Meeting him tête-à-tête is, as we shall see later, a curious experience. In 1966, writing for *Look*, Betty Rollin described Carson off camera as "testy, defensive, preoccupied, withdrawn, and wondrously inept and uncomfortable with people." Nowadays, his off-camera manner is friendly and impeccably diplomatic. Even so, you get the impression that you are addressing an elaborately wired security system. If the conversation edges toward areas in which he feels ill at ease or unwilling to commit himself, burglar alarms are triggered off, defensive reflexes rise around him like an invisible stockade, and you hear the distant baying of guard dogs. In addition to his childhood, his private life, and his income, these no-trespassing zones include all subjects of political controversy, any form of sexual behavior uncountenanced by the law, and such matters of social concern as abortion and the legalization of marijuana. His smile as he steers you away from forbidden territory is genial and unfading. It is only fair to remember that he does not pretend to be a pundit, employed to express his own opinions; rather, he is a professional explorer of other people's egos. In a magazine article that was published with annotations by Carson, Fred de Cordova wrote, "He's reluctant to talk much about himself because he is essentially a private person." To this Carson added a marginal gloss, intended as a gag, that had an eerie ring of truth: "I will not even talk to myself without an appointment." He has asked all the questions and knows all the evasive, equivocal answers. When he first signed to appear on the "Tonight Show," he was quizzed by the press so relentlessly that he refused after a while to submit to further interrogation. Instead, he issued a list of replies that journalists could append to any questions of their choice:

1. Yes, I did.
2. Not a bit of truth in that rumor.
3. Only twice in my life, both times on Saturday.
4. I can do either, but I prefer the first.
5. No. Kumquats.
6. I can't answer that question.
7. Toads and tarantulas.
8. Turkestan, Denmark, Chile, and the Komandorskie Islands.
9. As often as possible, but I'm not very good at it yet. I need much more practice.
10. It happened to some old friends of mine, and it's a story I'll never forget.

EXTRACT from Carson-watching journal, January, 1976:

There is such a thing as the pleasure of the expected. Opening routine of "Tonight Show" provides it; millions would feel cheated if the ceremony were changed. The close shot of Big Ed McMahon as his unctuous baritone takes off on its steeply ascending glissando "Heeeeeeeere's Johnny!" Stagehands create gap in curtain. Carson enters in his ritual Apparel, style of which is Casual Square. Typical outfit: checked sports coat with two vents, tan trousers, pale-blue shirt with neat but ungaudy tie. Not for him the blue-jeaned, open-necked, safari-jacketed Hollywood ensemble: that would be too Casual, too Californian. On the other hand, no dark suits with vests: that would be too Square, too Eastern Seaboard. Carson must reflect what de Cordova possessively calls "our bread-basket belt"—the Midwest, which bore him (on October 23, 1925, in Corning, Iowa), and which he must never bore.

On his lips as he walks toward applauding audience is the only unassuming smirk in show business. He halts and swivels to the right (upper part of body turning as rigid vertical unit, like that of man in plaster cast) to acknowledge Big Ed's traditional act of obeisance, a quasi-Hindu bow with fingertips reverently joined. Then the leftward rotation, to accept homage from Doc Severinsen—lead trumpet and musical director, hieratically clad in something skintight and ragingly vulgar—which takes more bizarrely Oriental form: the head humbly bowed while the hands orbit each other. Music stops; applause persists. In no hurry, Carson lets it ride, facially responding to every nuance of audience behavior; e.g., shouts of greeting, cries of "Hi-yo!" When the ecstasy subsides, the exordium is over, and Carson begins the monologue, or address to the faithful, which must contain (according to one of his writers) between sixteen and twenty-two surefire jokes.

Tone of monologue is skeptical, tongue-in-cheek, ironic. Manner: totally relaxed, hitting bull's-eyes without seeming to take aim, TV's embodiment of "Zen in the Art of Archery." In words uttered to me by the late screenwriter Nunnally Johnson, "Carson has a delivery like a Winchester rifle." Theme: implicitly liberal, but careful to avoid the stigma of leftism. The unexpected impromptus with which he rescues himself from gags that bomb, thereby plucking triumph from disaster, are also part of the expected pleasure. "When it comes to saving a bad line, he is the master"—to quote a tribute paid in my presence by George Burns. Carson registers a gag's impact with instant, seismographical finesse. If the laugh is five per cent less than he counted on, he notes the failure and reacts to it ("Did they clear the hall? Did they have a drill?") before any critic could, usually garnering a double-strength guffaw as reward. Whatever spoils a line—ambiguous phrasing, botched timing, faulty enunciation—he is the first to expose it. Nobody spots flaws in his own work more swiftly than Carson, or capitalizes on them more effectively. Query: Is this becoming a dangerous expertise? In other words, out from under how many collapsed jokes can you successfully climb?

This evening's main attraction is Don (The Enforcer) Rickles, not so much the court jester of TV as the court hit man. Carson can cope superbly with garrulous guests who tell interminable stories (whether ponderously, owing to drink or downers, or manically, owing to uppers or illicit inhalations). Instead of quickly changing the subject, as many hosts would, he slaughters the offenders with pure politesse. Often, he will give them enough rope to hang themselves, allowing them to ramble on while he affects attentive interest. Now and then, however, he will let the camera catch him in the act of half-stifling a yawn, or raising a baffled eyebrow, or aiming straight at the lens a stare of frozen, I-think-I-am-going-mad incredulity. He prevents us from being bored by making his own boredom funny—a daring feat of comic one-upmanship. The way in which he uses the camera as a silent conspirator is probably Carson's most original contribution to TV technique. There is a lens permanently trained on him alone—a private pipeline through which he transmits visual asides directly to the viewer, who thus becomes his flattered accomplice. Once, talking to me on a somewhat tattered theme, the difference between stage and screen acting, Paul Newman made a remark that seemed obvious at the time but grows in wisdom the more I ponder it. "On the stage, you have to seek the focus of the audience," he said. "In movies, it's given to you by the camera." Among the marks of a star on television, as in the cinema, is his or her ability to grasp this truth and act on it. Seek, and you shall not find; grab, and it shall not be given unto you. Carson learned these rules early and is now their master practitioner.

Even the best-planned talk shows, however, run into doldrums; e.g., the guest who suffers from incontinent sycophancy, or whose third marriage has brought into his life a new sense of wonder plus three gratingly cute anecdotes about the joys of paternity, or who is a British comedian on his first, tongue-tied trip to the States, or whose conversational range is confined to plugging an upcoming appearance at Lake Tahoe. On such occasions, the ideal solution is: Bring on Rickles, king of icebreakers, whose chosen weapon is the verbal hand grenade. Rickles is an unrivalled catalyst (though I can already hear him roaring, "What do you mean, I'm a catalyst? I'm a Jew!"). Squatly built, rather less bald than Mussolini, his bulbous face running the gamut from jovial contempt to outright nausea, he looks like an extra in a crowd scene by Hieronymus Bosch. No one is immune from his misanthropy; he exudes his venom at host and guests alike. In a medium ruled by the censorious Superego, Rickles is the unchained Id. At his best, he breaks through the bad-taste barrier into a world of sheer outrage where no forbidden thought goes unspoken and where everything spoken is anarchically liberating. More deftly than anyone else, Carson knows how to play matador to Rickles' bull, inciting him to charge, and sometimes getting gored himself. At one point during this program, Rickles interrupts a question from Carson with an authentic conversation-stopper. "Your left eye is dancing!" he bellows, leaning forward and pointing a stubby finger. "That means you're self-conscious. Ever since you stopped drinking, your left eye dances." Even Carson is momentarily silenced. (I did not fully understand why until, at a subsequent meeting, Carson told me that there was one symptom by which he could infallibly recognize a guest who was on the brink of collapse, whether from fear, stimulants, or physical exhaustion. He called it "the dancing-eyeball syndrome." A famous example from the early nineteen-sixties: Peter O'Toole appeared on the show after forty-eight sleepless hours, spent filming and flying, and could not utter a coherent sentence. Carson ushered him offstage during the first commercial. "The moment he sat down, I could see his eyeballs were twitching," Carson said to me. "I recognized the syndrome at once. He was going to bomb.")

. . .

TESTIMONY of a Carson colleague:

My witness is Pat McCormick, who has been supplying Carson with material on and off for eighteen years and was a staff writer on the show from 1972 to 1977. Regarded as one of the most inventive gagmen in the business, he has also worked for Red Skelton, Danny Kaye, and others of note. McCormick, at forty-seven, is a burly, diffident man with hair of many colors: a reddish thatch on top, a gray mustache, and patches of various intermediate tints sprouting elsewhere on his head and face. Suitably resprayed, he might resemble a cross between Teddy Roosevelt and Zero Mostel. I have it on Ed McMahon's authority that McCormick takes the occasional drink, and that he once turned up at a script conference declaring, "I have lost my car, but I have tire marks on my hands." He gives me his account of a typical day on the "Tonight Show." "The writers—there are usually five of us—arrive at the studio around 9:30 A.M.," he says. "We've read the morning papers and the latest magazines. Once a week, we all get together for an ideas meeting, but most days we work separately, starting out with the monologue. I tend to specialize in fairly weird, uninhibited stuff. Johnny enjoys that kind of thing, and I just let it pour out. Like a line I came up with not long ago: 'If you want to clear your system out, sit on a piece of cheese and swallow a mouse.' Johnny finds his own ways of handling bum gags. When he's in a bad situation, I always wonder how the hell he'll get out of it, and he always surprises me."

Always? I remind McCormick of an occasion two days earlier, when a series of jokes had died like flies, and Carson had got a situation-saving laugh by remarking, "I now believe in reincarnation. Tonight's monologue is going to come back as a dog." That sounded to me like *echt* McCormick.

With a blush matching some of his hair, he admits to authorship of the line. He continues, "All the monologue material has to be on Johnny's desk by three o'clock. He makes the final selection himself. One of his rules is: Never tell three jokes running on the same subject. And, of course, he adds ideas of his own. He's a darned good comedy writer, you know."

One sometimes detects a vindictive glint in Carson's eye when a number of gags sink without risible trace, but McCormick assures me that this is all part of the act and causes no outbreaks of cold sweat among the writing team. "After the monologue," he goes on, "we work on the desk spot with Ed McMahon, which comes next in the show, or on sketches that need polishing, or on material for one of Johnny's characters."

Accustomed to thinking of Carson the host, we forget the range of Carson the actor-comedian. His current incarnations include the talkative crone Aunt Blabby (Whistler's mother on speed); the bungling turbanned clairvoyant named Carnac the Magnificent; Art Fern, described by McCormick as "the matinée-movie m.c. with patent-leather hair who'll sell *anything*"; and—a newer acquisition—Floyd Turbo, the man in the red shirt who speaks for the silent majority, rebutting liberal editorials with a vehemence perceptibly impaired by his inability to read from a TelePrompTer at more than dictation speed. Fans will recall Turbo's halting diatribe against the anti-gun lobby: "If God didn't want man to hunt, he wouldn't have given us plaid shirts. . . . I only kill in self-defense. What would *you* do if a rabbit pulled a knife on you? . . . Always remember: you can get more with a smile and a gun than you can with just a smile."

Everything for the evening's show must be rehearsed and ready for taping by five-thirty, apart from the central, imponderable element, on which all else depends: Carson's handling of the guests. Briefed by his aides, he knows the visitors' backgrounds, recent achievements, and immediate plans, and during the commercials he will listen to tactical suggestions from confreres like Fred de Cordova; but when the tape is running, he is the field commander, and his intuitions dictate the course of events. As he awaits his entrance cue, he is entitled to reflect, like Henry V on a more earthshaking occasion, "The day, my friends, and all things stay for me." McCormick, who now and then appears as a guest on the show, has this to say of Carson the interviewer: "He leans right in and goes with you, instead of leaning back and worrying about what the viewers are thinking. He never patronizes you or shows off at your expense. If you're getting a few pockets of laughter from the studio audience, he'll encourage you and feed you. He's an ideal straight man as well as a first-rate comedian, and that's a unique combination. Above all, there's a strand of his personality that is quite wild. He can do good bread-and-butter comedy any day of the week—like his Vegas routines or his banquet speeches—but he has this crazy streak that keeps coming through on the show, and when it does it's infectious. You feel anything could happen."

Example of Carson when the spirit of pure, eccentric play descends upon him and he obeys its bidding, wherever it may lead: During the monologue on May 11, 1977, he finds, as sometimes happens, that certain words are emerging from his mouth in slightly garbled form. He wrinkles his brow in mock alarm, shrugs, and presses on to the next sentence: "*Yetserday*, U.S. Steel announced . . ." He pauses, realizing what he has said, turns quizzically to McMahon, and observes, " 'Yesterday' is not a hard word to say." Facing the camera again, he goes on, "Yesterday—all my troubles seemed so far away . . ." Only now he is *singing*—singing, unaccompanied, the celebrated standard by John Lennon and Paul McCartney: "Now it looks as though they're here to stay. Oh, I believe in yesterday." By this time, the band, which was clearly taken by surprise, has begun to join in, at first raggedly but soon improvising a respectable accompaniment. Warming to his berserk task, Carson does not stop until he has reached the end of the chorus. He resumes the monologue: "Now, what was I talking about? Oh, yes. Yesterday . . ." But no sooner has the word passed his lips than Doc's combo, determined not to let him off the hook, strikes up the melody again. Undaunted, Carson plunges into the second chorus. Having completed it, he silences the musicians with a karate chop. There is loud applause, followed by an extended pause. Where can he go from here? Cautiously feeling his way, he continues, "*About twelve hours ago*, U.S. Steel announced . . ." And successfully finishes the gag. Everyone in the studio is laughing, not so much at the joke as at the sight of Carson on the wing. Grinning, he addresses McMahon.

CARSON: That's what makes this job what it is.

McMAHON: What is it?

CARSON (*frowning, genuinely puzzled*): I don't know.

McCormick on Carson the private man: "Don't believe those iceberg stories. Once, when I was going through a bad divorce and feeling pretty low, I was eating alone in a restaurant and Johnny came in with a bunch of people. I'm not one of his intimate friends, but as soon as he saw me he left his guests and sat with me for more than half an hour, giving me all kinds of comfort and advice."

FURTHER notes of a Carson-watcher (random samplings from October and November, 1976):

Where other performers go home to relax after the show, Carson goes to the show to relax. The studio is his den, his living space—the equivalent in the show-business world of an exclusive salon in the world of literature. He instantly reacts to any untoward off-camera occurrence—a script inadvertently dropped, a guitar string accidentally plucked, a sneeze from a far corner of the room—as most of us would react to comparably abnormal events in the privacy of our homes. *Mutatis* very much *mutandis,* the show could be seen as a TV version of "The Conning Tower," Franklin P. Adams' famous column in the *Tribune,* which was launched in 1914 and consisted mainly of anecdotes, aphorisms, and verses contributed by F.P.A.'s friends and correspondents. "The Conning Tower," like the "Tonight Show," was a testing ground for new talents, and many of the people it introduced to the public went on to become celebrities.

October 1st: Traditional two-hour retrospective to mark the fourteenth anniversary of Carson's enthronement as NBC's emperor of causerie. Choice of material is limited to the period since 1970, for, with self-destructive improvidence, the company erased all the earlier Carson tapes, including Barbra Streisand's first appearance as his guest and Judy Garland's last. Host's debonair entry is hailed with fifty-second ovation, which sounds unforced. I note the digital mannerisms (befitting one who began his career as a conjurer) that he uses to hold our attention during his patter. The right index finger is particularly active, now stabbing downward as if pressing computer buttons, now rising to flick at his ear, to tickle or scratch one side of his nose: constantly in motion, never letting our eyes wander. Thus he stresses and punctuates the gags, backed always by Big Ed's antiphonal laughter.

Well-loved bits are rerun. The portly comic Dom DeLuise attempts a feat of leg-erdemain in which three eggs are at risk, and carries it off without breakage. But the sight of unbroken eggs—and others on standby—provokes Carson to a spell of riot. He tosses the original trio at DeLuise, who adroitly juggles with them and throws them back; Carson retaliates with more eggs, aiming a few at McMahon for good measure. Before long, in classic slapstick style, he has expressionlessly cracked an egg over DeLuise's head and dropped another inside the front of his trousers, smashing it as it falls with a kindly pat on the belly. "You're insane!" the victim cries. "You guys are bananas!" He gives Carson the same treatment; McMahon joins in; and by the end the floor and the three combatants are awash with what Falstaff would have called "pullet-sperm." Looking back on the clip, Carson puckishly observes, "There's something about eggs. I went ape." The whole impromptu outburst would not have been funny if it had been initiated by someone like Buddy Hackett; it worked because of its incongruity with Carson's persona—that of a well-nurtured Midwestern lad, playful but not vulgar. ("Even though he's over fifty," Fred de Cordova once said to me, "there's a Peck's Bad Boy quality that works for Johnny, never against him.")

Other oddities from the program's past: Carson diving onto a mattress from a height of twenty feet; splitting a block of wood with his head on instructions from a karate champion; tangling with a sumo wrestler; cuddling a cheetah cub; permitting a tarantula to crawl up his sleeve. We also see Carson con-fronted by guests with peculiar skills—the bird mimic whose big items are the mallard in distress and the cry of the loon, for instance, and the obsessive spe-cialist whose act (one of the most memorable stunts ever recorded in a single take) consists of seven thousand dominoes arranged on end in a convoluted, interwoven pattern, involving ramps and tunnels, so that the first, when it is pushed, sets off a chain reaction that fells the remaining six thousand nine hundred and ninety-nine, which spell out—among other things—the DNA symbol and Carson's name. In addition, we get the parody of "Dragnet," that triumph of alliterative tongue-twisting in which Jack Webb, investigating the theft of a school bell, sombrely elicits from Carson the information that klepto-maniac Claude Cooper copped the clean copper clappers kept in the clothes closet. Best of all are the snippets from Carson's interviews with people aged ninety and upward, whom he addresses as exact equals, with care and without condescension, never patronizing them, and never afraid to laugh when they get a sentence back to front or forget the punch line of a joke; one such en-counter is with a woman of a hundred and three years, who is still a licensed driver. (Paul Morrissey, the movie director, who is watching the program with me, remarks, "Nobody else on TV treats old people with the perfect tact and af-

fection of Carson. He must have a very loving relationship with his parents.")
An NBC spokesman chips in with a resounding but meretricious statistic. The
Carson show, he says, has already been seen by more than four times the population of our planet. This presumably means that one person who has
watched the program a hundred times counts as a hundred people. Either that
or NBC is laying claim to extraterrestrial viewers. The ratings war being what it
is, anything is possible.

November 12th: After days of spot announcements and years of coaxing by
the network, Frank Sinatra makes his début on the show. Received like visiting
royalty, he gives the impression of swaggering even when seated. For once, the
host seems uneasy, overawed, too ready to laugh. Don Rickles is hurried on
unannounced to dissipate the atmosphere of obsequiousness, which he does
by talking to the singer like Mafia subaltern reporting to Godfather; at least this
is better than treating him as God. (I get memory flash of cable sent to me by
Gore Vidal when he agreed to accept my younger daughter as godchild:
"Always a godfather, never a god." For many people in entertainment business,
Sinatra is both.) When conversation again falters, Rickles declares to world
at large, "I'm a Jew, and he's an Italian, and *here*"—he thrusts at Carson a
face contorted with distaste, like diner finding insect in soup—"*here* we
have . . . *what?*" Rickles wraps up interview by saying that he truly admires
Sinatra, because "he stimulates excitement, he stimulates our industry, and"—
fixing Carson with glare of malign relish—"*he . . . makes . . . you . . . nervous.*"

Not long afterward, Carson had his revenge. While acting as guest host on
the show, Rickles broke the cigarette box on Carson's desk by striking it with his
clenched fist when a gag fell flat. The next night, Carson returned. As soon as
he sat down, he noticed the damage. "That's an heirloom," he said. "I've had it
for nine years." Informed that Rickles was the culprit, he picked up the debris
and rose, telling one of the cameras to follow him. (None of this was rehearsed.) He then left the "Tonight Show" studio, crossed the corridor outside,
and, ignoring the red warning lights, marched into the studio opposite, where
Rickles was at that moment halfway through taping the next episode of his
comedy series "CPO Sharkey." Walking straight into the middle of a shot,
Carson held out his splintered treasure to Rickles and sternly demanded both
restitution and an apology. The Enforcer was flabbergasted, as were his supporting cast, his producer, and his director. Carson was impenitent. "I really
shook him," he said to me later, with quiet satisfaction. "He was speechless."

TESTIMONY from the two NBC associates who are closest to Carson:

These are Fred de Cordova and Ed McMahon. De Cordova, who has been
Carson's producer for the past seven years, talks to me in the "Tonight Show"
bungalow at Burbank. He is a large, looming, beaming man with horn-rimmed
glasses, an Acapulcan tan, and an engulfing handshake that is a contract in it-

self, complete with small print and an option for renewal on both sides. Now in his mid-sixties, he looks like a cartoon of a West Coast producer in his early fifties. His professional record, dating back to 1933, is exceptional: Ten years in theatre with the Shubert organization, followed by a decade making movies in Hollywood. Thence into TV, where he worked (directing and/or producing) with Burns and Allen, George Gobel, Jack Benny, and the Smothers Brothers. In the magazine piece he wrote which appeared with notations by Carson, he said he now had "the last great job in show business," because the Carson program was "spontaneous" and "instantaneous." He explained that it wasn't technically live, in that taping preceded transmission; nevertheless, "practically speaking, we are the only continuing live show left." (For accuracy's sake, this phrase should be amended to read, "the only continuing nationwide nighttime quasi-live talk show left, apart from Merv Griffin's.") He went on to compare the program to a ballgame, played "in front of a jammed grandstand night after night." "To me," Carson noted in the margin, "it's like a salmon going up the Columbia River." Trying to define Carson's appeal, de Cordova wrote, "He's somebody's son, somebody's husband, somebody's father. He combines them all." Which sounds very impressive until you reflect that it applies to most of the adult male population. Carson circled this passage and made it slightly narrower in scope by adding to the first sentence, "and several people's exhusband." De Cordova's most telling point, at which no one could cavil, came later in the article. "We have no laugh track," he said. "We're naked." In an age when canned hilarity has all but usurped the viewer's right to an autonomous sense of humor, it is reassuring to read a statement like that.

On the wall behind de Cordova's desk hangs a chart showing the lineup of guests for weeks, and even months, ahead. Perennial absentees, long sought, never snared, include Elton John and Robert Redford. When de Cordova is asked why the list is so sparsely dotted with people of much intellectual firepower, he reacts with bewilderment: "That just isn't true. We've had some of the finest minds I know—Carl Sagan, Paul Ehrlich, Margaret Mead, Gore Vidal, Shana Alexander, Madalyn Murray O'Hair." This odd aggregation of names sprang from the lips of many other "Tonight Show" employees to whom I put that question, almost as if they were contractually bound to commit it to memory. Nobody, however, denied that there have been few latter-day guests with the political weight of Nelson Rockefeller, Hubert Humphrey, and John and Robert Kennedy, all of whom appeared with Carson in his earlier years. De Cordova continues, "I've heard it said that Johnny is intimidated by witty, intellectual women. Well, just who *are* these women? Apart from people like Shana, who've had a lot of TV experience, they tend to freeze on camera. We've so often been fooled by witty cocktail talkers who simply didn't transfer to television." Carson, he points out, is no numbskull; he reads extensively, with special emphasis on politics, and has more than an amateur knowledge of astronomy. Also of sports: "Ilie Nastase, Chris Evert, and Dwight Stones have all been very effective guests." But there are, he admits, certain categories of people who are unlikely to receive the summons to Burbank: "We don't have an official blacklist, but Johnny wouldn't have Linda Lovelace on the show, for example. Or anyone mixed up in a sexual scandal, like Elizabeth Ray. And no criminals, except reformed criminals—we turned down Clifford Irving, the guy who forged the Howard Hughes memoirs. Johnny prefers to look for non-celebrities who'll make human-interest stories. We subscribe to fifty-seven newspapers from small towns and cities all over the country, and that's where we find some of our best material." He goes on to say, "In the monologue, Johnny will attack malfeasance, illiberal behavior, Constitutional abuses. But then compassion sets in. He was the first person to *stop* doing anti-Nixon jokes." (Ten years ago, Henry Morgan said of Carson, "He believes that justice is some kind of entity that is palpable. He talks about it as if he were talking about a chair.") Does the monologue suffer from network censorship? "The problem doesn't come up, because Johnny has an in-built sense of what his audience will take," de Cordova says. "He's the best self-editor I've ever known." This, as we shall see, was a somewhat disingenuous reply.

Lunch with the bulky, eternally clubbable McMahon in the Polo Lounge of the Beverly Hills Hotel. Born in Detroit, Big Ed is now in his mid-fifties, and has worked with Carson for two decades, including five years as his announcer on "Who Do You Trust?" NBC gives him eight weeks' annual vacation with full pay, and he makes a great deal of money on the side from night-club appearances, real-estate investments, and commercials for a variety of products, chief among them beer and dog food. Even so, he is well aware that, as he says to me, "the 'Tonight Show' is my staple diet, my meat and potatoes—I'm realistic enough to know that everything else stems from that." In 1972, when the show moved from New York to Los Angeles, McMahon left his wife and four children, after twenty-seven years of marriage, to go with it. (Divorce followed soon afterward; McMahon remarried in 1976.) He has known his place, and kept to it without visible resentment, since 1965, when the notorious Incident of the Insect Repellent showed him exactly where he stood. "Johnny was demonstrating an anti-mosquito spray," he says, "and just before using it he said he'd heard that mosquitoes only went for really passionate people. Acting on instinct, I stuck out my arm and slapped it. It wrecked Johnny's gag, and I had to apologize to him during the next break. That taught me never to go where he's going. I have to get my comedy in other areas. Before the show, I do the audience warmup, and even there I have to avoid any topical material he might be using in the monologue."

This being a show day, McMahon eats and drinks frugally (cold cuts and beer). Both he and Carson have drastically reduced their alcoholic intake over the past few years. On camera, Carson sips coffee and cream (no sugar), and McMahon makes do with iced tea. McMahon denies the rumor that Carson has become anti-social because of his abstinence: "If it's a big affair, you'll maybe find him in a corner, talking one to one, but in a small group he can be the life of the party, doing tricks, killing everybody." One of the unauthorized biographies of Carson contains a story about a surprise birthday party to which his second wife, Joanne, invited all his close friends. "There were about eight people there," an unnamed guest is quoted as saying, "and I think it was a shock to all of us." Pooh-poohing this yarn, McMahon counters by telling me about a surprise party he gave for Carson in 1962: "I built it up by pretending it was being held in his honor by *TV Guide* and he really had to go. He finally gave in. I said I'd drive him down there, and he began bitching as soon as he got in the car. So I suggested stopping off at my place for a preliminary drink, and he agreed. I'd arranged for the other cars to be parked out of sight, in case he recognized them. What happened was that he walked straight into the arms of about fifty friends and relatives who'd come from all over to see him. He had tears in his eyes. That was the first time I saw him touched."

Professionally, McMahon most enjoys the tête-à-tête at Carson's desk which follows the monologue: "Sometimes he develops a real resistance to bringing out the first guest. I see something goofy in his eyes. It means that he wants us to go on rapping together, so we play back and forth, getting wilder and wilder, until maybe the guest has gone home and it's time for the first commercial."

I read to him some remarks made by the columnist Rex Reed, who described Carson as "the most over-rated amateur since Evelyn and her magic violin" and continued, "The most annoying thing about Carson is his unwillingness to swing, to trust himself or his guests. . . . He never looks at you; he's too busy (1) watching the audience to see if they are responding, and (2) searching the face of his producer for reassurance."

McMahon finds these comments inexplicable. "Johnny can get absolutely spellbound by his guests," he says. "You'll see him lean his chin on his hand and really drink them in. And as for that stuff about not swinging—did the guy ever watch him with Tony Randall or Buck Henry or Orson Bean? He's always going off into unplanned areas and uncharted places. Other people have clipboards full of questions and use them like crutches. Johnny never uses any. And he loves meeting new comics and feeding them lines, the way he did with Steve Martin and Rodney Dangerfield when hardly anyone had heard of them. Naturally, he likes to get laughs himself. That's part of the job. A few nights ago, Tony Bennett was on the show, talking about his childhood and how his family hoped he'd achieve fabulous things when he grew up. Johnny listened for a long while and then said, quite deadpan, 'My parents wanted me to be a sniper.' Another time, he asked Fernando Lamas why he'd gone into movies, and Lamas said, 'Because it was a great way to meet broads.' I loved Johnny's comeback. He just nodded and said, 'Nietzsche couldn't have put it more succinctly.' And, of course, there are the famous ad-libs that everyone remembers, like when Mr. Universe was telling him how important it was to keep fit—'Don't forget, Mr. Carson, your body is the only home you'll ever have'—and Johnny said, 'Yes, my home *is* pretty messy. But I have a woman who comes in once a week.' " McMahon confirms my impression that Carson was daunted by Sinatra. He adds, "And he's always a little bit overawed by Orson Welles. But there was one time when we were both nervous. I came on as a guest to plug a film I'd just made, and we had a rather edgy conversation. When the interview was over, Johnny came out from behind his desk to shake hands and revealed to the world that he had no pants on. I was so anxious to get off that I didn't even notice." How long, I ask, will Carson stay with the show? "He'll still be there in 1980," says McMahon confidently.

THE year 1977, for Carson-watchers, was one in which the "Tonight Show," while retaining all its sparkle and caprice, gained not an inch in intellectual stature. It is one thing to say, as Carson often does, that he is not a professional controversialist. It is quite another to avoid controversy altogether.

February 2nd: Appearance of Alex Haley to talk about "Roots." (During the previous night's monologue, Carson used a curiously barbed phrase to account for the success of ABC's televised adaptation of Haley's best-seller. "Give the people what they want," he said. "Hatred, violence, and sex." It was difficult to tell whether the gibe was aimed at the rival network or at the book itself. One wondered, too, why he thought it amusing to add, "My great-great-great-great-grandfather was a runaway comedian from Bangladesh.") In 1967, when Haley was working for *Playboy*, he conducted a lengthy interview with Carson. In the course of it, Carson attacked the C.I.A. for hiring students to compile secret reports on campus subversives, condemned "the kind of corporate espionage and financial hanky-panky that goes on in business," supported the newly insurgent blacks in demanding "equality for all," and said, "It's ludicrous to declare that it's wrong to have sex with anyone you're not married to." Moreover, he summed up the war in Vietnam as "stupid and pointless." He seldom voiced these opinions with much vehemence on the show. Ten years later, with the war safely over, he welcomed Jane Fonda as his guest and congratulated her on having lived to see her views on Vietnam fully justified by history. With considerable tact, Ms. Fonda not only resisted the temptation to address her host as Johnny-come-lately but refrained from reminding him that when she most needed a television outlet for her ideas the doors of the "Tonight Show" studio were closed to her.

To return to February 2nd: Haley takes the initiative by asking Carson how far back he can trace his own roots. He replies that he knows who his grandparents were, and was personally very close to his father's parents, both of whom survived into their nineties. Of his pedigree before that, he confesses total ignorance. Haley thereupon shakes him by producing a heavy, leather-bound volume with a golden inscription on the cover: "Roots of Johnny Carson—A Tribute to a Great American Entertainer." Haley has signed the fly-leaf, "With warm best wishes to you and your family from the family of Kunta Kinte." Carson is obviously stirred. "I was tremendously moved that Alex had found time to do all this research in the middle of his success," he said to me afterward, and I learned from McMahon that this was only the second occasion on which he had seen the boss tearful. Although Haley was the instigator, the work was in fact carried out by the Institute of Family Research, in Salt Lake City. The people there first heard of the project on the evening of Saturday, January 29th, when Haley called them up and told them that the finished book had to be ready for presentation to Carson in Los Angeles the following Wednesday. "That gave us two working days to do a job that would normally take us two months," a spokesman for the Institute told me. "What's more, we had to do it in absolute secrecy, without any access to the person involved." A task force of fifteen investigators toiling round the clock for forty-eight hours just managed to beat the deadline. The result of their labors—consisting of genealogical charts going back to the sixteenth century, biographical sketches of Carson's more prominent forebears, and anecdotes from the family's history—ran to more than four hundred pages. The gesture cost Haley (or his publishers) approximately five thousand dollars. Carson lent me the book, a massive quarry of data, from which I offer a few chippings:

(1) Earliest known Carson ancestor: Thomas Kellogg, on the paternal side of the family, born c. 1521 in the English village of Debdon, Essex. The first Kelloggs to cross the Atlantic were Daniel (born 1630) and his wife, Bridget, who settled in Connecticut. By the early nineteenth century, we find offshoots of the clan widely dispersed in Indiana and Nebraska, and it was Emiline, of the Nebraska Kelloggs, who married Marshall Carson, great-grandfather of Johnny. Marshall (born c. 1833) was allured by gold, and staked a profitless claim in the western part of Nebraska. Along with Emiline, he moved to Iowa, where by dying in 1922 he narrowly failed to become a nonagenarian. That was the year in which his grandson Homer Loyd Carson married a girl named Ruth Hook. John William Carson (born 1925) was the second child of this union, flanked by an elder sister, Catherine, and a younger brother, Dick.

(2) On his mother's side, Carson's first authenticated forebear is Thomas Hooke, a seventh great-grandfather, who sailed from London to Maryland in 1668. Most of his maternal roots, however, lead back to Ireland, whence two of his fifth great-grandfathers embarked for the States in the middle years of the eighteenth century.

(3) His family tree is laden with hardworking farmers. Decennial census sheets from 1840 to 1900 show Carson progenitors tilling the land in Maine, Ohio, Indiana, Nebraska, and Iowa.

(4) As far as anyone knows, Johnny and Kit Carson are no more closely related than Edward and Bonwit Teller. Johnny's background nonetheless con-

tains two figures of some regional celebrity. One is Captain James Hook (maternal branch), who is reputed, but not proved, to have served with Washington at Valley Forge. In a private quarrel, Captain Hook lost a sliver of his ear to a man who pulled a knife on him. Being unarmed, Hook riposted by tearing off a much larger piece of his assailant's ear with his teeth. The other Carson ancestor of note is Judge James Hardy (paternal branch), a whimsical but beloved dispenser of justice in mid-nineteenth-century Iowa.

(5) Judge Hardy's son Samuel, who died in 1933, at the age of eighty-five, was a skilled amateur violinist. Otherwise, in all the four previous centuries of the Carson family saga there is no sign of anyone with an interest in the arts or a talent for entertainment.

February 10th: Significant how many of the failed gags in Carson's monologues miss their target because they are based on the naïve assumption that the studio audience has read the morning papers. One often gets the feeling that Carson is doubly insulated against reality. Events in the world outside Burbank and Bel Air impinge on him only when they have been filtered through magazines and newspapers and then subjected to a second screening by his writers and researchers. Hence his uncanny detachment, as of a man sequestered from the everyday problems with which most of us grapple. In fifteen years, barely a ripple of emotional commitment has disturbed the fishpond smoothness of his professional style. We are watching an immaculate machine. Some find the spectacle inhuman. "He looks plastic," said Dorothy Parker in 1966. On the other hand, Shana Alexander told me with genuine admiration, "He's like an astronaut, a Venusian, a visitor from another planet, someone out of 'Star Trek.' "

Two reflections on tonight's monologue. First, drawing on the latest Nielsen report, Carson informs us that during the icebound month of January the average American family watched television for seven hours and sixteen minutes per day. A fearsome statistic. No wonder they have so little time for newspapers. Second, he knocks the Senate for allowing its members' salaries to be raised to fifty-seven thousand five hundred dollars a year. The joke gives off a whiff of bad taste, coming, as it does, from a man who earns more than that every week. Whatever Carson's failings may be, they do not include a lack of chutzpah.

April 1st: Nice to hear Ethel Merman on the show, blasting out "Ridin' High" as if calling the cattle home across the sands of D flat major. But I wonder whether Carson would (or could) have done what Merv Griffin, of all people, did earlier in the evening; namely, devoted most of a ninety-minute program to a conversation with Orson Welles, which was conducted on what by talk-show standards was a respectably serious level. In 1962, when Carson took over the stewardship of the "Tonight Show," America was about to enter one of the grimmest and most divisive periods in its history, marked by the assassinations of the Kennedy brothers and Martin Luther King, the ghetto insurrections, the campus riots, the Vietnam war. Is it arguable that during this bad time Carson became the nation's chosen joker because, in Madison Avenue terms, he was guaranteed to relieve nervous strain and anxiety more swiftly and safely (ask your doctor) than any competing brand of wag? Now that the country's headaches have ceased to throb so painfully, its viewers may be ready for a more substantial diet than any that Carson, at the moment, cares to provide.

April 7th: Characteristic but in no way exceptional duologue between Carson and Buck Henry, the screenwriter and occasional actor. Whenever they meet on the show, their exchanges are vagrant, ethereal, unhurried, as if they were conversing in a limbo borrowed from a play by Samuel Beckett.

CARSON: Do you believe in plastic surgery?

HENRY: Absolutely. It's important, I think, to move things about judiciously.

CARSON: They're talking about freezing people and then reviving them in hundreds of years' time.

HENRY (*nods for a while, until a thought strikes him*): But suppose you died of freezing to death? (*Pause.*) I think it would be frightening to come back.

CARSON: If you could come back as somebody else, who would it be?

HENRY (*unhesitatingly*): Miss Teen-Age America.

CARSON: Where do you get ideas for your work?

HENRY: Oh, everyday places. Looking through keyholes.

CARSON: Eugene O'Neill got his ideas from his family.

HENRY: I expect to get a short monograph out of mine. (*Pause.*)

CARSON: You have a strange turn of mind.

Carson brings up a newspaper story about a California woman who was recently interred, in accordance with a clause in her will, at the wheel of her Ferrari.

HENRY: Yes. It's reasonable to be married—or I may mean buried—in a Ferrari.

CARSON: How do you want to go?

HENRY (*very slowly*): Very slowly. With a jazz band playing in the background. I want to be extremely old. I want to be withered beyond recall.

CARSON: But if you lived to be a hundred and fifty, how would you kill time for the last seventy years?

HENRY (*contemplatively*): You'd read a lot. I don't know what the real fun things to do would be after a hundred and twenty. I think the normal activities that come to mind would probably cripple you.

There was also some adagio talk about quarks and their relationship to other subatomic particles, but Henry declined to expand on the subject, perhaps feeling that it might be over our heads.

May 11th: Advice from Carson on longevity: "If you must smoke, don't do it orally." And, more cryptically: "You can add years to your life by wearing your pants backwards."

June 15th: He chats with someone who has attained longevity. Clare Ritter, an impoverished widow from Florida in her late seventies, discloses that her life's ambition is to make a trip to Egypt. In order to achieve it, she sells waste aluminum, which she collects by ransacking garbage cans.

CARSON: How much is this trip going to cost?

MRS. RITTER: Three thousand dollars.

CARSON: And how much have you saved so far?

MRS. RITTER: About half of it.

Carson volunteers to give her the rest himself. A graceful (and, I am assured, unpremeditated) gesture.

July 19th: Seated at the desk with McMahon, Carson says, "If you decide to ban your kids from watching TV, here's what they can do instead." He picks up a sheaf of humorous suggestions submitted by his writers, scans the first page, shows by his reaction that he finds it unfunny, and drops it on the floor. (This, like what ensues, is unplanned and impromptu.) He inspects page 2, raises his eyebrows, shows it to McMahon, drops *that* on the floor; goes on to page 3, gives McMahon a glimpse of it, whereupon both men shake their heads, and it, too, ends up on the floor. At this point, Carson starts to chuckle to himself. "How about *this*?" he says, and page 4 is tossed away, to be joined in rapid succession by a dozen, by *two* dozen more pages, falling faster and faster (the chuckle is by now uncontrollable), in a blizzard of rejection that does not stop until he has discarded every sheet of what was obviously planned as a solid five-minute comedy routine. On network TV, this is just not done. You do not throw away an expensive script in full view of a national audience unless you can ad-lib something funnier to take its place. Carson offers us nothing in exchange except what he alone can supply: the spectacle of Carson being Carson, acting on impulse, surrendering to whim, and, as ever, getting away with it. (No claim is made for the above escapade as archive material, or as anything more than a specimen of Carson in average form on an average night. I record it to illustrate how, in the right hands, pure behavior becomes pure television. Like Shakespeare's Parolles, Carson can say, "Simply the thing I am shall make me live.")

Later in this show, Albert Finney, an actor who has temporarily turned his hand to lyric-writing and his voice to singing, plugs his first L.P., declaring with brooding self-satisfaction that his songs derive from "the spring well" of personal experience. The number with which he favors us constitutes more of a threat to English grammar ("What has become of you and I?") than to Charles Aznavour, who seems to be Finney's model. The last guest is Madeline Kahn, who discusses the psychological ups and downs of her career as an actress. Carson responds with a rare flash of self-revelation. "I've had a little therapy myself," he says, "to cut down the hills and get out of the valleys."

August 4th: President Carter has recommended that it should not be a criminal offense to be found in possession of an ounce or less of marijuana.

CARSON: The trouble is that nobody in our band knows what an ounce or less means.

DOC SEVERINSEN: It means you're about out.

JANUARY 18, 1977: My first solo encounter with Carson. We are to meet at the Beverly Hills Hotel for an early luncheon in the Polo Lounge. I prepare for my date by looking back on Carson's pre–"Tonight Show" career. It is not a story of overnight success. At the time of his birth in Corning, Iowa, his father was a lineman for an electricity company. It was a peripatetic job, and the family moved with him through several other Iowa hamlets. When Johnny was eight, they settled in Norfolk, Nebraska, a town of some ten thousand, where Carson senior got a managerial post with the local light-and-power company. "When one meets Johnny's parents, one understands him," Al Capp has said. "They're almost the definitive Nebraska mother and father. Radiantly decent, well-spoken. The kind that raised their kids to have manners. Of all the television hosts I've faced, Carson has the most old-fashioned manners." By contemporary standards, he had a strict—even rigorous—upbringing, not calculated to encourage extrovert behavior. His brother Dick (now director of the "Merv Griffin Show") was once quoted as saying, "Put it this way—we're not Italian. Nobody in our family ever says what they really think or feel to anyone else." Except, I would add, in moments of professional crisis, when Johnny Carson can express himself with brusque and unequivocal directness. In 1966, for instance, the first three nights of a cabaret engagement he played in Miami were spoiled by a backstage staff too inexperienced to handle the elaborate sound effects that his act required. Carson accused his manager, Al Bruno, who had looked after his business affairs for almost ten years, of responsibility for the fiasco, and fired him on the spot. Again, there was the case of Art Stark, who described himself to an interviewer in 1966 as "Johnny's best friend." He had every reason to think so: for nearly a decade he had been Carson's producer, first on "Who Do You Trust?" and then on the "Tonight Show." He was the star's closest confidant, and when, in 1967, Carson embarked on a legal struggle with NBC for control of the show, including the right to hire and fire, he repeatedly assured Stark that, whatever the outcome, Stark's job would be safe. Having won the battle, however, Carson summoned Stark to his apartment and announced without preamble that he wanted another producer, unconnected with NBC. Dumbfounded, Stark asked when he would have to quit. "Right now," said Carson.

When Carson was twelve, he picked up, at a friend's house, a conjuring manual for beginners called "Hoffman's Book of Magic." Its effect on him has been compared to the impact on the youthful Keats of Chapman's Homer. ("Chapman hit it in the bottom of the ninth to tie the game against Milwaukee," said the man who made the comparison, a former Carson writer. "Little Johnny Keats was standing behind the center-field fence and the ball landed smack on his head.") Carson immediately wrote off for a junior magician's kit. He worked hard to master the basic skills of the trade, and, having tried out his tricks on his mother's bridge club, he made his professional début, billed as The Great Carsoni, before a gathering of Norfolk Rotarians. For this he received three dollars—the first of many such fees, for the kid illusionist was soon in demand at a variety of local functions, from firemen's picnics to county fairs. As a student at Norfolk High, he branched out into acting and also wrote a comic column for the school newspaper.

Digressive flash forward: In 1976, Carson was invited back to Norfolk to give the commencement address. Immensely gratified, he accepted at once. He took great pains over his speech, and when he delivered it, on May 23rd, the school auditorium was packed to the roof. In the front row, alongside his wife, brother, and sister, sat his parents, to whom he paid tribute for having "backed me up and let me go in my own direction." He also thanked one of his teachers, Miss Jenny Walker, who had prophetically said of him in 1943, "You have a fine sense of humor and I think you will go far in the entertainment world." In case anyone wondered why he had returned to Norfolk, he explained, "I've come to find out what's on the seniors' minds and, more important, to see if they've changed the movie at the Granada Theatre" (where, I have since discovered, Carson was working as a part-time usher when the manager interrupted the double feature to announce that the Japanese had bombed Pearl Harbor). He went on to recall that he had been chosen to lead the school's scrap-metal drive: "Unfortunately, in our zeal to help the war effort, we sometimes appropriated metal and brass from people who did not know they were parting with it." He continued, "I was also a member of the Thespians. I joined because I thought it meant something else. Then I found out it had to do with acting." In the manner expected of commencement speakers, he offered a little advice on coping with life in the adult world. Though his precepts were homespun to the point of platitude, they were transparently sincere and devoid of conventional pomposity. The main tenets of the Carson credo were these: (1) Learn to laugh at yourself. (2) Never lose the curiosity of childhood: "Go on asking questions about the nature of things and how they work, and don't stop until you get the answers." (3) Study the art of compromise, which implies a willingness to be convinced by other people's arguments: "Stay loose. In marriage, above all, compromise is the name of the game. Although"—and here he cast a glance at his third wife—"you may think that my giving advice on marriage is like the captain of the Titanic giving lessons on navigation." (4) Having picked a profession, feel no compulsion to stick to it: "If you don't like it, stop doing it. Never continue in a job you don't enjoy." (On the evidence, it would be hard to fault Carson for failing to practice what he preached.) A question-and-answer session then took place, from which I append a few excerpts:

Q: How do you feel about Norfolk nowadays?

CARSON: I'm very glad I grew up in a small community. Big cities are where alienation sets in.

Q: Has success made you happy?

CARSON: I have very high ups and very low downs. I can all of a sudden be depressed, sometimes without knowing why. But on the whole I think I'm relatively happy.

Q: Who do you admire most, of all the guests you've interviewed?

CARSON: People like Carl Sagan, Paul Ehrlich, Margaret Mead . . . (*He recites the official list, already quoted, of Most Valued Performers.*)

Q: In all your life, what are you proudest of?

CARSON: Giving a commencement address like this has made me as proud as anything I've ever done.

The applause at the end was so clamorous that Carson felt compelled to improvise a postscript. "If you're happy in what you're doing, you'll like yourself," he said. "And if you like yourself, you'll have inner peace. And if you have that, along with physical health, you will have had more success than you could possibly have imagined. I thank you all very much." He left the stage to a further outburst of cheers, having established what may be a record for speakers on such occasions: throughout the evening, he had made no reference to the deity, the flag, or the permissive society; nor had he used the phrase "this great country of ours."

After graduating from Norfolk, in 1943, Carson enrolled in the Navy's V-12 program, but training did not start until the fall, so he filled in time by hitch-hiking to California. There, in order to gain access to the many entertainments that were offered free of charge to servicemen, he stopped off at an Army-Navy store and prematurely bought himself a naval cadet's uniform. Thus attired, he danced with Marlene Dietrich at the Hollywood Stage Door Canteen. Later, he travelled south to see Orson Welles give a display of magic in San Diego, where he responded to the maestro's request for a volunteer from the audience and ecstatically permitted himself to be sawed in half. That night, he was arrested by two M.P.s and charged with impersonating a member of the armed forces—an offense that cost him fifty dollars in bail. After induction, he attended the midshipmen's school at Columbia University and served in the Pacific aboard the battleship Pennsylvania. Never exposed to combat, he had plenty of time to polish his conjuring skills. In 1946, discharged from the Navy, he entered the University of Nebraska, where he majored in English and moonlighted as a magician, by now earning twenty-five dollars per appearance. In need of an as-sistant, he hired a girl student named Jody Wolcott; he married her in 1948. (To dispose, as briefly as possible, of Carson's marital history: The liaison with Jody produced three sons—Chris, Ricky, and Cory—and was finally dissolved, after four years of separation, in 1963. "My greatest personal failure," Carson has said, "was when I was divorced from my first wife." In August, 1963, he married Joanne Copeland, aged thirty, a diminutive, dark-haired model and oc-casional actress. They parted company in 1970 but were not legally sundered until two years later, when the second Mrs. Carson was awarded a settlement of nearly half a million dollars, in addition to an annual hundred thousand in alimony. She had by then moved from New York to Los Angeles. Shortly after-ward, Carson migrated to the West Coast, bringing the show with him. Between these two events she discerns a causal connection. She has also de-clared that when, at a Hollywood party, Carson first met his next wife-to-be, "she was standing with her back to him, and he went right up to her, thinking it was me." On matters such as this, Carson's lips are meticulously sealed. All we know—or need to know—is that on September 30, 1972, during a gaudy celebration at the Beverly Hills Hotel in honor of his tenth anniversary on the "Tonight Show," he stepped up to the microphone and announced that at one-thirty that afternoon he had married Joanna Holland. Of Italian lineage, and a model by profession, she was thirty-two years old. They are still together. It is difficult to see how Carson could have mistaken her, even from behind, for her predecessor. She could not be sanely described as diminutive. Dark-haired, yes; but of medium height and voluptuous build. The third Mrs. Carson is the kind of woman, bright and *molto simpatica*, whom you would expect to meet not in Bel Air but at a cultural soirée in Rome, where—as like as not—she would be more than holding her own against the earnest platonic advances of Michelangelo Antonioni.)

Carson's post-college career follows the route to success traditionally laid down for a television—What? Personality-cum-comedian-cum-interviewer? No single word yet exists to epitomize his function, though it has had many practitioners, from Steve Allen, the archetypal pioneer, to the hosts of the latest and grisliest giveaway shows. In Carson's case, there are ten steps to stardom. (1) A multi-purpose job (at forty-seven dollars and fifty cents a week) as disc jockey, weather reporter, and reader of commercials on an Omaha radio station, where he breaks a precedent or two; e.g., when he is required to conduct pseudo-interviews, consisting of answers prerecorded by minor celebrities and distributed to small-town d.j.s with a list of matching questions, he flouts custom by ignoring the script. Instead of asking Patti Page how she began performing, he says, "I understand you're hitting the bottle pretty good, Patti—when did you start?," which elicits the taped reply "When I was six, I used to get up at church socials and do it." (2) A work-hunting foray, in 1951, to San Francisco and Los Angeles, which gets him nowhere except back to Omaha. (3) A sudden summons, later in the same year, from a Los Angeles television station, KNXT, offering him a post as staff announcer, which he accepts, at a hundred and thirty-five dollars a week. (4) A Sunday-afternoon show of his own ("KNXT *cautiously* presents 'Carson's Cellar' "), produced on a weekly budget of twenty-five dollars, plus fifty for Carson. It becomes what is known as a cult success (a golden phrase, which unlocks many high-level doors), numbering among its fans—and subsequently its guests—such people as Fred Allen, Jack Benny, and Red Skelton. (5) Employment, after thirty weeks of "Carson's Cellar," as a writer and supporting player on Skelton's CBS-TV show. (6) The Breakthrough, which occurs in 1954 and is brought about, in strict adherence to the "Forty-second Street" formula, by an injury to the star: Skelton literally knocks himself out while rehearsing a slapstick routine, and Carson, at roughly an hour's notice, triumphantly replaces him. (7) The Breakdown: CBS launches "The Johnny Carson Show," a half-hour program that goes through seven directors, eight writers, and thirty-nine weeks of worsening health before expiring, in the spring of 1956. (8) Carson picks self up, dusts self off, starts all over again. On money borrowed from his father, he moves from the West Coast to New York, where he joins the Friars Club, impresses its show-business membership with his cobra-swift one-liners, makes guest appearances on TV, and generally repairs his damaged reputation until (9) he is hired by ABC, in 1957, to run its quiz program "Who Do You Trust?," on which he spends the five increasingly prosperous years that lead him to (10) the "Tonight Show," and thence to the best table in the Polo Lounge, where he has been waiting for several minutes when I arrive, precisely on time.

He is making copious notes on a pad. I ask what he is writing. He says he has had an idea for tonight's monologue. In Utah, yesterday, the convicted murderer Gary Gilmore, who had aroused national interest by his refusal to appeal against the death sentence passed upon him, got his wish by facing a firing squad—Utah being a state where the law allows condemned criminals to select the method by which society will rid itself of them. Thus, the keepers of the peace have shot a man to death at his own urgent request. Carson's comment on this macabre situation takes the form of black comedy. Since justice must be seen to be done, why not let the viewing public in on the process of choice? Carson proposes a new TV show, to be called "The Execution Game." It would work something like this: Curtains part to reveal the death chamber, in the middle of which is an enormous wheel, equipped with glittering lights and a large golden arrow, to be spun by the condemned man to decide the nature of his fate. For mouth-watering prizes—ranging from a holiday for two in the lovely Munich suburb of Dachau to a pair of front-row seats at the victim's terminal throes—members of the audience vie with one another to guess whether the arrow will come to rest on the electric chair, the gas chamber, the firing squad, the garrote, or the noose.

This routine seems to me apt and mordant, and I tell Carson that I look forward to seeing it developed this evening. (Footnote: I looked in vain. The January 18th edition of the "Tonight Show" contained no mention of Gary Gilmore's execution apart from a terse and oddly sour sentence—"Capital punishment is a great deterrent to monologues"—inserted without buildup or comic payoff in Carson's opening spiel. A couple of nights later, one of his guests was Shelley Winters, who burst into an attack on the death penalty, using the Gilmore case as her springboard. Carson showed a distinctly nervous reluctance to commit himself; indeed, he shied away from the subject, and cut the discussion short by saying, "There are no absolutes." Yet I had seen him writing a piece that implied fairly bitter opposition to the process of judicial killing. What had happened? I called up Fred de Cordova, who admitted, after some hesitation, that he had disliked the "Execution Game" idea and that the network had backed him up. There had been a convulsive row with Carson, but in the end "Johnny saw reason" and the item was dropped. Hence his remark, meaningless except to insiders, about capital punishment's being "a great deterrent to monologues"; and so much for de Cordova's description of Carson as a supreme "self-editor" who never needed censorship.)

A believer in eating only when one is hungry, Carson orders nothing more than a salad and some mineral water. "I gave up drinking a couple of years ago," he says. "I couldn't handle it." He adds that we can chat until two o'clock, when he must be off to Burbank. He doesn't know who is lined up to appear tonight. This prompts an obligatory question: Which guests has he coveted and failed to corral? "Cary Grant, of course. But straight actors often get embarrassed on the show. They say they feel naked. Their business is to play other people, and it bugs them to have to speak as themselves. Naturally, I'd be glad to have Henry Kissinger. And it was a great sorrow to me when Charles Laughton, whom we'd been after for ages, died a few days before he was scheduled to appear. But on the whole I'm pretty content to have had a list of guests like Paul Ehrlich, Gore Vidal, Carl Sagan, Madalyn Murray O'Hair . . ." He flips through the familiar roster. "And it gives me a special kick to go straight from talking to that kind of person into an all-out slapstick routine." He runs over his rules for coping with fellow-comedians on the program: "You have to lay back and help them. Never compete with them. I learned that from Jack Benny. The better they are, the better the show is." (In more immature days, Carson's technique was less self-effacing. The late Jack E. Leonard told a reporter in 1967, "You say a funny line on Griffin, and he laughs and says, 'That's brilliant.' Carson repeats it, scavenging, hunting all over for the last vestiges of the joke, trying desperately to pull a laugh of his own out of it.") Carson continues, "When people get outrageous, you have to capitalize on their outrageousness and go along with it. The only absolute rule is: Never lose control of the show."

To stay in control is the hardest trick of all, especially when the talk veers toward obscenity; you have to head it off, preferably with a laugh, before it crashes through the barrier of public acceptance. At times, you have to launch a preëmptive strike of salaciousness in order to get an interview started. "Not long ago, a movie starlet came on the show with gigantic breasts bulging out of a low-cut dress," Carson says. "The audience couldn't look at anything else. If I'd ignored them, nobody would have listened to a word we said. There was only one thing to do. As soon as she sat down, I stared straight at her cleavage and said, 'That's the biggest set of jugs I ever saw.' It got a tremendous laugh. 'Now that we've got that out of the way,' I said, 'let's talk.' "

High on his list of favorite guests is Don Rickles, though he feels that Rickles has sadly mishandled his own TV career: "He went in for situation comedy and tried to be lovable. And he failed every time. What he needed—and I've told him this over and over again—was a game show called something like 'Meet Don Rickles,' where he could be himself and insult the audience, the way Groucho did on 'You Bet Your Life.' " Although Carson himself is less acid than he used to be, he is still capable of slapping down visitors who get uppish with him. "There was one time," he recalls, "when we had Tuesday Weld on the program, and she started behaving rather snottily. I finally asked her something innocuous about her future plans, and she said she'd let me know 'when I'm back on the show next year.' I was very polite. I just said that I hadn't scheduled her again quite that soon." Beyond doubt, Carson's least beloved subjects are British comedians, of whom he says, "I find them unfunny, infantile, and obsessed with toilet jokes. They're lavatory-minded." (It is true that British comics sometimes indulge, on TV, in scatological—and sexual—humor that would not be permitted on any American network; but this kind of liberty, however it may be abused, seems to me infinitely preferable to the restrictiveness that prevented Buddy Hackett, Carson's principal guest on February 1, 1977, from completing a single punch line without being bleeped.) I throw into the conversation my own opinion, which is that to shrink from referring to basic physical functions is to be truly infantile; to make good jokes about them, as about anything else, is evidence of maturity. It is depressing to reflect that if Rabelais were alive today he would not be invited to appear on the "Tonight Show."

Carson once said, "I've never seen it chiseled in stone tablets that TV must be uplifting." I ask him how he feels about his talk-show competitor Dick Cavett. His answer is brisk: "The trouble with Dick is that he's never decided what he wants to be—whether he's going for the sophisticated, intellectual viewer or for the wider audience. He falls between two stools. It gets so that you feel he's apologizing if he makes a joke." In reply to the accusation that his own show is intellectually jejune, Carson has this to say: "I don't want to get into big debates about abortion, homosexuality, prostitution, and so forth. Not because I'm afraid of them but because we all know the arguments on both sides, and they're circular. The fact is that TV is probably not the ideal place to discuss serious issues. It's much better to read about them." With this thought—self-serving but not easily refutable—he takes his leave.

FEBRUARY 10, 1977: The Hasty Pudding Club at Harvard has elected Carson its Man of the Year. There have been ten previous holders of the title, among them Bob Hope, Paul Newman, Robert Redford, James Stewart, Dustin Hoffman, and Warren Beatty. Delighted by the honor, because it is untainted by either lobbying or commercialism, Carson will fly to Harvard in two weeks' time to receive his trophy. While he is there, he will attend the opening night of "Cardinal Knowledge," the hundred-and-twenty-ninth in the series of all-male musicals presented by Hasty Pudding Theatricals, which claims to be the oldest dramatic society in the United States. I am to travel with Carson on what will be his first trip to Harvard. To give me details of the program of events that the Pudding people have prepared for him, he asks me to his home in Bel Air, where I present myself at 11 A.M. It is roughly five minutes by car from the Beverly Hills Hotel, and was built in 1950 for the director Mervyn LeRoy. Carson bought it five years ago, and, like many places where West Coast nabobs dwell, it is about as grand as a house can be that has no staircase. When you turn in at the driveway, a voice issuing from the wall sternly inquires your name and business; if your reply pacifies it, iron gates swing open to admit you.

I am welcomed by Joanna Carson's secretary, a lively young woman named Sherry Fleiner, part of whose job consists of working with Mrs. C. for a charitable organization known as SHARE—Share Happily And Reap Endlessly—which raises funds for the mentally retarded. (Other than a married couple who act as housekeepers, the Carsons have no live-in servants.) Proffering Carson's apologies, Miss Fleiner says that he is out on the tennis court behind the house, halfway through a closely fought third set. While awaiting match point, I discreetly case the joint, which has (I learn from Miss Fleiner) six bed-rooms. Except where privacy is essential, the walls are mainly of glass, and there is window-to-window carpeting with a zebra-stripe motif. Doors are infrequent. In accordance with local architectural custom, you do not leave one room to enter another, you move from one living area to the next. In the reading area (or "library") I spot a photograph of four generations of Carsons, the eldest being my host's grandfather Christopher Carson, who died two years ago at the age of ninety-eight, and I recall Carson's saying to me, in that steely, survivor's voice of his, "One thing about my family—we have good genes." On a wall nearby hangs a portrait of Carson by Norman Rockwell, the perfect artist for this model product of Middle American up-bringing. Other works of art, scattered through the relaxing, ingesting, and greeting areas, reveal an eclectic, opulent, but not barbarously spendthrift taste; e.g., a well-chosen group of paintings by minor Impressionists; a camel made out of automobile bumpers by John Kearney and (an authentic rarity) a piece of sculpture by Rube Goldberg; together with statues and graphic art from the Orient and Africa. Over the fireplace in the relaxing area, a facile portrait of Mrs. Carson, who deserves more eloquent brushwork, smilingly surveys the swimming pool.

Having won his match, Carson joins me, his white sporting gear undarkened by sweat, and leads me out of the house to a spacious octagonal office he has built alongside the tennis court. This is his command module. It contains ma-chinery for large-screen TV projection, and a desk of Presidential dimensions, bristling with gadgets. On a built-in sofa lies a cushion that bears the embroi-dered inscription "IT'S ALL IN THE TIMING." Coffee is served, and Carson offers me one of his cigarettes, which I refuse. He says that most people, even hardened smokers, do the same, and I do not find this surprising, since the brand he fa-vors is more virulent and ferociously unfiltered than any other on the market. He briefs me on the impending Harvard visit—a day and a half of sightseeing, speechmaking, banquets, conferences, seminars, and receptions that would tax the combined energies of Mencken, Mailer, and Milton Berle—and then throws himself open to me for further questioning.

Q: When you're at home, whom do you entertain?

CARSON: My lawyer, Henry Bushkin, who's probably my best friend. A few doctors. One or two poker players. Some people I've met through tennis, which is my biggest hobby right now—though I'm still interested in as-tronomy and scuba diving. And, of course, a couple of people who work on the show. But the point is that not many of my friends are exclusively show-business.

Q: Why do you dislike going to parties?

CARSON: Because I get embarrassed by attention and adulation. I don't know how to react to them in private. Swifty Lazar, for instance, sometimes embarrasses me when he praises me in front of his friends. I feel much more comfortable with a studio audience. On the show, I'm in control. Socially, I'm not in control.

Q: On the show, one of the things you control most strictly is the expression of your own opinions. Why do you keep them a secret from the viewers?

CARSON: I hate to be pinned down. Take the case of Larry Flynt, for example. [Flynt, the publisher of the sex magazine *Hustler*, had recently been convicted on obscenity charges.] Now, I think *Hustler* is tawdry, but I also think that if the First Amendment means what it says, then it protects Flynt as much as anyone else, and that includes the American Nazi movement. As far as I'm concerned, people should be allowed to read and see whatever they like, provided it doesn't injure others. If they want to read pornography until it comes out of their ears, then let them. But if I go on the "Tonight Show" and defend *Hustler*, the viewers are going to tag me as that guy who's into pornography. And that's going to hurt me as an entertainer, which is what I am.

Q: In private life, who's the wittiest man you've ever known?

CARSON: The wittiest would have to be Fred Allen. He appeared on a show I had in the fifties, called "Carson's Cellar," and I knew him for a while after that—until he died, in 1956. But there's an old vaudeville proverb—"A comic is a man who says funny things, and a comedian is a man who says things funny." If that's a valid distinction, then Fred was a comic, whereas Jonathan Winters and Mel Brooks are comedians. But they make me laugh just as much.

Before I go, Carson takes me down to a small gymnasium beneath the module. It is filled with gleaming steel devices, pulleys and springs and counterweights, which, together with tennis, keep the star's body trim. In one corner stands a drum kit at which Buddy Rich might cast an envious eye. "That's where I work off my hostilities," Carson explains. He escorts me to my car, and notices that it is fitted with a citizens-band radio. "I had one of those damned things, but I ripped it out after a couple of weeks," he says. "I just couldn't bear it—all those sick anonymous maniacs shooting off their mouths."

I understand what he means. Most of what you hear on CB radio is either tedious (truck drivers warning one another about speed traps) or banal (schoolgirls exchanging notes on homework), but at its occasional—and illegal—worst it sinks a pipeline to the depths of the American unconscious. Your ears are assaulted by the sound of racism at its most rampant, and by masturbation fantasies that are the aural equivalent of rape. The sleep of reason, to quote Goya's phrase, brings forth monsters, and the anonymity of CB encourages the monsters to emerge. Not often, of course; but when they do, CB radio becomes the dark underside of a TV talk show. No wonder Carson loathes it.

FEBRUARY 24, 1977: Morning departure from Los Angeles Airport of flight bearing Boston-bound Carson party, which consists of Mr. and Mrs. C., Mr. and Mrs. Henry Bushkin, and me. Boyish-looking, with an easy smile, a soft voice, and a modest manner, Bushkin, to whom I talked a few days earlier, is a key figure in Carson's private and professional life. "Other stars have an agent, a personal manager, a business manager, a P.R. man, and a lawyer," he told me. "I serve all those functions for Johnny." Bushkin was born in the Bronx in 1942. He moved to the West Coast five years ago and swiftly absorbed the ground rules of life in Beverly Hills; e.g., he is likely to turn up at his desk in a cardigan and an open-necked shirt, thus obeying the precept that casualness of office attire increases in direct ratio to grandeur of status. He first met Carson through a common friend in 1970, when he was working for a small Manhattan law firm that specialized in show-business clients. At that time, Carson lived at the United Nations Plaza, where one of his neighbors was David (Sonny) Werblin, formerly the driving force behind the Music Corporation of America and (until 1968) the president of the New York Jets. In 1969, Werblin had drawn up a plan whereby he and Carson would form a corporation, called Raritan Enterprises, to take over the entire production of the "Tonight Show," which would then be rented out to NBC for a vast weekly fee. Rather than risk losing Carson, the network caved in and agreed to Raritan's terms. "As the tax laws were in the late sixties, when you could pay up to ninety per cent on earned income, the Raritan scheme had certain advantages," Bushkin explained to me. "But there were handicaps that Johnny hadn't foreseen. Werblin had too many outside interests—for one thing, he owned a good-sized racing stable—and Johnny found himself managing the company as well as starring in the show, because his partner wasn't always there. When a major problem came up, he'd suddenly discover that Werblin had taken off for a month in Europe and couldn't be reached. Around 1972, Johnny decided that the plan wasn't working, and that's when he asked me to represent him. Not to go into details, let's just say that Werblin was painlessly eliminated from the setup. By that time, the maximum tax on earned income was down to fifty per cent, and that removed the basic motive for the corporate arrangement. So the show reverted to being an NBC operation. But Johnny went back with a much better financial deal than he had in 1969." When Bushkin came to Beverly Hills, in 1973, his life already revolved around Carson's. "It took about three years for our relationship to get comfortable, because Johnny isn't easy to know," he went on. "But now we're the best of friends, and so are our wives. The unwritten rule for lawyers is: Don't get too friendly with clients. But this is an unusual situation. This is Carson, and Carson's my priority."

Ed McMahon, I remarked, had predicted that Carson would stay with the "Tonight Show" until 1980. "I'll bet you that he's still there in 1984," Bushkin said.

If Carson can hold on as long as that, it would be churlish of NBC to unseat him before he reaches retiring age, in 1990.

5:30 P.M.: We land at Boston. Frost underfoot. Carson, following his new President's example, totes his suit (presumably the tuxedo required for tomorrow's festivities) off the plane. He murmurs to me, "If someone could get Billy Carter to sponsor a carry-off suitcase, they'd make a fortune." He walks through popping flashbulbs and a fair amount of hand-held-camera work to be greeted by Richard Palmer and Barry Sloane, undergraduate co-producers of the Hasty Pudding show, who look bland, businesslike, and utterly untheatrical; i.e., like co-producers. Waiting limos take Carsons and Bushkins to the Master's Residence at Eliot House, where they are to spend the night. I repair to my hotel.

8:30 P.M.: Pudding people give dinner for Carson and his entourage at waterfront restaurant called Anthony's Pier 4. When I announce destination, my cabdriver says, "That's the big Republican place. Gold tablecloths. Democrats like checked tablecloths. They go to Jimmy's Harbor Side." Décor at Anthony's features rustic beamery and period prints. Tablecloths definitely straw-colored, though cannot confirm that this has political resonance. Carson (in blue sports jacket, white shirt, and discreetly striped tie) sits beside wife (in brown woollen two-piece, with ring like searchlight on left hand) at round table with Bushkins, Pudding officials, and short, heavily tanned man with vestigial hair, dark silk suit, smoke-tinted glasses, and general aspect of semi-simian elegance. This, I learn, is David Tebet, the senior vice-president of NBC, whose suzerainty covers the Carson show, and who in May, 1977, will celebrate his twenty-first anniversary with the network. Of the three men who wield influence over Carson (the others being Bushkin and Fred de Cordova), Tebet is ultimately the most powerful. "It's a terrible thing to wish on him," Frank Sinatra once said of Tebet, "but it's too bad he's not in government today." In 1975, Robert D. Wood, then president of CBS-TV, described Tebet as "the ambassador of all NBC's good will—he sprinkles it around like ruby dust." With characteristic effusiveness, de Cordova has declared that the dust-sprinkler's real title should be "vice-president in charge of caring." In 1965, Carson came to the conclusion that he had to quit the "Tonight Show," because the daily strain was too great, but Tebet persuaded him to stay; what tipped the scale was the offer of an annual paid vacation of six weeks. Ten years later, Carson said he had a feeling that when he died a color TV set would be delivered to his graveside and "on it will be a ribbon and a note that says, 'Have a nice trip. Love, David.' "

During dinner, although wine is served, Carson drinks only coffee. He talks about "Seeds," a Wasp parody of "Roots," dealing with history of orthodox Midwestern family, which was recently broadcast on the "Tonight Show." Concept was his, and he is pleased with how it came out, though he regrets loss of one idea that was cut; viz., scene depicting primitive tribal ceremony at which the hyphen is ritually removed from Farrah Fawcett-Majors.

"He looks so mechanical," mutters a Pudding person on my right. "Like a talking propelling pencil." Same fellow explains to me that the club is divided into social and theatrical compartments. Former was founded in 1795; latter did not develop until 1844, when first show was presented, establishing an annual tradition that has persisted—apart from two inactive years in each of the World Wars—ever since. Pudding performers have included Oliver Wendell Holmes, William Randolph Hearst, Robert Benchley (star of "Below Zero," 1912), and Jack Lemmon. Tomorrow's production, which is to play a month at Pudding theatre, followed by quick tour to New York, Washington, and Bermuda, will cost a hundred thousand dollars. Revenue from box office and from program advertising, plus aid from wealthy patrons, will insure that it breaks even. (Undergraduates provide words, music, and cast; direction, choreography, and design are by professionals.) Publicity accruing from Carson's presence will boost ticket sales; thus, his visit amounts to unpaid commercial for show.

Another Pudding functionary tells me that club also bestows award on Woman of the Year—has, in fact, been doing so since 1951. First recipient was Gertrude Lawrence, Bette Midler got the nod in 1976, and last week Elizabeth Taylor turned up to collect the trophy for 1977. "She is genuinely humble," my informant gravely whispers. After dinner, Carson and wife are interviewed in banqueting salon of restaurant by local TV station. Mrs. C. is asked, "Did you fall in love with the private or the public Johnny Carson?" She replies, "I fell in love with both." Before further secrets of the confessional can be extracted, camera runs out of tape, to her evident relief.

February 25, 1977: Dining hall of Eliot House is crowded at 8:45 A.M. University band, with brass section predominant, lines up and plays "Ten Thousand Men of Harvard" as Carson (black-and-white checked sports jacket) leads his party in to breakfast. His every move is followed, as it will be all day, by television units, undergraduate film crew, and assorted press photographers. Asked by TV director whether sound system is to his liking, Carson says he has no complaints, "except I thought the microphone under the bed was pushing it a bit." Member of Harvard band achieves minor triumph of one-upmanship by conning Carson into inscribing and autographing autobiography of Dick Cavett.

Fast duly broken, party embarks on walking tour of Harvard Yard and university museums. Hundreds of undergraduates join media people in the crush around Carson, and police cars prowl in their wake to protect the star from terrorist assaults or kidnap attempts. Weather is slate-clouded and icy; Mrs.

Carson and Mrs. Bushkin both wear mink coats. Climax of tour is meeting with John Finley, internationally eminent classical scholar and treasure of Harvard campus, Eliot Professor of Greek Literature Emeritus and Master of Eliot House Emeritus, whose study is in the Widener Library. (During previous week, I called Professor Finley to find out how he felt about forthcoming encounter with Carson. "At first, I thought it was an asinine idea," he said. "I've never seen the man on television—as a matter of fact, I've spent most of my life with my nose plunged into classical texts. But, after all, how important is one's time, anyway?") Carson is properly deferential in the presence of this agile septuagenarian. Eavesdropping on their conversation, I hear Professor Finley say, "Writing is like an artesian well that we sink to find the truth." He talks about Aristotle, getting little response, and then tries to clarify for Carson the distinction drawn by Lionel Trilling between sincerity and authenticity, in literature and in life. "President Carter is an example of sincerity," he explains. "But whether he has authenticity—well, that's another matter. I'm not sure that Trilling would have been much impressed." Cannot imagine what Carson is making of all this.

12:30 P.M.: Luncheon in Carson's honor at the A.D. Club, described to me by reliable source as "the second-stuffiest in Harvard." (First prize goes, by general consent, if not by acclamation, to the Porcellian Club. Choice of venue today is dictated by fact that co-producers of Pudding show are members of A.D. and not of Porcellian.) Atmosphere is robustly patrician enough to warm heart of late Evelyn Waugh: sprigs of Back Bay dynasties sprawl in leather armchairs beneath group photographs of their forebears. Club clearly deserves title of No. 2; it could not conceivably try harder. Members cheer as Carson enters, flanked by Bushkin and Tebet. (This is a strictly stag sodality.) About twenty guests present, among them Professor Finley and Robert Peabody, son of former governor of Massachusetts and vice-president of Pudding Theatricals—a bouncing two-hundred-and-fifty-pound lad much cherished by Pudding enthusiasts for his comic talent in drag. Carson, still rejecting grape in favor of bean, wears blue sweater, dark slacks, and burgundy patent-leather shoes. When meal is consumed, he makes charming speech of thanks, in which he regrets that life denied him the opportunity of studying under Prof. Finley. (Later, rather less lovably, he is to tell drama students at Pudding Club that from his lunchtime chat with Finley "I learned a hell of a lot more about Aristotle than I wanted to know.")

2 P.M.: Carson is driven to Pudding H.Q. on Holyoke Street—narrow thoroughfare jammed with fans, through whom club officials have to force a way to the entrance. Upstairs, in red-curtained reception room, Carson is to hold seminar with thirty handpicked undergraduates who are studying the performing arts. This select bunch of initiates sits in circle of red armchairs. Carson takes his place among them and awaits interrogation. Standard of questions, dismal for allegedly high-powered assembly, seldom rises above gossip level; e.g.:

Q: As a regular viewer, may I ask why you have switched from wearing a Windsor knot to a four-in-hand?

CARSON: Well, I guess that's about all we have time for. [Questioner presses for reply.] Just between ourselves, it's a defense mechanism.

Q: Did Jack Paar have someone like Ed McMahon to work with?

CARSON: No. A psychiatrist worked with Jack Paar. The last time I saw Paar was in Philadelphia. He was sitting on a curb and he had a swizzle stick embedded in his hand. I removed it.

Q: I've noticed that people don't always laugh at your monologue. Why is that?

CARSON: Well, we don't actually *structure* it to go down the toilet. But we work from the morning papers and sometimes the audience isn't yet aware of what's happened in the news.

Q: How do you really feel about Jimmy Carter?

CARSON: The Carter Administration is perfect comedy material. And I think he rented the family. I don't believe Lillian is his mother. I don't believe Billy is his brother. They're all from Central Casting.

Q: Do you normally watch the show when you get home?

CARSON: No. I'd get worn out from seeing it all over again. If we're breaking in a new character, I'll watch.

Q [first of any substance]: Has the "Tonight Show" done anything more important than just brighten up the end of the day?

CARSON: I'd say it was quite important to let people hear the opinions of people like Paul Ehrlich, Carl Sagan, Gore Vidal, Margaret Mead . . . [Vide supra, passim.] We've also taken an interest in local politics. One year, there were eleven candidates for Mayor of Burbank, and we had to give them all equal time. That was pretty public-spirited. But what's important? I think it's important to show ordinary people doing extraordinary things. Like we once had a Japanese guy from Cleveland who wanted to be a cop but he was too short, so his wife had been hanging him up every night by his heels. And it's important to help people live out their fantasies, like when I pitched to Mickey Mantle on the show, or when I played quarterback for the New York Jets. But a lot of the time TV is judged by the wrong standards. If Broadway comes up with two first-rate new plays in a season, the critics are delighted. That's a good season. But on TV they expect that every week. It's a very visible medium to jump on. And there's another thing that isn't generally realized. If you're selling hard goods—like soap or dog food—you simply can't afford to put on culture. Exxon, the Bank of America—organizations like that can afford to do it. But they aren't selling hard goods, and that's what the "Tonight Show" has to do. [Applause for candor. This is the nearest approach to hard eloquence I have heard from Carson, and he sells it to great effect.]

Q: What is Charo really like?

This reduces Carson to silence, bringing the seminar to a close.

4:30 P.M.: Cocktail party for Carson at Club Casablanca, local haunt crowded to point just short of asphyxiation. Star and companions have changed into evening dress. Carson tells me how Prof. Finley sought to explain to him eternal simplicities of Aristotle's view of life, and adds, "He's out of touch with the real world." Subject for debate: By what criteria can Carson's world be said to be closer to reality than Aristotle's? Or, for that matter, than Professor Finley's? Carson group and non-acting Pudding dignitaries then proceed on foot to nearby bistro called Ferdinand's for early dinner. Eating quite exceptional softshell crabs, I sit next to Joanna C., who has flashing eyes and a quill-shaped Renaissance nose. Her mother's parents came from northern Italy; her father's family background is Sicilian. She introduced Carson to what is now his favorite Manhattan restaurant, an Italian place named Patsy's, and her immediate ambition is to coax him to visit Italy. Eying her husband (who must be well into his second gallon of coffee since breakfast), she tells me that the only time she has seen him cry was at the funeral of Jack Benny, who befriended and helped him from his earliest days in TV. She doesn't think he will still be on the "Tonight Show" when he's sixty (i.e., in 1985). "Of course, everybody wants him to act," she continues. "He was offered the Steve McQueen part in 'The Thomas Crown Affair,' and Mel Brooks begged him to play the Gene Wilder part in 'Blazing Saddles.' He read the script twice. Then he called Mel from Acapulco and said, 'I read it in L.A. and it wasn't funny, and it's even less funny in Mexico.' "

David Tebet, seated opposite, leans across table and tells me what he does. His voice is a serrated baritone growl. From what I gather, he is a combination of talent detector, ego masseur (of NBC stars), and thief (of other networks' stars). Has been quoted as saying that he judges performers by "a thing called gut reaction," and that he understands "their soft underbellies." To a thing called my surprise, he adds that these qualities of intestinal intuition help to keep stars reassured. According to an article in the *Wall Street Journal,* a two-thousand-year-old samurai sword hangs over the door of his New York office. Am not certain that this would have reassuring effect on me. It may, however, explain enigmatic remark of Bob Hope, who once referred to Tebet as "my Band-Aid." Razor-edged weapon is part of huge Tebet art collection (mainly Oriental but also including numerous prints and lithographs by Mucha, Klimt, Schiele, Munch, et al.), much of which adorns his NBC suite. Tebet claims this makes actors feel at home. But at whose home?

7 P.M.: Back to Pudding Club for pre-performance press conference. I count five movie and/or TV cameras, eight microphones, about thirty photographers, and several dozen reporters, all being jostled by roughly a hundred and fifty guests, gate-crashers, and ticket-holders diverted from route to auditorium by irresistible surge of Carson-watchers. Bar serves body-temperature champagne in plastic glasses; Carson requests slug of water.

Reporter asks what he thinks of Barbara Walters' million-dollar contract with ABC News.

He replies, "I think Harry Reasoner has a contract out for Barbara Walters." Press grilling is routine stuff, except for:

Q: What would you like your epitaph to be?

CARSON [after pause for thought]: I'll be right back.

Laughter and applause for this line, the traditional cliché with which talk-show hosts seque into commercial break. Subsequent research reveals that Carson has used it before in answer to same question. Fact increases my respect for his acting ability. That pause for thought would have fooled Lee Strasberg.

8 P.M.: Join expectant crowd in Pudding theatre, attractive little blue auditorium with three hundred and sixty-three seats. Standees line walls. In fat program I read tribute to "that performer who has made the most outstanding contribution to the entertainment profession during the past years—Johnny Carson." Article also states that in the fifties he wrote for "The Red Skeleton Show"—ideal title, I reflect, for Vincent Price Special—and concludes by summing up Carson's gifts in a burst of baroque alliteration: "Outspoken yet disciplined, he is a pool of profanity, a pit of profundity." Audience by now buzzing with impatience to hear from pool (or pit) in person.

Co-producer Palmer takes the stage and, reading from notes, pays brief homage to "a performer whose wit, humor, and showmanship rank him among America's greatest—ladies and gentlemen, Mr. Johnny Carson!" Band plays "Tonight Show" theme as Carson walks down the aisle and clambers up to shake Palmer's hand. Standing ovation greets him. Co-producer Sloane emerges from wings and solemnly presents him with small golden pudding pot. Ovation persists—three hundred and sixty-three seats are empty. When it and the spectators have subsided, Carson holds up his hands for silence and then makes speech precisely right for occasion. (Without notes, of course, as befits man who, if program is to be believed, has "liberated the airwaves from scripted domination.") He begins by saying that it is gratifying to hear so much applause without anyone's brandishing a sign marked "Applause." He thanks the club for the honor bestowed on him, even though (he adds) "I understand that this year the short list for the award was me, Idi Amin, and Larry Flynt." He expresses special gratitude for the hospitality extended to his wife and to him by

Eliot House: "It's the first time I've scored with a chick on campus since 1949." He has never visited the university before. However, it has played a small but significant role in his family history: "My Great-Uncle Orville was here at Harvard. Unfortunately, he was in a jar in the biology lab." Widening his focus, he throws in a couple of comments on the state of the nation. Apropos of the recent and groundless panic over immunizing the population against a rumored epidemic of swine flu: "Our government has finally come up with a cure for which there is no known disease." And a nostalgic shot at a familiar target: "I hear that whenever anyone in the White House tells a lie, Nixon gets a royalty." End of address. Sustained cheers, through which Carson returns, blinking in a manner not wholly explicable by the glare of the spotlights, to his seat.

"Cardinal Knowledge," the Pudding musical, at last gets under way. It's a farrago of melodramatic intrigue, with seventeenth-century setting and plethora of puns; e.g., characters called Barry de Hatchet and Viscount Hugh Behave. (How far can a farrago go?) Am pleased by high standard of performance, slightly dismayed by lack of obscenity in text. No need to dwell on show, except to praise Robert Peabody, mountainously flirtatious as Lady Della Tory, and Mark Szpak, president of Pudding Theatricals, who plays the heroine, Juana deBoise, with a raven-haired Latin vivacity that puts me in mind of the youthful Lea Padovani. Or the present Mrs. Carson.

10:15 P.M.: Intermission not yet over. Carson at bar, still on caffeine, besieged by mass of undergraduates, all of whom receive bright and civil answers to their questions. He has now been talking to strangers for thirteen hours (interrupted only by Act I of show) with no loss of buoyancy. "For the first time in my life," he remarks to me, "I know what it's like to be a politician."

Midnight has passed before the curtain falls and he makes his exit, to renewed acclamation. One gets the impression that the audience is applauding not just an admired performer but—why shun simplicities?—a decent and magnanimous man.

TWO thoughts in conclusion:

(1) If the most we ask of live television is entertainment within the limits set by commercial sponsorship, then Carson, week in, week out, is the very best we shall get. If, on the other hand, we ask to be challenged, disturbed, or provoked at the same time that we are entertained, Carson must inevitably disappoint us. But to blame him for that would be to accuse him of breaking a promise he never made.

(2) Though the written and rehearsed portions of what Carson does can be edited together into an extremely effective cabaret act, the skill that makes him unique—the ability to run a talk show as he does—is intrinsically, exclusively televisual. Singers, actors, and dancers all have multiple choices:

they can exercise their talents in the theatre, on TV, or in the movies. But a talk-show host can only become a more successful talk-show host. There is no place in the other media for the gifts that distinguish him—most specifically, for the gift of re-inventing himself, night after night, without rehearsal or repetition. Carson, in other words, is a grand master of the one show-business art that leads nowhere. He has painted himself not into a corner but onto the top of a mountain.

Long—or, at least, as long as the air at the summit continues to nourish and elate him—may he stay there.

(1978)

TRUMAN CAPOTE

THE DUKE IN HIS DOMAIN

MOST Japanese girls giggle. The little maid on the fourth floor of the Miyako Hotel, in Kyoto, was no exception. Hilarity, and attempts to suppress it, pinked her cheeks (unlike the Chinese, the Japanese complexion more often than not has considerable color), shook her plump peony-and-pansy-kimonoed figure. There seemed to be no particular reason for this merriment; the Japanese giggle operates without apparent motivation. I'd merely asked to be directed toward a certain room. "You come see Marron?" she gasped, showing, like so many of her fellow-countrymen, an array of gold teeth. Then, with the tiny, pigeon-toed skating steps that the wearing of a kimono necessitates, she led me through a labyrinth of corridors, promising, "I knock you Marron." The "l" sound does not exist in Japanese, and by "Marron" the maid meant Marlon—Marlon Brando, the American actor, who was at that time in Kyoto doing location work for the Warner Brothers–William Goetz motion-picture version of James Michener's novel "Sayonara."

My guide tapped at Brando's door, shrieked "Marron!," and fled away along the corridor, her kimono sleeves fluttering like the wings of a parakeet. The door was opened by another doll-delicate Miyako maid, who at once succumbed to her own fit of quaint hysteria. From an inner room, Brando called, "What is it, honey?" But the girl, her eyes squeezed shut with mirth and her fat little hands jammed into her mouth, like a bawling baby's, was incapable of reply. "Hey, honey, what *is* it?" Brando again inquired, and appeared in the doorway. "Oh, hi," he said when he saw me. "It's seven, huh?" We'd made a seven-o'clock date for dinner; I was nearly twenty minutes late. "Well, take off your shoes and come on in. I'm just finishing up here. And, hey, honey," he told the maid, "bring us some ice." Then, looking after the girl as she scurried off, he cocked his hands on his hips and, grinning, declared, "They kill me. They really kill me. The kids, too. Don't you think they're wonderful, don't you love them—Japanese kids?"

The Miyako, where about half of the "Sayonara" company was staying, is the most prominent of the so-called Western-style hotels in Kyoto; the majority of its rooms are furnished with sturdy, if commonplace and cumbersome, European chairs and tables, beds and couches. But, for the convenience of Japanese guests who prefer their own mode of décor while desiring the prestige of staying at the Miyako, or of those foreign travellers who yearn after authentic atmosphere yet are disinclined to endure the unheated rigors of a real Japanese inn, the Miyako maintains some suites decorated in the traditional manner, and it was in one of these that Brando had chosen to settle himself. His quarters consisted of two rooms, a bath, and a glassed-in sun porch. Without the overlying and underlying clutter of Brando's personal belongings, the rooms would have been textbook illustrations of the Japanese penchant for an ostentatious barrenness. The floors were covered with tawny *tatami* matting, with a discreet scattering of raw-silk pillows; a scroll depicting swimming golden carp hung in an alcove, and beneath it, on a stand, sat a vase filled with tall lilies and red leaves, arranged just so. The larger of the two rooms—the inner one—which the occupant was using as a sort of business office where he also dined and slept, contained a long, low lacquer table and a sleeping pallet. In these rooms, the divergent concepts of Japanese and Western decoration—the one seeking to impress by a lack of display, an absence of possession-exhibiting, the other intent on precisely the reverse—could both be observed, for Brando seemed unwilling to make use of the apartment's storage space, concealed behind sliding paper doors. All that he owned seemed to be out in the open. Shirts, ready for the laundry; socks, too; shoes and sweaters and jackets and hats and ties, flung around like the costume of a dismantled scarecrow. And cameras, a typewriter, a tape recorder, an electric heater that performed with stifling competence. Here, there, pieces of partly nibbled fruit; a box of the famous Japanese strawberries, each berry the size of an egg. And books, a deep-thought cascade, among which one saw Colin Wilson's "The Outsider" and various works on Buddhist prayer, Zen meditation, Yogi breathing, and Hindu mysticism, but no fiction, for Brando reads none. He has never, he professes, opened a novel since April 3, 1924, the day he was born, in Omaha, Nebraska. But while he may not care to read fiction, he does desire to write it, and the long lacquer table was loaded with overfilled ashtrays and piled pages of his most recent creative effort, which happens to be a film script entitled "A Burst of Vermilion."

In fact, Brando had evidently been working on his story at the moment of my arrival. As I entered the room, a subdued-looking, youngish man, whom I shall call Murray, and who had previously been pointed out to me as "the fellow that's helping Marlon with his writing," was squatted on the matting fumbling through the manuscript of "A Burst of Vermilion." Weighing some pages on his hand, he said, "Tell ya, Mar, s'pose I go over this down in my room, and maybe we'll get together again—say, around ten-thirty?"

Brando scowled, as though unsympathetic to the idea of resuming their endeavors later in the evening. Having been slightly ill, as I learned later, he had spent the day in his room, and now seemed restive. "What's this?" he asked, pointing to a couple of oblong packages among the literary remains on the lacquer table.

Murray shrugged. The maid had delivered them; that was all he knew. "People are always sending Mar presents," he told me. "Lots of times we don't know who sent them. True, Mar?"

"Yeah," said Brando, beginning to rip open the gifts, which, like most Japanese packages—even mundane purchases from very ordinary shops—were beautifully wrapped. One contained candy, the other white rice cakes, which proved cement-hard, though they looked like puffs of cloud. There was no card in either package to identify the donor. "Every time you turn around, some Japanese is giving you a present. They're crazy about giving presents," Brando observed. Athletically crunching a rice cake, he passed the boxes to Murray and me.

Murray shook his head; he was intent on obtaining Brando's promise to meet with him again at ten-thirty. "Give me a ring around then," Brando said, finally. "We'll see what's happening."

Murray, as I knew, was only one member of what some of the "Sayonara" company referred to as "Brando's gang." Aside from the literary assistant, the gang consisted of Marlon Brando, Sr., who acts as his son's business manager; a pretty, dark-haired secretary, Miss Levin; and Brando's private makeup man. The travel expenses of this entourage, and all its living expenses while on location, were allowed for in the actor's contract with Warner Brothers. Legend to the contrary, film studios are not usually so lenient financially. A Warner man to whom I talked later explained the tolerance shown Brando by saying, "Ordinarily we wouldn't put up with it. All the demands he makes. Except—well, this picture just *had* to have a big star. Your star—that's the only thing that really counts at the box office."

Among the company were some who felt that the social protection supplied by Brando's inner circle was preventing them from "getting to know the guy" as well as they would have liked. Brando had been in Japan for more than a month, and during that time he had shown himself on the set as a slouchingly dignified, amiable-seeming young man who was always ready to coöperate with, and even encourage, his co-workers—the actors particularly—yet by and large was not socially available, preferring, during the tedious lulls between scenes, to sit alone reading philosophy or scribbling in a schoolboy notebook. After the day's work, instead of accepting his colleagues' invitations to

join a group for drinks, a plate of raw fish in a restaurant, and a prowl through
the old geisha quarter of Kyoto, instead of contributing to the one-big-family,
houseparty bonhomie that picture-making on location theoretically generates,
he usually returned to his hotel and stayed there. Since the most fervent of
movie-star fans are the people who themselves work in the film industry,
Brando was a subject of immense interest within the ranks of the "Sayonara"
group, and the more so because his attitude of friendly remoteness produced,
in the face of such curiosity, such wistful frustrations. Even the film's director,
Joshua Logan, was impelled to say, after working with Brando for two weeks,
"Marlon's the most exciting person I've met since Garbo. A genius. But I don't
know what he's like. I don't know anything about him."

THE maid had reëntered the star's room, and Murray, on his way out, almost
tripped over the train of her kimono. She put down a bowl of ice and, with a
glow, a giggle, an elation that made her little feet, hooflike in their split-toed
white socks, lift and lower like a prancing pony's, announced, "Appapie!
Tonight on menu appapie."

Brando groaned. "Apple pie. That's all I need." He stretched out on the floor
and unbuckled his belt, which dug too deeply into the swell of his stomach.
"I'm supposed to be on a diet. But the only things I want to eat are apple pie and
stuff like that." Six weeks earlier, in California, Logan had told him he must
trim off ten pounds for his role in "Sayonara," and before arriving in Kyoto he
had managed to get rid of seven. Since reaching Japan, however, abetted not
only by American-type apple pie but by the Japanese cuisine, with its delicious
emphasis on the sweetened, the starchy, the fried, he'd regained, then doubled
this poundage. Now, loosening his belt still more and thoughtfully massaging
his midriff, he scanned the menu, which offered, in English, a wide choice of
Western-style dishes, and, after reminding himself "I've *got* to lose weight," ordered soup, beefsteak with French-fried potatoes, three supplementary vegetables, a side dish of spaghetti, rolls and butter, a bottle of *sake,* salad, and cheese
and crackers.

"And appapie, Marron?"

He sighed. "With ice cream, honey."

Though Brando is not a teetotaller, his appetite is more frugal when it comes
to alcohol. While we were awaiting the dinner, which was to be served to us in
the room, he supplied me with a large vodka on the rocks and poured himself
the merest courtesy sip. Resuming his position on the floor, he lolled his head
against a pillow, drooped his eyelids, then shut them. It was as though he'd
dozed off into a disturbing dream; his eyelids twitched, and when he spoke, his
voice—an unemotional voice, in a way cultivated and genteel, yet surprisingly
adolescent, a voice with a probing, asking, boyish quality—seemed to come
from sleepy distances.

"The last eight, nine years of my life have been a mess," he said. "Maybe the last two have been a little better. Less rolling in the trough of the wave. Have you ever been analyzed? I was afraid of it at first. Afraid it might destroy the impulses that made me creative, an artist. A sensitive person receives fifty impressions where somebody else may only get seven. Sensitive people are so vulnerable; they're so easily brutalized and hurt just because they *are* sensitive. The more sensitive you are, the more certain you are to be brutalized, develop scabs. Never evolve. Never allow yourself to feel anything, because you always feel too much. Analysis helps. It helped me. But still, the last eight, nine years I've been pretty mixed up, a mess pretty much. . . ."

THE voice went on, as though speaking to hear itself, an effect Brando's speech often has, for, like many persons who are intensely self-absorbed, he is something of a monologuist—a fact that he recognizes and for which he offers his own explanation. "People around me never say anything," he says. "They just seem to want to hear what I have to say. That's why I do all the talking." Watching him now, with his eyes closed, his unlined face white under an overhead light, I felt as if the moment of my initial encounter with him were being re-created. The year of that meeting was 1947; it was a winter afternoon in New York, when I had occasion to attend a rehearsal of Tennessee Williams' "A Streetcar Named Desire," in which Brando was to play the role of Stanley Kowalski. It was this role that first brought him general recognition, although among the New York theatre's cognoscenti he had already attracted attention, through his student work with the drama coach Stella Adler and a few Broadway appearances—one in a play by Maxwell Anderson, "Truckline Café," and another as Marchbanks opposite Katharine Cornell's Candida—in which he showed an ability that had been much praised and discussed. Elia Kazan, the director of "A Streetcar Named Desire," said at that time, and has recently repeated, "Marlon is just the best actor in the world." But ten years ago, on the remembered afternoon, he was still relatively unknown; at least, I hadn't a clue to who he might be when, arriving too early at the "Streetcar" rehearsal, I found the auditorium deserted and a brawny young man stretched out atop a table on the stage under the gloomy glare of work lights, solidly asleep. Because he was wearing a white T-shirt and denim trousers, because of his squat gymnasium physique—the weight-lifter's arms, the Charles Atlas chest (though an opened "Basic Writings of Sigmund Freud" was resting on it)—I took him for a stagehand. Or did until I looked closely at his face. It was as if a stranger's head had been attached to the brawny body, as in certain counterfeit photographs. For this face was so very untough, superimposing, as it did, an almost angelic refinement and gentleness upon hard-jawed good looks: taut skin, a broad, high forehead, wide-apart eyes, an aquiline nose, full lips with a relaxed, sensual expression. Not the least suggestion of Williams' unpoetic

Kowalski. It was therefore rather an experience to observe, later that afternoon, with what chameleon ease Brando acquired the character's cruel and gaudy colors, how superbly, like a guileful salamander, he slithered into the part, how his own persona evaporated—just as, in this Kyoto hotel room ten years afterward, my 1947 memory of Brando receded, disappeared into his 1957 self. And the present Brando, the one lounging there on the *tatami* and lazily puffing filtered cigarettes as he talked and talked, was, of course, a different person—bound to be. His body was thicker; his forehead was higher, for his hair was thinner; he was richer (from the producers of "Sayonara" he could expect a salary of three hundred thousand dollars, plus a percentage of the picture's earnings); and he'd become, as one journalist put it, "the Valentino of the bop generation"—turned into such a world celebrity that when he went out in public here in Japan, he deemed it wise to hide his face not only by wearing dark glasses but by donning a surgeon's gauze mask as well. (The latter bit of disguise is not so *outré* in Japan as it may sound, since numerous Asians wear such masks, on the theory that they prevent the spreading of germs.) Those were some of the alterations a decade had made. There were others. His eyes had changed. Although their *caffè-espresso* color was the same, the shyness, any traces of real vulnerability that they had formerly held, had left them; now he looked at people with assurance, and with what can only be called a pitying expression, as though he dwelt in spheres of enlightenment where they, to his regret, did not. (The reactions of the people subjected to this gaze of constant commiseration range from that of a young actress who avowed that "Marlon is really a very *spiritual* person, wise and very sincere; you can see it in his eyes" to that of a Brando acquaintance who said, "The way he looks at you, like he was so damn sorry for you—doesn't it make you want to cut your throat?") Nevertheless, the subtly tender character of his face had been preserved. Or almost. For in the years between he'd had an accident that gave his face a more conventionally masculine aspect. It was just that his nose had been broken. And, maneuvering a word in edgewise, I asked, "How did you break your nose?"

". . . by which I don't mean that I'm *always* unhappy. I remember one April I was in Sicily. A hot day, and flowers everywhere. I like flowers, the ones that smell. Gardenias. Anyway, it was April and I was in Sicily, and I went off by myself. Lay down in this field of flowers. Went to sleep. That made me happy. I was happy *then*. What? You say something?"

"I was wondering how you broke your nose."

He rubbed his nose and grinned, as though remembering an experience as happy as the Sicilian nap. "That was a long time ago. I did it boxing. It was when I was in 'Streetcar.' We, some of the guys backstage and me—we used to go down to the boiler room in the theatre and horse around, mix it up. One night, I was mixing it up with this guy and—crack! So I put on my coat and walked around to the nearest hospital—it was off Broadway somewhere. My nose was really busted. They had to give me an anesthetic to set it, and put me to bed. Not that I was sorry. 'Streetcar' had been running about a year and I was sick of it. But my nose healed pretty quick, and I guess I would've been back in the show practically right away if I hadn't done what I did to Irene Selznick." His grin broadened as he mentioned Mrs. Selznick, who had been the producer of the Williams play. "There is one shrewd lady, Irene Selznick. When she wants something, she wants it. And she wanted me back in the play. But when I heard she was coming to the hospital, I went to work with bandages and iodine and mercurochrome, and—Christ!—when she walked in the door, I looked like my head had been cut off. At the least. And *sounded* as though I were dying. 'Oh, Marlon,' she said, 'you poor, *poor* boy!' And I said, 'Don't you worry about anything, Irene. I'll be back in the show tonight!' And she said, 'Don't you dare! We can manage without you for—for—well, a *few* days more.' 'No, no,' I said. 'I'm O.K. I want to work. Tell them I'll be back tonight.' So she said, 'You're in no condition, you poor darling. I *forbid* you to come to the theatre.' So I stayed in the hospital and had myself a ball." (Mrs. Selznick, recalling the incident recently, said, "They didn't set his nose properly at all. Suddenly his face was quite different. Kind of tough. For months afterward, I kept telling him, 'But they've *ruined* your face. You must have your nose broken again and reset.' Luckily for him, he didn't listen to me. Because I honestly think that broken nose made his fortune as far as the movies go. It gave him sex appeal. He was too beautiful before.")

Brando made his first trip to the Coast in 1949, when he went out there to play the leading role in "The Men," a picture dealing with paraplegic war veterans. He was accused, at the time, of uncouth social conduct, and criticized for his black-leather-jacket taste in attire, his choice of motorcycles instead of Jaguars, and his preference for obscure secretaries rather than movie starlets; moreover, Hollywood columnists studded their copy with hostile comments concerning his attitude toward the film business, which he himself summed up soon after he entered it by saying, "The only reason I'm here is that I don't yet have the moral courage to turn down the money." In interviews, he repeatedly stated that becoming "simply a movie actor" was the thing furthest from his thoughts. "I may do a picture now and then," he said on one occasion, "but mostly I intend to work on the stage." However, he followed "The Men," which was more of a *succès d'estime* than a commercial triumph, by re-creating Kowalski in the screen treatment of "A Streetcar Named Desire," and this role, as it had done on Broadway, established him as a star. (Defined practically, a movie star is any performer who can account for a box-office profit regardless of the quality of the enterprise in which he appears; the breed is so scarce that there are fewer than ten actors today who qualify for the title. Brando is one of them; as a box-office draw, male division, he is perhaps outranked only by William Holden.) In the course of the last five years, he has played a Mexican revolutionary ("Viva Zapata!"), Mark Antony ("Julius Caesar"), and a motorcycle-mad juvenile delinquent ("The Wild One"); earned an Academy Award in the role of a dockyard thug ("On the Waterfront"); impersonated Napoleon ("Désirée"); sung and danced his way through the part of an adult delinquent ("Guys and Dolls"); and taken the part of the Okinawan interpreter in "The Teahouse of the August Moon," which, like "Sayonara," his tenth picture, was partly shot on location in Japan. But he has never, except for a brief period in summer stock, returned to the stage. "Why should I?" he asked with apathy when I remarked on this. "The movies have a greater potential. They can be a factor for good. For moral development. At least some can—the kind of movies I want to do." He paused, seemed to listen, as though his statement had been tape-recorded and he were now playing it back. Possibly the sound of it dissatisfied him; at any rate, his jaw started working, as if he were biting down on an unpleasant mouthful. He looked off into space suddenly and demanded, "What's so hot about New York? What's so hot about working for Cheryl Crawford and Robert Whitehead?" Miss Crawford and Whitehead are two of New York's most prominent theatrical producers, neither of whom has had occasion to employ Brando. "Anyway, what would I be in?" he continued. "There aren't any parts for me."

Stack them, and the playscripts offered him in any given season by hopeful Broadway managements might very well rise to a height exceeding the actor's own. Tennessee Williams wanted him for the male lead in each of his last five plays, and the most recent of these, "Orpheus Descending," which was pending production at the time of our talk, had been written expressly as a costarring vehicle for Brando and the Italian actress Anna Magnani. "I can explain very easily why I didn't do 'Orpheus,' " Brando said. "There are beautiful things in it, some of Tennessee's best writing, and the Magnani part is great; she stands for something, you can understand her—and she would wipe me off the stage. The character I was supposed to play, this boy, this Val, he never takes a stand. I didn't really know what he was for or against. Well, you can't act a vacuum. And I told Tennessee. So he kept trying. He rewrote it for me, maybe a couple of times. But—" He shrugged. "Well, I had no intention of walking out on any stage with Magnani. Not in that part. They'd have had to mop me up." Brando mused a moment, and added, "I think—in fact, I'm sure—Tennessee has made a fixed association between me and Kowalski. I mean, we're friends and he knows that as a person I am just the opposite of Kowalski, who was everything I'm against—totally insensitive, crude, cruel. But still Tennessee's image of me is confused with the fact that I played that part. So I don't know if he could write for me in a different color range. The only reason I did 'Guys and Dolls' was to work in a lighter color—yellow. Before that, the brightest color I'd played was red. From red down. Brown. Gray. Black." He crumpled an empty cigarette package and bounced it in his hand like a ball. "There aren't any parts for me on the stage. Nobody writes them. Go on. Tell me a part I could do."

In the absence of vehicles by worthy contemporaries, might he not favor the work of older hands? Several responsible persons who appeared with him in the film had admired his reading of Mark Antony in "Julius Caesar," and thought him equipped, provided the will was there, to essay many of the Mount Everest roles in stage literature—even, possibly, Oedipus.

Brando received reminders of this praise blankly—or, rather, he seemed to be indulging his not-listening habit. But, sensing silence again, he dissolved it: "Of course, movies *date* so quickly. I saw 'Streetcar' the other day and it was already an old-fashioned picture. Still, movies do have the greatest potential. You can say important things to a lot of people. About discrimination and hatred and prejudice. I want to make pictures that explore the themes current in the world today. In terms of entertainment. That's why I've started my own independent production company." He reached out affectionately to finger "A Burst of Vermilion," which will be the first script filmed by Pennebaker Productions— the independent company he has formed.

And did "A Burst of Vermilion" satisfy him as a basis for the kind of lofty aims he proposed?

He mumbled something. Then he mumbled something else. Asked to speak more clearly, he said, "It's a Western."

He was unable to restrain a smile, which expanded into laughter. He rolled on the floor and roared. "Christ, the only thing is, will I ever be able to look my friends in the face again?" Sobering somewhat, he said, "Seriously, though, the first picture *has* to make money. Otherwise, there won't be another. I'm nearly broke. No, no kidding. I spent a year and two hundred thousand dollars of my own money trying to get some writer to come up with a decent script. Which used my ideas. The last one, it was so terrible I said I can do better myself. I'm going to direct it, too."

Produced by, directed by, written by, and starring. Charlie Chaplin has managed this, and gone it one better by composing his own scores. But professionals of wide experience—Orson Welles, for one—have caved in under a lesser number of chores than Brando planned to assume. However, he had a ready answer to my suggestion that he might be loading the cart with more than the donkey could haul. "Take producing," he said. "What does a producer do except cast? I know as much about casting as anyone does, and that's all producing is. Casting." In the trade, one would be hard put to it to find anyone who concurred in this opinion. A good producer, in addition to doing the casting— that is, assembling the writer, the director, the actors, the technical crew, and the other components of his team—must be a diplomat of the emotions, smoothing and soothing, and, above all, must be a skilled mechanic when it comes to dollars-and-cents machinery. "But seriously," said Brando, now excessively sober, " 'Burst' *isn't* just cowboys-and-Indians stuff. It's about this Mexican boy—hatred and discrimination. What happens to a community when those things exist."

"Sayonara," too, has moments when it purports to attack race prejudice, telling, as it does, the tale of an American jet pilot who falls in love with a Japanese music-hall dancer, much to the dismay of his Air Force superiors, and also to the dismay of her employers, though the latter's objection is not the racial unsuitability of her beau but simply that she has a beau at all, for she is a member of an all-girl opera company—based on a real-life counterpart, the Takarazuka Company—whose management promotes a legend that offstage its hundreds of girls lead a conventlike existence, unsullied by male presences of any creed or color. Michener's novel concludes with the lovers forlornly bidding each other *sayonara,* a word meaning farewell. In the film version, however, the word, and consequently the title, has lost significance; here the fadeout reveals the twain of East and West so closely met that they are on their way to the matrimonial bureau. At a press conference that Brando conducted upon his Tokyo arrival, he informed some sixty reporters that he had contracted to do this story because "it strikes very precisely at prejudices that serve to limit our progress toward a peaceful world. Underneath the romance, it attacks prejudices that exist on the part of the Japanese as well as on our part," and also he was doing the film because it would give him the "invaluable opportunity" of working under Joshua Logan, who could teach him "what to do and what not to do."

But time had passed. And now Brando said, with a snort, "Oh, 'Sayonara,' I love it! This wondrous hearts-and-flowers nonsense that was supposed to be a serious picture about Japan. So what difference does it make? I'm just doing it for the money anyway. Money to put in the kick for my own company." He pulled at his lip reflectively and snorted again. "Back in California, I sat through twenty-two hours of script conferences. Logan said to me, 'We welcome any suggestions you have, Marlon. Any changes you want to make, you just make them. If there's anything you don't like—why, rewrite it, Marlon, write it your own way.' " Brando's friends boast that he can imitate anybody after fifteen minutes' observation; to judge by the eerie excellence with which he mimicked Logan's vaguely Southern voice, his sad-eyed, beaming, aquiver-with-enthusiasm manner, they are hardly exaggerating. "*Rewrite?* Man, I rewrote the whole damn script. And now out of that they're going to use maybe eight lines." Another snort. "I give up. I'm going to walk through the part, and that's that. Sometimes I think nobody knows the difference anyway. For the first few days on the set, I tried to act. But then I made an experiment. In this scene, I tried to do everything wrong I could think of. Grimaced and rolled my eyes, put in all kinds of gestures and expressions that had no relation to the part I'm supposed to be playing. What did Logan say? He just said, 'It's wonderful! Print it!' "

A phrase that often occurs in Brando's conversation, "I only mean forty per cent of what I say," is probably applicable here. Logan, a stage and film director of widely recognized and munificently rewarded accomplishments ("Mister

Roberts," "South Pacific," "Picnic"), is a man balanced on enthusiasm, as a bird is balanced on air. A creative person's need to believe in the value of what he is creating is axiomatic; Logan's belief in whatever project he is engaged in approaches euphoric faith, protecting him, as it seems designed to do, from the nibbling nuisance of self-doubt. The joy he took in everything connected with "Sayonara," a film he had been preparing for two years, was so nearly flawless that it did not permit him to conceive that his star's enthusiasm might not equal his own. Far from it. "Marlon," he occasionally announced, "says he's never been as happy with a company as he is with us." And "I've never worked with such an exciting, inventive actor. So pliable. He takes direction beautifully, and yet he always has something to add. He's made up this Southern accent for the part; I never would have thought of it myself, but, well, it's exactly right— it's perfection." Nevertheless, by the night I had dinner in Brando's hotel room Logan had begun to be aware that there was something lacking in his rapport with Brando. He attributed it to the fact that at this juncture, when most of the scenes being filmed concentrated on Japanese background (street crowds, views, spectacles) rather than actors, he had not yet worked with Brando on material that put either of them to much of a test. "That'll come when we get back to California," he said. "The interior stuff, the dramatic scenes. Brando's going to be great—we'll get along fine."

THERE was another reason for Logan's inability, at that point, to give his principal player the kind of attention that might have established closer harmony: he was in serious disharmony with the very Japanese elements that had contributed most to his decision to make the picture. Long infatuated with the Japanese theatre, Logan had counted heavily on interlacing "Sayonara" with authentic sequences taken from the classic Kabuki theatre, the masked Nō dramas, the Bunraku puppet plays; they were to be, so to say, the highbrow-lights of the film. And to this end Logan, along with William Goetz, the producer, had been in negotiation for over a year with Shochiku, the gigantic film company that controls a major part of Japan's live theatrical activities. The ruler of the Shochiku empire is a small, unsmiling eminence in his eighties, known as Mr. Otani; he has a *prénom*, Takejiro, but there are few men alive on such familiar terms that they would presume to use it. The son of a butcher (and therefore, in Japan's Buddhist society, a member of the outcast group), Otani, together with a brother now dead, founded Shochiku and nurtured it to the point where, for the last four years, its payroll has been the biggest of any single company in Japan. A tycoon to rival Kokichi Mikimoto, the late cultured-pearl potentate, Otani casts a cloaklike shadow over the entire Japanese entertainment industry; in addition to having monopolistic control of the classic theatre, he owns the country's most extensive chain of movie houses and music halls, produces many films, and has a hand in radio and television. From Otani's vantage point, any transactions with the Messrs. Logan and Goetz must have looked like very small *sake*. However, he was at first in sympathy with their project, largely because he was impressed by the fervor of Logan's veneration for Kabuki, Nō, and Bunraku, the three unquestionably genuine gems in the old man's crown, and the ones closest to his heart. (According to some specialists, these ancient arts owe their continued health mainly to his generosity.) But Otani is not all philanthropist; when Shochiku's negotiations with the "Sayonara" management were supposedly concluded, the former had given the latter, for a handsome price, franchise to photograph scenes in Tokyo's famed Kabuki Theatre, and for a still handsomer honorarium, permission to make free use of the Kabuki troupe, the Nō plays and players, and the Bunraku puppeteers. Shochiku had also agreed to the participation of its own all-girl opera company—a necessary factor in the production of the film, since the Takarazuka troupe depicted in the novel had deeply resented Michener's "libel" and refused any coöperation whatever. Logan, leaving for Japan, was so elated he could have flown there under his own power. "Otani's given us carte blanche, and this is going to be it, the real thing," he said. "None of that fake Kabuki, that second-rate stuff, but the real thing—something that's never been put in a picture before." And was not destined to be; for, across the wide Pacific, Logan and his associates had a personal Pearl Harbor awaiting them. Otani is seldom seen; he usually appears in the person of bland assistants, and as Logan and Goetz disembarked from their plane, a group of these informed the film-makers that Shochiku had made an error in its financial reckoning; the bill was now much higher than the initial estimate. Producer Goetz objected. Otani, certain that he held the stronger cards (after all, here were these Hollywood people in Japan, accompanied by an expensive cast, an expensive crew, and expensive equipment), replied by raising the tab still more. Whereupon Goetz, himself a businessman as tough as tortoise shell, ended the negotiations and told his director they would have to make up their own Kabuki, Nō, Bunraku, and all-girl opera company from among unattached, free-lancing artists.

Meanwhile, the Tokyo press was publicizing the contretemps. Several papers, the *Japan Times* among them, implied that Shochiku was to be censured for having "acted in bad faith"; others, taking a pro-Shochiku, or perhaps simply an anti-"Sayonara," line, expressed themselves as delighted that the Americans would not have the opportunity to "degrade our finest artistic traditions" by representing them in a film version of "a vulgar novel that is in no way a compliment to the Japanese people." The papers antagonistic to the "Sayonara" project especially relished reporting the fact that Logan had cast a Mexican actor, Ricardo Montalban, in the part of a ranking Kabuki performer (Kabuki is traditionally an all-male enterprise; the grander, more difficult roles are those of women, played by female impersonators, and Montalban's assignment was to portray one such) and then had had the "effrontery" to try

and hire a genuine Kabuki star to substitute for Montalban in the dance sequences, which, one Japanese writer remarked, was much the same as "asking Ethel Barrymore to be a stand-in." All in all, the local press was touchily
interested in what was taking place down in Kyoto—the city, two hundred and
thirty miles south of Tokyo, in which, because of its plethora of historic temples, its photogenic blue hills and misty lakes, and its carefully preserved old-
Japan atmosphere, with elegant geisha quarter and paper-lantern-lighted
streets, the "Sayonara" staff had decided to take most of their location shots.
And, all in all, down in Kyoto the company was encountering as many difficulties as its ill-wishers could have hoped for. In particular, the Americans were
finding it a problem to muster nationals willing to appear in their film—an interesting phenomenon, considering how desirous the average Japanese is of
having himself photographed. True, the movie-makers had rounded up a rag-
bag-picking of Nō players and puppeteers not under contract to Shochiku, but
they were having the devil's own time assembling a presentable all-girl opera
company. (These peculiarly Japanese institutions resemble a sort of single-sex,
innocent-minded Folies-Bergère; oddly, few men attend their performances,
the audiences being, on the whole, as all-girl as the cast.) In the hope of bridg-
ing this gap, the "Sayonara" management had distributed posters advertising
a contest to select "the one hundred most beautiful girls in Japan." The affair,
for which they expected a big turnout, was scheduled to take place at two
o'clock on a Thursday afternoon in the lobby of the Kyoto Hotel. But there
were no winners, because there were no contestants; none showed up.
Producer Goetz, one of the disappointed judges, resorted next, and with some
success, to the expedient of luring ladies out of Kyoto's cabarets and bars.
Kyoto—or, for that matter, any Japanese city—is a barfly's Valhalla.
Proportionately, the number of premises purveying strong liquor is higher
than in New York, and the diversity of these saloons—which range from cozy
bamboo closets accommodating four customers to many-storied, neon-hued
temples of fun featuring, in accordance with the Japanese aptitude for imitation, cha-cha bands and rock 'n' rollers and hillbilly quartets and *chanteuses
existentialistes* and Oriental vocalists who sing Cole Porter songs with
American Negro accents—is extraordinary. But however low or however de-
luxe the establishment may be, one thing remains the same: there is always
on hand a pride of hostesses to cajole and temper the clientele. Great numbers
of these sleekly coifed, smartly costumed, relentlessly festive *jolies jeunes filles*
sit sipping Parfaits d'Amour (a syrupy violet-colored cocktail currently fashionable in these surroundings) while performing the duties of a poor man's
geisha girl; that is, lightening the spirits, without necessarily corrupting the
morals, of weary married men and tense, anxious-to-be-amused bachelors. It
is not unusual to see four to a customer. But when the "Sayonara" officials
began to try to corral them, they had to contend with the circumstance that
nightworkers, such as they were dealing with, have no taste for the early

rising that picture-making demands. To acquire their talents, and see that the ladies were on the set at the proper hour, certain of the film's personnel did everything but distribute engagement rings.

Still another annoyance for the makers of "Sayonara" involved the United States Air Force, whose coöperation was vital, but which, though it had previously promised help, now had fits of shilly-shallying, because it gravely objected to one of the basic elements of the plot—that during the Korean War some American Air Force men who married Japanese were shipped home. This, the Air Force complained, may have been the *practice*, but it was not official Pentagon policy. Given the choice of cutting out the offending premise, and thereby removing a sizable section of the script's entrails, or permitting it to remain, and thereby forfeiting Air Force aid, Logan selected surgery.

Then, there was the problem of Miss Miiko Taka, who had been cast as the Takarazuka dancer capable of arousing Air Force Officer Brando's passion. Having first tried to obtain Audrey Hepburn for the part, and found that Miss Hepburn thought not, Logan had started looking for an "unknown," and had come up with Miss Taka, poised, pleasant, an unassuming, quietly attractive nisei, innocent of acting experience, who stepped out of a clerking job with a Los Angeles travel bureau into what she called "this Cinderella fantasy." Although her acting abilities—as well as those of another "Sayonara" principal, Red Buttons, an ex-burlesque, ex-television jokester, who, like Miss Taka, had had meagre dramatic training—were apparently causing her director some concern, Logan, admirably undaunted, cheerful despite all, was heard to say, "We'll get away with it. As much as possible, I'll just keep their faces straight and their mouths shut. Anyway, Brando, he's going to be so great *he'll* give us what we need." But, as for giving, "I give up," Brando repeated. "I'm going to give up. I'm going to sit back. Enjoy Japan."

AT that moment, in the Miyako, Brando was presented with something Japanese to enjoy: an emissary of the hotel management, who, bowing and beaming and soaping his hands, came into the room saying "Ah, Missa Marron Brando—" and was silent, tongue-tied by the awkwardness of his errand. He'd come to reclaim the "gift" packages of candy and rice cakes that Brando had already opened and avidly sampled. "Ah, Missa Marron Brando, it is a missake. They were meant for derivery in another room. Aporogies! Aporogies!" Laughing, Brando handed the boxes over. The eyes of the emissary, observing the plundered contents, grew grave, though his smile lingered—indeed, became fixed. Here was a predicament to challenge the rightly renowned Japanese politesse. "Ah," he breathed, a solution limbering his smile, "since you rike them very much, you muss keep one box." He handed the rice cakes back. "And they"—apparently the rightful owner—"can have the other. So, now everyone is preased."

It was just as well that he left the rice cakes, for dinner was taking a long while to simmer in the kitchen. When it arrived, I was replying to some inquiries Brando had made about an acquaintance of mine, a young American disciple of Buddhism who for five years had been leading a contemplative, if not entirely unworldly, life in a settlement inside the gates of Kyoto's Nishi-Honganji Temple. The notion of a person's retiring from the world to lead a spiritual existence—an Oriental one, at that—made Brando's face become still, in a dreaming way. He listened with surprising attention to what I could tell him about the young man's present life, and was puzzled—chagrined, really—that it was not all, or at all, a matter of withdrawal, of silence and prayer-sore knees. On the contrary, behind Nishi-Honganji's walls my Buddhist friend occupied three snug, sunny rooms brimming with books and phonograph records; along with attending to his prayers and performing the tea ceremony, he was quite capable of mixing a Martini; he had two servants, and a Chevrolet, in which he often conveyed himself to the local cinemas. And, speaking of that, he had read that Marlon Brando was in town, and longed to meet him. Brando was little amused. The puritan streak in him, which has some width, had been touched; his conception of the truly devout could not encompass anyone as *du monde* as the young man I'd described. "It's like the other day on the set," he said. "We were working in a temple, and one of the monks came over and asked me for an autographed picture. Now, *what* would a monk want with my autograph? A picture of me?"

He stared questioningly at his scattered books, so many of which dealt with mystical subjects. At his first Tokyo press conference, he had told the journalists that he was glad to be back in Japan, because it gave him another chance to "investigate the influence of Buddhism on Japanese thought, the determining cultural factor." The reading matter on display offered proof that he was adhering to this scholarly, if somewhat obscure, program. "What I'd like to do," he presently said, "I'd like to talk to someone who *knows* about these things. Because—" But the explanation was deferred until the maid, who just then skated in balancing vast platters, had set the lacquer table and we had knelt on cushions at either end of it.

"Because," he resumed, wiping his hands on a small steamed towel, the usual preface to any meal served in Japan, "I've seriously considered—I've very *seriously* thought about—throwing the whole thing up. This business of being a successful actor. What's the point, if it doesn't evolve into anything? All right, you're a success. At last you're *accepted,* you're welcome everywhere. But that's it, that's all there is to it, it doesn't lead anywhere. You're just sitting on a pile of candy gathering thick layers of—of *crust.*" He rubbed his chin with the towel, as though removing stale makeup. "Too much success can ruin you as surely as too much failure." Lowering his eyes, he looked without appetite at the food that the maid, to an accompaniment of constant giggles, was distributing on the plates. "Of course," he said hesitantly, as if he were slowly turning over a coin to study the side that seemed to be shinier, "you can't *always* be a failure. Not and survive. Van Gogh! There's an example of what can happen when a person never receives any recognition. You stop relating; it puts you outside. But I guess success does that, too. You know, it took me a long time before I was aware that that's what I was—a big success. I was so absorbed in myself, my own problems, I never looked around, took account. I used to walk in New York, miles and miles, walk in the streets late at night, and never *see* anything. I was never sure about acting, whether that was what I really wanted to do; I'm still not. Then, when I was in 'Streetcar,' and it had been running a couple of months, one night—dimly, dimly—I began to hear this roar. It was like I'd been asleep, and I woke up here sitting on a pile of candy."

Before Brando achieved this sugary perch, he had known the vicissitudes of any unconnected, unfinanced, only partly educated (he has never received a high-school diploma, having been expelled before graduation from Shattuck Military Academy, in Faribault, Minnesota, an institution he refers to as "the asylum") young man who arrives in New York from more rural parts—in his case, Libertyville, Illinois. Living alone in furnished rooms, or sharing underfurnished apartments, he had spent his first city years fluctuating between acting classes and a fly-by-night enrollment in Social Security; Best's once had him on its payroll as an elevator boy. A friend of his, who saw a lot of him in those pre-candy days, corroborates to some extent the rather somnambulistic portrait Brando paints of himself. "He was a brooder, all right," the friend has said. "He seemed to have a built-in hideaway room and was always rushing off to it to worry over himself, and gloat, too, like a miser with his gold. But it wasn't all Gloomsville. When he wanted to, he could rocket right out of himself. He had a wild, kid kind of fun thing. Once, he was living in an old brownstone on Fifty-second Street, near where some of the jazz joints are. He used to go up on the roof and fill paper bags with water and throw them down at the stiffs coming out of the clubs. He had a sign on the wall of his room that said, 'You Ain't Livin' If You Don't Know It.' Yeah, there was always something jumping in that apartment—Marlon playing the bongos, records going, people around, kids from the Actors' Studio, and a lot of down-and-outers he'd picked up. And he could be sweet. He was the least opportunistic person I've ever known. He never gave a damn about anybody who could help him; you might say he went out of his way to avoid them. Sure, part of that—the kind of people he didn't like and the kind he did, both—stemmed from his insecurities, his inferiority feelings. Very few of his friends were his equals—anybody he'd have to *compete* with, if you know what I mean. Mostly they were strays, idolizers, characters who were dependent on him one way or another. The same with the girls he took out. Plain sort of somebody's-secretary-type girls—nice enough but nothing that's going to start a stampede of competitors." (The last-mentioned preference of Brando's was true of him as an adolescent, too, or so his grandmother has said. As she put it, "Marlon always picked on the cross-eyed girls.")

The maid poured *sake* into thimble-size cups, and withdrew. Connoisseurs of this palely pungent rice wine pretend they can discern variations in taste and quality in over fifty brands. But to the novice all *sake* seems to have been brewed in the same vat—a toddy, pleasant at first, cloying afterward, and not likely to echo in your head unless it is devoured by the quart, a habit many of Japan's *bons vivants* have adopted. Brando ignored the *sake* and went straight for his filet. The steak was excellent; Japanese take a just pride in the quality of their beef. The spaghetti, a dish that is very popular in Japan, was not; nor was the rest—the conglomeration of peas, potatoes, beans. Granted that the menu was a queer one, it is on the whole a mistake to order Western-style food in Japan, yet there arise those moments when one retches at the thought of more raw fish, sukiyaki, and rice with seaweed, when, however temptingly they may be prepared and however prettily presented, the unaccustomed stomach revolts at the prospect of eel broth and fried bees and pickled snake and octopus arms.

As we ate, Brando returned to the possibility of renouncing his movie-star status for the satisfactions of a life that "led somewhere." He decided to compromise. "Well, when I get back to Hollywood, what I *will* do, I'll fire my secretary and move into a smaller house," he said. He sighed with relief, as though he'd already cast off old encumbrances and entered upon the simplicities of his new situation. Embroidering on its charms, he said, "I won't have a cook or maid. Just a cleaning woman who comes in twice a week. But"—he frowned, squinted, as if something were blurring the bliss he envisioned—"wherever the house is, it has to have a *fence.* On account of the people with pencils. You don't know what it's like. The people with pencils. I need a fence to keep them out. I suppose there's nothing I can do about the telephone."

"Telephone?"

"It's tapped. Mine is."

"Tapped? Really? By whom?"

He chewed his steak, mumbled. He seemed reluctant to say, yet certain it was so. "When I talk to my friends, we speak French. Or else a kind of bop lingo we made up."

Suddenly, sounds came through the ceiling from the room above us—footfalls, muffled voices like the noise of water flowing through a pipe. "Sh-h-h!" whispered Brando, listening intently, his gaze alerted upward. "Keep your voice down. *They* can hear everything." They, it appeared, were his fellow-actor Red Buttons and Buttons' wife, who occupied the suite overhead. "This place is made of paper," he continued, in tiptoe tones, and with the absorbed countenance of a child lost in a very earnest game—an expression that half explained his secretiveness, the looking-over-his-shoulder, coded-bop-for-telephones facet of his personality that occasionally causes conversation with him to assume a conspiratorial quality, as though one were discussing subversive topics in perilous political territory. Brando said nothing; I said nothing. Nor did Mr. and Mrs. Buttons—not anything distinguishable. During the siege of silence, my host located a letter buried among the dinner plates, and read it while he ate, like a gentleman perusing his breakfast newspaper. Presently, remembering me, he remarked, "From a friend of mine. He's making a documentary, the life of James Dean. He wants me to do the narration. I think I might." He tossed the letter aside and pulled his apple pie, topped with a melting scoop of vanilla ice cream, toward him. "Maybe not, though. I get excited about something, but it never lasts more than seven minutes. Seven minutes exactly. That's my limit. I never know why I get up in the morning." Finishing his pie, he gazed speculatively at my portion; I passed it to him. "But I'm really considering this Dean thing. It could be important."

James Dean, the young motion-picture actor killed in a car accident in 1955, was promoted throughout his phosphorescent career as the All-American "mixed-up kid," the symbol of misunderstood hot-rodding youth with a switch-blade approach to life's little problems. When he died, an expensive film in which he had starred, "Giant," had yet to be released, and the picture's press agents, seeking to offset any ill effects that Dean's demise might have on the commercial prospects of their product, succeeded by "glamorizing" the tragedy, and, in ironic consequence, created a Dean legend of rather necrophilic appeal. Though Brando was seven years older than Dean, and professionally more secure, the two actors came to be associated in the collective movie-fan mind. Many critics reviewing Dean's first film, "East of Eden," remarked on the well-nigh plagiaristic resemblance between his acting mannerisms and Brando's. Off-screen, too, Dean appeared to be practicing the sincerest form of flattery; like Brando, he tore around on motorcycles, played bongo drums, dressed the role of rowdy, spouted an intellectual rigmarole, cultivated a cranky, colorful newspaper personality that mingled, to a skillfully potent degree, plain bad boy and sensitive sphinx.

"No, Dean was never a friend of mine," said Brando, in response to a question that he seemed surprised to have been asked. "That's not why I may do the narration job. I hardly knew him. But he had an *idée fixe* about me. Whatever I did he did. He was always trying to get close to me. He used to call up." Brando lifted an imaginary telephone, put it to his ear with a cunning, eavesdropper's smile. "I'd listen to him talking to the answering service, asking for me, leaving messages. But I never spoke up. I never called him back. No, when I—"

The scene was interrupted by the ringing of a real telephone. "Yeah?" he said, picking it up. "Speaking. From where? . . . Manila? . . . Well, I don't know anybody in Manila. Tell them I'm not here. No, when I finally met Dean," he said, hanging up, "it was at a party. Where he was throwing himself around, acting the madman. So I spoke to him. I took him aside and asked him didn't he know he was sick? That he needed help?" The memory evoked an intensified version of Brando's familiar look of enlightened compassion. "He listened to me. He knew he was sick. I gave him the name of an analyst, and he went. And at least his *work* improved. Toward the end, I think he was beginning to find his own way as an actor. But this glorifying of Dean is all wrong. That's why I believe the documentary could be important. To show he wasn't a hero; show what he really was—just a lost boy trying to find himself. That ought to be done, and I'd like to do it—maybe as a kind of expiation for some of my own sins. Like making 'The Wild One.' " He was referring to the strange film in which he was presented as the Führer of a tribe of Fascistlike delinquents. "But. Who knows? Seven minutes is my limit."

From Dean the conversation turned to other actors, and I asked which ones, specifically, Brando respected. He pondered; though his lips shaped several names, he seemed to have second thoughts about pronouncing them. I suggested a few candidates—Laurence Olivier, John Gielgud, Montgomery Clift, Gérard Philipe, Jean-Louis Barrault. "Yes," he said, at last coming alive, "Philipe is a good actor. So is Barrault. Christ, what a wonderful picture that was—'Les Enfants du Paradis'! Maybe the best movie ever made. You know, that's the only time I ever fell in love with an actress, somebody on the screen. I was mad about Arletty." The Parisian star Arletty is well remembered by international audiences for the witty, womanly allure she brought to the heroine's part in Barrault's celebrated film. "I mean, I was really in *love* with her. My first trip to Paris, the thing I did right away, I asked to meet Arletty. I went to see her as though I were going to a shrine. My ideal woman. Wow!" He slapped the table. "Was that a mistake, was that a disillusionment! She was a tough article."

The maid came to clear the table; *en passant*, she gave Brando's shoulder a sisterly pat, rewarding him, I took it, for the cleaned-off sparkle of his plates. He again collapsed on the floor, stuffing a pillow under his head. "I'll tell you," he said, "Spencer Tracy is the kind of actor I like to watch. The way he holds back, *holds* back—then darts in to make his point, darts back. Tracy, Muni, Cary Grant. They know what they're doing. You can learn something from them."

Brando began to weave his fingers in the air, as though hoping that gestures would describe what he could not precisely articulate. "Acting is such a tenuous thing," he said. "A fragile, shy thing that a sensitive director can help lure out of you. Now, in movie-acting the important, the *sensitive* moment comes around the third take of a scene; by then you just need a whisper from the director to crystallize it for you. Gadge"—he was using Elia Kazan's nickname—"can usually do it. He's wonderful with actors."

Another actor, I suppose, would have understood at once what Brando was saying, but I found him difficult to follow. "It's what happens inside you on the third take," he said, with a careful emphasis that did not lessen my incomprehension. One of the most memorable film scenes Brando has played occurs in the Kazan-directed "On the Waterfront"; it is the car-ride scene in which Rod Steiger, as the racketeering brother, confesses he is leading Brando into a death trap. I asked if he could use the episode as an example, and tell me how his theory of the "sensitive moment" applied to it.

"Yes. Well, no. Well, let's see." He puckered his eyes, made a humming noise. "That was a seven-take scene, and I didn't like the way it was written. Lot of dissension going on there. I was fed up with the whole picture. All the location stuff was in New Jersey, and it was the dead of winter—the cold, Christ! And I was having problems at the time. Woman trouble. That scene. Let me see. There were seven takes because Rod Steiger couldn't stop crying. He's one of those actors loves to cry. We kept doing it over and over. But I can't remember just when, just how it crystallized itself for me. The first time I saw 'Waterfront,' in a projection room with Gadge, I thought it was so terrible I walked out without even speaking to him."

A month earlier, a friend of Brando's had told me, "Marlon always turns against whatever he's working on. Some element of it. Either the script or the director or somebody in the cast. Not always because of anything very rational—just because it seems to comfort him to be dissatisfied, let off steam about something. It's part of his pattern. Take 'Sayonara.' A dollar gets you ten he'll develop a hoss on it somewhere along the line. A hoss on Logan, maybe. Maybe against Japan—the whole damn country. He loves Japan *now*. But with Marlon you never know from one minute to the next."

I was wondering whether I might mention this supposed "pattern" to Brando, ask if he considered it a valid observation about himself. But it was as though he had anticipated the question. "I ought to keep my mouth shut," he said. "Around here, around 'Sayonara,' I've let a few people know the way I feel. But I don't always feel the same way two days running."

IT was ten-thirty, and Murray called on the dot.

"I went out to dinner with the girls," he told Brando, his telephone voice so audible that I could hear it, too; it spoke above a blend of dance-band rumble and barroom roar. Obviously he was patronizing not one of the more traditional, cat-quiet Kyoto restaurants but, rather, a place where the customers wore shoes. "We're just finishing. How about it? You through?"

Brando looked at me thoughtfully, and I, in turn, at my coat. But he said, "We're still yakking. Call me back in an hour."

"O.K. Well . . . O.K. Listen. Miiko's here. She wants to know did you get the flowers she sent you?"

Brando's eyes lazily rolled toward the glassed-in sun porch, where a bowl of asters was centered on a round bamboo table. "Uh-huh. Tell her thanks very much."

"Tell her yourself. She's right here."

"No! Hey, wait a minute! Christ, *that's* not how you do it." But the protest came too late. Murray had already put down the phone, and Brando, reiterating "*That's* not how you do it," blushed and squirmed like an embarrassed boy.

The next voice to emanate from the receiver belonged to his "Sayonara" leading lady, Miss Miiko Taka. She asked about his health.

"Better, thanks. I ate the bad end of an oyster, that's all. Miiko? . . . Miiko, that was very *sweet* of you to send me the flowers. They're beautiful. I'm looking at them right now. Asters," he continued, as though shyly venturing a line of verse, "are my favorite flowers. . . ."

I retired to the sun porch, leaving Brando and Miss Taka to conduct their conversation in stricter seclusion. Below the windows, the hotel garden, with its ultra-simple and *soigné* arrangements of rock and tree, floated in the mists that crawl off Kyoto's waterways—for it *is* a watery city, crisscrossed with shallow rivers and cascading canals, dotted with pools as still as coiled snakes and mirthful little waterfalls that sound like Japanese girls giggling. Once the imperial capital and now the country's cultural museum, such an aesthetic treasure house that American bombers let it go unmolested during the war, Kyoto is surrounded by water, too; beyond the city's containing hills, thin roads run like causeways across the reflecting silver of flooded rice fields. That evening, despite the gliding mists, the blue encircling hills were discernible against the night, for the upper air had purity; a sky was there, stars were in it, and a scrap of moon. Some portions of the town could be seen. Nearest was a neighborhood of curving roofs, the dark façades of aristocratic houses fashioned from silky wood yet austere, northern, as secret-looking as any stone Siena palace. How brilliant they made the street lamps appear, and the doorway lanterns casting keen kimono colors—pink and orange, lemon and red. Farther away was a modern flatness—wide avenues and neon, a skyscraper of raw concrete that seemed less enduring, more perishable, than the papery dwellings stooping around it.

Brando completed his call. Approaching the sun porch, he looked at me looking at the view. He said, "Have you been to Nara? Pretty interesting."

I had, and yes, it was. "Ancient, old-time Nara," as a local cicerone unfailingly referred to it, is an hour's drive from Kyoto—a postcard town set in a show-place park. Here is the apotheosis of the Japanese genius for hypnotizing nature into unnatural behavior. The great shrine-infested park is a green salon where sheep graze, and herds of tame deer wander under trim pine trees and, like Venetian pigeons, gladly pose with honeymooning couples; where children yank the beards of unretaliating goats; where old men wearing black capes with mink collars squat on the shores of lotus-quilted lakes and, by clapping their hands, summon swarms of fish, speckled and scarlet carp, fat, thick as trout, who allow their snouts to be tickled, then gobble the crumbs that the old men sprinkle. That this serpentless Eden should strongly appeal to Brando was a bit surprising. With his liberal taste for the off-trail and not-overly-trammelled, one might have thought he would be unresponsive to so ruly, subjugated a landscape. Then, as though apropos of Nara, he said, "Well, I'd like to be married. I want to have children." It was not, perhaps, the non sequitur it seemed; the gentle safety of Nara just could, by the association of ideas, suggest marriage, a family.

"You've got to have love," he said. "There's no other reason for living. Men are no different from mice. They're born to perform the same function. Procreate." ("Marlon," to quote his friend Elia Kazan, "is one of the gentlest people I've ever known. Possibly the gentlest." Kazan's remark had meaning

when one observed Brando in the company of children. As far as he was concerned, Japan's youngest generation—lovely, lively, cherry-cheeked kids with
bowlegs and bristling bangs—was always welcome to lark around the
"Sayonara" sets. He was good with the children, at ease, playful, appreciative;
he seemed, indeed, their emotional contemporary, a co-conspirator. Moreover,
the condoling expression, the slight look of dispensing charitable compassion,
peculiar to his contemplation of some adults was absent from his eyes when he
looked at a child.)

Touching Miss Taka's floral offering, he went on, "What other reason is there
for living? Except love? That has been my main trouble. My inability to love anyone." He turned back into the lighted room, stood there as though hunting
something—a cigarette? He picked up a pack. Empty. He slapped at the pockets
of trousers and jackets lying here and there. Brando's wardrobe no longer
smacks of the street gang; as a dresser, he has graduated, or gone back, into an
earlier style of outlaw chic, that of the prohibition sharpie—black snap-brim
hats, striped suits, and sombre-hued George Raft shirts with pastel ties.
Cigarettes were found; inhaling, he slumped on the pallet bed. Beads of sweat
ringed his mouth. The electric heater hummed. The room was tropical; one
could have grown orchids. Overhead, Mr. and Mrs. Buttons were again bumping about, but Brando appeared to have lost interest in them. He was smoking,
thinking. Then, picking up the stitch of his thought, he said, "I can't. Love anyone. I can't trust anyone enough to give myself to them. But I'm ready. I want
it. And I may, I'm almost on the point, I've really got to . . ." His eyes narrowed,
but his tone, far from being intense, was indifferent, dully objective, as though
he were discussing some character in a play—a part he was weary of portray-
ing yet was trapped in by contract. "Because—well, what else is there? That's
all it's all about. To love somebody."

(At this time, Brando was, of course, a bachelor, who had, upon occasion, indulged in engagements of a quasi-official character—once to an aspiring authoress and actress, by name Miss Blossom Plumb, and again, with more public
attention, to Mlle. Josanne Mariani-Bérenger, a French fisherman's daughter.
But in neither instance were banns ever posted. One day last month, however,
in a sudden and somewhat secret ceremony at Eagle Rock, California, Brando
was married to a dark, sari-swathed young minor actress who called herself
Anna Kashfi. According to conflicting press reports, either she was a
Darjeeling-born Buddhist of the purest Indian parentage or she was the
Calcutta-born daughter of an English couple named O'Callaghan, now living
in Wales. Brando has not yet done anything to clear up the mystery.)

"Anyway, I have *friends*. No. No, I don't," he said, verbally shadowboxing.
"Oh, sure I do," he decided, smoothing the sweat on his upper lip. "I have a
great many friends. Some I don't hold out on. I let them know what's happening. You have to trust somebody. Well, not all the way. There's nobody I rely on
to tell *me* what to do."

I asked if that included professional advisers. For instance, it was my under-standing that Brando very much depended on the guidance of Jay Kanter, a young man on the staff of the Music Corporation of America, which is the agency that represents him. "Oh, Jay," Brando said now. "Jay does what I tell *him* to. I'm alone like that."

The telephone sounded. An hour seemed to have passed, for it was Murray again. "Yeah, still yakking," Brando told him. "Look, let *me* call *you*. . . . Oh, in an hour or so. You be back in your room? . . . O.K."

He hung up, and said, "Nice guy. He wants to be a director—eventually. I was saying something, though. We were talking about friends. Do you know how I make a friend?" He leaned a little toward me, as though he had an amusing se-cret to impart. "I go about it very gently. I circle around and around. I circle. Then, gradually, I come nearer. Then I reach out and touch them—ah, so gen-tly . . ." His fingers stretched forward like insect feelers and grazed my arm. "Then," he said, one eye half shut, the other, à la Rasputin, mesmerically wide and shining, "I draw back. Wait awhile. Make them wonder. At just the right moment, I move in again. Touch them. Circle." Now his hand, broad and blunt-fingered, travelled in a rotating pattern, as though it held a rope with which he was binding an invisible presence. "They don't know what's happening. Before they realize it, they're all entangled, involved. I have them. And suddenly, sometimes, I'm all *they* have. A lot of them, you see, are people who don't fit anywhere; they're not accepted, they've been hurt, crippled one way or an-other. But I want to help them, and they can focus on me; I'm the duke. Sort of the duke of my domain."

(A past tenant on the ducal preserve, describing its seigneur and his subjects, has said, "It's as though Marlon lived in a house where the doors are never locked. When he lived in New York, the door always *was* open. Anybody could come in, whether Marlon was there or not, and everybody did. You'd arrive and there would be ten, fifteen characters wandering around. It was strange, be-cause nobody seemed to really know anybody else. They were just there, like people in a bus station. Some type asleep in a chair. People reading the tabs. A girl dancing by herself. Or painting her toenails. A comedian trying out his night-club act. Off in a corner, there'd be a chess game going. And drums—bang, boom, bang, boom! But there was never any drinking—nothing like that. Once in a while, somebody would say, 'Let's go down to the corner for an ice-cream soda.' Now, in all this Marlon was the common denominator, the only connecting link. He'd move around the room drawing individuals aside and talking to them alone. If you've noticed, Marlon can't, *won't*, talk to two people simultaneously. He'll never take part in a *group* conversation. It always has to be a cozy tête-à-tête—one person at a time. Which is necessary, I sup-pose, if you use the same kind of charm on everyone. But even when you know that's what he's doing, it doesn't matter. Because when *your* turn comes, he makes you feel you're the only person in the room. In the world. Makes you feel that you're under his protection and that your troubles and moods concern him deeply. You have to believe it; more than anyone I've known, he radiates *sincerity*. Afterward, you may ask yourself, 'Is it an act?' If so, what's the point? What have you got to give him? Nothing except—and this *is* the point—affection. Affection that lends him authority over you. I sometimes think Marlon is like an orphan who later on in life tries to compensate by becoming the kindly head of a huge orphanage. But even outside this institution he wants everybody to love him." Although there exist a score of witnesses who might well contradict the last opinion, Brando himself is credited with having once informed an interviewer, "I can walk into a room where there are a hundred people—if there is *one* person in that room who doesn't like me, I know it and have to get out." As a footnote, it should be added that within the clique over which Brando presides he is esteemed as an intellectual father, as well as an emotional big brother. The person who probably knows him best, the comedian Wally Cox, declares him to be "a creative philosopher, a very deep thinker," and adds, "He's a real liberating force for his friends.")

BRANDO yawned; it had got to be a quarter past one. In less than five hours he would have to be showered, shaved, breakfasted, on the set, and ready for a makeup man to paint his pale face the mulatto tint that Technicolor requires.

"Let's have another cigarette," he said as I made a move to put on my coat.

"Don't you think you should go to sleep?"

"That just means getting up. Most mornings, I don't know why I do. I can't face it." He looked at the telephone, as though remembering his promise to call Murray. "Anyway, I may work later on. You want something to drink?"

Outside, the stars had darkened and it had started to drizzle, so the prospect of a nightcap was pleasing, especially if I should have to return on foot to my own hotel, which was a mile distant from the Miyako. I poured some vodka; Brando declined to join me. However, he subsequently reached for my glass, sipped from it, set it down between us, and suddenly said, in an offhand way that nonetheless conveyed feeling, "My mother. She broke apart like a piece of porcelain."

I had often heard friends of Brando's say, "Marlon worshipped his mother." But prior to 1947, and the première of "A Streetcar Named Desire," few, perhaps none, of the young actor's circle had met either of his parents; they knew nothing of his background except what he chose to tell them. "Marlon always gave a very colorful picture of home life back in Illinois," one of his acquaintances told me. "When we heard that his family were coming to New York for the opening of 'Streetcar,' everybody was very curious. We didn't know what to expect. On opening night, Irene Selznick gave a big party at '21.' Marlon came with his mother and father. Well, you can't imagine two more attractive people. Tall, handsome, charming as they could be. What impressed me—I think it amazed everyone—was Marlon's attitude toward them. In their presence, he wasn't the lad we knew. He was a model son. Reticent, respectful, very polite, considerate in every way."

Born in Omaha, Nebraska, where his father was a salesman of limestone products, Brando, the family's third child and only son, was soon taken to live in Libertyville, Illinois. There the Brandos settled down in a rambling house in a countrified neighborhood; at least, there was enough country around the house to allow the Brandos to keep geese and hens and rabbits, a horse, a Great Dane, twenty-eight cats, and a cow. Milking the cow was the daily chore that belonged to Bud, as Marlon was then nicknamed. Bud seems to have been an extroverted and competitive boy. Everyone who came within range of him was at once forced into some variety of contest: Who can eat fastest? Hold his breath longest? Tell the tallest tale? Bud was rebellious, too; rain or shine, he ran away from home every Sunday. But he and his two sisters, Frances and Jocelyn, were devotedly close to their mother. Many years later, Stella Adler, Brando's former drama coach, described Mrs. Brando, who died in 1954, as "a very beautiful, a heavenly, lost, girlish creature." Always, wherever she lived, Mrs. Brando had played leads in the productions of local dramatic societies, and always she had longed for a more brightly footlighted world than her surroundings provided. These yearnings inspired her children. Frances took to painting; Jocelyn, who is at present a professional actress, interested herself in the theatre. Bud, too, had inherited his mother's theatrical inclinations, but at seventeen he announced a wish to study for the ministry. (Then, as now, Brando searched for a belief. As one Brando disciple once summed it up, "He needs to find something in life, something in himself, that is permanently true, and he needs to lay down his life for it. For such an intense personality, nothing less than that will do.") Talked out of his clerical ambitions, expelled from school, rejected for military service in 1942 because of a trick knee, Brando packed up and came to New York. Whereupon Bud, the plump, towheaded, unhappy adolescent, exits, and the man-sized and very gifted Marlon emerges.

Brando has not forgotten Bud. When he speaks of the boy he was, the boy seems to inhabit him, as if time had done little to separate the man from the hurt, desiring child. "My father was indifferent to me," he said. "Nothing I could do interested him, or pleased him. I've accepted that now. We're friends now. We get along." Over the past ten years, the elder Brando has supervised his son's financial affairs; in addition to Pennebaker Productions, of which Mr. Brando, Sr., is an employee, they have been associated in a number of ventures, including a Nebraska grain-and-cattle ranch, in which a large percentage of the younger Brando's earnings was invested. "But my mother was everything to me. A whole world. I tried so hard. I used to come home from school . . ." He hesitated, as though waiting for me to picture him: Bud, books under his arm, scuffling his way along an afternoon street. "There wouldn't be anybody home. Nothing in the icebox." More lantern slides: empty rooms, a kitchen. "Then the telephone would ring. Somebody calling from some bar. And they'd say, 'We've got a lady down here. You better come get her.' " Suddenly, Brando was silent. In the silence the picture faded, or, rather, became fixed: Bud at the telephone. At last, the image moved again, leaped forward in time. Bud is eighteen, and: "I thought if she loved me enough, trusted me enough, I thought, then we can be together, in New York; we'll live together and I'll take care of her. Once, later on, that really happened. She left my father and came to live with me. In New York, when I was in a play. I tried so hard. But my love wasn't enough. She couldn't care enough. She went back. And one day"—the flatness of his voice grew flatter, yet the emotional pitch ascended until one could discern, like a sound within a sound, a wounded bewilderment—"I didn't care any more. She was there. In a room. Holding on to me. And I let her fall. Because I couldn't take it any more—watch her breaking apart, in front of me, like a piece of porcelain. I stepped right over her. I walked right out. I was indifferent. Since then, I've been indifferent."

The telephone was signalling. Its racket seemed to rouse him from a daze; he stared about, as though he'd wakened in an unknown room, then smiled wryly, then whispered, "Damn, damn, damn," as his hand lurched toward the telephone. "Sorry," he told Murray. "I was just going to call you. . . . No, he's leaving now. But look, man, let's call it off tonight. It's after one. It's nearly two o'clock. . . . Yeah. . . . Sure thing. Tomorrow."

Meanwhile, I'd put on my overcoat, and was waiting to say good night. He walked me to the door, where I put on my shoes. "Well, *sayonara*," he mockingly bade me. "Tell them at the desk to get you a taxi." Then, as I walked down the corridor, he called, "And listen! Don't pay too much attention to what I say. I don't always feel the same way."

IN a sense, this was not my last sight of him that evening. Downstairs, the Miyako's lobby was deserted. There was no one at the desk, nor, outside, were there any taxis in view. Even at high noon, the fancy crochet of Kyoto's streets had played me tricks; still, I set off through the marrow-chilling drizzle in what I hoped was a homeward direction. I'd never before been abroad so late in the city. It was quite a contrast to daytime, when the central parts of the town, caroused by crowds of fiesta massiveness, jangle like the inside of a *pachinko* parlor, or to early evening—Kyoto's most exotic hours, for then, like night flowers, lanterns wreathe the side streets, and resplendent geishas, with their white ceramic faces and their ballooning lacquered wigs strewn with silver bells, their hobbled wiggle-walk, hurry among the shadows toward meticulously tasteful revelries. But at two in the morning these exquisite grotesques are gone, the cabarets are shuttered; only cats remained to keep me company, and drunks and red-light ladies, the inevitable old beggar-bundles in doorways, and, briefly, a ragged street musician who followed me playing on a flute a medieval music. I had trudged far more than a mile when, at last, one of a hundred alleys led to familiar ground—the main-street district of department stores and cinemas. It was then that I saw Brando. Sixty feet tall, with a head as huge as the greatest Buddha's, there he was, in comic-paper colors, on a sign above a theatre that advertised "The Teahouse of the August Moon." Rather Buddha-like, too, was his pose, for he was depicted in a squatting position, a serene smile on a face that glistened in the rain and the light of a street lamp. A deity, yes; but, more than that, really, just a young man sitting on a pile of candy.

(1957)

A PRYOR LOVE

SKIN FLICK

WINTER, 1973. Late afternoon: the entr'acte between dusk and darkness, when the people who conduct their business in the street—numbers runners in gray chesterfields, out-of-work barmaids playing the dozens, adolescents cultivating their cigarette jones and lust, small-time hustlers selling "authentic" gold wristwatches that are platinum bright—look for a place to roost and to drink in the day's sin. Young black guy, looks like the comedian Richard Pryor, walks into one of his hangouts, Opal's Silver Spoon Café. A greasy dive with an R & B jukebox, it could be in Detroit or in New York, could be anywhere. Opal's has a proprietor—Opal, a young and wise black woman, who looks like the comedian Lily Tomlin—and a little bell over the door that goes *tink-a-link,* announcing all the handouts and gimmes who come to sit at Opal's counter and talk about how needy their respective asses are.

Black guy sits at the counter, and Opal offers him some potato soup—"something nourishing," she says. Black guy has moist, on-the-verge-of-lying-or-crying eyes and a raggedy Afro. He wears a green fatigue jacket, the kind of jacket brothers brought home from 'Nam, which guys like this guy continue to wear long after they've returned home, too shell-shocked or stoned to care much about their haberdashery. Juke—that's the black guy's name—is Opal's baby, flopping about in all them narcotics he's trying to get off of by taking that methadone, which Juke and Opal pronounce "metha*don*"—the way two old-timey Southerners would, the way Juke and Opal's elders might have, if they knew what that shit was, or was for.

Juke and Opal express their feelings for each other, their shared view of the world, in a lyrical language, a colored people's language, which tries to atomize their anger and their depression. Sometimes their anger is wry: Opal is tired of hearing about Juke's efforts to get a job, and tells him so. "Hand me that jive about job training," she says. "You trained, all right. You highly skilled at not working." But that's not entirely true. Juke has submitted himself to the rigors of "rehabilitation." "I was down there for about three weeks, at that place, working," Juke says. "Had on a suit, tie. Shaving. Acting crazy. Looked just like a fool in the circus." Pause. "And I'm fed up with it." Pause. "Now I know how to do a job that don't know how to be done no more." Opal's face fills with sadness. Looking at her face can fill your mind with sadness. She says, "For real?" It's a rhetorical question that black people have always asked each other or themselves when they're handed more hopelessness: Is this for real?

Night is beginning to spread all over Juke and Opal's street; it is the color of a thousand secrets combined. The bell rings, and a delivery man comes in, carting pies. Juke decides that everyone should chill out—he'll play the jukebox, they'll all get down. Al Green singing "Let's Stay Together" makes the pie man and Juke do a little finger-snapping, a little jive. Opal hesitates, says, "Naw," but then dances anyway, and her shyness is just part of the fabric of the day, as uneventful as the delivery man leaving to finish up his rounds, or Opal and Juke standing alone in this little restaurant, a society unto themselves.

The doorbell's tiny peal. Two white people—a man and a woman, social workers—enter Opal's. Youngish, trenchcoated. And the minute the white people enter, something terrible happens, from an aesthetic point of view. They alienate everything. They fracture our suspended disbelief. They interrupt our identification with the protagonists of the TV show we've been watching, which becomes TV only when those social workers start hassling our Juke, our Opal, equal halves of the same resilient black body. When we see those white people, we start thinking about things like credits, and remember that this is a television play, after all, written by the brilliant Jane Wagner, and played with astonishing alacrity and compassion by Richard Pryor and Lily Tomlin on "Lily," Tomlin's second variety special, which aired on CBS in 1973, and which remains, a little over a quarter of a century later, the most profound meditation on race and class that I have ever seen on a major network.

"We're doing some community research and we'd like to ask you a few questions," the white woman social worker declares as soon as she enters Opal's. Juke and Opal are more than familiar with this line of inquiry, which presumes that people like them are always available for questioning—servants of the liberal cause. "I wonder if you can tell me, have you ever been addicted to drugs?" the woman asks Juke.

Pryor-as-Juke responds instantly. "Yeah, I been addicted," he says. "I'm addicted right now—don't write it down, man, be cool, it's not for the public. I mean, what I go through is private." He is incapable of making "Fuck you" his first response—or even his first thought. Being black has taught him how to allow white people their innocence. For black people, being around white people is sometimes like taking care of babies you don't like, babies who throw up on you again and again, but whom you cannot punish, because they're babies. Eventually, you direct that anger at yourself—it has nowhere else to go.

Juke tries to turn the questioning around a little, through humor, which is part of his pathos. "*I* have some questions," he tells the community researchers, then tries to approximate their straight, white tone: "Who's Pigmeat Markham's Mama?" he asks. "Wilt Chamberlain the tallest colored chap you ever saw?"

When the white people have left and Juke is about to leave, wrapped in his thin jacket, he turns to Opal and says, "You sweet. You a sweet woman. . . . I'll think aboutcha." His eyes are wide with love and need, and maybe fear or madness. "Be glad when it's spring," he says to Opal. Pause. "Flower!"

"Lily" was never shown again on network television, which is not surprising, given that part of its radicalism is based on the fact that it features a white female star who tries to embody a black woman while communicating with a black man about substantive emotional matters, and who never wears anything as theatrically simple as blackface to do it; Tomlin plays Opal in whiteface, as it were. Nevertheless, "Juke and Opal," which lasts all of nine minutes and twenty-five seconds, and which aired in the same season in which "Hawaii Five-O," "The Waltons," and "Ironside" were among television's top-rated shows, remains historically significant for reasons other than the skin game.

As Juke, Richard Pryor gave one of his relatively few great performances in a project that he had not written or directed. He made use of the poignancy that marks all of his great comedic and dramatic performances, and of the vulnerability—the pathos cradling his sharp wit—that had seduced people into loving him in the first place. Tomlin kept Pryor on the show over objections from certain of the network's executives, and it may have been her belief in him as a performer, combined with the high standards she set for herself and others, that spurred on the competitive-minded Pryor. His language in this scene feels improvised, confessional, and so internalized that it's practically nonverbal: not unlike the best of Pryor's own writing—the stories he tells when he talks shit into a microphone, doing standup. And as he sits at Opal's counter we can see him falling in love with Tomlin's passion for her work, recognizing it as the passion he feels when he peoples the stage with characters who might love him as much as Tomlin-as-Opal seems to now.

ALTHOUGH Richard Pryor was more or less forced to retire in 1994, eight years after he discovered that he had multiple sclerosis ("It's the stuff God hits your ass with when he doesn't want to kill ya—just slow ya down," he told *Entertainment Weekly* in 1993), his work as a comedian, a writer, an actor, and a director amounts to a significant chapter not only in late-twentieth-century American comedy but in American entertainment in general. Pryor is best known now for his work in the lackadaisical Gene Wilder buddy movies or for

abominations like "The Toy." But far more important was the prescient commentary on the issues of race and sex in America that he presented through
standup and sketches like "Juke and Opal"—the heartfelt and acute social observation, the comedy that littered the stage with the trash of the quotidian as it
was sifted through his harsh and poetic imagination, and that changed the very
definition of the word "entertainment," particularly for a black entertainer.

The subject of blackness has taken a strange and unsatisfying journey
through American thought: first, because blackness has almost always had to
explain itself to a largely white audience in order to be heard, and, second, because it has generally been assumed to have only one story to tell—a story of
oppression that plays on liberal guilt. The writers behind the collective modern
ur-text of blackness—James Baldwin, Richard Wright, and Ralph Ellison—all
performed some variation on the theme. Angry but distanced, their rage blan-
keted by charm, they lived and wrote to be liked. Ultimately, whether they
wanted to or not, they in some way embodied the readers who appreciated
them most—white liberals.

Richard Pryor was the first black American spoken-word artist to avoid this.
Although he reprised the history of black American comedy—picking what he
wanted from the work of great storytellers like Bert Williams, Redd Foxx,
Moms Mabley, Nipsey Russell, LaWanda Page, and Flip Wilson—he also
pushed everything one step further. Instead of adapting to the white perspective, he forced white audiences to follow him into his own experience. Pryor
didn't manipulate his audiences' white guilt or their black moral outrage. If he
played the race card, it was only to show how funny he looked when he tried to
shuffle the deck. And as he made blackness an acknowledged part of the
American atmosphere he also brought the issue of interracial love into the
country's discourse. In a culture whose successful male Negro authors wrote
about interracial sex with a combination of reverence and disgust, Pryor's
gleeful, "fuck it" attitude had an effect on the general population which
Wright's "Native Son" or Baldwin's "Another Country" had not had. His best
work showed us that black men like him and the white women they loved were
united in their disenfranchisement; in his life and onstage, he performed the
great, largely unspoken story of America.

"I love Lily," Pryor said in a *Rolling Stone* interview with David Felton, in 1974,
after "Juke and Opal" had aired and he and Tomlin had moved on to other
things. "I have a thing about her, a little crush. . . . I get in awe of her. I'd seen
her on 'Laugh-In' and shit, and something about her is very sensual, isn't it?"

Sensuality implies a certain physical abandonment, an acknowledgment of
the emotional mess that oozes out between the seams that hold our public selves
together—and an understanding of the metaphors that illustrate that disjunction. (One of Tomlin's early audition techniques was to tap-dance with taps taped

to the soles of her bare feet.) It is difficult to find that human untidiness—what Pryor called "the madness" of everyday life—in the formulaic work now being done by the performers who ostensibly work in the same vein as Pryor and Tomlin. Compare the rawness of the four episodes of a television show that Pryor co-wrote and starred in for NBC in 1977 with any contemporary HBO show by Tracey Ullman (who needs blackface to play a black woman): the first Pryor special opens with a closeup of his face as he announces that he has not had to compromise himself to appear on a network-sponsored show. The camera then pulls back to reveal Pryor seemingly nude but with his genitalia missing.

Pryor's art defies the very definition of the word "order." He based his style on digressions and riffs—the monologue as jam session. He reinvented standup, which until he developed his signature style, in 1971, had consisted largely of borscht-belt-style male comedians telling tales in the Jewish vernacular, regardless of their own religion or background. Pryor managed to make blacks interesting to audiences that were used to responding to a liberal Jewish sensibility—and, unlike some of his colored colleagues, he did so without "becoming" Jewish himself. (Dick Gregory, for example, was a political comedian in the tradition of Mort Sahl; Bill Cosby was a droll Jack Benny.) At the height of his career, Pryor never spoke purely in the complaint mode. He was often baffled by life's complexities, but he rarely told my-wife-made-me-sleep-on-the-sofa jokes or did "bits" whose sole purpose was to "kill" an audience with a boffo punch line. Instead, he talked about characters—black street people, mostly. Because the life rhythm of a black junkie, say, implies a certain drift, Pryor's stories did not have badda-bing conclusions. Instead, they were encapsulated in a physical attitude: each character was represented in Pryor's walk, in his gestures—which always contained a kind of vicarious wonder at the lives he was enacting. Take, for instance, his sketch of a wino in Peoria, Illinois—Pryor's hometown and the land of his imagination—as he encounters Dracula. In the voice of a Southern black man, down on his luck:

> Hey man, say, nigger—you with the cape. . . . What's your name, boy? Dracula? What kind of name is that for a nigger? Where you from, fool? Transylvania? I know where it is, nigger! You ain't the smartest motherfucker in the world, even though you is the ugliest. Oh yeah, you a ugly motherfucker. Why you don't get your teeth fixed, nigger? That shit hanging all out your mouth. Why you don't get you an orthodontist? . . . This is 1975, boy. Get your shit together. What's wrong with your natural? Got that dirt all in the back of your neck. You's a filthy little motherfucker, too. You got to be home 'fore the sun come up? You ain't lyin', motherfucker. See your ass during the day, you liable to get arrested. You want to suck what? You some kind of freak, boy? . . . You ain't suckin' nothing here, junior.

Pryor's two best comedy albums, both of which were recorded during the mid to late seventies—"Bicentennial Nigger" and "That Nigger's Crazy"—are not available on CD, but his two concert films, "Richard Pryor Live in Concert" and "Richard Pryor—Live on the Sunset Strip," which were released in 1979 and 1982, respectively, are out on video. The concert films are excellent examples of what the *Village Voice* critic Carrie Rickey once described as Pryor's ability to "scare us into laughing at his demons—our demons—exorcising them through mass hyperventilation." "Pryor doesn't tell jokes," she wrote, "he tells all, in the correct belief that without punch lines, humor has *more* punch. And pungency." Taken together, the concert films show the full panorama of Pryor's moods: brilliant, boring, insecure, demanding, misogynist, racist, playful, and utterly empathetic.

BEFORE Richard Pryor, there were only three aspects of black maleness to be found on TV or in the movies: the suave, pimp-style blandness of Billy Dee Williams; the big-dicked, quiet machismo of the football hero Jim Brown; and the cable-knit homilies of Bill Cosby. Pryor was the first image we'd ever had of black male fear. Not the kind of Stepin Fetchit noggin-bumpin'-into-walls fear that turned Buckwheat white when he saw a ghost in the "Our Gang" comedies popular in the twenties, thirties, and forties—a character that Eddie Murphy resuscitated in a presumably ironic way in the eighties on "Saturday Night Live." Pryor was filled with dread and panic—an existential fear, based on real things, like racism and lost love. (In a skit on "In Living Color," the actor Damon Wayans played Pryor sitting in his kitchen and looking terrified, while a voiceover said, "Richard Pryor—afraid of absolutely everything.")

"Hi. I'm Richard Pryor." Pause. "Hope I'm funny." That was how he introduced himself to audiences for years, but he never sounded entirely convinced that he cared about being funny. Instead, Pryor embodied the voice of injured humanity. A satirist of his own experience, he revealed what could be considered family secrets—secrets about his past, and about blacks in general, and about his relationship to the black and white worlds he did and did not belong to. In the black community, correctness, political or otherwise, remains part of the mortar that holds lives together. Pryor's comedy was a high-wire act: how to stay funny to a black audience while satirizing the moral strictures that make black American life like no other.

The standard approach, in magazine articles about Pryor, has been to comment on his anger—in an imitation-colloquial language meant to approximate Pryor's voice. "Richard Pryor said it first: *That nigger's crazy*," begins a 1978 article in *People* magazine. And Pryor had fun with the uneasiness that the word "nigger" provoked in others. (Unlike Lenny Bruce, he didn't believe that if you said a word over and over again it would lose its meaning.) Take his great "Supernigger" routine: "Look up in the sky, it's a crow, it's a bat. No, it's Supernigger! Yes, friends, Supernigger, with X-ray vision that enables him to see through everything except Whitey."

In 1980, in the second of three interviews that Barbara Walters conducted with Richard Pryor, this exchange took place:

WALTERS: When you're onstage . . . see, it's hard for me to say. I was going to say, you talk about niggers. I can't . . . you can say it. I can't say it.

PRYOR: You just said it.

WALTERS: Yeah, but I feel so . . .

PRYOR: You said it very good.

WALTERS: . . . uncomfortable.

PRYOR: Well, good. You said it pretty good.

WALTERS: O.K.

PRYOR: That's not the first time you said it. *(Laughter.)*

Pryor's anger, though, is actually not as interesting as his self-loathing. Given how much he did to make black pride part of American popular culture, it is arresting to see how at times his blackness seemed to feel like an ill-fitting suit. One gets the sense that he called himself a "nigger" as a kind of preëmptive strike, because he never knew when the term would be thrown at him by whites, by other blacks, or by the women he loved. Because he didn't match any of the prevailing stereotypes of "cool" black maleness, he carved out an identify for himself that was not only "nigger" but "sub-nigger." In "Live on the Sunset Strip" he wears a maraschino-red suit with silk lapels, a black shirt, and a bow tie. He says, "Billy Dee Williams could hang out in this suit and look cool." He struts. "And me?" His posture changes from cocky to pitiful.

Pryor believed that there was something called unconditional love, which he alone had not experienced. But to whom could he, a "sub-nigger," turn for that kind of love? The working-class blacks who made him feel guilty for leaving them behind? His relatives, who acted as if it were their right to hit him up for cash because he'd used their stories to make it? The white people who felt safe with him because he was neurotic—a quality they equated with intelligence? The women who married him for money or status? The children he rarely saw? He was alienated from nearly everyone and everything except his need. This drama was what made Pryor's edge so sharp. He acted out against his fantasy by testing it with rude, brilliant commentary. A perfect role for Pryor might have been Dostoyevsky's antihero, Alexei, in "The Gambler," whose bemused nihilism affects every relationship he attempts. (Pryor once told Walters that he saw people "as the nucleus of a great idea that hasn't come to be yet.") That antiheroic anger prevents him from just telling a joke. He tells it through clenched teeth. He tells it to stave off bad times. He tells it to look for love.

HIS LIFE, AS A BIT

Black guy named Richard Pryor, famous, maybe a little high, appears on the eleventh Barbara Walters special, broadcast on May 29, 1979, and says this about his childhood, a sad house of cards he has glued together with wit:

PRYOR: It was hell, because I had nobody to talk to. I was a child, right, and I grew up seeing my mother . . . and my aunties going to rooms with men, you understand. . . .

WALTERS: Your grandmother ran a house of prostitution or a whorehouse.

PRYOR: Three houses. Three.

WALTERS: Three houses of prostitution. She was the chief madam.

PRYOR: . . . There were no others.

WALTERS: O.K. . . . Who believed in you? Who cared about you?

PRYOR: Richard Franklin Lennox Thomas Pryor the Third.

The isolation that Richard Pryor feels is elaborated on from time to time, like a bit he can't stop reworking. The sad bit, he could call it, if he did bits anymore, his skinny frame twisting around the words to a story that goes something like this: Born in Peoria, on December 1, 1940. "They called Peoria the model city. That meant it had the niggers under control." Grew up in one of the whorehouses on North Washington Street, which was the house of his paternal grandmother, Marie Carter Pryor Bryant. "She reminded me of a large sunflower—big, strong, bright, appealing," Pryor wrote in his 1995 memoir, "Pryor Convictions." But "she was also a mean, tough, controlling bitch."

Pryor called his father's mother "Mama," despite the fact that he had a mother, Gertrude. When Richard's father, Buck Carter, met Gertrude, she was already involved in Peoria's nefarious underworld, and she soon began working in Marie's whorehouse. Everything in Richard Pryor's world, as he grew up, centered on Marie, and he never quite recovered from that influence. "I come from criminal people," he told one radio interviewer. At the age of six, he was sexually abused by a young man in the neighborhood (who, after Richard Pryor became Richard Pryor, came to his trailer on a film set and asked for his autograph). And Pryor never got over the division he saw in his mother: the way she could separate her emotional self from her battered body and yet was emotionally damaged anyway.

"At least, Gertrude didn't flush me down the toilet, as some did," Pryor wrote in his memoir. "The only person scarier than God was my mother. . . . One time Buck hit Gertrude, and she turned blue with anger and said 'Okay, motherfucker, don't hit me no more. . . . Don't stand in front of me with fucking undershorts on and hit me, motherfucker.' Quick as lightning, she reached out with her finger claws and swiped at my father's dick. Ripped his nutsack off. I was just a kid when I saw this." Pryor records the drama as a born storyteller would—in the details. And the detail that filters through his memory most clearly is the rhythm of Gertrude's speech, its combination of profanity and rhetoric. Not unlike a routine by Richard Pryor.

Pryor soon discovered humor—the only form of manipulation he had in his community of con artists, hookers, and pimps. "I wasn't much taller than my Daddy's shin when I found that I could make my family laugh," Pryor wrote.

> I sat on a railing of bricks and found that when I fell off on purpose everyone laughed, including my grandmother, who made it her job to scare the shit out of people. . . . After a few more minutes of falling, a little dog wandered by and poo-pooed in our yard. I got up, ran to my grandmother, and slipped in the dog poop. It made Mama and the rest laugh again. Shit, I was really onto something then. So I did it a second time. "Look at that boy! He's crazy!" That was my first joke. All in shit.

When Pryor was ten years old, his mother left his father and went to stay with relatives in Springfield, Illinois, but Pryor stayed with his grandmother. In a biography by John and Dennis Williams, Pryor's teacher Marguerite Yingst Parker remembered him as "perpetually exhausted, sometimes lonely, always likable. . . . He was a poor black kid in what was then a predominantly white school, who didn't mingle with his classmates on the playground." Pryor often got through the tedium of school by entertaining his classmates. Eventually, Parker struck a deal with him: if he got to school on time, she would give him a few minutes each week to do a routine in front of the class. Not long afterward, Pryor met Juliette Whittaker, an instructor at the Carver Community Center. "He was about eleven, but looked younger because he was such a skinny little boy. And very bright," she recalled in the Williams book. "We were rehearsing 'Rumpelstiltskin' and he was watching. He asked if he could be in the play. I told him we only had one part left, and he said, 'I don't care. I'll take anything. I just want to be in the play.' . . . He took the script home and, unbeknownst to anybody, he memorized the entire thing."

When Pryor was in the eighth grade, a teacher who was fed up with his classroom routines asked him to leave school. He slowly became absorbed into the mundane working-class life that Peoria had to offer, taking a job at a packing plant, running errands. When he was seventeen, he discovered that the black woman he was seeing had also been sleeping with his father. Then, in an attempt to escape, Pryor enlisted in the Army, in 1958. He was stationed in Germany, where he was involved in a racial incident: a young white soldier laughed too hard about the painful black parts in the Douglas Sirk film "Imitation of Life," and Pryor and a number of other black inductees beat and stabbed him. Pryor went to jail, and when he was discharged, in 1960, he returned to his grand-mother's twilight world of street life and women for hire.

Pryor had some idea of what he wanted to be: a comedian like the ones he had seen on TV, particularly the black comedians Dick Gregory and Redd Foxx. He began performing at small venues in Peoria, telling topical jokes in the ca-dence of the time: "You know how to give Mao Tse-tung artificial respiration? No. Good!" The humor then "was kind of rooted in the fifties," the comedian and actor Steve Martin told me. "Very straight jokes, you know. The dominant theme on television and in the public's eye was something Catskills. Jokes. Punch lines." And it was within that form that Pryor began to make a name for himself in the local clubs.

But Pryor was ambitious, and his ambition carried him away from Peoria. In 1961, he left behind his first wife and their child, "because I could," and began working the night-club circuit in places like East St. Louis, Buffalo, and Youngstown, Ohio. In 1963, he made his way to New York. "I opened *Newsweek* and read about Bill Cosby," Pryor told David Felton. "That fucked me up. I said, 'God damn it, this nigger's doin' what *I'm* fixin' to do. I want to be the only nigger, ain't no room for two niggers.' " In New York, Pryor began appear-ing regularly at Café Wha?. By 1966, he had begun to make it nationally. He appeared on a show hosted by Rudy Vallee called "On Broadway Tonight." Then on Ed Sullivan, Merv Griffin, and Johnny Carson—appearing each time with marcelled hair and wearing a black suit and tie that made him look like an undertaker. But his jokes were like placards that read "Joke": "When I was young I used to think my people didn't like me. Because they used to send me to the store for bread and then they'd move." Or "I heard a knock on the door. I said to my wife, 'There's a knock on the door.' My wife said, 'That's pecul-yar, we ain't got no door.' "

He was fêted as the new Bill Cosby by such show-business luminaries as Bobby Darin and Sid Caesar, and other comedians and writers counselled him to keep it that way: "Don't mention the fact that you're a nigger. Don't go into such bad taste," Pryor remembers being told by a white writer called Murray Roman. "They were gonna try to help me be nothin' as best they could," he said in the *Rolling Stone* interview. "The life I was leading, it wasn't me. I was a robot. Beep. Good evening, ladies and gentlemen, welcome to the Sands Hotel. Maids are funny. Beep. . . . I didn't feel good. I didn't feel I could tell anybody to kiss my ass, 'cause I didn't have no ass, you dig?"

A drug habit kicked in. Then, in 1967, while Pryor was doing a show in Las Vegas, he broke down. "I looked out at the audience," Pryor wrote. "The first person I saw was Dean Martin, seated at one of the front tables. He was staring right back at me. . . . I checked out the rest of the audience. They were staring at me as intently as Dean, waiting for that first laugh. . . . I asked myself, Who're they looking at, Rich? . . . And in that flash of introspection when I was unable to find an answer, I crashed. . . . I finally spoke to the sold-out crowd: 'What the fuck am I doing here?' Then I turned and walked off the stage."

He was through with what he'd been doing: "I was a Negro for twenty-three years. I gave that shit up. No room for advancement."

IN the following years—1968 through 1971—Pryor worked on material that became more or less what we know today as the Richard Pryor experience. A close friend, the comedian and writer Paul Mooney, took him to the looser, more politicized environs of Berkeley, and Pryor holed up there and wrote.

The black folklorist and novelist Zora Neale Hurston once wrote that, although she had "landed in the crib of negroism" at birth, it hadn't occurred to her until she left her home town that her identity merited a legitimate form of intellectual inquiry. It was only after Pryor had left Peoria and wrested a certain level of success from the world that he was able to see his own negroism, and what made it unique. As Mel Watkins writes, in his book "On the Real Side: Laughing, Lying, and Signifying," after Pryor moved to Berkeley and met the writers Cecil Brown and Ishmael Reed he discovered that "accredited intellectuals" could share "his affection and enthusiasm for the humor and lifestyles of common black folks." Pryor also discovered Malcolm X's speeches and Marvin Gaye's album "What's Going On." Both taught him how to treat himself as just another character in a story being told. He distanced himself from the more confessional Lenny Bruce—whose work had already influenced him to adopt a hipper approach to language—and "Richard Pryor" became no more important than the winos or junkies he talked about.

Pryor began to reconstruct himself first through the use of sound—imagining the sound of Frankenstein taking LSD, for example, or a baby "being birthed." His routines from this time regularly involved gurgles, air blown through pursed lips, beeps. He also began playing with individual words. He would stand in front of an audience and say "God damn" in every way he could think to say it. Or he'd say, "I feel," in a variety of ways that indicated the many different ways he could feel. And as he began to understand how he felt he began to see himself, to create his body before his audience. He talked about the way his breath and his farts smelled, what he wanted from love, where he had been, and what America thought he was.

In those years, Pryor began to create characters that were based on his own experience; he explored the territory and language of his family and his childhood—that fertile and unyielding ground that most artists visit again and again. The producer George Schlatter, who watched Pryor's transformation at a number of clubs in the late sixties and the early seventies, told me, "Richard grew up in a whorehouse. The language he used, he was entitled to it. Now the kids coming up, they use the word 'fuck' and that becomes the joke. Richard used the word 'fuck' on the way to the joke. It was part of his vocabulary. It was part of his life experience." As Pryor began to recall his relatives' voices, he became able to see them from the outside, not without a certain degree of fondness. "My aunt Maxine could suck a neckbone, it was a work of art," he'd say. Or:

> My father was one of them eleven-o'clock niggers. [Voice becoming more high-pitched] "Say, say, where you going, Richard? Say, huh? Well, nigger, you ain't ask nobody if you could go no place. What the fuck, you a man now, nigger? Get a job. I don't give a fuck where you go, be home by eleven. You understand eleven, don't you, nigger? *You can tell time, can't you?* . . . Eleven o'clock, bring your ass here. I don't mean down the street singing with them niggers, either. I ain't getting you ass out of jail no more, motherfucker. That's right. [Pause] And bring me back a paper."

Pryor's routines became richer in depth, in imagination—rather like the characters Edgar Lee Masters created for his brilliant, problematic "Spoon River Anthology." But the most popular and best-known of Pryor's characters—Mudbone, an old black man from Tupelo, Mississippi, whom Pryor created in 1975—also shows how a Pryor character can be *too* well drawn, too much of a crossover tool. Mudbone spoke with a strong Southern dialect and his tales were directly descended from the slave narratives that told (as the critic Darryl Pinckney described them) "of spirits riding people at night, of elixirs dearly bought from conjure men, chicken bones rubbed on those from whom love was wanted." From "Mudbone Goes to Hollywood":

OLD NEGRO MAN'S VOICE: There was an old man name was Mudbone. . . . And he used to sit right here in front of the barbecue shop and he'd dip snuff . . . and he'd spit. . . . He'd been in a great love affair. That right. He had a woman—he loved her very much—he had to hurt her though 'cause she fucked around on him. He said he knew she was fucking around 'cause I'd leave home and go to work and come back home, toilet seat be up. . . . So I set a little old trap for her there. Went to work early, you know, always did get up early, 'cause I like to hear the birds and shit. . . . So this particular morning, went on to work. Set my trap for this girl. She was pretty, too. Loved her. Sweet as she could be. Breast milk like Carnation milk. So I nailed the toilet seat down and doubled back and I caught that nigger trying to lift it up. So, say, Well, nigger, send your soul to heaven, 'cause your ass is mine up in here.

Mudbone was the character that Pryor's audiences requested again and again. But, as Pauline Kael noted in her review of "Live on the Sunset Strip," Pryor became tired of him: "Voices, ostensibly from the audience, can be heard. One of them calls, 'Do the Mudbone routine,' and, rather wearily, saying that it will be for the last time, Pryor sits on a stool and does the ancient storyteller

[who] was considered one of his great creations. And the movie goes thud. . . . Pryor looks defeated."

And he should: Mudbone was the trick he turned and got tired of turning—a safe woolly-headed Negro, a comic version of Katherine Anne Porter's old Uncle Jimbilly. Compare Mudbone, for example, to the innovative and threatening "Bicentennial Nigger" character: "Some nigger two hundred years old in blackface. With stars and stripes on his forehead, lips just a-shining." "Battle Hymn" theme music, and Pryor's voice becomes Stepin Fetchit–like. "But he happy. He happy, 'cause he been here two hundred years. . . . Over here in America. 'I'm so glad you'll took me out of Dahomey.' " Shuckin' and jivin' laugh. " 'I used to could live to be a hundred and fifty, now I dies of the high blood pressure by the time I'm fifty-two.' "

BY 1973, Richard Pryor had become a force in the entertainment industry. He now appeared regularly in such diverse venues as Redd Foxx's comedy club in Central L.A., where the clientele was mostly black, and the Improv, on Sunset Strip, which was frequented by white show-business hipsters. And he behaved as badly as he wanted to wherever he wanted to—whether with women, with alcohol, or with drugs. "I got plenty of money but I'm still a nigger," he told a radio interviewer. He had become Richard Pryor, the self-described "black greasy motherfucker," whose new style of entertainment was just one of many innovations of the decade—in music (Sly and the Family Stone and the Average White Band), in acting (Lily Tomlin and Ronnee Blakley), and in directing (Martin Scorsese and Hal Ashby). Cultural rebellion and political activism defined hip in Hollywood then—an era that is all too difficult to recall now.

"The idea of a black guy going out and saying he fucked a white woman was outrageous . . . but funny," Schlatter told me. "White women dug Richard because he was a naughty little boy, and they wanted some of that. He was talking about real things. Nobody was talking below the waist. Richard went right for the lap, man."

Pryor had directed a film called "Bon Appétit" a few years before—the footage is now lost. "The picture opened with a black maid having her pussy eaten at the breakfast table by the wealthy white man who owned the house where she worked," he recalled in "Pryor Convictions." "Then a gang of Black Panther types burst into the house and took him prisoner. As he was led away, the maid fixed her dress and called, 'Bon appétit, baby!' "

Each time someone asked why "that nigger was crazy," Pryor upped the ante by posing a more profound question. On a trip to a gun shop with David Felton in the early seventies, for example, Pryor asked the salesman, "How come all the targets are black?" The salesman smiled, embarrassed. "Uh, I don't know, Richard," he said, shaking his head. "I just—" "No, I mean I always wondered about that, you know?" Pryor said.

Pryor's edginess caught the attention of Mel Brooks, who was already an established Hollywood figure, and in 1972 Brooks hired him to work on a script called "Black Bart," the story of a smooth, Gucci-wearing black sheriff in the eighteen-seventies American West. This was to be Pryor's real crossover gig, not only as a writer but as an actor, but the leading role eventually went to Cleavon Little. Whatever the reason for not casting Pryor (some people who were involved with the movie told me that no one could deal with his drinking and his drug use), there are several scenes in the film (renamed "Blazing Saddles") that couldn't have been written by anyone else. One scene didn't make it in. It shows a German saloon singer, Lili von Dyke, in her darkened dressing room with Bart, whom she is trying to seduce.

LILI: Here, let me sit next to you. Tell me, *schatzi*, is it true vat zey say about the way you people are gifted? . . . Oh, oh, it's twue, it's twue, it's twue, it's twue.

BART: Excuse me, you're sucking my arm.

Pryor's best performances (in films he didn't write himself) date from these years. There is his poignant and striking Oscar-nominated appearance in Sidney J. Furie's 1972 film, "Lady Sings the Blues." As the Piano Man to Diana Ross's Billie Holiday, Pryor gives a performance that is as emotional and as surprising as his work in "Juke and Opal." And then there is his brilliant comic turn as Sharp-Eye Washington, the disreputable private detective in Sidney Poitier's 1974 film, "Uptown Saturday Night"—a character that makes use of Pryor's ability to convey paranoia with his body: throughout the movie, he looks like a giant exclamation point. And as Zeke Brown, in "Blue Collar," Paul Schrader's 1978 film about an automobile plant in Detroit, Pryor gives his greatest sustained—if fraught—film performance. In an interview with the writer Kevin Jackson, Schrader recalls his directorial début:

There were . . . problems. Part of it was to do with Richard's style of acting. Being primarily versed in stand-up comedy he had a creative life of between three and four takes. The first one would be good, the second would be real good, the third would be terrific, and the fourth would probably start to fall off. . . . The other thing Richard would do when he felt his performance going flat was to improvise and change the dialogue just like he would have done in front of a live audience, and he would never tell me or anyone what he was going to do.

Generally, though, Pryor had a laissez-faire attitude toward acting. One always feels, when looking at the work that he did in bad movies ranging from "You've Got to Walk It Like You Talk It or You'll Lose That Beat," in 1971, to "Superman III," released twelve years and twenty-seven films later, that Pryor had a kind of contempt for these mediocre projects—and for his part in them. Perhaps no character was as interesting to Richard Pryor as Richard Pryor. He certainly didn't work hard to make us believe that he was anyone other than himself as he walked through shameful duds like "Adiós Amigo." On the other hand, his fans paid all the love and all the money in the world to see him be himself: they fed his vanity, and his vanity kept him from being a great actor.

IN September, 1977, Lily Tomlin asked Pryor to be part of a benefit at the Hollywood Bowl to oppose Proposition Six, a Californian anti-gay initiative. Onstage, Pryor started doing a routine about the first time he'd sucked dick. The primarily gay members of the audience hooted at first—but they didn't respond well to Pryor's frequent use of the word "faggot." Pryor's rhythm was thrown off. "Shit . . . this is really weird," he exploded. "This is an evening about human rights. And I am a human being. . . . I just wanted to test you to your motherfucking *soul.* I'm doing this shit for *nuthin'.* . . . When the niggers was burning down Watts, you motherfuckers was doin' what you wanted to do on Hollywood Boulevard . . . didn't give a shit about it." And as he walked offstage: "You Hollywood faggots can kiss my happy, *rich* black ass."

Pryor liked to tell the truth, but he couldn't always face it himself. Although he spent years searching for an idealized form of love, his relationships were explosive and short-lived. From 1969 to 1978, he had three serious relationships or marriages—two with white women, one with a black woman—and two children. There were also affairs with film stars such as Pam Grier and Margot Kidder, and one with a drag queen. He was repeatedly in trouble for beating up women and hotel clerks. His sometimes maudlin self-involvement when a woman left him rarely involved any kind of development or growth. It merely encouraged the self-pity that informed much of his emotional life.

By the late seventies, Pryor was freebasing so heavily that he left his bedroom only to go to work and even then only if he could smoke some more on the set. He was even more paranoid than he'd always been and showed very little interest in the world. The endless cycle of dependence—from the drinking to the coke to the other drugs he needed to come down from the coke—began to destroy his health. Then, in 1980, he tried to break the cycle by killing himself. He wrote his own account of the episode, in "Pryor Convictions":

After free-basing without interruption for several days in a row, I wasn't able to discern one day from the next. . . . "I know what I have to do," I mumbled. "I've brought shame to my family. . . . I've destroyed my career. I know what I have to do." . . . I reached for the cognac bottle on the table in front of me and poured it all over me. Real natural, methodical. As the liquid soiled my body and clothing, I wasn't scared. . . . I was in a place called There. . . . I picked up my Bic lighter. . . . WHOOSH! I was engulfed in flame. . . . Sprinting down the driveway, I went out the gates and ran down the street. . . . Two cops tried to help me. My hands and face were already swollen. My clothes burnt in tatters. And my smoldering chest smelled like a burned piece of meat. . . . "Is there?" I asked. "Is there what?" someone asked. "Oh Lord, there is no help for a poor widow's son, is there?"

Pryor was in critical condition at the Sherman Oaks Community Hospital for seven weeks. When Jennifer Lee—a white woman, whom he married a year later—went to visit him, he described himself as a "forty-year-old burned-up nigger." And, in a sense, Pryor never recovered from his suicide attempt. "Live on the Sunset Strip," which came out three years later, is less a pulled-together performance than the performance of a man trying to pull himself together. He could no longer tell the truth. He couldn't even take the truth. And, besides, people didn't want the truth (a forty-year-old burned-up nigger). They wanted Richard Pryor—"sick," but not ill.

WHITE HONKY BITCH

Jennifer Lee was born and grew up in Ithaca, New York, one of three daughters of a wealthy lawyer. In her twenties, she moved to L.A. to become an actress, had affairs with Warren Beatty and Roman Polanski, and appeared in several B movies. She met Pryor in 1977, when she was hired to help redecorate his house. "We sat on an oversized brass bed in Richard's house," she wrote in an article for *Spin* magazine. "He was blue—heartsick over a woman who was 'running game' on him. He was putting a major dent in a big bottle of vodka. You could feel the tears and smell the gardenias, even with hip, white-walled nasal passages." Since that day, she told me, laughing, as we sat in the garden at the Château Marmont, in L.A., last winter, she has always been "the head bitch."

As Jennifer talked with me that afternoon, dressed in black leather pants and a black blazer, her white skin made even whiter by her maroon lipstick, I thought of the photographs I had seen of her with Pryor, some of which were reproduced in her 1991 memoir, "Tarnished Angel." These images were replaced by others: the white actress Shirley Knight berating Al Freeman, Jr., in the film version of Amiri Baraka's powerful play, "Dutchman," and Diane Arbus's haunting photograph of a pregnant white woman and her black husband sitting on a bench in Washington Square in the sixties. Then I thought of Pryor's routines on interracial sex. From "Black Man, White Woman":

Don't ever marry a white woman in California. A lot of you sisters probably saying "Don't marry a white woman anyway, nigger." [Pause] Shit. . . . Sisters look at you like you killed yo' Mama when you out with a white woman. You can't laugh that shit off, either. [High-pitched, fake-jovial voice] "Ha ha she's not with me."

From a routine entitled "Black & White Women":

There really is a difference between white women and black women. I've dated both. Yes, I have. . . . Black women, you be suckin' on their pussy and they be like, "Wait, nigger, shit. A little more to the left, motherfucker. You gonna suck the motherfucker, get down." You can fuck white women and if they don't come they say, "It's all right, I'll just lay here and use a vibrator."

Pryor was not only an integrationist but an integrationist of white women and black men, one of the most taboo adult relationships. The judgments that surround any interracial couple: *White girls who are into black dudes are sluts. White dudes aren't enough for them; only a big-dicked black guy can satisfy them. Black dudes who are into white girls don't like their kind. And, well, you know how they treat their women: they abuse them; any white girl who goes out with one is a masochist.* The air in America is thick with these misconceptions, and in the seventies it was thicker still. Plays and films like "A Taste of Honey," "A Patch of Blue," "Deep Are the Roots," "All God's Chillun' Got Wings," and "The Great White Hope" gave a view of the black man as both destroyer and nursemaid to a galaxy of white women who were sure to bring him down. But no real relationships exist in these works. The black male protagonists are more illustration than character. (Though they make excellent theatrical agitprop: what a surplus of symbols dangles from their mythic oversized penises!) In his work, Pryor was one of the first black artists to unknot the narrative of that desire and to expose it. In life he had to live through it as painfully as anyone else.

When Jennifer Lee first slept with Pryor, she told me, she touched his hair and he recoiled: its texture was all the difference in the world between them. That difference is part of the attraction for both members of interracial couples. "Ain't no such thing as an ugly white woman," says a character in Eldridge Cleaver's 1968 polemic, "Soul on Ice." In some ways Pryor found it easier to be involved with white women than with black women: he could blame their misunderstandings on race, and he could take advantage of the guilt they felt for what he suffered as a black man.

Yet, while Pryor may have felt both attracted by and ashamed of his difference from Lee, he also pursued her through all his drug blindness and self-absorption because he saw something of himself in her. "What no one gets," Lee told me, "is that one of the ways Richard became popular was through women falling in love with him—they saw themselves in him, in his not fitting in, the solitude of it all, and his willingness to be vulnerable as women are. And disenfranchised, of course, as women are." That black men and white women were drawn to each other through their oppression by white men was a concept I had first seen expressed in the feminist Shulamith Firestone's book "The Dialectic of Sex." There is a bond in oppression, certainly, but also a rift because of it—a contempt for the other who marks you as different—which explains why interracial romance is so often informed by violence. Cleaver claimed that he raped white women because that was the only kind of empowerment he could find in his brutal world. At times, Pryor directed a similar rage at Jennifer Lee, and she, at times, returned it.

LIFE in the eighties: Pryor gets up. Does drugs. Drives over to the Comedy Store to work out a routine. Has an argument with Jennifer after a party.

Maybe they fly to Hawaii. Come back in a week or so. Some days, Pryor is relaxed in his vulnerability. Other days, he tries to throw her out of the car. Richard's Uncle Dickie says about Jennifer, who is from an Irish family, "Irish are niggers turned inside out." Richard says about Jennifer, "The tragedy was that Jennifer could keep up with me." And she did. They married in 1981. They divorced in 1982.

With Lee, Pryor took the same trajectory that he had followed with many women before her. He began with a nearly maudlin reverence for her beauty and ended with paranoia and violence. In "Tarnished Angel," Lee describes Pryor photographing her as she was being sexually attacked by a drug dealer he hung out with—a lowlife in the tradition of the people he had grown up with. Pryor could be brutally dissociative and sadistic, especially with people he cared about: he did not separate their degradation from his own. He was also pleased when Lee was jealous of the other women he invariably became involved with. And when she left him, she claims, he stalked her.

Pryor got married again in 1986, to Flynn Be-Laine, two years after she'd given birth to his son Steven. Lee moved back to New York, where she wrote a challenging review of Pryor's film "Jo Jo Dancer, Your Life Is Calling," for *People*:

> Well, Richard, you blew it. I went to see "Jo Jo Dancer." . . . I went looking for the truth, the real skinny. Well, guess what? It wasn't there. . . . How sad. After all, it was you who was obsessed by the truth, be it onstage or in your private life. . . . You had no sacred cows. That's why I fell in love with you, why I hung in through the wonder and madness. . . . Listen to your white honky bitch, Richard: Ya gotta walk it like you talk it or you'll lose that beat.

But later the same year, when Lee interviewed Pryor for *Spin*, they had reached a kind of détente:

LEE: What about the rage, the demons?

PRYOR: They don't rage much anymore.

LEE: Like a tired old monster?

PRYOR: Very tired. He hath consumed me.

LEE: Has this lack of rage quieted your need to do standup?

PRYOR: Something has. I'm glad it happened *after* I made money.

Pryor had gone sober in 1983 and he soon recognized that, along with alcohol, he needed to relinquish some of the ruthless internal navigations that had given his comedy its power. He performed live less and less. There were flashes of the old brilliance: on Johnny Carson, for example, when he responded to false rumors that he had AIDS. And when his public raised its fickle refrain— "He's sick, he's washed up"—he often rallied, but in the last eight years of his performing life he became a more conventional presence.

Pryor divorced Flynn in 1991, and in 1994 he placed a call to Jennifer. He was suffering from degenerative multiple sclerosis, he told her, and wouldn't be able to work much longer. "He said, 'My life's a mess. Will you help me out?' " she recalls. "I thought long and hard about it. . . . I wasn't sure it would last, because Richard loves to manipulate people and see them dance. But, see, he can't do that anymore, because he finally bottomed. That's the only reason Richard is allowing his life to be in any kind of order right now."

Lee came back to Pryor in July of that year. "When I got there, he was in this ridiculous rental for, like, six thousand dollars a month," she told me. "Five bedrooms, seven bathrooms. Honey, it was classic. You couldn't write it better." Lee helped him to find a smaller house in Encino, and she has cared for him since then. He has two caregivers and is bathed and dressed in a collaborative effort that has shades of Fellini. He spends his days in a custom-made wheelchair, while others read to him or give him physical or speech therapy. Every Friday, he goes to the movies. According to Lee, he can speak well when he wants to, but he doesn't often want to. "Sometimes he'll say, 'Leave me the fuck alone, Jenny,' " she tells me, laughing. "Just the other day, Richard was sitting, staring out the window, and his caregiver said, 'Mr. Richard, what are you thinking about?' He said, 'I'm thinking about how much money I pay all you mother-fuckers.' " He doesn't see his children much, or his other ex-wives, or the people he knew when he still said things like "I dig show business. I do. . . . I wake up every morning and I kiss it. Show business, you fine bitch."

BLUE MOVIE

"Was that corny?" Lily Tomlin said to me one afternoon last winter when I told her I'd heard that certain CBS executives hadn't wanted her to kiss Pryor good night at the close of "Lily," back in 1973. After all, Pryor was then a disreputable black comic with an infamous foul mouth, and Lily Tomlin had just come from "Laugh-In," where she had attracted nationwide attention. Tomlin kissed him anyway, and it was, I think, the first time I had ever seen a white woman kiss a black man—I was twelve—and it was almost certainly the first time I had ever seen Richard Pryor.

Tomlin and I were sitting with Jane Wagner, her partner and writer for thirty years, in a Cuban restaurant—one of their favorite places in Los Angeles. Tomlin and Wagner were the only white people there.

"We just loved Richard," Tomlin told me. "He was the only one who could move you to tears. No one was funnier, dearer, darker, heavier, stronger, more radical. He was everything. And his humanity was just glorious."

"What a miracle 'Juke and Opal' got on," Wagner said. "The network treated us as if we were total political radicals. I guess we were. And they hated Richard. They were so threatened by him."

CBS had insisted that Tomlin and Wagner move "Juke and Opal" to the end of the show, so that people wouldn't switch channels in the middle, bringing down the ratings. "It threw the whole shape of the show off," Tomlin recalled in a 1974 interview. "It made 'Juke and Opal' seem like some sort of Big Message, which is not what I intended. . . . I wasn't out to make any, uh, heavy statements, any real judgments."

"Everybody kept saying it wasn't funny, but we wanted to do little poems. I mean, when you think of doing a drug addict in prime time!" Wagner told me. And what they did *is* a poem of sorts. It was one of the all too few opportunities that Tomlin had to showcase, on national television, the kind of performance she and Pryor pioneered.

"Lily and Richard were a revolution, because they based what they did on real life, its possibilities," Lorne Michaels, the producer of "Saturday Night Live," told me. "You couldn't do that kind of work now on network television, because no one would understand it. . . . Lily and Richard were the exemplars of a kind of craft. They told us there was a revolution coming in the field of entertainment, and we kept looking to the left, and it didn't come."

IT is odd to think that Richard Pryor's period of pronounced popularity and power lasted for only a decade, really—from 1970 to 1980. But comedy is rock and roll, and Pryor had his share of hits. The enormous territory he carved out for himself remains more or less his own. Not that it hasn't been scavenged by other comedians: Eddie Murphy takes on Pryor's belligerent side, Martin Lawrence his fearful side, Chris Rock his hysteria, Eddie Griffin his ghoulish goofiness. But none of these comedians approaches Pryor's fundamental strangeness, vulnerability, or political intensity. Still, their work demonstrates the power of his influence: none of them would exist at all were it not for Richard Pryor. The actor Richard Belzer described him to me as "the ultimate artistic beacon." "It was like he was the sun and we were planets," Belzer said. "He was the ultimate. He took socially complex situations and made you think about them, and yet you laughed. He's so brilliantly funny, it was revelatory. He's one of those rare people who define a medium."

According to Lee, Pryor has been approached by a number of artists who see something of themselves in him. Damon Wayans and Chris Rock wanted to star in a film version of Pryor's life. The Hughes Brothers expressed interest in making a documentary. In 1998, the Kennedy Center gave Pryor its first Mark Twain Prize, and Chevy Chase, Whoopi Goldberg, Robin Williams, and others gathered to pay tribute to him. Pryor's written acceptance of the award, however, shows a somewhat reluctant acknowledgment of his status as an icon: "It is nice to be regarded on par with a great white man—now that's funny!" he wrote. "Seriously, though, two things people throughout history have had in common are hatred and humor. I am proud that, like Mark Twain, I have been able to use humor to lessen people's hatred!"

In some ways, Pryor probably realizes that his legendary status has weakened the subversive impact of his work. People are quick to make monuments of anything they live long enough to control. It's not difficult to see how historians will view him in the future. An edgy comedian. A Mudbone. But will they take into account the rest of his story: that essentially American life, full of contradictions; the life of a comedian who had an excess of both empathy and disdain for his audience, who exhausted himself in his search for love, who was a confusion of female and male, colored and white, and who acted out this internal drama onstage for our entertainment.

(1999)

GONE FOR GOOD

THE photograph shows a perfectly arrested moment of joy. On one side—the left, as you look at the picture—the catcher is running toward the camera at full speed, with his upraised arms spread wide. His body is tilting toward the center of the picture, his mask is held in his right hand, his big glove is still on his left hand, and his mouth is open in a gigantic shout of pleasure. Over on the right, another player, the pitcher, is just past the apex of an astonishing leap that has brought his knees up to his chest and his feet well up off the ground. Both of *his* arms are flung wide, and he, too, is shouting. His hunched, airborne posture makes him look like a man who has just made a running jump over a sizable object—a kitchen table, say. By luck, two of the outreaching hands have overlapped exactly in the middle of the photograph, so that the pitcher's bare right palm and fingers are silhouetted against the catcher's glove, and as a result the two men are linked and seem to be executing a figure in a manic and difficult dance. There is a further marvel—a touch of pure fortune—in the background, where a spectator in dark glasses, wearing a dark suit, has risen from his seat in the grandstand and is lifting his arms in triumph. This, the third and central Y in the picture, is immobile. It is directly behind the overlapping hand and glove of the dancers, and it binds and recapitulates the lines of force and the movements and the theme of the work, creating a composition as serene and well ordered as a Giotto. The subject of the picture, of course, is classical—the celebration of the last out of the seventh game of the World Series.

This famous photograph (by Rusty Kennedy, of the Associated Press) does not require captioning for most baseball fans or for almost anyone within the

Greater Pittsburgh area, where it is still prominently featured in the art collec-
tions of several hundred taverns. It may also be seen, in a much enlarged ver-
sion, on one wall of the office of Joe L. Brown, the general manager of the
Pittsburgh Pirates, in Three Rivers Stadium. The date of the photograph is
October 17, 1971; the place is Memorial Stadium, in Baltimore. The catcher is
Manny Sanguillen, of the Pirates, and his leaping teammate is pitcher Steve
Blass, who has just defeated the defending (and suddenly former) World
Champion Baltimore Orioles by a score of 2–1, giving up four hits.

I am not a Pittsburgher, but looking at this photograph never fails to give me
pleasure, not just because of its aesthetic qualities but because its high-
bounding happiness so perfectly brings back that eventful World Series and that
particular gray autumn afternoon in Baltimore and the wonderful and inex-
pungible expression of joy that remained on Steve Blass's face after the game
ended. His was, to be sure, a famous victory—a close and bitterly fought pitchers' battle against the Orioles' Mike Cuellar, in which the only score for seven innings had been a solo home run by the celebrated Pirate outfielder Roberto
Clemente. The Pirates had scored again in the eighth, but the Orioles had responded with a run of their own and had brought the tying run around to third
base before Blass shut them off once and for all. The win was the culmination of
a stirring uphill fight by the Pirates, who had fallen into difficulties by losing the
first two games to the Orioles; Steve Blass had begun their comeback with a
wonderfully pitched three-hit, 5–1 victory in the third game. It was an outstanding Series, made memorable above all by the play of Roberto Clemente,
who batted .414 over the seven games and fielded his position with extraordinary zeal. He was awarded the sports car as the most valuable player of the
Series, but Steve Blass was not far out of the running for the prize. After that last
game, Baltimore manager Earl Weaver said, "Clemente was great, all right, but
if it hadn't been for Mr. Blass, *we* might be popping the corks right now."

I remember the vivid contrast in styles between the two stars in the noisy,
floodlit, champagne-drenched Pirate clubhouse that afternoon. Clemente, at
last the recipient of the kind of national attention he had always deserved but
had rarely been given for his years of brilliant play, remained erect and removed, regarding the swarming photographers with a haughty, incandescent
pride. Blass was a less obvious hero—a competent but far from overpowering
right-hander who had won fifteen games for the Pirates that year, with a most
respectable 2.85 earned-run average, but who had absorbed a terrible pounding by the San Francisco Giants in the two games he pitched in the National
League playoffs, just before the Series. His two Series victories, by contrast,
were momentous by any standard—and, indeed, were among the very best
pitching performances of his entire seven years in the majors. Blass, in any
case, celebrated the Pirates' championship more exuberantly than Clemente,
exchanging hugs and shouts with his teammates, alternately smoking a cigar
and swigging from a champagne bottle. Later, I saw him in front of his locker

with his arm around his father, Bob Blass, a plumber from Falls Village, Connecticut, who had once been a semi-pro pitcher; the two Blasses, I saw, were wearing identical delighted, non-stop smiles.

Near the end of an article I wrote about that 1971 World Series, I mentioned watching Steve Blass in batting practice just before the all-important seventh game and suddenly noticing that, in spite of his impending responsibilities, he was amusing himself with a comical parody of Clemente at the plate: "Blass . . . then arched his back, cricked his neck oddly, rolled his head a few times, took up a stance in the back corner of the batter's box, with his bat held high, and glared out at the pitcher imperiously—Clemente, to the life." I had never seen such a spirited gesture in a serious baseball setting, and since then I have come to realize that Steve Blass's informality and boyish play constituted an essential private style, as original and as significant as Clemente's eagle-like pride, and that each of them was merely responding in his own way to the challenges of an extremely difficult public profession. Which of the two, I keep wondering, was happier that afternoon about the Pirates' championship and his part in it? Roberto Clemente, of course, is dead; he was killed on December 31, 1972, in Puerto Rico, in the crash of a plane he had chartered to carry emergency relief supplies to the victims of an earthquake in Nicaragua. Steve Blass, who is now thirty-three, is out of baseball, having been recently driven into retirement by two years of pitching wildness—a sudden, near-total inability to throw strikes. No one, including Blass himself, can cure or explain it.

THE summer of 1972—the year after his splendid World Series—was in most respects the best season that Steve Blass ever had. He won nineteen games for the Pirates and lost only eight, posting an earned-run average of 2.48—sixth-best in the National League—and being selected for the N.L. All-Star team. What pleased him most that year was his consistency. He went the full distance in eleven of the thirty-two games he started, and averaged better than seven and a half innings per start—not dazzling figures (Steve Carlton, of the Phillies, had thirty complete games that year, and Bob Gibson, of the Cards, had twenty-three) but satisfying ones for a man who had once had inordinate difficulty in finishing games. Blass, it should be understood, was not the same kind of pitcher as a Carlton or a Gibson. He was never a blazer. When standing on the mound, he somehow looked more like a journeyman pitcher left over from the nineteen-thirties or forties than like one of the hulking, hairy young flingers of today. (He is six feet tall, and weighs about one hundred and eighty pounds.) Watching him work, you sometimes wondered how he was getting all those batters out. The word on him among the other clubs in his league was something like: Good but not overpowering stuff, excellent slider, good curve, good change-up curve. A pattern pitcher, whose slider works because of its location. No control problems. Intelligent, knows how to win.

I'm not certain that I saw Blass work in the regular season of 1972, but I did see him pitch the opening game of the National League playoffs that fall against the Cincinnati Reds, in Pittsburgh. After giving up a home run to the Reds' second batter of the day, Joe Morgan, which was hit off a first-pitch fastball, Blass readjusted his plans and went mostly to a big, slow curve, causing the Reds to hit innumerable rainmaking outfield flies, and won by 5–1. I can still recall how Blass looked that afternoon—his characteristic, feet-together stance at the outermost, first-base edge of the pitching rubber, and then the pitch, delivered with a swastika-like scattering of arms and legs and a final lurch to the left—and I also remember how I kept thinking that at any moment the sluggers of the Big Red Machine would stop overstriding and overswinging against such unintimidating deliveries and drive Blass to cover. But it never happened—Blass saw to it that it didn't. Then, in the fifth and deciding game, he returned and threw seven and one-third more innings of thoughtful and precise patterns, allowing only four hits, and departed with his team ahead by 3–2—a pennant-winning outing, except for the fact that the Pirate bullpen gave up the ghost in the bottom of the ninth, when a homer, two singles, and a wild pitch entitled the Reds to meet the Oakland A's in the 1972 World Series. It was a horrendous disappointment for the Pittsburgh Pirates and their fans, for which no blame at all could be attached to Blass.

My next view of Steve Blass on a baseball diamond came on a cool afternoon at the end of April this year. The game—the White Sox vs. the Orioles—was a close, 3–1 affair, in which the winning White Sox pitcher, John McKenzie, struck out seventeen batters, in six innings. A lot of the Sox struck out, too, and a lot of players on both teams walked—more than I could count, in fact. The big hit of the game was a triple to left center by the White Sox catcher, David Blass, who is ten years old. His eight-year-old brother, Chris, played second, and their father, Steve Blass, in old green slacks and a green T-shirt, coached at third. This was a late-afternoon date in the Upper St. Clair (Pennsylvania) Recreation League schedule, played between the White Sox and the Orioles on a field behind the Dwight D. Eisenhower Elementary School—Little League baseball, but at a junior and highly informal level. The low, *low* minors. Most of the action, or inaction, took place around home plate, since there was not much bat-on-ball contact, but there was a shrill non-stop piping of encouragement from the fielders, and disappointed batters were complimented on their overswings by a small, chilly assemblage of mothers, coaches, and dads. When Chris Blass went down swinging in the fourth, his father came over and said, "The sinker down and away is *tough*." Steve Blass has a longish, lightly freckled face, a tilted nose, and an alert and engaging expression. At this ballgame, he looked like any young suburban father who had caught an early train home from the office in order to see his kids in action. He looked much more like a commuter than like a professional athlete.

Blass coached quietly, moving the fielders in or over a few steps, asking the shortstop if he knew how many outs there were, reminding someone to take his hands out of his pockets. "Learning the names of all the kids is the hard part," he said to me. It was his second game of the spring as a White Sox coach, and between innings one of the young outfielders said to him, "Hey, Mr. Blass, how come you're not playing with the Pirates at Three Rivers today?"

"Well," Blass said equably, "I'm not *in* baseball anymore."

"Oh," said the boy.

Twilight and the end of the game approached at about the same speed, and I kept losing track of the count on the batters. Steve Blass, noticing my confusion, explained that, in order to avert a parade of walked batters in these games, any strike thrown by a pitcher was considered to have wiped out the balls he had already delivered to the same batter; a strike on the 3–0 count reconverted things to 0–1. He suddenly laughed. "Why didn't they have that rule in the N.L.?" he said. "I'd have lasted until I was fifty."

, Then it was over. The winning (and undefeated) White Sox and the losing Orioles exchanged cheers, and Karen Blass, a winning and clearly undefeated mother, came over and introduced me to the winning catcher and the winning second baseman. The Blasses and I walked slowly along together over the thick new grass, toting gloves and helmets and Karen's fold-up lawn chair, and at the parking lot the party divided into two cars—Karen and the boys homeward bound, and Steve Blass and I off to a nearby shopping center to order one large cheese-and-peppers-and-sausage victory pizza, to go.

BLASS and I sat in his car at the pizza place, drinking beer and waiting for our order, and he talked about his baseball beginnings. I said I had admired the relaxed, low-key tenor of the game we had just seen, and he told me that his own Little League coach, back in Connecticut—a man named Jerry Fallon—had always seen to it that playing baseball on his club was a pleasure. "On any level, baseball is a tough game if it isn't really fun," Blass said. "I think most progress in baseball comes from enjoying it and then wanting to extend yourself a little, wanting it to become more. There should be a feeling of 'Let's go! Let's keep on with this!' "

He kept on with it, in all seasons and circumstances. The Blasses' place in Falls Village included an old barn with an interestingly angled roof, against which young Steve Blass played hundreds of one-man games (his four brothers and sisters were considerably younger) with a tennis ball. "I had all kinds of games, with different, very complicated ground rules," he said. "I'd throw the ball up, and then I'd be diving into the weeds for pop-ups or running back and calling for the long fly balls, and all. I'd always play a full game—a made-up game, with two big-league teams—and I'd write down the line score as I went along, and keep the results. One of the teams always had to be the Indians. I was a *total* Indians fan, completely buggy. In the summer of '54, when they won that record one hundred and eleven games, I managed to find every single box score in the newspapers and clip it, which took some doing up where we lived. I guess Herb Score was my real hero—I actually pitched against him once in Indianapolis, in '63, when he was trying to make a comeback—but I knew the whole team by heart. Not just the stars but all the guys on the bench, like George Strickland and Wally Westlake and Hank Majeski and the backup third baseman, Rudy Regalado. My first big-league autograph was Hank Majeski."

Blass grew up into an athlete—a good sandlot football player, a second-team All-State Class B basketball star, but most of all a pitcher, like his father. ("He was wilder than hell," Blass said. "Once, in a Canaan game, he actually threw a pitch over the backstop.") Steve Blass pitched two no-hitters in his junior year at Housatonic Regional High School, and three more as a senior, but there were so many fine pitchers on the team that he did not get to be a starter until his final year. (One of the stars just behind him was John Lamb, who later pitched for the Pirates; Lamb's older sister, Karen, was a classmate of Steve's, and in time she found herself doubly affiliated with the Pirate mound staff.)

The Pittsburgh organization signed Steve Blass right out of Housatonic High in 1960, and he began moving up through the minors. He and Karen Lamb were married in the fall of 1963, and they went to the Dominican Republic that winter, where Steve played for the Cibaeñas Eagles and began working on a slider. He didn't quite make the big club when training ended in the spring, and was sent down to the Pirates' Triple A club in Columbus, but the call came three weeks later. Blass said, "We got in the car, and I floored it all the way across Ohio. I remember it was raining as we came out of the tunnel in Pittsburgh, and I drove straight to Forbes Field and went in and found the attendant and put my uniform on, at two in the afternoon. There was no *game* there, or anything—I just had to see how it looked."

We had moved along by now to the Blasses' house, a medium-sized brick structure on a hillside in Upper St. Clair, which is a suburb about twelve miles southeast of Pittsburgh. The pizza disappeared rapidly, and then David and Chris went off upstairs to do their homework or watch TV. The Blass family room was trophied and comfortable. On a wall opposite a long sofa there was, among other things, a plaque representing the J. Roy Stockton Award for Outstanding Baseball Achievement, a Dapper Dan Award for meritorious service to Pittsburgh, a shiny metal bat with the engraved signatures of the National League All-Stars of 1972, a 1971 Pittsburgh Pirates World Champions bat, a signed photograph of President Nixon, and a framed, decorated proclamation announcing Steve Blass Day in Falls Village, Connecticut: "Be it known that this twenty-second day of October in the year of our Lord 1971, the citizens of Falls Village do set aside and do honor with pride Steve Blass, the tall skinny kid from Falls Village, who is now the hero of baseball and will be our hero always." It was signed by the town's three selectmen. The biggest picture in the room hung over the sofa—an enlarged color photograph of the Blass family at the Father-and-Sons Day at Three Rivers Stadium in 1971. In the photo, Karen Blass looks extremely pretty in a large straw hat, and all three male Blasses are wearing Pirate uniforms; the boys' uniforms look a little funny, because in their excitement each boy had put on the other's pants. Great picture.

Karen and Steve pointed this out to me, and then they went back to their arrival in the big time on that rainy long-ago first day in Pittsburgh and Steve's insisting on trying on his Pirate uniform, and they leaned back in their chairs and laughed about it again.

"With Steve, everything is right out in the open," Karen said. "Every accomplishment, every stage o f the game—you have no idea how much he loved it, how he enjoyed the game."

That year, in his first outing Blass pitched five scoreless innings in relief against the Braves, facing, among others, Hank Aaron. In his first start, against the Dodgers in Los Angeles, he pitched against Don Drysdale and won, 4–2. "I thought I'd died and gone to Heaven," Blass said to me.

He lit a cigar and blew out a little smoke. "You know, this thing that's happened has been painted so bad, so tragic," he said. "Well, I don't go along with that. I know what I've done in baseball, and I give myself all the credit in the world for it. I'm not bitter about this. I've had the greatest moments a person could ever want. When I was a boy, I used to make up those fictitious games where I was always pitching in the bottom of the ninth in the World Series. Well, I really *did* it. It went on and happened to me. Nobody's ever enjoyed winning a big-league game more than I have. All I've ever wanted to do since I was six years old was to keep on playing baseball. It didn't even have to be major-league ball. I've never been a goal-planner—I've never said I'm going to do this or that. With me, everything was just a continuation of what had come before. I think that's why I enjoyed it all so much when it did come along, when the good things did happen."

All this was said with an air of summing up, of finality, but at other times that evening I noticed that it seemed difficult for Blass to talk about his baseball career as a thing of the past; now and then he slipped into the present tense—as if it were still going on. This was understandable, for he was in limbo. The Pirates had finally released him late in March ("out-righted" him, in baseball parlance), near the end of the spring-training season, and he had subsequently decided not to continue his attempts to salvage his pitching form in the minor leagues. Earlier in the week of my visit, he had accepted a promising job with Josten's, Inc., a large jewelry concern that makes, among other things, World Series rings and high-school graduation rings, and he would go to work for them shortly as a travelling representative in the Pittsburgh area. He was out of baseball for good.

PITCHING consistency is probably the ingredient that separates major-league baseball from the lesser levels of the game. A big-league fastball comes in on the batter at about eighty-five or ninety miles an hour, completing its prescribed journey of sixty feet six inches in less than half a second, and, if it is a strike, generally intersects no more than an inch or two of the seventeen-inch-wide plate, usually near the upper or lower limits of the strike zone; curves and sliders arrive a bit later but with intense rotation, and must likewise slice off only a thin piece of the black if they are to be effective. Sustaining this kind of control over a stretch of, say, one hundred and thirty pitches in a seven- or eight-inning appearance places such excruciating demands on a hurler's body and psyche that even the most successful pitchers regularly have games when they simply can't get the job done. Their fastball comes in high, their curves hang, the rest of their prime weapons desert them. The pitcher is knocked about, often by an inferior rival team, and leaves within a few innings; asked about it later, he shrugs and says, "I didn't have it today." He seems unsurprised. Pitching, it sometimes appears, is too hard for *anyone*. Occasionally, the poor performance is repeated, then extended. The pitcher goes into a slump. He sulks or rages, according to his nature; he asks for help; he works long hours on his motion. Still he cannot win. He worries about his arm, which almost always hurts to some degree. Has it gone dead? He worries about his stuff. Has he lost his velocity? He wonders whether he will ever win again or whether he will now join the long, long list—the list that awaits him, almost surely, in the end—of suddenly slow, suddenly sore-armed pitchers who have abruptly vanished from the big time, down the drain to oblivion. Then, unexpectedly, the slump ends—most of the time, that is—and he is back where he was: a winning pitcher. There is rarely an explanation for this, whether the slump has lasted for two games or a dozen, and managers and coaches, when pressed for one, will usually mutter that "pitching is a delicate thing," or—as if it explained anything—"he got back in the groove."

In spite of such hovering and inexplicable hazards, every big-league pitcher knows exactly what is expected of him. As with the other aspects of the game, statistics define his work and—day by day, inning by inning—whether he is getting it done. Thus, it may be posited as a rule that a major-league hurler who gives up an average of just over three and a half runs per game is about at the middle of his profession—an average pitcher. (Last year, the National League and the American League both wound up with a per-game earned-run average of 3.62.) At contract-renewal time, earned-run averages below 3.30 are invariably mentioned by pitchers; an E.R.A. close to or above the 4.00 level will always be brought up by management. The select levels of pitching proficiency (and salary) begin below the 3.00 line; in fact, an E.R.A. of less than 3.00 certifies true quality in almost exactly the same fashion as an over-.300 batting average for hitters. Last year, both leagues had ten pitchers who finished up below 3.00, led by Buzz Capra's N.L. mark of 2.28 and Catfish Hunter's 2.49 in the A.L. The best season-long earned-run average of the modern baseball era was Bob Gibson's 1.12 mark, set in 1968.

Strikeouts are of no particular use in defining pitching effectiveness, since there are other, less vivid ways of retiring batters, but bases on balls matter. To put it in simple terms, a good, middling pitcher should not surrender more than three or four walks per game—unless he is also striking out batters in considerable clusters. Last year, Ferguson Jenkins, of the Texas Rangers, gave up only forty-five walks in three hundred and twenty-eight innings pitched, or an average of 1.19 per game. Nolan Ryan, of the Angels, walked two hundred and two men in three hundred and thirty-three innings, or 5.4 per game; however, he helped himself considerably by fanning three hundred and sixty-seven, or just under ten men per game. The fastball is a great healer.

At the beginning of the 1973 season, Steve Blass had a lifetime earned-run average of 3.25 and was averaging 1.9 walks per game. He was, in short, an extremely successful and useful big-league pitcher, and was understandably enjoying his work. Early that season, however, baseball suddenly stopped being fun for him. He pitched well in spring training in Bradenton, which was unusual, for he has always been a very slow starter. He pitched on opening day, against the Cards, but threw poorly and was relieved, although the Pirates eventually won the game. For a time, his performance was borderline, but his few wins were in sloppy, high-scoring contests, and his bad outings were marked by streaks of uncharacteristic wildness and ineffectuality. On April 22nd, against the Cubs, he gave up a walk, two singles, a homer, and a double in the first inning, sailed through the second inning, and then walked a man and hit two batsmen in the third. He won a complete game against the Padres, but in his next two appearances, against the Dodgers and the Expos, he survived for barely half the distance; in the Expos game, he threw three scoreless innings, and then suddenly gave up two singles, a double, and two walks. By early June, his record was three wins and three losses, but his earned-run average suggested that his difficulties were serious. Bill Virdon, the Pirate manager, was patient and told Blass to take all the time he needed to find himself; he reminded Blass that once—in 1970—he had had an early record of two and eight but had then come back to finish the season with a mark of ten and twelve.

What was mystifying about the whole thing was that Blass still had his stuff, especially when he warmed up or threw on the sidelines. He was in great physical shape, as usual, and his arm felt fine; in his entire pitching career, Blass never experienced a sore arm. Virdon remained calm, although he was clearly puzzled. Some pitching mechanics were discussed and worked on: Blass was sometimes dropping his elbow as he threw; often he seemed to be hurrying his motion, so that his arm was not in synchronization with his body; perhaps he had exaggerated his peculiar swoop toward first base and thus was losing his power. These are routine pitching mistakes, which almost all pitchers are guilty of from time to time, and Blass worked on them assiduously. He started again against the Braves on June 11th, in Atlanta; after three and one-third innings he was gone, having given up seven singles, a home run, two walks, and a total of five runs. Virdon and Blass agreed that a spell in the bullpen seemed called for; at least he could work on his problems there every day.

Two days later, the roof fell in. The team was still in Atlanta, and Virdon called Blass into the game in the fifth inning, with the Pirates trailing by 8–3. Blass walked the first two men he faced, and gave up a stolen base and a wild pitch and a run-scoring single before retiring the side. In the sixth, Blass walked Darrell Evans. He walked Mike Lum, throwing one pitch *behind* him in the process, which allowed Evans to move down to second. Dusty Baker singled, driving in a run. Ralph Garr grounded out. Davey Johnson singled, scoring another run. Marty Perez walked. Pitcher Ron Reed singled, driving in two more runs, and was wild-pitched to second. Johnny Oates walked. Frank Tepedino singled, driving in two runs, and Steve Blass was finally relieved. His totals for the one and one-third innings were seven runs, five hits, six bases on balls, and three wild pitches.

"It was the worst experience of my baseball life," Blass told me. "I don't think I'll ever forget it. I was embarrassed and disgusted. I was totally unnerved. You can't imagine the feeling that you suddenly have no *idea* what you're doing out there. You have no business being there, performing that way as a major-league pitcher. It was kind of scary."

None of Blass's appearances during the rest of the '73 season were as dreadful as the Atlanta game, but none of them were truly successful. On August 1st, he started against the Mets and Tom Seaver at Shea Stadium and gave up three runs and five walks in one and two-thirds innings. A little later, Virdon gave him a start in the Hall of Fame game at Cooperstown; this is a meaningless annual exhibition, played that year between the Pirates and the Texas Rangers, but Blass was as wild as ever and had to be relieved after two and one-third innings. After that, Bill Virdon announced that Blass would probably not start another game; the Pirates were in a pennant race, and the time for patience had run out.

Blass retired to the bullpen and worked on fundamentals. He threw a lot, once pitching a phantom nine-inning game while his catcher, Dave Ricketts, called the balls and strikes. At another point, he decided to throw every single day in the bullpen, to see if he could recapture his groove. "All it did was to get me very, very tired," Blass told me. He knew that Virdon was not going to use him, but whenever the Pirates fell behind in a game, he felt jumpy about the possibility of being called upon. "I knew I wasn't capable of going in there," he said. "I was afraid of embarrassing myself again, and letting down the club."

On September 6th, the Pirate front office announced that Danny Murtaugh, who had served two previous terms as the Pirates' manager, was replacing Bill Virdon at the helm; the Pirates were caught up in a close, four-team division race, and it was felt that Murtaugh's experience might bring them home. One of Murtaugh's first acts was to announce that Steve Blass would be given a start. The game he picked was against the Cubs, in Chicago, on September 11th. Blass, who had not pitched in six weeks, was extremely anxious about this test; he walked the streets of Chicago on the night before the game, and could not get to sleep until after five in the morning. The game went well for him. The Cubs won, 2–0, but Steve gave up only two hits and one earned run in the five innings he worked. He pitched with extreme care, throwing mostly sliders. He had another pretty good outing against the Cardinals, for no decision, and then started against the Mets, in New York, on September 21st, but got only two men out, giving up four instant runs on a walk and four hits. The Mets won, 10–2, dropping the Pirates out of first place, but Blass, although unhappy about his showing, found some hope in the fact that he had at least been able to get the ball over the plate. "At that point," he said, "I was looking for even a little bit of success—one good inning, a few real fastballs, anything to hold on to that might halt my negative momentum. I wanted to feel I had at least got things turned around and facing in the right direction."

The Mets game was his last of the year. His statistics for the 1973 season were three wins and nine defeats, and an earned-run average of 9.81. That figure and his record of eighty-four walks in eighty-nine innings pitched were the worst in the National League.

I went to another ballgame with Steve Blass on the night after the Little League affair—this time at Three Rivers Stadium, where the Pirates were meeting the Cardinals. We sat behind home plate, down near the screen, and during the first few innings a lot of young fans came clustering down the aisle to get Steve's autograph. People in the sections near us kept calling and waving to him. "Everybody has been great to me, all through this thing," Blass said. "I don't think there are too many here who are thinking, 'Look, there's the wild man.' I've had hundreds and hundreds of letters—I don't know how many— and not one of them was down on me."

In the game, Bob Gibson pitched against the Pirates' Jerry Reuss. When Ted Simmons stood in for the visitors, Blass said, "He's always hit me pretty good. He's really developed as a hitter." Then there was an error by Richie Hebner, at third, on a grounder hit by Ken Reitz, and Blass said, "Did you notice the batter take that big swing and then hit it off his hands? It was the swing that put Richie back on his heels like that." Later on, Richie Zisk hit a homer off Gibson, on a three-and-two count, and Blass murmured, "The high slider is one of *the* hittable pitches when it isn't just right. I should know."

The game rushed along, as games always do when Gibson is pitching. "You know," Blass said, "before we faced him we'd always have a team meeting and we'd say, 'Stay out of the batter's box, clean your spikes—anything to make him slow up.' But it never lasted more than an inning or two. He makes you play his game."

A little later, however, Willie Stargell hit a homer, and then Manny Sanguillen drove in another run with a double off the left-field wall ("*Get* out of here!" Steve said while the ball was in flight), and it was clear that this was not to be a Gibson night. Blass was enjoying himself, and it seemed to me that the familiarities and surprises of the game had restored something in him. At one point, he leaned forward a little and peered into the Pirate dugout and murmured, "Is Dock Ellis over in his regular corner there?," but for the most part he kept his eyes on the field. I tried to imagine what it felt like for him not to be down in the dugout.

I had talked that day to a number of Blass's old teammates, and all of them had mentioned his cheerfulness and his jokes, and what they had meant to the team over the years. "Steve's humor in the clubhouse was unmatched," relief pitcher Dave Giusti said. "He was a terrific mimic. Perfect. He could do Robert Kennedy. He could do Manny Sanguillen. He could do Roberto Clemente—not just the way he moved but the way he talked. Clemente loved it. He could do rat sounds—the noise a rat makes running. Lots of other stuff. It all made for looseness and togetherness. Because of Steve, the clubhouse was never completely silent, even after a loss." Another Pirate said, "Steve was about ninety per cent of the good feeling on this club. He was always up, always agitating. If a player made a mistake, Steve knew how to say something about it that would let the guy know it was O.K. Especially the young guys—he really understood them, and they put their confidence in him because of that. He picked us all up. Of course, there was a hell of a lot less of that from him in the last couple of years. We sure missed it."

For the final three innings of the game, Blass and I moved upstairs to general manager Joe Brown's box. Steve was startled by the unfamiliar view. "Hey, you can really see how it *works* from here, can't you?" he said. "Down there, you've got to look at it all in pieces. No wonder it's so hard to play this game right."

In the Pirates' seventh, Bill Robinson pinch-hit for Ed Kirkpatrick, and Blass said, "Well, *that* still makes me wince a little." It was a moment or two before I realized that Robinson was wearing Blass's old uniform number. Robinson fanned, and Blass said, "Same old twenty-eight."

The Pirates won easily, 5–0, with Jerry Reuss going all the way for the shutout, and just before the end Steve said, "I always had trouble sleeping after pitching a real good game. And if we were home, I'd get up about seven in the morning, before anybody else was up, and go downstairs and make myself a cup of coffee, and then I'd get the newspaper and open it to the sports section and just— Just soak it all in."

We thanked Joe Brown and said good night, and as we went down in the elevator I asked Steve Blass if he wanted to stop off in the clubhouse for a minute and see his old friends. "Oh, no," he said. "No, I couldn't do that."

AFTER the end of the 1973 season, Blass joined the Pirates' team in the Florida Instructional League (an autumn institution that exists mostly to permit the clubs to look over their prime minor-league prospects), where he worked intensively with a longtime pitching coach, Don Osborn, and appeared in three games. He came home feeling a little hopeful (he was almost living on such minimal nourishments), but when he forced himself to think about it he had to admit that he had been too tense to throw the fastball much, even against rookies. Then, in late February, 1974, Blass reported to Bradenton with the other Pirate pitchers and catchers. "We have a custom in the early spring that calls for all the pitchers to throw five minutes of batting practice every day," he told me. "This is before the rest of the squad arrives, you understand, so you're just pitching to the other pitchers. Well, the day before that first workout I woke up at four-thirty in the morning. I was so worried that I couldn't get back to sleep— and all this was just over going out and throwing to *pitchers*. I don't remember what happened that first day, but I went out there very tense and anxious every time. As you can imagine, there's very little good work or improvement you can do under those circumstances."

The training period made it clear that nothing had altered with him (he walked twenty-five men in fourteen innings in exhibition play), and when the club went North he was left in Bradenton for further work. He joined the team in Chicago on April 16th, and entered a game against the Cubs the next afternoon, taking over in the fourth inning, with the Pirates down by 10–4. He pitched five innings, and gave up eight runs (three of them unearned), five hits, and seven bases on balls. The Cubs batted around against him in the first inning he pitched, and in the sixth he gave up back-to-back home runs. His statistics for the game, including an E.R.A. of 9.00, were also his major-league figures for the year, because late in April the Pirates sent him down to the Charleston (West Virginia) Charlies, their farm team in the Class AAA International League. Blass did not argue about the decision; in fact, as a veteran with more than eight years' service in the majors, he had to agree to the demotion before the parent club could send him down. He felt that the Pirates and Joe Brown had been extraordinarily patient and sympathetic in dealing with a baffling and apparently irremediable problem. They had also been generous, refusing to cut his salary by the full twenty per cent permissible in extending a major-league contract. (His pay, which had been ninety thousand dollars in 1973, was cut to seventy-five thousand for the next season, and then to sixty-three thousand this spring.) In any case, Blass wanted to go. He needed continuous game experience if he was ever to break out of it, and he knew he no longer belonged with a big-league club.

The distance between the minors and the majors, always measurable in light-years, is probably greater today than ever before, and for a man making the leap in the wrong direction the feeling must be sickening. Blass tries to pass off the experience lightly (he is apparently incapable of self-pity), but one can guess what must have been required of him to summon up even a scrap of the kind of hope and aggressive self-confidence that are prerequisites, at every level, of a successful athletic performance. He and Karen rented an apartment in Charleston, and the whole family moved down when the school year ended; David and Chris enjoyed the informal atmosphere around the ballpark, where they were permitted to shag flies in batting practice. "It wasn't so bad," Blass told me.

But it was. The manager of the Charlies, Steve Demeter, put Blass in the regular starting rotation, but he fared no better against minor-leaguers than he had in the big time. In a very brief time, his earned-run average and his bases-on-balls record were the worst in the league. Blass got along well with his teammates, but there were other problems. The mystery of Steve Blass's decline was old stuff by now in most big-league-city newspapers, but as soon as he was sent down, there was a fresh wave of attention from the national press and the networks, and sportswriters for newspapers in Memphis and Rochester and Richmond and the other International League cities looked on his arrival in town as a God-given feature story. Invariably, they asked him how much money he was earning as a player; then they asked if he thought he was worth it.

The Charlies did a lot of travelling by bus. One day, the team made an eight-hour trip from Charleston to Toledo, where they played a night game. At eleven that same night, they reboarded the bus and drove to Pawtucket, Rhode Island, for their next date, arriving at about nine in the morning. Blass had started the game in Toledo, and he was so disgusted with his performance that he got back on the bus without having showered or taken off his uniform. "We'd stop at an all-night restaurant every now and then, and I'd walk in with a two-day beard and my old Charleston Charlies uniform on, looking like go-to-hell," Blass said. "It was pretty funny to see people looking at me. I had some books along, and we had plenty of wine and beer on the bus, so the time went by somehow." He paused and then shook his head. "*God,* that was an awful trip," he said.

By early August, Blass's record with Charleston was two and nine, and 9.74. He had had enough. With Joe Brown's permission, he left the Charlies and flew West to consult Dr. Bill Harrison, of Davis, California. Dr. Harrison is an optometrist who has helped develop a system of "optometherapy," designed to encourage athletes to concentrate on the immediate physical task at hand—hitting a ball, throwing a strike—by visualizing the act in advance; his firm was once retained by the Kansas City Royals baseball team, and his patients have included a number of professional golfers and football players. Blass spent four days with him, and then rejoined the Pirates, this time as a batting-practice pitcher. He says now that he was very interested in Dr. Harrison's theories but that they just didn't seem to help him much.

In truth, nothing helped. Blass knew that his case was desperate. He was almost alone now with his problem—a baseball castaway—and he had reached the point where he was willing to try practically anything. Under the guidance of pitching coach Don Osborn, he attempted some unusual experiments. He tried pitching from the outfield, with the sweeping motion of a fielder making a long peg. He tried pitching while kneeling on the mound. He tried pitching with his left foot tucked up behind his right knee until the last possible second of his delivery. Slow-motion films of his delivery were studied and compared with films taken during some of his best games of the past; much of his motion, it was noticed, seemed extraneous, but he had thrown exactly the same way at his peak. Blass went back and corrected minute details, to no avail.

The frustrating, bewildering part of it all was that while working alone with a catcher Blass continued to throw as well as he ever had; his fastball was alive, and his slider and curve shaved the corners of the plate. But the moment a batter stood in against him he became a different pitcher, especially when throwing a fastball—a pitcher apparently afraid of seriously injuring somebody. As a result, he was of very little use to the Pirates even in batting practice.

Don Osborn, a gentle man in his mid-sixties, says, "Steve's problem was mental. He had mechanical difficulties, with some underlying mental cause. I don't think anybody will ever understand his decline. We tried everything—I didn't know anything else to do. I feel real bad about it. Steve had a lot of guts to stay out there as long as he did. You know, old men don't dream much, but just the other night I had this dream that Steve Blass was all over his troubles and could pitch again. I said, 'He's ready, we can use him!' Funny . . ."

It was probably at this time that Blass consulted a psychiatrist. He does not talk about it—in part out of a natural reticence but also because the Pirate front office, in an effort to protect his privacy, turned away inquiries into this area by Pittsburgh writers and persistently refused to comment on whether any such therapy was undertaken. It is clear, however, that Blass does not believe he gained any profound insights into possible unconscious causes of his difficulties. Earlier in the same summer, he also experimented briefly with transcendental meditation. He entered the program at the suggestion of Joe Brown, who also enrolled Dave Giusti, Willie Stargell, pitcher Bruce Kison, and himself in the group. Blass repeated mantras and meditated twice a day for about two months; he found that it relaxed him, but it did not seem to have much application to his pitching. Innumerable other remedies were proposed by friends and strangers. Like anyone in hard straits, he was deluged with unsolicited therapies, overnight cures, naturopathies, exorcisms, theologies, and amulets, many of which arrived by mail. Blass refuses to make jokes about these nostrums. "Anyone who takes the trouble to write a man who is suffering deserves to be thanked," he told me.

Most painful of all, perhaps, was the fact that the men who most sympathized with his incurable professional difficulties were least able to help. The Pirates were again engaged in a close and exhausting pennant race fought out over the last six weeks of the season; they moved into first place for good only two days before the end, won their half-pennant, and then were eliminated by the Dodgers in a four-game championship playoff. Steve Blass was with the team through this stretch, but he took no part in the campaign, and by now he was almost silent in the clubhouse. He had become an extra wheel. "It must have been hell for him," Dave Giusti says. "I mean *real* hell. I never could have stood it."

When Blass is asked about this last summer of his baseball career, he will only say that it was "kind of a difficult time" or "not the most fun I've had." In extended conversations about himself, he often gives an impression of an armored blandness that suggests a failure of emotion; this apparent insensitivity about himself contrasts almost shockingly with his subtle concern for the feelings of his teammates and his friends and his family, and even of strangers. "My overriding philosophy is to have a regard for others," he once told me. "I don't want to put myself over other people." He takes pride in the fact that his outward, day-to-day demeanor altered very little through his long ordeal. "A person lives on," he said more than once, smiling. "The sun will come up tomorrow." Most of all, perhaps, he sustained his self-regard by not taking out his terrible frustrations on Karen and the boys. "A ballplayer learns very early that he can't bring the game home with him every night," he said once. "Especially when there are young people growing up there. I'm real proud of the fact that this thing hasn't bothered us at home. David and Chris have come through it all in fine shape. I think Karen and I are closer than ever because of this."

Karen once said to me, "Day to day, he hasn't changed. Just the other morning, he was out working on the lawn, and a couple of the neighbors' children came over to see him. Young kids—maybe three or four years old. Then I looked out a few minutes later, and there was a whole bunch of them yelling and rolling around on the grass with him, like puppies. He's always been that way. Steve has worked at being a man and being a father and a husband. It's something he has always felt very strongly about, and I have to give him all the credit in the world. Sometimes I think I got to hate the frustration and pain of this more than he did. He always found something to hold on to—a couple of good pitches that day, some little thing he had noticed. But I couldn't always share that, and I didn't have his ability to keep things under control."

I asked if maintaining this superhuman calm might not have damaged Steve in some way, or even added to his problems.

"I don't know," she said. "Sometimes in the evening—once in a great while—we'd be sitting together, and we'd have a couple of drinks and he would relax enough to start to talk. He would tell me about it, and get angry and hurt. Then he'd let it come out, and yell and scream and pound on things. And I felt that even this might not be enough for him. He would never do such a thing outside. Never." She paused, and then she said, "I think he directed his anger toward making the situation livable here at home. I've had my own ideas about Steve's pitching, about the mystery, but they haven't made much difference. You can't force your ideas on somebody, especially when he is doing what he thinks he has to do. Steve's a very private person."

STEVE Blass stayed home last winter. He tried not to think much about baseball, and he didn't work on his pitching. He and Karen had agreed that the family would go back to Bradenton for spring training, and that he would give it one more try. One day in January, he went over to the field house at the University of Pittsburgh and joined some other Pirates there for a workout. He threw well. Tony Bartirome, the Pirate trainer, who is a close friend of Steve's, thought he was pitching as well as he ever had. He told Joe Brown that Steve's problems might be over. When spring training came, however, nothing had altered. Blass threw adequately in brief streaks, but very badly against most batters. He hit Willie Stargell and Manny Sanguillen in batting practice; both players told him to forget it. They urged him to cut loose with the fastball.

Joe Brown had told Blass that the end of the line might be approaching. Blass agreed. The Pirate organization had been extraordinarily patient, but it was, after all, in the business of baseball.

On March 24th, Steve Blass started the second game of a doubleheader against the White Sox at Bradenton. For three innings, he escaped serious difficulty. He gave up two runs in the second, but he seemed to throw without much tension, and he even struck out Bill Melton, the Chicago third baseman, with a fastball. Like the other Pirates, Dave Giusti was watching with apprehensive interest. "I really thought he was on his way," he told me. "I was encouraged. Then, in the fourth, there were a couple of bases on balls and maybe a bad call by the ump on a close pitch, and suddenly there was a complete reversal. He was a different man out there."

Blass walked eight men in the fourth inning and gave up eight runs. He threw fifty-one pitches, but only seventeen of them were strikes. Some of his pitches were close to the strike zone, but most were not. He worked the count to 3–2 on Carlos May, and then threw the next pitch behind him. The booing from the fans, at first scattered and uncomfortable, grew louder. Danny Murtaugh waited, but Blass could not get the third out. Finally, Murtaugh came out very slowly to the mound and told Blass that he was taking him out of the game; Dave Giusti came in to relieve his old roommate. Murtaugh, a peaceable man, then charged the home-plate umpire and cursed him for the bad call, and was thrown out of the game. Play resumed. Blass put on his warmup jacket and trotted to the outfield to run his wind sprints. Roland Hemond, the general manager of the White Sox, was at Bradenton that day, and he said, "It was the most heartbreaking thing I have ever seen in baseball."

Three days later, the Pirates held a press conference to announce that they had requested waivers from the other National League clubs, with the purpose of giving Blass his unconditional release. Blass flew out to California to see Dr. Bill Harrison once more, and also to visit a hypnotist, Arthur Ellen, who has worked with several major-league players, and has apparently helped some of them, including Dodger pitcher Don Sutton, remarkably. Blass made the trip mostly because he had promised Maury Wills, who is now a baserunning consultant to several teams, that he would not quit the game until he had seen Mr. Ellen.

Blass then returned to Bradenton and worked for several days with the Pirates' minor-league pitching coach, Larry Sherry, on some pitching mechanics. He made brief appearances in two games against Pirate farmhands, and threw well. He struck out some players with his fastball. After the second game, he showered and got into his Volkswagen and started North to join his family, who had returned to Pittsburgh. It was a good trip, because it gave him time to sort things out, and somewhere along the way he decided to give it up. The six-day waiver period had expired, and none of the other clubs had claimed him. He was encouraged about his pitching, but he had been encouraged before. This time, the fastball had been much better, and at least he could hold on to that; maybe the problem had been mechanical all along. If he came back now, however, it would have to be at the minor-league level, and even if he made it back to the majors, he could expect only three or four more years before his effectiveness would decline because of age and he would have to start thinking about retirement. At least *that* problem could be solved now. He didn't want to subject Karen to more of the struggle. It was time to get out.

OF all the mysteries that surround the Steve Blass story, perhaps the most mysterious is the fact that his collapse is unique. There is no other player in recent baseball history—at least none with Blass's record and credentials—who has lost his form in such a sudden and devastating fashion and been totally unable to recover. The players and coaches and fans I talked to about Steve Blass brought up a few other names, but then they quickly realized that the cases were not really the same. Some of them mentioned Rex Barney, a Dodger fastball pitcher of the nineteen-forties, who quit baseball while still a young man because of his uncontrollable wildness; Barney, however, had only one good year, and it is fair to say that he never *did* have his great stuff under control. Dick Radatz, a very tall relief pitcher with the Red Sox a decade ago, had four good years, and then grew increasingly wild and ineffective. (He is said to have once thrown twenty-seven consecutive balls in a spring-training game.) His decline, however, was partially attributable to his failure to stay in shape. Von McDaniel, a younger brother of Lindy McDaniel, arrived suddenly as a pitcher with the Cardinals, and disappeared just as quickly, but two years' pitching hardly qualifies as a record. There have been hundreds of shiningly promising rookie pitchers and sluggers who, for one reason or another, could not do their thing once they got up to the big time. Blass's story is different. It should also be understood that his was not at all the somewhat commonplace experience of an established and well-paid major-league star who suffers through one or two mediocre seasons. Tom Seaver went through such a slump last summer. But Seaver's problems were only relatively serious (his record for 1974 was 11–11), and were at least partly explicable (he had a sore hip), and he has now returned to form. Blass, once his difficulties commenced, was helpless. Finally, of course, one must accept the possibility that a great many players may have suffered exactly the same sort of falling off as Blass for exactly the same reasons (whatever they may be) but were able to solve the problem and continue their athletic careers. Sudden and terrible batting and pitching slumps are mysterious while they last; the moment they end, they tend to be forgotten.

What happened to Steve Blass? Nobody knows, but some speculation is permissible—indeed, is perhaps demanded of anyone who is even faintly aware of the qualities of Steve Blass and the depths of his suffering. Professional sports have a powerful hold on us because they display and glorify remarkable physical capacities, and because the artificial demands of games played for very high rewards produce vivid responses. But sometimes, of course, what is happening on the field seems to speak to something deeper within us; we stop cheering and look on in uneasy silence, for the man out there is no longer just another great athlete, an idealized hero, but only a man—only ourself. We are no longer at a game. The enormous alterations of professional sport in the past three decades, and especially the prodigious inflation of franchises and salaries, have made it evident even to the most thoughtless fan that the play he has come to see is serious indeed, and that the heart of the game is not physical but financial. Sport is no longer a release from the harsh everyday American business world but its continuation and apotheosis. Those of us (fans and players alike) who return to the ballpark in the belief that the game and the rules are unchanged—merely a continuation of what we have known and loved in the past—are deluding ourselves, perhaps foolishly, perhaps tragically.

Blass once told me that there were "at least seventeen" theories about the reason for his failure. A few of them are bromides: He was too nice a guy. He became smug and was no longer hungry. He lost the will to win. His pitching motion, so jittery and unclassical, at last let him down for good. His eyesight went bad. (Blass is myopic, and wears glasses while watching television and driving. He has never worn glasses when pitching, which meant that Pirate catchers had to flash him signals with hand gestures rather than with finger waggles; however, he saw well enough to win when he was winning, and his vision has not altered in recent years.) The other, more serious theories are sometimes presented alone, sometimes in conjunction with others. Answers here become more gingerly.

He was afraid of injury—afraid of being struck by a line drive.

Blass was injured three times while on the mound. He cracked a thumb while fielding a grounder in 1966. He was struck on the right forearm by a ball hit by Joe Torre in 1970, and spent a month on the disabled list. While trying for his twentieth victory in his last start in 1972, he was hit on the point of the elbow of his pitching arm by a line drive struck by the Mets' John Milner; he had to leave the game, but a few days later he pitched that first playoff game for the Pirates and won it handily. (Blass's brother-in-law, John Lamb, suffered a fractured skull when hit by a line drive in spring training in 1971, and it was more than a year before he recovered, but Blass's real pitching triumphs all came after that.)

He was afraid of injuring someone—hitting a batter with a fastball.

Blass did hit a number of players in his career, of course, but he never caused anyone to go on the disabled list or, for that matter, to miss even one day's work. He told me he did not enjoy brushing back hitters but had done so when it was obviously called for. During his decline, he was plainly unable to throw the fastball effectively to batters—especially to Pirate batters in practice. He says he hated the idea of hitting and possibly sidelining one of his teammates, but he is convinced that this anxiety was the result of his control problems rather than the cause.

He was seriously affected by the death of Roberto Clemente.

There is no doubt but that the sudden taking away of their most famous and vivid star affected all the Pirates, including Steve Blass. He and Clemente had not been particularly close, but Blass was among the members of the team who flew at once to Puerto Rico for the funeral services, where Blass delivered a eulogy in behalf of the club. The departure of a superstar leaves an almost visible empty place on a successful team, and the leaders next in line—who in this case would certainly include Steve Blass—feel the inescapable burden of trying to fill the gap. A Clemente, however, can never be replaced. Blass never pitched well in the majors after Clemente's death. This argument is a difficult one, and is probably impossible to resolve. There are Oedipal elements here, of course, that are attractive to those who incline in such a direction.

He fell into a slump, which led to an irreparable loss of confidence.

This is circular, and perhaps more a description of symptoms than of the disability itself. However, it is a fact that a professional athlete—and most especially a baseball player—faces a much more difficult task in attempting to regain lost form than an ailing businessman, say, or even a troubled artist; no matter how painful his case has been, the good will of his associates or the vagaries of critical judgment matter not at all when he tries to return. All that matters is his performance, which will be measured, with utter coldness, by the stats. This is one reason that athletes are paid so well, and one reason that fear of failure—the unspeakable "choking"—is their deepest and most private anxiety. Steve Blass passed over my questions about whether he had ever felt this kind of fear when on the mound. "I don't think pitchers, by their nature, allow themselves to think that way," he said. "To be successful, you turn that kind of thought away." On the other hand, he often said that two or three successive well-pitched games probably would have been all he needed to dissipate the severe tension that affected his performances once things began to go badly for him. They never came.

The remaining pieces of evidence (if, indeed, they have any part in the mystery) have been recounted here. Blass is a modest man, both in temperament and in background, and his success and fame were quite sudden and, to some degree, unexpected. His salary at the beginning of 1971—the year of his two great Series wins—was forty thousand dollars; two years later, it was ninety thousand, and there were World Series and playoff checks on top of that. Blass was never thought of as one of the great pitchers of his time, but in the late sixties and early seventies he was probably the most consistent starter on the Pirate staff; it was, in fact, a staff without stars. On many other teams, he would have been no more than the second- or third-best starter, and his responsibilities, real and imagined, would have been less acute.

I took some of these hard questions to Blass's colleagues. Danny Murtaugh and Bill Virdon (who is now the Yankees' pilot) both expressed their admiration for Blass but said they had no idea what had happened to him. They seemed a bit brusque about it, but then I realized, of course, that ballplayers are forever disappearing from big-league dugouts; the manager's concern is with those who remain—with today's lineup. "I don't know the answer," Bill Virdon told me in the Yankee clubhouse. "If I did, I'd go get Steve to pitch for me. He sure won a lot of big games for us on the Pirates."

Joe Brown said, "I've tried to keep my distance and not to guess too much about what happened. I'm not a student of pitching and I'm not a psychologist. You can tell a man what to do, but you can't *make* him do it. Steve is an outstanding man, and you hate to quit on him. In this business, you bet on character. Big-league baseball isn't easy, yet you can stand it when things are going your way. But Steve Blass never had a good day in baseball after this thing hit him."

Blass's best friends in baseball are Tony Bartirome, Dave Giusti, and Nelson King (who, along with Bob Prince, is part of the highly regarded radio-and-television team that covers the Pirate games).

Tony Bartirome (*He is forty-three years old, dark-haired, extremely neat in appearance. He was an infielder before he became a trainer, and played one season in the majors—with the Pirates, in 1952*): "Steve is unique physically. He has the arm of a twenty-year-old. Not only did he never have a sore arm but he never had any of the stiffness and pain that most pitchers feel on the day after a game. He was always the same, day after day. You know, it's very important for a trainer to know the state of mind and the feelings of his players. What a player is *thinking* is about eighty per cent of it. The really strange thing is that after this trouble started, Steve never showed any feelings about his pitching. In the old days, he used to get mad at himself after a bad showing, and sometimes he threw things around in the clubhouse. But after this began, when he was taken out of a game he only gave the impression that he was happy to be out of there—relieved that he no longer had to face it that day. Somehow, he didn't show any emotion at *all*. Maybe it was like his never having a sore arm. He never talked in any detail about his different treatments—the psychiatry and all. I think he felt he didn't need any of that—that at any moment he'd be back where he was, the Blass of old, and that it all was up to him to make that happen."

Dave Giusti (*He is one of the great relief pitchers in baseball. He earned a B.A. and an M.A. in physical education at Syracuse. He is thirty-five—dark hair, a mustache, and piercing brown eyes*): "Steve has the perfect build for a pitcher—lean and strong. He is remarkably open to all kinds of people, but I think he has closed his mind to his inner self. There are central areas you can't infringe on with him. There is no doubt that during the past two years he didn't react to a bad performance the way he used to, and you have to wonder why he couldn't apply his competitiveness to his problem. Karen used to bawl out me and Tony for not being tougher on him, for not doing more. Maybe I should have come right out and said he seemed to have lost his will to fight, but it's hard to shock somebody, to keep bearing in on him. You're afraid to lose a friend, and you want to go easy on him because he is your friend.

"Last year, I went through something like Steve's crisis. The first half of the season, I was atrocious, and I lost all my confidence, especially in my fastball. The fastball is my best pitch, but I'd get right to the top of my delivery and then something would take over, and I'd know even before I released the ball that it wasn't going to be in the strike zone. I began worrying about making big money and not performing. I worried about not contributing to the team. I worried about being traded. I thought it might be the end for me. I didn't know how to solve my problem, but I knew I *had* to solve it. In the end, it was talking to people that did it. I talked to everybody, but mostly to Joe Brown and Danny and my wife. Then, at some point, I turned the corner. But it was talking that did it, and my point is that Steve can't talk to people that way. Or won't.

"Listen, it's tough out there. It's hard. Once you start maintaining a plateau, you've got to be absolutely sure what your goals are."

Nellie King (*A former pitcher with the Pirates. He is friendly and informal, with an attractive smile. He is very tall—six-six. Forty-seven years old*): "Right after that terrible game in Atlanta, Steve told me that it had felt as if the whole world was pressing down on him while he was out there. But then he suddenly shut up about it, and he never talked that way again. He covered it all up. I think there *are* things weighing on him, and I think he may be so angry inside that he's afraid to throw the ball. He's afraid he might kill somebody. It's only nickel psychology, but I think there's a lost kid in Steve. I remember that after the '71 Series he said, 'I didn't think I was as good as this.' He seemed truly surprised at what he'd done. The child in him is a great thing—we've all loved it—and maybe he was suddenly afraid he was losing it. It was being forced out of him.

"Being good up here is *so* tough—people have no idea. It gets much worse when you have to repeat it: 'We know you're great. Now go and do that again for me.' So much money and so many people depend on you. Pretty soon you're trying so hard that you can't function."

I ventured to repeat Nellie King's guesses about the mystery to Steve Blass and asked him what he thought.

"That's pretty heavy," he said after a moment. "I guess I don't have a tendency to go into things in much depth. I'm a surface reactor. I tend to take things not too seriously. I really think that's one of the things that's *helped* me in baseball."

A smile suddenly burst from him.

"There's one possibility nobody has brought up," he said. "I don't think anybody's ever said that maybe I just lost my control. Maybe your control is something that can just go. It's no big thing, but suddenly it's gone." He paused, and then he laughed in a self-deprecating way. "Maybe that's what I'd like to believe," he said.

ON my last morning with Steve Blass, we sat in his family room and played an imaginary ballgame together—half an inning of baseball. It had occurred to me that in spite of his enforced and now permanent exile from the game, he still possessed a rare body of precise and hard-won pitching information. He still knew most of the hitters in his league, and, probably as well as any other pitcher around, he knew what to pitch to them in a given situation. I had always wanted to hear a pitcher say exactly what he would throw next and why, and now I invited Blass to throw against the Cincinnati Reds, the toughest lineup of hitters anywhere. I would call the balls and strikes and hits. I promised he would have no control problems.

He agreed at once. He poured himself another cup of coffee and lit up a Garcia y Vega. He was wearing slacks and a T-shirt and an old sweater (he had a golfing date later that day), and he looked very young.

"O.K.," he said. "Pete Rose is leading off—right? First of all, I'm going to try to keep him off base if I can, because they have so many tough hitters coming up. They can bury you before you even get started. I'm going to try to throw strikes and not get too fine. I'll start him off with a slider away. He has a tendency to go up the middle, and I'll try to keep it a bit away."

Rose, I decided, didn't offer. It was ball one.

"Now I'll throw him a sinking fastball, and still try to work him out that way. The sinking fastball tends to tail off just a little."

Rose fouled it into the dirt.

"Well, now we come back with another slider, and I'll try to throw it inside. That's just to set up another slider *outside*."

Rose fouled that one as well.

"We're ahead one and two now—right?" Blass said. "Well, this early in the game I wouldn't try to throw him that slow curve—that big slop off-speed pitch. I'd like to work on that a couple of times first, because it's early and he swings so well. So as long as I'm ahead of him, I'll keep on throwing him sliders—keep going that way."

Rose took another ball, and then grounded out on a medium-speed curveball.

Joe Morgan stood in, and Blass puffed on his cigar and looked at the ceiling.

"Joe Morgan is strictly a fastball hitter, so I want to throw him a *bad* fastball to start him off," he said. "I'll throw it in the dirt to show it to him—get him geared to that kind of speed. Now, after ball one, I'll give him a medium-to-slow curveball and try to get it over the plate—just throw it for a strike."

Morgan took: one and one.

"Now I throw him a *real* slow curveball—a regular rainbow. I've had good luck against him with that sort of stuff."

And so it went. Morgan, I decided, eventually singled to right on a curve in on the handle—a lucky hit—but then Blass retired his next Cincinnati hitter, Dan Driessen, who popped out on a slider. Blass laid off slow pitches here, so Sanguillen would have a chance to throw out Morgan if he was stealing.

Johnny Bench stood in, with two out.

"Morgan won't be stealing, probably," Blass said. "He won't want to take the bat out of Bench's hands." He released another cloud of cigar smoke, thinking hard. "Well, I'll start him out with a good, tough fastball outside. I've got to work very carefully to him, because when he's hot he's capable of hitting it out anytime."

Ball one.

"Well, the slider's only been fair today. . . . I'll give him a slider, but away—off the outside."

Swinging strike. Blass threw another slider, and Bench hit a line single to left, moving Morgan to second. Tony Perez was the next batter.

"Perez is not a good high, hard fastball hitter," Blass said. "I'll begin him with that pitch, because I don't want to get into any more trouble with the slider and have him dunk one in. A letter-high fastball, with good mustard on it."

Perez took a strike.

"Now I'll do it again, until I miss—bust him up and in. He has a tendency to go after that kind of pitch. He's an exceptional offspeed hitter, and will give himself up with men on base—give up a little power to get that run in."

Perez took, for a ball, and then Blass threw him an intentional ball—a very bad slider inside. Perez had shortened up on the bat a little, but he took the pitch. He then fouled off a fastball, and Blass threw him another good fastball, high and inside, and Perez struck out, swinging, to end the inning.

"Pretty good inning," I said. "Way to go." We both laughed.

"Yes, you know that *exact* sequence has happened to Perez many times," Blass said. "He shortens up and then chases the pitch up here."

He was animated. "You know, I can almost *see* that fastball to Perez, and I can see his bat going through it, swinging through the pitch and missing," he said. "That's a good feeling. That's one of the concepts of Dr. Harrison's program, you know—visualization. When I was pitching well, I was doing that very thing. You get so locked in, you see yourself doing things before they happen. That's what people mean when they say you're in the groove. That's what happened in that World Series game, when I kept throwing that big slop curveball to Boog Powell, and it really ruined him. I must have thrown it three out of four pitches to him, and I just *knew* it was going to be there. There's no doubt about it—no information needed. The crowd is there, this is the World Series, and all of a sudden you're locked into something. It's like being plugged into a computer. It's 'Gimme the ball, *boom!* Click, click, click . . . *shoom!*' It's that good feeling. You're just flowing easy."

(1975)

LADY WITH A PENCIL

K ATHARINE White, who joined the staff of *The New Yorker* in August of 1925, six months after it was founded, by Harold Ross, agreed with her boss on many things, but she would not have agreed with the sentiment he expressed at the end of a letter he wrote to her in 1938, when she was in Maine and he was enduring the final, dragging throes of a New York summer—"the worst period of the year, with nothing on hand and no one seeming to do anything," he wrote. The letter closed, "I read a dozen stories today and all were junk. . . . An editor's life is certainly a life of disappointment. Yours sincerely, H. W. Ross." Ross famously saw failure and disappointment lurking everywhere, and he seemed to almost enjoy feeling embattled; his beleaguered vigilance was part of what made him charming, irritating, and successful. Katharine White, who was Katharine Sergeant Angell at the beginning of her *New Yorker* career, had an editor's life, too, and she knew that stories might not work and that writers might be unpredictable and unreliable, but she worried more about her writers' disappointments than about her own; to her, an editor's life was one of constantly renewed fulfillment.

In some ways, Katharine White's ambitions for the magazine surpassed Ross's: she pushed him to publish serious poetry (while also attempting to keep the flame of light verse alive as the supply of talented practitioners dwindled over the years); she had adventurous tastes, and enlarged the scope of both the magazine's fiction and the factual pieces; and she saw that the magazine's sense of humor, in its writing and in its cartoons, could be raised above the level of a "comic paper," which is how Ross sometimes referred to his magazine. Before she was hired, as a manuscript reader, she had written a handful of magazine articles and held several jobs unrelated to journalism or the literary world. Her background was much like that of many women in publishing today. She had grown up in an upper-middle-class suburb of Boston, with a prosperous father and an aunt who was an early graduate of Smith and had worked as a teacher. (Katharine's mother had died when she was six years old.) She had attended one of Boston's best private schools for girls, and had graduated from Bryn Mawr, one of the few colleges organized around the militant belief that a woman's place was in the world. She was married to a promising attorney, a graduate of Harvard Law School. Katharine's privilege put her in the way of certain opportunities, but just as important was a kind of good luck: like thousands of other young and youngish people—when she was hired, she was thirty-two and was the mother of two small children—in New York in the nineteen-twenties, she was in the right place at the right time. What's inspiring about her life and career is how much she did with that luck, how thoroughly she transformed the place and the time she was in. What's even more remarkable is that it didn't seem to occur to her not to.

Within months, she became indispensable to Ross, and soon there was no part of the magazine she wasn't involved in. The collaboration was an unlikely one. Ross had grown up in Colorado and Utah, and had left school at the age of thirteen. For several years, he worked as a tramp newspaperman all over the country, and during the First World War he was an editor and reporter in France for *The Stars and Stripes,* the Army newspaper. He played poker, he swore, and he dated actresses. But, though Ross was self-educated, he was not unsophisticated; and Katharine's sophistication was the kind that allowed her to see the promise of Ross's vision, which at that time was far from obvious, and to help him clarify and improve it. As William Shawn, the editor of the magazine after Ross's death, in 1951, wrote in her obituary, in 1977, "More than any other editor except Harold Ross himself, Katharine White gave *The New Yorker* its shape, and set it on its course."

WHEN I came to work at *The New Yorker,* in 1978, in the magazine's typing pool, I knew very little about Katharine White—only that she had been married to E. B. White and, before they were married, had encouraged Ross to hire him as a staff writer; that she was an "important" fiction editor (not that I knew then what editors actually did, or what made one important); and that she was, by her first marriage, the mother of Roger Angell, another important fiction editor, whose office was at the other end of the building from the typing pool, and whose lunch I sometimes ordered when I filled in at the receptionist's desk on my floor (chicken salad on white toast, black coffee, vanilla ice cream). And I knew that Roger's—Mr. Angell's—office had once been his mother's office. (After Katharine White retired, at the end of 1960, her office—a prime piece of real estate—was left vacant for several years. This is an extreme case of a practice that was not uncommon by the time I got here: letting the "meaning" drain out of an office, so its future inhabitants wouldn't get any big ideas about who they were. But when Roger moved into her office, in the mid-seventies, after another editor retired, the meaning drained right back in. He says that a psychiatrist once told him that his being an editor and occupying his mother's office was "the greatest piece of active sublimation in my experience.")

Though Katharine White was officially held in high esteem around the magazine when I began working there, the message that came through when her name was mentioned was decidedly mixed. Most of what I knew about her I'd learned from Brendan Gill's "Here at The New Yorker," which had been published three years earlier. Mrs. White was eighty-two and was in poor health when the book came out, and Gill's descriptions of her and several of her colleagues so pained her that she made sure her annotated copy was included in the collection of books and personal papers she bequeathed to Bryn Mawr. Still, Gill did credit her with helping to invent the magazine, and he called her Ross's "intellectual conscience."

Harrison Kinney, in his fat new biography of James Thurber, writes, "Nearly all descriptions of Katharine sooner or later include the adjective 'formidable.' " This is true, except for the "nearly" part. The word is so loaded when it is applied to women that for some years I was, I think, afraid to find out what it was loaded *with*. The magazine was by then an institution, and fitting in—disappearing, if possible—was encouraged, and I wanted to fit in, so when people at the office used that word to describe Katharine White ("forbidding" cropped up a lot, too), and spoke of being afraid, even terrified, of her, I absorbed their ambivalence without examining it.

The grudging quality that always came through in conversation is in the books, too. They give with one hand while taking away, subtly, with the other. "She took care to make her weight felt at every turn" is how Gill summarizes her influence at the magazine, and in his wording there is a hint of something furtive and not quite right, as in, say, "She took care to wipe her fingerprints off the gun." Scott Elledge, E. B. White's biographer, acknowledges Katharine White's influence on twentieth-century letters by listing the writers she brought to the magazine—the roster includes Thurber, Vladimir Nabokov, Marianne Moore, John O'Hara, Mary McCarthy, Clarence Day, S. N. Behrman, Jean Stafford, William Maxwell, Ogden Nash, Irwin Shaw, Nadine Gordimer, John Cheever, and John Updike—but he, too, seems to be made nervous by Katharine White's tremendous strengths. He writes, "The qualities that made her seem formidable . . . were essentially intellectual—along with her straight-backed, one might almost say regal, carriage." In the very next sentence you can almost hear him breathe a sigh of relief as he chivalrously rushes to rescue her from the brink of smart-woman purgatory: "These qualities were softened, however, by her equally evident and appealing femininity." Even her own biographer, Linda H. Davis, whose "Onward and Upward," published in 1987, gives Katharine her due in many respects and is the most valuable source of information about her life, suffers occasionally from a tone of lamentation over her imperfections. (The title of Davis's book is right on the money, though: "Onward and Upward," a phrase borrowed from the Unitarians, was a heading that Katharine cooked up for the magazine, and it's as good a description as any of her modus vivendi.)

It wasn't until recently, when I took another look into Katharine White's life, that I uncovered my own prejudices about her, and I realized that the main impression I had formed from my first reading of Davis's book (and it's no fault of the book), nine years ago, was of the recently divorced Katharine Angell's marrying E. B. White without telling her children, and of their finding out about it two days later, when a relative read the news in Walter Winchell's column. This shocks me now as much as it did when I first learned of it—Roger was nine then, and his sister, Nancy (now Nancy Angell Stableford), who was going on thirteen, says that her mother never satisfactorily explained the lapse—but what shocks me more is how much my judgment of her as a mother affected my judgment of her as an editor, in a way that it never would have if she had been a man, and a father.

ANOTHER double-edged word often used to describe Katharine White is "aristocratic." No doubt this has something to do with her appearance; even at a time when people in general dressed more formally than they do now, Katharine White stood out in her beautifully tailored clothes and Sally Victor hats. She was a small woman, only a couple of inches over five feet, and she had big gray eyes. She had long brown hair (by the forties, it had turned gray), which she always had done at the Frances Fox Institute, and which she wore in a bun held together with bone hairpins. "She was terribly handsome," William Maxwell says. "I never saw her in any way in disarray." Mary D. Kierstead, who began working at the magazine in 1948 and became a fiction reader in 1957, says that evidence of Katharine White's great taste and style was everywhere—in the way she dressed, in the objects in her house, and in how she planted her garden—and the result, she says, was a feeling not of "nasty neatness" but of inviting comfort, a sense that everything was somehow just right. Her ability to express strong opinions about the way things should be done was everywhere in her work: she never had the title of executive editor but she had, with Ross's blessing, executive authority. Maxwell, who retired from The New Yorker in the mid-seventies, was a fiction editor for forty years, and was a colleague of Katharine White's for twenty-five of them. He says, "What was remarkable about her was that she was always reaching out toward writers who were not characteristic of the magazine. If there was a distance they couldn't quite bridge"—he cites Nabokov, with his fondness for neologisms and archaisms—"she found a way to bridge it."

Maxwell goes on to recall, "She had a sense of what was good for the magazine as a whole. She'd rip the magazine to pieces if something came in that was topical, even though it was early Monday morning"—the day the magazine went to press. "She was aware of the importance of making *The New Yorker* seem up to date. And it was important. She was continually interested in what was happening in the city." Her interests were political, social, literary, cultural. (And culinary—I saw a memo she wrote to Lois Long in 1929, asking her to check out the food buyer at Macy's as a possible Profile subject.) Maxwell says she was always writing to her congressman; Roger Angell remembers his parents sweeping out of the house at night, dressed up to go to the theatre or a dinner party.

Joseph Mitchell is an admirer of Katharine White's and was an office friend (together they decided that the two greatest American books were Mark Twain's "Life on the Mississippi" and Sarah Orne Jewett's "The Country of the Pointed Firs"). Mitchell says, "She was so of the moment. She reminded me in a weird way—her worldliness, though that isn't the word at all—of Colette. She was a very good writer. There's a kind of comedy to it, a way of looking at the world. The humor barely peeps out, and consequently you remember it."

Between 1958 and 1970, Katharine White wrote fourteen gardening columns for the magazine (which E. B. White collected in book form after her death), and they owe their existence, in a sense, to an event in her life that she was not entirely happy about. In 1938, E. B. White decided that he could no longer be a writer if being a writer meant living in New York City, and that year the Whites moved to a Maine farmhouse they had bought five years earlier. Katharine continued working half time for *The New Yorker;* every day, her secretary in the office mailed her a huge packet of manuscripts, galleys, letters, and books, and every day Katharine mailed back a packet of marked-up manuscripts and galleys, memos, and opinions. Years later, she protested Brendan Gill's assertion that she had been "reluctant" to leave her job. She said that her years in Maine, where she spent a lot of time in her garden, had, among their other benefits, laid the groundwork for her writing. She said that she had been sad to leave, but not reluctant. Ross, however, was more than sad to see the Whites go. He did his best to keep Katharine informed about what was going on in the office, and he continued to rely on her judgment as much as the distance between them permitted. And he hoped they would return.

Ross got his wish five years later, during the war. The Whites came back to New York, and Katharine resumed her editorial duties in the office. She was no longer the head of the fiction department, for she had resigned that position in 1938, but her involvement in the magazine was total, and remained so for the next fourteen years. In 1956, she became the head of the fiction department again for a short time, and in 1957 she and her husband left New York for good and moved back to their farm. Katharine took on the role of consulting editor for three years, and then retired. But her interest in the magazine never died: she read every issue until failing eyesight made that impossible, and made a point of letting writers—and not just her own writers—know when she particularly liked a piece of theirs.

. . . .

IN a letter that Katharine wrote to Ross from Maine in 1940, she added this postscript: "When you get long memos not written on my beautiful office type-writer, it means Mr. White is trying to write. He told me hearing me batting away made him feel uncreative, when he was struggling to put words on paper! . . . So I just shut up, and take to pencil." Not surprisingly, the solici-tousness and understanding that marked Katharine's relationships with her writers also extended to Andy—as E. B. White had been known to one and all since his college days. Andy came first, and the household always revolved around his needs. The marriage was by all accounts a loving one, although the match appeared to be almost as unlikely as the professional partnership be-tween Katharine and Ross.

Katharine was seven years older than Andy. When they married, she was, at thirty-seven, a well-paid editor with many responsibilities, both personal and professional, and he was, at thirty, a writer of still small reputation who had never been married; when it came to romantic entanglements, he desired the romance but dreaded the entanglement. One person who knew the Whites said of his relationship with Katharine, "He didn't play hard to get—he *was* hard to get, though very happy once got." She admired him as a writer and found him funny, and he admired her as an editor and found her funny, too, in a different way. He told his biographer, Scott Elledge, about a discussion he and Katharine had one morning:

> I don't remember how ivy got into the discussion but potted plants have never been far removed from Katharine's thoughts. Anyway, when I heard the word "ivy," I said petulantly, "Oh, let the ivy rest!" K's whole manner changed. Instead of slamming the ball back over the net at me, she replied in a mild and thoughtful voice: "That sounds like the name of an English country house."
>
> At this point, I decided that she was the girl for me and the hell with the ob-stacles. So, after some badgering, she agreed to it, and we spent the rest of the day getting married.

Katharine's relative lack of irony made some people think she was humor-less; her husband, whose self-consciousness was often debilitating to him, found great charm, and probably great relief, in her directness.

If Katharine was like a cross between Eleanor Roosevelt and Jane Austen, Andy was in many ways like a character he himself created, in his first chil-dren's book, "Stuart Little." Stuart is a mouse, the son of human parents in New York City, and he leaves his family and goes off on a quest to find Margalo, the bird he has fallen in love with. White, the youngest of six children, was slight of build, mouselike in his vulnerability and lack of confidence, and Stuart-like in his perpetual sensitivity to romance and to nature. He was boyish and romantic to the end of his life (and became better-looking as he got older and his hair and his mustache turned from brown to white), and he never felt more at home than he did at his farm, surrounded by animals. Stuart never finds Margalo, but Andy and Katharine found each other, and their devotion did not diminish with time. A week after they were married, he wrote to her that he was filled with hope, because she was "the person to whom I return" and "the recurrent phrase in my life." He went on, "I realized that so strongly one day a couple of weeks ago when, after being away and among people I wasn't sure of and in circumstances I had doubts about, I came back and walked into your office and saw how real and incontrovertible you seemed. I don't know whether you know just what I mean or whether you experience, ever, the same feeling; but what I mean is, that being with you is like walking on a very clear morning—definitely the sensation of belonging there." Forty-eight years later, in response to a letter of condolence he had received after Katharine's death, he wrote, "She seemed beautiful to me the first time I saw her, and she seemed beautiful when I gave her the small kiss that was goodbye."

KATHARINE White was very private, and, Linda Davis points out, "Much of her time was spent alone in a room—reading, writing, and editing. . . . That time spent alone prohibits us from knowing certain things about Katharine White's inner life. Some things she did not communicate." True enough—and certain aspects of her private life were so unusual, and would be considered just as unusual even now, that you can't help wanting to know what she made of them. Katharine divorced her first husband, Ernest Angell, in 1929 (after spending the requisite three months in Reno), and a few months later she married Andy White. She and Ernest had joint custody of the children, but Roger and Nancy's home was with their father, on the Upper East Side; their mother's apartment, in the Village, where she lived with Andy and their new baby, Joel, who was born in 1930, was a place they went to on weekends. On the subject of this unconventional arrangement there is only silence. Her pieces for the magazine—the gardening columns, fourteen years' worth of children's-book reviews, a couple of brief reminiscences—are full of autobiographical and personal references, and the voice is vivid and conversational, yet the emotions of the person behind the voice remain fairly well hidden. But in her papers at Bryn Mawr and in those in *The New Yorker*'s files, which are now housed in some thousand boxes in the New York Public Library, across the street from the magazine's offices, Katharine White left a lengthy, detailed record of the part of her life that mattered most to her—her life as an editor.

READING the memos and letters that went back and forth between Harold Ross and Katharine White through the years made me giddy with a feeling of discovery, as if I'd suddenly hit upon the structure of *The New Yorker*'s DNA—almost as if I'd been present at the creation. I could only scratch the surface of the archives, but every folder I opened had something *alive* in it—a blast of criticism, a burst of humor, an odd phrase, a gripe, an idea, a forceful opinion. I'd been to the archives at Bryn Mawr, and I got the same sense of life in the letters there, but largely through indirection, for most of the letters there were written *to* Katharine. Her sense of humor was expressed in her correspondents' eager attempts to appeal to it, her devotion in their expressions of gratitude to her and concern for her. (Katharine's letters at Bryn Mawr are often about her health, a subject that occupied a sizable space in her thoughts as a young woman and preoccupied her more and more as she got older. In 1975, Jean Stafford wrote to her, "Our correspondence, yours and mine, could be the subject of a thesis with the title, perhaps, of 'The Medical Histories of One Contemporary American Emancipated Woman Fiction Editor and One Contemporary American Emancipated Woman Fiction Writer: An In-Depth Look at Orthopaedic and Allergic, etc. Problems among Literary Women of the Twentieth Century.' " Enough said.)

In Katharine's own letters, handwritten second thoughts often sidle in next to the first, typewritten ones. A letter to an old friend goes over the ground of meeting and becoming engaged to Ernest Angell in neutral fashion: "On my eighteenth birthday, just before I entered Bryn Mawr, Ernest proposed to me and we became engaged, and stayed so for five years before he was through Harvard and law school and he had found a job in Cleveland." End of paragraph. But then, in neat script, comes "Such early commitments just don't work." Katharine, with an eye on future scholars, often attached notes to the letters. To a cranky late-thirties memo from Ross she appends this typed note: "A wonderfully censorious and funny memo to me from Ross. One of the chores I had had to do always was read every word of the X issue (just out), point out faults, repetitions, typos, merits, and failings. . . . Apparently my reports (or *a* report) became too burdensome and worst of all carried queries I should have asked of someone else. I was rebuked." She adds, in her own hand, "The wonderful thing about my relationship with Ross was that he could be utterly outspoken with me and I to him but we never got mad at each other. I felt just as free to tell him he was 'crazy' as he felt free to call me 'crazy.' "

The memos in the Public Library's archives have exactly that kind of openness and honesty, and that confiding tone, and a basic understanding of each other that saw them through their constant misunderstandings. Like the repartee between Cary Grant and Rosalind Russell in "His Girl Friday," and between William Powell and Myrna Loy in "The Thin Man," the exchanges between Ross and Katharine White carry a romantic electrical charge—the romance coming from how close these two came to the heady ideal, hardly ever achieved between men and women at work, of complete equality.

Ross to White: "I did not intend you to take Sifton's memorandum seriously. I sent it as a curiosity."

White to Ross: "I can't really believe that I'm to reject this poem for the reasons you give. What's more I don't care to. . . . I really think you are wrong from the literary point of view and hope you will reconsider."

Ross to White: "Tell Guiterman he not only got the statue cleaned up but the word 'hell' in the New York Times, which is a much greater accomplishment."

White to Ross: "In general I might say that this book is fascinating, informative, and awful."

Ross to White: "Not only, to my astonishment, does Fowler use no point after Mrs but he has a little piece on the use of the period after abbreviations (or constructions) that amazes me for its impracticability. It is so revolutionary that Edgar Hoover would punch him as a red if he were alive and showed up over here."

White to Ross (in 1934): "I am going to suggest something which I think at first will give you all the horrors. It is that we get a radio for this office."

White to Ross, on a pink routing slip:

> Mr. Ross—
> "Of all mean words this tongue doth know
> The meanest of these is 'I told you so.' "
>   KSW

The three-by-five pink "to-from" slip, stalwart transmitter of pithy directives and opinions and jokes at the magazine for more than half a century, is now slated for extinction—an unspeakable development to those of us with ancient blood ties to our office supplies. Seeing this last one, from the early thirties, reminded me of a note that Harriet Walden, who was Katharine's secretary for several years before her retirement (and my boss in the typing pool), and afterward remained her liaison to the magazine, showed me recently. Their correspondence was warm and affectionate, but Katharine was once swept away by a paper-induced panic. In 1964, she wrote, "Dear Harriet: Please never again send this horrible special white paper now required in the office. It can't be used in this household. Please try to order, and we'll pay for, yellow paper of the old sort. . . . As EBW says, it's a serious matter—like taking away a violinist's bow, one that he has used all his life. It's *crippling* to every writer I've talked to. KSW." This note was written on—the congregation will please rise—a little pink routing slip.

What really stands out in the White-Ross correspondence I saw is how adult these two people were, how well they listened to each other, how naturally it seemed to come to them to treat each other as equals. Joseph Mitchell says, "I *liked* the way she got along with Mr. Ross. I never knew two people who were put together so well. They became an extraordinary pair." It was a collaboration that Katharine somehow took in stride; and though the partnership was a model one, it has never come close to being repeated at the magazine. For three decades, Katharine White was the only female editor on the premises. In a 1944 note to Ross about the artist Helen Hokinson, who was vacillating between renewing her contract with *The New Yorker* and going into newspaper syndication, Katharine seems to enjoy confiding the pleasure she takes in her position. She told him she spoke to Hokinson about the "disadvantages of her being typed as woman page stuff, and the slight stigma attached to the artistic merit of any work by women, which is done for an exclusively feminine audience," and adds, "I told her I thought she ought to feel it as much of a comedown as I would feel it if I had to give up being an editor of *The New Yorker* for being an editor of a fashion magazine." The respect she and Ross had for each other bred a loyalty that was free of fear, and it made good work possible—and good work was what both of them were interested in above all else. Perhaps this is where Katharine's "formidableness" comes in; as Gardner Botsford, an editor at the magazine from the forties on, puts it, in his own pithy, pink-slip way, "She was someone whose standards and capabilities were so much higher than your own that you just sat down and shut up." Katharine's work was her life to such an extent that the day after she married Andy White she was at her desk, banging out memos to Ross (and still signing them K. S. Angell): a suggestion for Robert Benchley's theatre column, a memo about a Peter Arno cover.

Having grown up with the idea that good taste was not something you exercised so much as it was something you didn't violate, I had assumed that Katharine White's much lauded good taste in editorial matters was reined-in and backward-looking, more concerned with what the magazine shouldn't be doing than with what it could be doing, but in memo after memo she pushes Ross (and, later, Shawn) to widen the embrace of the magazine and to move it forward. There are ideas for Profiles of national, not just local, figures; long lists of writers who might be good for book reviews; countless memos on writers she's tracking and pursuing; suggestions for covers and cartoons; a checklist of tired cartoon ideas to watch out for and squelch. There was a long memo to Ross about the editing of fiction: she listed twenty-seven names, all of them contributors who had complained, with varying degrees of vehemence, about being overedited, and she urged Ross to go easy with his queries, and told him that several important writers, including Faulkner and Hemingway, refused to submit their fiction to *The New Yorker* for fear of Ross's tampering. There are endless ideas for Talk of the Town stories, and fairly endless criticisms of published ones: on one tear sheet, she underlined a lead sentence that read, "Every now and then we run across an announcement so staggering to our reason that we have to go off somewhere and lie down for a week," and wrote next to it, "This is getting pretty neurotic." Most striking of all was a memo of "random thoughts" which a number of modern press critics would be all too pleased to have written: "Talk lacks *news*, lacks any digging for facts on important things and too much digging for facts on stereotyped quaint or curious, but dull and trivial, people and places—quaint shops, queer and unimportant people, people who have lived longer or made buttons longer or collected more queer collections than anyone else, etc. It's all singularly devitalized. We have too many long dullish personality stories about people who are well enough to tell about but are not the people in the news one wants to know about. Why, for example, couldn't we have found out who wrote 'Washington Merry-Go-Round,' which everyone is crazy to know, instead of publishing a long story on the doctor of the Fire Dept. (This was a good story by the way—I don't mean he wasn't worth writing about, but only cite him as not being a hot news personality.) . . . Also, I still believe in calling in for occasional meetings people like Benchley, Long, Sullivan, Markey and Mosher—someone on sports, etc. We're no longer a lively group of people working for the love of it—we're a bedraggled, institutionalized scattered force, each working in our little rut." The memo is dated August 27, 1931.

Katharine seems to have perfected the rhetorical use of the gone-to-hell-in-a-handbasket motif in 1931. That fall, in a detailed memo to James M. Cain, who, before he went on to write "Double Indemnity" and "The Postman Always Rings Twice," served a stint as managing editor, she wrote, "Dear Mr. Cain: I wish to register a strong protest on the present telephone service. I don't think I have ever known it so bad in the history of the magazine."

OVER and over, when I talked to writers who had worked with Katharine White, I heard tales of endless encouragement and support. (Not that she was uncritical—she did not spare Nabokov her anxiety about the subject matter of "Lolita," and she told Mary McCarthy that she felt "The Group" was "too much a social document and too little a novel.") She was always honest with her writers, always in touch with them, and always eager to see their next story or poem. When I spoke to William Maxwell, I asked him what Katharine White was like to work with. He had been a contributor of short stories to the magazine before he joined the staff, and she had been his first editor. He said, "The strongest impression I have of her is that she was maternal."

Our conversation took place before I began rooting around at Bryn Mawr and the Public Library, when I was still trying to square the conflicting images I had of her—the nurturing, encouraging editor and the mother who basically gave up her children—and I said, "It's funny; as an editor she was maternal, and as a mother she was editorial."

"I think that's not even to be wondered at," he said. If you have a creative life, you can only do so much, he explained—something he, too, had had to come to terms with. "If you give it in one place, it has to be taken away from another."

Maxwell's response to my puzzlement was so matter-of-fact that I didn't realize until later that he hadn't really explained the contradiction—he had just restated it as a fact of life. But that was the whole point: we were looking at the same thing in different ways, as men and women have been brought up to do. Men tend to see their lives, regardless of the balance of the various parts, as a unified whole, but the prevailing metaphor for women of my generation has failure built into it: we are said to "juggle" the various parts of our lives, and the only possible outcome if we concentrate on one ball in particular is that we drop the others. But this is not how Katharine White saw her life—partly because she could afford not to, by hiring people to juggle for her, but mainly because she just didn't think that way. When I started looking at her life as she looked at it—and as she lived it—it suddenly seemed all of a piece.

Roger Angell grew up with *The New Yorker:* his mother and Andy White, he told me, "talked about Ross all the time—he was like another person at the dinner table." Roger sold his first story to the magazine fifty-two years ago, at the age of twenty-three, and he has now been a fiction editor here for forty years. (He and his mother overlapped for only a matter of a few months, but he did inherit a number of her writers.) Needless to say, he has spent a lot more time than I have sorting out the apparent contradictions in his mother's life and their effect on his life. By now, he seems to see her as she would have wanted to be seen—as someone who was actively, passionately engaged in what she was doing. "All the signs of her work were around her wherever she went," he said. "She carried one of those big brown portfolios—it was stuffed with galleys and manuscripts, and she always had brown pencils scattered around, and big erasers and eraser scrubbings and cigarette ashes. If she was formidable, if people were scared of her, it was because she was so good at what she did, and she knew so much, and she was in the middle of everything—not because she'd been given power but because she assumed that this was where she belonged, because she cared so much."

Roger leaned forward to make his next point: "She was intensely, *intensely* interested in the work. It was the main event of her life—*The New Yorker,* and *New Yorker* writers, and what was in the magazine. It wasn't a matter of power. It was about what was on the page or what could be on the page if something worked out."

Roger's wife, Carol, had told me that Katharine White was a better mother-in-law than mother. Roger brought this up, and said he agreed with Carol. His mother had great difficulty expressing emotion directly, he said, and her way of showing affection to her children was to worry about them. "I think a source of endless pain for her was that she'd given up her children," he said. "I think she tried to make up for what she perceived as her defection as a mother by worrying about us more than any mother had ever worried. She was this way with her writers—she'd worry about her writers' health, money, happiness, their success, their children. She was a terrific worrier—she was a major-league worrier—and for an editor to be a major-league worrier is a wonderful thing."

In Roger's assessment of the gifts that his mother had brought to her work was, I thought, also an acknowledgment that he had come to appreciate what was best about her and had found a way to live with the rest—and that he had been able to learn from her gifts. He said, "I know I have a basic feeling that definitely came from my mother: Has this been done as well as it can be done? Has the writer done what he wants to do here?"

Maxwell, who learned editing mostly from Katharine White, said much the same thing. "There are two kinds of editor—a yes editor and a no editor. Katharine was a yes editor." And it's not easy to convey a yes while you're say-

ing no—which is what an editor has to say most of the time. Katharine knew
the difficulty and the importance of getting this equation right, and it was at
the heart of her approach to her work. In a self-critical letter that she wrote to
a friend who had praised one of her gardening columns—a piece that frowned
on certain schools of flower arranging—Katharine conveyed this, and also
managed to tip her hat, with characteristic generosity, to one of her writers.
The piece, she wrote, "had the great disadvantage of being an attack or knocking down and, as Marianne Moore once wisely said in a lecture to students, it's
too easy to be against and much harder and more useful to be for—only she
said it much better."

(1996)

DEALING WITH ROSEANNE

ONCE upon a time, in 1985, Johnny Carson introduced the freshest new comic voice on the Los Angeles comedy-club scene, a thirty-two-year-old Denver housewife, to his "Tonight Show" audience. Backstage, before going on, the comedienne opened a letter she'd written to herself years before, when she'd imagined this moment of triumph. Part of it said, "This is the beginning of your life, for She who is and is not yet." Then Carson said, "Please welcome Roseanne Barr!" and the nation took its first look at the radical feminist disguised as a faux naïf who would become an iconoclast the like of which had never been seen before on TV. She was a bulky five feet four, in flats and black slacks, with a gardenia corsage pinned to her black-and-orange jacket. She chewed gum as she smiled. She gave a girlish little wave of her left hand, and in a voice as affectless as her salute said, "Oh, hi. I been married thirteen years, and lemme tell you, it's a thrill to be out of the house. I never get out of the house. I stay home all the time. I never do anything fun 'cause I'm a housewife. I hate the word 'housewife.' I prefer to be called 'domestic goddess.' "

The laughs during her monologue were often longer than the jokes. "Do you guys like that guy Stephen King that writes those really scary books?" she asked the audience. "Well, now he has come out with the scariest book he ever, ever wrote. It is *so* scary. It's about a husband with a mind of his own." On video, the audience's shock is audible: there is a gasp, then applause, then cheering. Roseanne laughs along with the viewers. "Oh, don't get tense, ladies. It's just a fantasy. It could never really happen." It had taken Roseanne five years to perfect the six minutes of material and the ungrammatical jazz of her delivery, which steered her début expertly to its final punch. "Still, stuff bugs me," she said. "This bugs me the worst. That's when the husband thinks that the wife knows where everything is, huh? Like they think the uterus is a track-ing device. He comes in: 'Hey, Roseanne! Roseanne! Do we have any Cheetos left?' Like he can't go over and lift up that sofa cushion himself."

From that moment, Roseanne was out of the house and into the fantasy life of the nation; her very presence was a provocation. Her body (she sometimes tipped the scales at more than two hundred pounds) and her unladylike talk made her America's bourgeois nightmare come to comic life. "Roseanne," the show she minted from the strong, bright part of her splintered personality, has been beamed around the world on prime-time television since 1988 and is going into its eighth—and probably final—year. The onetime waitress, who was working for a dollar and a half an hour plus tips in Denver when she began doing her standup act, now earns a little more than a million dollars for each of the twenty-five episodes she does in a season. Her production company, Full Moon & High Tide, negotiated a deal with ABC to produce up to four series. Roseanne figures that by the end of the century she should be worth around a billion dollars. On being asked in public recently about her stature as the most powerful woman in American entertainment, Roseanne feigned modesty and said, "What about Oprah?" In private, though, during a week I spent with her in L.A. this spring, Roseanne contended, "I'm way more up there than Oprah. I have commitments for solid pay-or-play series; and nobody—no man or woman—has that. Just me." Roseanne also has a screenwriting deal with Miramax. She won the fierce competition for the rights to co-produce (with Warner Bros.) an American version of Jennifer Saunders' hugely successful British sitcom "Absolutely Fabulous." She is refining contract arrangements to co-produce "Planet Hollywood Squares," a weekly version of the famous quiz show, and a late-night comedy show. And within three years Roseanne's Big Food Diner, which she started in Eldon, Iowa, during her interlude with hus-band No. 2, the comedian Tom Arnold, will be expanded to a string of diners across America. (They will feature "the real food that everybody likes," from her own calorie-crammed recipes.) Finally, Roseanne is planning to start a line of clothing for large women and has already made some of the designs. "Very simple and tailored things," she says. "No big swans and shit like that on them."

Commercial success has allowed Roseanne to win for herself, her comedy, and her feminist agenda what had previously been allowed only to a handful of great American funnymen, such as Charlie Chaplin and Woody Allen: the con-trol of her product. Most comedians are hostile sharpshooters loudly proclaim-ing their innocence, but Roseanne has got where she is by biting the hands that have fed her—family, feminism, and Hollywood. She simply can't see a bound-ary without crossing it. Her divorces, her disputed history as an abused child, her public excesses—what she calls those "Prozac moments," as when she botched the singing of "The Star-Spangled Banner" at a baseball game—have fed the tabloids and sometimes obscured her gift. Roseanne has the rare markings of a true renegade comic spirit. Recently, two months before her third marriage—to her twenty-eight-year-old bodyguard/driver, Ben Thomas—she showed off the scar of her in-vitro pregnancy on the David Letterman show. The scar made news; but, in a way, the gesture was much more than a prank. The comic's job is to bare wounds to a world that won't admit its own. "The hollow and full run together," Roseanne has written of her paradoxical nature; and the genuine zany has no choice but to express this dividedness as a way of mastering it. "I am an overweight overachiever with a few dandy compulsive-obsessive disorders and a little problem with self-mutilation," she writes in a 1994 autobiography, "My Lives." "Like vampires and night creatures, we wander the earth, alone, haunted, not owning a body, just temporarily inhabiting one. Crazy all the way."

Roseanne holds nothing back: whatever emotion overtakes her, she expresses. "I'm pure id," she says. When *TV Guide* said that the current season of "Roseanne" lacked "the touch of Tom Arnold" (Arnold had been the show's co-executive producer), Roseanne called up the "Tonight Show" and got Jay Leno to cut his monologue short so she could rebut the remarks. "I've had the Tom Arnold touch, and, let me tell you, what he lacked in size he made up for in speed," she told the nation. To the charge of falling ratings, she fumed, "Did it ever occur to anybody that it was simply because of complications with my in-vitro fertilization and doctors ordering me to lay on my back for twelve weeks of my pregnancy and that during those times *I wasn't even on the show?*" Roseanne was in fine and fearless fury. "O.K., well I think what they're really mad about is that I'm a woman calling the shots; and that I was a waitress; and that I was a maid; and I never went past the ninth grade, and I *still* do a better show than any of them. And I just want to say now I'm back in full force and I've even fired the head writer who in my absence let my show go to hell. And it felt so great to fire yet another overpaid, undertalented man that the press cannot wait to give credit for *my* work. So in conclusion I would like to say that anybody who has a problem with that can kiss my ass!" At this point, Leno tried politely to approach Roseanne and segue into the next part of the show. "I'm not done! I'm not done!" she said, pushing him away and turning back to Mr. and Mrs. America. "And after that," she said, "they can kiss my baby's ass, too!" It was great television, and an exemplary lesson in Roseanne's roaring high dudgeon: If you can't stand the heat, stay out of her face.

Rage is Roseanne's ozone. She exudes it. She creates it. "It isn't a choice," Roseanne says. "You don't decide 'I'm going to be offensive or do something that upsets people.' It just happens." When Roseanne addressed the National Association of College Broadcasters not long ago, she began by saying, "Some of you have absolutely no talent and don't know what you're doing at all, have no point of view, and don't care. I predict that you're the ones who will be successful." The broadcasting wanna-bes laughed. Roseanne, as usual, was making the unacceptable irresistible. Because of the sexual politics of previous eras, the comediennes to whom Roseanne sees herself linked—Mae West, Judy Holliday, Lucille Ball—got their way by cunning indirection. But Roseanne prefers the head butt to the bon mot. She can rumble. Matt Berry, a standup comedian who performed with Roseanne in the Denver clubs and now works as a writer on her show, remembers the time that fifty bikers and their girlfriends came to a gig. "She used to have a line in her act where she goes, 'I really hate bikers. You know, they all got tobacco juice in their beards. They piss on the side of the road. And the men are even worse!' " he says. "She walks out. Sees all these bikers. Big, burly guys. She looks at the comics in the back. 'Should I do it?' We're yelling, 'Do it!' She did it. They fuckin' loved her. They went nuts."

Roseanne has reclaimed for female comedy the phallic aggression which is traditionally associated with male humor, whose totem, the Fool's sceptre, is actually the penis. Even Roseanne's physical posture—she has discarded the apologetic feminine stance onstage, and plants her feet firmly apart—suggests phallic power, which is, she insists, "really womb power that men stole." "A man standing with his legs apart is impersonating a woman," Roseanne explains, assuming the erect birth posture. "Men all have womb envy. We don't have penis envy." She goes on, "My psychic penis is way larger than any man's. My attitude is, I have a vagina and therefore I have the bigger penis." Roseanne stated her position most succinctly in her rough-and-tumble standup days, when, she says, "I was the filthiest act ever. I would do anything." She'd end her set by saying, "People say to me, 'You're not very feminine.' Well, they can *suck my dick.*"

IN her comedy, Roseanne is unrelenting, which translates in psychological terms as inconsolable. Laughter is her revenge on a childhood she characterizes as a "roiling nightmare of Dickensian struggle." Roseanne was born in 1952, into a poor Jewish family living among Mormons in Salt Lake City. She remembers praying "either make me retarded or make me a Mormon," and explains, "They all seemed so happy; they didn't see the ugliness I did." Roseanne's grandmother Bobbe Mary lost all her relatives in the Nazi concentration camps, and ran an apartment house for survivors of the Holocaust; Roseanne remembers that her mother, who was born in Utah, lived in constant fear of being exterminated. "Her hobbies," Roseanne writes, "were being a credit to her race and hiding in the basement." This is not comic hyperbole. "Our mother would say, 'They'll come for us,' " Roseanne says. "I remember her taking us down to the basement if someone just came and knocked on the door. I really, truly believed that if anybody found out we were Jewish they would kill us." But, she says, "I knew Jews were allowed to live safely in New York." This knowledge came from "The Ed Sullivan Show" and the Jewish comedians on it. "It was like Radio Free America," she says. "I loved them all—Totie Fields, Jack Carter, Buddy Hackett. But the comedian who really moved me was Richard Pryor. I knew that he was inside the stereotype and fighting against it, that he was going to blow it up from the inside. I got that immediately. I thought, By God, I'm going to do the same thing being a woman.'"

All the oppression and self-loathing that male authority perpetrates against women seem to have coalesced, one way or another, in her. She claims to have twenty-one separate personalities, and four years ago went public with the accusation that her parents abused her (which they deny). According to family lore, as an infant Roseanne screamed so frantically and jammed her fist in her mouth so consistently that she rubbed the skin off her nose and had to be put in a tiny restraining jacket. At sixteen, after she was hit by a car (her head was impaled on the hood ornament), she was institutionalized for a year, and when she got out she often had a recurring nightmare that she could not wake up. "I was horrified that people would think I was dead and bury me alive," Roseanne says. She also turned her fury recklessly on herself—cutting herself, burning herself, and abusing her body by alternately starving and gorging it. Nonetheless, in the midst of a chaotic family atmosphere Roseanne learned that the way to survive was to be fierce and funny. Her father, whom she characterizes in her books as a bully and a slob, had grown up wanting to be a comedian. "So I just kind of grew a part of me that was very aggressive in a comedic way," Roseanne says. "Because if I was to dare to be aggressive and it wasn't funny, I would be hurt badly. But if it was funny he would laugh. It was really weird." Laughter became both a seduction and a defense—a way for Roseanne to call attention to herself and to create a buffer of space around herself. "He taught me that comedy was mightier than the pen *and* the sword," Roseanne says. "We would always have contests, showdowns, and I would always win. Even if it was anti-male, anti-him, he would say, 'Good one.' "

In 1971, when she was eighteen, Roseanne had an illegitimate daughter, Brandi ("My father spat at me; he *spat* at me!"), whom she gave up for adoption and with whom she was reunited a few years ago. (Brandi now works on Roseanne's show.) That same year, Roseanne left home and met her first husband, Bill Pentland, who was a motel night clerk in Georgetown, Colorado, where Roseanne was prep cooking and washing dishes in a restaurant. By the time she was twenty-six she was caring for three children under the age of four (Jessica, 1975; Jennifer, 1976; and Jake, 1978) in a house that occupied six hundred square feet. As she later joked, "I breed well in captivity."

In reality, she didn't. She worked variously as a window dresser, a maid, a waitress, and a prostitute, and gradually began to write comedy. Roseanne calls her emergence a "slow dawning." "I aspired to be Gertrude Stein, or Dylan Thomas, or some poetess tragically and forlornly trying to scrape some piece of misery off the sole of my soul and write some touching little fat girl shit about it," she wrote in her first book, "Roseanne: My Life as a Woman" (1989), "until . . . I heard Lord Buckley, and Lenny Bruce, and understood the jazz of words alone." In 1980, when Roseanne went to work as a cocktail waitress at Bennigan's, which became known to the regulars as Rosie's, she found her arena. "I'd go, 'That's six bucks for the drinks, another three bucks for me to take them off the tray and give them to ya,' " she says. "I'd shortchange 'em. Eat food off their plates. They always laughed. This one guy goes, 'Well, Roseanne, do you know anybody that is married and does not want to get divorced and wants to fool around with somebody else who is married, who has a lot of money, who likes to have a lot of sex and be taken care of?' And I go, 'Well, yeah. Your wife.' " At Bennigan's, Roseanne "felt like a star"; and, more important, she was at liberty. From eight at night to two in the morning, she worked the room, fending off the male come-ons with "the meanest comebacks imaginable." It was at Bennigan's that Roseanne first learned of the Comedy Works, a club where aspiring comics could test their material. "That's when it hit me that the place was invented only for me to go and do it," she says. "I always knew. Totally always. That I was gonna be a comic and I was gonna have my own show and I was gonna be as rich as Bill Cosby." To Pentland (who is now on good terms with Roseanne; last year he had a walk-on part in her show), Roseanne's almost messianic sense of her calling was "like somebody saying they're gonna win the lottery." He made her a mike stand from a screwdriver and a broom handle so she could practice her delivery in their living room; but he was skeptical. "I was happy to see her get a hobby that fulfilled her," he says. "My sense of it at that time was that Roseanne wanted to be more than a performer—she wanted to be a political voice."

As Roseanne writes, "I began to tell the truth about my life—because I couldn't tell the truth off the stage. And very quickly, the world began to blow apart." The first time Roseanne went onstage and pronounced her rebellion—what she calls "a huge, cosmic 'NO' "—she felt "chilled and free and redeemed. I had decided to Stand Up." Roseanne took her newfound freedom to the outer limits. She had one gig as an m.c. at a strip club. "I had a woman partner," Roseanne says, speaking of a cohort named Susan Bublitz. "Me and her would go on there and of course we'd see the strippers downstairs afterwards. I swear one had a flattop under her wig. Puts on muscle shirt, sweatpants, Nikes. A butch cat. Me and Susan were onstage one night. I thought it was hilarious. I go, 'We'd like to do our impressions of the strippers for ya.' All these drunk fuckers are goin' 'Take it off!' So we start makin' out. And I go, 'Don't you know these women are fuckin' dykes, and they *hate* you?' On Friday and Saturday nights at midnight, they made me and Susan eat bananas. Then they'd have the guys in the audience vote on which one of us was the winner. I'd just take the banana, peel it, and eat it. Susan'd be like—I'd watch her—doing the whole thing. She won every night. And I'd go, 'Fuck you. *I* swallowed!' "

Roseanne had also begun working at the radical Woman to Woman bookstore (where, she says, she kept men out with a baseball bat), reading in women's history, and lecturing on feminist ethics. She recalls one lecture on pornography that she gave with a black woman in Wyoming, when the local feminists didn't want to hear Roseanne's class analysis and she and her partner were "sort of run out of there on a rail." "They were kind of O.K. when it was about oppression of women," she says. "But when we talked about women as oppressors of other races, they didn't want to hear it."

Roseanne carried the ideological battles at the bookstore into her private war over comedy. "I used to always get up and go, 'Why are we talking to women who go to college and learn how to talk like men? Go talk to the women on welfare, if you want a fuckin' grassroots movement,' " she says. In a letter to a lesbian comedienne whose act disgusted her, she wrote:

> I'm going all over this town with stories about what my life experience as a woman has been. I performed at a lesbian coffeehouse and received the stunned oxen look from all of the women/womyn/chicks there. . . . I'm going to be a comic, and I'm gonna talk about what I know, and . . . I have a place and a reason for being in this movement. Deal with me. The subtle bigotry I feel from lesbians (not all of them) infuriates me. If some comic can stand up and tell about growing up Catholic, or Jewish or Wasp, then I can tell my story about growing up straight. . . . Besides the fact that I'm married to a man, and have children, I'm the most radical woman in this town, dig it, and your heterophobia is boring. Separate your issues. If this is a woman's movement then it's only dealing with about 10% of the world's women. . . . I am one of the other 90%—deal with that. Aside from your het bigotry, you also have the attitude of otherness with black and Jewish women. Deal with it. You don't let me do my shit in front of you, and the boys don't let me do it for them. What a movement.

"The act didn't work well at the beginning," Roseanne says of finding her female comic voice in those early days, but she did have her inspired moments. "I remember Lenny Bruce said Jackie Kennedy was climbing out of the limo in Dallas to save her own ass. That's Lenny, the archetypal male comic. My joke was: I'm a woman and I know that was never, never true. She wasn't climbing out to save her own ass. She sees her husband's brains sliding down the back of the car, and she's going out there because she's trying to clean up the mess!" That particular joke was a turning point for Roseanne. She told it in a jazz club, and there was shocked recognition in the laughter she got. "I knew right then that I had hooked into exactly what I see and what I feel and the way to use language to express it," Roseanne says. Nothing now was sacred, not even the sisterhood. "I don't know why lesbians hate men," she used to joke. "They don't have to fuck them."

During her academic feminist phase, Roseanne also did a bit about breast feeding: "Contrary to popular belief, breasts are not on our body to sell stereos and cars; they're to feed children." The second time she performed it at the Comedy Works, a woman in the first row picked up her chair and turned it so that her back was to Roseanne. "I just snapped," Roseanne says. "That was when I believed in this sisterhood-feminist shit and didn't know what the real world was about. I go, 'What are you doing!' I left my text. 'Are you trying to tell your husband, "Don't worry. I'll still blow you. I won't listen to that big bad woman"?' And then I got silence. They banned me. They wouldn't let me work at the club anymore." Undaunted, she organized a protest of feminist comediennes in Boulder called Take Back the Mike and was finally reinstated without having to change her act. The victory taught Roseanne one basic maneuver of comic attack: "Don't keep secrets. Tell on 'em. Because they're weak, they can't live in the light of day."

Looking back on that difficult period now, Roseanne says, "I had to make a choice between being radical and being mainstream. I made a conscious decision that I was never going to talk that academic feminist language again. It's all about white male élitist horseshit. So I went back to the way people I grew up with, the people like me, talk. And why wouldn't we be heard? I just talk louder, and I'm heard. I'm also discredited a lot." Roseanne's rejection of manners and clean language is both a critique of and a revenge on the decorum of patriarchy, which assures that women collude in their own destruction. "I love the word 'fuck,' " she says. "It's a verb, a noun, everything, and it's just infused with intense feeling and passion, you know, negative and positive. And women aren't supposed to say it, so I try to say it as much as I can." She goes on, "When I was a teen-ager, my mother had this book called 'Fascinating Womanhood.' I opened it to a page that said, 'Watch your little girl and see how she gets her way with your husband. She snaps her head and shakes her curls. You need to emulate that. You do that if you want your way with your husband.' So he'll buy ya a friggin' toaster! I was just freaked out by it. My mother's havin' a meeting once a week with these ladies, and they talk about doin' this shit. It was so ugly, so horrible, and I'm like 'I'm never gonna get married.' One chapter was called 'Domestic Goddess': you know, you cook for him, you clean for him, you're his fuckin' slave, and you're supposed to do it all with a smile. And I just remember sitting there over breakfast with my sister and the whole thing came crashing together."

Like Chaplin discovering his bowler hat and cane, when Roseanne found the character of Domestic Goddess she found her idiom and her popularity. The first time she did the new act, in Kansas City, she got a standing ovation. Lois Bromfield, a comedienne who performed with Roseanne in the early days and has become a writer on Roseanne's show, explains, "She hit that nerve of the woman in the Midwest whom nobody spoke to. They'd had no one to relate to—not for a long time."

ROSEANNE'S studio is just over the leafy foothills of Coldwater Canyon and Laurel Canyon, which wind down from fashionable Beverly Hills into the smoggy lumpen sprawl of the Valley. Here, only walking distance from her soundstage, in Studio City, is the America Roseanne speaks for: McDonald's,

Winchell's doughnuts, Blockbuster Video, and Du-Par's Restaurant ("Breakfast Served All Day"), where waitresses stand on sore feet and make wisecracks, the way Roseanne herself once did.

At nine o'clock on a Monday morning, the cast and crew straggle in, and about ten minutes before the first reading of this week's script is to begin, Roseanne's stretch limo slinks into view. Her driver, who calls her Boss, opens the door for her. She is dressed in a denim skirt and pea-green hiking boots with cleated rubber soles, topped incongruously with frilly white socks. "Jesus Christ, I'm tired," she says as she emerges.

Although Roseanne is pregnant with the son she has decided to name simply Buck ("He's too macho to have a middle name"), her face and her presence have no lustre. Without eyeliner, lipstick, and blusher, which are applied only on taping days, Roseanne's definition is muted and vague. Her face has little mobility. In fact, despite her obvious intelligence and authority, there is something cadaverous about Roseanne, a deadness that only rage and laughter can banish. (She seems to love combat precisely because it makes her feel more alive.) The most cursory encounter with Roseanne and the climate of free-floating anxiety and hate in which she operates gives credence to her claims of child abuse. Something has been murdered in her; and this is palpable in the flatness of her voice, the slouch of her body, the quicksilver shifts of mood from bombast to gloom, the timidity and detachment behind her eyes. Over the last few years, Roseanne has undergone some well-publicized cosmetic operations: the breasts she used to joke about ("Actually, I only have one breast. I just part it down the middle") have been reduced; she's had a stomach tuck and a nose job. ("My face was so bad," she said. "Every time I looked in the mirror, I looked like my dad, and I couldn't stand it.") But, despite all these changes, nothing can erase the evidence of her soul's unease.

Inside the cavernous soundstage, the sets of the show are spread around like rooms in a behemoth doll's house. A table has been set up in the middle of the studio for the show's director, Gail Mancuso; the current head writer, Eric Gilliland; and members of the cast, who trickle in from the kitchen, where coffee, doughnuts, and smoked salmon are on tap. Behind the table, a number of director's chairs have been lined up for the writers, who mill around holding copies of the new show—"The Blaming of the Shrew," by Lawrence Broch. This episode of "Roseanne" is something of a rarity, because it was written solo instead of group-written, or "gang-banged"—the writers' term for the collaborative process in which the scenes are divided among teams of writers. Still, the group has been polishing Broch's work for a week prior to this first reading. Behind the writers' chairs is an entire bank of tarpaulined theatre seats that will hold the audience when the show is taped on Thursday, but today they seat only me and the parents of Ashley Johnson, a precocious and talented eleven-year-old who is to play Lisa, the "shrew" of the piece, with whom D.J., Roseanne's fictional son, is to have his first date.

Roseanne pulls up a chair between John Goodman, who plays her husband, Dan Conner, and Laurie Metcalf, who plays her neurotic fictional sister, Jackie. Ranged around the table are Michael Fishman (D.J.), Michael O'Keefe (Jackie's reticent husband, Fred), Johnny Galecki (the erstwhile boyfriend of Roseanne's younger fictional daughter, Darlene; Darlene herself—the hilarious Sara Gilbert—is at Yale, where she is an art major), and Ellen DeGeneres, who is making a guest appearance on this episode, as an inept therapist trying to give marriage guidance to Jackie and Fred.

Roseanne remembers the first time she took a seat at a production read-through, before she'd wrested control of her show from the producers. "They had, like, extras and the crew people sitting at the far end of the table, and the stars up at the other end of the table," she recalls. "I remember walking in and going, 'Oh, Jesus Christ! Everything in the men's world is exactly like the Army. Everything's militaristic. Rank.' I thought, How am I gonna do it? I was really into being an anarchist then. So I sat at the end with the crew guys. The producers were so pissed! But I wanted to make the statement that this show wasn't about corporate America, it wasn't about corporate thinking, it was about people, the American people."

Now Roseanne greets the assembled table with "Happy Purim," and everyone laughs. To Roseanne, the calm here is the calm of a battlefield after the bodies have been removed. "Everybody's banned," she says. "And they have been since the third show. Banned." That is, the network is banned; the advertisers are banned; even the owners of the show, Carsey-Werner, are banned from Roseanne's space. According to Marcy Carsey—who, along with her partner, Tom Werner, has produced "The Cosby Show," "Cybill," and "Grace Under Fire"—Roseanne walked off the show "five or six times" during the first thirteen episodes. Carsey prefers to think of their absence from Roseanne's set as a choice rather than a requirement. "We made a judgment; I don't know if it was right or not," Carsey says. "We thought that part of the thing Roseanne was doing was acting out against authority, which she saw as us. So we thought— like the good parents we are sometimes—that when somebody is acting out like that you stay away for a while. We talked to the writers, went over stories, edited rough cuts. We just weren't on the set."

Part of the battle between Roseanne and her producers has been about the ownership of the show. Although Roseanne may own the show's success, she does not completely own its origins. In 1987, Roseanne had craftily designed her first HBO special as a kind of pilot to present her trailer-trash character to the networks, even briefly going into a backstage double-wide to deal with her beer-swilling couch potato of a husband and her bumptious kids. Roseanne wanted to create a TV sitcom around her domestic-goddess character, and her agents had her taking meetings all over town. Meanwhile, quite independently, Carsey-Werner was developing a show about a working mother. "We were looking for the outrageous voice that could be the center of the show," Carsey says. "We pitched it to Roseanne. But the fact is that that show was in development. She was cast in the role, and she brought a lot to the role."

Roseanne, however, is her own greatest creation, and the imperialism of her fame extends to the show, which she sees as incontrovertibly hers. She wanted to run it her way. Martin Luther announced his revolution by nailing ninety-five theses to the church door; Roseanne announced hers by posting a one-page broadsheet, which is now framed in the makeup room of her trailer, on her dressing-room door. She prophesied that the show would be a hit (it went to No. 1 after the ninth episode), and the document served notice on the company to behave or be gone. It said,

THESE ARE THE PEOPLE WHO ARE GOING TO BE FIRED IF THEY'RE NOT NICE TO ME. PEOPLE WHO *I* AM BOSS OF—EVERYBODY 'CAUSE *I* GOT MY OWN TV SHOW. ALL PRODUCERS, ALL WRITERS, ALL SUBJECT TO CHANGE.

Below was a long list that Roseanne had graded and, she says, continued to grade every week. Those in her good graces got a check by their names; those in bad odor got "applicable" written beside theirs. Some, who were on probation, got "not applicable as yet."

Seven years on, Roseanne finds this memento of those embattled early days "hilarious." She still has skirmishes with her writers, but the worst one was the first. In the inaugural script for the show, written by Matt Williams, a former producer-writer on "Cosby" who is credited as the creator of "Roseanne" (and who refused to be interviewed for this article), Roseanne was the passive second banana. "The sister was my character," Roseanne says. "And I was like June Cleaver: 'And then what happened, darling?'"

Roseanne claims that the producers were going behind her back to Goodman and Metcalf to suggest they do the show without her, and says she was shocked that Williams had demoted her defiant character to a feed. "We had a war from Day One," she says. "He goes, 'Well, I don't think people will like you.' And I go, 'Well, if they don't like me, why did I get this show?'" The show was then called "Life and Stuff," and that was another point of loud contention. "I go, 'What are you tellin' me? It's called "Life and Stuff"? Kiss my ass! It's called "Roseanne."' He just went insane, and I went insane, too." Roseanne kept rewriting Williams's scripts. She recalls one of their shouting matches at the ABC offices, when Williams tipped over a table: "He goes, 'I'm not your fucking scribe! I write what's meaningful to me! I'm a fuckin' writer! I'm an artist!' And I'd be like, 'Well, not on this show, by God. You're gonna write what I tell you to write.'" Roseanne characterizes her fury as "so strong I could've sucked out his will to live with my nostrils." Williams and Roseanne crossed their Rubicon, which she describes in "My Lives," on the fourth episode. In a love scene with John Goodman, Roseanne refused to say, "Well, you're my equal in bed, but that's it."

"That is not a woman's voice," Roseanne said. "And I'm not gonna say it."

"You will say it as written," Williams replied.

What followed was one of the high-water marks in the annals of entertainment intransigence: Roseanne's infamous sit-in—or, rather, bed-in. "I said, 'When this show goes to No. 1, you're fuckin' outta here.' I didn't have anything. They had fifteen lawyers. They come stand around me: 'Say the line, Roseanne, as written.' I say, 'No, I'm not gonna fuckin' say it.' It was so horrible." Pentland, who had quit his thirty-thousand-dollar-a-year job with the post office after Roseanne's success, was at home minding their three kids when Roseanne's SOS came from the studio. "It was like talking to someone in a bunker over a military telephone," Pentland says. "Carsey-Werner's attorneys were down there saying, 'You're in breach of contract. You're going to lose the show.' We renewed our faith in that call. We'd lived broke, and we could do it again if we had to. We decided that if we let them win she would lose control of everything she'd been working for. Once they couldn't bluff, they lost their ability to intimidate her. It was kind of like the Cuban missile crisis, when Dean Rusk said, 'The other guy blinked.' From that moment on, she had control of the show and made it into a much better product."

ROSEANNE'S neurotic TV family was the first one to put America in contact with something resembling real life in the working-class world—a place where children are difficult, parents have real emotional and financial problems, and there's a discrepancy between what American society promises and what it delivers. The message of "Roseanne" flies in the face of the vision of consumer contentment conjured by the show's advertisers, who currently cough up about a quarter of a million dollars per thirty seconds to be on during her show, the fourth-highest rate on ABC (after the Super Bowl, the Academy Awards, and "Home Improvement").

"Working-class people have to work really, really hard for just the smallest thing, so they're stronger," Roseanne says. "They're more into God, more into community, more into family than middle-class people are. Totally. Middle-class people are fearful of losing. So everything is about a fear of loss. When everything's based on money, everything's for sale, including their integrity and their morals." Over the years, the Conners' struggles have provided Roseanne and her writers with opportunities to discuss racism, unemployment, lesbianism, abortion, aging, and masturbation, among many other issues. ("On my show, I'm the boss," Roseanne said in a special episode that brought her together with many of the famous TV moms of earlier eras; "and Father Knows Squat.") In the story that the actors are reading today, D.J. is in thrall to Lisa, a pint-size bundle of assertiveness who is Roseanne in miniature. Lisa calls D.J. "doofus," complains about her corsage for the dance, and generally rules the roost. Dan doesn't like seeing D.J. bossed around; Roseanne, of course, loves it. "If a boy is pushing a girl around, he's trying to keep her *down*," Roseanne explains to Dan. "But if a girl is pushing a boy around, she's trying to elevate herself. Can't you see that? Boys bullying girls is a step backwards. But girls bullying boys—now, that's the future." D.J. and Lisa skip school, go to Chicago, and are brought home by Dan, who then enlists Roseanne both to punish D.J. for his truancy and to offer some sound parental advice about equality in relationships. Meanwhile, in the subplot, Jackie and Fred are in therapy, discussing their relationship.

As the episode is read—and read well—by the cast, the writers cheer the script on. There is nothing more ravishing to a writer than to hear words sweated out in private get laughs in public. It's like planning a party and hoping that it turns into a blast; the anxiety is that a good time won't be had by all. Here "all" means Roseanne. A dip in the collective response at the first reading might cause Roseanne to draw a haphazard line through a speech or a page— a gesture that in a nanosecond may wipe out a good part of a writer's weekly work. So the writer's non-stop hee-hawing—a kind of laughter that combines exhaustion, hopefulness, and fear—is to an outsider's ear slightly frantic and unreal. Sometimes an actor gives the words an unexpected spin, and then the tension momentarily collapses. The room is suddenly gleeful, hooting it up, thrilled by the promise of the writers' collective mischief. Today, Roseanne is enjoying things—especially Ashley Johnson's no-nonsense Lisa, who clocks all the different haircuts of the Conner men standing by the door and says, "Man, who gets drunk and cuts this family's hair?" And later, when Jackie gets on her high horse and says to Roseanne, "I'm just waiting to hear you say 'You may be right, Jackie,'" Roseanne's comeback, the writers agree, is a "classic Roseanne line": "Yeah, and I'm waiting for chocolate air." The phrase brings the house down and earns the kind of look from Roseanne that the writers are always watching for—that wide-eyed twinkle that says nothing short of nuclear attack will make her part with the words.

AFTER the reading, the writers amble back to their warrens in Building 3, some four hundred yards away from the studio, while Roseanne and Gail Mancuso get to work on the therapist scene. After a couple of passes at it, DeGeneres looks over at Roseanne and says, "I'm completely mirroring Jackie's emotions, which I think is so wrong for a shrink."

"I hate headshrinkers so much," Roseanne says. That statement leads to a discussion of psychiatrists' fees. DeGeneres says hers is ninety dollars an hour. "Is that what they cost?" Roseanne asks, taking a sudden detour down memory lane. "Mine was three-fifty. It was about that good. My first one, I remember, used to fall asleep. While we were all talkin'. Community mental-health association. My little sister was only about six, and she didn't want to be involved in the family therapy. She brought her toothbrush and knitting. She'd sit there and knit and then take her toothbrush out and rub it on the wall. Every one of us would do something to signal that we weren't interested. We had the cheesiest."

But Roseanne's subsequent therapy has brought her some measure of understanding. In "My Lives" she challenges the notion, promoted by her family in various interviews, that the abuse in her household was just ordinary family horseplay. (Roseanne claims that her sisters were both abused, too; they deny it.) Roseanne writes, "Everyone's Dad sticks his hand down his daughters' pants, squeezes their tits, their ass, their legs. *Every* twelve-year-old gets photographed with a movie camera by her father while she's in the tub. . . . *All* fathers talk sexually all the time to their daughters, don't they? *All* mothers hold pillows over their children's faces until they black out or pretend to, and stare at their children with hatred-edged eyes. There were no boundaries." Roseanne remembers watching her parents being interviewed on "60 Minutes": "They said they didn't molest their children. They were a family of fanny pinchers. . . . What they were saying was—and this is exactly how it was in my childhood—We're gonna pinch your fannies as much as we want even if it makes you horrifically uncomfortable and scared and destroys everything in you." She goes on, "That's how they think. They're trying to use the semantics of language to cover up what they do, which is why I'm so into naming things. It's not 'fanny-pinching'—it's naked ass-grabbing. There's a big fuckin' difference."

Roseanne's parents, Helen and Jerry Barr, have not been in contact with Roseanne except by lawyer since her public statement about their child abuse. Roseanne now says she is "at peace" with herself about it. In 1987, in her first HBO special, Roseanne thanked her parents for letting their children "say whatever we wanted as long as it was funny." In one "Roseanne" episode, there is a moving moment when her father has died, and Roseanne is left alone beside his coffin at the funeral home. Roseanne takes out a piece of paper on which she has written her last goodbye, which turns out to be an indictment. "O.K.—I'm angry at you for lying to me my whole life," she says. "I'm angry that I didn't ever know who you really were. I'm mad that when I was a kid you ignored me and when you did give me any attention it was usually violent. I'm mad that you left us alone with a crazy mother. I'm mad that because of you I grew up distrustful of men and I couldn't even trust my own husband for the first five years we were married." Roseanne concludes, "So, Dad, I'm forgiving you, just because I need to move on with my life. And I forgive myself for being so damn angry." She lifts the lid of the coffin, places her list of grievances inside, and, at the door, turns back and says, "Thank you for your humor. I love you. G'bye." The speech, which Roseanne says she wrote, sums up the blessings and the barbarity of the Barr family. But the scene also demonstrates how Roseanne negotiates her survival. She literally deposits her grievances with someone else and walks away. In life, she does the same thing. Instead of being persecuted, Roseanne persecutes; instead of being shamed, she attacks; instead of being annihilated, she annihilates.

Roseanne recalls that her first family target was her Uncle Sherman, who used to denigrate her grandmother's cooking while scarfing it. "I'd say things to my uncle like 'Well, if you don't like the soup, why do you eat five bowls of it?' " she says. "He'd laugh. My mother would laugh—until one day he got mad and said, 'You've got a smart mouth, little girl.' And I said, 'Well, yeah, but just because you can't answer me.' You know, the way kids do. My grandmother turned around and said, 'Shut up. You have to respect him. He's your elder.' And I remember this huge catharsis in my head, like 'Oh, well, women aren't supposed to defend themselves against men. There's always some sort of threat if you do.' And I just thought about that forever and ever. I always understood that the women in my family were not assuming any of the power that was inherently theirs. They apologized for it. It always appalled me, and it still appalls me." But in those days if Roseanne wasn't venting her aggression in jokes, she couldn't express anger or deal with problematic situations at home except in a cartoonish play voice. "I always defined it as a play voice till I went into therapy and found out it's a person," Roseanne says, of the personality she calls Cindy, who is, she says, "probably the person who most saved my life." Roseanne goes on, "One time I was hosting 'Saturday Night Live.' I wanted to do a sketch with Cindy in it, 'cause I was getting real brave and I'd been in therapy for a couple of years and I thought I would be able to handle it. So I allowed her to come through, and the other actors were real scared, 'cause you can sort of tell it's not a character. It's a person."

AT the end of the DeGeneres scene, Roseanne settles into a leather armchair perched on a wooden trolley and calls over some of her assistants, pointing in the direction of the Conners' kitchen. "Girls," she says, "pull me over there." The sight of Roseanne being lugged across the studio strikes everybody, including Roseanne, as amusing. "This is the port-a-throne," she says. She passes the time between setups talking with the crew, hankering out loud for Swensen's Sticky Chewy Chocolate ice cream, and casting a beady eye over the script of each scene after it has been rehearsed. Roseanne's line "In this family we solve our own problems. No psychiatrists. No therapists . . . no pediatricians" is sent back to the Big Room for more work. "If I don't get it, the public won't get it. I'm dumber than they are," she says. And the line at the end of Act I also displeases her. D.J. has been grounded after being AWOL with Lisa in Chicago. "You like him going with Lisa," Dan needles Roseanne, in the act's final beat. "And if it doesn't work out with her, I hear Squeaky Fromme is up for parole soon." Goodman gets a laugh from the crew, but Roseanne thinks the reference is passé. She says, "We're gonna dump that. I need a better line."

"Are there any great women criminals anymore?" Goodman asks.

"Yeah, me," Roseanne says.

Roseanne sidles up to the script supervisor, Hayden Ghaffary, whose job it is to relay Roseanne's notes directly to the head writer, in the Big Room, and tosses the script on the lectern. "Act II, Scene 2," Roseanne says to her. "I want it beat everywhere. It's sappy shit." In sitcom slang, "beat" means to better a line, which is what the writers, working in teams, spend most of their waking hours trying to do. Their private term for this enterprise is "feeding the monster."

Roseanne employs more writers for her show than are employed on any other sitcom, and she mixes standup comics in with TV writers, to give the comics on-the-job training in commercial storytelling. This "comedy college" consists of a relatively young, morose group made up mostly of men. The actors keep a cordial distance from them; the burnout rate here is high, and the brass are loath to fraternize with the enlisted men. (Eight of the twenty-four writers assembled for the run-through will not return for Roseanne's eighth season.) "I have six kids," says Dave Raether, a veteran of three seasons. "I have dinner with my family maybe once every three weeks." But the compensation for the fourteen-hour days is a king's ransom. Even a mid-level writer who stays for a few years will have made his million, or close to it; and the head writer, Eric Gilliland, who is thirty-two, will make two and a half million dollars this year, whether he finishes the season or not.

At noon, when the writers are summoned from their compound to take their first look at the episode on its feet, they follow the show from set to set. All the while, of course, they laugh. Beside me, William Lucas Walker, an executive story editor, is watching Roseanne closely and making marks in his script. A wavy line means that a joke needs work; a small check means a titter; a large check means a boff, or big laugh; and an "R" means Roseanne laughed. ("Here's how you can tell if it's funny," Roseanne explained later. "If I say it and nobody laughs, it's not funny.") For the writers, every day is a war of attrition, but when a big joke stays in, like one that Walker got into the pot-smoking episode—where Dan, in a wave of sixties nostalgia, recalls the slogan "Today is the first day of the rest of your life," and Roseanne says, "Who ever knew it was going to be such a long, bad day?"—the battle seems worth the effort. "If I write a play," Walker explains, "thirty million people aren't going to laugh at a joke I wrote."

Once the run-through is over, a sudden entropy envelops the place. Roseanne disappears into her trailer for meetings, and without her gravitational pull the studio loses its sense of agitation and fun. The actors go home; the writers drift back to their offices, complaining about cuts. "The show's O.K.," says Walker, beckoning to one of the writers. "But it'll be a lot stronger by Thursday." Danny Zuker approaches, dressed in shorts, his shirttail dangling underneath a jean jacket. Walker introduces him to me as the Mel Brooks of the staff.

"I can't believe you guys can laugh all week at the stuff you've written," I say.

"It's easy once you sell your soul," Zuker says.

. . .

AT nine-thirty on Tuesday morning, Ghaffary is on the phone to Gilliland, who is in the writers' main building. The actors are called for ten, but it's clear from the urgency in Ghaffary's voice that Roseanne is already on the premises. "There was a slight logic problem, and Roseanne found a way to fix it," Ghaffary says. "Page twelve. Before D.J. and Lisa leave. She's cut everything after that speech until page fifteen. She wants some sort of conflict before they exit, and she would like that before the run-through. In an hour."

"I need a rewrite!"

Roseanne's voice precedes her, and, like her body, it takes up space. She looms into view wearing a black beret and a turquoise T-shirt that says "It Must Be Venus Envy." "Roseanne is just an explosion," says the writer Lois Bromfield. The male writers may privately curse Roseanne's abrasive blasts, but the women on the staff are thrilled by them. "If she threw scripts at people and called the head writer 'boy'—all things I've seen her do—and she was wrong, Roseanne would be insane," Bromfield says. "But here's the incredible part. She's almost always right." Roseanne's concern of the moment is a short trailer-park scene, for an episode that is to be taped along with "The Blaming of the Shrew" on Thursday. Roseanne has donated a walk-on part for a charity auction, and, paying fifteen hundred dollars for the privilege, Sharon Stone has bought it. "Can we get a rewrite?" Roseanne asks Ghaffary, and then grabs the phone from her to speak directly to Gilliland. "Did you hear all this stuff about the rules she's got?" Roseanne says about Stone's Thursday schedule. "It's unbelievable. She'll be here at one-thirty to acclimate. Two hours for makeup. Can you dig that? And she wants a tight pink beautician's outfit. Two hours for makeup! I said, 'Just tell her to get up out of bed and come down. That's what she should look like.' Is that hilarious? Do you love that? So, we won't be able to start the show till seven-thirty."

Later, inside the tidy calm of her trailer, Roseanne's persona softens. There is a punch-in lock on her trailer door, a bodyguard outside talking on the limousine's car phone. "For me, as a woman, the only place on earth that's ever existed that I don't feel all the male oppression is just inside my little office," she says. Roseanne, the star and executive producer of her show, puts her job description this way: "I'm a real good editor. I just edit down to get to the jokes quicker. You'll notice that yesterday I did a lot of general editing; today I started on the jokes. I always make sure that everybody else has their jokes, and then, on Wednesday, I do mine. My jokes." Roseanne has always written jokes. "It's like automatic writing. It's all unconscious. Comedy's about the unconscious," she says. "If you can tap into that. It's only about four or five times a year that I can do that." But the gruelling production schedule can't wait for Roseanne's unconscious to kick in, and therefore she needs writers. This haunts and infuriates her, and makes for an uneasy alliance with the help. Earlier in the morning, as I stood watching Roseanne rehearse, a writer, unknown to me and asking for anonymity, whispered, "She doesn't write the show. She never has written the show. In general, when she does decide to participate, like this week, because you're here, she's the source of very bad ideas that the writers have to circumnavigate to make the show any good at all."

Roseanne dismisses this kind of vitriol as typical male folderol. "They're so horrified of their mothers' power that they have to spend their whole life diminishing it," she says. In any case, the argument about creative ownership of the show is academic: Roseanne owns the mill and the charisma. And she treats the writers as extensions of herself. "I give them a big speech in the beginning," Roseanne says, and, without much coaxing, launches into it: "The world is run by women, contrary to what you believe—especially the family, especially the working-class family. These women that we're doing the show about, they make no compromises. They don't kowtow to men like middle-class women do." But Roseanne says it's hard to find men or women who can write about a working-class milieu. "This is the best group I've ever had," she says. "But, by virtue of the fact that they're male, they can only write what they've seen about women. So I try to get women in here, and they can't do it, either. In order to get power in Hollywood, or anywhere in the world, they've had to emulate men. They sound like male voices. The thing that's always missing in the stuff they write for me is the anarchy and the fight. They don't get it. Because they're so fucking damaged—if you want the bottom line—that they cannot see a woman as anything but a big, loving, nurturer sex thing. I see it in their work. When I get tougher with them, I get back castration and mutilation jokes. I'm like, 'Now I have to go back there and baby these fuckers along to get a decent joke out of them that has a woman's point of view.' " She goes on, "I had to find a place where they loved me as well as feared me. It's like being Big Mama. I always have to have my tit out for every fuckin' one of 'em, you know. I resent it. It's a big drain."

Roseanne's notion of mothering includes the knowledge that "they like to be spanked." And although Roseanne claims that her tongue-lashings are "an act"—part of the negotiating skills she's had to learn to get the best work from her writers—they also express her very real ambivalence. Kevin Abbott, one of the show's senior producer-writers, who will not be back next year, recalls how Roseanne spoke to the writers in March, at the first reading after Rob Ulin was deposed and Gilliland was promoted to replace him: "She starts off, 'I just want to say for all of you who don't know—Rob is dead; Eric is doing a great job. I'm really happy right now. And if I don't like the next one, I'll fire you, too. No, no, I don't mean that . . . I'm just sayin' . . .' She'd say something nice and immediately undercut it with something vicious. The writers were just staring at her with no idea of how to react. 'I really wanted to say something nice,' she said. 'But I just can't. It all just keeps coming out mean.' At one point, somebody laughed, and she turned and said, 'Don't laugh unless I tell you to!' So then there's a dead silence. Finally, Matt Berry goes, 'Can we laugh now?' She has a real love-hate relationship with writers. She really resents whatever they bring her."

Part of Roseanne's behavior can be explained by the comic's natural competitiveness. "I can't ever let anybody be funnier than me," she says. "I guess 'cause of my father, or something in my childhood. I just feel like this is *war*." But Roseanne's ferocity may come down to something else. "They frighten me," she says of the writers, comparing herself to a lion tamer. "I always have my whip. If I didn't have my whip and my chair in front of me, I wouldn't go into that goddam cage. They scare the shit out of me. I'm not lying. And not just men. Women scare me, too, especially the women that are out here. They don't even know that everything they're doing is against themselves."

Today, a young woman writer is ushered into the trailer to be interviewed by Roseanne, and Roseanne is cordial but reserved. The writer seems genuinely awed to be in Roseanne's presence, but rallies to roll her credits: "Uncle Buck," "Out All Night," "Pride & Joy." Roseanne cuts in to ask if she has children. No, she says, but her sister does, and they're darling. Roseanne asks when she could start, saying, "I do need women on the show. I especially need women committed to doin' the stuff that women really do." She suggests that the writer do a few scenes for the show, and then there is some flimflammery about writing commitments: the writer doesn't have the time just now, but she promises something within a few weeks, and leaves. The interview has lasted perhaps five minutes. Afterward, as Roseanne is herding me toward the door, she says, "See, that's what happens. Almost uniformly, always what happens with women. They come to interview for the job, but they don't want the job. They tell you they're not going to do it by saying what she said. Then you're real nice to them so they don't sell a story about you to the *Enquirer.*" Roseanne laughs, and adds, "When I realized that I couldn't find any women writers, I went to my women friends who were comics, who'd got pretty well beaten down in the comedy clubs tryin' to say things as women. I got 'em, and I go, 'I want you to say the worst shit you always wanted to say. Send me stuff that just shocks me and scares me every single day and I'll tone it down.' That's how I got 'Absolutely Fabulous.' I'm using these women comics. They're just awesome." (The pilot, written by Jennifer Saunders and Roseanne, with Lois Bromfield, Ruby Wax, and Cynthia Mort, is being completed as we speak.)

At the door, she says, "Women like the one I just interviewed and most of the women I see don't have any ambition. They're satisfied if two or three of their jokes get into a show. Anyone who shows up and wants to stick her neck out and take the shit that comes from that, man, I'd take them in a second. It pisses me off, because when I was home with my three kids, and I was going to do standup, I'd get up and sit in a closet with a flashlight on 'cause my husband was asleep to write the shit I had to write. And so do a lot of women have to do that." She opens the trailer door to the glare of the afternoon. "So, if you just don't have the time right now," she says, "fuck you."

. . .

OVER at the writers' compound, Dave Raether sits at his computer trying to focus the wandering minds of his comic team, who are sprawled on sofas in one of the joke rooms. A former journalist from Minnesota, Raether is the only one here who isn't a standup comedian. Matt Berry, Allan Stephan, Ed Yeager, and even Bromfield, the room's missing ingredient, who is off polishing the "AbFab" pilot, were all veterans of comedy-club circuits, and old publicity photographs of their standup selves are the only decorations on the walls. To describe the group's method of comic creation as "improvisation" doesn't do the process justice. It's more like throwing food at a wall and whatever sticks is what stays in the script. At this particular moment, the room is trying to find words for an exchange between Jackie and Roseanne about therapy.

"Is there anything about the therapist?" Raether asks. "How nice she was? How fucked up she was? Is there something that the therapist did that's funny?"

"Something about the room," says Yeager, a trim man with thinning hair who was with Roseanne in her Denver days. " 'You think that office was designed to make you feel comfortable.' "

" 'Very much like this kitchen,' " Yeager says.

" 'They must have the same designer,' " Stephan says.

" 'Must have the same designer,' " Raether repeats, turning back to his computer. "That's a good setup. O.K. Let's get some more jokes out of that."

As the afternoon wears on, Raether focusses his team on the last of their jokes to beat, where Roseanne and Dan try to talk to D.J. about being led around by Lisa. He reads the group in: " 'Well, what your mom means is, we know why you keep going out with her.' D.J.: ' 'Cause she tells me to.' " Raether looks up. "He's under her spell," he says.

" 'I put him under a spell,' " Stephan says. " 'She casts her spell. . . .' 'Dominating little bitch' won't work, will it?"

The room laughs, and Raether says, "That's sort of the joke. She's the sorcerer."

" 'Check his pupils, Dan. See if they're dilated.' "

" 'We need an exorcist.' "

" 'Check his balls.' "

" 'We need an exorcist.' " Raether laughs. "Good."

"Suddenly we're comin' alive here," Matt Berry says.

"How many have we got, Dave?" Stephan asks.

"Four," Raether says.

Stephan presses on. " 'And I thought they broke the mold with me,' " he says.

"Is there a twist?" Raether asks. "A different way of saying it? Roseanne fucks up the saying, makes it bigger."

"Wait a minute," Yeager says. " 'After I was made, they broke the mold.' "

" 'Apparently they fixed my broken mold,' " Raether says.

"There you go," Stephan says. "Go for it."

"I'd try it," Matt Berry says. "What the hell. If they don't get it . . ."

It's time to pitch to the Big Room.

THE Big Room houses a well-polished table and three senior producer-writers, who, by this hour in the afternoon, have lost some of their shine. Gilliland, whose shoulder-length hair and square-rimmed glasses make him a dead ringer for Mike in "Doonesbury," is slumped in the middle of the table with his head on the script, and Miriam Trogdon, a supervising producer, sits across from him with a row of empty Evian bottles lined up in front of her; at the end of the table is Kevin Abbott. Outside, palm fronds rustle in the bright day; inside, the Big Room has the crepuscular gloom of a writer's den. An amanuensis types every agreed-upon new joke into a portable computer, and the revision is instantaneously projected above him on a TV monitor.

"When I go in to pitch, I just enjoy it so much," Raether told me. "It's like performing. You know you're always going to get laughs." Raether takes a black leather swivel chair near Abbott, and the rest of his group belly up to the big table. They are beating the line "The whole time at the therapist's office, Fred just sat there like a bump on a log." Raether's first option draws a dead silence; undaunted, he launches into his second: "Roseanne says, 'Well, maybe you should have sent him to a tree surgeon.' "

"Oh, my God," says Gilliland.

Raether looks up from his pages. "We knew that one wouldn't—"

Gilliland cuts in, "I appreciate the joke of it."

Raether tries another: " 'Fred just sat there like a deer in headlights.' 'Well, all I can say, Jackie, is buckle up and hit the gas.' "

After a few more options, Gilliland stops him. "O.K. Those are good offers. We got enough here. We'll take the deer-in-headlights joke."

Next is the broken mold joke, which earns a "very funny" from Gilliland. The team is excused; another cadre enters. "Pitchy-poo," says Trogdon, and the process resumes. Afterward, the Big Room continues its weeding. There are setups to be clarified, lines to be cut. Gilliland is a patient man with a baby face and a permanently forlorn look. His idea of a good time is to listen to a Cubs game and read the paper in his garden on his day off. "The big trick in writing is to keep Roseanne herself separate from Roseanne Conner," Gilliland says. "I think Roseanne is more daunting. Roseanne Conner is more lovable—strong but wise, good, fair, and just."

On a break, Gilliland goes into the writers' snack room, which has shelves overflowing with M&M's, Pop-Tarts, Raisinets, Twix, and Starburst, and an icebox full of soda—enough sugar to keep the writers in orbit for weeks. A producer and her ten-year-old daughter come in, and the little girl ogles the candy like Pinocchio at the fair. She makes a beeline for the M&M's. "She thinks this is life," her mother says.

"If this isn't life," Gilliland says, "I'm screwed."

· · ·

"WEDNESDAY is a low-energy day, because the actors don't want to give out before a performance," says Raether, standing outside the bungalow where he and his posse are taking a break from the morning's rewrites. "Usually, on Wednesday, the Big Room is working on next week's script."

"The Big Room," Berry says. "The power that goes on there is almost addictive."

"Yeah," Raether says. "Because you're around very interesting people. Five or six standups for fourteen hours a day. Really, really funny."

Bill Walker leans out a window near the Big Room. "She just yelled she wants a hundred jokes per page!" he shouts. The doors of the other bungalows open. "Ten jokes per comic per scene!" The words are repeated and passed on, and then the writers, like firemen responding to a station-house alarm, emerge from their rooms. They know the drill. They head for the main office and cluster around a TV monitor that is hooked up to the soundstage and trained on Roseanne. Big Mama is watching them, and she is not pleased. "I want it in an hour," Roseanne growls into the camera's eye. On second thought, she wants them front and center at Stage 2: "Now!"

Later, the standups are asked to Roseanne's trailer to pitch their options directly to her. "I guess it's like going to the principal's office," Roseanne says. "But they're excited. That's why I brought 'em down and let 'em sit there for two hours before they went into my room. I have to baby them along; and when you baby 'em along you get good things."

When the writers emerge forty minutes later, Raether says, "As I'm walking to the trailer, I'm thinking, This is the worst person in the world. But afterward I'm thinking, She's a riot. What a fun person. She started laughing at the glazed-ham joke. She could not stop laughing."

"Jackie accuses Roseanne of being bossy," Berry explains. "And her comeback is 'Bossy! Is a farmer who turns a pig into a glazed ham bossy?' "

"She's laughing," Raether says. "We're all laughing. It just seemed like the funniest possible joke."

"That's the way it should be," Stephan says. "You have her immediate reaction. It's a better system than her sending notes and notes coming back to her. That way, she never sees the choices."

"She worked on words with us," Berry says. "We had a great time."

ON the day of the taping, everything broadcasts Roseanne's sovereignty. Each friend or special guest who enters the studio is tagged with a royal-blue wristband saying "Roseanne" and "Void if removed from wrist." A dozen or so stony-faced enforcers in suits rim the playing area and Roseanne's dressing room. Although Roseanne is easy with the actors during rehearsals and perky with DeGeneres and Stone for their photo opportunities together, there is nothing rollicking or accessible about her today. "Before I perform, I cast a circle—a magic circle—around myself," she says. Its mojo is palpable. She gives no eye contact, makes no gestures of acknowledgment, moves to her own beat. With one exception: when Stephan arrives, Roseanne recounts the morning's victory over a reporter, explaining, "I said to him, 'It's way better around here since we got rid of His Highness King Shit' "—Tom Arnold. "And then he asks, 'Are you upset that they're moving you to Wednesdays at eight?' And I go, 'They can move it to eight, they can move it to nine, or they can shove it up their ass for all I care. I'm getting paid the same.' I loved it. It was real fun. I got some great lines off about Rob gettin' fired. He goes, 'Did you bring in somebody else?' 'Nope,' I go. 'This is a blue-collar show. We fire from the top, not like white-collar shows, where they fire from the bottom.' "

About half an hour before showtime, the audience files in and the writers assemble near a soundproof booth just above the bleachers. They have their own monitor to watch. Broch, the original author of the episode, is there with his fiancée; Berry brings his two towheaded children; Walker arrives with a friend. Renee Kurtz, an ABC executive, and Raether, Abbott, Trogdon, and the others all cram into the booth, too.

The opening of the show sails along on wave after wave of laughter. In Roseanne's fourteen speeches there are eleven jokes, and all of them score. "I liked that scene," Raether says, applauding. "Especially my work." But in the next scene, when Dan and Roseanne argue about whether D.J. should be allowed to go to the lake with Lisa, Raether can be heard bleating, "Aaargh!" Roseanne has muffed a joke and won't reshoot it. "Screw it," she says. "It's gone." The audience cheers Roseanne's outburst, but inside the booth the writers seethe.

"Another brilliant, well-thought-out editorial decision," says Abbott from the back.

But soon there's joy in the room again as the audience howls at DeGeneres's psychotherapist scene.

"She's trimmed some stuff out of here," Abbott says.

Miriam Trogdon looks at him. "Who did?"

"Who do you think?"

The big charge for the writers in the second act is watching Roseanne's glazed-ham joke bomb.

"We worked on her all day trying to take that thing away from her," says Tim Doyle, another producer-writer.

"She picked *that* one?" Trogdon asks.

But all is forgiven when Roseanne makes the line about "chocolate air" sing. The audience rocks with laughter, and someone says to Trogdon, who coined it, "That's a great line. Major."

"I love hearing the writers in the room—'That's mine.' 'That's mine,' " Renee Kurtz says.

"At home, I say it for nearly all the jokes," Berry says. "My daughter goes, 'Daddy, how do I know which ones are yours?' I say, 'The ones that you're laughing at, those are mine. The others are Danny Zuker's.' "

At the post mortem in the writers' booth, Broch is hugged by his fiancée, Berry is hugged by his daughter, and Walker hugs his script. "She can make anything work," he says. "She can make a straight line funny. Just her behavior."

Roseanne moves briefly among the cast and crew, then unceremoniously disappears. The comic fireworks that the writers have planned all week are a kind of Roman candle that dazzles and dies too soon. Some of them wander over to the Canyon Restaurant's bar to savor their victories and mourn their losses before they begin to climb next week's mountain.

"You hate all the intimidation and all the mental games she puts you through," Abbott says. "But I will say one thing. The reason the show's been good over the years is because the writers are afraid to bring crap to the table. You watch the head writers go, 'We got to get something better here.' They're afraid to bring a joke that's anything less than the best you can get." He goes on, "When I leave at the end of the year, I'm really going to be sad. It will be kind of closing the door on a piece of television history. She's one of a kind."

"ALL I do is read about serial killers," Roseanne says four days later, seated in the parlor of her Brentwood Hills house, a huge Alpine-Tudor-style chalet. (She has essentially turned this house over to her kids; she and Ben Thomas live in a smaller, adjacent white brick house.) "Every book I have is about serial killers and abnormal psychology. That's where I get my comedy." She glances up at a gallery overlooking the parlor. With its dark wood beams and mottled light filtering through the surrounding trees, the room has a shadowy, brooding aura that fits Roseanne's mood. She continues, "When everything is corrupt and filthy and brutal and psychotic, you will be, too. And that will be considered normal. That's what I find funny. The things that are normal are horrific and horrifying to me."

By her own admission, Roseanne has a "criminal mentality." She says, "If I hadn't found comedy, I'd probably be out killing people." When her jokes score, she says, they "kill." And she prefers to be called "killer bitch" rather than "feminist." Roseanne says, "It's like this: I gave birth to ya, and I can take ya out, too. I think that's what makes me a bit different from other women. Because I'll beat the shit out of them, and not just verbally. I'm not opposed to violence. In fact, I think it's great. I think women should be more violent, kill more of their husbands. I like the fight. If people are comin' at you, you don't just sit there and lay down and go, 'Oh, bless you.' That's not in the human arsenal. To say that women should do that is to say women aren't human."

The warrior spectacle that Roseanne makes of herself in Hollywood, she explains, is meant to call into question the supremacy of middle-class liberal women like Jodie Foster, Susan Sarandon, and Meryl Streep, all of whom Roseanne considers "talented and fuckin' deluded." She says, "They don't have any subtext to anything they say. They're all just upset about salaries, or something that feminism was about twenty-five years ago. They're rewarded for making the women's movement appear to be lost in time. And they don't even know it. I want them to shut the fuck up and get out of the way of the real women that are doin' something. I'd like to see 'em go down to goddam South Central and talk to those women. Let's hear what they have to say about violence in America. Let's not hear from Jodie Foster, for chrissake!" Roseanne continues, "These type of women are just translators. And they are, in effect, castrated females—excuse me, but that's what they are. They're just too middle-class white." Once Roseanne reaches a certain threshold of anger, her mood lifts; her voice and body become animated. "Jodie Foster," Roseanne says, her eyes aglitter. "I hate everything she stands for, and everyone gathered around her to help her stand for it. It's a big fat fuckin' lie. Let's not be who we are. Let's hide behind our art. ('Nell' . . . I gotta do 'Nell' onstage sometime.) Let's oppress everybody who is exactly like us. Make it even harder for them to be who they are. In her fuckin' Armani with her tits hangin' out. And constantly rewarded and rewarded. And by who? The power structure that she totally speaks for."

For a Carnegie Hall appearance Roseanne plans to do next February, she wants to open with a screen image of Streep, Foster, and Sarandon which dissolves into her singing "Streetwalker Blues." She giggles at the thought of it. "It's a horrible song," she says, and, naturally, begins to sing:

> I've got nipples on my titties
> Big around as both my thumbs
> I've got somethin' between my legs
> That makes a dead man come.

The script for the new act is a neatly typed pile of ideas, which is stashed in a large mahogany desk in the main house. Roseanne has another office and another big desk in an outbuilding on the premises. Both are calm, well-ordered spaces, dominated by tanks of exotic tropical fish. Roseanne will take six months to write and refine the material. She pulls out a page and reads, "It's not like in fairy tales; most guys are pigs. Like where the prince kisses the princess and she wakes up. Hey, in real life most guys, even if she didn't wake up, they'd still fuck her." Roseanne laughs. "It's so mean. I like it when it's mean," she says. "You want to get people moved or pissed, or something. Feel something. I like it when guys scream back at me, 'Bullshit, Roseanne!' "

Maybe because her lawyer will soon be arriving to discuss fallout from her divorce, or maybe because her rant against the actresses has tapped into Roseanne's bottomless reservoir of anger, she pulls out a section called "Tom Arnold." "I'm on a gag order. I can't say nothin' about him," she says, and fixes me with a glance. "But I can tell jokes." She sits down in her upholstered swivel chair. "Like this one: When you get married, all you hear is 'I'm the man. I wear the pants. I'm the man, I'll make all the decisions.' Yeah—till the divorce. 'What am I gonna do? How will I survive? I have to live the way I was accustomed.' How much do you need to have a shitty studio apartment with orange shag carpet that smells like piss, man? How much do you need for that? To have shelves made out of bricks you stole, and beer and pizza in your fridge? How much do you need to keep your stale water in your bong? That's what you were accustomed to, man. Fuck you, get a job. How're you gonna live? Just like before. Like a fuckin' pig. Sell stories to the *Enquirer,* like you used to. Put on your fuckin' Iowa sweatshirt and get fuckin' to it."

Later, in her other office, part of which is now an art studio, Roseanne pulls a big cardboard box out of a cupboard and sits cross-legged on the floor to pick through the flotsam and jetsam of fifteen years of hectic life: jottings on menus and in manuscript, "Roseanne" scripts and character sketches, and feminist feuilletons like "Big Mama Rag," "Celtic Healing Goddesses," and "Points of Unity"—the last a detailed document Roseanne wrote for the Woman to Woman bookstore. One of her earliest joke ideas, with "Write this up as a big story" scrawled across it, goes like this: "Boys like a good listener. Boys like to win at games. Boys like to think they're smarter than you. Boys don't respect a girl who gives in to them, so you go around practicing virginal behavior: being docile, being quiet, a gracious loser. But that's only till you get a man. Then you must start being the real you, if you ever were, and spend all your time trying to change him from someone who'd want to live with a stupid loser with no sex drive." Roseanne chuckles to herself as she reads.

"That's a hard thing to say."

"Yeah," she says. "But it's true."

Roseanne fishes out the mimeographed program she wrote for her comedy protest Take Back the Mike. Her bio reads, "Roseanne Barr—Person of Ceremonies: an adorably angry/vicious comic, wife of ten years, mother of three, affectionately referred to as 'castrating bitch' by many male colleagues." Pages of scribbled notions from the early eighties are churned up, a kind of grab bag of griefs being willed into good times:

· I have a song in my heart: Schubert's death waltz.
· My husband's given me the best years of his life. '76 and '77.
· I undress to motivational tapes.
· If you can't say something nice, I would probably like you.
· "Dance as though you're making love." "You mean you want me to go off and dance alone."

Roseanne rummages for a while, then pushes herself up and finds a chair. "While I'm alive on this earth, I'm going to create my own reality," she says.

"I'm not gonna fit it around me. I'm not gonna cut myself anymore to fit theirs. That's in all things I do, including my language."

After next year, when "Roseanne" goes off the air, she will be at large. "I know I have bigger things to do besides this," she says. She has joked about running for President. ("We need new blood in the White House—every twenty-eight days.") Her millions, as she says, "don't make me vote any different, they don't make me dress any better," but they do give her clout. She has a ten-year plan: she sees herself as a children's-rights advocate, and she is talking about setting up a foundation. "I feel that because I got all this I'm supposed to do that," she says. "That's the tradeoff." She also fancies herself a TV mogul. Roseanne plans to either own a network or align herself with one, to program shows that "only empower women." She tells me, "It may appear like a pipe dream now, but you should keep the quote for when I do own a network, and then you can say I said so in '95."

Whatever happens, Roseanne's greatest achievement has been her own salvation. "*God, freeze the family hands, lips, the thousand diseases of us this time, in this generation,*" she prays at the end of "My Lives." "*Spare me my grandchildren—as you have spared me.*" When I ask Roseanne why she wants another child, she says, "I want to keep doing it until I get it a hundred per cent right." She feels she has destroyed the neurotic family pattern that made her who she is. And if that has indeed come to pass, then the blessings of her life and her laughter have been engineered by the same fierce principle: without a killing, no feast. Roseanne stares at the battered cardboard box. "It's amazing that I got away with it, isn't it?" she says.

(1995)

MALCOLM GLADWELL

THE COOLHUNT

BAYSIE Wightman met DeeDee Gordon, appropriately enough, on a coolhunt. It was 1992. Baysie was a big shot for Converse, and DeeDee, who was barely twenty-one, was running a very cool boutique called Placid Planet, on Newbury Street in Boston. Baysie came in with a camera crew—one she often used when she was coolhunting—and said, "I've been watching your store, I've seen you, I've heard you know what's up," because it was Baysie's job at Converse to find people who knew what was up and she thought DeeDee was one of those people. DeeDee says that she responded with reserve—that "I was like, 'Whatever' "—but Baysie said that if DeeDee ever wanted to come and work at Converse she should just call, and nine months later DeeDee called. This was about the time the cool kids had decided they didn't want the hundred-and-twenty-five-dollar basketball sneaker with seventeen different kinds of high-technology materials and colors and air-cushioned heels anymore. They wanted simplicity and authenticity, and Baysie picked up on that. She brought back the Converse One Star, which was a vulcanized, suède, low-top classic old-school sneaker from the nineteen-seventies, and, sure enough, the One Star quickly became the signature shoe of the retro era. Remember what Kurt Cobain was wearing in the famous picture of him lying dead on the ground after committing suicide? Black Converse One Stars. DeeDee's big score was calling the sandal craze. She had been out in Los Angeles and had kept seeing the white teen-age girls dressing up like *cholos*, Mexican gangsters, in tight white tank tops known as "wife beaters," with a bra strap hanging out, and long shorts and tube socks and shower sandals. DeeDee recalls, "I'm like, 'I'm telling you, Baysie, this is going to hit. There are just too many people wearing it. We have to make a shower sandal.' " So Baysie, DeeDee, and a designer came up with the idea of making a retro sneaker-sandal, cutting the back off the One Star and putting a thick outsole on it. It was *huge*, and, amazingly, it's still huge.

Today, Baysie works for Reebok as general-merchandise manager—part of the team trying to return Reebok to the position it enjoyed in the mid-nineteen-eighties as the country's hottest sneaker company. DeeDee works for an advertising agency in Del Mar called Lambesis, where she puts out a quarterly tip sheet called the *L Report* on what the cool kids in major American cities are thinking and doing and buying. Baysie and DeeDee are best friends. They talk on the phone all the time. They get together whenever Baysie is in L.A. (DeeDee: "It's, like, how many times can you drive past O. J. Simpson's house?"), and between them they can talk for hours about the art of the coolhunt. They're the Lewis and Clark of cool.

What they have is what everybody seems to want these days, which is a window on the world of the street. Once, when fashion trends were set by the big couture houses—when cool was trickle-down—that wasn't important. But sometime in the past few decades things got turned over, and fashion became trickle-up. It's now about chase and flight—designers and retailers and the mass consumer giving chase to the elusive prey of street cool—and the rise of coolhunting as a profession shows how serious the chase has become. The sneakers of Nike and Reebok used to come out yearly. Now a new style comes out every season. Apparel designers used to have an eighteen-month lead time between concept and sale. Now they're reducing that to a year, or even six months, in order to react faster to new ideas from the street. The paradox, of course, is that the better coolhunters become at bringing the mainstream close to the cutting edge, the more elusive the cutting edge becomes. This is the first rule of the cool: The quicker the chase, the quicker the flight. The act of discovering what's cool is what causes cool to move on, which explains the triumphant circularity of coolhunting: because we have coolhunters like DeeDee and Baysie, cool changes more quickly, and because cool changes more quickly, we need coolhunters like DeeDee and Baysie.

DeeDee is tall and glamorous, with short hair she has dyed so often that she claims to have forgotten her real color. She drives a yellow 1977 Trans Am with a burgundy stripe down the center and a 1973 Mercedes 450 SL, and lives in a spare, Japanese-style cabin in Laurel Canyon. She uses words like "rad" and "totally," and offers non-stop, deadpan pronouncements on pop culture, as in "It's all about Pee-wee Herman." She sounds at first like a teen, like the same teens who, at Lambesis, it is her job to follow. But teen speech—particularly girl-teen speech, with its fixation on reported speech ("so she goes," "and I'm like," "and he goes") and its stock vocabulary of accompanying grimaces and gestures—is about using language less to communicate than to fit in. DeeDee uses teen speech to set herself apart, and the result is, for lack of a better word, *really* cool. She doesn't do the teen thing of climbing half an octave at the end of every sentence. Instead, she drags out her vowels for emphasis, so that if she mildly disagreed with something I'd said she would say "Maalcolm" and if she strongly disagreed with what I'd said she would say "Maaalcolm."

Baysie is older, just past forty (although you would never guess that), and went to Exeter and Middlebury and had two grandfathers who went to Harvard (although you wouldn't guess that, either). She has curly brown hair and big green eyes and long legs and so much energy that it is hard to imagine her asleep, or resting, or even standing still for longer than thirty seconds. The hunt for cool is an obsession with her, and DeeDee is the same way. DeeDee used to sit on the corner of West Broadway and Prince in SoHo—back when SoHo was cool—and take pictures of everyone who walked by for an entire hour. Baysie can tell you precisely where she goes on her Reebok coolhunts to find the really cool alternative white kids ("I'd maybe go to Portland and hang out where the skateboarders hang out near that bridge") or which snowboarding mountain has cooler kids—Stratton, in Vermont, or Summit County, in Colorado. (Summit, definitely.) DeeDee can tell you on the basis of the *L Report*'s research exactly how far Dallas is behind New York in coolness (from six to eight months). Baysie is convinced that Los Angeles is not happening right now: "In the early nineteen-nineties a lot more was coming from L.A. They had a big trend with the whole Melrose Avenue look—the stupid goatees, the shorter hair. It was cleaned-up after-grunge. There were a lot of places you could go to buy vinyl records. It was a strong place to go for looks. Then it went back to being horrible." DeeDee is convinced that Japan *is* happening: "I linked onto this future-technology thing two years ago. Now look at it, it's huge. It's the whole resurgence of Nike—Nike being larger than life. I went to Japan and saw the kids just bailing the most technologically advanced Nikes with their little dresses and little outfits and I'm like, 'Whoa, this is trippy!' It's performance mixed with fashion. It's really superheavy." Baysie has a theory that Liverpool is cool right now because it's the birthplace of the whole "lad" look, which involves soccer blokes in the pubs going superdressy and wearing Dolce & Gabbana and Polo Sport and Reebok Classics on their feet. But when I asked DeeDee about that, she just rolled her eyes: "Sometimes Baysie goes off on these tangents. *Man,* I love that woman!"

I used to think that if I talked to Baysie and DeeDee long enough I could write a coolhunting manual, an encyclopedia of cool. But then I realized that the manual would have so many footnotes and caveats that it would be unreadable. Coolhunting is not about the articulation of a coherent philosophy of cool. It's just a collection of spontaneous observations and predictions that differ from one moment to the next and from one coolhunter to the next. Ask a coolhunter where the baggy-jeans look came from, for example, and you might get any number of answers: urban black kids mimicking the jailhouse look, skateboarders looking for room to move, snowboarders trying not to look like skiers, or, alternatively, all three at once, in some grand concordance.

Or take the question of exactly how Tommy Hilfiger—a forty-five-year-old white guy from Greenwich, Connecticut, doing all-American preppy clothes— came to be the designer of choice for urban black America. Some say it was all about the early and visible endorsement given Hilfiger by the hip-hop auteur Grand Puba, who wore a dark-green-and-blue Tommy jacket over a white Tommy T-shirt as he leaned on his black Lamborghini on the cover of the hugely influential "Grand Puba 2000" CD, and whose love for Hilfiger soon spread to other rappers. (Who could forget the rhymes of Mobb Deep? "Tommy was my nigga / And couldn't figure / How me and Hilfiger / used to move through with vigor.") Then I had lunch with one of Hilfiger's designers, a twenty-six-year-old named Ulrich (Ubi) Simpson, who has a Puerto Rican mother and a Dutch-Venezuelan father, plays lacrosse, snowboards, surfs the long board, goes to hip-hop concerts, listens to Jungle, Edith Piaf, opera, rap, and Metallica, and has working with him on his design team a twenty-seven-year-old black guy from Montclair with dreadlocks, a twenty-two-year-old Asian-American who lives on the Lower East Side, a twenty-five-year-old South Asian guy from Fiji, and a twenty-one-year-old white graffiti artist from Queens. That's when it occurred to me that maybe the reason Tommy Hilfiger can make white culture cool to black culture is that he has people working for him who are cool in both cultures simultaneously. Then again, maybe it *was* all Grand Puba. Who knows?

One day last month, Baysie took me on a coolhunt to the Bronx and Harlem, lugging a big black canvas bag with twenty-four different shoes that Reebok is about to bring out, and as we drove down Fordham Road, she had her head out the window like a little kid, checking out what everyone on the street was wearing. We went to Dr. Jay's, which is the cool place to buy sneakers in the Bronx, and Baysie crouched down on the floor and started pulling the shoes out of her bag one by one, soliciting opinions from customers who gathered around and asking one question after another, in rapid sequence. One guy she listened closely to was maybe eighteen or nineteen, with a diamond stud in his ear and a thin beard. He was wearing a Polo baseball cap, a brown leather jacket, and the big, oversized leather boots that are everywhere uptown right now. Baysie would hand him a shoe and he would hold it, look at the top, and move it up and down and flip it over. The first one he didn't like: "*Oh*-kay." The second one he hated: he made a growling sound in his throat even before Baysie could give it to him, as if to say, "Put it back in the bag—now!" But when she handed him a new DMX RXT—a low-cut run/walk shoe in white and blue and mesh with a translucent "ice" sole, which retails for a hundred and ten dollars—he looked at it long and hard and shook his head in pure admiration and just said two words, dragging each of them out: "No *doubt*."

Baysie was interested in what he was saying, because the DMX RXT she had was a girls' shoe that actually hadn't been doing all that well. Later, she explained to me that the fact that the boys loved the shoe was critical news, because it suggested that Reebok had a potential hit if it just switched the shoe to the men's section. How she managed to distill this piece of information from the crowd of teen-agers around her, how she made any sense of the two dozen shoes in her bag, most of which (to my eyes, anyway) looked pretty much the same, and how she knew which of the teens to really focus on was a mystery. Baysie is a Wasp from New England, and she crouched on the floor in Dr. Jay's for almost an hour, talking and joking with the homeboys without a trace of condescension or self-consciousness.

Near the end of her visit, a young boy walked up and sat down on the bench next to her. He was wearing a black woollen cap with white stripes pulled low, a blue North Face pleated down jacket, a pair of baggy Guess jeans, and, on his feet, Nike Air Jordans. He couldn't have been more than thirteen. But when he started talking you could see Baysie's eyes light up, because somehow she knew the kid was the real thing.

"How many pairs of shoes do you buy a month?" Baysie asked.

"Two," the kid answered. "And if at the end I find one more I like I get to buy that, too."

Baysie was onto him. "Does your mother spoil you?"

The kid blushed, but a friend next to him was laughing. "Whatever he wants, he gets."

Baysie laughed, too. She had the DMX RXT in his size. He tried them on. He rocked back and forth, testing them. He looked back at Baysie. He was dead serious now: "Make sure these come out."

Baysie handed him the new "Rush" Emmitt Smith shoe due out in the fall. One of the boys had already pronounced it "phat," and another had looked through the marbleized-foam cradle in the heel and cried out in delight, "This is bug!" But this kid was the acid test, because this kid knew cool. He paused. He looked at it hard. "Reebok," he said, soberly and carefully, "is trying to get *butter.*"

In the car on the way back to Manhattan, Baysie repeated it twice. "Not better. *Butter!* That kid could totally tell you what he thinks." Baysie had spent an hour coolhunting in a shoe store and found out that Reebok's efforts were winning the highest of hip-hop praise. "He was so *fucking* smart."

IF you want to understand how trends work, and why coolhunters like Baysie and DeeDee have become so important, a good place to start is with what's known as diffusion research, which is the study of how ideas and innovations spread. Diffusion researchers do things like spending five years studying the adoption of irrigation techniques in a Colombian mountain village, or developing complex matrices to map the spread of new math in the Pittsburgh school system. What they do may seem like a far cry from, say, how the Tommy Hilfiger thing spread from Harlem to every suburban mall in the country, but it really isn't: both are about how new ideas spread from one person to the next.

One of the most famous diffusion studies is Bruce Ryan and Neal Gross's analysis of the spread of hybrid seed corn in Greene County, Iowa, in the nineteen-thirties. The new seed corn was introduced there in about 1928, and it was superior in every respect to the seed that had been used by farmers for decades. But it wasn't adopted all at once. Of two hundred and fifty-nine farmers studied by Ryan and Gross, only a handful had started planting the new seed by 1933. In 1934, sixteen took the plunge. In 1935, twenty-one more followed; the next year, there were thirty-six, and the year after that a whopping sixty-one. The succeeding figures were then forty-six, thirty-six, fourteen, and three, until, by 1941, all but two of the two hundred and fifty-nine farmers studied were using the new seed. In the language of diffusion research, the handful of farmers who started trying hybrid seed corn at the very beginning of the thirties were the "innovators," the adventurous ones. The slightly larger group that followed them was the "early adopters." They were the opinion leaders in the community, the respected, thoughtful people who watched and analyzed what those wild innovators were doing and then did it themselves. Then came the big bulge of farmers in 1936, 1937, and 1938—the "early majority" and the "late majority," which is to say the deliberate and the skeptical masses, who would never try anything until the most respected farmers had tried it. Only after they had been converted did the "laggards," the most traditional of all, follow suit. The critical thing about this sequence is that it is almost entirely interpersonal. According to Ryan and Gross, only the innovators relied to any great extent on radio advertising and farm journals and seed salesmen in making their decision to switch to the hybrid. Everyone else made his decision overwhelmingly because of the example and the opinions of his neighbors and peers.

Isn't this just how fashion works? A few years ago, the classic brushed-suède Hush Puppies with the lightweight crêpe sole—the moc-toe oxford known as the Duke and the slip-on with the golden buckle known as the Columbia—were selling barely sixty-five thousand pairs a year. The company was trying to walk away from the whole suède casual look entirely. It wanted to do "aspirational" shoes: "active casuals" in smooth leather, like the Mall Walker, with a Comfort Curve technology outsole and a heel stabilizer—the kind of shoes you see in Kinney's for $39.95. But then something strange started happening. Two Hush Puppies executives—Owen Baxter and Jeff Lewis—were doing a fashion shoot for their Mall Walkers and ran into a creative consultant from Manhattan named Jeffrey Miller, who informed them that the Dukes and the Columbias weren't dead, they were dead chic. "We were being told," Baxter recalls, "that there were areas in the Village, in SoHo, where the shoes were selling—in resale shops—and that people were wearing the old Hush Puppies. They were going to the ma-and-pa stores, the little stores that still carried them, and there was this authenticity of being able to say, 'I am wearing an original pair of Hush Puppies.' "

Baxter and Lewis—tall, solid, fair-haired Midwestern guys with thick, shiny wedding bands—are shoe men, first and foremost. Baxter was working the cash register at his father's shoe store in Mount Prospect, Illinois, at the age of thirteen. Lewis was doing inventory in his father's shoe store in Pontiac, Michigan, at the age of seven. Baxter was in the National Guard during the 1968 Democratic Convention, in Chicago, and was stationed across the street from the Conrad Hilton downtown, right in the middle of things. Today, the two men work out of Rockford, Michigan (population thirty-eight hundred), where Hush Puppies has been making the Dukes and the Columbias in an old factory down by the Rogue River for almost forty years. They took me to the plant when I was in Rockford. In a crowded, noisy, low-slung building, factory workers stand in long rows, gluing, stapling, and sewing together shoes in dozens of bright colors, and the two executives stopped at each production station and described it in detail. Lewis and Baxter know shoes. But they would be the first to admit that they don't know cool. "Miller was saying that there is something going on with the shoes—that Isaac Mizrahi was wearing the shoes for his personal use," Lewis told me. We were seated around the conference table in the Hush Puppies headquarters in Rockford, with the snow and the trees outside and a big water tower behind us. "I think it's fair to say that at the time we had no idea who Isaac Mizrahi was."

By late 1994, things had begun to happen in a rush. First, the designer John Bartlett called. He wanted to use Hush Puppies as accessories in his spring collection. Then Anna Sui called. Miller, the man from Manhattan, flew out to Michigan to give advice on a new line ("Of course, packing my own food and thinking about 'Fargo' in the corner of my mind"). A few months later, in Los Angeles, the designer Joel Fitzpatrick put a twenty-five-foot inflatable basset hound on the roof of his store on La Brea Avenue and gutted his adjoining art gallery to turn it into a Hush Puppies department, and even before he opened—while he was still painting and putting up shelves—Pee-wee Herman walked in and asked for a couple of pairs. Pee-wee Herman! "It was total word of mouth. I didn't even have a sign back then," Fitzpatrick recalls. In 1995, the company sold four hundred and thirty thousand pairs of the classic Hush Puppies. In 1996, it sold a million six hundred thousand, and that was only scratching the surface, because in Europe and the rest of the world, where Hush Puppies have a huge following—where they might outsell the American market four to one—the revival was just beginning.

The cool kids who started wearing old Dukes and Columbias from thrift shops were the innovators. Pee-wee Herman, wandering in off the street, was an early adopter. The million six hundred thousand people who bought Hush Puppies last year are the early majority, jumping in because the really cool people have already blazed the trail. Hush Puppies are moving through the country just the way hybrid seed corn moved through Greene County—all of which illustrates what coolhunters can and cannot do. If Jeffrey Miller had been wrong—if cool people hadn't been digging through the thrift shops for Hush Puppies—and he had arbitrarily decided that Baxter and Lewis should try to convince non-cool people that the shoes were cool, it wouldn't have worked. You can't convince the late majority that Hush Puppies are cool, because the late majority makes its coolness decisions on the basis of what the early majority is doing, and you can't convince the early majority, because the early majority is looking at the early adopters, and you can't convince the early adopters, because they take their cues from the innovators. The innovators do get their cool ideas from people other than their peers, but the fact is that they are the last people who can be convinced by a marketing campaign that a pair of suède shoes is cool. These are, after all, the people who spent hours sifting through thrift-store bins. And why did they do that? Because their definition of cool is doing something that nobody else is doing. A company can intervene in the cool cycle. It can put its shoes on really cool celebrities and on fashion runways and on MTV. It can accelerate the transition from the innovator to the early adopter and on to the early majority. But it can't just manufacture cool out of thin air, and that's the second rule of cool.

At the peak of the Hush Puppies craziness last year, Hush Puppies won the prize for best accessory at the Council of Fashion Designers' awards dinner, at Lincoln Center. The award was accepted by the Hush Puppies president, Louis Dubrow, who came out wearing a pair of custom-made black patent-leather Hush Puppies and stood there blinking and looking at the assembled crowd as if it were the last scene of "Close Encounters of the Third Kind." It was a strange moment. There was the president of the Hush Puppies company, of Rockford, Michigan, population thirty-eight hundred, sharing a stage with Calvin Klein and Donna Karan and Isaac Mizrahi—and all because some kids in the East Village began combing through thrift shops for old Dukes. Fashion was at the mercy of those kids, whoever they were, and it was a wonderful thing if the kids picked you, but a scary thing, too, because it meant that cool was something you could not control. You needed someone to find cool and tell you what it was.

WHEN Baysie Wightman went to Dr. Jay's, she was looking for customer response to the new shoes Reebok had planned for the fourth quarter of 1997 and the first quarter of 1998. This kind of customer testing is critical at Reebok, because the last decade has not been kind to the company. In 1987, it had a third of the American athletic-shoe market, well ahead of Nike. Last year, it had sixteen per cent. "The kid in the store would say, 'I'd like this shoe if your logo wasn't on it,' " E. Scott Morris, who's a senior designer for Reebok, told me. "That's kind of a punch in the mouth. But we've all seen it. You go into a shoe store. The kid picks up the shoe and says, 'Ah, man, this is nice.' He turns the shoe around and around. He looks at it underneath. He looks at the side and he goes, 'Ah, this is Reebok,' and says, 'I ain't buying this,' and puts the shoe down and walks out. And you go, 'You was just digging it a minute ago. What happened?' " Somewhere along the way, the company lost its cool, and Reebok now faces the task not only of rebuilding its image but of making the shoes so cool that the kids in the store *can't* put them down.

Every few months, then, the company's coolhunters go out into the field with prototypes of the upcoming shoes to find out what kids really like, and come back to recommend the necessary changes. The prototype of one recent Emmitt Smith shoe, for example, had a piece of molded rubber on the end of the tongue as a design element; it was supposed to give the shoe a certain "richness," but the kids said they thought it looked overbuilt. Then Reebok gave the shoes to the Boston College football team for wear-testing, and when they got the shoes back they found out that all the football players had cut out the rubber component with scissors. As messages go, this was hard to miss. The tongue piece wasn't cool, and on the final version of the shoe it was gone. The rule of thumb at Reebok is that if the kids in Chicago, New York, and Detroit all like a shoe, it's a guaranteed hit. More than likely, though, the coolhunt is going to turn up subtle differences from city to city, so that once the coolhunters come back the designers have to find out some way to synthesize what was heard, and pick out just those things that all the kids seemed to agree on. In New York, for example, kids in Harlem are more sophisticated and fashion-forward than kids in the Bronx, who like things a little more colorful and glitzy. Brooklyn, meanwhile, is conservative and preppy, more like Washington, D.C. For reasons no one really knows, Reeboks are coolest in Philadelphia. In Philly, in fact, the Reebok Classics are so huge they are known simply as National Anthems, as in "I'll have a pair of blue Anthems in nine and a half." Philadelphia is Reebok's innovator town. From there trends move along the East Coast, trickling all the way to Charlotte, North Carolina.

Reebok has its headquarters in Stoughton, Massachusetts, outside Boston— in a modern corporate park right off Route 24. There are basketball and tennis courts next to the building, and a health club on the ground floor that you can look directly into from the parking lot. The front lobby is adorned with shrines for all of Reebok's most prominent athletes—shrines complete with dramatic action photographs, their sports jerseys, and a pair of their signature shoes— and the halls are filled with so many young, determinedly athletic people that when I visited Reebok headquarters I suddenly wished I'd packed my gym clothes in case someone challenged me to wind sprints. At Stoughton, I met with a handful of the company's top designers and marketing executives in a long conference room on the third floor. In the course of two hours, they put one pair of shoes after another on the table in front of me, talking excitedly about each sneaker's prospects, because the feeling at Reebok is that things are finally turning around. The basketball shoe that Reebok brought out last winter for Allen Iverson, the star rookie guard for the Philadelphia 76ers, for ex-

ample, is one of the hottest shoes in the country. Dr. Jay's sold out of Iversons
in two days, compared with the week it took the store to sell out of Nike's new
Air Jordans. Iverson himself is brash and charismatic and faster from foul line
to foul line than anyone else in the league. He's the equivalent of those kids in
the East Village who began wearing Hush Puppies way back when. He's an innovator, and the hope at Reebok is that if he gets big enough the whole company can ride back to coolness on his coattails, the way Nike rode to coolness
on the coattails of Michael Jordan. That's why Baysie was so excited when the
kid said Reebok was trying to get *butter* when he looked at the Rush and the
DMX RXT: it was a sign, albeit a small one, that the indefinable, abstract thing
called cool was coming back.

When Baysie comes back from a coolhunt, she sits down with marketing experts and sales representatives and designers, and reconnects them to the
street, making sure they have the right shoes going to the right places at the
right price. When she got back from the Bronx, for example, the first thing she
did was tell all these people they had to get a new men's DMX RXT out, *fast*, because the kids on the street loved the women's version. "It's hotter than we realized," she told them. The coolhunter's job in this instance is very specific.
What DeeDee does, on the other hand, is a little more ambitious. With the *L
Report*, she tries to construct a kind of grand matrix of cool, comprising not
just shoes but everything kids like, and not just kids of certain East Coast urban
markets but kids all over. DeeDee and her staff put it out four times a year, in six
different versions—for New York, Los Angeles, San Francisco, Austin-Dallas,
Seattle, and Chicago—and then sell it to manufacturers, retailers, and ad agencies (among others) for twenty thousand dollars a year. They go to each city
and find the coolest bars and clubs, and ask the coolest kids to fill out questionnaires. The information is then divided into six categories—You Saw It Here
First, Entertainment and Leisure, Clothing and Accessories, Personal and
Individual, Aspirations, and Food and Beverages—which are, in turn, broken
up into dozens of subcategories, so that Personal and Individual, for example,
includes Cool Date, Cool Evening, Free Time, Favorite Possession, and on and
on. The information in those subcategories is subdivided again by sex and by
age bracket (14–18, 19–24, 25–30), and then, as a control, the *L Report* gives
you the corresponding set of preferences for "mainstream" kids.

Few coolhunters bother to analyze trends with this degree of specificity.
DeeDee's biggest competitor, for example, is something called the *Hot Sheet*, out
of Manhattan. It uses a panel of three thousand kids a year from across the
country and divides up their answers by sex and age, but it doesn't distinguish
between regions, or between trendsetting and mainstream respondents. So
what you're really getting is what *all* kids think is cool—not what cool kids
think is cool, which is a considerably different piece of information. Janine
Misdom and Joanne DeLuca, who run the Sputnik coolhunting group out of
the garment district in Manhattan, meanwhile, favor an entirely impressionis-

tic approach, sending out coolhunters with video cameras to talk to kids on the ground that it's too difficult to get cool kids to fill out questionnaires. Once, when I was visiting the Sputnik girls—as Misdom and DeLuca are known on the street, because they look alike and their first names are so similar and both have the same *awesome* New York accents—they showed me a video of the girl they believe was the patient zero of the whole eighties revival going on right now. It was back in September of 1993. Joanne and Janine were on Seventh Avenue, outside the Fashion Institute of Technology, doing random street interviews for a major jeans company, and, quite by accident, they ran into this nineteen-year-old raver. She had close-cropped hair, which was green at the top, and at the temples was shaved even closer and dyed pink. She had rings and studs all over her face, and a thick collection of silver tribal jewelry around her neck, and vintage jeans. She looked into the camera and said, "The sixties came in and then the seventies came in and I think it's ready to come back to the eighties. It's totally eighties: the eye makeup, the clothes. It's totally going back to that." Immediately, Joanne and Janine started asking around. "We talked to a few kids on the Lower East Side who said they were feeling the need to start breaking out their old Michael Jackson jackets," Joanne said. "They were joking about it. They weren't doing it yet. But they were going to, you know? They were saying, 'We're getting the urge to break out our Members Only jackets.' " That was right when Joanne and Janine were just starting up; calling the eighties revival was their first big break, and now they put out a full-blown videotaped report twice a year which is a collection of clips of interviews with *extremely* progressive people.

What DeeDee argues, though, is that cool is too subtle and too variegated to be captured with these kind of broad strokes. Cool is a set of dialects, not a language. The *L Report* can tell you, for example, that nineteen-to-twenty-four-year-old male trendsetters in Seattle would most like to meet, among others, King Solomon and Dr. Seuss, and that nineteen-to-twenty-four-year-old female trendsetters in San Francisco have turned their backs on Calvin Klein, Nintendo Gameboy, and sex. What's cool right now? Among male New York trendsetters: North Face jackets, rubber and latex, khakis, and the rock band Kiss. Among female trendsetters: ska music, old-lady clothing, and cyber tech. In Chicago, snowboarding is huge among trendsetters of both sexes and all ages. Women over nineteen are into short hair, while those in their teens have embraced mod culture, rock climbing, tag watches, and bootleg pants. In Austin-Dallas, meanwhile, twenty-five-to-thirty-year-old women trendsetters are into hats, heroin, computers, cigars, Adidas, and velvet, while men in their twenties are into video games and hemp. In all, the typical *L Report* runs over one hundred pages. But with that flood of data comes an obsolescence disclaimer: "The fluctuating nature of the trendsetting market makes keeping up with trends a difficult task." By the spring, in other words, everything may have changed.

The key to coolhunting, then, is to look for cool people first and cool things later, and not the other way around. Since cool things are always changing, you can't look for them, because the very fact they are cool means you have no idea what to look for. What you would be doing is thinking back on what was cool before and extrapolating, which is about as useful as presuming that because the Dow rose ten points yesterday it will rise another ten points today. Cool people, on the other hand, are a constant.

When I was in California, I met Salvador Barbier, who had been described to me by a coolhunter as "the Michael Jordan of skateboarding." He was tall and lean and languid, with a cowboy's insouciance, and we drove through the streets of Long Beach at fifteen miles an hour in a white late-model Ford Mustang, a car he had bought as a kind of ironic status gesture ("It would look good if I had a Polo jacket or maybe Nautica," he said) to go with his '62 Econoline van and his '64 T-bird. Sal told me that he and his friends, who are all in their mid-twenties, recently took to dressing up as if they were in eighth grade again and gathering together—having a "rally"—on old BMX bicycles in front of their local 7-Eleven. "I'd wear muscle shirts, like Def Leppard or Foghat or some old heavy-metal band, and tight, tight tapered Levi's, and Vans on my feet—big, like, checkered Vans or striped Vans or camouflage Vans—and then wristbands and gloves with the fingers cut off. It was total eighties fashion. You had to look like that to participate in the rally. We had those denim jackets with patches on the back and combs that hung out the back pocket. We went without I.D.s, because we'd have to have someone else buy us beers." At this point, Sal laughed. He was driving really slowly and staring straight ahead and talking in a low drawl—the coolhunter's dream. "We'd ride to this bar and I'd have to carry my bike inside, because we have really expensive bikes, and when we got inside people would freak out. They'd say, 'Omigod,' and I was asking them if they wanted to go for a ride on the handlebars. They were like, 'What is wrong with you. My boyfriend used to dress like that in the eighth grade!' And I was like, 'He was probably a lot cooler then, too.' "

This is just the kind of person DeeDee wants. "I'm looking for somebody who is an individual, who has definitely set himself apart from everybody else, who doesn't look like his peers. I've run into trendsetters who look completely Joe Regular Guy. I can see Joe Regular Guy at a club listening to some totally hardcore band playing, and I say to myself 'Omigod, what's that guy doing here?' and that totally intrigues me, and I have to walk up to him and say, 'Hey, you're really into this band. What's up?' You know what I mean? I look at everything. If I see Joe Regular Guy sitting in a coffee shop and everyone around him has blue hair, I'm going to gravitate toward him, because, hey, what's Joe Regular Guy doing in a coffee shop with people with blue hair?"

We were sitting outside the Fred Segal store in West Hollywood. I was wearing a very conservative white Brooks Brothers button-down and a pair of Levi's, and DeeDee looked first at my shirt and then my pants and dissolved into laughter: "I mean, I might even go up to *you* in a cool place."

Picking the right person is harder than it sounds, though. Piney Kahn, who works for DeeDee, says, "There are a lot of people in the gray area. You've got these kids who dress ultra funky and have their own style. Then you realize they're just running after their friends." The trick is not just to be able to tell who is different but to be able to tell when that difference represents something truly cool. It's a gut thing. You have to somehow just *know.* DeeDee hired Piney because Piney clearly *knows:* she is twenty-four and used to work with the Beastie Boys and has the formidable self-possession of someone who is not only cool herself but whose parents were cool. "I mean," she says, "they named me after a *tree.*"

Piney and DeeDee said that they once tried to hire someone as a coolhunter who was not, himself, cool, and it was a disaster.

"You can give them the boundaries," Piney explained. "You can say that if people shop at Banana Republic and listen to Alanis Morissette they're proba-bly not trendsetters. But then they might go out and assume that everyone who does that is not a trendsetter, and not look at the other things."

"I mean, I myself might go into Banana Republic and buy a T-shirt," DeeDee chimed in.

Their non-cool coolhunter just didn't have that certain instinct, that sense that told him when it was O.K. to deviate from the manual. Because he wasn't cool, he didn't know cool, and that's the essence of the third rule of cool: You have to be one to know one. That's why Baysie is still on top of this business at forty-one. "It's easier for me to tell you what kid is cool than to tell you what things are cool," she says. But that's all she needs to know. In this sense, the third rule of cool fits perfectly into the second: the second rule says that cool cannot be manufactured, only observed, and the third says that it can only be observed by those who are themselves cool. And, of course, the first rule says that it cannot accurately be observed at all, because the act of discovering cool causes cool to take flight, so if you add all three together they describe a closed loop, the hermeneutic circle of coolhunting, a phenomenon whereby not only can the uncool not see cool but cool cannot even be adequately described to them. Baysie says that she can see a coat on one of her friends and think it's not cool but then see the same coat on DeeDee and think that it is cool. It is not pos-sible to be cool, in other words, unless you are—in some larger sense—already cool, and so the phenomenon that the uncool cannot see and cannot have de-scribed to them is also something that they cannot ever attain, because if they did it would no longer be cool. Coolhunting represents the ascendancy, in the marketplace, of high school.

Once, I was visiting DeeDee at her house in Laurel Canyon when one of her *L Report* assistants, Jonas Vail, walked in. He'd just come back from Niketown on Wilshire Boulevard, where he'd bought seven hundred dollars' worth of the latest sneakers to go with the three hundred dollars' worth of skateboard shoes he'd bought earlier in the afternoon. Jonas is tall and expressionless, with a peacoat, dark jeans, and short-cropped black hair. "Jonas is good," DeeDee says. "He works with me on everything. That guy knows more pop culture. You know: What was the name of the store Mrs. Garrett owned on 'The Facts of Life'? He knows all the names of the *extras* from eighties sitcoms. I can't believe someone like him exists. He's fucking unbelievable. Jonas can spot a cool person a *mile* away."

Jonas takes the boxes of shoes and starts unpacking them on the couch next to DeeDee. He picks up a pair of the new Nike ACG hiking boots, and says, "All the Japanese in Niketown were really into these." He hands the shoes to DeeDee.

"Of *course* they were!" she says. "The Japanese are all into the tech-looking shit. Look how exaggerated it is, how bulbous." DeeDee has very ambivalent feelings about Nike, because she thinks its marketing has got out of hand. When she was in the New York Niketown with a girlfriend recently, she says, she started getting light-headed and freaked out. "It's cult, cult, cult. It was like, 'Hello, are we all drinking the Kool-Aid here?' " But this shoe she loves. It's Dr. Jay's in the Bronx all over again. DeeDee turns the shoe around and around in the air, tapping the big clear-blue plastic bubble on the side—the visible Air-Sole unit—with one finger. "It's so fucking rad. It looks like a platypus!" In front of me, there is a pair of Nike's new shoes for the basketball player Jason Kidd.

I pick it up. "This looks . . . cool," I venture uncertainly.

DeeDee is on the couch, where she's surrounded by shoeboxes and sneakers and white tissue paper, and she looks up reprovingly because, of course, I don't get it. I *can't* get it. "Beyooond cool, Maalcolm. Beyooond cool."

(1997)

ADAM GOPNIK

MAN GOES TO SEE A DOCTOR

LATELY, a lot of people in New York—why, I'm not entirely sure—have been sending me clippings about the decline and fall of psychoanalysis. Most of the reasons given for its disappearance make sense: people are happier, busier; the work done by the anti-Freudian skeptics has finally taken hold of the popular imagination, so that people have no time for analytic longueurs and no patience with its mystifications. Along with those decline-and-fall pieces, though, I've also been sent—and in this case I don't entirely want to know why—a lot of hair-raising pieces about mental illness and its new therapies: about depressions, disasters, hidden urges suddenly (or brazenly) confessed and how you can cure them all with medicine. Talking is out, taking is in. When I go back to New York, some of my friends seem to be layered with drugs, from the top down, like a pousse-café: Rogaine on top, then Prozac, then Xanax, then Viagra. . . . In this context, my own experience in being doctored for mental illness seems paltry and vaguely absurd, and yet, in its way, memorable.

I was on the receiving end of what must have been one of the last, and easily one of the most unsuccessful, psychoanalyses that have ever been attempted—one of the last times a German-born analyst, with a direct laying on of hands from Freud, spent forty-five minutes twice a week for six years discussing, in a small room on Park Avenue decorated with Motherwell posters, the problems of a "creative" New York neurotic. It may therefore be worth recalling, if only in the way that it would be interesting to hear the experiences of the last man mesmerized or the last man to be bled with leeches. Or the last man—and there must have been such a man as the sixteenth century drew to a close and the modern age began—to bring an alchemist a lump of lead in the sincere belief that he would take it home as gold.

So it happened that on a night in October, 1990, I found myself sitting in a chair and looking at the couch in the office of one of the oldest, most patriarchal, most impressive-looking psychoanalysts in New York. He had been recommended to me by another patient, a twenty-year veteran of his couch. The choice now presents itself of whether to introduce him by name or by pseudonym, a choice that is more one of decorum than of legal necessity (he's dead). To introduce him by name is, in a sense, to invade his privacy. On the other hand, not to introduce him by name is to allow him to disappear into the braid of literature in which he was caught—his patients liked to write about him, in masks, theirs and his—and from which, at the end, he was struggling to break free. He had, for instance, written a professional article about a well-known patient, in which the (let's say) playwright who had inspired the article was turned into a painter. He had then seen this article, and the disputes it engendered, transformed into an episode in one of the playwright's plays, with the playwright-painter now turned into a novelist, and then the entire pas de deux had been turned by a colleague into a further psychoanalytic study of the exchange, with the occupations altered yet again—the playwright-painter-novelist now becoming a poet—so that four layers of disguise (five, as I write this) gathered around one episode in his office. "Yes, but I received only one check" was his bland response when I pointed this out to him.

His name, I'll say, was Max Grosskurth, and he had been practicing psychoanalysis for almost fifty years. He was a German Jew of a now vanishing type—not at all like the small, wisecracking, scared Mitteleuropean Jews that I had grown up among. He was tall, commanding, humorless. He liked large, blooming shirts, dark suits, heavy handmade shoes, club ties. He had a limp, which, in the years when I knew him, became a two-legged stutter and then left him immobile, so that our last year of analysis took place in his apartment, around the corner from the office. His roster of patients was drawn almost exclusively from among what he liked to call creative people, chiefly writers and painters and composers, and he talked about them so freely that I sometimes half expected him to put up autographed glossies around the office, like the ones on the wall at the Stage Deli. ("Max—Thanks for the most terrific transference in Gotham! Lenny") When we began, he was eighty, and I had crossed thirty.

I've read that you're not supposed to notice anything in the analyst's office, but that first evening I noticed it all. There was the couch, a nice Charles Eames job. On one wall there was a Motherwell print—a quick ink jet—and, opposite, a framed poster of one of the Masaccio frescoes in Santa Maria del Carmine in Florence. I was instantly impressed. The two images seemed to position him (and me) between Italian humanism, in its first, rocky, realistic form, at one end, and postwar New York humanism, in its jumpy, anxiety-purging form, at the other. On a bookshelf beside him were nothing but bound volumes of a psychoanalytic journal, rising to the ceiling. (He had edited that journal for a time. "Let me give you some counsel," he said to me much later. "Editing never means anything.")

He was lit by a single shaded bulb, just to his left, in that kind of standing brass lamp with a long arcing neck. This put his face in a vaguely sinister half light, but, with his strong accent and the sounds of traffic out on Park Avenue and a headlight occasionally sweeping across the room, the scene had a comforting European melancholia, as though directed by Pabst.

Why was I there? Nothing interesting: the usual mixture of hurt feelings, confusion, and incomprehension that comes to early-arriving writers when the thirties hit. John Updike once wrote that, though the newcomer imagines that literary New York will be like a choir of angels, in fact it is like the Raft of the Medusa—and he was wrong about this only in that the people on the Raft of the Medusa still have hope. In New York, the raft has been adrift now for years, centuries, and there's still no rescue boat in sight. The only thing left is to size up the others and wait for someone to become weak enough to eat.

I spilled out my troubles; told him of my sense of panic, anxiety; perhaps wept. He was silent for a minute—not a writer's minute, a real one, a long time.

"Franz Marc was a draftsman of remarkable power," he said at last: the first words of my analysis. His voice was deep and powerful, uncannily like Henry Kissinger's: not quacky, pleading Viennese but booming, arrogant German.

The remark about Franz Marc was not *quite* apropos of nothing—he knew me to be an art critic—but very near. (Franz Marc was the less famous founder of the German Expressionist movement called Der Blaue Reiter; Kandinsky was the other.) He must have caught the alarmed look in my eyes, for he added, more softly, "There are many worthwhile unexplored subjects in modern art." Then he sat up in his chair—swallowed hard and pulled himself up—and for a moment I had a sense of just how aged he was.

"You put me in mind," he said—and suddenly there was nothing the least old in the snap and expansive authority of his voice—"you put me in mind of Norman Mailer at a similar age." (This was a reach, or raw flattery; there is nothing about me that would put anyone in mind of Norman Mailer.) " 'Barbary Shore,' he thought, would be the end of him. What a terrible, terrible, terrible book it is. It was a great blow to his narcissism. I recall clearly attending dinner parties in this period with my wife, an extremely witty woman, where everyone was mocking poor Norman. My wife, an extremely witty woman . . ." He looked at me as though, despite the repetition, I had denied it; I tried to look immensely amused, as though reports of Mrs. Grosskurth's wit had reached me in my crib. "Even my wife engaged in this banter. In the midst of it, however, I held my peace." He rustled in his chair, and now I saw why he had sat up: he suddenly became a stiff, living pillar, his hands held before him, palms up—a man holding his peace in the middle of banter flying around the dinner table. A rock of imperturbable serenity! He cautiously settled back in his chair. "Now, of course, Norman has shown great resourcefulness and is receiving extremely large advances for his genre studies of various American criminals."

From the six years of my analysis, or therapy, or whatever the hell it was, there are words that are as permanently etched in my brain as the words "E pluribus unum" are on the nickel. "Banter" and "genre studies" were the first two. I have never been so grateful for a *mot juste* as I was for the news that Mrs. Grosskurth had engaged in banter, and that Norman Mailer had made a resourceful turn toward genre studies. Banter, that was all it was: criticism, the essential competitive relations of writers in New York—all of it was *banter*, engaged in by extremely witty wives of analysts at dinner parties. And all you had to do was . . . refuse to engage in it! Hold your peace. Take no part! Like him— sit there like a rock and let it wash over you.

And then there was the wacky perfection of his description of the later Mailer, with its implications of knowing (not firsthand certainly; Mailer, as far as I know, had never been his patient) the inside story: he had, under stress, found appropriate genre subjects. American criminals. The whole speech, I thought, was so profound that it could be parsed and highlighted like one of those dog-eared assigned texts you find on the reserve shelf in undergraduate libraries: Artists suffered from *narcissism*, which made them susceptible to *banter*, which they could overcome by *resourcefulness*, which might lead them to—well, to take up *genre studies*. ("Genre studies," I was to discover, was Grosskurthese for "journalism." He often indulged in strangely Johnsonian periphrases: once, talking about Woody Allen, he remarked, "My wife, who was an extremely witty woman, was naturally curious to see such a celebrated wit. We saw him in a cabaret setting. I recall that he was reciting samples of his writings in a state of high anxiety." It took me days of figuring—what kind of reading had it been? a kind of Weimar tribute evening?—to realize that Dr. and Mrs. Grosskurth had gone to a night club and heard the comedian's monologue.)

I came away from that first session in a state of blissful suspended confusion. Surely this wasn't the way psychoanalysis was supposed to proceed. On the other hand, it was much more useful—and interesting, too—to hear that Norman Mailer had rebounded by writing genre studies than it was to hear that my family was weird, for that I knew already. I felt a giddy sense of relief, especially when he added, sardonically, "Your problems remind me of"—and here he named one of the heroes of the New York School. "Fortunately, you suffer neither from impotence nor alcoholism. That is in your favor." And that set the pattern of our twice- and sometimes thrice-weekly encounters for the next five years. He was touchy, prejudiced, opinionated, impatient, often bored, usually high-handed, brutally bigoted. I could never decide whether to sue for malpractice or fall to my knees in gratitude for such an original healer.

Our exchanges hardened into a routine. I would take the subway uptown at six-thirty; I would get out at Seventy-seventh Street, walk a couple of blocks uptown, and enter his little office, at the corner of Park Avenue, where I would join three or four people sitting on a bench. Then the door opened, another neurotic—sometimes a well-known neurotic, who looked as though he wanted to hide his face with his coat, like an indicted stockbroker—came out, and I went in. There was the smell of the air-conditioner.

"So," he would say. "How are you?"

"Terrible," I would say, sometimes sincerely, sometimes to play along.

"I expected no less," he would say, and then I would begin to stumble out the previous three or four days' problems, worries, gossip. He would clear his throat and begin a monologue, a kind of roundabout discussion of major twentieth-century figures (Freud, Einstein, and, above all, Thomas Mann were his touchstones), broken confidences of the confessional, episodes from his own life, finally snaking around to an abrupt "So you see . . ." and some thunderously obvious maxim, which he would apply to my problems—or, rather, to the nonexistence of my problems, compared with real problems, of which he'd heard a few, you should have been here then.

For instance: I raised, as a problem, my difficulty in finishing my book, in writing without a deadline. I raised it at length, circuitously, with emotion. He cleared his throat. "It is commonplace among writers to need extreme arousal. For instance, Martin Buber." I riffled through my card catalogue: wasn't he the theologian? "He kept pornography on the lecture stand with him, in order to excite him to a greater performance as a lecturer. He would be talking about 'I and thou,' and there he would be, shuffling through his papers, looking at explicit photographs of naked women." He shook his head. "This was really going very far. And yet Buber was a very great scholar. It was appropriate for his approach. It would not be appropriate for you, for it would increase your extreme overestimation of your own role."

Mostly, he talked about what he thought it took to survive in the warfare of New York. He talked about the major figures of New York literary life—not necessarily his own patients but writers and artists whose careers he followed admiringly—as though they were that chain of forts upstate, around Lake George, left over from the French and Indian War: the ones you visited as a kid, where they gave you bumper stickers. There was Fort Sontag, Fort Frankenthaler, Fort Mailer. "She is very well defended." "Yes, I admire her defenses." "Admirably well defended." Once, I mentioned a famous woman intellectual who had recently got into legal trouble: hadn't she been well defended? "Yes, but the trouble is that the guns were pointing the wrong way, like the British at Singapore." You were wrung out with gratitude for a remark like that. I was, anyway.

It was his theory, in essence, that "creative" people were inherently in a rage, and that this rage came from their disappointed narcissism. The narcissism could take a negative, paranoid form or a positive, defiant, arrogant form. His job was not to cure the narcissism (which was inseparable from the creativity) but, instead, to fortify it—to get the drawbridge up and the gate down and leave the Indians circling outside, with nothing to do but shoot flaming arrows harmlessly over the stockade.

He had come of age as a professional in the forties and fifties, treating the great battlers of the golden age of New York intellectuals, an age that, seen on the couch—a seething mass of resentments, jealousies, and needs—appeared somewhat less golden than it did otherwise. "How well I recall," he would begin, "when I was treating"—and here he named two famous art critics of the period. "They went to war with each other. One came in at ten o'clock. 'I must reply,' he said. Then at four-thirty the other one would come in. 'I must reply,' he would say. 'No,' I told them both. 'Wait six months and see if anyone recalls the source of this argument.' They agreed to wait. Six months later, my wife, that witty, witty woman, held a dinner party and offered some pleasantry about their quarrel. No one understood; no one even remembered it. And this was in the days when *ARTnews* was something. I recall what Thomas Mann said. . . ." Eventually, abruptly, as the clock on the wall turned toward seven-thirty, he would say, "So you see . . . this demonstrates again what I always try to tell you about debates among intellectuals."

I leaned forward, really wanting to know. "What is that, Doctor?" I said.

"*No one cares.* People have troubles of their own. We have to stop now." And that would be it.

I would leave the room in a state of vague, disconcerted disappointment. *No one cares?* No one cares about the hard-fought and brutally damaging fight for the right sentence, the irrefutable argument? And: *People have troubles of their own?* My great-aunt Hannah could have told me that. *That* was the result of half a century of presiding over the psyches of a major moment in cultural history? And then, fifteen minutes later, as I rode in a cab downtown my heart would lift—would fly. That's right: *No one cares! People have troubles of their own!* It's O.K. That doesn't mean you shouldn't do it; it means you should do it, somehow, for its own sake, without illusions. Just write, just live, and don't care too much yourself. No one cares. It's just *banter.*

SOMETIMES his method of bringing me to awareness—if that was what he was doing—could be oblique, not to say bizarre. There was, for instance, the Volestein Digression. This involved a writer whose name was, shall we say, Moses Volestein. Dr. G. had once read something by him and been fascinated by his name. "What a terrible name," he said. "*Vole.* Why would a man keep such a terrible name?" His name didn't strike me as a burden, and I said so.

"You are underestimating the damage that this man's name does to his psy-chic welfare," he replied gravely. "It is intolerable."

"I don't think he finds it intolerable."

"You are wrong."

Then, at our next meeting: "Your resistance to my discussion of Volestein's name at our last session is typical of your extreme narcissistic overestimation. You continue to underestimate the damage a name like that does to the human psyche."

"Doctor, surely you overestimate the damage such a name does to the human psyche."

"You are wrong. His family's failure to change this name suggests a deep denial of reality." He pursued Volestein's name through that session and into the next, and finally I exploded.

"I can't believe we're spending another hour discussing Moses Volestein's funny name!" I said. "I mean, for that matter, some people might think my own name is funny."

He considered. "Yes. But your name is merely very ugly and unusual. It does not include a word meaning a shrewlike animal with unpleasant associations for so many people. It is merely very ugly."

And then I wondered. My name—as natural to me as the sound of my own breathing? I had volunteered that it might be peculiar, out of some mixture of gallantry and point-scoring. But my hurt was enormous. My wife, who had kept her own name when we married—out of feminist principle, I had thought—said, "Yes, when we met I couldn't believe it. I wouldn't go out with you for a week because of it." It was a shock as great as any I had received, and as salutary. Had he obsessed on Volestein with the intention of making me face Gopnik, in all its oddity, and then, having faced it, grasp some ironic wisdom? *I had a funny name.* And then the corollary: people could have funny names and go right on working. They might never even notice it. Years later, online, I found myself on a list of writers with extremely funny names—I suppose this is what people do with their time now that they are no longer in psychoanalysis—and I was, amazingly, happy to be there. So that was one score. Even your name could be absurd and you wouldn't know it. And the crucial addition: it didn't matter. Indifference and armor could get you through anything.

SOMETIMES Dr. Grosskurth would talk about his own history. He was born in Berlin before the First World War, at a time when German Jews were German above all. His mother had hoped that he would become a diplomat. But he had decided to study medicine instead, and particularly psychiatry; he was of that generation of German Jews who found in Freud's doctrines what their physicist contemporaries found in Einstein's. He had spoken out against the Nazis in 1933 and had been forced to flee the country at a moment's notice. One of his professors had helped him get out. (He was notably unheroic in his description of this episode. "It was a lesson to me to keep my big mouth shut" was the way he put it.) He fled to Italy, where he completed medical school at the University of Padua.

He still loved Italy: he ate almost every night at Parma, a restaurant nearby, on Third Avenue, and spent every August in Venice, at the Cipriani. One spring, I recall, I announced that my wife and I had decided to go to Venice.

He looked at me tetchily. "And where will you stay?" he asked.

"At this *pensione*, the Accademia," I said.

"No," he said. "You wish to stay at the Monaco, it is a very pleasant hotel, and you will have breakfast on the terrace. That is the correct hostel for you."

I reached into my pockets, where I usually had a stubby pencil, and searched them for a stray bit of paper—an American Express receipt, the back of a bit of manuscript paper—to write on.

"No, no!" he said, with disgust. My disorderliness was anathema to his Teutonic soul. "Here, I will write it down. Oh, you are so chaotic. Hand me the telephone." I offered him the phone, which was on a small table near his chair, and he consulted a little black book that he took from his inside right jacket pocket. He dialled some long number. Then, in a voice even deeper and more booming than usual—he was raised in a time when long-distance meant long-distance—he began to speak in Italian.

"*Sì, sono Dottore Grosskurth.*" He waited for a moment—genuinely apprehensive, I thought, for the first time in my acquaintance with him—and then a huge smile, almost a big-lug smile, broke across his face. They knew him.

"*Sì, sì,*" he said, and then, his voice lowering, said, "No," and something I didn't understand; obviously, he was explaining that Mrs. Grosskurth had died. "*Pronto!*" he began, and then came a long sentence beginning with my name and various dates in *giugno*. "*Sì, sì.*" He put his hand over the receiver. "You wish for a bath or a shower?" he demanded.

"Bath," I said.

"Good choice," he said. It was the nearest thing to praise he had ever given me. Finally, he hung up the phone. He looked at the paper in his hand and gave it to me.

"There," he said. "You are reserved for five nights, the room has no view of the canal, but, actually, this is better, since the gondola station can be extremely disturbing. You will eat breakfast on the terrace, and there you will enjoy the view of the Salute. Do not eat dinner there, however. I will give you a list of places." And, on an "Ask Your Doctor About Prozac" pad, he wrote out a list of restaurants in Venice for me. (They were mostly, I realized later, after I got to know Venice a bit, the big old, fifties-ish places that a New York analyst would love: Harry's Bar, Da Fiore, the Madonna.)

"You will go to these places, order the spaghetti *vongole*, and then . . ."

"And then?"

"And then at last you will be happy," he said flatly.

. . .

HE was so far from being an orthodox Freudian, or an orthodox anything, that I was startled when I discovered how deep and passionate his attachment to psychoanalytic dogma was. One day, about three years in, I came into his office and saw that he had a copy of *The New York Review of Books* open. "It is very sad," he began. "It is very sad indeed, to see a journal which was once respected by many people descend into a condition where it has lost the good opinion of all reasonable people." After a few moments, I figured out that he was referring to one of several much discussed pieces that the literary critic Frederick Crews had written attacking Freud and Freudianism.

I read the pieces later myself and thought them incontrovertible. Then I sat down to read Freud, for the first time—"Civilization and Its Discontents," "Totem and Taboo," "The Interpretation of Dreams"—and was struck at once by the absurdity of the arguments as arguments and the impressive weight of humane culture marshalled in their support. One sensed that one was in the presence of a kind of showman, a brilliant essayist, leaping from fragmentary evidence to unsupported conclusion, and summoning up a whole body of psychological myth—the Id, the Libido, the Ego—with the confidence of a Disney cartoonist drawing bunnies and squirrels. I found myself, therefore, in the unusual position of being increasingly skeptical of the therapeutic approach to which I fled twice a week for comfort. I finally got up the courage to tell Grosskurth this.

"You therefore find a conflict between your strongest intellectual convictions and your deepest emotional gratification needs?" he asked.

"Yes."

He shrugged. "Apparently you are a Freudian."

This seemed to me a first-rate exchange, honors to him, but I couldn't let it go. My older sister, a professor of psychology at Berkeley, regarded Freud as a comic relic (I had told her about my adventures in psychoanalysis), and in the midst of the *New York Review* debate she wrote one of the most devastating of the anti-Freud letters to the editor. She even made a passing, dismissive reference to the appeal of "figures of great personal charisma"—I knew what *that* was about—and then stated, conclusively, that there was nothing to be said in defense of psychoanalysis that couldn't also be said in defense of magic or astrology. ("She is very well defended, your sister," Grosskurth said.)

On behalf of his belief, Grosskurth would have said—did say, though over time, if not in these precise words—that while Freud may have been wrong in all the details, his central insight was right. His insight was that human life is shaped by a series of selfish, ineradicable urges, particularly sexual ones, and that all the other things that happen in life are ways of toning down these urges and giving them an "acceptable" outlet. An actual, undramatic but perilous world of real things existed, whose essential character was its indifference to human feelings: this world of real things included pain, death, and disease, but also many things unthreatening to our welfare. His project—the Freudian project, properly understood—was not to tell the story of our psyche, the curious drawing-room comedy of Id and Ego and Libido, but just the opposite: to drain the drama from all our stories. He believed that the only thing to do with the knowledge of the murderous rage within your breast was not to mythologize it but to put a necktie on it and heavy shoes and a dark-blue woollen suit. Only a man who knew that, given the choice, he would rape his mother and kill his father could order his spaghetti *vongole* in anything like peace.

There was, however, a catch in this argument, or so I insisted in the third year of my analysis, over several sessions and at great length. Weren't the well-defended people he admired really the ones at the furthest imaginable remove from the real things, the reality, whose worth he praised so highly? Did Susan Sontag actually have a better grasp of things-as-they-are than anyone else? Would anybody point to Harold Brodkey as a model of calm appraisal of the scale of the world and the appropriate place of his ego in it? Wasn't the "enormous narcissistic overestimation" of which he accused me inseparable from the "well-defended, internalized self-esteem" he wanted me to cultivate? The people who seemed best defended—well, the single most striking thing about them was how breathtakingly out of touch they were with the world, with other people's feelings, with the general opinion of their work. You didn't just have to be armored by your narcissism; you could be practically entombed in it, so that people came knocking, like Carter at King Tut's tomb, and you'd still get by. Wasn't that a problem for his system, or, anyway, for his therapy?

"Yes," he said coldly.

"Oh," I said, and we changed the subject.

MY friends were all in therapy, too, of course—this was New York—and late at night, over a bottle of red wine, they would offer one "insight" or another that struck me as revelatory: "My analyst helped me face the recurring pattern in my life of an overprotectiveness that derives from my mother's hidden alcoholism," or "Mine helped me see more clearly how early my father's depression shaped my fears," or "Mine helped me see that my reluctance to publish my personal work is part of my reluctance to have a child." What could I say? "Mine keeps falling asleep, except when we discuss Hannah Arendt's sex life, about which he knows quite a lot."

His falling asleep was a problem. The first few years I saw him, he still had a reasonably full schedule and our sessions were usually late in the day; the strain told on him. As I settled insistently (I had decided that if I was going to be analyzed I was going to be analyzed) into yet one more tiresome recital of grievances, injustices, anxieties, childhood memories, I could see his long, big, partly bald head nodding down toward the knot of his tie. His eyes would flutter shut, and he would begin to breathe deeply. I would drone on—"And so I think that it was my mother, really, who first gave me a sense of the grandiose. There was this birthday, I think my sixth, when I first sensed . . ."—and his chin would nestle closer and closer to his chest, his head would drop farther, so that I was looking right at his bald spot. There was only one way, I learned, after a couple of disconcerting weeks of telling my troubles to a sleeping therapist, to revive him, and that was to gossip. "And so my mother's relationship with my father reminds me—well, in certain ways it reminds me of what people have been saying about Philip Roth's divorce from Claire Bloom," I would say abruptly, raising my volume on the non sequitur.

Instantly, his head would jerk straight up, his eyes open, and he would shake himself all over like a Lab coming out of the water. "Yes, what are they saying about this divorce?" he would demand.

"Oh, nothing, really," I would say, and then I would wing it for a minute, glad to have caught his attention.

Unfortunately, my supply of hot literary gossip was very small. So there were times (and I hope that this is the worst confession I will ever have to make) when I would invent literary gossip on the way uptown, just to have something in reserve if he fell asleep, like a Victorian doctor going off to a picnic with a bottle of smelling salts, just in case. ("Let's see: what if I said that Kathy Acker had begun an affair with, oh, V. S. Pritchett—that would hold *anybody's* interest.") I felt at once upset and protective about his sleeping. Upset because it was, after all, my nickel, and protective because I did think that he was a great man, in his way, and I hated to see him dwindling: I wondered how long he would go on if he sensed that he was dwindling.

Not long ago, I read, in a book about therapy, a reference to a distinguished older analyst who made a point of going to sleep in front of his patients. Apparently, Grosskurth—for who else could it have been?—was famous for his therapeutic skill in falling asleep as you talked. It was tactical, even strategic.

Or was he just an old man trying to keep a practice going for lack of anything better to do, and doing anything—sleeping, booking hotel rooms, gossiping, as old men do—so that he would not have to be alone? Either limitlessly shrewd or deeply pathetic: which was it? Trying to answer that question was one of the things that kept me going uptown.

As we went on into our fourth and fifth years, all the other problems that I had brought to him became one problem, *the* New York problem. Should my wife—should we—have a baby? We agonized over it, in the modern manner. Grosskurth listened, silently, for months, and finally pronounced.

"Yes, you must go ahead and have a child. You will enjoy it. The child will try your patience repeatedly, yet you will find that there are many pleasures in child-rearing." He cleared his throat. "You will find, for instance, that the child will make many amusing mistakes in language."

I looked at him, a little dumbfounded—that was the best of it?

"You see," he went on, "at about the age of three, children begin to talk, and naturally their inexperience leads them to use language in surprising ways. These mistakes can really be *extremely* amusing. The child's errors in language also provide the kinds of anecdotes that can be of value to the parents in a social setting." It seemed an odd confidence on which to build a family—that the child would be your own live-in Gracie Allen, and you could dine out on his errors—but I thought that perhaps he was only defining, so to speak, the minimal case.

So we did have the child. Overwhelmed with excitement, I brought him pictures of the baby at a week old. ("Yes," he said dryly, peering at my Polaroids, "this strongly resembles a child.") And, as my life was changing, I began to think that it was time to end, or anyway wind down, our relationship. It had been six years, and, for all that I had gained—and I thought that I had gained a lot: if not a cure, then at least enough material to go into business as a blackmailer—I knew that if I was to be "fully adult" I should break my dependence. And he was growing old. Already aged when we began, he was now, at eighty-five or six, becoming frail. Old age seems to be a series of lurches, rather than a gradual decline. One week he was his usual booming self, the next week there was a slow deliberateness in his gait as he came to the office door. Six months later, he could no longer get up reliably from his chair, and once fell down outside the office in my presence. His face, as I helped him up, was neither angry nor amused, just doughy and preoccupied, the face of a man getting ready for something. That was when we switched our sessions to his apartment, around the corner, on Seventy-ninth Street, where I would ring the bell and wait for him to call me in—he left the door open, or had it left open by his nurse, whom I never saw. Then I would go inside and find him—having been helped into a gray suit, blue shirt, dark tie—on his own sofa, surrounded by Hofmann and Miró engravings and two or three precious Kandinsky prints.

About a month into the new arrangement, I decided to move to Europe to write, and I told him this, in high spirits and with an almost breathless sense of advancement: I was going away, breaking free of New York, starting over. I thought he would be pleased.

To my shock, he was furious—his old self and then some. "Who would have thought of this idea? What a self-destructive regression." Then I realized why he was so angry: despite all his efforts at fortification, I had decided to run away. Fort Gopnik was dropping its flag, dispersing its troops, surrendering its territory—all his work for nothing. Like General Gordon come to reinforce Khartoum, he had arrived too late, and failed through the unforgivable, disorganized passivity of the natives.

In our final sessions, we settled into a non-aggression pact. ("Have we stopped too soon, Doctor?" I asked. "Yes," he said dully.) We talked neutrally, about art and family. Then, the day before I was to leave, I went uptown for our last session.

It was a five-thirty appointment, in the second week of October. We began to talk, amiably, like old friends, about the bits and pieces of going abroad, visas and vaccinations. Then, abruptly, he began to tell a long, meandering story about his wife's illness and death, which we had never talked about before. He kept returning to a memory he had of her swimming back and forth in the hotel pool in Venice the last summer before her death.

"She had been ill, and the Cipriani, as you are not aware, has an excellent pool. She swam back and forth in this pool, back and forth, for hours. I was well aware that her illness was very likely to be terminal." He shook his head, held his hands out, dealing with reality. "As soon as she had episodes of dizziness and poor balance, I made a very quick diagnosis. Still, back and forth she swam."

He stopped; the room by now had become dark. The traffic on Seventy-ninth Street had thickened into a querulous, honking rush-hour crowd. He was, I knew, too shaky on his feet to get up and turn on the lights, and I thought that it would be indelicate for me to do it—they were his lights. So we sat there in the dark.

"Naturally, this was to be the last summer that we spent in Venice. However, she had insisted that we make this trip. And she continued to swim." He looked around the room, in the dark—the pictures, the drawings, the bound volumes, all that was left of two lives joined together, one closed, the other closing.

"She continued to swim. She had been an exceptional athlete, in addition to being, as you know, an extremely witty woman." He seemed lost in memory for a moment, but then, regaining himself, he cleared his throat in the dark, professionally, as he had done so many times before.

"So you see," he said, again trying to make the familiar turn toward home. And then he did something that I don't think he had ever done before: he called me by my name. "So you see, Adam, in life, in life . . ." And I rose, thinking, Here at our final session—no hope of ever returning, my bag packed and my ticket bought to another country, far away—at last, the truth, the point, the thing to take away that we have been building toward all these years.

"So you see, Adam, in retrospect . . ." he went on, and stirred, rose, on the sofa, trying to force his full authority on his disobedient frame. "In retrospect, life has many worthwhile aspects," he concluded quietly, and then we had to stop. He sat looking ahead, and a few minutes later, with a goodbye and a handshake, I left.

Now I was furious. I was trying to be moved, but I would have liked to be moved by something easier to be moved by. That was all he had to say to me, *Life has many worthwhile aspects?* For once, that first reaction of disappointment stuck with me for a long time, on the plane all the way to Paris. All these evenings, all that investment, all that humanism, all those Motherwell prints—yes, all that money, my money—for that? *Life has many worthwhile aspects?* Could there have been a more fatuous and arrhythmic and unmemorable conclusion to what had been, after all, *my* analysis, my only analysis?

Now, of course, it is more deeply engraved than any other of his words. In retrospect, life has many worthwhile aspects. Not all or even most aspects. And not beautiful or meaningful or even tolerable. Just *worthwhile*, with its double burden of labor and reward. Life has *worth*—value, importance—and it takes a while to get there.

I came back to New York about a year later and went to see him. A woman with a West Indian accent had answered when I called his number. I knew that I would find him declining, but still, I thought, I would find him himself. We expect our fathers to take as long a time dying as we take growing up. But he was falling away. He was lying on a hospital bed, propped up, his skin as gray as pavement, his body as thin and wasted as a tree on a New York street in winter. The television was on, low, tuned to a game show. He struggled for breath as he spoke.

He told me, very precisely, about the disease that he had. "The prognosis is most uncertain," he said. "I could linger indefinitely." He mentioned something controversial that I had written. "You showed independence of mind." He turned away, in pain. "And, as always, very poor judgment."

In New York again, five months later, I thought, I'll just surprise him, squeeze his hand. I walked by his building, and asked the doorman if Dr. Grosskurth was in. He said that Dr. Grosskurth had died three months before. For a moment I thought, Someone should have called me, one of his children. Yet they could hardly have called all his patients. ("But I was special!" the child screams.) Then I stumbled over to Third Avenue and almost automatically into Parma, the restaurant that he had loved. I asked the owner if he knew that Dr. Grosskurth had died, and he said yes, of course: they had had a dinner, with his family and some of his friends, to remember him, and he invited me to have dinner, too, and drink to his memory.

I sat down and began an excellent, solitary dinner in honor of my dead psychoanalyst—seafood pasta, a Venetian dish, naturally—and, in his memory, chewed at the squid. (He liked squid.) The waiter brought me my bill, and I paid it. I still think that the owner should at least have bought the wine. Which shows, I suppose, that the treatment was incomplete. ("They should have paid for your wine?" "It would have been a nice gesture, yes. It would have happened in Paris." "You are hopeless. I died too soon, and you left too early. The analysis was left unfinished.")

The transference wasn't completed, I suppose, but something—a sort of implantation—did take place. He is inside me. In moments of crisis or panic, I sometimes think that I have his woollen suit draped around my shoulders, even in August. Sometimes in ordinary moments I almost think that I have become him. Though my patience is repeatedly tried by my child, I laugh at his many amusing mistakes in language—I have even been known to repeat these mistakes in social settings. I refer often to the sayings of my wife, that witty, witty woman. On the whole, I would say that my years in analysis had many worthwhile aspects.

(1998)

SHOW DOG

I F I were a bitch, I'd be in love with Biff Truesdale. Biff is perfect. He's friendly, good-looking, rich, famous, and in excellent physical condition. He almost never drools. He's not afraid of commitment. He wants children—actually, he already has children and wants a lot more. He works hard and is a consummate professional, but he also knows how to have fun.

What Biff likes most is food and sex. This makes him sound boorish, which he is not—he's just elemental. Food he likes even better than sex. His favorite things to eat are cookies, mints, and hotel soap, but he will eat just about anything. Richard Krieger, a friend of Biff's who occasionally drives him to appointments, said not long ago, "When we're driving on I-95, we'll usually pull over at McDonald's. Even if Biff is napping, he always wakes up when we're getting close. I get him a few plain hamburgers with buns—no ketchup, no mustard, and no pickles. He loves hamburgers. I don't get him his own French fries, but if I get myself fries I always flip a few for him into the back."

If you're ever around Biff while you're eating something he wants to taste— cold roast beef, a Wheatables cracker, chocolate, pasta, aspirin, whatever—he will stare at you across the pleated bridge of his nose and let his eyes sag and his lips tremble and allow a little bead of drool to percolate at the edge of his mouth until you feel so crummy that you give him some. This routine puts the people who know him in a quandary, because Biff has to watch his weight. Usually, he is as skinny as Kate Moss, but he can put on three pounds in an instant. The holidays can be tough. He takes time off at Christmas and spends it at home, in Attleboro, Massachusetts, where there's a lot of food around and no pressure and no schedule and it's easy to eat all day. The extra weight goes to his neck. Luckily, Biff likes working out. He runs for fifteen or twenty minutes twice a day, either outside or on his Jog-Master. When he's feeling heavy, he runs longer, and skips snacks, until he's back down to his ideal weight of seventy-five pounds.

Biff is a boxer. He is a show dog—he performs under the name Champion Hi-Tech's Arbitrage—and so looking good is not mere vanity; it's business. A show dog's career is short, and judges are unforgiving. Each breed is judged by an explicit standard for appearance and temperament, and then there's the incalculable element of charisma in the ring. When a show dog is fat or lazy or sullen, he doesn't win; when he doesn't win, he doesn't enjoy the ancillary benefits of being a winner, like appearing as the celebrity spokesmodel on packages of Pedigree Mealtime with Lamb and Rice, which Biff will be doing soon, or picking the best-looking bitches and charging them six hundred dollars or so for his sexual favors, which Biff does three or four times a month. Another ancillary benefit of being a winner is that almost every single weekend of the year, as he travels to shows around the country, he gets to hear people applaud for him and yell his name and tell him what a good boy he is, which is something he seems to enjoy at least as much as eating a bar of soap.

PRETTY soon, Biff won't have to be so vigilant about his diet. After he appears at the Westminster Kennel Club's show, this week, he will retire from active show life and work full time as a stud. It's a good moment for him to retire. Last year, he won more shows than any other boxer, and also more than any other dog in the purebred category known as Working Dogs, which also includes Akitas, Alaskan malamutes, Bernese mountain dogs, bullmastiffs, Doberman pinschers, giant schnauzers, Great Danes, Great Pyrenees, komondors, kuvaszok, mastiffs, Newfoundlands, Portuguese water dogs, Rottweilers, St. Bernards, Samoyeds, Siberian huskies, and standard schnauzers. Boxers were named for their habit of standing on their hind legs and punching with their front paws when they fight. They were originally bred to be chaperones—to look forbidding while being pleasant to spend time with. Except for show dogs like Biff, most boxers lead a life of relative leisure. Last year at Westminster, Biff was named Best Boxer and Best Working Dog, and he was a serious contender for Best in Show, the highest honor any show dog can hope for. He is a contender to win his breed and group again this year, and is a serious contender once again for Best in Show, although the odds are against him, because this year's judge is known as a poodle person.

Biff is four years old. He's in his prime. He could stay on the circuit for a few more years, but by stepping aside now he is making room for his sons Trent and Rex, who are just getting into the business, and he's leaving while he's still on top. He'll also spend less time in airplanes, which is the one part of show life he doesn't like, and more time with his owners, William and Tina Truesdale, who might be persuaded to waive his snacking rules.

Biff has a short, tight coat of fox-colored fur, white feet and ankles, and a patch of white on his chest roughly the shape of Maine. His muscles are plainly sketched under his skin, but he isn't bulgy. His face is turned up and pushed in, and has a dark mask, spongy lips, a wishbone-shaped white blaze, and the earnest and slightly careworn expression of a small-town mayor. Someone once told me that he thought Biff looked a little bit like President Clinton. Biff's face is his fortune. There are plenty of people who like boxers with bigger bones and a stockier body and taller shoulders—boxers who look less like marathon runners and more like weight-lifters—but almost everyone agrees that Biff has a nearly perfect head.

"Biff's head is his father's," William Truesdale, a veterinarian, explained to me one day. We were in the Truesdales' living room in Attleboro, which overlooks acres of hilly fenced-in fields. Their house is a big, sunny ranch with a stylish pastel kitchen and boxerabilia on every wall. The Truesdales don't have children, but at any given moment they share their quarters with at least a half-dozen dogs. If you watch a lot of dog-food commercials, you may have seen William—he's the young, handsome, dark-haired veterinarian declaring his enthusiasm for Pedigree Mealtime while his boxers gallop around.

"Biff has a masculine but elegant head," William went on. "It's not too wet around the muzzle. It's just about ideal. Of course, his forte is right here." He pointed to Biff's withers, and explained that Biff's shoulder-humerus articulation was optimally angled, and bracketed his superb brisket and forelegs, or something like that. While William was talking, Biff climbed onto the couch and sat on top of Brian, his companion, who was hiding under a pillow. Brian is an English toy Prince Charles spaniel who is about the size of a teakettle and has the composure of a hummingbird. As a young competitor, he once bit a judge—a mistake Tina Truesdale says he made because at the time he had been going through a little mind problem about being touched. Brian, whose show name is Champion Cragmor's Hi-Tech Man, will soon go back on the circuit, but now he mostly serves as Biff's regular escort. When Biff sat on him, he started to quiver. Biff batted at him with his front leg. Brian gave him an adoring look.

"Biff's body is from his mother," Tina was saying. "She had a lot of substance."

"She was even a little extreme for a bitch," William said. "She was rather buxom. I would call her zaftig."

"Biff's father needed that, though," Tina said. "His name was Tailo, and he was fabulous. Tailo had a very beautiful head, but he was a bit fine, I think. A bit slender."

"Even a little feminine," William said, with feeling. "Actually, he would have been a really awesome bitch."

THE first time I met Biff, he sniffed my pants, stood up on his hind legs and stared into my face, and then trotted off to the kitchen, where someone was cooking macaroni. We were in Westbury, Long Island, where Biff lives with Kimberly Pastella, a twenty-nine-year-old professional handler, when he's working. Last year, Kim and Biff went to at least one show every weekend. If they drove, they took Kim's van. If they flew, she went coach and he went cargo. They always shared a hotel room.

While Kim was telling me all this, I could hear Biff rummaging around in the kitchen. "Biffers!" Kim called out. Biff jogged back into the room with a phony look of surprise on his face. His tail was ticking back and forth. It is cropped so that it is about the size and shape of a half-smoked stogie. Kim said that there was a bitch downstairs who had been sent from Pennsylvania to be bred to one of Kim's other clients, and that Biff could smell her and was a little out of sorts. "Let's go," she said to him. "Biff, let's go jog." We went into the garage, where a treadmill was set up with Biff's collar suspended from a metal arm. Biff hopped on and held his head out so that Kim could buckle his collar. As soon as she leaned toward the power switch, he started to jog. His nails clicked a light tattoo on the rubber belt.

Except for a son of his named Biffle, Biff gets along with everybody. Matt Stander, one of the founders of *Dog News*, said recently, "Biff is just very, very personable. He has a je ne sais quoi that's really special. He gives of himself all the time." One afternoon, the Truesdales were telling me about the psychology that went into making Biff who he is. "Boxers are real communicators," William was saying. "We had to really take that into consideration in his upbringing. He seems tough, but there's a fragile ego inside there. The profound reaction and hurt when you would raise your voice at him was really something."

"I *made* him," Tina said. "I made Biff who he is. He had an overbearing personality when he was small, but I consider that a prerequisite for a great performer. He had such an *attitude!* He was like this miniature *man!*" She shimmied her shoulders back and forth and thrust out her chin. She is a dainty, chic woman with wide-set eyes and the neck of a ballerina. She grew up on a farm in Costa Rica, where dogs were considered just another form of livestock. In 1987, William got her a Rottweiler for a watchdog, and a boxer, because he had always loved boxers, and Tina decided to dabble with them in shows. Now she makes a monogrammed Christmas stocking for each animal in their house, and she watches the tape of Biff winning at Westminster approximately once a week. "Right from the beginning, I made Biff think he was the most fabulous dog in the world," Tina said.

"He doesn't take after me very much," William said. "I'm more of a golden retriever."

"Oh, he has my nature," Tina said. "I'm very strong-willed. I'm brassy. And Biff is an egotistical, self-centered, selfish person. He thinks he's very important and special, and he doesn't like to share."

BIFF is priceless. If you beg the Truesdales to name a figure, they might say that Biff is worth around a hundred thousand dollars, but they will also point out that a Japanese dog fancier recently handed Tina a blank check for Biff. (She immediately threw it away.) That check notwithstanding, campaigning a show dog is a money-losing proposition for the owner. A good handler gets three or four hundred dollars a day, plus travel expenses, to show a dog, and any dog aiming for the top will have to be on the road at least a hundred days a year. A dog photographer charges hundreds of dollars for a portrait, and a portrait is something that every serious owner commissions, and then runs as a full-page ad in several dog-show magazines. Advertising a show dog is standard procedure if you want your dog or your presence on the show circuit to get well known. There are also such ongoing show-dog expenses as entry fees, hair-care products, food, health care, and toys. Biff's stud fee is six hundred dollars. Now that he will not be at shows, he can be bred several times a month. Breeding him would have been a good way for him to make money in the past, except that whenever the Truesdales were enthusiastic about a mating they bartered Biff's service for the pick of the litter. As a result, they now have more Biff puppies than Biff earnings. "We're doing this for posterity," Tina says. "We're doing it for the good of all boxers. You simply can't think about the cost."

On a recent Sunday, I went to watch Biff work at one of the last shows he would attend before his retirement. The show was sponsored by the Lehigh Valley Kennel Club and was held in a big, windy field house on the campus of Lehigh University, in Bethlehem, Pennsylvania. The parking lot was filled with motor homes pasted with life-size decals of dogs. On my way to the field house, I passed someone walking an Afghan hound wearing a snood, and someone else wiping down a Saluki with a Flintstones beach towel. Biff was napping in his crate—a fancy-looking brass box with bright silver hardware and with luggage tags from Delta, USAir, and Continental hanging on the door. Dogs in crates can look woeful, but Biff actually likes spending time in his. When he was growing up, the Truesdales decided they would never reprimand him, because of his delicate ego. Whenever he got rambunctious, Tina wouldn't scold him—she would just invite him to sit in his crate and have a time-out.

On this particular day, Biff was in the crate with a bowl of water and a gourmet Oinkeroll. The boxer judging was already over. There had been thirty-three in competition, and Biff had won Best in Breed. Now he had to wait for several hours while the rest of the working breeds had their competitions. Later, the breed winners would square off for Best in Working Group. Then, around dinnertime, the winner of the Working Group and the winners of the other groups—sporting dogs, hounds, terriers, toys, non-sporting dogs, and herding dogs—would compete for Best in Show. Biff was stretched out in the crate with his head resting on his forelegs, so that his lips draped over his ankle like a café curtain. He looked bored. Next to his crate, several wire-haired fox terriers were standing on tables getting their faces shampooed, and beyond them a Chihuahua in a pink crate was gnawing on its door latch. Two men in white shirts and dark pants walked by eating hot dogs. One of them was gesturing and exclaiming, "I thought I had good dachshunds! I thought I had *great* dachshunds!"

Biff sighed and closed his eyes.

While he was napping, I pawed through his suitcase. In it was some dog food; towels; an electric nail grinder; a whisker trimmer; a wool jacket in a lively pattern that looked sort of Southwestern; an apron; some antibiotics; baby oil; coconut-oil coat polish; boxer chalk powder; a copy of *Dog News;* an issue of *ShowSight* magazine, featuring an article subtitled "Frozen Semen—Boon or Bain?" and a two-page ad for Biff, with a full-page, full-color photograph of him and Kim posed in front of a human-size toy soldier; a spray bottle of fur cleanser; another Oinkeroll; a rope ball; and something called a Booda Bone. The apron was for Kim. The baby oil was to make Biff's nose and feet glossy when he went into the ring. Boxer chalk powder—as distinct from, say, West Highland–white-terrier chalk powder—is formulated to cling to short, sleek boxer hair and whiten boxers' white markings. Unlike some of the other dogs, Biff did not need to travel with a blow dryer, curlers, nail polish, or detangling combs, but, unlike some less sought-after dogs, he did need a schedule. He was registered for a show in Chicago the next day, and had an appointment at a clinic in Connecticut the next week to make a semen deposit, which had been ordered by a breeder in Australia. Also, he had a date that same week with a bitch named Diana who was about to go into heat. Biff has to book his stud work after shows, so that it doesn't interfere with his performance. Tina Truesdale told me that this was typical of all athletes, but everyone who knows Biff is quick to comment on how professional he is as a stud. Richard Krieger, who was going to be driving Biff to his appointment at the clinic in Connecticut, once told me that some studs want to goof around and take forever but Biff is very businesslike. "Bing, bang, boom," Krieger said. "He's in, he's out."

"No wasting of time," said Nancy Krieger, Richard's wife. "Bing, bang, boom. He gets the job done."

After a while, Kim showed up and asked Biff if he needed to go outside. Then a handler who is a friend of Kim's came by. He was wearing a black-

and-white houndstooth suit and was brandishing a comb and a can of hair spray. While they were talking, I leafed through the show catalogue and read some of the dogs' names to Biff, just for fun—names like Aleph Godol's Umbra Von Carousel and Champion Spanktown Little Lu Lu and Ranchlake's Energizer O'Motown and Champion Beaverbrook Buster V Broadhead. Biff decided that he did want to go out, so Kim opened the crate. He stepped out and stretched and yawned like a cat, and then he suddenly stood up and punched me in the chest. An announcement calling for all toys to report to their ring came over the loudspeaker. Kim's friend waved the can of hair spray in the direction of a little white poodle shivering on a table a few yards away and exclaimed, "Oh, no! I lost track of time! I have to go! I have to spray up my miniature!"

TYPICALLY, dog contestants first circle the ring together; then each contestant poses individually for the judge, trying to look perfect as the judge lifts its lips for a dental exam, rocks its hindquarters, and strokes its back and thighs. The judge at Lehigh was a chesty, mustached man with watery eyes and a grave expression. He directed the group with hand signals that made him appear to be roping cattle. The Rottweiler looked good, and so did the giant schnauzer. I started to worry. Biff had a distracted look on his face, as if he'd forgotten something back at the house. Finally, it was his turn. He pranced to the center of the ring. The judge stroked him and then waved his hand in a circle and stepped out of the way. Several people near me began clapping. A flash-bulb flared. Biff held his position for a moment, and then he and Kim bounded across the ring, his feet moving so fast that they blurred into an oily sparkle, even though he really didn't have very far to go. He got a cookie when he finished the performance, and another a few minutes later, when the judge wagged his finger at him, indicating that Biff had won again.

You can't help wondering whether Biff will experience the depressing let-down that retired competitors face. At least, he has a lot of stud work to look forward to, although William Truesdale complained to me once that the Truesdales' standards for a mate are so high—they require a clean bill of health and a substantial pedigree—that "there just aren't that many right bitches out there." Nonetheless, he and Tina are optimistic that Biff will find enough suitable mates to become one of the most influential boxer sires of all time. "We'd like to be remembered as the boxer people of the nineties," Tina said. "Anyway, we can't wait to have him home."

"We're starting to campaign Biff's son Rex," William said. "He's been living in Mexico, and he's a Mexican champion, and now he's ready to take on the American shows. He's very promising. He has a fabulous rear."

Just then, Biff, who had been on the couch, jumped down and began pacing. "Going somewhere, honey?" Tina asked.

He wanted to go out, so Tina opened the back door, and Biff ran into the back yard. After a few minutes, he noticed a ball on the lawn. The ball was slippery and a little too big to fit in his mouth, but he kept scrambling and trying to grab it. In the meantime, the Truesdales and I sat, stayed for a moment, fetched ourselves turkey sandwiches, and then curled up on the couch. Half an hour passed, and Biff was still happily pursuing the ball. He probably has a very short memory, but he acted as if it were the most fun he'd ever had.

(1995)

FORTY-ONE FALSE STARTS

T HERE are places in New York where the city's anarchic, unaccommo-
dating spirit, its fundamental, irrepressible aimlessness and heedless-
ness have found especially firm footholds. Certain transfers between subway
lines, passageways of almost transcendent sordidness; certain sites of torn-
down buildings where parking lots have silently sprung up like fungi; certain
intersections created by illogical confluences of streets—these express with
particular force the city's penchant for the provisional and its resistance to
permanence, order, closure. To get to the painter David Salle's studio, walking
west on White Street, you have to traverse one of these disquieting intersections—that of White and Church Streets and an interloping Sixth
Avenue—which has created an unpleasantly wide expanse of street to cross,
interrupted by a wedge-shaped island on which a commercial plant nursery
has taken up forlorn and edgy residence, surrounding itself with a high wire
fence and keeping truculently irregular hours. Other businesses that have
arisen around the intersection—the seamy Baby Doll Lounge, with its sign offering "Go-Go Girls"; the elegant Ristorante Arquá; the nameless grocery and
Lotto center; the dour Kinney parking lot—have a similar atmosphere of in-
sularity and transience. Nothing connects with anything else, and everything
looks as if it might disappear overnight. The corner feels like a no man's land
and—if one happens to be thinking about David Salle—looks like one of his
paintings.

Salle's studio, on the second floor of a five-story loft building, is a long room
lit with bright, cold overhead light. It is not a beautiful studio. Like the streets
outside, it gives no quarter to the visitor in search of the picturesque. It doesn't

even have a chair for the visitor to sit in, unless you count a backless, half-broken metal swivel chair Salle will offer with a murmur of inattentive apology. Upstairs, in his living quarters, it is another story. But down here everything has to do with work and with being alone.

A disorderly profusion of printed pictorial matter covers the surfaces of tables in the middle of the room: art books, art journals, catalogues, brochures mingle with loose illustrations, photographs, odd pictures ripped from magazines. Scanning these complicated surfaces, the visitor feels something of the sense of rebuff he feels when looking at Salle's paintings, a sense that this is all somehow none of one's business. Here lie the sources of Salle's postmodern art of "borrowed" or "quoted" images—the reproductions of famous old and modern paintings, the advertisements, the comics, the photographs of nude or half-undressed women, the fabric and furniture designs that he copies and puts into his paintings—but one's impulse, as when coming into a room of Salle's paintings, is to politely look away. Salle's hermeticism, the private, almost secretive nature of his interests and tastes and intentions, is a signature of his work. Glancing at the papers he has made no effort to conceal gives one the odd feeling of having broken into a locked desk drawer.

On the walls of the studio are five or six canvases, on which Salle works simultaneously. In the winter of 1992, when I began visiting him in his studio, he was completing a group of paintings for a show in Paris in April. The paintings had a dense, turgid character. Silk-screen excerpts from Indian architectural ornament, chair designs, and photographic images of a woman wrapped in cloth were overlaid with drawings of some of the forms in Duchamp's "The Bride Stripped Bare by Her Bachelors, Even," rendered in slashing, ungainly brushstrokes, together with images of coils of rope, pieces of fruit, and eyes. Salle's earlier work had been marked by a kind of spaciousness, sometimes an emptiness, such as Surrealist works are prone to. But here everything was condensed, impacted, mired. The paintings were like an ugly mood. Salle himself, a slight, handsome man with shoulder-length dark hair, which he wears severely tied back, like a matador, was feeling bloody-minded. He was going to be forty the following September. He had broken up with his girlfriend, the choreographer and dancer Karole Armitage. His moment was passing. Younger painters were receiving attention. He was being passed over. But he was also being attacked. He was not looking forward to the Paris show. He hated Paris, with its "heavily subsidized aestheticism." He disliked his French dealer. . . .

2

In a 1991 interview with the screenwriter Becky Johnston, during a discussion of what Johnston impatiently called "this whole Neo-Expressionist Zeitgeist Postmodernist Whatever-you-want-to-call-it Movement" and its habit of "constantly looking backward and reworking or recontextualizing art history," the painter David Salle said, with disarming frankness, "You mustn't underestimate the extent to which all this was a process of educating ourselves. Our generation was pathetically educated, just pathetic beyond imagination. I was better educated than many. Julian"—the painter Julian Schnabel—"was totally uneducated. But I wasn't much better, frankly. We had to educate ourselves in a hundred different ways. Because if you had been hanging around the Conceptual artists all you learned about was the Frankfurt School. It was as if nothing existed before or after. So part of it was the pledge of self-education—you know, going to Venice, looking at great paintings, looking at great architecture, looking at great furniture—and having very early the opportunity to kind of buy stuff. That's a form of self-education. It's not just about acquisition. It was a tremendous explosion of information and knowledge."

To kind of buy stuff. What is the difference between buying stuff and kind of buying it? Is "kind of buying" buying with a bad conscience, buying with the ghost of the Frankfurt School grimly looking over your shoulder and smiting its forehead as it sees the money actually leave your hand? This ghost, or some relative of it, has hung over all the artists who, like Salle, made an enormous amount of money in the eighties, when they were still in their twenties or barely into their thirties. In the common perception, there is something unseemly about young people getting rich. Getting rich is supposed to be the reward for hard work, preferably arriving when you are too old to enjoy it. And the spectacle of young millionaires who made their bundle not from business or crime but from avant-garde art is particularly offensive. The avant-garde is supposed to be the conscience of the culture, not its id.

3

All during my encounter with the artist David Salle—he and I met for interviews in his studio, on White Street, over a period of two years—I was acutely conscious of his money. Even when I got to know him and like him, I couldn't dispel the disapproving, lefty, puritanical feeling that would somehow be triggered each time we met, whether it was by the sight of the assistant sitting at a sort of hair-salon receptionist's station outside the studio door; or by the expensive furniture of a fifties corporate style in the upstairs loft, where he lives; or by the mineral water he would bring out during our talks and pour into white paper cups, which promptly lost their takeout-counter humbleness and assumed the hauteur of the objects in the Design Collection of the Museum of Modern Art.

Salle was one of the fortunate art stars of the eighties—young men and women plucked from semi-poverty and transformed into millionaires by genies disguised as art dealers. The idea of a rich avant-garde has never sat well with members of my generation. Serious artists, as we know them or like to think of them, are people who get by but do not have a lot of money. They live with second or third wives or husbands and with children from the various marriages, and they go to Cape Cod in the summer. Their apartments are filled with faded Persian carpets and cat-clawed sofas and beautiful and odd objects bought before anyone else saw their beauty. Salle's loft was designed by an architect. Everything in it is sleek, cold, expensive, unused. A slight sense of quotation mark hovers in the air, but it is very slight—it may not even be there—and it doesn't dispel the atmosphere of dead-serious connoisseurship by which the room is dominated.

4

During one of my visits to the studio of the artist David Salle, he told me that he never revises. Every brushstroke is irrevocable. He doesn't correct or repaint, ever. He works under the dire conditions of performance. Everything counts, nothing may be taken back, everything must always go relentlessly forward, and a mistake may be fatal. One day, he showed me a sort of murdered painting. He had worked on it a little too long, taken a misstep, killed it.

5

The artist David Salle and I are sitting at a round table in my apartment. He is a slight, handsome man of thirty-nine, with dark shoulder-length hair, worn tightly sleeked back and bound with a rubber band, accentuating his appearance of quickness and lightness, of being sort of streamlined. He wears elegant, beautifully polished shoes and speaks in a low, cultivated voice. His accent has no trace of the Midwest, where he grew up, the son of second-generation Russian Jewish parents. It has no affectation, either. He is agreeable, ironic, a little detached. "I can't remember what we talked about last time," he says. "I have no memory. I remember making the usual artist's complaints about critics, and then saying, 'Well, that's terribly boring, we don't want to be stuck talking about that'—and then talking about that. I had a kind of bad feeling about it afterward. I felt inadequate."

6

The artist David Salle and I met for the first time in the fall of 1991. A few months earlier, we had spoken on the telephone about a mystifying proposal of his: that I write the text for a book of reproductions of his paintings, to be published by Rizzoli. When I told him that there must be some mistake, that I was not an art historian or an art critic, and had but the smallest acquaintance with his work, he said no, there wasn't a mistake. He was deliberately looking for someone outside the art world, for an "interesting writer," who would write an unconventional text. As he talked, I found myself reluctant to say no to him then and there, even though I knew I would eventually have to refuse. Something about the man made me say I would think about it. He then said that to acquaint me with his work and with himself he would send some relevant writings. A few days later, a stylish package arrived, preceded by a telephone call from an assistant at Salle's studio to arrange the details of delivery. It contained three or four exhibition catalogues, several critical articles, and various published interviews, together with a long interview that was still in typescript but was bound in a hard black cover. It was by the screenwriter Becky Johnston, who, I later learned, was an "interesting writer" Salle had previously approached to do the Rizzoli book. She had done the interview in preparation for the text but had never written it.

7

David Salle's art has an appearance of mysterious, almost preternatural originality, and yet nothing in it is new; everything has had a previous life elsewhere—in master paintings, advertising art, comics, photographs. Other artists have played the game of appropriation or quotation that Salle plays—Duchamp, Schwitters, Ernst, Picabia, Rauschenberg, Warhol, Johns—but none with such reckless inventiveness. Salle's canvases are like bad parodies of the Freudian unconscious. They are full of images that don't belong together: a woman taking off her clothes, the Spanish Armada, a kitschy fabric design, an eye.

8

David Salle is recognized as the leading American postmodernist painter. He is the most authoritative exemplar of the movement, which has made a kind of mockery of art history, treating the canon of world art as if it were a gigantic, dog-eared catalogue crammed with tempting buys and equipped with a helpful twenty-four-hour-a-day 800 number. Salle's selections from the catalogue have a brilliant perversity. Nothing has an obvious connection to anything else, and everything glints with irony and a sort of icy melancholy. His jarring juxtapositions of incongruous images and styles point up with special sharpness the paradox on which this art of appropriated matter is poised: its mysterious, almost preternatural appearance of *originality*. After one looks at a painting by Salle, works of normal signature-style art—paintings done in a single style with an intelligible thematic—begin to seem pale and meagre, kind of played out. Paintings like Salle's—the unabashed products of, if not vandalism, a sort of cold-eyed consumerism—are entirely free of any "anxiety of influence." For all their borrowings, they seem unprecedented, like a new drug or a new crime. They are rootless, fatherless and motherless.

9

The artist David Salle has given so many interviews, has been the subject of so many articles, has become so widely inscribed as an emblematic figure of the eighties art world that it is no longer possible to do a portrait of him simply from life. The heavy shadow of prior encounters with journalists and critics falls over each fresh encounter. Every writer has come too late, no writer escapes the sense of Bloomian belatedness that the figure of Salle evokes. One cannot behave as if one had just met him, and Salle himself behaves like the curator of a sort of museum of himself, helpfully guiding visitors through the exhibition rooms and steering them toward the relevant literature. At the Gagosian Gallery, on Madison Avenue, where he exhibits, there is a two-and-a-half-foot-long file drawer devoted exclusively to published writings about Salle's art and person.

My own encounter with Salle was most heavily shadowed by the interviews he had given two writers, Peter Schjeldahl and Becky Johnston. Reading their dialogues with him was like listening to conversations between brilliant characters in a hastily written but inspired play of advanced ideas and intense, slightly mysterious relationships.

1 0

The spectre of wrongdoing hovers more luridly over visual art than over literature or music. The forger, the pornographer, and the fraud are stock figures in the allegory that constitutes the popular conception of the art world as a place of exciting evil and cunning. The artist David Salle has the distinction of being associated with all three crimes. His paintings are filled with "borrowed" images (twice he has settled out of court with irked owners); often contain drawings of naked or half-undressed women standing or lying in indecent, if not especially arousing, positions; and have an appearance of messy disjunction that could be dismissed (and has been dismissed by Hilton Kramer, Robert Hughes, and Arthur Danto) as ineptitude palming itself off as advanced art. Most critics, however, have without hesitation accepted Salle's work as advanced art, and some of them—Peter Schjeldahl, Sanford Schwartz, Michael Brenson, Robert Rosenblum, and Lisa Liebmann, for example—have celebrated its transgressive quality and placed his paintings among the works that most authoritatively express our time and are apt to become its permanent monuments.

1 1

Unlike David Salle's enigmatic, difficult art, his life is the banal story of a boy who grew up in Wichita, Kansas, in a poorish Jewish family, took art lessons throughout his childhood, went to art school in California, came to New York, and became rich and famous overnight.

12

During an interview with the artist David Salle, published in 1987, the critic and poet Peter Schjeldahl said to him:

> I've noticed, looking at your work attentively for six years or so, a repeating phenomenon, that of going away from seeing your things extremely stimu- lated and with vivid memories, and thought processes that seem to continue on their own, but eventually they get attenuated and fall apart, leaving a rather sour residue. If I haven't seen something by you for a while, I can start to think that I'm overliking it. . . . Then, when I see something new, some- thing good by you, there is an immediate freshening, an immediate dropping away of that mood of depression.

I recognize in Schjeldahl's feelings about Salle's work an echo of my own feel- ings about Salle the man. When I haven't seen him for several weeks or months, I begin to sour on him, to think I'm overliking him. Then I see him again, and I experience Schjeldahl's "immediate freshening." As I write about him now—I haven't seen him for a month—I feel the return of the antago- nism, the sense of sourness. Like the harsh marks Salle makes over the softer images he first applies to his canvas, they threaten to efface the benign, admir- ing feelings of the interviews.

13

It is rare to read anything about the artist David Salle in which some allusion isn't made to the question of whether his work is pornographic and whether his depictions of women are humiliating and degrading. Images of women with panties down around their ankles who are pulling blouses over their heads, or women standing bent over with outthrust naked buttocks, or women lying naked on tables with their legs spread recur in Salle's paintings and have become a kind of signature of his work. The images are monochrome—they are copied from black-and-white photographs—and the pudenda are usually so heavily shaded as to foreclose prurience. To anyone who has seen any of the unambiguously dirty pictures of art history—Courbet's "The Origin of the World," say, or Balthus's "The Guitar Lesson"—the idea of Salle as a pornogra- pher is laughable. However, the poses of Salle's women are unsettling. Someone has stage-directed them—someone with a very cold eye and with def- inite and perhaps rather unpleasant ideas, someone who could well be taking photographs for a girlie magazine, maybe a German girlie magazine. As it hap- pens, some of Salle's images of women are, in fact, derived from the files of an

American girlie magazine called *Stag*, for which he briefly worked in the art department (the magazine was on the verge of folding when he left, and he helped himself to cartons of photographs, mostly of women but also of car and airplane crashes); others are copied from photographs he took himself of hired models.

1 4

In a review of a show of David Salle's paintings, drawings, and watercolors at the Menil Collection, in Houston, in 1988, Elizabeth McBride wrote, "He indulges himself in degrading, depersonalizing, fetishistic images of women which constitute . . . a form of obscenity. . . . Paintings such as these are a way of giving permission for degrading actions. This work has all the cold beauty and the immorally functional power of a Nazi insignia." Of the same show Susan Chadwick wrote, "Salle's work . . . is even more mean-spirited, more contemptuous, and more profoundly misogynist than I had realized. . . . That brings us to the difficult question concerning art that is socially bad. Art that presents a message which is in some way wrong, bad, evil, corrupting, immoral, inhumane, destructive, or sick. What can be done about negative artists? I cringe when I see parents bringing their young children through this show at the Menil on weekends."

1 5

In the winter of 1992, I began a series of interviews with the artist David Salle. They were like sittings for a portrait with a very practiced sitter. Salle has given many—dozens of—interviews. He is a kind of interview addict. But he is remarkably free of the soul-sickness that afflicts so many celebrities, who grow overly interested in the persona bestowed on them by journalism. Salle cultivates the public persona, but with the detachment of someone working in someone else's garden. He gives good value—journalists come away satisfied—but he does not give himself away. He never forgets, and never lets the interviewer forget, that his real self and his real life are simply not on offer. What is on offer is a construct, a character who has evolved and is still evolving from Salle's ongoing encounters with writers. For Salle (who has experimented with sculpture, video, and film) the interview is another medium in which to (playfully) work. It has its careerist dimension, but he also does it for the sport. He once told me that he never makes any preparatory drawings for or revises anything in his paintings. Every stroke of the brush is irrevocable; nothing can be changed or retracted. A few false moves and the painting is ruined, unsalvageable. The same sense of tense improvisation pervades Salle's answers to interviewers' questions. He looks ahead to the way his words will read in print and chooses them with a kind of fearless carefulness. He also once told me of how

he often gets lost as he paints: "I have to get lost so I can invent some way out."
In his interviews, similarly, moments of at-a-lossness become the fulcrum for
flights of verbal invention. Sometimes it almost seems as if he were provoking
the interviewer to put him on the spot, so that he can display his ingenuity in
getting off it.

16

During recent talks I had with the painter David Salle, who was one of the
brightest art stars of the eighties, he would tell me—sometimes in actual
words, sometimes by implication—that the subject of his declining reputation
in the art world was of no real interest to him. That this was not where his real
life lay but was just something to talk about with an interviewer.

17

Writers have traditionally come to painters' ateliers in search of aesthetic
succor. To the writer, the painter is a fortunate alter ego, an embodiment of
the sensuality and exteriority that he has abjured to pursue his invisible,
odorless calling. The writer comes to the places where traces of making can
actually be seen and smelled and touched expecting to be inspired and enabled, possibly even cured. While I was interviewing the artist David Salle, I
was coincidentally writing a book that was giving me trouble, and although
I cannot pin it down exactly (and would not want to), I know that after each
talk with Salle in his studio something clarifying and bracing did filter down
to my enterprise. He was a good influence. But he was also a dauntingly productive artist, and one day, as I walked into the studio and caught a glimpse
of his new work, I blurted out my envious feelings. In the month since we
last met, he had produced four large, complex new paintings, which hung
on the walls in galling aplomb—while I had written maybe ten pages I
wasn't sure I would keep. To my surprise, instead of uttering a modest disclaimer or reassuring words about the difference between writing and painting, Salle flushed and became defensive. He spoke as if I were accusing him,
rather than myself, of artistic insufficiency; it appears that his productivity
is a sensitive subject. His detractors point to his large output as another sign
of his lightweightness. "They hold it up as further evidence that the work is
glib and superficial," Salle said.
    "If work comes easily, it is suspect."
    "But it *doesn't* come easily. I find it extremely difficult. I feel like I'm beating
my head against a brick wall, to use an image that my father would use. When
I work, I feel that I'm doing everything wrong. I feel that it can't be this hard for
other people. I feel that everyone else has figured out a way to do it that allows
him an effortless, charmed ride through life, while I have to stay in this horri-

ble pit of a room, suffering. That's how it feels to me. And yet I know that's not the way it appears to others. Once, at an opening, an English critic came up to me and asked me how long I had worked on the five or six paintings I was showing. I told her, and she said, 'Oh, so fast! You work so fast.' She was a representative of the new, politically correct, anti-pleasure school of art people. I could easily visualize her as a dominatrix. There was some weird sexual energy there, unexpressed. I immediately became defensive."

"I just realized something," I said. "Everyone who writes or paints or performs is defensive about everything. I'm defensive about not working fast *enough*."

In a comradely spirit, Salle later showed me a painting that had failed. It was a painting he had dwelled on a little too long, had taken a fatal misstep with, and had spoiled. I was shocked when I saw it. I had seen it in its youth and bloom a few months earlier; it had shown a ballet couple in a stylized pose radiantly smiling at each other, a mordant parody of a certain kind of dance photography popular in the nineteen-fifties. (Its source was a photograph in a fifties French dance magazine.) Now the man's face was obliterated. It looked as if someone had angrily thrown a can of gray paint at it. "It's a reject, a failed painting. It's going to be cut up," Salle said, as if speaking of a lamed horse that was going to be taken out and shot.

"It was so fine when I saw it first."

"It wasn't fine. It never worked. It's so bad. It's so much worse than I remembered. It's one of the worst things I've done in years. The image of the couple is so abrasive, so aggressive. I tried to undercut it by painting out the man's face. It was even more obnoxious than hers. But when I did that I was on a course of destruction."

1 8

The painter David Salle, like his art, which refuses to narrate, even though it is full of images, declines to tell a story about himself, even though he makes himself endlessly available for interviews and talks as articulately as any subject has ever talked. Salle has spoken with a kind of rueful sympathy of the people who look at his art of fragmentary, incongruous images and say it is too complicated, too much trouble to figure out, and turn away. He, of all people, should know what they are feeling, since his work, and perhaps his life as well, is about turning away. Nothing is ever resolved by Salle, nothing adds up, nothing goes anywhere, everything stops and peters out.

1 9

On an afternoon in April, 1992, the painter David Salle and I sat on a pristine yellow fifties corporate-style sofa in his loft, on White Street, looking at a large horizontal painting that was hanging there, a work he had kept for himself from a group of what he calls "the tapestry paintings," done between 1988 and 1991. The painting made me smile. It showed a group of figures from old art—the men in doublets and in hats with plumes, the women in gowns and wearing feathers in their hair—arranged around a gaming table, the scene obviously derived from one of de La Tour's tense dramas of dupery: and yet not de La Tour, exactly, but a sardonic pastiche of sixteenth- and seventeenth-century Dutch and Italian genre styles. In the gesture for which Salle is known, he had superimposed on the scene incongruous-seeming fragments: two dark monochrome images of bare-breasted women holding wooden anatomy dolls, a sketchily rendered drawing of a Giacometti sculpture, a drawing of a grimacing face, and a sort of Abstract Expressionist rectangle of gray paint with drips and spatters obliterating a man's leg. As if participating in the joke of their transplantation from Baroque to postmodernist art, the costumed men and women had set their faces in comically rigid, exaggerated expressions. When I asked Salle what paintings he had had in mind when he made his pastiche, he gave me an answer that surprised me—and then didn't surprise me. One of the conditions of Salle's art is that nothing in it be original; everything must come from previously made work, so even a pastiche would have to be a pastiche done by someone else. In this case, it was an anonymous Russian tapestry-maker, whose work Salle had found reproduced in a magazine and had copied onto his canvas. The tapestry paintings, perhaps more richly and vividly than any of Salle's other groups of work, illustrate the paradox on which his art is poised—that an appearance of originality may be achieved through dumb copying of the work of others. Salle has been accused of all kinds of bad things by his detractors (Hilton Kramer, Robert Hughes, and Arthur Danto, the most prominent of the critics who hate his work, have all said that he can't draw), but no one has ever accused him—no one can accuse him—of being derivative. His work has always looked like new art and, as time goes on and his technique and certain of his recurrent images have grown familiar, like art by David Salle. The tapestry paintings—there are more than ten of them—were a culmination. They have an energy, an invention, a kind of gorgeousness, and an atmosphere of success, of having pulled something off against heavy odds, that set them apart from Salle's other works. It is no wonder that he wanted to keep a memento of his achievement.

But now the achievement only seemed to fuel Salle's bitterness, his sense of himself as "someone who is no longer current," who is "irrelevant after having been relevant." He looked away from the painting and said, "The younger artists want to kill you off. They just want to get rid of you. You're in their way. I haven't been the artist who is on young artists' minds for a long time. It has been six or seven years since I was the artist who was on young artists' minds. That's how fast it moves. The artists young artists have on their minds are people I've barely heard of. I'm sure there are young artists who think I'm dead." I laughed, and he joined me. Then, his bitterness returning, Salle said, "I feel that I've just gotten started, marshalled my forces, done the research, and learned enough about painting to do something interesting. What I do used to matter to others—for reasons that may not have had anything to do with its merit. But now, when I feel I have something to say, no one wants to hear it. There has always been antagonism to my work, but the sense of irritation and annoyance has stepped up. 'What, *you're* still around?' "

20

In an interview with the screenwriter Becky Johnston, in 1991, the artist David Salle, during a discussion of his childhood, in Wichita, Kansas, gave this answer to a question about his mother:

> You know, I don't really remember her very well. I just remember that she had a lovely gray skirt and a pink blouse with French cuffs and she had her monogram embroidered on the skirt in pink thread. She worked in the dress store [where Salle's father worked as a buyer, window dresser, and advertising-layout man]—she was a saleswoman on the floor—and she dressed very chicly. I remember her then—which was when I was about six—and then I remember her ten or fifteen years later when she worked at night as a cashier in the accounting department of the J. C. Penney store, and she was completely, utterly changed: she wore brown or beige double-knit pants suits. And I honestly don't remember what happened to her in between. I have no images of her in between. In my mind, she just went from being this very chic, very lovely, kind of slightly elevated person, to being this horrible drudge. Then, some years later, she changed back again.

In an interview with me, in 1992, Salle returned to this memory and told me how upset his mother had been when she read a version of it in an essay by Henry Geldzahler, which appeared in the catalogue of Salle's photographs of naked or partly naked women posed in strange positions. "I had been hesitant to send the catalogue to my mother because of the imagery," Salle told me. "It never occurred to me that something in the *text*, which is innocuous, would upset her. But when she called me up she was in tears."

21

In the introduction to a book-length interview with the artist David Salle, published in 1987 by Random House, the critic and poet Peter Schjeldahl writes, "My first reaction on meeting this twenty-seven-year-old phenom was, I'm afraid, a trifle smug. Simply, he was so transparently, wildly ambitious—even by the standards of his generation, whose common style of impatient self-assurance I had begun to recognize—that I almost laughed at him."

When I was interviewing the artist David Salle, an acutely intelligent, reserved, and depressed man, he would tell me about other interviews he was
giving, and once he showed me the transcript of a conversation with Barbaralee
Diamonstein (it was to appear in a book of interviews with artists and art-world
figures published by Rizzoli), which was marked by a special confrontational
quality and an extraordinary air of liveliness. It was as if the interviewer had
provoked the artist out of his usual state of skeptical melancholy and propelled
him into a younger, less complex, more manic version of himself.

There is a passage, for example, in which Diamonstein confronts Salle with a
piece of charged personal history. "From what I have read, you worked as a layout man at what was referred to as a porn magazine. Is that true?" Salle says
yes. "How much did it affect your sensibility? I think you should address the
issue and get rid of it one way or the other," Diamonstein sternly says. Salle,
disconcerted, lamely points out that actually he wasn't a layout man but a
paste-up person at the porn magazine. Still floundering, he irrelevantly adds
that he and the other young men in the art department were "pretty stoned
most of the time." Diamonstein continues to push Salle on the question of
what the experience of working at a men's magazine called *Stag* meant to him.
"So, did this affect your sensibility by either informing you, giving you a skill?
Repelling you, amusing you? Finding it absurd, interesting—how did you
react? How did you ever get there in the first place?"

Salle begins to see a way out of the impasse. "A friend of mine worked there,"
he says. "It was just a job on one level, but 'absurd/interesting' describes it
pretty well. Nobody there took it very seriously. It wasn't *shameful*—people who
worked there didn't tell their families they did something else. At least, I don't
think so. I just remembered there was one guy who worked there because his
father worked there—they were both sitting there all day airbrushing tits and
ass. Like father, like son, I guess."

Diamonstein meets this with an inspiration of her own. "You could have had
a job at *Good Housekeeping,* too," she points out.

"Well, I only worked there for about six months," a momentarily crushed
Salle retorts. Then he finds his tone again: "There has been so much made of it.
Even though I had no money, I quit as soon as I could. You know, this assump-
tion of *causality* assigned to the artist's life like plot points in a play is really
nutty. Do people think I learned about tits and ass working on *Stag* magazine?
Do I seem that pathetic?"

In an essay published in the *Village Voice* in 1982, the critic Peter Schjeldahl
wrote of his initial reaction to the work of David Salle, who was to become "my
personal favorite among current younger artists":

When I first encountered Salle's work, two or three years ago, its vertiginous mix of blatancy ("storytelling" pictures) and elusiveness (the "story" was impossible to figure out) made me a little sick. I was also rattled by the frequent use of pornographically posed female nudes. It now seems to me hardly conceivable that in his determined excavation of the culture's most charged pictorial matter, Salle would not have availed himself of these ritualized vehicles of male fantasy. But it made me so nervous that I rather comically felt a surge of relief when in last year's show Salle presented a male nude. What may have been even more shocking was Salle's cavalierly offhand exploitation of classically modernist pictorial devices, those sacred signs. He was using them like cheap tools, without even the upside-down respect accorded by satirical irony (as in Lichtenstein). I itched to dislike this stuff.

Then it started to get me. It was like a welling, congested, sentimental weepiness without an object, as emotions triggered by images of, say, a depressed-looking girl smoking in bed and some unspecific tragedy in a crowded street sought cathartic resolution, in vain. It was an abstracted sensation of dislocation, yearning, and loss that started resonating with my sense of what both art and life are like here in the late twentieth century. Suddenly Salle's harsh artifice seemed heroic, an earnest of authenticity—without ceasing to seem perverse, against the grain.

2 4

One day, the artist David Salle and I talked about Thomas Bernhard's novel "The Loser."

"I'm a third of the way through it," I said, "and at first I was excited by it, but now I'm a little bored. I may not finish it."

"It's so beautiful and so pessimistic," Salle said.

"Yes, but it doesn't hold your interest the way a nineteenth-century novel does. I'm never bored when I'm reading George Eliot or Tolstoy."

"I am," Salle said.

I looked at him with surprise. "And you're *not* bored when you're reading Bernhard?"

"I'm bored by plot," Salle said. "I'm bored when it's all written out, when there isn't any shorthand."

2 5

In the fall of 1991, I attended a book party for the writer Harold Brodkey given by the painter David Salle in his loft, in Tribeca. The first thing I saw on walking into the room was Brodkey and Norman Mailer in conversation. As I approached, I heard them jovially talking about the horrible reviews each had just received, like bad boys proudly comparing their poor marks. The party took place early in my acquaintance with Salle, and this fragment of conversation was a sort of overture to talks I later had with him about his sense of himself as a bad boy of art and about his inability to stop picking at the sore of his own bad reviews. He is an artist who believes in the autonomy of art, who sees the universe of art as an alternative to the universe of life, and who despises art that has a social agenda. But he is also someone who is drawn to the world of popular criticism, to the bazaar where paintings and books and performances are crudely and carelessly rated, like horses or slaves, and who wants to be one of the Chosen even as he disdains the choosers; in other words, he is like everybody else. Only the most pathologically pure-hearted writers, artists, and performers are indifferent to how their work is received and judged. But some hang more attentively than others on the words of the judges. During my talks with Salle, he kept returning to the subject of his reception, like an unhappy moth helplessly singeing itself on a light bulb. "I don't know why I keep talking about this," he would say. "This isn't what is on my mind. I don't care that much. I spend a disproportionate amount of time complaining to you about how I am perceived. Every time we finish one of these talks, I have a pang of regret. I feel that all I do is complain about how badly I'm treated, and this is so much not what I want to be talking about. But for some reason I keep talking about it."

2 6

David Salle is one of the best-received and best-rewarded of the artists who came to prominence in the nineteen-eighties, but he is not one of the happiest. He is a tense, discontented man, with a highly developed sense of irony.

2 7

In several of David Salle's paintings, a mysterious dark-haired woman appears, raising a half-filled glass to her lips. Her eyes are closed, and she holds the glass in both hands with such gravity and absorption that one can only think she is taking poison or drinking a love potion. She is rendered in stark black-and-white and wears a period costume—a dress with a sort of Renaissance aspect. The woman disturbs and excites us, the way people in dreams do whom we know we know but can never quite identify. David Salle himself has some of the enigmatic vividness of the drinking woman. After many interviews with him, I feel that I only *almost* know him, and that what I write about him will have the vague, vaporous quality that our most indelible dreams take on when we put them into words.

2 8

One of the leitmotivs of a series of conversations I had in 1992 and 1993 with the painter David Salle was his unhappiness over the current reception of his work. "I don't think anyone has written a whole essay saying my work is passé," he said. "It's more a line here and there. It's part of the general phenomenon called eighties-bashing. The critics who have been negative all along, like Robert Hughes and Hilton Kramer, have simply stepped up their negativity. The virulence of the negativity has grown enormously in the past couple of years. The reviews by Hughes and Kramer of my '91 show were weirdly, personally insulting. The two of them were always negative, but now it was as if they smelled blood and were moving in for the kill."

I told Salle I would like to read those reviews, and a few days later his assistant sent them to me. Salle had not exaggerated. Hughes and Kramer seemed beside themselves with dislike and derision; their reviews had an almost hysterical edge. "The exhibition of new paintings by David Salle at the Gagosian Gallery . . . has one tiny merit," Hughes wrote in *Time* on April 29, 1991. "It reminds you how lousy and overpromoted so much 'hot' 'innovative' American art in the 1980's was. If Julian Schnabel is Exhibit A in our national wax museum of recent duds, David Salle is certainly Exhibit B." He went on:

> Yet is there a duller or more formula-ridden artist in America than Salle in 1991 as he approaches the Big Four-Oh? . . . Drawing, as anyone who has seen a few Salles knows, is not what the artist does. He never learned to do it, and probably never will. He is incapable of making an interesting mark. . . . Thus his pictures enable critics to kvetch soulfully about the dissociation of signs and meanings, and to praise what all good little deconstructors would call their "refusal of authoritarian closure," meaning, roughly, that they don't mean anything in particular. It's as though those who bet on him can't bear to face the possibility that his work was vacuous to begin with. . . . The Gagosian Gallery . . . has even hired a guard to stand at the entrance to the room in which Salle's six new paintings are displayed, presumably in case some collector from the bottom of the waiting list is seized by the impulse to grab one of those tallowy objects from the wall and make a run for it. Ten minutes into the show, your heart goes out to that guard. Eight hours a day, five days a week, of this!

Kramer had wrung his hands in the New York *Observer* of April 15th:

> About some art exhibitions nowadays, we hardly know whether to laugh or cry. Their pretensions, not to mention the atmosphere of piety surrounding them, are undeniably laughable. Yet their artistic realization is at once so barren and so smug—and offers so few of the satisfactions we look to art to bring us—that the sense of comedy they elicit turns, almost before we know it, to feelings of grief and depression. . . .
>
> Consider the David Salle exhibition that is currently occupying the lush precincts of the Gagosian Gallery. . . .
>
> In the 80's, a taste for the raunchy and outrageous functioned in the fash-

ionable art world very much the way junk bonds functioned in the financial markets, and it was no accident that the artists who produced art of this sort often found their most enthusiastic patrons among the collectors who were the principal beneficiaries of such junk-bond enterprises. These collectors often knew very little about the art that had been created in the past—in the days, that is, before they made their first fortunes. For such collectors, art history began the day they first walked into Leo Castelli's or Mary Boone's. In that world, the Old Masters were Jasper Johns and Andy Warhol, and artists like David Salle, who had been nominated to succeed those exalted talents, were guaranteed a sensational success.

The hostility and snobbery of both Hughes and Kramer toward the collectors of Salle's work is worthy of note. This kind of insult of the consumer has no equivalent in book or theatre or movie reviewing. That is probably because the book/play/film reviewer has some fellow feeling with the buyers of books and theatre and film tickets, whereas the art reviewer usually has no idea what it is like to buy a costly painting or sculpture. He is, per financial force, a mere spectator in the tulipomaniacal drama of the contemporary art market, and he tends to regard the small group of people rich enough to be players as if they were an alien species, quite impervious to his abuse. As for the collectors, they repay the critics for their insults by ignoring their judgments: they go right on buying—or, at any rate, they don't immediately stop buying—the work of artists who get bad reviews. Eventually, critical consensus (the judgments of museum curators form a part of it) is reflected in the market, and in time collectors bow to its will, but at the moment they were not bowing to Hughes's and Kramer's opinions and were continuing to trade in Salles. Salle smarted under the attacks but continued to make money.

29

I once asked the artist David Salle if he had read an article in *The New Republic* by Jed Perl (who also frequently writes for Hilton Kramer's *The New Criterion*) about how the wrong artists are celebrated and how the really good artists are obscure. The article was entitled "The Art Nobody Knows," with the subhead "Where Is the Best American Art to Be Found? Not in the So-Called Art World." It articulated the antagonism of an older generation toward the art stars of the eighties, and complained of the neglect suffered by a group of serious artists, who had been quietly working and, over the years, "making the incremental developments that are what art is all about." The world of these artists, Perl said, was "the real art world," as opposed to the world of Salle and Schnabel and Cindy Sherman. Perl held up two artists—the sculptor Barbara Goodstein and the painter Stanley Lewis, whose work "is rarely seen by anybody beyond a small circle of admirers"—as examples of the neglected "real artist." "What happens to an artist whose development receives so little public recognition?" he asked. "Can artists keep on doing their damnedest when the wide world doesn't give a damn?"

Salle said that he had not read the article and that it sounded interesting. "I have always wanted to know what Jed Perl likes," he said. "Maybe he's right. Maybe these *are* the good artists." He asked me to send him the article, and I did so. The next time we met, he greeted me with it in his hand and an amused look on his face. "What a pity they illustrated it," he said. "Without the illustrations, you might think Perl was onto something. But when you see the work you just have to laugh. It's so *tiny*."

3 0

I used to visit the artist David Salle in his studio and try to learn the secret of art from him. What was he doing, in his enigmatic, allusive, aggressive art? What does any artist do when he produces an art work? What are the properties and qualities of authentic art, as opposed to ersatz art? Salle is a contemplative and well-spoken man, and he talked easily and fluently about his work and about art in general, but everything he said only seemed to restate my question. One day, he made a comment on the difference between collages done by amateurs and collages done by artists which caused my ears to prick up. It occurred to me that a negative example—an example of something that wasn't art—could perhaps be instructive. Accordingly, on my next visit with Salle I took with me three collages I had once made for my own pleasure. At the time, Salle was himself making collages, in preparation for a series of paintings featuring images of consumer products of the fifties. He was going to copy his collages in oil paint on large canvases, but they already looked like works of art. "Why are your collages art and mine not?" I asked him.

Salle propped up my collages and regarded them closely. At last, he said, "There's nothing that says your collages aren't art. They're art if you declare them to be so."

"Yes, that's the Duchamp dictum. But I don't declare them to be so. Don't you remember the distinction you drew between collages made by amateurs and collages made by artists?"

"I was speaking generally," Salle said.

I realized that he was being delicate, that he didn't want to voice his true opinion of my collages. I assured him that I hadn't brought the collages to be praised, that I had no investment in them, that I had brought them only in order to engage him in a discussion. "Please say anything that occurs to you."

"Stuff occurs to me, but I don't want to say it. It might sound mean-spirited."

Eventually, Salle conquered enough of his reluctance to make a few mild criticisms of the composition of my collages, and to say that his own collages were composed along simple principles that any art-school freshman would recognize. Looking back on the incident, I see that Salle had also seen what any first-year student of psychology would have seen—that, for all my protests to the contrary, I *had* brought my art to him to be praised. Every amateur harbors the fantasy that his work is only waiting to be discovered and acclaimed; a second fantasy—that the established contemporary artists must (also) be frauds—is a necessary corollary.

31

I once visited the artist David Salle in his studio, on White Street, when he was making preparatory collages for a series of paintings based on consumer products, and he told me that he had noticed himself being obsessively drawn to two images: watches and shoes. They had seemed meaningful to him—he had been cutting pictures of watches and shoes out of newspapers and magazines—but he hadn't known why. The meaning of the watches remained obscure, he said, but a few days earlier he had cracked the code of the shoes. "The shoe as presented in the selling position isn't the thing. The thing is underneath the shoe. *It's the idea of being stepped on.*" Salle's sense of himself as being stepped on—by people who are jealous of him, by people who feel superior to him, by people who don't like his sexual politics, by people who find his work too much trouble to decipher—has become a signature of his public persona.

32

There is a kind of man who is always touchingly and a little irritatingly mentioning his wife—touchingly because one is moved by the depth of his affection, and irritatingly because one feels put down by the paragon who inspires it. During the two years I interviewed the artist David Salle, he was always mentioning the dancer and choreographer Karole Armitage, with whom he had lived for seven years. Although Salle and Armitage had separated a few months before our talks began, he would speak about her as if he were still under her spell. They had met in 1983, and had become a famous couple. She had been a lead dancer in the Merce Cunningham company, and had then formed her own avant-garde company. Her choreography was a kind of version in dance of what Salle was doing in painting: an unsettling yoking of incongruous elements. (The fusion of classical ballet with punk-rock music was Armitage's initial postmodernist gesture.) That Salle should become her collaborator—painting sets and designing costumes for her ballets—seemed almost inevitable. The first product of the Armitage-Salle collaboration was a ballet called "The Mollino Room," performed at the Metropolitan Opera House in May, 1986, which had been commissioned by American Ballet Theatre, and in which Baryshnikov himself danced. In an article entitled "The Punk Princess and the Post-modern Prince," published in *Art in America*, Jill Johnston wonderfully wrote of the première, "It attracted a capacity audience of art world luminaries and suburban bankers or whoever they were in their tuxedos and jewels and wild satisfied looks of feeling they were at just the right place that opening evening in Manhattan." As events proved, however, the bankers were in the wrong place. The ballet got terrible reviews, as did Armitage's subsequent ballets "The Tarnished Angels" and "The Elizabethan Phrasing of the Late Albert Ayler," both staged at the Brooklyn Academy in 1987. "Little talent, much pretension. Any other comment might seem superfluous," the *Times* dance critic Anna Kisselgoff wrote of Armitage on the latter occasion.

"The dance world is controlled by one person, Anna Kisselgoff," Salle told me bitterly. "She controls it internationally as well as locally. A good review from Anna will get you a season in France, and a bad review will cancel it. Karole was literally run out of town by Anna. She can't work in New York anymore." Armitage now lives and works in Los Angeles and abroad.

Salle and Armitage have remained close friends; they talk frequently on the telephone and meet whenever she comes to New York. Salle speaks of her with a kind of reverence for the rigor and extremity of her avant-gardism. She and her dancers represent to him the purest form of artistic impudence and intransigence. "During the seven years I was with Karole, I lived a different life from that of any artists I know," he told me. "I lived her life. She would probably tell you she lived mine. At any rate, during those years I was more involved with her work than with my own. Her work was about being on the edge, performed by people who enjoyed being on the edge, for an audience who wanted to be on the edge. Her life was much more urgent and alive and crisis-oriented. The performing arts are like that. When I was with Karole, artists seemed boring to me—staid and self-satisfied. Stolid, like rocks in a stream. Very few people had her inquisitiveness and restlessness, her need for stimulation in the deepest sense. When I was with Karole, artists seemed almost bovine to me, domestic, house-oriented, safe."

Salle and I were talking in his sleek, cold, obsessively orderly loft on White Street, furnished with nineteen-fifties corporate-style sofas and chairs, and I asked him if Armitage had helped furnish the place.

"No," he said. "I wasn't with her when I bought the loft. She moved in a few years later. I came to see this place through her eyes. Through her eyes it was intimidating and alienating. There was no place for her in it."

"Was there an area that she took possession of, that became her own domain?"

"No, not really. Because there was no way to divide it. She had a desk—sort of where that painting is. There was a country house in upstate New York. I bought it because she liked it. It was an old house, and she had a romantic feeling about it. But we never had time to go there."

3 3

In a long interview with the artist David Salle by the screenwriter Becky
Johnston, there is a passage about the painting tradition of the female nude in
Western art and about Salle's sense of himself as not belonging to that tradition. "It would be interesting," Johnston says, "to try to point out what is different about your nude women from the parade of nude women which has
gone by."

"Well, we both agree there's a difference," Salle says. "It feels like a complete
break."

"Absolutely. But I want to know what you think that break is."

Salle struggles to answer and gives up. "I'm not getting anywhere. I know it's
different, but I don't know why. I don't know how to express it in words. What
do you think?"

Johnston says shrewdly, "I think the difference between the nude woman
in your paintings and those in others is that *she's not a woman.* She's a representative of something else. She's a stand-in for your view. I don't think
that's true of most of the women in art. And I don't think it's a sexual obsession with women which motivates your use of the nude, as it does, say,
Picasso's. It's much deeper, more personal and subjective. That's my opinion."

Salle doesn't protest, and Johnston goes on to ask him, "If you had to describe it—and I know this is asking you to generalize, but feel free to do so
wildly—what's 'feminine' to you?"

Salle stops to consider. "I have the feeling that if I were to start talking about
what I think is feminine, I would list all the qualities I can think of."

3 4

David Salle is a slight, handsome man of forty-one, who wears his dark shoulder-
length hair pulled back and bound with a rubber band, though sometimes he
will absently pull off the rubber band and let the hair fall around his thin, not
always cleanly shaven face. In 1992 and 1993, I would visit him at his studio,
and we would talk about his work and his life. I did not find what he said about
his work interesting (I have never found anything any artist has said about his
work interesting), but when he talked about his life—especially about his life as
an unsettling presence in the art world and his chronic feeling of being misunderstood—that was something else. Then his words took on the specificity,
vividness, and force that had drained out of them when he talked about art.
But even so I felt dissatisfied with the portrait of the artist that was emerging
for me—it seemed too static—and one day I said to him, "I keep thinking there
should be some action."

"Action?"

"Yes. Something should happen. There has been some action—I've been to your studio and to your loft and to your drawing show and to the dinner afterward—but I want more."

"We'll think of something," Salle said.

"What if I watched you paint?"

"We could try it, though I think it would be pretty boring, like being around a film set. A lot of waiting around." Salle then recalled artists he had seen on TV as a child, who painted and talked to the audience. "My friend Eric Fischl tells me there's a whole raft of them on TV now—wildly entertaining, creepy guys who paint and talk a blue streak. Fischl is an expert on TV painters. He says there's a guy on TV who is the fastest painter in the world. It's a funny thing to think about. Painting, like theatre, is about illusion, and I think it might be shocking to see how undramatic the process is through which the illusions are created."

"We could go to a museum together."

Salle said he had already done that with a journalist—Gerald Marzorati, for an article in *ARTnews*. "We went to the Met. I was badly hung over, and it only magnified the pathetic limitations of what I had to say about other art. We were looking at these Rembrandts, and I didn't have anything to say about them. It came down to 'They sure are good.' "

I never watched Salle paint (his talk about the TV artists somehow took care of that), but I did go to a museum with him once—to the Met, to see the Lucian Freud show. I had had a rather cumbersome journalistic idea. Robert Hughes, who had written scathingly about Salle, had called Freud "the best realist painter alive," and I imagined doing a set piece in which Salle would make acidic comments on a favorite of Hughes's as a sort of indirect revenge. I called up Salle and put the idea to him. Salle said he'd be glad to go to the Freud show, but couldn't oblige me with my set piece, since he didn't hate Freud's work—he admired it, and had even "quoted" from it in his own work. At the show, Salle moved through the rooms very quickly. He could tell at a glance what he wanted to look at and what he didn't, and mostly he didn't. He strode past paintings, only occasionally pausing to stand before one. He lingered appreciatively before a small nude owned by a film actor—"Ah, the Steve Martin," he said when he spotted it—and a large painting of Freud's family and friends in his studio, flanked by a studio sink and a massive scented geranium with many dead leaves. What Salle said about the paintings that captured his interest was technical in character; he spoke of strategies of composition and of the depositing of paint on canvas. Of the well-known painting of Freud's mother lying down, Salle said, "It has the same palette as 'Whistler's Mother'—a ravishing palette." In the last rooms of the show, where the provocative large paintings of the overweight performance artist Leigh Bowery were hanging, Salle permitted himself a negative comment. "That's completely unremarkable," he said of "Naked Man, Back View," a huge painting of a seated, naked Bowery. He added, "Freud is adored for being 'bad'—by the same people who hate my work because I'm 'bad.' "

I recalled a conversation I'd once had with Salle about Francis Bacon. Salle had been speaking about his own work, about his images of women—"They're all kind of dire, they have a dire cast," he said—and I had asked him, speaking of dire, whether Bacon had been an influence. "You're not the first person to ask me that," Salle said. "Several people have observed that to me. Bacon is actually not an artist I'm interested in, but lately I've been thinking about him a lot in attempting to defend myself against certain criticisms. If you turned these criticisms around and levelled them against Bacon, it would be absurd. No one would ever say these things about Bacon. And it's purely because his work is homosexual and mine is heterosexual. The same attitudes transposed are incorrect."

"Why are dire images done by a homosexual more correct than those done by a heterosexual?"

"Because in art politics to be homosexual is, a priori, more correct than to be heterosexual. Because to be an artist is to be an outsider, and to be a gay artist is to be a double outsider. That's the correct condition. If you're a straight artist, it's not clear that your outsiderness is legitimate. I know this is totally absurd, that I'm making it sound totally absurd. But the fact is that in our culture it does fall primarily to gays and blacks to make something interesting. Almost everything from the straight white culture is less interesting, and has been for a long time."

3 5

After the opening of a show of David Salle's drawings at the uptown Gagosian Gallery in March, 1992, a celebratory dinner was held at a suavely elegant restaurant in the East Seventies, and as the evening proceeded I was struck by the charm and gaiety of the occasion. The ritual celebrations of artistic achievement—the book parties, the opening-night parties, the artists' dinners—give outward form to, and briefly make real, the writer's or performer's or painter's fantasy that he is living in a world that wishes him well and wants to reward him for his work. For a few hours, the person who has recently emerged from the "horrible pit," as Salle once called it, of his creative struggles is lulled into forgetting that the world is indifferent to him and intent only on its own pleasures. Occasionally, the world is pleased to applaud and reward an artist, but more often than not it will carelessly pass him by. And what the world gives, it delights in taking away: the applauded and rewarded artist does not remain so; the world likes to reverse itself. What gives the book party or the opening-night party or the artist's dinner its peculiar feverish glitter is the lightly buried consciousness of the probable bad fate that awaits the artist's offering.

Since shows of painters' drawings are considered relatively minor affairs, the dinner was a small one (for about twenty people) and had a more relaxed and less complicated atmosphere than a full-scale show would have elicited.

The restaurant was a very expensive and a very good one; we ordered carefully and ate seriously. Salle, who was wearing a kind of sailor's blouse, sat quietly and calmly and watchfully, like a boy at a birthday party. I retain an image of Sabine Rewald, a curator at the Metropolitan, who looks like a Vermeer, lifting a spoonful of pink sorbet to her mouth and smiling happily. My table partners—Robert Pincus-Witten, an art critic and emeritus professor of art history, who is now a director at Gagosian, and Raymond Foye, another director, who also publishes tiny, strange books of exotica, such as the poems of Francis Picabia—were masters of the art of intimate, complicit table talk. Our host, Larry Gagosian, was absent. He was out of town; the opening was evidently not important enough for him to fly in for.

Two years later, the opening, at the Gagosian downtown gallery, of a Salle show of eight large "Early Product Paintings," based on images in fifties advertising, was something else again. This was a high-stakes show—each painting was priced at around a hundred thousand dollars—and an entire restaurant had been hired for the artist's dinner. Things were no longer simple. Things were very complicated. The restaurant, filled with artists, writers, performers, filmmakers, collectors, critics, gallery owners, hangers-on, hummed with a sense of intrigue and with the threat of something not coming off. Gagosian, a tall, dark-skinned, gray-haired man in his late forties, with a deadpan manner, walked through the room casting looks here and there, like Rick in "Casablanca" checking the house. Pincus-Witten and Foye, again on duty, skimmed about on anxious, obscure errands. Salle (playing the Paul Henreid role?) wore a dark jacket over a tieless white shirt, and jeans, and was only slightly more reserved, detached, and watchful than usual. I left before the Vichy police came. The image I retain from this occasion, like Sabine Rewald's pink sorbet from the previous one (though it comes from the opening proper), is the sight of a tall, thin man in a gray suit, who stood in the center of the gallery and stood out from everyone else because of the aura of distinction that surrounded him. He had a face with clever, European features, but it was his bearing that was so remarkable. He carried himself like a nobleman; you expected to look down and see a pair of greyhounds at his feet. Throughout the opening, he had his arm around a young black man with an elaborate tribal hairdo. He was the painter Francesco Clemente, another of Gagosian's hundred-thousand-dollar-a-picture artists, and another of the painters who came to prominence in the nineteen-eighties. Unlike Salle, however, he has not yet seen his star fall.

During a series of talks I had with Salle, over a two-year period, he was always careful to say nothing bad about fellow-painters—even his comments on Julian Schnabel, with whom he had had a public falling out, were restrained. But I gathered from a few things he let drop about Clemente's charmed life in art that it was a bitter reminder of everything his own wasn't. "What I've been circling around trying to find a way to ask," Salle once told me, "is the simple question 'How is it that some people are basically taken seriously and others are basically not taken seriously?' " In spite of the money he makes from his art, in spite of the praise sometimes bordering on reverence he has received from advanced critics (Peter Schjeldahl, Sanford Schwartz, Lisa Liebmann, Robert Rosenblum, Michael Brenson, for example), Salle feels that admission into the highest rank of contemporary painting has been denied him, that he will always be placed among the second-stringers, that he will never be considered one of the big sluggers.

3 6

The artist David Salle, in a 1990 catalogue of his prints called the "Canfield Hatfield" series (A. J. Liebling wrote about Hatfield in "The Honest Rain-maker"), wrote, "Professor Canfield Hatfield was a supposedly real-life character who figured prominently in racetrack operations and betting schemes of all types in this country in the first part of the twentieth century. Among the Professor's many activities to promote belief in a higher system of control over seemingly random events were his exploits as a paid maker of rain for drought-stricken communities in the West—a high-wager kind of job and by extension a useful metaphor for the relationship between risk, hope, and fraud that enter into any art-making or rain-making situation."

3 7

The lax genre of personality journalism would not seem to be the most congenial medium for a man of David Salle's sharp, odd mind and cool, irritable temperament. And yet this forty-one-year-old painter has possibly given more interviews than any other contemporary artist. Although the published results have, more often than not, disappointed him, they have not deterred him from further fraternization with the press; when I was interviewing him, in 1992 and 1993, he would regularly mention other interviews he was giving. One of them—an interview with Eileen Daspin, of the magazine W—turned out badly. Salle lost his subject's wager that the interviewer's sympathetic stance wasn't a complete sham, and had to endure the vexation of reading a piece about himself that shimmered with hostility and turned his words against him. "It can't be easy being David Salle in the 1990's," Daspin wrote, in the October, 1993, issue. "He is definitely out. Like fern bars and quiche. A condition that's a little hard to take after having been one of the genius artist boy wonders of the Eighties." This was the style and tone of the article. Salle himself sounded petulant and egotistical. ("I was completely ignored by the same people at the beginning of my career who then celebrated me and who are now happy to ignore me.")

A month or so later, Salle told me of his feelings about the article. "I read it very, very quickly, in disgust, and threw the magazine in the trash. I had been ambushed. I should have known better. I have no one to blame but myself. She gave off plenty of signals that should have raised alarms. It led to my saying some interesting things—except I said them to the wrong person."

"It interests me that you always take responsibility for the interview—that if you don't like it, you blame yourself rather than the interviewer."

"Oh, I can blame her," Salle said. "I didn't do it single-handed. She did it. She kept saying 'What does it feel like to be a has-been? Don't you feel bad being put in the position of a has-been?' and I kept saying—with a misguided sense of pedagogical mission—'Well, you have to understand that this has a context and a history and a trajectory.' I was talking about the tyranny of the left. But it came out with her saying merely how angry and unhappy I was about being a has-been. All the pains I took to explain the context had gone for nothing."

"She made you sound like a very aggressive and unpleasant person."

"Maybe I am. I was trying out the thesis that the art world lionizes bullies. In any case, I'm reaching the point where I'm resigned to being misinterpreted. Instead of seeing this as a bad fate that befell me through no fault of my own, I now see it as a natural state of affairs for an artist. I almost don't see how it can be otherwise."

"Then why do you give all these interviews?"

Salle thought for a moment. "It's a lazy person's form of writing. It's like writing without having to write. It's a form in which one can make something, and I like to make things."

I remembered something Salle had once made that had failed, like the *W* interview, and that he had destroyed in disgust, as he had destroyed his copy of the magazine. It was a painting of two ballet dancers.

3 8

The artist David Salle—as if speaking of another person—once talked to me about his impatience. "I have a way of making people feel that they don't have my attention, that I have lost interest and turned away. People I'm close to have complained about it."

"And then?"

"I get even more impatient."

"Is it that your thoughts wander?"

"I start thinking that my life is going to be over soon. It's that simple. I don't have that much time left. I felt this way when I was twenty."

Salle had recently turned forty. He had noticed—without drawing the almost too obvious inference—that he was cutting images of watches out of newspapers and magazines. One day, after arriving a little late for an appointment with me, he apologized and then told me that he used to be obsessively punctual. "I had to train myself not to arrive exactly on the dot. It was absurd and unseemly to be so punctual. It was particularly unseemly for an artist to be so punctual."

I asked Salle what his punctuality had been about.

"I think it had to do with focussing so much on people's expectations of me. But it was also because I myself hate to wait. For all my, I'm sure, bottomless inconsiderateness of other people, I'm always empathizing with the other person. I empathize with the torturer. I find it very easy to empathize with Robert Hughes when he writes of his aversion to my work. I feel I know exactly what he's thinking and why. It's a kind of arrogance, I know, but I feel sorry for him. He doesn't know any better. I had to learn to be late and I had to learn to be cruel, to exude hostility. But it's not really my nature. I do it badly, because it's not who I am."

3 9

Toward the end of a long series of interviews with the artist David Salle, I received this letter from him:

> After the many hours of trying to step outside of myself in order to talk about who or what I am, I feel that the only thing that really matters in art and in life is to go against the tidal wave of literalism and literal-mindedness—to insist on and *live* the life of the imagination. A painting has to be the experience, instead of pointing to it. I want to have and to give *access to feeling.* That is the riskiest and only important way to connect art to the world—to make it alive. Everything else is just current events.
>
> Most of our conversations, I think, were about how this idea has a special frequency which is easily drowned out by the din of the moment. That is, we talked, or I talked, mostly about its being "drowned out." But the important thing is not really the "underdogness" of it—but just the feeling itself.

4 0

To write about the painter David Salle is to be forced into a kind of parody of his melancholy art of fragments, quotations, absences—an art that refuses to be any one thing or to find any one thing more interesting, beautiful, or significant than another.

4 1

One day, toward the end of a conversation I was having with the painter David Salle in his studio, on White Street, he looked at me and said, "Has this ever happened to you? Have you ever thought that your real life hasn't begun yet?"

"I think I know what you mean."

"You know—soon. Soon you'll start your real life."

(1994)

NICHOLAS LEMANN

THE REDEMPTION

"It's quite fascinating," said Joe. "This big honor, the biggest in the world, can happen to a man almost overnight. What was Coolidge when he was nominated for the vice-presidency? He'd been governor of Massachusetts and settled the police strike. What was Harding? Well, Harding isn't a good example, because he'd not only been governor of his state but United States senator as well. But look at the other side, the Democrats. Wilson, a governor and a college president. Cox? Nobody. Franklin Roosevelt, the fellow that ran for vice-president, I used to know him slightly. At least I met him at dances when I was in college. A typical New York snob, I always thought."
—*John O'Hara, "Ten North Frederick."*

I MET George W. Bush once by accident back in the early seventies, at Harvard. I must have been a freshman or a sophomore. Some home-town friends of mine from New Orleans, Grant and Margot Thomas, were in Cambridge for a few years because Grant was getting a master's degree, and I used to drop by their apartment all the time. To me, it was a warm island of Southern gaiety in a sour sea of ambition and after-the-revolution ill will. Life had a light and charming cast there. The Thomases had a dog named Layla, and their neighbors, who were the authors of the Curious George books, would appear occasionally to deliver fond mock-chastisings in a Mitteleuropa accent. One afternoon when I was there, the doorbell rang and a guy came up the stairs: George Bush.

I remember having two thoughts. One was that he looked like a standard-issue boarding-school boy turned business-school student. He was wearing wide-wale corduroy trousers, an Izod polo shirt with the collar turned up, a crewneck sweater, and Sperry Top-siders—the uniform of the day for his group. He had curly brown hair worn just a little longer, but not much, than you could wear it at your first job. The second thought was that he must be the son of the head of the Republican National Committee. This was, on the one hand, just about the worst credential you could present in Cambridge at that moment, but, on the other hand, being the son of a definite somebody always registered as a plus at Harvard. One of the things you were socialized to do there was to notice that kind of signifier of position, and affect not to notice. So we greeted each other with meaningful blankness. I, in my Army fatigues, T-shirt, long hair, and big round glasses, would have come across to him as being as deeply not his type as he did to me. The famous Bush charm was not on display. After a few minutes, I said I had to go.

I mention all this because it was very much at the top of the agenda the next time I came face to face with George Bush, which was a few days before Christmas, in the hamlet of Derry, New Hampshire. At one end of town, outside the office of the local newspaper, sat a big bus, which had been got up in the manner of the conveyance of a travelling musical act, with a painting of an eagle on one side and a landscape on the other. A small clutch of people, some of them members of a Texas Rangers security detail, stood outside. Soon Bush emerged from the newspaper office, and I introduced myself. He gave me an appraising look. "You're Henry Thomas's friend," he said. "I saw him last night, at the Christmas party at the Mansion"—the Governor's Mansion, in Austin. "Didn't you teach with him at the Chinquapin School?"

What Bush does with people is establish a direct, personal connection—a vector of just-you-and-me. One aspect of it is that everybody gets a nickname, which thenceforth becomes the fixative in the relationship, the instant way of establishing that there's this special thing going on between Bush and the other person. My friend Grant Thomas was born Henry Grant Thomas, Jr., so, somewhere back in the mists of time in the private-school and country-club world of Houston, where they first met, he became, to Bush, and to Bush only, Henry. Chinquapin was a school in Texas for poor kids where Grant taught for a year, during the period when Bush was in the Air National Guard. I had registered, therefore, as an old friend of Grant's, probably from the South, probably a liberal, but possibly at least the kind who goes beyond hypocritical preachiness. Not exactly right, but in the ballpark. He motioned for me to get on the bus.

Inside, the long channel of space had been divided into two parts, a dressing room in back and a living room in front, where eight or ten people could sit on upholstered couches. A few aides were inside, and a few local Republican politicians, and another reporter, from the newspaper in Nashua. I was going to interview Bush as the bus travelled from Derry to Manchester, a few miles away, where he would give a speech at a high school.

Bush looked great. He was wearing a wool jacket that perfectly hugged his back and shoulders, a white shirt with some kind of crosshatched texture in the fabric, black ostrich-skin cowboy boots emblazoned with his initials, and a belt with a nicely worked silver buckle. The curly dark hair of long ago had matured into a close-cropped gray pelt like a Roman emperor's. He was trim and golden. His face had that middle-aged patrician's quality of being creased in a way that somehow connotes success.

HE began the interview by questioning me. Hadn't I recently published a book on education and testing? It was obvious that in his mind this book had been filed under "Respectable but Too Liberal." Didn't I want people's S.A.T. scores to be readjusted to account for their backgrounds? I said I didn't. Well, then, what did I want? He was looking to identify the thing that he knew he disagreed with. I said I was for a national achievement test, based on national curriculum standards. That was it. "You've got your opinion, I've got mine," he said, and then he went on to explain that a national test was unnecessary because of a long-running government-financed program called the National Assessment of Educational Progress—a program that everybody inside the education world and almost nobody outside of it knows about. He grinned. "And now that I've won that argument . . ." He and the appreciative audience in the bus broke out laughing. He stretched out and put his boots up on the couch.

The interview, in other words, began with the quality of an amiably competitive game. Bush wasn't just going to sit back and let me ask him questions; he was going to take the initiative, establish a teasing, givin'-you-shit vibe, and score a quick point off me, as if to show that he wasn't an easy mark for the kind of tricky public-policy questions that I had probably come to ask. Now that all that had been established, we could begin.

But, even then, that competitive feeling hung heavy in the air. Sometimes Bush would answer a question by going into what I knew to be a well-used string of sentences from one of his speeches—the unspoken part of the answer being "See, I stayed on message and didn't let you trip me up." Or he'd jump in, mid-question, with a quick, triumphant answer, as if to say that he'd been ready for that one. When a question began with a premise, he'd often challenge the premise. When he detected an allusion to a public criticism of him, he'd declare his critics to be wrong. While he was answering, he was also ascending a rising curve of nomenclatural informality which began with "Nicholas" and quickly made its way to "Nick." He seemed happiest when he could come in with a quick, sure answer. Once, I asked what he'd want written on his Presidential tombstone. Instantly: "He came, he said, he accomplished."

There was something jarring between the tone of Bush's prospective Presidency, as he sketched it out—in which he would lead by the example of his personal probity, heal the partisan sickness that grips Washington, and solve problems in a practical, positive way—and his aggressive, ironic manner. Or,

when there wasn't this curious dissonance, there was instead a nearly instantaneous switching back and forth between serious and comic modes. The feeling was: We don't really have to be all official and sombre with each other, do
we? Can't we be real—which inevitably means a high quotient of kidding—instead? Here's an example:

ME: What do you do about the pure, horrible human-rights-abuse case happening in some corner of the world with no real strategic import to the United
States?

BUSH: And Rwanda's a great example of what you're referring to. There will be
times when the United States can lend its prestige and help and wealth to
help ameliorate a situation. But people should understand that I will commit
troops only where our strategic interests are involved. And, as you said,
there's no strategic importance to the United States.

ME: Was Somalia (*pronounced with a long "a"*) a mistake?

BUSH: Somalia (*pronounced with a short "a"*). Please, Nick. *(Mock-serious shocked
look—he'd scored another point.)* You know, I have to get every single word—
I'm a leader, I have to be correct a hundred per cent of the time. *(General
laughter in the front of the bus.)* I haven't unleashed my great line yet, which
is that my mother taught me not to be a know-it-all. *(Pause for a perfect beat,
quick innocent glance around the room.)* I didn't let her down. *(More laughter.
Bush acknowledges it with a broad smile, then turns serious again.)* You know,
it's an interesting question. What makes it interesting, of course, is that
Somalia was during my dad's Administration. And I try to avoid putting myself in a position where, you know, the headlines scream "BUSH CRITICIZES
FATHER." I think the big mistake, of course, is to change any humanitarian
relief mission into a political mission. Which is what the Clinton Administration did. The idea of getting troops in to distribute food and then get
them out of there is a reach, as far as I'm concerned, but I don't want to
second-guess.

What didn't happen in the interview was this: Bush's thinking about a question for a minute (or at least giving the appearance that he was), and then offering what came across as a considered, custom-tailored answer. Instead, the
couple of times when we got onto unplowed ground, he'd come back with a
non sequitur. I asked Bush about his position in favor of abolishing inheritance
taxes (something all the Republican candidates except John McCain are for). It
rarely comes up in the campaign, so I thought I might get a fresh answer:

ME: Let me ask you a question about the inheritance tax, or the death tax, which
you've repeatedly called—

BUSH (*jumping in*): Eight-year phaseout.

ME: More of a conceptual question. If you abolish it, over eight years or however many years, don't you wind up with a country that looks more like an aristocracy, because—

BUSH (*jumping in again*): No. Because I think wealth would be more likely to be dissipated, without the trusts and the legal documents that are formed to protect a wasted generation from squandering their granddaddy's lucre.

ME: So if you just give it to them instead of putting it in trust, then that would sort of solve that problem?

BUSH: Well, I think it's more likely that people who are unable to—I mean, I think people would spend their money. I do. Now, this inheritance situation for the, as you said, in quotes, the aristocracy, is: The trusts are pretty well protected by the laws, the tax laws. It's quite the opposite of what you said. The current law has tied up tons of wealth.

This seemed to me rooted more in some deep and long-standing well of emotion about no-good trust-fund kids than in logic, because even without inheritance taxes rich people can set up trusts. But I didn't get a chance to pursue it, because we had arrived in Manchester, early.

BUSH motioned for the bus driver to pull over at a Dunkin' Donuts and went inside, pulling me along. He shook the hand of everyone in the place, saying, in each case, "I'm George Bush. I'm askin' for your vote." When there weren't any hands left, we sat at a table and continued the interview for a while, in multitasking mode—Bush shifting between talking to me, talking to the people at the adjoining tables, and greeting anybody who came up to say hello.

When the possibilities of Dunkin' Donuts seemed to have been exhausted, Bush turned back to the three or four of us who were sitting with him and said, "Here's what we've learned. Two things. One, how many people there are in New Hampshire with a Texas connection. So far today, two. The other is—we ran into a Hispanic lady from Estado de Chihuahua—how many people from Mexico there are here."

It was time to get back on the bus. My interview was plainly over. I asked Bush what I should do now. "Usually what we do with guys like you is drop 'em on the road about a third of the way there," he said, with a little smile, "but you can ride with us to the high school." So I sat and watched while Bush chatted with the other people on the bus. He was relaxed and happy, but hardly at rest. His face was like a library of human mugging—eyebrow raises, cheek blowouts, lip purses, mock grimaces, feints of surprise, and, of course, the famous smirk, which, in this context, seemed to be just one aspect of an all-out effort, requiring the service of all body parts, not to be dull, rather than a way of appearing superior. At one point, he and the New Hampshire politicians got into a discussion of whether the Texas Rangers should re-sign Aaron Sele, the former Boston Red Sox pitcher who had just become a free agent. Bush shot me a glance that indicated that he reckoned the name Aaron Sele would be unfamiliar to someone like me. (True.) "Baseball player, Nicky." Evidently Bush's search for a nickname for me had now found its end point.

We all went into the high school, where Bush gave a short speech to wild applause and then held a press conference. Back on the bus, he indicated me, with a nod of his head, to the other people in the living room. "This guy says to me, 'You should talk about N.A.E.P. in there,' " Bush said. "But if I did that not a single person would know what I was talking about!" He'd scored again, but this time the levelling of a charge that everybody knew to be outlandish, a fable representing my impracticality, seemed to mean that I was being fitted out for a pleasant if somewhat distant spot in the Bush emotional universe.

As we drove on to Hudson for a reception, I moved back to the "follow car" with the advance people. Soon we arrived at the house of a Republican stalwart named Rhona Charbonneau. It was a dark, cozy place, decorated with enormous displays of tchotchkes—figurines, model cars, baseballs, commemorative dishes—and filled with a happy, expectant crowd of Party people. On the dining-room table was a cake in the shape of the White House. Bush's father, when he was President, had once done a similar event here, and so had Barbara Bush.

Bush took up a place that had been made for him, with a microphone and a spotlight, on a stair landing in the living room. He glanced around, shooting little arrows of recognition to faces he knew, and then he gave a short speech. It was the one he always gives, with slight situational variations. He begins by talking about his wife, Laura, and his twin daughters, Barbara and Jenna. He says that Laura used to be a public-school librarian and that now "her most important job title isn't First Lady, it's Mom." He says that his daughters didn't want him to run for President, but he is doing it anyway because he is worried about children "who can't access the American dream." And then you can tell that he's working around to the end when he brings up his twin daughters again. The last bit is a mock oath of office in which he says that when he takes office he'll put his hand on the Bible, laying one hand out palm down to demonstrate, and swear, raising the other hand, to restore honor and dignity to the office. The final words, delivered with his hand raised, are "So help me God!"

Speaking from a podium isn't Bush's natural métier. He tends to amble to the stage, rather than making a big kapow entrance. His gestures seem overrehearsed and a little awkward; for example, his standard emphasis move is to bend his knees slightly, tilt back the upper half of his body, throw out his palms, and deliver the line with a too predictable punch. His voice isn't a fabulous instrument, either: the range of tone and volume is too flat; it lacks richness and roundness. You can sense him itching to connect individually, to get back to having fun, as he speaks. At the Charbonneau house, while he was talking he spotted me standing against a wall. If there's such a thing as winking invisibly, that's what he did, and then he said to the audience, "There are some folks, really decent folks in this country, who want to have a national test. Not me!"

The big payoff was not the speech but the aftermath. Bush stepped down into the living room and started greeting people. Now he was almost glowing with the pleasure of being down in the room with his folks: pulling his face close to other faces, draping his arms across shoulders, kissing old ladies, registering exaggerated surprise or hilarity in response to what he was told, remembering the names of people who hadn't expected to have their names remembered. With the men, baseball came up a lot; with the women, his mother. In this and most other rooms, he was maybe the second-handsomest man—handsome enough to be magnetic, but short of the dangerous territory of being pretty or overtly sexual. He made you feel drawn to him, without feeling so strongly drawn to him that it was frightening. He went through the house person by person by person, interminably, making the sale every time. You could see how this scene, endlessly repeated all over the country in 1999, could have caused the world of Republican Party organizers to give him its heart.

When Bush finally left, he spotted me standing, a little expectantly, next to the door of the bus. "Nicky, you want to ride with us?" he said. "C'mon." So I got back on, positioning myself in the narrow spot between the front and back rooms of the bus. Bush signed baseballs for some of the local politicians and then gave some interview time to the reporter from Nashua. After a while, the bus pulled up at a hotel where he was going to be the dinner speaker. He had changed out of his jacket and tie during the day. Now he had to change back. To get to the dressing room, he had to brush past me, and as he did he said, sarcastically, "Nicky, I can't tell you what a pleasure it's been."

I moved up toward the door of the bus so that I could get off. In a moment, Bush reemerged from the back room. He was shaving with an electric razor. "So who you writing this article for, Nicky?" he asked me. I told him it was for *The New Yorker*—though we both knew he knew. "*The Noooo Yawkuh*," he said, rolling it out endlessly in a kind of Texan-imitating-an-upper-class-Brit accent. "I can't believe any of their readers would be interested in what I have to say." He grinned—yet another score. Then suddenly he was serious. "Do you know how they got my grade transcript?" I said I didn't. "Let me tell you, some people at Yale heard about that. The little girl who did that is the same little girl who asked me about mooning somebody."

He was referring to an episode a couple of months earlier in which someone from *The New Yorker* called to ask about a rumor that he had mooned the opposition at a Yale-Princeton football game in the sixties. I thought the way out of this moment would be to go back to the Nicky-and-the-Governor game we had developed, in which I was supposed to play the city slicker as comic foil. "What's mooning, Governor?"

But Bush was not in the mood for jokes. His face was flushed and hard. "Mooning's when you drop your pants and show somebody your rear end," he said, "and the answer's no." And then, as suddenly as the storm had come on, it passed. Bush finished shaving, shook my hand, reminded me that he'd seen Henry Thomas at the Mansion the previous evening, and stepped off the bus. The last time I saw him, he was working his way through a vast hotel dining room, bathed in the golden light of a television crew, shaking every single hand.

THE official story of George W. Bush's life, often repeated, is one of redemption: On his fortieth birthday, Bush dramatically renounces alcohol, his religious faith begins to deepen, and he embarks on a journey to his political destiny. It might help explain him better, though, to accept the premise but change the terms: Bush's redemption, indeed his whole story, makes more sense if understood as an interplay of class and personality and locale, rather than of God and man.

Whenever George W. Bush discusses his father, he visibly changes. The grinning, let's-have-fun look is gone. He alternates between two stances: deep reverence, and blustery anger at those who have done the old man wrong. In George W. Bush's world, George H. W. Bush—President Bush—is a godlike figure, held in genuine awe.

George H. W. Bush was born, in 1924, into a tightly enclosed, rich, influential group: high-Protestant, English-stock, boarding-schooled, Ivy-Leagued finance capitalists. To outsiders, members of this group look like easy inheritors, but from the inside one of the group's prime characteristics is felt to be a preoccupation—obsession even—with competition, the competition being usually limited, though, to its own membership. Within the group, George H. W. Bush was the guy who always won, the effortless possessor of the subculture's most prized (though unquantifiable) qualities: character, leadership, athleticism, and devotion to public service. Even his emigration to Midland, Texas, in the late nineteen-forties, was, in context, more a daring move than it was a self-exile or a spurning of his Wall Street destiny. In the pages of this magazine forty years ago, John Bainbridge marvelled at "the scores of eager, hard-driving young men, many of them graduates of Yale, Princeton, or other Eastern universities, who have flowed to Midland." Bainbridge's first example was Bush, identified as the son of a Connecticut senator.

George W. Bush grew up in Midland and Houston, but he was a member of the Texas Raj—a circle of Liedtkes and Bakers and Mosbachers, Texans who had educational and financial ties to the Eastern Seaboard élite—and, evi-

dently, it was expected that he, the firstborn son, would, whether finally resident in Texas or not, take up a position in his powerful ancestral subculture.
But this proved to be unexpectedly difficult, in a way that Bush couldn't have
failed to find painful. He lived in Midland until he was thirteen, by all accounts
happily (except for the tragedy of his younger sister's death from leukemia).
Then the family moved to Houston. Then he was sent East to the family schools,
Andover and Yale.

Bush almost immediately became a recognizable version of what he is today,
a hail fellow well met with a talent for establishing a jovial connection with an
unusually large number of people. The lead item on his Andover résumé was
head cheerleader. He was neither an outstanding student nor an outstanding
athlete, as his father had been. Also, he doesn't seem to have liked boarding
school. "Andover was cold and distant and difficult," Bush says in his new autobiography, "A Charge to Keep." "In every way, it was a long way from
home . . . forlorn is the best word to describe my sense of the place and my initial attitude. . . . It was a hard transition."

Clay Johnson, then another Texan at Andover and still one of the people
closest to Bush, told me that when the time came to apply to college the guidance counsellor at Andover told both of them that they really ought to consider
applying to the University of Texas as well as to Yale, the school they had in
mind—"which I took offense at," Johnson said. The implication was that they
might not be able to cut it at Yale. Yale evidently didn't agree, because it accepted both boys (those were the days when more than three dozen members of
every Andover graduating class got in), and they became roommates.

Just recently, the question of Bush's attitude toward Yale has become complicated. In 1978, when Bush was running unsuccessfully for Congress from
Midland, his opponents beat up on him for his Eastern education. In 1994,
when he was running successfully for governor of Texas, he took an anti-Yale
position. Now that he's running for President, he and his friends are emphasiz-
ing his positive feelings about Yale. "George *loved* Yale," another old roommate,
Terry Johnson, told me. "He was a fish totally in water. He thrived at Yale."

Still, even his friends will agree that over the years the Bush-Yale relationship has been bumpy. He has a well-known antipathy toward the other most famous member of the class of '68, Strobe Talbott, the Deputy Secretary of State,
who was the perfectly promising and eternally networking young man that
Bush wasn't. During the nineteen-eighties, he came to believe that his father
should get an honorary degree from Yale. He would grouse about what was
taking them so long, and then, when the degree was finally granted, in 1991,
he reported to his friends, furiously, that at the official reception the wife of the
president of the university, Helen Whitney, a documentary filmmaker, had refused to be in the same room with the President of the United States. In 1993,
he initially refused to make a twenty-fifth-reunion contribution to Yale, although in the end Clay Johnson talked him into it.

One may reconcile these accounts by surmising that Bush personally may have had a hell of a good time at Yale but he was also aware that the tide of the institution was running against his type. The leading item on his résumé there was being president of Delta Kappa Epsilon, the hardest-partying, baddest-boy, most athlete-venerating of the campus fraternities. He had two run-ins with the police as an undergraduate, once when he stole a Christmas wreath from a New Haven storefront for the Deke house, and again when he and a group of friends tore down the Princeton goalposts after a football game. He was quoted as a public figure in the Yale *Daily News* (Strobe Talbott, chairman) only in connection with the Dekes' practice of branding a Delta into each pledge's back ("There's no scarring mark physically or mentally," he said). And, as at Andover, he got to know lots and lots of people and made an unusual number of close friendships.

After Bush's class was admitted, Yale's new president, Kingman Brewster, Jr., a liberal-reformist New England patrician, brought in an insurrectionary new director of admissions, only twenty-nine years old, named R. Inslee Clark, Jr. Clark set about making Yale more of a national institution dominated by public-school graduates who were picked for their academic abilities. He made so many people mad that he lasted only five years in the job, but by that time the revolution was substantially complete. A good way of encapsulating the abrupt change from Old Yale to New Yale is this: George H. W. Bush is the eldest of four brothers. All four went to Yale. George W. Bush is the eldest of four brothers, too. He is the only one who went to Yale.

In the Old Yale, George W. Bush would have been a familiar and lovable figure, someone who felt entirely comfortable there. Living with a set of roommates from Andover, planning vaguely to go into business, being obviously talented at personal relations, being an unserious student, a Republican, the son, grandson, and cousin of dozens of Yalies—all of which applied to Bush—would have put him right at the center of the Yale experience. By the time Bush graduated, it put him at the periphery. In the fall of his junior year, the *Daily News* reported that fewer than two hundred and twenty-five people had attended the annual rush meeting at Delta Kappa Epsilon, down from more than four hundred the year before.

What was interesting about the change at Yale—which was part of a change along the same lines in the whole American élite—was that, while everybody agreed that something big had happened, they disagreed over what the something was. To most of the New Yale people, it was the advent of meritocracy, a system in which brains would be put in their rightful place atop the list of human attributes, and the deserving, not the inheritors, would get the rewards. To Old Yale people like Bush and his friends, the change looked more political—good old Republican Yale moving to the left. Terry Johnson told me that a graduate teaching assistant had declared to a class he was in, after the Watts riots of 1965, "The solution's simple. It's income redistribution. That solves the problem." Johnson—like Bush, an unusually fit and handsome middle-aged man—shook his head. "Not 'We have to focus on core things that will solve the problem. Skills. Education. Discipline.' No. Just 'Take from the rich and give to the poor.' There was a lot of that then." When he's in an anti-Yale mood, Bush talks about its being populated with "élitists" and "snobs." That would make him one of the ones being looked down upon. In the venue in which his birth entitled him to noble rank, unexpected events had now made him into a populist.

YALE was still Old enough, though, that it was assumed, without being stated, that most of the students didn't need to think about getting a job, because before they got there they already belonged to a network that could take care of that for them. Even in this context, Bush stood out as unusually undirected. Sam Chauncey, in those days a young Yale administrator who knew Bush, says, "I vividly remember sitting with him on the fence at Davenport College, and he said, 'I just don't have the foggiest idea what I want to do.' " Anyway, at that moment most Yale boys thought about life after graduation mainly as a short-term question of how to avoid going off to fight in the Vietnam War. A member of Bush's Yale crowd named George Carpenter got kicked out for a year for excessive hell-raising, which meant he temporarily lost his student deferment. He was drafted, sent to Vietnam, and killed in action. "That made it real to us," another of Bush's close friends from Yale, Roland Betts, says.

Bush returned to Houston and joined an Air National Guard unit that was well populated with children of prominent Texans who were looking for a respectable alternative to the front lines. Five years after finishing Yale, Bush applied to the University of Texas law school, which turned him down, and Harvard Business School, which accepted him. (Bush, a man with a long memory for slights, told me that when he became governor he "decided to have a little fun with the University of Texas folks. I said I didn't get in. Somehow the University of Texas overlooked the potential of George W. Bush, who now approved its budget.") At Harvard, as at Yale, he stood out for being fun-loving, gregarious, and unambitious.

Then he moved to his childhood home, Midland, and became an oilman—an unusual choice for a graduate of Harvard Business School in the seventies. Back then, the cult of the entrepreneur was almost unimaginably smaller than it is now; if you were smart and ambitious you went to work for a big corporation or, more likely, a consulting firm or an investment bank. In going to Midland, Bush wasn't participating in a tiny but distinct East Coast vogue of the day, either, as his father had done in going there. He was going home, and following in his father's footsteps.

Bush seems to have felt some impulse to conduct his life almost point by point as his father had. He went to Andover. He went to Yale. At an unusually young age, while still in college, he became engaged to a society belle from home, just as his father had. He became a military pilot. He went into the oil business in Midland financed by family connections, even giving the company he started a strikingly similar name to the one his father had started (George H. W. Bush: Zapata; George W. Bush: Arbusto—same language, same number of syllables, other end of the alphabet). He ran for Congress.

But at every step things didn't work out as well as they had for the old man. Andover was difficult. He did not conquer Yale. His fiancée, Cathy Wolfman, broke off their engagement. His military experience did not come anywhere near qualifying him as a hero, as his father's had. When his oil company made an initial public offering, only a million two hundred thousand dollars of the six million dollars in stock sold. He ran a strong race for Congress, but he lost. A lot of the explanation for the difference between the experience of the younger Bush and that of the elder lies in the individuals, but it's also true that they changed the rules on George W. Bush. By the time he was out of adolescence, he was part of a displaced élite. Over one generation, the Eastern Seaboard part of his world dramatically altered the qualities it valued. It made these changes without becoming any less competitive than it always had been; in fact, it probably became more competitive. All these changes worked against him personally. In that endless series of competitions, he kept coming up short. It was not merely in the spiritual sense that George W. Bush needed redemption.

Several years ago, Karl Rove, the strategist who has guided every detail of Bush's political career, brought to his attention a book by Myron Magnet called "The Dream and the Nightmare: The Sixties' Legacy to the Underclass," which was published in 1993. The book seems to have made a strong impression on Bush: Rove brought Magnet down to Austin in 1998 to talk to Bush's entire senior staff, then to Bush; and Bush talks about Magnet's book more often than he does the work of other anti-sixties authors, such as Marvin Olasky, whom Rove brought to his attention, and David Horowitz, whom Bush found on his own. Magnet blames just the kind of new academic liberals who were rising at Yale when Bush was there for the problems of the poor in America today: they challenged the moral verities so successfully as to engender, at the very opposite end of the socioeconomic scale, a disastrous wholesale change in the direction of permissiveness and relativism. "What I remember him telling me at lunch was that he'd been through the sixties," Magnet told me. "Been there, done that. It was extremely destructive. The culture was at the root of a huge proportion of America's problems, especially the underclass." So the sixties had done something much worse than push him aside. They had ruined the lives of millions of ordinary Americans, and even, it seems, been responsible for his own wild years, even though Bush was never self-consciously a sixties person. That would lend both an aspect of personal account-settling and a large social purpose to Bush's intent in 2000 to wrest national power from the élitists and the snobs.

. . .

BUSH never really made it in the oil business. His company got washed out in the bust of the mid-eighties. He merged it with a bigger company owned by two family friends from Ohio, and then sold that company to an outfit known for putting people with famous names on its board. In a world where money is how they keep score, he put in more than a decade, in very good times as well as bad ones, with unusual access to capital at favorable terms because of his family connections, and at the end of it he had amassed only a few hundred thousand dollars—chicken feed for an independent oilman. Being an entrepreneur wasn't what redeemed him. Instead, it was a combination of two things: Texas, and a new relation to his father which was much more workable than trying to follow him.

Bush fit in in Texas, culturally, politically, and socially, far more comfortably than he had in the Northeast. The whole package that being *le Texan homme moyen sensuel* entails—the business-venerating conservative politics, the devout non-High Church Christianity (Bush switched from Episcopalian to Methodist after he married), the reverence for sports and military heroes, the cowboy boots, the Western art, the bass fishing, the country music, the practicality, the friendliness to strangers, the endless deadpan ironic joking, the relatively low level of concern with the fine gradations of social status—was perfect for Bush. Unlike his father a generation earlier, it required no adjustment on his part to become a Texan, and no leap of imagination on Texas's part to think of him as one.

As Bush's oil business was sinking, in the late eighties, his father was starting a Presidential campaign. That was fortuitous timing. Bush moved to Washington and took up a post as a kind of official kibbitzer at the Bush for President office. He didn't have specific responsibilities; his job was to look out single-mindedly for his father's interests, travel and make speeches on his behalf, and keep an eye on the hired campaign staff, especially the campaign manager, Lee Atwater. He'd sit in his office with the door open, his boots up on the desk, a tin of Copenhagen snuff near at hand, gathering intelligence and, when necessary, kicking a little butt, just to make sure the staff knew they were subordinate to the President. The idea was that George W. Bush was especially useful to his father because he was tougher, more conservative, more political, and had a better instinct for the public mood. Having failed in his years of efforts to be exactly like his father, he now succeeded at a different project: making up for the elder Bush's shortcomings, chiefly excessive gentlemanliness, and avenging his losses. It wasn't exactly a dignified role, because it required playing the boss's son very heavily, well into middle age; Jeb Bush, by contrast, though seven years younger, was in Florida patiently building up an independent political base.

When the election was over and Bush had moved back to Texas, he'd still pop up to Washington sometimes and set errant employees of his father's straight, particularly if he suspected them of self-aggrandizement—the best-known example being the role he played in persuading John Sununu to resign as White House chief of staff. Not long ago, I went to see Sununu, who's an intensely proud man, to ask him what had really happened, and he took pains to emphasize that quitting was his own decision, that George W. Bush was only one of several people who had talked with him about it, and that Jeb was the Bush son with whom he generally discussed political matters. But, yes, they had talked: "He fell on the side of those who were encouraging me not to stay," Sununu said. "I've tried to think back to that conversation. I don't recall exact quotes. Being a buffer, taking lightning for the President—that analogy came up in some of my conversations. It was a very amicable conversation."

AFTER Sununu was gone, Bush tried, in vain, to put a little more fire in the belly of the 1992 reëlection campaign (Lee Atwater had died)—for example, by hunting around for evidence of incompetence by Ross Perot's computer company. He even moved back to Washington briefly. But by that time Bush's redemption had taken another enormous step forward. Just after the 1988 election, he found out that Eddie Chiles, an old friend of his father's from the oil business, wanted to sell the Texas Rangers. Bush seems to have regarded this as a political opportunity as much as a business opportunity—a way of putting himself before the public so that he could run for office. In 1989, he told Laurence I. Barrett, of *Time*, "My biggest liability in Texas is the question 'What's the boy ever done? So he's got a famous father and ran a small oil company. He could be riding on Daddy's name if he ran for office.' Now I can say, 'I've done something—here it is.' "

Because his record as a businessman in Midland was not confidence-inspiring, Bush, even though he was the son of the sitting President, did not have the ability to raise a lot of investment capital in Texas. What he did have was that special ability to make extraordinarily loyal friends. The biggest investors in the Rangers deal were his old Deke friend from Yale, Roland Betts, and Betts's partner, Tom Bernstein, former financiers of a string of Disney movies, and later the founders of the Chelsea Piers sports complex in Manhattan. Bush is often portrayed as having been set up with the Rangers by Richard Rainwater, the Forth Worth–based big daddy of Texas investing, but the real story is more interesting: Bush pitched Rainwater on the Rangers deal; Rainwater turned him down; Peter Ueberroth, then the commissioner of baseball, interceded with Rainwater, because he thought it wouldn't look good for Bush to buy the Rangers with out-of-town money, and persuaded him to get involved. Rainwater then recruited a bottom-fishing Dallas investor named Rusty Rose to join the investor group as a co-manager so that Bush wouldn't be solely responsible for running the team. In 1989, Bush took out a bank loan to buy a six-hundred-thousand-dollar stake in the Rangers, which he sold nine years later for fifteen million dollars. In 1990, Bush sold the last of his oil stock (shortly before the company reported a big quarterly loss) and used the proceeds to pay off his loan.

In the management of the Rangers, Rusty Rose was the financial guy; Bush was the public face of the team, in charge of dealing with fans and the press and politicians. This was especially important because part of what made the deal attractive to investors was the prospect of getting the citizens of Arlington, Texas, to approve a tax surcharge that would help pay for the construction of a new stadium for the Rangers.

Bush travelled around Texas, endlessly making speeches about the Rangers (meanwhile making himself known, too), and, most nights when the team was playing, sitting in an open owner's box down next to the field, grinning, shaking hands with fans, cheering for the Rangers, razzing their opponents, and handing out baseball cards that he'd had made with his picture on them. He was the head cheerleader again, and he was good at it.

Meanwhile, he was already in heavy consultation with Karl Rove, whom he had met back in the seventies, in Houston, through his father. He had thought about running for governor of Texas in 1990, and had decided not to, because Betts and the other investors wanted him to see through the turnaround of the Rangers, and because there would be negative synergy between his campaign and his father's Presidency. In 1994, with the elder Bush out of office and the Rangers thriving in their new stadium, he did run, and his brother Jeb ran for governor of Florida, too.

Bush's opponent was Ann Richards, who was probably best known nationally for making a speech at the 1988 Democratic National Convention in which she made fun of his father for having been "born with a silver foot in his mouth." Though popular in polls, Richards was an improbable figure as governor of Texas; she was a liberal and relatively inexperienced in politics. Texas is the most conservative big state—Karl Rove sent me a paper he wrote in 1997 neatly demonstrating that Republicans hold a substantial natural electoral advantage there.

Rove arranged a series of tutorials in Texas governance for Bush, and together they picked four campaign themes: education, juvenile justice, tort reform, and welfare reform. He relentlessly stuck to them; he had what's known in the trade as good message discipline. Richards's strategy was to get him to lose his well-advertised temper by constantly taunting him about the lightness of his record. He never did. In a Republican landslide year, he won by eight points—but his younger brother, who had been planning his political life for much longer, just barely lost, having staked out a place for himself that was too far to the right for Florida voters. Somewhat to the surprise of the Bush circle, George, not Jeb, was suddenly the leading politician in the family.

· · ·

IN discussions of George W. Bush's Presidential candidacy, it is often pointed out that Texas has a weak governorship—a grace note that gets struck a little too quickly and dutifully. The Texas constitution was adopted in 1876—in other words, just as the yoke of Reconstruction was being thrown off. T. R. Fehrenbach (who, by the way, has advised Bush on education) writes in "Lone Star," the standard history of Texas, that the governor "was left awesome responsibilities but few powers." The legislature is permitted to meet for only a hundred and forty days every other year. Many offices that are filled by gubernatorial appointment in other states are independently elected in Texas, so the governor doesn't have a cabinet. The lieutenant governor, who presides over the state senate and chairs the board that prepares the budget, is more powerful than the governor. One state-government budget analyst made a count for me of the number of people who report to the governor of Texas, and came up with a hundred and thirty-seven. Bush's budget director, Albert Hawkins, estimated the number at about two hundred. By contrast, the governor of Arkansas has fourteen hundred people working for him; the mayor of Chicago, forty-two thousand people.

The backlash against Reconstruction created not just a weak governorship but a one-party system—no Republicans. Together, these led to a tradition of pragmatic, conservative consensus politics in which the business-civic establishment, pursuing economic development as its overriding goal, has an ongoing power that doesn't fluctuate much with each election cycle. Today Texas is a two-party state, but the old style remains. The governor (in particular, Bush) will even campaign for legislators of the opposing party who have been supportive during the session.

The constitution gives Texas governance a particular flavor. Practically everything happens during the biennial legislative session—January through late May or early June in odd-numbered years—and the plupart of practically everything happens at the very end of the session. The citizen-legislators descend on Austin from far and wide (Texas is larger than France), and the vicinity of the capital takes on the atmosphere of a caravansary: jammed hotels and bars, drinking, parties, gossip, intrigue, love affairs, all building up to the end-of-session climax.

Bush did not govern in the Washington-executive manner, in which the head of state begins the year by issuing a great blueprint for all government policy and spending. He opened his governorship by issuing a "budget policy message" of three double-spaced pages, rather than a budget. Still, his first session was a big success. He made himself an ally, even a protégé, of the speaker, Pete Laney, and the lieutenant governor, Bob Bullock—both Democrats. He was friendly and accessible to the legislators, as Richards had not been. He'd take them to ballgames or invite them for a meal at the Mansion. The Texas economy was better than it had been for a long time. In the areas of all four campaign promises, the legislature passed major bills, and all four bills were distinctly influenced by Bush, even if they weren't his, exactly.

Bush's signature issue, education, is a perfect example of the Texas way. Education reform in Texas began in the mid-eighties, when a Democratic governor appointed Ross Perot, who was then a Republican, to run a commission on Texas schools. Since then, and especially since a series of lawsuits forced the legislature to equalize funding between school districts, education reform has been the big item in every session of the legislature.

Texas has supported education reform partly because the business interests, terrified by the oil busts of the eighties, want a state economy built around a literate and numerate workforce. There aren't any teachers' unions in Texas, only "associations," which removes from the equation some of the automatic conservative suspicion of public education. Also, Texas has a much less entrenched class system than the East does. Everybody at least pretends to be just a generation away from small-town lower-middle-class life, which revolves around high-school sports. Considering the size of the state, there still aren't a lot of private schools. The typical prosperous Texan has a better feeling for the problems of a kid in public school than the typical prosperous New Yorker. This is evidently the case with Bush, who went to Texas public schools and who learned in the East what it feels like to be branded as inferior in school. Nobody would accuse him of having developed a mastery of all areas of Texas public policy, but he did learn the ins and outs of education.

The over-all effect of all those years of education-reform efforts in Texas has been to create a much more centralized system, of the kind that Bush accused me of liking. Under a "Robin Hood" law, the rich districts have to give serious money to the poor ones. The state has produced central curriculum standards, and has commissioned tests specifically based on them. Every student in the public schools has to take the Texas tests in reading and math from the third through eighth grades. The scores are tabulated by race and class; each district has to maintain, at a certain level, not just its average scores but the scores of its black, Hispanic, and poor students or suffer hard consequences. And minority scores have gone up dramatically.

Bush did not invent this accountability system, but he has supported it strongly. When the right made runs against curriculum standards, state tests, and the keeping of separate data for minority students so that districts could be forced to take measures to raise their performance, Bush defended the system. He could pick out a conservative cause or two to push for each session, such as providing state financing to charter schools, and get credit for the over-all results produced by the more liberal aspects of education reform while maintaining his conservative credentials.

. . .

IN his second session as governor, Bush, high on the success of the first session, tried something much more ambitious, and he failed. As a matter of holy writ, Texas has no state income tax. The schools have to rely mainly on property taxes, which have been rising fast. Bush wanted to shift the tax burden dramatically away from property taxes, which would help both middle-class homeowners and big oil companies (three-fifths of property-tax revenues come from business). He picked up an idea that Charls Walker, a Washington corporate super-lobbyist (and native Texan), has been pushing for years—a value-added tax on goods and services—as the way to make up the revenue lost from property-tax cuts. This would have been an achievement of a different order of magnitude from the first session's, because now Bush was trying to initiate a major policy on his own, not accelerate and modify the course of actions that Bullock and Laney and the legislature were already taking.

However, Bush hadn't anticipated how furious the opposition would be from those in the business-civic establishment who would have seen their taxes go up. Pete Laney, the speaker, appointed a special committee on property-tax reform, which simply shelved Bush's bill and wrote a new version, which Bush endorsed and campaigned for. It passed in the House, but the Senate passed a much weaker version, and in conference—after a typically frenetic end-of-session fiesta of lobbying, including individual pleas to members by Bush—it died.

Bush was able to save face by getting a much smaller property-tax cut passed, which wound up not having much net effect on most homeowners' bills. The episode shows a major weakness on his part—he couldn't pass what was by far the biggest proposal of his governorship—but it also shows some strengths. He didn't brood or sulk. He got something. And he pushed to make sure that the tax cut was directed at ordinary homeowners, which he didn't have to do. Still, the failure of the tax bill was a big loss. Sam Howe Verhovek, writing in the *Times* at the end of the session, called it "the first big setback of his gubernatorial term" and suggested that the defeat would hurt Bush if he made a run for the Presidency in 2000.

But then, curiously, it didn't matter. Right after the session ended, Bush began showing up in national polls as the most popular of the possible Republican Presidential candidates. Under the obsessively detailed direction of Karl Rove, he put himself on display to the key elements of the Party—speaking at fund-raisers around the country, working Republican governors' meetings, campaigning for senators and congressmen, forging alliances with such important Christian conservatives as Pat Robertson and Ralph Reed. In 1998, he ran for reëlection and crushed his liberal Democratic opponent, Garry Mauro. Not very long after his second inauguration, Bush, whose entire official experience in public life consisted of one term as governor of a state with a weak governorship, had been essentially anointed as the Republican nominee.

BUSH spent 1998 and 1999 winning over a tough-minded, committed group of political insiders, the kind of people who know that they're going to bet on a horse in the Republican Presidential campaign. If you were one of those people in late 1998 and you looked at George W. Bush, you would see a man who not only just got reëlected governor of the second-biggest state in the country with almost seventy per cent of the vote but who led the entire Republican ticket in Texas—seventeen other people—to victory. That's right: there are no Democratic statewide officeholders in Texas today. You would see a man who had cut deeply into constituencies the Republicans have trouble with, notably women (Bush got sixty-five per cent of the female vote in 1998) and Hispanics (forty-nine per cent). Twenty-seven per cent of registered Democrats voted for Bush, which brings to mind the possibility that he could have a Ronald Reagan-like appeal to swing voters nationally. You might have met George Bush, seen him perform at a fund-raiser or been brought down to Austin by Rove for a meeting with him, at which he'd have been more impressive than you'd expected him to be—mature, sincere, and decently well versed, apparently no longer the hotheaded kid of his father's Presidential campaigns.

Counterposed to all this was the Party's grim situation in Washington, where the Republicans had bet very heavily on President Clinton's impeachment, had lost seats in the congressional elections, and had watched in horror after the elections as first Newt Gingrich and then his successor as Speaker of the House, Bob Livingston, melted down in public. If you were looking for somebody who was the opposite of Newt Gingrich, you couldn't do much better than Bush: he was normal, he was fit, he was middle-of-the-country, he wasn't frighteningly ambitious, he was faithful to his wife, as an officeholder he made deals not war, he was comforting not scary, and, if you thought about it, maybe Gingrich had been a little too brainy and bookish all along.

This non-primary primary fed on itself. Bush's fund-raising operation officially opened for business on March 7, 1999. Within a month, it had raised six million dollars just in contributions at the thousand-dollar maximum, from early bet-placers, Texas friends, loyal names from Bush family Rolodexes, lobbyists, baseball friends, Yale friends, Andover friends, friends of Bush's Republican governor friends—a great outpouring of love, during times so good that it was easy for the members of the professional-managerial-entrepreneurial class and their families to write thousand-dollar checks. (By the end of 1999, when the Bush fund-raising total stood at sixty-three million dollars, nearly eighty-five per cent of the total had come in the form of five-hundred-dollar and thousand-dollar contributions.) Bush's enormous fund-raising success sent a signal that loosened more endorsements from Republican politicians in the states and in Congress. The contributions and the endorsements generated awestruck press attention and scared opponents like Elizabeth Dole and Dan Quayle out of the race long before a vote had been cast.

During the last six months of 1999, Bush delivered a series of speeches that touched on all the main policy areas of the federal government. What emerged in the highest relief from these were two slogans that denoted the main distinctive theme of his campaign: "compassionate conservatism" and "prosperity with a purpose." These stick in the mind because no Presidential candidate in decades has dared to run on compassion, or even mention it prominently. Even today, only a Republican could do it—coming from a Democrat, people would think that higher taxes were on the way.

For Bush, though, compassion has a lot of political benefits. It instantly puts to rest the question of what his message is. It helps to position him as a moderate for the general election. It wins over the liberal press, assuages Republican women who find the Gingrich–Tom DeLay–Dick Armey wing of the Party too struttingly confrontational, and appeals to minority voters. The non-obvious constituency for compassionate conservatism is evangelicals, with whom the imagery of love and redemption and higher purpose resonates.

Inside the Republican Party, compassionate conservatism—the idea, if not the precise slogan—long predates Bush's interest. In 1983, at the height of the Reagan revolution, an Indiana congressman named Dan Coats, a former aide to Dan Quayle, conservative and devoutly Christian, began to push for a distinctly Republican way of running anti-poverty programs (as an alternative to simply abolishing them). The idea would be to fund groups that promote "values," because they can turn people's lives around by getting them to give up self-destructive behavior. Most of these groups have a religious affiliation. In the nineties, after Coats had been elected to the Senate, he started the Project for American Renewal, which brought together Christian groups, conservative politicians, and intellectuals (mostly Catholic) interested in a revival of "civil society." Bush's chief speechwriter, Mike Gerson, used to work for Coats. Bush's chief domestic-affairs adviser, Stephen Goldsmith, who just stepped down as mayor of Indianapolis, started a program there called the Front Porch Alliance, run by a former Coats aide, that funded religious anti-poverty programs. Bush made his big compassionate-conservatism speech last summer at a Front Porch Alliance event in Indianapolis.

These ideas appeal deeply to Bush. They have three hooks, all powerful for him: the recognition of the force of religious faith, especially as an influence on behavior; the implication, which runs through most of the faith-based social-program literature, that the liberal élitists took a crack at the country's social problems in the sixties and botched the job; and the extension of Bush's own life story to millions of troubled people at the other end of American society.

Faith-based social programs offer a very Bush mixture of redemption (for the devout poor) and competition (with liberal do-gooders).

It doesn't necessarily follow, though, that the rhetoric of compassionate conservatism would unerringly lead to a major change in direction for the federal government. The main mechanism for compassionate conservatism would be government grants to faith-based social programs—some of which already get government grants and have for years. It's possible to make a lot of fuss about compassionate conservatism without changing existing policy much. The test will come once Bush is in office. (The same goes for Al Gore, who has also endorsed the idea of new government help for faith-based social programs.)

THE truth is that although Bush may turn out to be another Reagan in his ability to attract voters, it's already obvious that he isn't going to be another Reagan in the sense of trying to revolutionize the national polity. Even prospectively, he doesn't propose anything dramatic. He says constantly that he wants to do a few things and do them well. He likes to describe himself as a problem solver. He wants to increase the defense budget, but only modestly, much less than the Republican right would like. In foreign policy, he would be a "fierce free trader," but that's what Clinton has been. He would do less humanitarian intervention abroad (no Haitis in the Bush Administration), but he would be a strong internationalist. He would tilt slightly toward Taiwan, but not enough to disrupt trade with China. He would cut the top income-tax rate, but not to the extent that Reagan did. He would protect Social Security. On education, he has a lot of small ideas that don't seem to add up to the kind of major commitment of government resources that Texas undertook on his watch.

What George W. Bush really offers us is himself. When Republicans talk about him, what you hear is an intense loathing for Bill Clinton, and an equally intense desire to take back the White House. Things about Bush that might ordinarily appear unremarkable—that may, in fact, be true of you and most people you know—are rhetorically elevated to Presidential qualifications by the implied comparison with Clinton. Bush is happily and faithfully married. He has close friends. He is "comfortable in his own skin." He wants to be President, but he doesn't *need* to be President. He doesn't read polls and conduct focus groups before every move he makes. When there is a decision to make, he chooses the option that he thinks represents the right thing to do. He would conduct the Presidency with the principles of dignity and honor in mind.

Bush's opponents and the press have put a lot of effort into finding some Presidentially disqualifying datum about him: he may have used cocaine, he doesn't know the names of world leaders. Actually, the main argument against him is hiding in plain sight: compared with other Presidents, he just hasn't done very much in his life. If (I'd guess when) he takes office this time next year, he'll come to the Presidency with a lighter résumé than anybody has in at least a hundred years: Helping to manage a professional sports franchise and a term and a half as governor of Texas. Openly admitted drift before that. No experience handling a crisis or solving a major conflict. Good political instincts and a gift for connecting with people. A decent, trustworthy guy. Not especially knowledgeable or curious, but a quick study. Growing. That's it.

The idea of Bush as President runs counter to the American tradition of giving the job to someone who has spent a lifetime being outstanding. The tradition encompasses even the Presidents we think of as lightweights: Harry Truman had held political office for more than twenty years before he became President, in 1945; Warren Harding was in public life from 1899 until he became President, in 1921; John F. Kennedy was a member of Congress (first the House, then the Senate) from 1947 until he became President, in 1961. Ronald Reagan rose from obscurity to become a prominent actor, the head of a labor union, a two-term governor of California, and a three-time Presidential candidate before he took office. George H. W. Bush was the kind of person friends were predicting would one day be President practically from his teenage years onward. Dwight Eisenhower spent his whole life in public service and organized the conquest of Europe. George W. Bush's ascension would represent the apotheosis of an ordinary man.

KARL Rove has a riff, which he gives to anybody who will listen, entitled "It's 1896." Every national political reporter has heard it, to the extent that it induces affectionate eye-rolling when it comes up. "It's 1896" is based on Rove's reading of the work of a small school of conservative revisionist historians of the Gilded Age (that is, historians who love the Gilded Age), one of whom, Lewis Gould, taught a graduate course that Rove took at the University of Texas.

Here's the theory, delivered at Rove's mile-a-minute clip: "Everything you know about William McKinley and Mark Hanna"—the man elected President in 1896 and his political Svengali—"is wrong. The country was in a period of change. McKinley's the guy who figured it out. Politics were changing. The economy was changing. We're at the same point now: weak allegiances to parties, a rising new economy."

Interested, I went to the library and read up on McKinley. There are a couple of big differences between this campaign and the one in 1896: it was a recession campaign run on economic issues, and McKinley's main proposal, high protectionist tariffs, runs opposite to Bush's position on the same issue. But the similarities are indeed striking—so striking as to make you wonder whether Rove deliberately followed the Hanna-McKinley playbook as he coached

George W. Bush through his astonishingly rapid transformation from aimless Presidential son to putative President.

McKinley was a man with an "amiable disposition" and a "winning demeanor," great at political handshaking events, who was elected and then reëlected governor of the most important state between the coasts, Ohio. He was unusually popular, for a Republican, with urban workers and ethnic minorities. When he ran into financial trouble, his rich friends took up a collection and bailed him out. He even proposed a big reduction in Ohio property taxes.

Mark Hanna, who devoted himself full time to making McKinley President, engineered a "front-porch campaign," involving a staged procession of prominent visitors to McKinley's home in Canton, which worked so well that McKinley was able to lock up the Republican nomination early. Then Hanna systematically raised much more money than any previous Presidential campaign ever had, and used it to fund an unprecedentedly heavy media campaign (in the form of widely distributed pamphlets) and a massive organizational effort in the states. And, in winning, McKinley ushered in a period in which the Republicans, as the Party representing business prosperity in the new industrial age, controlled the White House right up to the Great Depression, with the exception of Woodrow Wilson's two terms.

Lewis Gould has noted hopefully that McKinley is rising into the middle ranks of Presidential greatness, but the main event of his Presidential term, the Spanish-American War, caught him flat-footed. George W. Bush represents the hope not so much of a redirection of the federal government as of another Republican restoration, one that would put the White House back in the hands of the party of business and—by bringing suburban, female, and minority voters into the Republican coalition—perhaps do so for a good long time.

For Bush himself, it would be a restoration in more than just that way. People who know him say he's itching to take on Al Gore in the general election. When Bush talks about Gore, he does so in a way that makes it clear that he has him pegged as a member of the liberal-intellectual coterie that rose to power in the sixties, at Yale and elsewhere. He has been quoted more than once as saying that he realized Gore didn't have the right touch when he read an interview Gore gave to Louis Menand for *The New Yorker*—an interview in which Gore dropped the name Merleau-Ponty. Bush told an old friend who had lunch with him in Austin last spring that he can't wait to go "*mano a mano*" with Gore. When asked to state succinctly the difference between Gore and himself, he'll usually say that he went to San Jacinto Junior High School, in Midland, Texas, and Gore went to St. Albans, in Washington, D.C. It's going to be a regular guy versus an archetypal member of the new élite—no contest.

But, of course, George W. Bush is not just a non-member of the new élite; he's a fully born-in member of the old élite. If not his class, certainly his family, discussed in almost genetic terms, is an explicit part of the argument for his candidacy. It has to be: imagine how thin his claim on the Presidency would be without the family connection. Many of the people around Bush believe that the American people realize they made a mistake in denying George H. W. Bush a second term in 1992, and now they have a chance to remedy it. "People remember the integrity and rectitude of his father, of his family," C. Boyden Gray, an old Bush Administration hand, told me. "He comes by that by virtue of having the name Bush."

A couple of months before I travelled with Bush in New Hampshire, I was granted a brief telephone interview. His sharpest, most alive answer by far came in response to the question of what lesson he had taken from his father's defeat in 1992. "First lesson, polls change," he said. "I take nothing for granted. Second, we've got a strategy for the timing of policy speeches. It's important to have a strategy and set the debate. In many ways, they didn't spend the capital wisely. It was reactive in many ways. It wasn't necessarily my dad's fault. It was a two-front war. You die a death of a thousand cuts in politics. Buchanan inflicted a lot of cuts, and then Perot picked it up. He got defined as somebody who didn't care about the domestic economy and how people were doing at home. They defined him before he could define himself."

Bush is obviously out to rectify those mistakes. If his father was too politically passive, too concerned with foreign affairs, too unconnected to people's daily lives, well, George W. Bush is going to be the opposite on every count. In fact, if the 2000 election is a replay of 1992, the roles, as cast by George W. Bush, will be reversed: Gore, the essence-of-Washington, excessively loyal Vice-President, surrounded by high-priced, self-serving political consultants, plays George H. W. Bush. Bush, the politically gifted, empathetic, cunning Southern governor, with his cadre of totally loyal and subservient aides, plays Bill Clinton. The result would be elaborately satisfying. A Bush would be back in the White House. Those ethereal qualities that Bush's class thinks of as innate to its members—good character and leadership—would be enshrined as more important than earnest book learning. And George W. Bush would have progressed from trying to emulate his father, to protecting him from his shortcomings, to, finally, outdoing him, which might have been the idea all along.

(2000)

GORE WITHOUT A SCRIPT

T OWARD the end of his political career, Senator Albert Gore, Sr., wrote a
couple of books, one on the eve of the 1970 Senate campaign and the
other, which was longer and told a bit more "with the bark on," as they say in
Tennessee, a couple of years later. To read them now is to be taken back to a
time in American politics when notes were struck that nobody strikes anymore.

Senator Gore grew up on a struggling farm in the hills of middle Tennessee.
In the evenings, the family would sit around a kerosene lamp, and the father
would talk about his hero—William Jennings Bryan, the Great Commoner.
Senator Gore managed to cobble together an education for himself over many
years, by working his way first through a local teachers' college, then a night
law school conducted at the Y.M.C.A. in Nashville. It was there that he met his
wife, Pauline, who was working her way through Vanderbilt Law School by
waiting on tables in a coffee shop in the evenings. Gore's first full-time job, as a
schoolteacher, paid seventy-five dollars a month.

The Depression hit the Gore family very hard. Senator Gore's father, fearing
for the stability of the local banks in Smith County, Tennessee, divided his savings among three of them. All three failed, and he lost everything. When the
future Senator's father went to sell his crops that year, he made eighty-nine dollars, and Gore remembered the scene of "grown men who were so desperate
the tears streamed down their cheeks as they stood with me at the window to
receive their meager checks for a full year's work." During that time, George
H. W. Bush, the father of this year's other Presidential candidate, was a student

at Greenwich Country Day School, to which he was driven every morning by his family's chauffeur.

Salvation arrived, in the form of Franklin Roosevelt and the New Deal. F.D.R. brought electricity to rural Tennessee. F.D.R. proposed higher taxes on corporations and the rich. F.D.R. made a speech about the South in which he said, "When you come right down to it, there is little difference between the feudal system and the fascist system." Gore was elected to the United States Congress, and later to the Senate, where he fought constantly against tax cuts, privatization, tight money, Wall Street, and the Federal Reserve Board. When, for example, he heard that John F. Kennedy, the newly elected President, was going to appoint a Wall Street man, C. Douglas Dillon, as Secretary of the Treasury, he retreated to his farm in Carthage, Tennessee, and wrote Kennedy a blistering letter, warning that "such an appointment would be a signal that you had given up the goals of a truly Democratic Administration." Gore's oldest granddaughter, Karenna Gore Schiff, remembers him once introducing her to a new farmhand who hesitated to shake her hand because his was dirty. Gore laughed and motioned for her to shake hands anyway, advising her to say, "That's all right—I'm a Democrat."

Gore lost his seat in 1970, to a rising young man of the Republican Party, Bill Brock. The race was widely seen as a last hurrah for old-fashioned Southern populism. In Tennessee, the Democratic Party, which had dominated state politics for all of living memory, and which, indeed, had practically been invented in Tennessee (Andrew Jackson lived within a hundred miles of where Senator Gore was born), seemed to have expired practically overnight. In 1966, the Republicans took one of Tennessee's Senate seats. In 1970, they took the other, and the governorship, too. The old dream of Southern liberals, which animates Senator Gore's writings, was that if they could ever kill off the Jim Crow system blacks and poor whites could make common, populist cause against the Bourbons and their moneyed allies in New York. Now Jim Crow was dead, and the opposite was happening: the white South was going Republican. Gore saw his last race as a primal struggle between good and evil; in his post-defeat book, he approvingly quotes David Halberstam, who wrote, in *Harper's*, of Brock's campaign slogan, "Bill Brock Believes": "Believes is the code word for Nigger."

From the Democratic point of view, the Party was the victim of its own success. By taxing and spending, it had managed to get some money into the hands of the flat-busted country farmers of the Depression South. Now they were doing better, beyond their dreams, really, and a lot of their children weren't farmers anymore. They had gone to college, thanks to programs the Democrats had passed, and modern industry had come to the South, thanks to the Democrats' ending segregation and building dams and power plants and highways (Albert Gore was the chief sponsor of the bill that created the interstate-highway system), and they had white-collar jobs and were living in new houses in the suburbs—and voting Republican.

Not long ago in Nashville, I went to see James Neal, the former Watergate prosecutor, who has been a friend of the Gore family since the nineteen-fifties and is now the lawyer for Al Gore, in the matter of his fund-raising in 1996. He told me that when he was growing up—the son of a middle-Tennessee farmer, in a house with no indoor plumbing—his father used to point out to him a man named Roark who lived in their part of the country, and say, "Look, son! There's a Republican!" Neal was telling me this story in his office, on the twentieth floor of a plate-glass Nashville skyscraper. He was wearing bluejeans and scuffed boots and chewing on an unlit cigar that looked about a foot long. "He must have pointed that guy out to me twenty times," Neal said. "It was like he was a man with two heads. Now I see these people out in Brentwood who drive a Lexus, who belong to my country club, and they curse the government. And I sit and listen to them! Drive a Lexus and condemn the party that got you there. That's what it amounts to."

If you drive the fifty miles from Nashville out to Carthage, the plain little town that is still the Gore family seat, you see that almost everything built in the last forty years is grander than almost everything built before then, and that the new construction—the malls and the subdivisions—is creeping out toward Carthage. Nissan and Saturn have built factories not too far away, something inconceivable in the stone-agrarian South of the Depression. In the 1996 Presidential election, the hapless Dole-Kemp ticket was just one point behind in Al Gore's old congressional district.

This isn't just a regional story, or one of particular interest because of who is running for President. Most of the dominant national politicians of the past decade are people whose formative experience as young politicians was in figuring out how to play the South's abrupt and dramatic shift from Democratic to Republican. This is the story of George H. W. Bush's political life, and of George W. Bush's, and of Jeb Bush's, and of Newt Gingrich's and Dick Armey's and Tom DeLay's—they were in the rising group; and then in the falling group, the one that had to deal with the foundation's being knocked out from under it, are Bill Clinton and Al Gore. Gore's entire political life has been about trying to survive within a tradition that he was born into and watched die. In that situation, you either become very, very nimble or very, very careful. Al Gore himself once wrote, "I grew up in a determinedly political family, in which I learned at an early age to be very sensitive—too sensitive, perhaps—to what others were thinking, and to notice carefully—maybe too carefully—the similarities and differences between my way of thinking and that of the society around me."

At least in his writings, Albert Gore, Sr., always insisted that the South could be the most liberal region of the country and that the post-civil-rights return to economic populism was still on the way. In one of his books, though, he did make a concession to changing times. He proposed passing the torch to a new type of populist:

This reconstruction of our country from within calls for guidance by men who live neither in the memories of the past nor in the emotions of the present; it calls for guidance by men who are pre-eminently thinkers, men who, let it be said very simply, are concerned with a future-oriented understanding of things—it calls for guidance, if you will, by the intellectuals who over the years have voiced many of the latent convictions and beliefs of the poor and downtrodden.

Al Gore was intimately involved in his father's last campaign and therefore in the final bitterness of it. He travelled with the old man. When his father decided that he needed to buy television ads, Gore appeared in them, wearing a military uniform and being told, "Son, always love your country." Although Gore's service in Vietnam is usually held up as an example of his devotion to his father—he enlisted in part because it seemed required by the 1970 campaign—Halberstam's article in *Harper's* suggests that the father might actually have liked the idea of running a campaign alongside a son who refused to go to Vietnam. But when changing times took out the elder Gore the younger one had to play his ambitions quite differently. What the father wrote about the advent of an emotionless, intellectual, futurist strain of populist would have been the script—and, beneath Al Gore's many protective layers, it remains the script, as I discovered when I was able to talk with him. He displayed a degree of thoughtfulness and study, and also of abstraction from the daily world, that is astonishing in a Presidential candidate in mid-campaign.

IN the middle of June, Al Gore unveiled a new theme for his Presidential campaign in a speech at the New-York Historical Society, on the West Side of Manhattan. If you haven't spent time in the vicinity of a sitting Vice-President of the United States—in White House lingo, a V-POTUS—it's surprising how much apparatus is involved. Air Force Two sits on the runway at La Guardia, city streets get closed off, police are everywhere outside and Secret Service everywhere inside. You have to arrive an hour ahead of time. Dogs have to sniff you before you can sit in the audience. This has the effect of raising the ante on Gore, wherever he goes—you feel that for all this trouble you should get a big payoff.

But on this particular day, after the audience had been assembled and had sat waiting for a good while in the auditorium, Gore merely ambled onstage from the wings, accompanied by Robert Rubin, the former co-chairman of Goldman, Sachs and former Secretary of the Treasury, who is now with Citigroup, and who also ambled. The Democratic Party had made peace with Wall Street. Gore's new campaign theme was Prosperity and Progress. There was a logo behind the lectern with those words printed repeatedly across a map of the United States. Gore sat in a chair, motionless as a wax figure, while Rubin introduced him, stressing the role Gore had played in a project that his father had not considered very worthy during his officeholding days: eliminating the federal deficit.

I had been watching Gore speak all spring. He has held elective office continuously for twenty-four years, so he has an enormous amount of experience at this. Still, it obviously doesn't come naturally to him. He is poised, he has a rich, booming voice, but he doesn't often "inhabit the role," in the acting sense; instead, every move seems calculated and practiced. I kept thinking of that early scene in "Terminator 2," when Arnold Schwarzenegger, as a cyborg, walks into a biker bar, and a digital readout flashes across the inside of his eyelids, giving height, weight, and build of each person he sees. Similarly, you can see Gore read a situation, pause while the script flashes, formulate his response— and then react. He has an odd quality of taking in what he's seeing with an almost digitalized exactitude (that's why, in private, he's supposed to be a gifted mimic), while appearing to be oblivious. Rubin, at one point in his introduction, glanced fondly over at Gore. Gore froze, got the readout (*Introducer interacting with V-POTUS. Must respond*), smiled broadly, and then went back into the waxworks.

Gore has two basic modes when he gives speeches. One is meant to play as "high energy" and the other as statesmanlike. In high-energy mode, he speaks in a Southern accent and takes the stage at a trot. He pivots his body from side to side, bouncing a little on the balls of his feet, and gestures with both hands; all this makes it look as if his hands were controlled by one puppeteer and his body by another. In statesmanlike mode, he has no accent, he walks, and he stands behind a lectern making rolling gestures with one hand. On this day, he was in a kind of enhanced version of statesmanlike: he spoke more peppily than usual, and he used a teleprompter, but his face was like a block and his rhetoric was full of village-elder words like "discipline," "conscience," "decency," "security," "responsibility," and "trust." Then, at the end, he pumped it up a little. When he perorates, Gore slows down his delivery and lowers his voice to a stage whisper. "We will win this fight!" he said. "We will not rest! Hear me now!" When he finished, the song "You Ain't Seen Nothing Yet" came loudly over the speaker system and he walked out from behind the lectern and shook hands for a while. The speech he had delivered was to the word identical with the text his staff had handed out. It was impossible to leave the room with the feeling that you had been brought into the intimate presence of the real Al Gore.

Gore went off somewhere for the rest of the afternoon, and after dinner he flew to Scranton, Pennsylvania, the next leg of the Prosperity and Progress tour. The event on his schedule was one of the great boilerplate items in Presidential politics, a rally at an airport hangar. I arrived before Gore, in a plane the campaign had chartered for the travelling press. Some of us joined a good-sized crowd in the hangar, and others of us decided to skip the event and go out for dinner. A loudspeaker was playing the kind of up-tempo, glass-rattling anthems that you hear over the sound system at major-league baseball games. Most of the people there were white, middle-aged, and middle class, and they didn't seem at all put out to be waiting around in a hangar for Gore to arrive. It's not every day that you see the Vice-President of the United States up close.

One reason Gore had come here was that there was a very close local race for state representative, a special election that would put the Democrats one seat away from a majority in the Pennsylvania legislature, and that would affect redistricting. There was a podium set up, and the candidate for state representative got up and spoke. His name was Jim Wansacz, and he was twenty-eight years old—just about the same age as Al Gore when he made his first run for office. Wansacz's father had held the same seat years earlier, and now the son was trying to get it back. He seemed impossibly young and raw, out of place in the suit he was wearing, like a boy at his First Communion. He got up and spoke, hoarsely, with a desperate energy, waving his arms, about how much he loved his mother and father—he didn't seem to feel the need, and neither did the audience, for public-policy talk. As he got a little way into how wonderful his parents were, he started to cry. Then he changed the subject to Al Gore. "He came to *our* area!" Wansacz shouted. "He cares about the same issues *we* care about!"

It turned out that several of the politicians in the hangar that night were the scions of political families. Besides Jim Wansacz and Al Gore, there was an Eisenhower (a distant cousin of Dwight) who was running for state attorney general, and two sons of Bob Casey, the former governor of Pennsylvania (he died earlier this year), one of whom is Pennsylvania's auditor general, the other of whom is running for the U.S. House of Representatives. It was possible to imagine, watching the scene, that the dreams of Albert Gore, Sr., had come true: the children of the miners and factory workers and farmers of his day had become teachers and firefighters, and they were still Democrats. And the children of the old populist politicians were New Democrats, but still fighting, delivering a new kind of public goods to their people, preschool and prescription drugs instead of electricity and running water and banks that wouldn't fail.

Air Force Two landed, taxied, and parked so as to be perfectly framed in the doorway of the hangar, fifty yards away. Various people emerged from the plane, limousines materialized on the runway, the ballpark music came up, and then there was a long, long pause. Finally, Gore appeared in the doorway of the plane. He stopped, waved, walked down the stairway, and then ran at a dead sprint across the runway to the hangar. It may sound corny, but if you were there it was really exciting, the spotlighted Vice-President running toward you. The crowd cheered, and Gore mounted the podium. He seemed relaxed and happy, even though it must have been a brutally long day for him. In a deep Southern accent, he said that Tipper says hello and that they had just celebrated their thirtieth wedding anniversary. Had anybody else been married thirty years? That's great. And we just became grandparents for the first time. Any other grandparents here?

Gore was speaking into a handheld microphone, without a script, lustily promising things—prescription-drug benefits, family leave, better-behaving H.M.O.s, better schools, help with college tuition. "Ah'm just gettin' warmed up," he said after a few minutes. "Ah think ah'm gon' take mah coat off." And on and on he went with the strong economy and the way he was gon' put Medicare in a lockbox where Congress couldn't mess with it. In the windup, he let his voice break a little and pranced across the stage, and then he plunged into the crowd to shake hands.

A limousine pulled near to drive Gore away. He handshook his way over to it, and somebody opened a door for him. Then something peculiar happened. Gore turned and looked back at the hangar and the podium, frozen for a long moment in silhouette against the spotlights. It was as if two invisible strings were pulling him in opposite directions, the limo and the hangar. Suddenly, with an air of wild release, he ran back to the podium, leaped up the stairs, spread his arms exultantly, and absorbed wave after gratifying wave of the unconditional love of the crowd. He dismounted and went back to the handshaking in a near-frenzy, circumnavigating the entire hangar, for twenty, thirty, forty minutes. Often when Gore appears in public, people start quietly slipping out of the room after a while. This time nobody was about to leave before he did.

Some of the reporters had a cynical interpretation of what we were seeing. The Gore campaign had hired a film crew to shoot this event for possible use in advertisements: never believe that Gore is capable of spontaneity. Even so, it was an electric moment, the only one I ever saw on the Gore campaign—the only one where Gore seemed like a real politician, instead of somebody trying very hard to play the part of a politician.

BY the next morning, the electricity was gone. The local bishop had cancelled a Gore event on health care scheduled for the following day at a Catholic hospital, because Gore favors legal abortion. The lead story in the Scranton *Times-Tribune* was about how, at the airport hangar, Gore had mistakenly referred to Jim Wansacz by his father's name, John. The *Times*, where Gore had stopped to meet with the senior editors and reporters on his way to the speech at the New-York Historical Society, as part of the kickoff of the Prosperity and Progress tour, printed excerpts of the conversation that made it clear he had come across poorly, having answered questions by delivering little speeches on tangentially related topics.

The Gore campaign had hastily lined up another hospital for the event, but there were protesters outside with signs saying "George W. Bush for President" and "Stop the Killing of Unborn Babies." The triumphant visit to Scranton had become the controversial visit to Scranton. Inside, Gore conducted a town meeting, the kind of event his staff thinks he's best at, with a group of doctors and nurses. His Southern accent was gone. Whenever he had to mention someone's name, he bore down on it, clearly trying to avoid his mistake of the night before. He seemed to be straining to connect. Every time somebody asked a question, Gore would walk over and stand close, making intense eye contact and nodding slowly to show that he understood. Then, after the question had been asked, he would stroll to the middle of the stage and deliver his answer to the whole audience. It was a technique that probably made theoretical sense, but it seemed awfully forced when you were watching it.

One doctor asked Gore about malpractice, beginning with an amiable dig—vintage locker-room-of-the-hospital stuff—about Gore's being a lawyer. You could see the readout on Gore's eyelids: *All doctors hate lawyers. Must reassure subject. V-POTUS not lawyer. V-POTUS journalist.* "Actually, I did not wind up becoming a lawyer," Gore said. "I wound up becoming a newspaper reporter." Actually, Gore left being a full-time newspaper reporter to go to law school, and then left law school to run for Congress. This is the kind of exaggeration he falls into when he's forcing his game, trying to ingratiate himself in a way that obviously isn't real—the kind that, if anybody catches him at it, can be presented as one of his "lies."

Before the event was scheduled to end, people stopped raising their hands. "I seem to have exhausted the questions and comments," Gore said evenly. He went into a few closing remarks, the ballpark music came up, he shook a few hands, and then he ducked out.

THE familiar idea that Gore is stiff in public but funny and relaxed in private is within range of the truth, yet it doesn't capture the full strangeness of the situation. On rare occasions, he can be wonderful in public. I caught a glimpse of that in Scranton. Gore's friends like to cite a few other examples. There was a tour of the Western states at the end of the 1992 Presidential campaign when every stop seemed to draw an adoring crowd, and you could feel the impending victory. There was his fiftieth-birthday party, at which k.d. lang, dressed in a tuxedo, vampily sang "Happy Birthday, Mr. Vice-President," parodying Marilyn Monroe's famous serenade to J.F.K., while Tipper Gore feigned jealousy and Gore feigned temptation (the joke being that lang is gay). There was the eloquent eulogy he delivered for his father, in 1998. Earlier this year, an old friend of his named Jerry Thompson, a columnist for the Nashville *Tennessean,* died during the runup to the New Hampshire primary, a crucial event for Gore. He cleared his schedule, flew to Nashville for two days, and delivered a great, heartfelt speech.

Gore can also be stiff and lifeless in private. "Every time you see him, it's almost like you're meeting him for the first time," one old friend says. He is incapable of making small talk. And it gets even stranger. A political consultant who had been involved in several winning Senate campaigns in the 1998 elections went up to Capitol Hill to watch his clients being sworn in when the new congressional session opened. Gore, as presiding officer of the Senate, appears at these ceremonies. At the first swearing-in, the consultant thought, Ah, finally I'm getting to see the famous loose, funny Gore, the genuinely attractive and charming figure. At the next swearing-in, Gore was precisely the same, joke for joke, gesture for gesture, as if his central processing unit were performing a subroutine that he had loaded in earlier in the day. The same thing happened at the next swearing-in, and the next, and the next—not the minutest variation. So there isn't as much difference between loose and funny and stiff and formal as it may appear.

Gore sometimes switches modes in midstream, too, in public and in private. He lacks any middle range. He'll be speaking animatedly, and then, as if a great, grinding railyard switch is being thrown, he'll abruptly shut down and become lifeless. What seems to trigger this is an internal risk sensor, which, once activated, causes him to become overwhelmingly cautious. An invitation to say something impolitic, to give an opinion on an issue where offending an interest group whose support he wants seems unavoidable, and he's gone, into a territory of bland, well-tested sloganeering.

The phenomenon is self-reinforcing. Gore's painfully high self-awareness, his impulse to think rather than feel his way through a situation, leads to an excessively controlled presentation. (Even when he is evidently at ease, he speaks very formally, as I found out when I met him.) People notice those qualities, and conclude that he's condescending, or not paying attention, or even being actively hostile. They react by finding little ways to zing him—the reporters who travel with him, palpably seething over how controlled the environment is, do this a lot, finding new exaggerations and material for "campaign in trouble" stories—and Gore then retreats even further. Besides being a good public speaker, a high-level politician has to have a capacity for brief face-to-face interactions that leave the other person all aglow, convinced that there's a real relationship there. Gore is able to do this, but often, inexplicably, he doesn't. A common story you hear about Gore involves somebody's meeting him, being charmed and impressed (nobody in politics has more earnestly good impulses), developing what feels like a friendship, and then having a painful encounter in which Gore has, without warning, become an automaton, a man who speaks in a sonorous official tone about the positions of the Clinton-Gore Administration, the way an adult would speak to a child, or who answers heartfelt correspondence with a form letter. Gore has a closer family life and fewer real friends than most Washington figures of his eminence; people who think of themselves as acquaintances, and think that Gore treats them as such, will sometimes be surprised to hear that he has described them to someone else as intimates.

. . .

ANOTHER thing the best politicians do is attract a cadre of true believers, who work for them in a spirit of nearly religious devotion. Gore has one person like this in his upper echelon of advisers—Leon Fuerth, his foreign-policy aide, who had early training as an engineer, is so precise, diligent, and guarded, speaking not just in perfect sentences but in perfect paragraphs, that he makes his boss look like Jim Carrey. Most of the others around Gore as he runs for President are professionals, people who have won their battle stars in the Democratic Party but have no special connection to him. Even his closest campaign adviser, Carter Eskew, who has known him since 1973 and was brought into the Presidential campaign only last spring in connection with a shakeup, made it clear when I talked to him that his personal relationship with Gore is on hold until November, and that for now he is hired help.

People who travel with a Presidential campaign often refer to it half jokingly as the "bubble," meaning that it is an extraordinarily controlled, unnatural environment, and you never quite know where it's taking you next, or what's going on in the outside world, and you're constantly being watched. It's an apt analogy, which might be extended by saying that Al Gore is a "bubble boy," like those immunodeficient kids who are a staple of *People* and made-for-TV movies. He has been an elected official in the federal government since he was twenty-eight years old. Even before he was a congressman, Gore was a young prince, widely seen by his family and close friends as a potential President.

Bill Kovach, the recently retired curator of the Nieman Foundation, at Harvard, who was originally a journalist in Tennessee, remembers meeting the sixteen-year-old Gore at the 1964 Democratic National Convention, in Atlantic City, and being drawn into a searching conversation by his older sister Nancy about how Al ought to play the question of serving in Vietnam, in light of his future political prospects. At Harvard, Gore wore neckties to class and called his teachers "sir" after everybody else had stopped doing so, made himself a protégé of one of the leading scholars of the American Presidency, Richard Neustadt, and wrote his undergraduate honors thesis (based mainly on interviews with upper-echelon figures in the Washington establishment) on the effect of television on the Presidency. Soon after Gore got to Congress, he began to look for national issues on which he could develop a reputation for stature. He was elected to the Senate, all of whose members have had the thought of being President flit across their minds, at the age of thirty-six. He first ran for President at the age of thirty-nine. The stakes have always been high, and because of the changing politics of the South, and of the nation, the risk has always been high, too. In the last thirty years, words that Albert Gore, Sr., took for granted as the staples of his political rhetoric, like "liberal" and "tax" and "government," have come to have negative connotations. Al Gore has lived a life devoid of incentives to let down his guard.

What he has done, perhaps in response, is to develop an intellectual quality that is rare in a politician, a tendency to understand the world in terms of abstract systems. The usual currency of politics is people. You meet with people all day long, people work for you, you stand at the lectern and speak to people, and that leads you to understand the world at large in terms of people, too. Worth is measured in aggregate numbers of people helped. History itself seems to turn on questions of alliances and coalitions and parties and elections. Gore just doesn't think this way. The readout always seems to be saying *Hit escape to go up one level.* So up and up and up he goes—and away and away and away—until he reaches a realm of cosmic understanding of the larger forces against which our petty affairs are played out. Gore is all transcendence and no immanence (and Bush is all immanence and no transcendence). "The world is a system, not a collection of individuals," I heard him say in one of his speeches (not an applause line, you can be sure). Who else would say this in a Presidential campaign, or even think it?

At this empyrean level, where almost none of day-to-day politics is conducted, Gore is the most impressive politician alive. The lack of connection between the drive to moral improvement that seems to be Gore's underlying motivation for being in politics and the careful positioning that has been a prerequisite to election as a Southern Democrat during his adult life disappears. He is free to be a crusader, who wants, quite literally, to rescue humanity (from its own mistakes, through the power of the disciplined mind). When Gore has to come down to the ground level of daily politics, he overcalculates, or he too obviously ingratiates, or he brutally attacks, or he sticks too closely to the script. But that doesn't mean there isn't a real Al Gore behind the opaque exterior. There is. You find him by going up and away.

THE earliest clear glimpse of Al Gore's mind is his Harvard undergraduate thesis, "The Impact of Television on the Conduct of the Presidency, 1947–1969." It's good! Gore, though usually a dull speaker, is almost never a dull writer. When he's sitting by himself at a desk, an organized intelligence goes to work. You don't get anecdotes or elegant turns of phrase, but the thoughts are crisp, and they march smartly along, and when a date or a fact is called for he chases it down. Already, in the thesis, a recognizable Gore is present: it is a work of technological determinism, in which systems are more powerful than people, even Presidents of the United States. You can almost feel Gore empathetically entering the situation of the television-challenged Lyndon Johnson and trying to figure out how somebody else equally uncomfortable with the medium might handle it better: by limiting exposure and weighing every word.

In the thesis, Gore makes it clear which medium, print or television, he prefers: in print, "personality factors and visual rhetoric are effectively screened out and the reader is forced to make judgments on the basis of logic and reason." So it shouldn't be surprising that, after college and Vietnam, he chose to take a job at the Nashville *Tennessean*. Old friends of Gore's describe this as the happiest time of his life, and the only time in his adulthood when he usually seemed at ease and readily made connections with other people (by Gore's, not general human, standards). Journalists know that their field is, counterintuitively, a refuge for shy, self-conscious people. Also, journalism provided an outlet for Gore's love of meticulous, systemic analysis and of moralism: he was an investigative reporter and an editorialist. (For a time while he was at the *Tennessean*, he had gone to Vanderbilt Divinity School.)

At the same time, Gore moved to the place where his family's political base was. The *Tennessean*'s editor and publisher, John Seigenthaler, Sr., one of a long line of substitute fathers Gore has acquired during his life, was more than just a newspaperman. He had been an aide to Robert Kennedy and was well connected in the Democratic Party; being his protégé put you into a network that extended into politics.

Bill Kovach remembers getting a call from Albert Gore, Sr., a few years into Al Gore's *Tennessean* period, when Kovach was living in Washington and working for the *Times.* Could he call Al and try to talk him into going to law school? The former Senator said he knew that Al loved his newspaper work, but it would be a shame for him to close off his options, to lose the chance to do something else later. Kovach made the call, and he and the Senator's son had a long talk, with Kovach invoking the names of sainted figures in journalism who had legal training, such as Anthony Lewis, and Gore sounding polite but unenthusiastic. He went, of course, but he still worked for the *Tennessean,* and when the congressman from his home district announced his retirement—the news was conveyed by Seigenthaler, who added, "You know what I think"—he dropped out to run, knowing that in that part of Tennessee once you win a congressional seat it's yours for life. He was elected in 1976, a year of redemption for the Gore family, because while Al was winning Bill Brock was losing the old Gore Senate seat to a Democrat, Jim Sasser.

As a congressman, Gore pursued a two-track strategy. First, he became an obsessively hardworking, risk-avoiding advocate for his constituents. He flew back to middle Tennessee nearly every weekend, and when he was there he would hold town meetings, often as many as five or six a day, to listen to his constituents' complaints. If you asked for a favor, it would be entered in a notebook, which Gore would consult while driving between towns so that he would remember to ask you if that problem with your Social Security check which we discussed a few months back had been taken care of.

The other track involved making his name on issues that were not directly related to his district—unlike his father, who had developed a national reputation as a fierce and partisan advocate on the issues that mattered most to the constituents. Right away, Gore got a seat on the House Interstate and Foreign Commerce Committee, and was active on the subcommittee on oversight and investigations. In the late seventies, investigating corporate misdeeds had a prestige that is difficult to recapture today. Gore turned the subcommittee into a venue for taking on business bad guys with a brittle, furious moral right-eousness. Not yet thirty, he presided over public hearings at which he warned the chairman of Gulf Oil that he was "on thin ice." He went after the contact-lens industry for overpricing, a chemical company for selling a carcinogenic flame retardant used in children's pajamas, and uranium producers for price fixing.

As time went on, Gore shifted his attention, in the great-world compartment of his congressional career, from investigations to arms control. Encountering Leon Fuerth, he signed up for a yearlong, one-on-one tutorial, complete with weekly meetings and a syllabus, and relentlessly mastered what is probably the most arcane topic in government—the topic that may be the most important to the future of humanity but is one of the least important to voters. Becoming an expert on nuclear arms gave Gore a national, and even international, reputa-tion. (Not an easy thing—can you name a junior congressman?) It also estab-lished him as the kind of centrist, pro-defense Democrat that the times seemed to demand, especially if you came from the South. And the arms-control de-bate was conducted in that very Gore realm—*Hit escape to go up one level*—where humans recede and technology and logic come to the fore.

In 1983, when Tennessee's senior senator, Howard Baker, announced his impending retirement from the Senate, Gore, who had been monitoring Baker's intentions since early in his House career, began planning his candi-dacy at once. He was elected easily, in 1984, and it seemed to be another seat he could hold for life, especially because he continued to visit home constantly and to avoid the kind of stands that had caused his father to lose. As he had in the House, Gore made himself into the kind of member who is more a promi-nent voice than a passer of bills, engendering in his colleagues more respect than love. In 1991, after he cast one of ten Democratic votes in favor of enter-ing the Gulf War, the Democratic leader, George Mitchell, barely even spoke to him for a time.

In 1987, just two years into his first Senate term, Gore decided to run for President. He was, obviously, not the front-runner, but there was no front-runner that year. (The Democrats wound up nominating Michael Dukakis.) Running was a brassy, but not all that risky, move for Gore. It was the début year for Super Tuesday, the many-state Southern primary designed to put the center of the Party back in control of the nominating process. Even if Gore didn't win, he would have positioned himself a few notches up in the Party hi-erarchy, and Super Tuesday gave him a real shot.

BUT Gore drew a remarkably harsh lesson (to the point of self-flagellation) from the only race he hasn't won: that he had debased himself in Presidential politics and now he was a man in need of spiritual redemption. He later wrote, "I began to doubt my own political judgment, so I began to ask the pollsters and professional politicians what they thought I ought to talk about. As a result, for much of the campaign I discussed what everybody else discussed, which too often was a familiar list of what the insiders agree are 'the issues.' " (This is an eerily precise description of what Gore has been doing—again—in his second Presidential race.) Now he needed to deepen himself.

Gore asked a group of his friends to set up a series of seminars for him, like the arms-control seminars with Leon Fuerth, only much more ambitious, with big-time thinkers, such as the economists Kenneth Arrow and Brian Arthur, flying to Washington to brief him. *Up one level!* By the end of it, Gore had a new, sweeping view of the world and its prospects. His main interest had noticeably shifted, from arms control to global warming, but the setup was familiar: mankind was in a morally dire situation of its own making, which could be solved through a combination of analytic mastery, spiritual guidance, and the use of technology in healthy ways instead of unhealthy ones.

He decided to write a book. In the summer of 1990, a proposal for a work by Gore about the environment made the rounds of publishers in New York, and John Sterling, the editor-in-chief of Houghton Mifflin, after a long talk with the impassioned Gore, made a deal to publish it. Gore turned in a first draft in July of 1991. Gore mythology has it that seeing his young son hit by an automobile after a baseball game in 1989 helped him decide not to run for President again in 1992. Although his son's accident was a searing experience and Gore devoted himself completely to the child's recovery, it's also the case that at the time he turned in the first draft of the book he still hadn't made up his mind about 1992. (By his own account he began writing the book in his son's hospital room.) Sterling and Gore agreed that the book needed substantial revision, and they soon realized that he couldn't possibly get it done and also run for President. Gore said he needed a little time to think about that. Then, in August, he called Sterling and said he had decided not to run, but he wanted the book to be published in January—before the diversions of Presidential politics. That schedule meant a brutal extra workload for everybody involved, especially Gore himself. But he met the deadline. He worked flat out for months, summoning up all of that furious, hungry, competitive diligence he has. And the book arrived in stores during the third week of January, 1992.

What transaction had just taken place, exactly? Had Gore given up a shot at the Presidency for the sake of the book, because the book was more important to him? Had he insisted on the killer rush because he wanted the book to function as an advertisement for his Vice-Presidential candidacy, or even as a means of late entry into the Presidential race if the other candidates faltered? Whatever was going on, the book that was meant to take him away from the calculations imposed by Presidential politics, that was meant to be renunciatory, brought him back in. Having attempted to free himself of his own "timidity of vision" and become an environmental crusader, Gore wound up in one of the most constrained jobs there is.

Though the book, "Earth in the Balance," was much made fun of by Republicans, it is an impressive and brave work. Rather than confine itself to matters of government policy, it ranges widely over all manner of historical, psychological, and religious matters. It is melodramatic, apocalyptic, and passionate, the work of a guarded man who has made a conscious decision—forced himself—to bare his soul on the printed page. As he writes, "I have become very impatient with my own tendency to put a finger to the political winds and proceed cautiously."

The soul that Gore bares in "Earth in the Balance" is a tormented one. The theme of self-criticism is nearly ever present, and Gore makes it clear that, aside from the facts of the case, he was drawn to the environmental crisis and the solving of it as a way of working out a crisis in his own life. As he puts it, "The search for truths about this ungodly crisis and the search for truths about myself have been the same search all along." He argues that every bad quality in people, singularly or collectively, manifests itself specifically in desecration of the earth. Conversely, the saving of the earth is possible only if we embrace—if he embraces, in particular—a different, better set of qualities. In the moral hierarchy that Gore creates in "Earth in the Balance," the lowest rung is occupied by cynicism, short-range thinking, and cheap manipulation of images and slogans, all of which he specifically attributes to politics. On the next rung there is logic and reason, but if, in the end, we are going to save the earth this, too, must be put aside in favor of a looser, freer, less controlling spirituality. Female qualities seem to be superior to male ones. In a long passage on dysfunctional families which has an autobiographical air, Gore posits a child who grows up "severely stressed by the demands of the dominant, all-powerful father." A little later, he suggests that this child "begins controlling his inner experience—smothering spontaneity, masking emotion, diverting creativity into robotic routine." Environmentalism somehow offers the promise of undoing all that damage and healing all that pain and making one genuine at last.

"Earth in the Balance" is not so much the work of an intellectual as the work of someone immensely impressed by intellectualism and intellectuals, who occupy the venerated position for him that baseball heroes do for Bush. Gore constantly seeks to demonstrate the breadth of material that he has mastered: the Bible, electrical engineering, mythology, psychology, history. In the footnotes, he mentions having constructed a master calendar correlating the great events of world history with major changes in weather and climate. Can there be anybody in public life who knows more than Gore does, or who so much wants us to see how much he knows? What is also striking about the book is how much it is taken up with a seemingly endless series of metaphors, alternatively high-dramatic, technological, showily erudite, and religio-spiritual. Sandpiles, holography, human skin, machines, the midlife crisis, Kristallnacht, and slavery are all brought in by Gore as points of comparison to environmental phenomena. One of the basic distinctions in literary theory—a subject of intense interest to Gore—is between metaphor and metonymy. Metaphor is implied comparison—the literary equivalent of a cutaway shot in a movie. Metonymy is the expression of a whole by reducing it to a part—the equivalent of a closeup. "My new car is a real thoroughbred!" is metaphoric; "I've got a new set of wheels" is metonymic. Gore communicates by comparing, not reducing—he thinks in metaphors. (And Bush thinks in metonyms.) Even when his intention is to shed all restraint and become passionate and direct, his mind is always taking him away, to something else that seems to him similar to the subject at hand.

IT is easy to forget, at this late and weary point in the Clinton Administration, and after so many years of Al Gore-is-stiff jokes and his endless attempts to defuse them (one year he had himself wheeled in to the Gridiron dinner on a handcart), how exciting his nomination as Vice-President was. His book was a big hit, he had an attractive and obviously close family, and he had national stature. He gave Clinton some much-needed ballast. But in hindsight the Vice-Presidency was a perilous role for Gore. It required him to suppress the full-throated passion to which he had pledged himself in "Earth in the Balance" and put him in close proximity to a man who, as a natural at the personal side of politics, might have been custom-designed to heighten his insecurities.

Clinton and Gore have treated each other rather well, though. Clinton gave Gore the things Vice-Presidents always want: a West Wing office, a one-on-one weekly lunch, and supervising authority over a few real issues (as opposed to funeral duty and the chairmanship of ceremonial commissions). Gore, conversely, played two roles, at least in the early years, both of which were quite useful to Clinton. Clinton has trouble taking a firm stand; Gore was the house moralist, the advocate for the option that would represent the unpopular, tough, but right thing to do. He was for imposing an energy tax, intervening early in Bosnia, allowing gays in the military, and balancing the budget. And he took on for the disorganized Clinton the management of big, complex, unglamorous tasks, the kind that involve great draughts of bureaucratic work without much political payoff. He managed the National Performance Review, better known as "Reinventing Government," which involved going through the entire federal government agency by agency and through the budget line by line. He represented the White House in the negotiations over the important but (to the public, anyway) terminally dull telecommunications act, which Congress passed in 1996. He set up three major and several minor bilateral commissions with the No. 2s in foreign governments, which then established subcommittees to discuss the details of government. Nobody has ever taken on such a big workload as Vice-President.

To understand how Gore did at these tasks, it's helpful to think again of the great grinding railyard switch being thrown. When offering his advice, he was preachy, but when he was in charge of something he was ministerial: diligent, careful, responsible, thorough, and politically clunky. The National Performance Review did save a lot of money, mainly by offering corporate-style early-retirement buyouts to civil servants, but Gore was notorious within the Administration for pushing to have an aggressively high savings figure attributed to it. In general, the parts of the review that required systematic understanding and hard work came to fruition and the parts that required political skill did not: the government's computer-buying procedures were modernized, but the Treasury couldn't be induced to turn the Bureau of Alcohol, Tobacco, and Firearms over to the F.B.I., where it belongs. Gore's Russia commission, similarly, did scads of useful work but wound up embarrassing him politically. Just days after his opposite number, Viktor Chernomyrdin, came to the United States for a chummy joint press conference with Gore in Washington, followed by a trip *à deux* to Silicon Valley, Chernomyrdin was fired by Boris Yeltsin. Gore was great at thorough, and not so great at adept.

The over-all picture of Gore as a government executive which emerges from people who have worked with him is that he always knows the material, that he is efficient and hard-driving, to the point sometimes of being peremptory with staff members who are late with something or haven't done it right, that his intentions are nothing but the best, but that he lacks "touch," or "feel." Clinton is legendary inside the government for improving on the prepared speech or talking points in the delivery; Gore is legendary for sticking rigidly to the script. In meetings, Clinton often guides the discussion to an inference that the staff didn't see in advance; Gore marches through the agenda in precise, orderly fashion, speaking in the technical language of a public-policy graduate seminar. Clinton hates being alone; Gore likes being alone, sitting in his office in front of the computer screen, sipping herbal tea. The mystical part of Clinton's soul finds its expression in actually doing the stuff you do in a government job, like making speeches and lobbying legislators and running meetings. The mystical part of Gore's soul finds its expression in ascending to a plane far above the one where daily politics is practiced. He is never happier than when meeting with the type of person he admires most—not another politician but an intellectual, cultural, or spiritual figure who has thought about the world in a new way, such as Carl Sagan, the astronomer, or Deborah Tannen, the linguist, or the Grateful Dead and the Dalai Lama (both brought to the White House for visits by a proud and delighted Gore), or Stephen Hawking, the theoretical physicist, or Daniel Hillis, the father of parallel computing, or Ian Player, the South African environmentalist who saved the white rhinoceros.

· · ·

AS Gore's White House years went on, he seemed to fall off the wagon he had proclaimed himself to be on by writing "Earth in the Balance." The old, guarded, politically risk-averse version of himself was more often on display. People around him thought that the Democratic rout in 1994 rattled him, and that Clinton's impeachment, coming, as it did, just on the verge of his own Presidential campaign, really rattled him. In both cases, he said in strategy meetings that the President was a kind of national father and that the country now was fatherless—which seemed to people listening to have more to do with the low moment's whisking Gore back to the primal moment of the loss of his own father, on the altar of political courage, in 1970, than with the practicalities of the situation at hand.

In 1997, when an international summit meeting on global warming was held in Kyoto—the issue to which Gore pledged himself utterly in "Earth in the Balance"—he temporized, under a barrage from his political aides, who saw the summit as a loser for him, until the last possible minute. In the end, he went, and he spent the long plane flight forcing his staff through a complete revision of the bland speech that had been written for him. Global warming is the toughest possible issue for Gore. Part of the solution is to convert coal-fired plants, some of the worst of which are in the Midwest, to natural gas, and to reduce auto emissions—and Gore cannot be elected President without carrying the Midwest and retaining the support of the A.F.L.-C.I.O., whose treasurer is the former head of the mine workers' union. In August of 1998, a delegation of heads of environmental groups called on Gore in the White House to urge him to do more on global warming. He lost his temper and shouted, "Name me one senator who'll support me on this!" He told his visitors he had become convinced that we have to have a major catastrophe before the American public will be ready to do anything about global warming.

The Democratic nomination appeared at first to be as safely Gore's as his House and Senate seats had been. When Bill Bradley's challenge looked as if it were unexpectedly going to take off, Gore had an intense, worried reaction, firing a significant portion of the campaign high command he had painstakingly assembled and moving sharply away from the centrist position he had built up over his years in public life. In 1995, Gore held a series of three dinners at the Vice-Presidential mansion to discuss race (Bradley was among the guests). Gore was typically guarded, but one might have surmised that he was rethinking some of the traditional Democratic positions. He had asked prominent thinkers on the topic, including Tamar Jacoby, a writer and editor who is now one of the nation's leading voices of opposition to affirmative action, to organize the dinners; after each one, Gore and Jacoby, along with Martin Peretz, the editor of *The New Republic* (and one of Gore's surrogate fathers), Peretz's wife, Anne, and Stanley Crouch, the fight-picking novelist-critic-musician—Peretz a wholehearted opponent of affirmative action, and Crouch a supporter with reservations—sat around sipping cognac when the other guests had left. Earlier this year, in a debate at the Apollo Theatre, in Harlem, Gore indignantly accused Bradley of harboring inner doubt about the one affirmative-action program that even people who love affirmative action are embarrassed about, a Federal Communications Commission tax break on sales of cable-television systems to (necessarily rich) minorities.

LEAVING aside impeachment, which after all had almost no negative impact on Democratic candidates in the last national elections, it would be hard to think of a more ideal set of circumstances under which to run for President than the ones Gore finds himself in this year. The economy is better than it has ever been. We are at peace. The Democratic Party has shed its McGovernite baggage. Gore's opponent has nowhere near his experience or his stamina or his impressive biography or his disciplined mind. But the people around Gore, and evidently the candidate himself, seem to believe that to present him to the voters as he really is—a serious man who at every juncture has pushed himself hard, who cares about doing right, who has developed passion and expertise, who has a sense of the world, who has devoted himself to public life—couldn't possibly work. Instead, the play is to develop a position on each issue that is more popular than George W. Bush's—a Social Security position, a prescription-drug position, a budget-surplus position—and to out-aggress Bush, work longer hours than he can work, go at him hard, rattle him, and force him into mistakes. The Gore people are hiding their guy, in other words, behind a wall of fine-grained political calculation. Most of what Gore says in public is in relation to Bush, rather than about himself. What would we see if he stopped doing that?

I interviewed Gore on Air Force Two one Saturday afternoon during a flight between a fund-raiser in San Francisco and a fund-raiser in Miami. The plane is set up, back to front, in this way: stewards and kitchen; press; security (more people than you'd expect); staff (fewer people than you'd expect); Vice-President's cabin. The press sits in first-class splendor, hoping, almost always in vain, that Gore will wander back for an informal chat. Everybody warned me that if I asked Gore any question about whatever was the issue of the moment—on that day, whether Janet Reno would appoint a special counsel to investigate his fund-raising activities in 1996—he would answer with bland press-conference rhetoric. So I decided to go as far in the other direction as I possibly could.

Somewhere in the middle of the flight, Chris Lehane, Gore's thin, determined press secretary, came and motioned me up to the front of the plane, and together we went into Gore's cabin. It was small and meticulously neat. There was a desk with a big executive-style chair on each side, and, on the other side of the cabin, a small sofa with a coffee table bolted to the floor in front of it. All the tabletops were perfectly clear.

Gore had us sit together on the sofa, so that we had to pivot to face each other. He was wearing white khakis, a green semi-casual buttoned shirt, and black polished cowboy boots—the uniform of a Sunbelt dad at a Saturday barbecue. Up close, his features, which look thick and blocky to an audience, have an almost porcelain delicacy. He has unusually white teeth and unusually blue eyes. I noticed that his fingernails were bitten to the quick.

Before the three dinners on race that he hosted, he had held a series of three dinners on metaphor, with a leading scholar acting as interlocutor at each one. I asked him why he's so interested in metaphor, mentioning both the dinners and the heavy use of metaphor in "Earth in the Balance."

Gore brightened. "Oh, you've read my book?" he said. "Oh, thank you!" He seemed genuinely pleased, almost to the point of being flustered. "You want some coffee? Water?" I said no, thanks. "Well, thanks for reading my book. I appreciate that. And for you to read it is different from"—readout: *Let's maybe not go there*—"I mean . . . well, anyway, thank you."

He paused for a long time to gather his thoughts, and when he spoke it was in deliberate, print-ready prose, delivered with just the faintest hint of a Southern accent. "The word 'metaphor' is just a highfalutin description of a very common, ubiquitous process by which all of us try to increase our understanding of the world around us," Gore said. "You move from the familiar to the unfamiliar. You use what you know as a tool for trying to better understand what you don't know." He paused again. "At the most basic level, right now, since we've just met, I'm using myself as a metaphor for you."

How so? I asked.

"What I know about human nature is rooted first and foremost in my own life experience, and since I don't know you very well I'm making assumptions about the way you approach life that inevitably begin from the experiences that I have had. And I daresay you're doing the same thing with me. It's not a complicated process, and even to call attention to it gives it more significance than it ought to have. But the point I'm trying to make is that often the word 'metaphor' is simply a shorthand description for a very common, run-of-the-mill intellectual tool that all of us use.

"I became interested in more complex metaphors and their explanatory power when I was writing 'Earth in the Balance.' In particular, in my effort to try to understand the origins of our modern world view, and its curious reliance on specialization and ever-narrower slices of the world around us into categories that are then themselves dissected, in an ongoing process of separation, into parts and subparts—a process that sometimes obliterates the connection to the whole and the appreciation for context and the deeper meanings that can't really be found in the atomized parts of the whole—and in exploring the roots of that way of looking at the world, I found a lot of metaphors in the seventeenth and eighteenth centuries that came directly from the scientific revolution into the world of politics and culture and sociology. And many of those metaphors are still with us."

Such as?

"The clockwork universe. The idea that all the world is a machine of moving parts that will eventually be completely understood by means of looking carefully at all the different gears and cogs in the wheels and then . . ." He trailed off; he seemed to be searching for an exact phrase, and as he did this he turned his head in profile, squeezed his eyes shut, and made a pointing gesture with his hand. Then, when the words came, he turned his head back to me and smiled engagingly. "When I compared the absolute number of new scientific insights that came in the first flush of the scientific revolution to the incredible flood of scientific insights that now pour out of every single discipline, every single day, it's astonishing. There's no comparison. And yet the migration of those explanatory metaphors, from the narrow niches of science into the broader public dialogue about how we live our lives and how we understand the human experience and how we can better solve the social problems that become more pressing with each passing decade—that migration is, has been, reduced to the barest trickle."

I started to interrupt to ask another question. "May I make this one final point here?" Gore said. He turned to Chris Lehane. "Give me something to draw with." Lehane didn't have anything, so I tore a piece of paper out of my notebook and gave it to Gore. He put the paper on the coffee table and, leaning over it, made an inscrutable diagram.

Gore showed me the page, which had four pairs of short vertical lines drawn on it, with the space between the lines in each pair varying. "If this"—the first pair—"represented the number of real innovations and brand-new understandings of scientific and mechanical relationships in the world that came after the Cartesian revolution, and all the work done in mathematics and mechanics, this"—the second pair, drawn above it, and spaced a little closer together—"might represent the appearance of analogous explanations in the way society looked at itself. By contrast, this number"—he pointed to the third pair of lines, which were extremely far apart, out at the edges of the piece of paper—"in the current accelerated scientific and technological revolution, wouldn't be represented on a piece of paper in the same scale." Gore then indicated the fourth pair of lines, which were set so close together they were practically touching. "And yet the number of the new insights that make their way into our dialogue with one another about the way our world operates, socially, politically, culturally—well, leave alone culturally, because I think artists have done their own work in communicating nonverbally about some of the insights. But the numbers here would be smaller.

"You see the point?" Gore said. He turned to Lehane again. "Get me the copy of *The New York Times* for today, the full copy. I want the Arts section." Back to me. "And so—well, anyway, I'm sorry. You go ahead."

Gore had strayed quite a bit from the strict definition of a metaphor. Instead, he seemed to mean, by metaphor, a new, unrelated, and probably more creative way of thinking about something drawn from another domain. I asked him whether he was interested in metaphors because he was looking for solutions to problems or because he was trying to figure out how best to communicate with the public.

"Both!"

Lehane returned with the newspaper. Gore pointed to a picture of a dog with the head of a sheep. He gave me a long, deep, direct look and a serious nod. "O.K.?" I asked him what he meant. He paused again in profile.

"Our language hasn't caught up with that artist," he said, turning back to me. "We are breaking apart the traditional boundaries between species. The day after tomorrow, the human genome will be completed in its first rough draft. That is a landmark on the road toward yet another new Promethean technological power, this time to rearrange the way in which life takes its various forms. And this artist seems to me to be saying, at least on one level, 'Here is something you'd better prepare yourself for.' Now, obviously, in the real world that's not going to happen"—meaning a dog with the head of a sheep. "At least I hope it's not going to happen. But something like it is happening already. And the image in that work of art communicates right now, more profoundly than anyone in the world of politics or sociology has been able to communicate, about the kinds of decisions that we have to prepare ourselves to make."

GORE gestured for another piece of paper, and when I gave one to him he bent over the coffee table again and began to draw another diagram. I was starting to wonder whether I ought to direct the conversation more or just keep listening.

The Vice-President worked diligently, like a good student at his desk. This second drawing was made up of a circle with twenty little dots floating inside it, connected by wavy lines. "Now, let me come back to your question." He walked me through Thomas Kuhn's theory of scientific revolutions, apologizing for the overused word "paradigm," and explained that every so often an unusually creative scientist finds a new way to connect the dots of unexplained data.

I started to interrupt. "Hold on," Gore said. He wasn't finished. He leaned forward and lightly touched my arm, to signal me to give him another minute. "That process goes on all the time. What is it that speeds up that process? If you can see a new pattern in one part of the world, it may be a pattern that is widely replicated in other parts of the world. In fact, that is the normal way these things happen. And there is a scientific phenomenon that is called the self-sameness principle. It appears in fractal theory. If you look at a map of the coastline of New Jersey, and then magnify it a hundred times, and then magnify that a thousand times, the basic design of the ins and outs of the coastline will be the same at every level of magnification. And they call that the self-sameness principle. I don't understand it. It's way beyond my depth. But I do believe that there's something about our world that—" He began another long pause. "I'm searching for the right word here—that *manifests* that self-sameness principle in a lot of different ways. And when we find a brand-new understanding of the world that comes out of a powerful new discovery in science, it often allows us to look at social and political matters and find ways to connect the dots that haven't made sense before."

I asked Gore where God fits into all this.

"Give me another piece of paper," he said. He drew a series of small circles, and then a bigger circle over in a corner of the page. "If you"—another pause—"if you are in an animist society, encumbered with a belief system that—now, that's a value judgment, but I will stand by it, I think that it's a confining belief system—if you believe that every object, living or inanimate, which populates your world has its own animating spirit, then intellectually, if you observe some mystery that you can't explain, you are going to be *less than curious* about the nature of that phenomenon, because you will most likely assume that that mystery is easily explainable in terms of the whims in the animating spirit of that object. If, on the other hand, you come to believe in a creator or a deity that is responsible for having set in motion or having created all of the universe, then"—he went back to the paper and drew a series of lines, connecting all the little circles to the bigger one—"you have a new power of curiosity, because you don't assume that there is a whimsical animating spirit that explains what you're observing. You're not afraid of that spirit world. You are God-fearing in the sense that you may have some notion of what duties you owe to the creator responsible for both yourself and the rest of the world, but you can look at the world around you without the same fear and trepidation that an animist has. And that can empower you to look for logical explanations for what's going on in your world."

In 1996, Gore gave a speech to the American Association for the Advancement of Science in which he proposed "distributed intelligence" as the best metaphor for the current historical moment. I asked him how that metaphor applied to government. He smiled, clearly pleased that I had read the speech. His face was animated and eager, almost shining.

"Here's how it works," he said. "Prior to our Constitution, almost all forms of government relied on a single processor of information, be it a king or a khan or a tsar. The decisions were all concentrated at a single place, from which some of them might have to be delegated, but the responsibility was still placed in a single point." Then he went into a detailed history of the development of parallel computer processing. It was an odd blend of Gore-as-teacher, lecturing me, wanting to confer his understanding, and Gore-as-student, wanting to demonstrate that he had mastered the material. He turned over the last sheet of paper I had given him and drew two circles, one with a single square in the center and arrows pointing in and out of it, the other with a dozen squares scattered in it.

"Now, take this phenomenon"—parallel processing—"as a metaphor and look at systems of government. Here's the King of England in 1776." He pointed to the circle that had a single square in the middle. "Whatever challenge the British Empire faced, the ultimate responsibility for making decisions was at the center. As the world became more complicated, the decisions that had to be made stacked up and the process became unwieldy. When our Constitution was written, the revolutionary insight at its core was that every single individual citizen ought to have the power to make meaningful decisions about the world immediately around him. The system we know as representative democracy would, in this analogy, be comparable to the software that makes it possible to have a simultaneous task order go out to all the citizens with suffrage—remembering that of course only white males were then so recognized—and in the regular election process the young nation endeavored to collect the results of all that information processing and assemble it at the center, in the Capitol building, with representatives bringing with them a rough approximation of what all the voters in their districts were thinking and feeling about the challenges that our nation had to confront." He indicated the second circle, the one containing many squares. "Does that make sense?" He touched my arm lightly again.

I told him I had read his father's books—on hearing this, he beamed again, and thanked me—and had been struck by how much the old man viewed the world through the lens of race and class. Was that a way of thinking that fit the South only in the past, or did it still make sense to him today?

Gore glanced at Chris Lehane. "We can find more time, if you need more time," Gore said. "Not on this flight, but afterward."

He thought for a minute, and then explained that race matters, in a way, less in the South today than in the rest of the country, because the civil-rights movement had put many Southerners, more than people in the rest of the country, through a real transformation. "They emerged from that experience far more enlightened about the true significance of race in our society, and far more able, as a result, to transcend it," he said. "The basic formula is not that complicated. It's a two-step process. You have to first establish absolute and genuine mutual respect for difference. And that respect for difference has to include both an appreciation for the unique suffering that has come about because of the difference, and the unique gifts and contributions that have come about because of the difference. And a basic appreciation for the unique perspective that is based on that difference. Then the second step is a transcendence of that difference to embrace all the elements that we have in common in the human spirit."

. . .

MY tape ran out—forty-five minutes had passed. I fumbled as I tried to turn it over, and Gore, after watching me for a while, told me how to accomplish the job properly. He had stopped speaking while the tape was not running, and as soon as I had it going again he resumed. "For those who have not been through that searing, transformative personal encounter with the civil-rights revolution a common mistake is to move directly to step two and bypass step one—in other words, to say, 'Can't we just get along?' To say, 'Let's transcend this essentially meaningless, artificial distinction called race.' And it's a noble, if naïve, thought. Worse than that, it can be"—another long pause while he searched for the right word—"disrespectful of the person of another race you're relating to, because it's all too easy for someone in the majority, in a culture shaped by the majority, in a political system largely controlled by the majority, to blithely ignore, or not notice, the profound differences in opportunity and privilege that are pervasive in the experience of someone in the minority in that culture. And if you, as a member of the majority, say, 'Let's just transcend this distinction,' without any apparent appreciation for what the distinction means in the life of the person you're trying to communicate with, all of your seeming good faith will come off as"—another pause—"contextual hostility."

I thought I could see what Gore was doing here. He was explaining, indirectly, subtly, and gently, why he had declined to accept the view of Northern friends of his, like Marty Peretz, that the country should drop affirmative action and pursue absolute color-blindness as an ideal. But he had also chosen—surely not by accident, since nothing Gore does is unconsidered—to answer only the race part of my question, not the class part. I asked him whether he agreed with his father's view that if we could ever get past the race issue we could have a politics of economic class.

"That's the last question," Chris Lehane said.

Gore thought again, and out came another perfectly formed answer. "My father's experience taught him that whenever economic hard times put pressure on those with low incomes and less valuable skills, the result was increased tension between whites and blacks. And therefore his determination to awaken, in whites and blacks alike, the common interest they had in changing policies and politics to empower themselves, and to change the economic royalism, as he would call it, of the Bourbons and their successors, drove him to a view of race that was"—pause—"perhaps too influenced by the enlightenment view." He stopped himself. "Let me rephrase that. Perhaps too influenced by the common liberal view of the time that race was first and foremost—that racism, excuse me, was first and foremost a logical mistake, which, once corrected, would dissolve and disappear. I don't believe that. At least, I believe that is true, but not the whole truth. It is a logical mistake, a way of thinking profoundly in error. But it is also a manifestation of a deeper vulnerability." An aide came into the cabin and handed Gore a slip of paper with a few words written on it. He glanced at it and turned back to me. "Let me ask you to pause for just five minutes, O.K.?"

I left the cabin and stood outside in the aisle. Gore still hadn't really answered the class part of the question. Here he was, a career government employee who refuses to invest in anything but U.S. Treasury instruments, spending a weekend away from home flying across the country from one fund-raiser to another fund-raiser while figuring out how to handle that week's crisis, which was his possible prosecution for overaggressive fund-raising. And Bush had managed to position himself, pretty successfully, as the populist in the race and Gore as the élitist! It was hard to imagine that the unlikeliness of this being the life of his father's son hadn't occurred to him, but he did not share with me whatever thoughts he had on that subject.

While I was waiting, an image flashed in my mind: Gore in breeches and a powdered wig, composing something at his desk with a quill pen. Perhaps it was a plan for an experiment with new agricultural methods on his land, or correspondence with a like-minded office-holder in another state, or a letter to a packet merchant requesting scientific instruments from France or philosophical texts from England. It also occurred to me that, whatever happens in this election, Gore's reaction will likely be just what it was after his previous Presidential race, in 1988. He'll want to redeem himself from his painful excursion into hard-nosed politics, with its blend of overcautious thought and overaggressive behavior, by launching a moral crusade—either from inside the White House or from private life.

Gore opened the door to the cabin and motioned me back in. When we sat down and he saw that the tape was running again, he picked up exactly where he had left off: "I think it is a mistake in thinking, a profound error. But it's also a manifestation of a deeper vulnerability in human nature, one that we are capable of transcending. But it is a persistent vulnerability." There was another long, searching pause. "My way of understanding this has come in large measure from Reinhold Niebuhr's work, and I'm not qualified to paraphrase it, but if I tried I would say it this way: Each of us has an inherent capacity for both good and evil. And if you prefer nonreligious language you could say that the lingering presence of nature red in tooth and claw that we carry with us from our evolutionary development gives us the capacity to strike out violently when we encounter a fearful difference—when we encounter a difference that inspires fear. Groups protect one another. Survival in the ancient past presumably depended on that ready impulse. But our spiritual nature—or, to describe it again in parallel terms, our evolutionary development—has also given us a much richer heritage with which we can overcome the impulse to evil, or violence, triggered by fear of difference."

By now Chris Lehane was employing nice but insistent the-interview-is-over body language. I was struck, naturally, by the lack of connection between our conversation and the accusatory thrust-and-parry, or rousing catchphrase-making, or after-dinner remarkese, in which people, including Gore, run for President. It was as if the Gore of the past hour were stored in a separate container. "One more thing," I said to Gore. "Everything we've been talking about is to some extent a counterpoint to how one conducts a Presidential campaign. How do you communicate what's in your soul to the American people, through the static of a Presidential campaign?"

Gore stood up and smiled genially, but I thought also ironically. "Are you talking about before this *New Yorker* interview appears? I think this article will completely eliminate that problem."

(2000)

DELTA NIGHTS

I T'S a damp Delta night in January, and we've pulled into Lambert, in Quitman County, Mississippi, at one time a modestly prosperous cotton town, now reduced to a rather curious thing. The railway station—stripped down and operated in an only-one-man-needs-to-run-it kind of way—is still functioning as an agricultural freight stop, more or less as it always has, but it seems to be the exception. The town center consists of two rows of Main Street–like buildings, vaguely Victorian in design, relics of nineteenth-century antebellum cotton commerce, almost all of them abandoned. One of these would have housed the barbershop, or the bank, or the post office. Now they're home to whomever, whatever, anybody, nobody. One was the Rexall drugstore. (The "x" in Rexall has broken off.) The feeling of the place is of impoverished improvisation, variations on a squatter's theme, and Lambert's empty buildings have been taken up by anyone who has the know-how to crack open a padlocked door and get the electricity turned on. As we pull in, flames leap out from a corner, the only light on a street without street lights: it's a barbecue, the pit constructed from fallen loose bricks, right out on the sidewalk. The town seems to be deadly desolate, and yet, weirdly, it is also busy with people.

It's Saturday night, and we're in the heart of the heart of the Delta, the homeland of the blues. Our drive began in Clarksdale, near the birthplace of Muddy Waters, and continued through the very crossroads where Robert Johnson, seventy-two years ago, was supposed to have done his legendary transaction with the Devil, exchanging his soul for a satanic facility on guitar. And for half an hour we've been on county highways, all straight lines and right angles, cutting through plowed fields of cotton and soybean, seeing no other vehicles, no people, no lights except the distant dull blue of a farmhouse television, and then this explosion of busyness, in this place near no place, an embellished dot on a road map. We park, get out. Main Street is thrumming— a heavy, amplified bass coming from behind a number of boarded-up store- fronts. We pick a solid, thickly painted door, which gives after I push against it, and it opens up to the sweet, acrid smell of a woodstove, a smoky array of blue and green lights dangling from an overhead pipe, and, atop a stage in the cor- ner, a sixty-year-old man in a two-piece suit and brown patent-leather shoes— Johnnie Billington playing electric guitar.

This is the first stop on a visit to Delta juke joints, and it's impossible not to be impressed by that profoundly unmodern, unreconstructed feeling that you still find in the South. I'm here because of an interest in Lucinda Williams, the Louisiana-born singer and writer, and although she isn't with me tonight (she's in Nashville, singing with the North Mississippi All Stars—as it happens, a Delta blues band), the Delta has served Williams as a highly personal, emo- tional reference library, something she keeps coming back to in her music, for images or metaphors or, sometimes, for its famous twelve-bar arrangements and its flattened blue notes. Williams is forty-seven, and, obsessively working and reworking a small collection of tunes, has created a concentrated reper- toire of around three dozen exceptionally powerful songs. For a thirty-five-year effort (Williams began playing when she was twelve), that works out to about a song a year, and it's still possible to see a live show in which she gets a little car- ried away—and she always seems to be on the verge of getting a little carried away—and hear almost the entire œuvre, as was the case about eighteen months ago at New York's Irving Plaza, when Williams's encores went on longer than the act, and the audience emerged, after nearly two and a half hours, thoroughly spent, not only by the duration of the program but also by the unforgiving rawness of the songs. They're unforgiving because they are so relentlessly about pain or longing or can't-get-it-out-of-your-head sexual de- sire, but most often they're about loss, and usually about losing some impossi- ble fuckup of a man, who has got more charm and charisma than a civilized society should allow, and who never lives up to any of the promises he made when he was drunk, on drugs, in lust, in love, incarcerated, in pain, insane, in rehab, or, in some other essential but frustratingly appealing romantic way, un- accountable. He's usually from Baton Rouge, Louisiana (and a bass player), or from Lafayette, Louisiana (and a bass player), or from Lake Charles, Louisiana (and a bass player), or maybe from Greenville, Mississippi (and a bass player), and the songs come across as both very Southern and also painfully autobio- graphical. Ouch! you think after you've heard Lucinda Williams for the first time, this girl has gone through some shit. Her songs are not traditional rock and roll, if only because they are more written, more preoccupied with the con- cerns of language and image, than most rock tunes. They're not country, al- though there is an occasional twangy country element. They're not folk, even

though "Car Wheels on a Gravel Road," her 1998 album (and her first commercial success), got a Grammy award for the best contemporary-folk record of
the year. And they're not blues, even though they are informed by something
that might be described as a blues attitude.

This quality of being both one thing and another (and yet another) is at the
heart of Williams's achievement—thus the knotty, contradictory labels she
gets stuck with, like the blackest white girl in Louisiana (or the white woman
with a black man's soul), or Raymond Carver with a guitar (because of her
stark narratives), or a female Hank Williams. At some point, I started asking
her colleagues to characterize her music and was met with a kind of stuttering
bafflement (gruff-speaking Gurf Morlix, for instance, who worked with
Williams for eleven years and wrote most of the guitar hooks on her songs,
paused for a long Marlboro Man, spit-out-your-tobacco minute and said, "Shit,
I never thought about it as anything except the music of a genius, but I don't
know what it is") until I was rebuked for even trying by Hobart Taylor, a champion of Williams going back almost to the days when she wore a granny dress
and sang on street corners: "Don't even go there," he said. "It's a trap."

Whatever this music gumbo might be, the blues remains one of its spicier in-
gredients—thus this visit to the Delta, where, after Johnnie Billington surren-
ders the stage to younger colleagues, including a teen-ager on bass who is
hunched over in pain from what people are saying is a degenerative spinal disease, and a keyboard player so diminutive that his head disappears behind the
piano, we wander out, get back into the car, and eventually find ourselves on a
long dirt road, a shortcut to some place where, if we're lucky, we might catch
the last set of Robert Walker, another aging giant of the blues. The woman in
the back seat with me is telling me that I need to be careful, that Saturday
nights in the Delta are wild. There have been gang killings, and trouble between whites and blacks, and it might be advisable for me to stick close, because, she says, whispering in a tone that is meant to be reassuring, she's got a
loaded pistol in her handbag, and, you know, hey, shit happens.

After miles of empty fields, a church appears on our right, a white clapboard
shoebox, resting atop brick stilts, nothing else in view, and then, a few minutes
later, we turn, and, just before the town of Bobo, we come upon the Holmes
Grocery & Diner, a square building with white bulbs draped across its awning
like Christmas lights, a gravel parking lot, and a big barn of a room in the back.

When Lucinda Williams was starting out, she sang "country blues" (unlike
the urban Chicago variety), the kind that would have originated in places like
this Bobo juke joint, and her first album, recorded in a single afternoon in
1978, consisted only of classics by the country-blues masters—Robert
Johnson and Memphis Minnie, of course, but also an ancient shuffling geezer
called Blind Pearly Brown, who used to play wizardly guitar sitting on a stool
on a street corner in Macon, Georgia, on Saturday afternoons, when six-year-
old Lucinda was a mesmerized member of the audience. And although the

blues are no longer a feature of her concerts—with the exception of a slow rendering of Howlin' Wolf's "Come to Me, Baby," which she performs as an encore, with a slippery sibilant last line ("Slide a little love in me") that transforms a simple tune, sung originally by a man, into a womanly erotic declaration—they seem always to be present in some way. This Holmes Grocery & Diner in Bobo, for instance, is remarkably similar to the juke joint pictured on the cover of Williams's "Car Wheels" CD, another shoebox in the country, with Christmas lights, looking utterly ordinary, pushed back into the corner of the photograph, behind a dirt road (in that inimitable Southern way, which finds its aesthetic not in what is pleasing or symmetrical or obvious but in the miserable thing that—indirect, off center, out of focus—is distinguished by its overwhelming authenticity).

The Holmes Grocery & Diner also calls to mind a song from that last CD, "2 Kool 2 Be 4-Gotten," a hymn to the Magic City juke joint, in Rosedale, Mississippi. (The title is written just as it appears on one of the juke joint's walls.) Again, the tune is not actually a blues number but something inspired by the blues, and while it seems to be musically evoking the place it describes—starting off with a slow percussion, the stress in the back, in a syncopated funk style, the drum just behind the beat (in a way that musicians often describe as a Southern sound), laid back, very cool, very juke—what Williams had in mind was the way Beat poets performed their work, with someone on drums and someone playing a bass, and a guy in front reading a poem, singsongy but still spoken. The tune is a recitation, a series of images: the signs mounted around the place ("House Rules, no exceptions. No bad language, no gambling, no fighting. Sorry, no credit. Don't ask"), the graffiti in the bathrooms, the gang rivalries ("June bug vs. hurricane"), and the essential amorality of a joint that's an escape, beyond accountability, and where shit happens.

The next morning, the birthday of Martin Luther King, Jr., I drive out to Rosedale, wanting to see the place that informed the song. Rosedale is built against the levee, the houses of the whites, west of the interstate, with driveways and lawns, and the homes of the blacks, on the other side, crowded, higgledy-piggledy, ramshackle, the timber of the porches and doorways disintegrating in the Mississippi air, an unchanged, unchanging picture that could have been taken any time in the last hundred years. This part of town is full of churches—the Gospel Temple, the Riverside United Baptist, the God's People in Unity, the Assembly of God—and I stop at one, a garish thing with turquoise walls and pink window frames and a white steeple, a great cotton candy of a place. I decide to join the well-dressed families, rushing across the parking lot, late for the eleven-o'clock service, and as I step inside everyone at the back turns to stare. I feel I've transgressed, and leave, but as I walk back to the car it occurs to me that I've been composing a selective, romanticized picture in my head. I made notes the night before, describing the highly sexual bump-and-grind dancing at the juke joint in Bobo, but I wrote nothing of the fact that half the people were fat, no-neck whites—croupiers and kitchen staff from the riverboat casinos. I note that, when we walked in, the band was playing "Mustang Sally" but not that it got bored and suddenly quit mid-tune, in seeming disgust at its audience. I describe Robert Walker, sitting against a wall, tired, possibly ill, a tall man in a draping white suit, white spats, with a Little Richard bouffant hairdo, a shiny white guitar, and a long melancholy face, but not the two white people who were sliding around the joint, "inconspicuously" trying to get the good angle in order to take his picture—this Delta postcard shot—including the man whose camera had an elaborate fashion-photo attachment, with a hooded white canopy above his flash, plus all sorts of high-tech gizmos spread across his table. And even in Lambert I noted the cheap-and-cheerful assortment of chairs, the cracked floors, the New Year's decorations that still hadn't been taken down, but not the banner stretched across the back of the stage: "Sponsored by the National Endowment for the Arts."

DADDY-GIRL

I am in Lucinda Williams's bedroom, and have been struck by a number of things. Above the headboard, and nailed to the wall, is a shiny, glitter-sprinkled, heart-shaped pink valentine from Jesus, who is depicted inside a diminishing succession of crucifixes, like so many Russian dolls, as pretty and effeminate, with a golden halo and dreamy blond hair. I don't think I've ever seen Jesus as a blond. Even so, it makes you wonder: Do you want God above your bed? There is a matching valentine alongside; in this one, Jesus is a brunet. Hanging on the wall by the bathroom is a similar arrangement, this one devoted to the Virgin Mary, a shrine of sorts, including an image that changes shape as you walk past: one moment it's the Virgin, and then—what do you know?—it's the Son of God! This house seems perfectly normal, almost suburban, from the outside—a two-story brick-and-wood affair, set back from the street, in a birch forest, in a semirural district of Nashville (Emmylou Harris lives two doors down)—but inside it's a floor-to-ceiling museum of Southern religious kitsch. There is a wall mounting of Jesus in a conch shell and another of Jesus inside a scallop; as you come up the stairs, you are met by a painting of exceptional ugliness, featuring an eye and a clock (the second hand pivots from a point in the pupil) and a piece of text, written in silver glitter, declaring that we love thee, O Lord, "at all times!" High on a kitchen wall is a cross that says "Bless Our Home," and if you look closely you can see a tiny amplifier, which, when triggered by the vibration of the screen door closing, plays a blast of a choir singing "Hallelujah!" On the refrigerator are magnetized bottle caps with a minuscule likeness of Jesus painted inside, decorated delicately with tiny gold stars and red glitter.

There are snakes. One has such oily-looking scales that I can't resist touching it. Several are rather abstract: stretched across the wall is a particularly crude thing that, in keeping with the governing aesthetic, is painted turquoise. (Many things in the house—including a Jesus night-light—are turquoise.) These are not actually snakes; they are serpents. Raving reverends, preaching the Gospel between bouts of gargling strychnine, walk barefoot atop serpents, not snakes. A joke, I assume. Or is it? Upstairs, in Lucinda's study, I discover that serpent handlers are a special interest, and she has photographs and books about people whom I can only regard—forgive me, O Lord—as insane weirdos.

What is her attitude toward all this? I can't tell; I'm not sure she knows. She owns photo collections of juke joints, hillbillies, cross-eyed Appalachian sharecroppers, rural pig guttings, preachers in a trance, the faithful showing off their fang scars, dumb-ass farmers displaying their guns, and Shelby Lee Adams portraits of sprawling families crowded onto buckling porches in places like Hooterville and Happy. At one moment, I wonder if she collects a certain kind of friend. During a five-day stay in Nashville, I meet a man named Dub Cornett, and then later both Lucinda and Richard Price, her boyfriend of nearly five years (and her bass player), whisper into my ear that Dub is from a family of backwoods hillbillies—"the real thing." On another evening, I'm introduced to a young songwriter named Hayseed, who stays with Williams when he has business in town but still lives with his Pentecostal family. He, too, I'm told, is "the real thing." I wouldn't think twice about them except that later, going over a press file of pieces about Williams, I notice that Dub and Hayseed were trotted out to meet journalists on some of those occasions, too. Is a point being made? The eccentric friends, whose authenticity is in their extreme Baptist intensity; the serpent handlers; the poison drinkers; the turquoise Jesus; the glittery Marys. Is this another illustration of that odd, indirect Southern aesthetic of miserable originality? (It might be white trash, but it's ours.)

Williams is of modest height (five feet four), and slim, almost preternaturally so—"It's the thing I share with my dad. I've always been a rake." Dad is the Arkansas poet Miller Williams, the beanpole figure you might have spotted reading at Bill Clinton's second Inauguration; his poems are hanging on the walls, including one written for Lucinda's boyfriend when he turned fifty:

> Year in, year out, most of us do our best
> To make a hundred, perfect on the test.
> The problems get harder, the teachers don't grade fair,
> But hell, the bell ain't rung and you're halfway there.

There's a room given over to exercise equipment—a weight machine, a stair-climbing machine, a dual-motion cycle machine, a rowing machine, a Nordic-

Track, an "abs-workout station"—but Williams seems not to use it. It's both new and noticeably untouched. So much kit, however, betrays a certain unease. The unease is evident in Williams's hair. It's streaked. It was dark brown (almost black) when I first met her, before she performed on "Saturday Night Live" last year. I've also seen it blond. When I eventually leave Nashville, and am reminded that I've forgone Williams's invitation to stay at her house ("You'd have been the first journalist to see me without makeup"), I suddenly appreciate how much time she puts into her looks. This is "the appearance thing," having to come across as attractive and sexy, to be, as she puts it, "someone you look at and say, 'Whoa, what a babe! I wouldn't mind . . .' " It is a preoccupation of a forty-seven-year-old only now breaking into a business that, committed to discovering the next Christina Aguilera, considers twenty-seven to be getting on. "I know I shouldn't be so bothered about this stuff," Williams says. "Politically, I know I shouldn't—what do I want to be, every guy's sex fantasy? But when you're in it, as I am, it's hard to ignore."

For all that, Williams's politics seem a bit sixties-ish ragbaggy. A characteristic Williams statement was her reply to a question put to her by *Rolling Stone* last December about her hopes for the next millennium: Lucinda, expressing a loathing for the boom economy, called for a stock-market crash and longed for a Depression, a peculiar dream for a woman who only now—that is, in the past eighteen months, say—has money in a bank account. In 1998, when the filmmaker Paul Schrader agreed to make a video for Lucinda's last album and flew down to Nashville to discuss possible ideas, he was struck by how badly this woman needed a break: here was someone in her mid-forties who was having trouble meeting the essential needs of food and shelter. (In the event, no video was made; no video has ever been made—another Williams tenet, MTV culture is a bad thing, although it's unclear if this arises out of a loathing for television or a paralyzing anxiety about appearing on it.) And last year, when I joined Lucinda in New Orleans, it was evident that the money troubles weren't quite over. We spent an afternoon shopping for old music posters—Fats Domino, for her brother, and Clifton Chenier, "King of Zydeco," for her friend Margaret Moser, a Louisiana-born music journalist—only to have Williams's credit card rejected.

IN many of these things—the ethic of dissent, the anti-establishment stance, the ease of doing without—her father's influence is unmistakable. Miller Williams, a man of indefatigable productivity, has twenty-nine books to his name, including twelve volumes of poetry. Lucinda has memories of his writing a poem every night after dinner, and he appears in the family photo albums very much playing the part, with an untrimmed beard and a black beret, flopped over a chair, writing verse on a yellow legal pad. Does a poet father make for a poetic, songwriting daughter? The answer must be yes, but it's not so obvious. Miller Williams sometimes performs with his daughter—he reads a poem, she sings, then he reads another poem—but you would be hard-pressed to hear a genetic link in their diction. And while Lucinda submits the text of her songs to him before she records them—there will be nothing for years, and suddenly the songs start arriving in the mail—his editorial interventions seem to be modest at most: she cites his objection, for instance, to the phrase "faded blue dress" in the song "He Never Got Enough Love." (She changed it to "sad blue dress.") You get the sense that what she wants is not Dad's advice but his approval, almost like a report card. Lucinda's friend Margaret Moser finds the whole thing peculiar—"this Daddy-girl thing," she calls it, this need to be patted on the back by a man who has nothing to do with the kind of rough-hewn, laconic cigarette ads for masculinity whom Lucinda has been consistently attracted to, although the disjunction that Moser describes is revealing in itself (and might well explain why so many of the Marlboro Men don't work out).

In any case, the idea of Daddy as a benign patriarchal pedagogue isn't a new thing; for much of Lucinda's life, that was his role. In 1969, when Lucinda was in the tenth grade, she was suspended from high school more than once—the first time for refusing to pledge allegiance to the flag—and her father eventually assumed the responsibility of completing her education. (He had already assumed the responsibility of her upbringing, having got custody of her and her two siblings after he divorced Lucinda's mother.) His solution to her education was to give her a reading list of a hundred great books, from the Iliad to "One Hundred Years of Solitude."

When I met Miller Williams, on a visit to Fayetteville, Arkansas, where he teaches at the university, I was interested in his account of Lucinda's suspension, an episode that must have been distressing in the extreme. I was wrong. Dad had been delighted—"just tickled pink!"—and he pointed out how the showdown involving Lucinda's refusal to pledge allegiance was similar to one of his own, twenty years before, when he was fired from McNeese State University for refusing to take the Louisiana loyalty oath required of state employees. But the parallels didn't stop there. Just after Lucinda was kicked out for being a dissident, he quit his job at Loyola University in an act of protest. The university, unhappy about a piece he had published as the editor of a new college literary magazine (a review of Anne Sexton's "Ballad of the Lonely Masturbator," which included too many graphic quotes), had insisted that it approve the contents of future issues before they were printed. This was censorship and not something Miller Williams could tolerate. An out-of-work father, an out-of-school daughter—what a peculiar family it must have been, I found myself thinking, but Miller, also the child of a dissident (a socialist Methodist minister so committed to challenging the status quo that he eventually questioned the Resurrection, discovered that he could no longer conduct the Easter service, and quit), wanted me to understand that this was the Williams way. On the drive from the airport, he bubbled over with more happy showdowns involving his daughter, including her recent confrontation with the producers of "Good Morning America" after they asked her to cut a verse from the song she was about to sing, "Right in Time," her paean to autoeroticism. The lines, Williams added, were not cut, and you could see him making a connection—her song about masturbation, his review about masturbation; like father, like daughter—and he chuckled merrily.

Lucinda never got a high-school diploma; for that matter, she never learned to read music, and although she later passed a college-entrance examination and was admitted to the University of Arkansas, she was bored by the rigors of formal education and was at a loss in harmony class. After one semester, she took her guitar and left Fayetteville, heading first for New Orleans, then for Austin, before settling in Houston—the folk scene of the early seventies.

When she returned, in 1977, four years later, it was under a doctor's orders. She had been singing so punishingly, in smoky clubs, on street corners, busking for rent, straining the rough, husky, untrained, almost Janis Joplin-like voice that characterized her early singing—a sound so sandpapery that Emmylou Harris described it as capable of peeling the chrome off a trailer hitch—that she was in danger of losing it altogether. Nodules had formed on her vocal cords. She was twenty-four. She had a notebook of songs, but no demos, no deals. And that was when she met Frank Stanford, the first of the men who would end up informing so much of the music she'd write for the next two decades.

BEAUTIFUL AS THE SUN

STANFORD, whose story still deserves a book (or a movie), was a precocious, original, highly accomplished poet, a huge personality, with an engine of charm and devastating good looks. "He was like Charlton Heston when he was a young man," Miller Williams tells me, recalling that, years before, Stanford had been admitted to a graduate writing workshop at the University of Arkansas while he was still a teen-age undergraduate, an unprecedented thing.

"He was as beautiful as the sun," the poet Carolyn (C. D.) Wright recalls when we meet to talk about Stanford. She ran a small press with him, the Lost Roads Publishers, and they were lovers, although Stanford was married to a painter, Ginny Stanford. "He had girlie curly hair and hazel eyes and big white teeth and a wide jaw and a wide mouth, which women loved. And men did, too. Everyone loved Frank. They couldn't help it." The writer Ellen Gilchrist knew him, she tells me, when I reach her in Mississippi, "very, very, very, very well," and representations of him are scattered throughout her short stories. "To know Frank then," she says, "was to see how Jesus got his followers. Everybody worshipped him."

Stanford was a Mississippi-born illegitimate child, abandoned at the Emory Home for Unwed Mothers, near Hattiesburg, a "convenience" run by one Sister White for politicians and businessmen. He was adopted by Dorothy Gilbert, who subsequently married Albert Franklin Stanford, an older man, a gentlemanly, worldly embodiment of the Old South. Albert Franklin Stanford built the levees along tributaries of the Mississippi, and this was where the boy passed his summers, alongside his much older "father," spending nights in tents on the levee, sitting in on the campfires the black laborers made, listening to their stories. The experience had a practical consequence. Stanford was working as a surveyor when Lucinda met him, in the spring of 1978, a quiet, enchanting figure who avoided cities and cultivated a manner of strangeness, appearing suddenly, unannounced, from out of the woods, smelling of earth, in suspenders and leather work boots. The experience also informed his poetry, and by then he had published nine volumes, and had just completed the four-hundred-and-fifty-page narrative poem "The Battlefield Where the Moon Says I Love You," a surreal account of a clairvoyant eleven-year-old's crusade for racial justice, with cameo appearances by movie stars and boxers ("I saw Sonny Liston crying in a short-order café"). Stanford's poems are distinguished by their easy, appealing voice—an intimate, companionable, please-stay-and-have-another-drink kind of voice—and a language that is local and highly vernacular, and that often features the speech of Mississippi blacks. "He evoked the Delta in his poems," Ellen Gilchrist recalls. "His poems *were* the Delta." There are images of women by campfires, of peas being shelled, of fingers smelling of backwater, of escaped convicts and people called Ray Baby and Born-in-the-Camp-with-Six-Toes. And there is Stanford's own half love affair with easeful Death, who appears in various guises—as a cool hipster in shiny loafers and a Cadillac, as a man in a bow tie running a hotel. Stanford was irresistible to the young singer, and she fell heavily in love.

Or so Lucinda concedes, more than twenty years after the event, embarrassed, awkward, in the company of her boyfriend, Richard Price, who has been, on every occasion I've seen them together, a paradigm of understanding, but who is unnerved by the Stanford story. "I just can't believe you fell for it," he says, the "it" being the easy charm, the good looks, the dark Byronic act. "I mean, you're so smart. How could you be so stupid?"

"It was just a fling," C. D. Wright tells me of Lucinda's relationship with Stanford. "And," she adds, sounding a little testy, "only because I was out of town at the time." But Stanford was having a lot of flings—more, it seems, than will ever be known, a frenzy of philandering. He was living with C. D. Wright while promising his wife that they'd get back together. ("He'd stop by every week," Ginny Stanford recalls in a piece published in the *New Orleans Review,* "to tell another lie.") And, by Wright's own count, he was making the same promise to six other women (a writer, a potter, a poet, a sculptor)—actually, maybe there were seven, if you include "that intense thing he was having in

New Orleans." Well, who knows how many? "In that last month," Ginny Stanford recalls, "he was seeing lots of people." Frank Stanford, Wright says, was one of the greatest liars she has ever known.

He had spent two weeks in Louisiana. This was in June. On the day he returned to Fayetteville, he sent flowers to Lucinda, who was out, and her father accepted them. Stanford went home and discovered there was a problem: for ten days, the woman he was living with and the wife he said he was returning to had been together, dismantling his lies. "There was a scene," C. D. Wright recalls, "and I'm not sure Frank had been rejected before. Suddenly, he wanted to go to his office. I didn't know why. We were all upset." The two women accompanied him and waited in the car. They learned later that he'd gone to pick up a pistol. They drove home. Then he went into the bedroom and shot himself three times. "That deadly duet," his wife recalls, of the gun and the moan: "Pop. *Oh!* Pop. *Oh!* Pop. *Oh!*"

Miller Williams got a call, asking him to help. "There was blood all over the bed and on the telephone," he says. "When you've had that much to do with someone's career, and someone so promising, and then to be asked to clean up after him—well, it was pretty tough." When he returned, exhausted, unspeakably sad, he found Lucinda waiting—she'd put the flowers in a vase. She hadn't heard the news.

At the funeral, she and her father stood back, out of the way. "And then after everyone had left," Miller Williams recalls, "and the coffin was lowered, and we were all by ourselves, we walked up to the grave, and Lucinda picked up a handful of dirt and sprinkled it across the coffin." (The act echoes a line in one of Stanford's last poems.) "And I remember thinking, Oh, Lucinda, God bless her, and I felt she was just going to disappear from the pain of it all. And, as we walked off, we turned, and there was a girl of about eighteen, very pretty, who had stood even further back—we hadn't seen her. And she then walked up and picked up a handful of dirt and threw it over the grave."

LUCINDA Williams wrote several songs about Stanford's death. "Pineola," an example of what her friend Hobart Taylor calls her documentary songs, is a heartfelt, angry rendition of the thing, more or less as it happened. There isn't much that was changed—Pineola for Fayetteville, Sonny for Frank, and a Pentecostal burial instead of a Catholic one. The song describes how Lucinda got the news ("When Daddy told me what happened"); her own flattened response ("I could not speak a single word. No tears streamed down my face. I just sat there on the living-room couch, staring off into space"); and the funeral, where Stanford's mother stood baffled by the hundreds of strangers who had shown up to mourn her adopted child's death. The song ends with a refrain about the handful of earth thrown onto the casket. Like several other Lucinda tunes of this time, "Pineola" is in what might be called a country style, reminiscent, say, of Bobbie Gentry's old AM radio favorite "Ode to Billie Joe." It's the song that hooked the novelist Annie Proulx, who heard it for the first time on the CD compilation accompanying the *Oxford American* Southern-music issue, and who described it as "the best alternative country song I'd heard in years."

"Sweet Old World" is a different kind of song—more ballad than short story—and its qualities are at the heart of the difficulty involved in articulating the value of any piece of music, which exists first as something in time, as sound and not as text. The difficulty is compounded with lyrical-seeming songs, if only because one part of their achievement is in language, a language that, once separated from the melody, can look banal. "Sweet Old World," written in the second person, is addressed to a suicide. Musically, it is characteristic of Williams's later songs. The more obvious, "pretty" harmonic elements are in the background (those sad, mournful Gurf Morlix licks, echoing the melody, played on guitar and violin), which allows Williams's voice to stand out up front, full of rough feelings and an abrasive sadness. The lyrics are a list of what the dead man is missing ("See what you lost when you left this world"), and consist of simple images arising out of the things we feel, see, smell: dancing with no shoes, the sensation of being touched by another's fingertips, the sound of your name called by a beloved, a train at night, the feeling of slipping a ring on your finger, the tingling of being kissed, the act of breathing. But because the song's images are of the senses it has an intimacy, even a seductive eroticism. This is perfectly understandable, given that it's being sung to a former lover, but was not something I appreciated until I saw it performed at an outdoor evening concert in Oxford, Mississippi, last year, when the air was swollen from a day of heavy thunderstorms. As a result, the music was rounder-sounding, cushioned, and the notes seemed to linger. There was a crowd of about five thousand crushed into the square. They weren't restless, exactly, but, having spent a day inside, amid reports that the concert might be cancelled, they had a pent-up attentiveness. The stars were coming out, but there was no breeze, just this heavy stillness, and then this tune, with its hip-rolling beat, which was about a suicide, after all. Slowly, people began dancing, everyone swaying, and hands were holding hips, and hands were slipping down trousers, and boys were kissing girls, and girls were kissing girls, slow, wet, slow-dance kisses, and, over to my left, just above Square Books, a couple were undoing their jeans, and, over on another balcony, just above the bar Proud Larry's, two women were holding each other so melodically that their embrace was virtually a sexual act. ("The shit we see people doing when we are onstage," Richard Price tells me later.) That night was the second night with the band for Greg Atticus Finch, a keyboard player who has since been dropped; he still remembers the tune that evening. " 'Sweet Old World,' " he said—in a burst of generosity remarkable for a person who has been banished from a band—"that song is simply the best ballad ever written. No one could write a better ballad than it. No one has written a better ballad. It just doesn't get any better."

Williams began writing both "Sweet Old World" and "Pineola" in 1979, the year after Stanford died. She had to wait thirteen years before they were released.

WHY so long? "Because," Williams says, "my career has been distinguished by other people, who have always been men, telling me what I should sound like." (To be fair, her first album consisted of all those blues numbers, and none of her own compositions, because that's what *she* thought the male producer wanted.) "Happy Woman Blues," her next album, was produced in 1980, and features "Sharp Cutting Wings," a mournful love tune (inspired by yet another poet) that has a characteristic Williams line: a series of love fantasies—of flying off with her poet lover, of being with him in a foreign country, of wanting no one to know them—that ends abruptly with her need for a small loan of "about a hundred dollars" (and there's something very exacting about that "about," as though it's just enough to pay last month's phone bill, score a Diet Coke and a turkey sandwich, and buy a Greyhound bus ticket). On the last day in the studio, the producer took it upon himself to introduce drums to Williams's string-band mix—not a bad sound, she felt, but it wasn't what she would have done, and wasn't something she was asked about. It was immaterial; the album made so little money that it's legitimate to ask if it was ever sold.

But no record made her any money, despite the fanatical efforts of so many people, including Hobart Taylor, who came upon Lucinda's playing at Anderson Fair or the Full Moon Café, and then embarked on a mission to make her known to the rest of the world. Taylor, a Houston journalist before he abandoned his career to promote Lucinda, helped her with the rent, paid for meals, and spent a modest inheritance on putting Lucinda up in the Chelsea Hotel in New York and producing a demo of ten songs, "Pineola" among them. Taylor failed to get a record company to take it. So, too, did David Hirshland, another dreamy disciple, who, like Taylor, abandoned his career (as a booking agent) so that he could throw himself into the cause. The result was another demo, this one paid for by CBS, whose executives then dithered, before confessing that they didn't know what it was and had no idea how to sell it: it was too much like country, according to the rock-and-roll executives; too much like rock and roll, according to the country executives. Williams, meanwhile, was working at a B. Dalton bookstore in a shopping mall near Glendale, driving a beat-up Saab that had a party trick of breaking down on the Harbor Freeway. When, four years later, she was finally taken up by a major record label, RCA, which was then run by Bob Buziak (who understood that Williams's music was neither one thing nor another and needed to be left alone), Buziak got fired, putting her into the hands of a producer who secretly believed she was a disco babe, a secret he didn't share with Williams herself until he had taken her already recorded songs and remixed them, adding a big bass here, a heavy drumbeat there, which, again, was not necessarily a bad sound, but it wasn't hers, and, this time, wasn't something she was going to put up with. She walked out on the deal, even though she was broke. She turned forty and was still broke when Mary Chapin Carpenter covered one of her tunes, "Passionate Kisses," and made it into a Grammy-winning hit. In many ways, it's the Lucinda Williams theme song, asking that essential question: I've waited so long, why can't I have everything now, dammit! Why can't I have a comfortable bed that won't hurt my back, and food for when I'm hungry, and clothes for when I'm cold, plus some pens that don't run out of ink (a poet's daughter, after all), and some quiet thinking time, and a big house full of friends, and a rock band, and a regular supply of passionate kisses?

WEEPING FITS

I'VE been studying Lucinda Williams's face—a youthful face, soft skin, few wrinkles, a face so much younger-looking than her age that waspish peers whisper that she must have submitted it to the surgeon's nip and tuck. (She hasn't.) Its dominant quality is its changeableness. This is a face full of weather—or, maybe, more accurately, it's akin to a weather report, a forecast of the personality you're going to see next. Now, the two of us in her living room, in the evening (Williams is an early-afternoon riser), her face is relaxed and expressive, and yields easily to a teasing, cackling laugh—a laugh that makes you feel appreciated and enjoyed. In concert, she has another face, and one that rarely gives up so much as a smile. It firms up, reveals little, and is at odds with the expressive songs she sings. It's a matter of control. Upheaval makes for these songs, and upheaval goes into the writing of them; she often works herself into such a state, reliving some awfulness, that she'll end up in a dark depression (Williams's depressions are legendary; "Am I too blue for you?" is the refrain of one song devoted to them; "When I cry like the sky like the sky sometimes, am I too blue?"), and these moments can be marked by weeping fits that go on for days. Williams now believes that the songs she writes when she has reached this therapeutic, unprotected rawness are her best, and that she has to go through this kind of trauma in order to write. But then these songs, once made, are performed with a fanatical sense of self-government; and that's what her face conveys then: discipline, containment, control.

She cried for days while writing the ballad "Little Angel, Little Brother," about her younger brother, an exceptional talent on the keyboard ("I see you now at the piano, your back a slow curve, playin' Ray Charles and Fats Domino while I sang all the words"), who has never realized his promise, owing to unhappiness or drink or that old Louisiana gift for self-destruction: "I see you sleeping in the car, curled up on the back seat, parked outside of a bar, an empty bottle at your feet, Little Angel, Little Brother." The song evokes some of the anguish of Lucinda's upbringing, among family members who were distinguished by their artistic ambitions but were held back or frustrated in some profound, soul-destroying way. Her brother also had the makings of a poet. (At fourteen, he'd voraciously read and reread all of Shakespeare.) Then, more disturbing, there was her mother, Lucy, who still had dreams of being a concert pianist when she met Miller Williams, but abandoned them after she quickly had three children, and struggled to bring them up, until, owing to mental illness or depression or something the family is uncomfortable talking about, she yielded her place to a nineteen-year-old undergraduate/housekeeper/caretaker/savior, whom her husband brought in to look after his confused offspring and whom he would eventually marry. (In a domestic cease-fire, the two women lived in the same house for five years.) And there was Miller Williams himself, who, for all his robust confidence, had spent years in an intellectual wilderness. By training and education, he was a biologist, but he had no aptitude for the sciences and kept moving from job to job, unable to secure tenure, until he abandoned both the university and his family and went to New York to work as a junior editor, sending home paltry sums set aside from his paltry salary.

Backstage, at the end of a concert last year at the House of Blues in New Orleans, I witnessed a Louisiana family reunion, which included Lucinda's mother, who had just moved back to the Crescent City ("Come see me," she told me, in a whisper. "I'm so lonely"); her brother Robert, who was also now living in New Orleans, driving a long-distance truck (and who was apprehensive about speaking to a journalist—his having been made the drunken self-destructive subject of "Little Angel, Little Brother" was plenty of attention, thank you very much); plus the much-loved Uncle Cecil, from Sulphur, Louisiana. As a child, Lucinda had seen so much of Uncle Cecil that she asked her mother if they'd lived in Sulphur, too, along with Lake Charles and Macon and a half-dozen other small college towns in the South. "No, no," her mother said, tellingly. "You're thinking of Iowa"—another town in Louisiana—"your grandmother's, where we went so often because we had no money for food and used to go there to eat." Lucinda's childhood was one of testing difficulty, and it is, she admits, an element in why she writes her particular songs of loss and neediness, some of which is touched on in "Car Wheels on a Gravel Road," her account of being a five-year-old in the South, with lyrics that evoke a time of tense domestic hush-hushness: of neighbors watching ("Pull the curtains back and look outside. Somebody somewhere don't know"); of parents' squabbling ("There goes the screen door slamming shut. You better do what you're told. When I get back the room better be picked up"); of a family's having a secret that others don't know ("Low hum of voices in the front seat. Stories nobody knows. Got folks in Jackson we're going to meet. Car wheels on a gravel road"). When Lucinda's father first heard the song, he sought out his daughter and apologized.

At one point, backstage, I felt I was seeing a comparably real-life illustration of the Williams first-person principle—the notion that her more serious fans engage with her music on a deeper, weirder level than they might with other songwriters' songs, because Lucinda's are believed to be so autobiographical. I'd seen the principle expressed in her fan mail, which I'd spent an evening reading in her company ("Miss Williams, did you ever get your heart stomped on by a guy named Alex? I figure you must have—or by an evil twin of his— since about every damn song in your incredible new album nails me straight in the heart"), and which featured confessions of exceptional pain that was either relieved, or relived, by a Williams song. (As the night wore on, and Lucinda kept failing to find a specific letter, one written by a d.j. who was committed to playing something by her every night, because "Sweet Old World" had stopped him from killing himself, you could see her face grow progressively darker— Weather alert!—as she skimmed confession after heartfelt confession, know- ing that she got this kind of mail because of the kind of song she wrote, and she wrote that kind of song because she went through Hell living a hurt or humil- iation, and then went through Hell reliving it when she wrote about it, and she hadn't written a thing now in three years, and she was dreading what she was going to have to go through again—Hell was beckoning.) There at the House of Blues, a fan, the cheerfully named Trish Blossom, had slipped past the tight se- curity, with a husband in tow, and had fixed on Lucinda. Trish Blossom was blond and tall and pretty, and came from the backwoods somewhere in Louisiana—she told this to me, adding that she didn't leave the woods ever, not for nobody, and she had come to New Orleans to see Lucinda, and here she was, and did Lucinda know that Trish Blossom never comes out for nobody, which all seemed a little nutty, but not threatening, I thought, until I glanced over at the husband and saw a face that had an unmistakable look of panic. ("Do you realize," he whispered, "how serious this is?") "She just needs love," Trish Blossom was saying, in a kind of trance. "Can't you see that she needs love? Nobody has loved her, and she has so much love to give, and I have so much love, and I will give her the love she needs." She eventually reached Williams, who handled the encounter expertly—this was a regular exchange. (The most recent involved a man who rushed the stage with a dozen roses, screaming "I love you, Lucinda!" before he was tackled and carried off, shouting, "I am not John Hinckley!") Lucinda gave Trish a hug, which became an embrace, but she came back for more ("I just can't let go") until Lucinda let herself be kissed on the lips, and reassured Trish that, yes, she was right, she just needed some love, and she was pleased that Trish had some to give her.

I'm not sure why first-person narratives—in songs, like Williams's, or even in fiction—invade the sentimental nervous system so effectively, but they provided me with a strategy for understanding Lucinda's music. It yields insights into a number of songs—the ones involving Frank Stanford, say, or something like "Drunken Angle," which was inspired by the death of Blaze Foley ("Blood spilled out from the hole in your heart, over the strings of your guitar, the worn-down places in the wood, that once made you feel so good"), a fellow Austin musician. (Foley was a two-hundred-and-fifty-pound subversive, antic, ferociously anti-commercial poet of folk rock—he celebrated the self-righteousness of his poverty by decorating his jeans, jacket, cowboy hat, and guitar with the same duct tape that held his boots together—who threatened a youth for stealing his own father's welfare checks until the boy shot Foley in the ribs, an act so enragingly pusillanimous that Foley chased the youth and eventually bled to death. You can see why Blaze Foley would appeal to Lucinda's accept-no-compromises world view. But it makes you wonder: Doesn't she know anyone besides bass players and dead men?)

The strategy is even more interesting in relation to Clyde Woodward, probably the most important love interest in Lucinda's life. Clyde, another bass player, who *almost* came from Louisiana, seems to have informed a dozen songs. But this is where the autobiographical approach gets complicated.

I'm sitting in Lucinda's house in Nashville, going through three meticulously organized volumes of photographs. Clyde appears regularly, a big fleshy man with a flap of dark hair and round cheeks and a barrel chest. Lucinda points out Clyde's characteristic pose—arms thrown out wide, a come-join-the-party look. There are pictures of the two of them in Austin. "That," Lucinda says, "is when Clyde persuaded me to pawn a rare twelve-string guitar so we could get food and beer" (whereupon the pawnshop burned down, a typical Clyde touch of fortune). There are pictures of them in New York; Clyde had come along ostensibly to be her manager, although he was jealous of her talent and was always getting in the way. (Clyde, in Lucinda's descriptions, comes across as a passionate, possessive, pig-headed, pugnacious sensualist—jealous and head-butting, but high entertainment.) There is another of Clyde helping her father build a porch in Fayetteville. "That was when we really had no money and nothing left to pawn." And another of Clyde in a kitchen, making gumbo, throwing a party, knocking back a beer, and suddenly Lucinda cries out, "Oh, my God! Oh, my God! Clyde is dead. And Frank is dead. What a thing. All my old boyfriends were in love with the idea of Louisiana, and they're dead!"

Like Stanford, Clyde was fascinated by death, but for Clyde death was an opponent in an elaborate game of combat, the only thing getting in the way of his kamikaze, nothing-can-stop-us approach to life. But Lucinda wasn't interested in dying; she had a career in mind, and so they broke up after four years. And then Clyde did die, more or less just like that, forty years old, jaundiced, anemic, skeletal beyond recognition, in a hospital in East Texas, trying to get back to Louisiana before his liver packed in—from excesses of all kinds. Clyde's last hours were spent with Lucinda's friend Margaret Moser (Lucinda was on a plane trying to reach him), as Moser read to him from a journal about Louisiana, which she had started compiling when she was living far away and feeling homesick. The journal had been Clyde's idea. Moser is from Louisiana. Clyde wasn't, although he was obsessed with the place and used to preach where to find its values: not in its open-air rock concerts, for instance, which you'd find anywhere, but in its parish dances, which you find nowhere else. Or in the dance halls along the road between Eunice and Opelousas. ("Inside, you'd be the only whites, and it would be packed shoulder to butt.") Or in its out-of-the-way crawfish farms, and its cockfights, and its gnarly French Catholicism. Or in odd things, like zydeco, which Clyde played. Or in its gumbo—for Clyde as much a metaphor as a food ("He saw God in a bowl of gumbo"): the spicy Delta hot pot that said, with its cayenne and its crawfish and its other crustaceans, this place and no other.

When Lucinda was growing up, Louisiana meant "backward." It was "country," and people made fun of her father's accent (even though, technically, his was not Louisiana but northeastern Arkansas), and he sometimes tried to disguise it. (My Louisiana father buried his accent deep, and told me once that much of his life was lived to prove that he could be more than a "hick" from a north-woods Louisiana paper-mill town, and I was struck by how the word "hick," very much his word, like "boondocks" and "sticks," was already dated and without force.) Clyde appeared in Lucinda's life when the perception of the place was shifting—in the way of these things, its hick, redneck ways are now the half-rebel expression of an inexplicably charismatic, bad-boy code of excess—and he helped her to recognize the shift. And she repaid him by writing a song about Lake Charles, her birthplace and his fantasy home, and where his ashes are now scattered. The song is the only one in her repertoire that affects her in unpredictable ways, and when she performs it she sometimes breaks down.

GOOD LIARS

THE South has a history of myth-makers, and at the heart of the Southern myth is a love affair with loss. It's what underlies the myth of the good Southern family; or the notion of the Southern gentleman, of honor and Old World grace and hospitality; or the filthy romance of the Confederate flag; or the sugary fables of "Gone with the Wind." These myths—still current, even if anachronistic, even if (like débutante balls and the languid luxury of a south-Georgia accent) *always* anachronistic—are among those cited by Edmund Wilson in "Patriotic Gore," in the pages of this magazine forty years ago, and offered up as examples of how the South is seen to have retained something that modernizing America no longer has. These were also illustrations of the way people from the North liked to think about the South then, units in the elaborate calculation to compensate for a place that was, when Wilson was writing, still synonymous with defeat and self-righteous pride and a kind of na-tionalized nationalistic bad judgment. In forty years, the South has changed, but mythmaking remains a habit of mind. I'm not sure that the myths Southerners fashion today are even necessarily that different—less obvious, sometimes subtle to the point of obscurity, but fundamentally founded on the principle that the South has got something that the rest of America doesn't have anymore. Some of this is in Lucinda Williams's songs ("I'm going back to the Crescent City, where everything's still the same"), although the myths she makes are more sophisticated and of her own private order—it's a vision in which Jack Kerouac meets Robert Johnson and General Robert E. Lee, and they form a blues band, singing lyrics dashed off by Eudora Welty, and after a blow-out, never-to-be-repeated concert they disappear at dawn on their Harleys, where they all die, driving far too fast, in a terrible accident. Like her Southern accent and her sense of "country," it's a vision built on her possession of uniqueness. And it was, I now realize, what drew me to the Delta on my own, and to Rosedale, looking for a juke joint that may no longer exist, and then, af-terward, heading down Mississippi State Highway No. 1, the river always on my right, the railroad tracks running parallel somewhere on my left, and the sky big and endless, and nothing else in view, except, every few miles, a white church, an adornment on the flood-flattened Delta horizon, surrounded by cars, having mysteriously drawn a crowd from a land that seemed to have no one on it.

What was I looking for? Something else, something personal, some remem-bered connection to a place, now lost, farther down the Delta, in Louisiana, in an oppressive, sulfur-stinking Civil War paper-mill town that, when I got there, later that day, would be proudly flying the Confederate flag on the birthday of M.L.K. It was where my family came from, and not all that far from where I was born, and in this I recognize now that, like Trish Blossom and the obsessive letter-writing fans, and like Lucinda's father, I'd personalized this woman's music—I had been tempted by its complex first-person, identify-with-me in-ducements—because in fact the songs that arise out of this landscape are not necessarily autobiographical at all; they merely seem to be so; they invite us to think them so. Good mythmakers are good liars. When Miller Williams sought out his daughter backstage, after listening to "Car Wheels on a Gravel Road," and apologized for her upbringing, he surprised Lucinda. ("Why, Daddy—that song's not about you!") And while "2 Kool 2 Be 4-Gotten," her tribute to the Magic City juke joint in Rosedale, is a recitation of juke-joint images, it is also a jumbly catalogue of all kinds of things you'd never see in such a place, includ-ing a man writhing around outside, claiming that he has decided to take up serpents and strychnine. What's he doing there? This is one of Williams's Pentecostal weirdos—an unlikely visitor to the wrong side of the tracks, even if the crowds inside now include no-neck white fatsos. In the same song, Robert Johnson (dead long before Lucinda Williams was born) is playing guitar in the corner, when, suddenly, an odd singsongy digressive poem pops up right in the middle, a non-sequitur remembrance of a self-destructive lover:

> Leaning against the railing of a Lake Charles bridge
> Overlooking the river, leaning over the edge
> He asked me: Would you jump into the water with me?
> I told him: No way, baby, that's your own death, you see?

Who is this person in love with death and what does he have to do with the Magic City juke joint? This is Clyde, the Lake Charles obsessive, and he has nothing to do with Magic City (both the key and the tempo change to accommodate his visit), but he enjoys a rightful role in a work that, I now understand, is more poem than song, a surrealistic invocation of Southernness not unlike the kitschy religious shrines and turquoise serpents and bottle-cap Christs in Lucinda's own house. It's a bit of mythmaking, by a poet of loss, about a place that's receding from experience, and that might never have been there in the first place. And Williams knows this. She has never been to Rosedale, Mississippi. She's never seen the Magic City juke joint, except in a picture book. For that matter, she's never been to a juke joint.

IN A MOOD

LUCINDA is in a mood. Margaret Moser warned me about these moods. ("She gets all hinky and starts honking like a mule, and then folds up her arms and presses her lips together, and won't look at anyone, and you can stare at her for the longest time and won't have any idea of what the fuck is going through her mind.") Her road manager, Paul Monahan, warned me about them, too, pointing out that he had been her manager for only the last part of her tour, seven months, and in that short time half a dozen people had been fired (including two bus drivers), until the final week, when the remaining band members were let go, too. ("She is the sweetest, most thoughtful, kindest person you'll ever meet. And then, suddenly, the pressure will freak her out, and she doesn't know why it's freaking her out, and she can see she's freaking out but can't do a thing about it.") I once saw the early warning signs of a tempest in the making, after a concert, as everyone was piling into the bus, preparing for the all-night journey ahead, an early-evening show at a festival in Dallas the next day, when Lucinda said she was unhappy with the mix that night, very, very unhappy—something wasn't right, the guitarists were too showoffy, the drummer was too much on top of the beat, something, whatever it was ("What the fuck is it?"), it wasn't working—and was short-tempered and unapproachable, a sudden change in personality that Richard, her boyfriend, recognized and adapted to, not getting too close, finding things to do in another part of the bus, avoiding eye contact, saying nothing, knowing that her questions didn't need answers, until he felt he could make his excuses, and, with relief expressing itself across his face, slipped out for a drink before the bus left.

Tonight, I'm not sure what it is. It's late and Lucinda hasn't eaten ("God damn it, I let my blood sugar fall"), and she's unhappy with Nashville—not to mention Austin, Houston, Los Angeles, and, especially, New York ("I fucking hate fucking New York," she says, eyeballing me provocatively, knowing that I live in the city, and when I don't reply she repeats it, "I fucking hate New York," and when I still don't respond she says it once more)—but it doesn't matter what subject we happen to settle on as we drive into town for a late dinner. Whatever it is, Lucinda is going to attack it.

We've reached the Sunset Grill, an upmarket Nashville music-business hangout, and have been joined by two friends, Vicky, a neighbor, who sits beside Lucinda, and Dub ("the real thing"), who "does something with Steve Earle," and there is talk of other musicians appearing later, and, nearby, the tables are filling up with sidemen arriving from a session with Merle Haggard. Lucinda's state of mind—the blood-sugar level modestly fortified by a bread roll—might now be described as more attitude than mood. She was in a similar way the last time she was here—again, that exhilarating capacity of hers, this tightrope shuffle, of always being on the verge of losing it—when she started ranting about the spinelessness of Nashville music, and, getting more and more worked up, and oblivious of the shushing noises her friends were making, flapping their hands, trying to make her shut up, went on to denounce the overproduced formulaic country sound of Faith Hill in an outburst that culminated in the cry "Oh, fuck Faith Hill"—the allure of those alliterating "f"s proving irresistible—only to realize that an unfazed Faith Hill was sitting at a table right behind her.

Tonight, though, it's anything, everything, the cost of living, the high price of rented accommodation, the yuppies who are driving out the artists, the Southern obsession with guns, the racks of them in the backs of pickup trucks, the nutcases who collect them (including the stepfather of her boyfriend), leading to a repellent horror of the things ("I wish they were all outlawed"), and sliding, somehow, into a denunciation of the Second World War, in which, Lucinda says, the United States should never have got involved, a sentiment that enrages Richard, and, before I realize it, the two of them are in an argument of considerable passion—with Lucinda insisting that she is not an existentialist but a nihilist and doesn't care about the future of unborn children. I'm feeling awkward and not quite wanting to listen too carefully when Richard, having worked himself into a seeming rage, tells her to fuck off. Just like that. "Lu," he says, and takes a breath for effect, "fuck off."

Vicky, the neighbor, sitting opposite, freezes with her mouth open, her fork of food suspended over her plate, staring at Richard with incredulity, and you can see she's about to ask him if he has just said what she thinks she's heard, when her question is rendered redundant because Richard repeats the imperative, with a second-person variation for stress, "Fuck you, Lucinda." Vicky takes a breath. "Richard Price," she says, using his full name in that scolding-mother way, "how dare you—" but she's shut down once more when Richard tells Lucinda that she'd do him and the whole room a great favor if she simply fucked off. And then he adds, "Fuck you, fuck you, fuck you." What are any of us to do? Vicky's hands are fluttering. You can see that she wants to walk out, but she can't do that because she's upset on behalf of her friend—she can't leave her here with someone who is telling her to fuck off, even if he's the man she lives with. In fact, Vicky's indignation has mounted in this way because, in the distress of the moment, she is looking at Richard and not to her side, where Lucinda is sitting. Lucinda, I am surprised to observe, is not upset. All night long, she's been oppressive company—relentlessly whiny and confrontational and negative—until finally she has provoked her boyfriend into being a bad-ass ("You can't fucking mess with the Hombre," he is saying now, punctuating his declaration with the inevitable refrain, "so fuck off, Lucinda"), and Lucinda is loving it. She is beaming. Vicky is telling Richard that he can't get away with this, when, against my better judgment, I interrupt her and say, "No, no, you don't understand, they're liking this, this is actually the way they are together, didn't you know?" and I look over to Lucinda and her eyes are glistening—they're shiny with pleasure—and she's looking at Richard with an unnerving intensity. Then she starts cackling, that rhythmic Lucinda laugh, easy and warm and deeply sexual.

What I find myself doing—inappropriately, of course—is rooting for them. The two of them have been seeing each other for nearly five years—the longest steady relationship in Lucinda's life—and, as a member of the audience witnessing the theatre of their being together, I've learned something of the trickiness of being Lucinda's guy. (It seems to work by inverting the conventional roles, so that Richard, for all his bad-ass Hombre attitude, is the patient one, the don't-worry-I'll-run-out-and-get-it one, the beck-and-call guy; in this household, there's no doubt who is wearing the trousers.) I saw them openly fighting once before, a tiff of a different order. This was in New Orleans, late, in a voodoo bar on Decatur Street. After a night of drinking and reminiscing by the river, Lucinda was suddenly in a mood. She was anxious, at two-thirty in the morning, that she hadn't written a song in three years. It was a curious time to be anxious, if only because, with concert dates booked for the next six months, there wasn't a lot she was going to be able to do to relieve her distress. The problem, it seemed, was that she was too happy. Richard didn't believe that this was a problem—happiness, he thought, was not a bad thing. But Lucinda wasn't listening. She was speaking longingly of her melancholy "Silver Lake period"— the time when, fourteen years before, living in a downtown apartment in Los

Angeles and, having just broken up with Clyde, alone, emotionally wounded, with little money and few distractions, she was focussed and wrote some of her best songs, one after the other: "Crescent City," "Passionate Kisses," "Changed the Locks," and "Side of the Road," a song that, describing a lover's need to be apart from her beloved ("I want to be alone . . . I want to see what it feels like to be without you, I want to know the touch of my own skin"), was starting to seem uncomfortably apposite. Richard persisted. You didn't need to be un-happy to write, he was saying: it's possible to be both creative *and* personally fulfilled—to have good food *and* good wine *and* money *and* good sex *and* write good songs. But Lucinda wasn't buying it (and was impatient with him and thinking something like, Oh, shut up, Richard, what do you know? You're just a bass player), and, again, I found myself wanting both of them to be happy, *please.*

I'm wanting her to be normal. But Lucinda isn't "normal." On some level, the person and the persona in her songs are related, as though her volatile character—this capacity for not knowing how to stop—is a manifestation of the same unguarded personality who can't stop herself from falling wholly in love, over and over again. Or, perhaps, another way of thinking of it: this woman, who has never held a job for any time, doesn't get up in the mornings, is routinely three or four hours late to appointments, who walks out of studios because she doesn't feel like singing that day, and has a knack for both tantrum and wonder, achieves a childlike intensity of emotion in her songs because on some level she isn't, even at the age of forty-seven, quite an adult. And I am probably not the only one who isn't in a hurry to see her grow up.

And then, wholly in character, persona and person still intertwined, last month Lucinda and her boyfriend decided to live apart, and Lucinda made plans to move into an airy loftlike apartment in downtown Nashville, not all that different from the airy apartment she once had in Silver Lake, and, alone now, with lots of space, and few distractions, she has started writing again. That happiness thing, who needs it?

(2000)

ABOUT THE EDITOR

DAVID REMNICK is the editor of *The New Yorker.* He won the Pulitzer Prize in 1994 for *Lenin's Tomb* and is also the author of *Resurrection* and *King of the World: Muhammad Ali and the Rise of an American Hero.* He lives in New York City with his wife and three children.

The Modern Library Editorial Board

Maya Angelou

·

Daniel J. Boorstin

·

A. S. Byatt

·

Caleb Carr

·

Christopher Cerf

·

Ron Chernow

·

Shelby Foote

·

Stephen Jay Gould

·

Vartan Gregorian

·

Charles Johnson

·

Jon Krakauer

·

Edmund Morris

·

Joyce Carol Oates

·

Elaine Pagels

·

John Richardson

·

Salman Rushdie

·

Arthur Schlesinger, Jr.

·

Carolyn See

·

William Styron

·

Gore Vidal

ABOUT THE TYPE

This book was set in Photina, a typeface designed
by José Mendoza in 1971. It is an elegant design
with high legibility, and its close character fit has
made it a popular choice for use in distinguished
magazines and art gallery publications.